D1522384

COLLECTED WORKS OF
BERNARD LONERGAN

VOLUME 23

EARLY WORKS ON THEOLOGICAL
METHOD 2

GENERAL EDITORS

Frederick E. Crowe and Robert M. Doran

COLLECTED WORKS
OF BERNARD
LONERGAN

Early Works on
THEOLOGICAL METHOD 2

translated by
Michael G. Shields

edited by
Robert M. Doran and
H. Daniel Monsour

Published for Lonergan Research Institute
of Regis College, Toronto
by University of Toronto Press
Toronto Buffalo London

ISBN 978-1-4426-4630-8 (cloth)
ISBN 978-1-4426-1435-2 (paper)

Printed on acid-free, 100% post-consumer recycled paper with
vegetable-based inks.

Requests for permission to quote from the Collected Works of
Bernard Lonergan should be addressed to University of Toronto Press.

Library and Archives Canada Cataloguing in Publication

Lonergan, Bernard J.F. (Bernard Joseph Francis), 1904–1984
Collected works of Bernard Lonergan / edited by Frederick E. Crowe and
Robert M. Doran

Includes bibliographical references and index.
Contents: v. 23. Early works on theological method 2 / translated by Michael G.
Shields ; edited by Robert M. Doran and H. Daniel Monsour.

ISBN 978-1-4426-4630-8 (v. 23 : bound).   ISBN 978-1-4426-1435-2 (v. 23 : pbk.)

1. Theology – 20th century.   2. Catholic Church.   I. Crowe, Frederick E.
II. Doran, Robert M., 1939–   III. Shields, Michael G.   IV. Monsour, Daniel, 1958–
V. Croken, Robert C., 1933–   VI. McShane, Philip, 1932–   VII. Lonergan Research
Institute   VIII. Title.

BX891.L595 1988   230   c880-933283

The Lonergan Research Institute gratefully acknowledges the generous contribution
of the Malliner Charitable Foundation, which has made possible the production of
this entire series.

University of Toronto Press acknowledges the financial assistance to its publishing
program of the Canada Council for the Arts and the Ontario Arts Council.

University of Toronto Press acknowledges the financial support for its publishing
activities of the Government of Canada through the Canada Book Fund.

Dedicated to the Memory of
Rev. Joseph Flanagan, S.J.

Contents

LATIN TEXT

General Editors' Preface

With volumes 23 and 24 in Collected Works of Bernard Lonergan, we turn to Lonergan's courses on method at the Gregorian University between 1959 and 1963. Volume 23 is concerned principally with three of these courses: 'De intellectu et methodo' (spring 1959), 'De systemate et historia' (fall 1959), and 'De methodo theologiae' (spring 1962). It also contains a report on a 1961 offering of 'De intellectu et methodo,' in which much of the material from the 1959 course of the same name was repeated but in which new material also appeared. Volume 24 will be devoted in part to an effort to reconstruct the two courses 'De methodo theologiae' that Lonergan taught in 1963. Also included in volume 24 will be a 1964 lecture, 'De notione structurae.' The basic documents composed at the time of the breakthrough in February 1965 to the notion of functional specialization will appear in volume 25.

A notion of the central thrust of these two volumes may be gleaned from what Lonergan writes in his 1977 lecture '*Insight* Revisited': 'The new challenge came from the *Geisteswissenschaften*, from the problems of hermeneutics and critical history, from the need of integrating nineteenth-century achievement in this field with the teachings of Catholic religion and Catholic theology. It was a long struggle that can be documented from my Latin and English writing during this period and from the doctoral courses I conducted *De intellectu et methodo, De systemate et historia,* and eventually *De methodo theologiae*. The eventual outcome has been the book, *Method*

in Theology.'[1] These two volumes join volume 22, *Early Works on Theologi-cal Method 1*, in providing some of the data of the documentation that Lonergan refers to. Other volumes – notably volumes 6 and 17 contain-ing philosophical and theological papers from this period, the preface and introduction to volume 11, *The Triune God: Doctrines*, and the first chapter in volume 12, *The Triune God: Systematics* – help in making the data avail-able for tracing Lonergan's development from *Insight* to *Method in Theology.* The material from the Trinity volumes dates from 1964, but there was also relevant material in the earlier versions: *Divinarum personarum conceptio ana-logica* of 1957 and 1959, and *De Deo Trino, Pars analytica* of 1961. Volume 22 contains material from three summer institutes on method in the 1960s: Regis College, Toronto (1962), Georgetown University (1964), and Boston College (1968). The website www.bernardlonergan.com contains audio re-cordings of the 1962 and 1968 institutes as well as both audio recordings and transcriptions of two more institutes that would be relevant for trac-ing this development: Regis College, Toronto (1969), and Boston College (1970), as well as a transcription of the lectures from Milltown Park, Dub-lin (1971); audio recordings of the latter institute will be uploaded to the site at some point. In the 1968, 1969, 1970, and 1971 institutes, Lonergan was reading from the manuscript of *Method in Theology*, as that manuscript moved closer each year to completion. In fact, by the time of the 1971 Dub-lin institute, he had already submitted the manuscript to the publishers.

The record, then, of the most relevant material as Lonergan made his way toward *Method in Theology* would include at least the following, in chron-ological order (the relevant volumes in the Collected Works are included):

1 *Divinarum personarum*, 1957, 1959, chapter 1: vol. 12
2 'De intellectu et methodo,' spring 1959: vol. 23
3 'De systemate et historia,' fall 1959: vol. 23
4 *De Deo Trino: Pars analytica*, preface and introduction, 1961: vol. 11
5 'De intellectu et methodo,' spring 1961: reported on in vol. 23
6 'De methodo theologiae,' spring 1962, vol. 23
7 'The Method of Theology,' Regis, summer 1962, vol. 22
8 'De methodo theologiae,' spring 1963: reconstructed from Loner-gan's lecture notes in vol. 24

---

1 Bernard Lonergan, '*Insight* Revisited,' *A Second Collection*, ed. Bernard J. Tyrrell and William F.J. Ryan (Toronto: University of Toronto Press, 1996) 277.

9 'De methodo theologiae,' fall 1963: reconstructed from Lonergan's
   lecture notes in vol. 24
10 *De Deo Trino: Pars dogmatica,* preface and introduction, 1964:
   vol. 11
11 *De Deo Trino: Pars systematica,* chapter 1, 1964: vol. 12
12 'The Method of Theology,' Georgetown, summer 1964: vol. 22
13 The breakthrough to functional specialization, 1965: www.
   bernardlonergan.com
14 'Transcendental Philosophy and the Study of Religion,' Boston College, summer 1968: vol. 22
15 Institute on *Method in Theology,* Regis, summer 1969: www.
   bernardlonergan.com
16 Institute on *Method in Theology,* Boston College, summer 1969: www.
   bernardlonergan.com
17 Institute on *Method in Theology,* Milltown Park, Dublin, summer 1969:
   www.bernardlonergan.com
18 *Method in Theology,* published 1972: scheduled to appear as vol. 14 in
   Collected Works of Bernard Lonergan

There are five chapters in the present volume. The first consists of a set
of notes compiled by students from the 1959 course 'De intellectu et methodo,' but approved by Lonergan and used by him again in teaching the same
course in 1961. The second consists of typed manuscripts found in the Lonergan Archives relevant to the 1959 course 'De systemate et historia.' The
third consists of transcriptions of handwritten material relevant to the same
course. The fourth presents a brief report on the 1961 course 'De intellectu
et methodo.' And the fifth presents the text of Lonergan's autograph of his
lecture notes for the 1962 course 'De methodo theologiae.'

There are also two appendices. The first contains a document from Lonergan's own hand relevant to 'De intellectu et methodo,' and the second
presents eleven manuscripts relevant mainly to 'De methodo theologiae'
but also to the other courses recorded here.

Once again, I thank my fellow General Editor, Frederick Crowe, for his
pioneering efforts in making available all the data that were used for the
editing of this volume. Michael Shields has once again provided us with
a superb translation of the Latin materials. A very special word of thanks
has to be reserved in this volume for Daniel Monsour, who returned to his
native Australia shortly after the basic editing tasks for this volume were
completed. I am deeply grateful to Danny for everything that he did for the

Collected Works project over the many years in which we worked together. I will miss his sure and steady contributions to these volumes.

As always, I am obliged to thank Marquette University for providing me with the wherewithal to continue my work on this project.

And finally, I am happy to be able to dedicate this volume to the memory of Rev. Joseph Flanagan, s.j., of Boston College. Fr Flanagan was particularly fond of the first item in the present volume. Almost every year, while I was attending the annual Lonergan Workshop at Boston College, he would at some point ask me, 'When are you going to get around to publishing "De intellectu et methodo"?' Within a few days of his death in May 2010, Michael Shields and I agreed that vol. 23 had to be dedicated to his memory. Lonergan Studies in North America will forever be deeply indebted to what Fr Flanagan did to make Boston College a vibrant center for the study and dissemination of Lonergan's work.

ROBERT M. DORAN
Marquette University

EARLY WORKS ON THEOLOGICAL
METHOD 2

De Intellectu et Methodo[1]

Supposita doctrina in opere *Insight*[2] tradita, ulterior fit gressus ad problema de methodo aliquomodo illuminandum. In qua quaestione maxima est necessitas philosophiae pro theologo. Si methodus est quam aptissima adaptatio mediorum in finem,[3] quando finis est scientia, finis, dum quaeritur,

Understanding and Method[1]

Presupposing what is explained in *Insight: A Study of Human Understanding*,[2] we move now to throw some light on the problem of method. On this question a theologian has the greatest need of philosophy. Method can be defined as the most fitting way of adapting means to an end;[3] but when the

---

1 [A 'Nota' at the end of this item in the original typescript indicates that these notes were prepared and arranged by students enrolled in the course 'De Intellectu et Methodo,' which Lonergan offered at the Gregorian University in the spring of 1959. Frederick Crowe indicates that the students were F. Rossi de Gasperis and P.J. Cahill. See Frederick E. Crowe, *Lonergan* (London: Geoffrey Chapman, 1992) 79, note 58. Appendix 1 below contains notes composed by Lonergan that are closely related to the first part of the present manuscript. Material in the notes within brackets is editorial. Most of the other notes are transferred from the compiled text.]

2 [Bernard Lonergan, *Insight: A Study of Human Understanding*, originally published London: Longmans, Green and Co., 1957; 5th ed., revised and augmented, vol. 3 in Collected Works of Bernard Lonergan, ed. Frederick E. Crowe and Robert M. Doran (Toronto: University of Toronto Press, 1992; repr. ed., 2005).]

3 [This definition of method is somewhat reminiscent of those found in *Insight*: 'A method is a set of directives that serve to guide a process towards a result' (p. 421; see also p. 423); '... in a generalized sense, there is a method if there is an intelligible set of directives that lead from a starting point that may be assumed to a goal that is to be obtained' (p. 450)]. Compare the later definition of *Method in Theology*: 'A method is a normative pattern of related and recurrent operations yielding cumulative and progressive results.' Bernard Lonergan, *Method in Theology* (Toronto: University of Toronto Press, 1996) 4. By 1965 Lonergan was to abandon any definition of method that

est ignotus, et tunc exsurgit problema de methodo, potius obscurum, unde a longe proficiscendum est.

1   De Notione Quaestionis

In hac parte agemus: de quaestione; de seriatione quaestionum; de ordinatione responsionum; de seriatione ordinationum responsionum; de criteriis novae ordinationis, seu de differentia inter diversas responsiones; de problematibus fundamenti, historicitatis, separationis.[4]

1.1 De quaestione

Quaestio exsistit quando adsunt rationes cogentes ad affirmandam et negandam unam eandemque propositionem.

Hoc non significat tamen quaestionem esse revera aliquid contradictorium; rationes autem requiruntur non pro una parte tantum, eaeque debent esse seriae.

Sic Gilbertus Porretanus: 'Ex affirmatione et eius contradictoria negatione quaestio constat. Non tamen omnis contradictio quaestio est. Cum enim altera (pars) nulla prorsus habere argumenta veritatis videtur ... aut cum neutra pars veritatis et falsitatis argumenta potest habere, tunc contradictio non est quaestio. Cuius vero utraque pars argumenta veritatis habere videtur, quaestio est.'[5]

Auctores mediaevales quaestiones colligebant[6] rationes pro utraque par-

end is knowledge, this end, while it is being pursued, is unknown. Thus, there arises the problem of method, a rather difficult one at that, and so we shall have to take a long run at it.

1   The Notion of Question

In this section we shall treat the following topics: the question; the serial arrangement of questions; the ordering of answers; the serial arrangement of the orderings of answers; criteria for new orderings, or the difference between divergent answers; the problems of foundation, of historicity, and of separation.[4]

1.1   The Question

A question exists when there are persuasive reasons for both affirming and denying one and the same proposition.

This does not mean, however, that a question is really something that is contradictory; but reasons, and serious ones, are required not for just one side but for both.

Thus, Gilbert de la Porrée: '... a question consists in an affirmation and its contradictory negation. Still, not every contradiction is a question. For when one side seems to be utterly without probative arguments ..., or when neither side is able to advance arguments that prove or disprove ..., then you have a contradiction that is not a question. But when both sides appear to have probative arguments, then there is a question.'[5]

Medieval authors would draw up lists of questions,[6] adducing reasons

---

might seem to be exclusively in terms of means and end. See 47300D0E060 in www.bernardlonergan.com, where 'thinking out the means to an end is a special case' of method conceived generally as 'an open pattern of recurrent and related operations' discovered by 'reflection on successful performance.']

4 [In the rest of this document Lonergan uses *chasma*, 'chasm,' instead of *separatio*.]

5 *Gilberti Porretae Commentaria in librum De Trinitate*, ML 64, 1258 A. See (Yves) M.-J. Congar, 'Le développement de la QUAESTIO,' in *Dictionnaire de théologie catholique* [henceforth: DTC] XV (29), s.v. 'Théologie,' 370–74, especially 371 [in English, *A History of Theology*, trans. and ed. Hunter Guthrie (Garden City, NY: Doubleday, 1968) 80–84, esp. 81–82.]

6 For example, Peter Abelard, *Sic et non*; ML 178, 1329–1610.

te excogitantes sive ex auctoritate Sacrae Scripturae sive Patrum. Technica quaestionis maxime elucet in operibus S. Thomae, ubi quoddam schema fixum habetur: generatim habentur tres rationes (circiter) pro una parte (= videtur quod non), deinde una ratio pro secunda parte (= sed contra est), deinde solutio (= respondeo dicendum), demum responsiones ad rationes contrarias (ad primum, etc.).

Optimum quoddam exemplum circa vim technicae quaestionis habetur in comparatione duorum articulorum, quae exhibet mutationem mentis Sancti Thomae: *Super II Sententiarum*, d. 28, q. 1, a. 2 (Utrum homo sine gratia possit vitare peccatum) et *De veritate*, q. 24, a. 12 (Utrum liberum arbitrium sine gratia in statu mortalis peccati vitare mortale peccatum possit), ubi enumerantur 23 'videtur quod non,' 11 'sed contra est,' atque totidem responsiones ad has 34 rationes, post longum 'respondeo dicendum.'[7]

Quaestiones tamen exsistebant antequam illa technica inveniretur; eas invenimus in ecclesia iam ab initio.

Maxima quaestio, iam ex primordiis reflexionis super revelationem, fuit utrum sint duo dei an unus Deus.

Sic Justinus, non explicite, sed per modum obiectionis ex Sacra Scriptura, ponit quaestionem: uni Deo gloria debetur; tamen et Christo gloria datur; quomodo haec duo simul componuntur? Ecce auctoritas a Tryphone Judaeo allata: 'Ego Dominus Deus: hoc nomen meum: et gloriam meam alteri non dabo, neque virtutes meas' (Is 42.8). Cui Justinus respondet:

> Sin ... ob eam causam, quod te existimaveris disputationem in
> eas angustias coniicere posse ut Scripturas inter se dicerem pu-
> gnare, errasti. Id enim numquam audebo nec cogitare nec dicere;
> sed si qua proponatur Scriptura quae eiusmodi esse videatur, et
> praetextum quasi esset alteri contraria praebeat; cum persuasum
> habeam nullam Scripturam alteri contrariam esse, fatebor potius
> me non intelligere quae dicuntur, et iis qui Scripturas inter se

for both sides drawn from the authority of scripture or the Fathers. The technique of the question reached its peak of development in the works of St Thomas Aquinas, who followed a regular pattern: first, there would be generally about three reasons for one side of the question (*videtur quod/ quod non*) followed by one reason for the other side (*sed contra*), then the solution (*respondeo dicendum*), and finally the answers to the contrary reasons (*ad primum, ad secundum,* etc.).

A prime example of the effectiveness of the technique of the question is to be found in the comparison between two articles, which shows a change of mind on the part of St Thomas: *Super II Sententiarum,* d. 28, q. 1, a. 2, 'Whether one without grace can avoid sin,' and *De veritate,* q. 24, a. 12, 'Whether free will without grace and in the state of mortal sin can avoid mortal sin,' in which there are enumerated 23 *videtur quod non*'s, 11 *sed contra*'s, and as many answers to these 34 arguments after a lengthy *respondeo dicendum.*[7]

Questions, of course, existed long before this technique was invented. Indeed we find them in the church from the very earliest times.

At the very beginning of theological reflection on the data of revelation the major question was whether there are two gods or only one.

Thus Justin, not explicitly but by way of handling an objection taken from scripture, poses this question: Glory is due to God alone; but glory is given to Christ also; how can these two be compatible? This was the argument from scripture advanced by the Jew Trypho: 'I am the Lord God: that is my name; my glory I give to no other, nor my praise to graven images' (Isaiah 42.8). Justin's reply is as follows:

> But if [you spoke these words] … because you thought you could bring our discussion to the point of getting me to assert that the scriptures contradict one another, you were quite mistaken. I would never dare to say or even think such a thing. Rather, if a scriptural passage which appears to be such be brought forward, and if there is a pretext [for saying] that it is contrary [to another], since I am entirely convinced that no scriptural passage contradicts another, I will instead confess that I do not understand what it says, and I will

7 [The article in *Super II Sententiarum* is quite short, with only 6 *videtur quod non*'s and a brief solution.]

pugnare suspicantur, ut idem potius ac ego sentiam, persuadere conabor.[8]

Sic Tertullianus contra Praxean: 'Ita duo negotia diaboli Praxeas Romae procuravit, prophetiam expulit et haeresin intulit; Paracletum fugavit, et Patrem crucifixit.'[9] Quaestio inde exsurgit ex patripassianismo Praxeae. Solutio tantum est in stabiliendo utrum et quo sensu sive Filius sive Spiritus sint Deus. Si quaeritur de Christo, Tertullianus respondet illum esse Deum. Citans initium evangelii Iohannaei, ipse ait: '… Sermo Dei, qui Filius dictus est, qui ipse Deus cognominatus est: "Et sermo erat apud Deum, et Deus erat Sermo."' (Io 1.1).[10] Si autem de Patre et de Filio simul quaeritur utrum sint Deus, tunc solutio Tertulliani est solutio verbalis: Pater est Deus; Filius est Dominus: 'Ergo … si Deus dixit, et Deus fecit; si alius Deus dixit et alius fecit, duo Dii praedicantur.'[11] Tertullianus difficultatem et ambiguitatem aggravat ex pluribus textibus Sacrae Scripturae: ex Ps. 44.7–8 (Deus ungens et Deus unctus), Is. 45.14 (Deus in Deo), Io 1.l (Deus apud Deum), Ps 109.1 (Deus sedens ad dexteram Dei), etc.

'Ergo,' inquis, 'provocabo te, ut hodie quoque ex auctoritate istarum Scripturarum constanter duos Deos et duos Dominos praedices.' Absit … Duos tamen Deos et duos Dominos numquam ex ore nostro proferimus: non quasi non et Pater Deus, et Filius Deus, et Spiritus Sanctus Deus, et Deus unusquisque; sed quoniam retro et duo Dii et duo Domini praedicabantur; ut, ubi venisset Christus, et Deus agnosceretur et Dominus vocaretur, quia Filius Dei et Domini … Itaque Deos omnino non dicam, nec Dominos; sed Apostolum sequar, ut si

try to persuade those who suspect that the bible may contradict itself to do the same.[8]

Tertullian, *Against Praxeas*: 'Praxeas took care of two pieces of business for the devil: he drove out prophecy and brought in heresy, he banished the Paraclete and crucified the Father.'[9] This question arises from Praxeas's patripassianism. The only solution is to determine whether and in what sense the Son and the Spirit are God. As for Christ, Tertullian's reply is that he is God. Citing the beginning of John's Gospel, he says: '… the Word of God whom scripture calls the Son and who is surnamed God – "and the Word was with God, and the Word was God"' (John 1.1).[10] However, if the questions are asked simultaneously whether the Father is God and the Son also is God, then Tertullian's solution is a verbal one: the Father is God; the Son is Lord: 'Therefore … if God spoke, God also made; if one God spoke and another made, two Gods are being spoken of.'[11] Tertullian compounds the difficulty and the ambiguity by quoting several texts from scripture: Psalm 44.7–8 [45.7], God anointing and God anointed; Isaiah 45.14, God in God; John 1.1, God with God; Psalm 109 [110].1, God seated at the right hand of God; etc.

> 'Therefore,' say you, 'I will charge you with consistently maintaining even today on the authority of the Bible that there are two Gods and two Lords.' Not at all! … we never speak of two gods or two lords; but it is not as if the Father is not God and the Son is not God and the Holy Spirit is not God and that each one is not God; but just that in the past two Gods and two Lords were spoken of; so that when Christ came he would be both acknowledged as God and addressed as Lord, because he is the Son of God and of the Lord … Therefore I will by no means say they are gods or lords; but I will follow the

---

8 Justin, *Dialogus cum Tryphone Judaeo,* 65; MG 6, 626 B–C.

9 Tertullian, *Adversus Praxean,* c. 1; ML 2, 156 A. [Lonergan quoted this text also in *The Triune God: Doctrines,* vol. 11 in Collected Works of Bernard Lonergan, trans. Michael G. Shields from *De Deo Trino: Pars dogmatica* (1964), ed. Robert M. Doran and H. Daniel Monsour (Toronto: University of Toronto Press, 2009) 86.]

10 Ibid. c. 7; ML 2, 162 B–C. [Lonergan quotes this text along with its surrounding sentences, thus providing a more ample indication of its context, in *The Triune God: Doctrines* 94.]

11 Ibid. c. 13; ML 2, 168 C.

pariter nominandi fuerint Pater et Filius, Deum Patrem appellem et Jesum Christum Dominum nominem …'[12]

Sic Hippolytus contra haeresin Noeti multos textus affert probantes unicitatem Dei: 'Si Christum confitemur Deum, igitur ipse est Pater, si est Deus; passus vero est Christus Deus, passus igitur est Pater. Pater enim erat ipse …'[13] Et iterum: 'Ipse Christus est Pater, ipse Filius; ipse passus est, ipse se excitavit a mortuis …'[14] Confutatio Hippolyti proficiscitur a Sacra Scriptura; et si negatur tritheismus,[15] non vitatur subordinationismus.[16]

Sic Origenes praeludit ad controversias arianas saec. IV: Pater est Deus per essentiam, Filius per participationem:

> Et hinc solvi potest illud, quod perturbat multos profitentes se Dei amantes esse ac verentes duos praedicare Deos, et propter hoc in falsa et impia dogmata incidentes … Dicendum enim est illis, quod *autotheos* quidem *ho theos* est, propter quod et Servator in precatione ad Patrem inquit: 'ut agnoscant te illum solum verum Deum'; quidquid vero est praeter hunc, qui *autotheos* dicitur, participatione et communione divinitatis illius deificatum, non ille *ho theos* sed *theos* magis proprie dicendum esse, quo nomine omnino primogenitus omnis creaturae, quippe qui cum primus sit apud ipsum, attrahens divinitatem ad seipsum, honorabilior est reliquis diis, qui sunt praeter ipsum, quorum *ho theos theos* est … Verus igitur *ho theos* est *ho Theos*: qui autem dii efformantur ad eius formam, velut imagines quaedam sunt primi exemplaris. Sed rursus multarum imaginum archetypa imago est ille *logos* qui est apud *ton theon*, in principio exsistens, quia sit apud *ton theon* semper manens '*theos*,' haudquaquam id habiturus

Apostle Paul, so that if the Father and the Son are both to be given a name, I will call the Father God and will name Jesus Christ Lord ...[12]

Hippolytus speaks in a similar way in his tract against the heresy of Noetus, citing a number of Noetus's texts proving the oneness of God: 'If we confess Christ to be God, then he is the Father, since he is God; but the God Christ suffered, therefore the Father suffered. For he himself was the Father ...'[13] Again: 'Christ himself is Father, he himself is Son; he suffered, and he raised himself from the dead ...'[14] Hippolytus's refutation begins from scripture; and if he does deny tritheism,[15] he does not avoid subordinationism.[16]

Origen, foreshadowing the Arian controversies of the fourth century, expresses this opinion: the Father is God by his essence, the Son by participation:

Here is the solution to that problem that upsets many who love God and are fearful of saying that there are two gods, and on account of this they fall into erroneous and impious doctrines ... We must say to them that The God, *ho theos*, is indeed *autotheos*, God himself, and accordingly the Savior in his prayer to the Father says, 'that they may acknowledge you, the one true God.' Whatever is divine, besides the one who is called *autotheos*, is deified through participating and sharing in his divinity, and is more properly called, not The God (*ho theos*), but God (*theos*). With this name he is the firstborn of all creation, in that he is the first after God, drawing divinity to himself, and of greater dignity than all other gods who exist besides him (for their God is the God [*ho theos*] ... *Ho theos*, therefore, is the true God; gods that are formed to his likeness are as images of the prime exemplar. But the archetype of many images is the Word, who in the be-

12 Ibid. c. 13; ML 2, 169 B – 170 B. [Parts of this text are quoted in *The Triune God: Doctrines* 324.]
13 Hippolytus, *Contra haeresin Noëti cuiusdam*, c. 2; MG 10, 806 B.
14 Ibid. c. 3; MG 10, 807 A.
15 Ibid. c. 11; MG 10, 818–19.
16 Ibid. cc. 8–10, MG 10, 815–18; cc. 13–15, MG 10, 819–26. [In *The Triune God: Doctrines*, Lonergan refers to the study by Gervais Aeby, *Les missions divines de saint Justin à Origène* (Fribourg en Suisse: Éditions universitaires, 1958) as a source providing evidence for a certain 'subordinationism' among the ante-Nicene writers, including Hippolytus.]

nisi *pros ton theon* esset, et haudquaquam *theos* mansurus nisi perpetuo permansisset in contemplatione paternae profunditatis.[17]

Solutio non vitat subordinationismum: solus Pater est *autotheos*; *logos* est
'*deuteros*' '*theos*.' Haec erit postea doctrina conservatorum inter Arianos,
dum alii sequentur novam scholam exegeseos Antiochenam. Eusebius Caesariensis sequetur Originem.

Sic Novatianus, in quaestionibus trinitariis, non vitat subordinationismum eo quod nondum cognoscitur *homoousios*: 'Est ergo Deus Pater omnium institutor et creator, solus originem nesciens, invisibilis, immensus,
immortalis, aeternus, unus Deus … Ex quo, quando ipse voluit, Sermo Filius natus est: qui … in substantia prolatae a Deo virtutis agnoscitur …'[18]

Cfr. etiam S. Dyonisium Romanum contra Sabellianos (DB 48–51),[19] et
infinitas quaestiones antenicaenas et postnicaenas, nec non quaestiones tri-
nitarias tempore Patrum Cappadocium.[20]

Ex quibus exemplis concludimus ea quae technice in mediaevo tractantur iam antea tractata esse, unde falso tam diversae videntur quaestiones
mediaevales ab iis quae in fontibus revelationis habentur. Revera fontes
quaestionum mediaevalium sunt scripturisticae et patristicae.

1.2 De seriatione quaestionum

Non tantum una datur quaestio. Etenim, una soluta, oritur alia. Quando
in Oriente determinatum est Filium esse Deum, orta est quaestio utrum
Spiritus Sanctus sit Deus (Conc. Constantinopolitanum I, 381), deinde qua-

ginning is with God, because he is with God abiding forever as God, and would in no way have this if he were not with God, and would in no way remain God if he did not remain in perpetual contemplation of the depths of the Father's being.[17]

This solution does not escape subordinationism: only the Father is *autotheos*; the *Logos* is '*deuteros*,' 'second, '*theos*,' 'god' [but not Divinity itself]. This will later become the doctrine of the conservatives among the Arians, while others will follow the new Antiochene school of exegesis. Eusebius of Caesarea will follow Origen.

Novatian, in dealing with trinitarian questions, did not avoid subordinationism either, since the term *homoousios* was still unknown: 'God the Father, therefore, is the author and creator of all things, who alone knows no beginning, is invisible, immense, immortal, eternal, one God ... From him, when he chose, the Word was born as Son: he whose substance is acknowledged as being of the power issuing from God ...'[18]

See also Pope Dionysius against the Sabellians (DB 48–51; DS 112–15; ND 301–303),[19] and the innumerable ante-Nicene and post-Nicene questions, as well as the trinitarian questions at the time of the Cappadocian Fathers.[20]

From these examples it is clear that those matters that were handled in a technical way in the Middle Ages had been dealt with long before. Hence, the difference between the medieval questions and those found in the sources of revelation is only apparent. In fact, the sources of the medieval questions are scriptural and patristic.

1.2 The Serial Arrangement of Questions

There is never just one question. For as soon as one is answered, another arises. When it had been determined in the East that the Son was God, the question arose whether the Holy Spirit was God (First Council of Constan-

---

17 Origen, *Commentariorum in Evangelium Johannis*, tomus 2, c. 2; MG 14, 110 A–C. [For Lonergan's citing of most of this text, see *The Triune God: Doctrines* 126, with the last sentence cited on p. 122.]
18 Novatian, *De Trinitate liber*, c. 31; ML 3, 949 A–B.
19 [On Pope Dionysius, see Lonergan, *The Triune God: Doctrines* 115.]
20 See August Hahn, *Bibliothek der Symbole und Glaubensregeln der Apostolisch-katholischen Kirche* (Breslau: Grass & Barth, 1842) [2nd ed., *Bibliothek der Symbole und Glaubensregeln der alten Kirche* (Breslau: E. Morgenstern, 1877); 3rd ed., 1897; reprint ed., Hildesheim: Georg Olms Verlagsbuchhandlung, 1962].

estiones ortae sunt de Christo Deo simul et homine (Conc. Ephesinum, 431), de duobus naturis in Christo (Conc. Chalcedonense, 451), de persona divina an humana in Christo (Conc. Constantinopolitanum II, 553; Conc. Constantinopolitanum III, 680–81, quod egit de duobus voluntatibus et operationibus Christi); deinde orta est quaestio de processione Spiritus Sancti a Patre et a Filio (schisma Photianum et Conc. Lugdunense II,1274; Concilium Florentinum, 1438–45).

Sic problematica theologiae Graecae occupavit Ecclesiam per plus millennium.

At in Occidente, Pelagiani, ut olim stoici, non defendebant aliquod cohaerens systema affirmationum, sed potius aliquam seriem fluidam positionum, quae omnes fundabantur in assertione fundamentali, cui numquam contradixissent, seu hominem ex diis petere atque expectare debere non virtutem, sed fortunam. Hic nucleus centralis plurimis seriebus quaestionum originem dedit de relatione inter gratiam et libertatem, inter praedestinationem et reprobationem, etc.

Reiecta una haeresi in oppositam confugiunt. Sic Augustinus scripsit *De libero arbitrio* contra Manichaeos, sed etiam *De gratia et libero arbitrio* et *De correptione et gratia* pro monachis Hadrumetanis. Protestantes Scripturam et religionem interiorem extollentes negant organizationem exteriorem Ecclesiae hierarchicae atque aspectum iuridicum et socialem-visibilem Ecclesiae; Catholici, reagentes contra Protestantismum, in exteriorizationem vitae Christianae incidunt aliquando. Modernistae extollunt crisin biblicam, quam e converso Catholici impugnant.

Facile est invenire rationes pro utraque parte, pro utroque cornu contradictionis. Mt 5.37 ait: 'Sit autem sermo vester, est, est; non, non; quod autem his abundantius est, a malo est'; 1 Cor 8.1 s. ait: 'Scientia inflat, caritas vero aedificat. Si quis autem se existimat scire aliquid, nondum cognovit quemadmodum oporteat eum scire.' Nisi hae affirmationes assumantur in conspectu quodam synthetico, oppositae rationes et difficultates non solvuntur.

S. Anselmus, loquens de quaestionibus sui temporis, notat quod, dum olim erant homines superbi reponentes totam efficaciam virtutis in libero arbitrio, nunc adsunt multi totaliter desperantes de libertate et de possibilitate componendi illam cum gratia et actione divina.[21] Ad eliminandam

tinople, 381), and subsequently the questions arose concerning Christ as both God and man (Council of Ephesus, 431), concerning the two natures in Christ (Council of Chalcedon, 451), whether Christ's person was divine or human (Second Council of Constantinople, 553; the Third Council of Constantinople, 680–81, dealt with the two wills and two sets of operations in Christ). Subsequently there arose the question about the procession of the Holy Spirit from the Father and the Son (the Photian Schism and the Second Council of Lyons, 1274; the Council of Florence, 1438–45).

Thus did the problematic of Greek theology occupy the church for over a thousand years.

Meanwhile in the West the Pelagians, like the Stoics before them, did not defend any coherent system of theses but had, rather, a fluid series of positions all based upon one fundamental assertion which they never would have contradicted, namely, that man ought to ask for or expect from the gods not virtue but good fortune. This central nucleus gave rise to several series of questions concerning the relationship between grace and freedom, predestination and damnation, and so forth.

In rejecting one heresy, one often goes to the opposite extreme. Augustine wrote *De libero arbitrio* against the Manicheans, but also wrote *De gratia et libero arbitrio* and *De correptione et gratia* for the monks of Hadrumetum. Protestants, in emphasizing the importance of scripture and interior religion, denied the external organization of a hierarchical church and the juridical aspect of a visible society; Catholics in reaction to this sometimes overemphasized the external aspect of Christianity. Modernists extolled biblical criticism, while Catholics on the contrary attacked it.

It is easy to find reasons for either side, for each horn of the contradiction. In Matthew 5.37 we read: 'Let your speech be Yes, Yes; or No, No. Anything more than this comes from the evil one.' And 1 Corinthians 8.1–2: 'Knowledge puffs up, love builds up. If anyone thinks he knows something, he does not yet know anything in the way he ought to.' Unless these affirmations are subsumed in some overall view or synthesis, contrary reasons and difficulties will go unsolved.

St Anselm, in speaking about questions of his own time, observes that while formerly men were proud and attributed the whole efficacy of virtue to free will, now many utterly despair of human liberty and of the possibility of combining it with God's grace and activity.[21] Anselm, who did much to

21 Anselm, *De concordia praescientiae et praedestinationis nec non gratiae Dei cum libero arbitrio*, q. 3, c. 1 [*al.* 11]; ML 158, 522.

hanc desperationem plurimum Anselmus, primus magnus speculativus mediaevalis.

S. Thomas, in *Quodlibeto* IV, q. 9, a. 3 (18), asserit quod și omnes quaestiones theologicas magistri in scholis solverent auctoritatibus, auditores quidem certissimi essent quod res ita est, at scholae essent vacuae intelligentia:

> Quaedam … disputatio ordinatur ad removendum dubitationem an
> ita sit; et in tali disputatione theologica maxime utendum est auctori-
> tatibus … Quaedam vero disputatio est magistralis in scholis non ad
> removendum errorem sed ad instruendum auditores ut inducantur
> ad intellectum veritatis quam intendit: et tunc oportet rationibus
> inniti investigantibus veritatis radicem, et facientibus scire quomo-
> do sit verum quod dicitur: alioquin si nudis auctoritatibus magister
> quaestionem determinet, certificabitur quidem auditor quod ita est,
> sed nihil scientiae vel intellectus acquiret et vacuus abscedet.[22]

Eodem modo Concilium Vaticanum (1870; DB 1796) aliquam imperfectam et analogicam mysteriorum intelligentiam et possibilem et fructuosissimam agnoscit; proinde qui utilitatem impugnet theologiae speculativae, aperte contra Vaticanum agit.

Unde, ubi aliqua quaestio, ibi seriatio aliqua quaestionum; ubi una responsio, ibi aliqua seriatio responsionum, quae multitudo responsionum debet ordinari.

1.3 De ordinatione responsionum

Ordinatio sit logica: scholastici raro adhibent methodum logicam in ordinandis responsionibus, at saepe praesupponitur implicite hic usus. Ulterior

eliminate this despair, was the first great speculative thinker of the Middle Ages.

St Thomas declares that if schoolmasters were to solve all questions by arguments from authority, their students would know with the utmost certitude what was true, but such schools would be quite bereft of understanding:

> One kind of argument is directed to removing doubts as to whether something is so. In such arguments in theology, one relies especially on the authorities that are recognized by the persons with whom one is disputing ... But another kind of argument is that of the teacher in the schools. It seeks not to remove error but to instruct the students so that they understand the truth that the teacher hopes to convey. In such cases it is important to base one's argument on reasons that go to the root of the truth in question, that make hearers understand how what is said is true. Otherwise, if the teacher settles a question simply by an appeal to authorities, the students will have their certitude that the facts are indeed as stated; but they will acquire no knowledge or understanding, and they will go away empty.[22]

In 1870 the [First] Vatican Council (DB 1796, DS 3016, ND 132) similarly recognized both the possibility and the fruitfulness of an imperfect and analogical understanding of the mysteries of faith; accordingly, impugning the usefulness of speculative theology clearly goes against Vatican I.

Thus, where there is a question, there is a serial arrangement of questions; and where there is an answer, there will be a serial arrangement of answers, and this multitude of answers itself has to be put in order.

1.3 The Ordering of Answers

An ordering should be logical. The Schoolmen rarely employ a logical method in ordering their answers, but the use of such a method is often implicitly

---

22 Thomas Aquinas, *Quaestiones quodlibetales* IV, q. 9, a. 3 (18). [Lonergan cites this text in *The Triune God: Systematics*, vol. 12 in Collected Works of Bernard Lonergan, trans. Michael G. Shields from *De Deo Trino: Pars systematica* (1964), ed. Robert M. Doran and H. Daniel Monsour (Toronto: University of Toronto Press, 2007) 8–9.]

tamen quaestio latet in hoc puncto: controvertitur enim quid logica ipsa sit; dici potest quod evolutio dogmatum est logica an illogica? agiturne in logica non de conceptibus, iudiciis, intelligibilibus veris, at tantum de vocibus, terminis, propositionibus, unde tantum de sensibilibus ordinandis?

Vere utilis esset clara et distincta notio ordinationis logicae. Ordinatio logica praesupponit multa responsa. Ordinatio est logica quatenus adhibetur technica derivationis circa terminos (definitiones) et propositiones, ita ut positis talibus terminis atque propositionibus, alii termini propositionesque sequantur. Termini autem et propositiones sunt primitivi et derivati. Derivata sunt quae ex aliis quacumque technica deductionis obtinentur, secundum multa possibilia systemata. Non derivata seu primitiva sunt quae ex aliis aliqua technica non obtinentur, nec hoc significat ea esse per se nota.

Unde primus gressus ordinationis logicae consistit in colligendis omnibus responsionibus actualibus atque introducenda technica derivationis separandis elementis primitivis (neque necessario evidentibus neque necessariis, sed iis quae tantum ex aliis non derivantur) ab elementis derivatis. Dein, simul sumptis terminis et propositionibus primitivis, iterum adhibita technica derivationis, devenitur ad omnes terminos atque propositiones derivatas possibiles (derivatio obiectiva). Sic obtinetur aliquod systema.

Systema est quaedam virtualis totalitas propositionum determinata ex terminis et propositionibus primitivis mediante sola technica derivationis.

Sic, per solam technicam derivationis, non potest obtineri ex verbis Sacrae Scripturae terminus *homoousios* adhibitus in Concilio Nicaeno. Certe, homo intelligens et rationabilis, legens Scripturam, potest capax esse videndi consubstantialitatem involvi in conceptionibus scripturisticis, at haec est alia quaestio, tangens intelligentiam et rationabilitatem, non puram technicam logicam.

In systemate logico omnes termini et propositiones primitivae et omnes termini et propositiones derivatae secundum eorum derivationem debent ordinari.

Euclides, v.gr., non pervenit ad systematis notionem. Eius conclusiones nequeunt demonstrari nisi recurrendo ad axiomata non Euclidea. V.gr. in casu anguli externi et interni efformati ab aliqua linea recta secante duas rectas parallelas, quod angulus exterior sit maior angulo interiori opposi-

presupposed. Yet a further question underlies this point, for the nature of logic itself is in dispute. Can it be said that the development of dogma is logical or illogical? Does not logic deal, not with concepts, judgments, and intelligible truths, but only with words, terms, and propositions, and hence only with the ordering of perceptible realities?

A clear and distinct notion of logical ordering would really be a useful thing to have. Logical ordering presupposes a multiplicity of answers. An ordering is logical inasmuch as it employs a technique of derivation regarding terms (definitions) and propositions, so that when certain terms and propositions are posited, other terms and propositions follow. Now, terms and propositions can be primitive or derived. They are derived when they are arrived at from other terms or propositions through some deductive technique, in accordance with many possible systems. Non-derived or primitive terms and propositions are those that are not arrived at from other terms and propositions by some such technique, but this does not mean that they are self-evident, *per se nota.*

From this it follows that the first step in logical ordering consists in collecting all actual answers and bringing in a technique of derivation by separating the primitive elements (not necessarily evident or necessary ones, but simply those that are not derived from others) from the derived elements. Next, if one takes together all the primitive terms and propositions, the technique of derivation is applied once again in order to arrive at all possible derived terms and propositions (objective derivation). Thus does one obtain a system.

A system is a virtual totality of propositions established from primitive terms and propositions by means of a technique of derivation alone.

Thus, through a technique of derivation alone the term *homoousios* used by the Council of Nicea cannot be obtained from the words of scripture. To be sure, an intelligent and reasonable person reading scripture can be capable of seeing that consubstantiality is involved in the scriptural concepts; but that is another question, having to do with understanding and reasonableness, not a purely logical technique.

In a logical system, all primitive terms and propositions and all derived terms and propositions must be ordered according to their derivation.

Euclid, for example, did not arrive at the notion of system. His conclusions cannot be demonstrated except by having recourse to non-Euclidean axioms. For instance, in the case of the exterior and interior angle formed by a straight line intersecting two straight parallel lines, the fact that the

to perspicitur quidem, at non demonstratur secundum principia Euclidea. Perspicitur quidem intelligibile in sensibili, at haec perspectio nequit logice iustificari, unde hodierni mathematici alia systemata extruunt.[23]

Ordinatio sit cohaerens, scilicet systema non debet continere simul et aliquam propositionem et ipsius contradictoriam. Neque obliviscenda est consideratio motus versus systema efformandum; cohaerentia debet inveniri in nisu ad hanc efformationem (v.gr. sicut adest in theologia dialectica Abaelardi, in *Sic et non*). Sic systema thesium theologicarum, prout adhuc hodie in manualibus invenitur, scilicet cum probationibus desumptis ex magisterio ecclesiastico, ex traditione patristica et theologica, ex Sacra Scriptura, ex rationibus theologicis et philosophicis, poterat esse optimum antequam exigentiae considerationis historicae sese imponerent. Nunc autem magis experimur necessitatem distinguendi adaequate methodum historicam a speculativa.

Propositiones ordinatae debent habere sensum realem: non sufficit enim ut inter se cohaereant, quod potest dari etiam inter pura entia rationis. Consequentiae alicuius quaestionis possunt esse fere infinitae. E contra usus metaphysicae in theologia debet aliquomodo limitari. Hoc praecise fit introducendo distinctionem inter ens reale et ens rationis. Haec distinctio supponit metaphysicam atque eius extensionem ad ordinem supernaturalem, sed simul limitat eius usum.

Sensus realis habetur in aliquo systemate quando determinari potest utrum affirmare aliquam propositionem et simul ipsius contradictoriam habeat aliquam consequentiam a parte rei. Unde, ut systema habeat sensum realem, gressus fit ex logica ad metaphysicam seu semanticam.

Sic Congar tria stadia theologiae agnoscit: theologiam Alcuini quae a grammatica regebatur, Abaelardi quae a dialectica, Gulielmi Altissiodor-

exterior angle is greater than the opposite interior angle is grasped but not demonstrated in accordance with Euclidean principles. The intelligible is grasped in the sensible data, but this grasp cannot be logically substantiated, and so mathematicians today set up other systems.[23]

An ordering should be coherent. This means that a system must not simultaneously contain a proposition and its contradictory. Nor must one fail to consider the movement towards forming a system; the coherence is to be found in the drive to form that system (as seen, for example, in Abelard's theological dialectic in his *Sic et non*). Thus, a system of theological theses such as those found in the current manuals, with proofs taken from the church's *magisterium*, from patristic and theological tradition, from scripture, and from theological and philosophical reasons, was able to be the best system available before the necessity of considering things historically made itself felt. Now we experience the need for an adequate distinction between historical and speculative methods.

Ordered propositions must have real meaning: coherence among propositions is not sufficient, since this can also obtain among purely conceptual beings, *entia rationis.* The consequences of any question can be virtually infinite. On the other hand, the use of metaphysics in theology has to be somewhat limited. This is done precisely by introducing the distinction between a real being and a conceptual being. This distinction presupposes metaphysics and its extension to the supernatural order, but at the same time limits its use.

A system has real meaning when it can be determined whether the simultaneous affirmation of a proposition and of its contradictory has some consequence in reality. Hence, for a system to have real meaning it must go beyond logic to metaphysics, or semantics.

Thus, Congar discerns three stages in theology: the theology of Alcuin, governed by grammar, that of Abelard, governed by dialectic, and that of William of Auxerre, Philip the Chancellor, and St Thomas, governed by

---

23 [On the logical limitations of Euclidean procedures, see also Bernard Lonergan, *Understanding and Being,* vol. 5 in the Collected Works of Bernard Lonergan, ed. Elizabeth A. Morelli and Mark D. Morelli (Toronto: University of Toronto Press, 1990) 23–28, and *Phenomenology and Logic: The Boston College Lectures on Mathematical Logic and Existentialism,* vol. 18 in Collected Works of Bernard Lonergan, ed. Philip J. McShane (Toronto: University of Toronto Press, 2001) 11–15. The statement that 'an ordering should be logical' is thus qualified, as much of what follows indicates. See the comments immediately below contrasting closed and open systems. Logic will yield to method and take its place within method.]

ensis, Philippi Cancellarii et S. Thomae quae a metaphysica.[24] Requiritur metaphysica ut constet de reali validitate alicuius systematis.

Primus qui insistit in correspondentiam inter nomina et realitatem est Eunomius, qui demonstrare conatur nullum medium exsistere inter positionem Nicaenam homoousianam et suam positionem Arianam extremam anhomoiosianam, et hoc contra tentativum Semi-Arianorum, ut Acacius vel Basilius Ancyrensis.[25]

Eadem totalitas diversimode ordinari potest systematibus aequivalentibus. Haec possibilis multiplicitas in ordinatione est maximi momenti. S.Thomas distinguit inter ordinationem secundum ea quae sunt priora quoad se (et tunc habentur systemata) et ordinationem secundum ea quae sunt priora quoad nos (et tunc incipimus a sensilibus). Sic, v.gr., in scientiis naturalibus incipitur cum observationibus ex sensibilibus, ex quibus hypotheses exstruuntur et theoriae conficiuntur. Sed in manualibus istarum scientiarum, sive mathematicarum, sive physicarum, sive chimicarum, initium fit ab istis theoriis, sic a tabula periodica elementorum (Mendeleev) in chimia, a theoriis Newtonianis vel Einsteinianis in physica, etc.

Scientiae empiricae fundantur in fide et in possibilitate perpetuae correctionis. Si aliqua lex empirice statuta per saecula semper verificatur et numquam impugnatur, habetur quaedam enormis verificatio empirica. Sic in chimia, in tabula periodica elementa non definiuntur per relationem quam habent ad experientiam sensibilem sed per relationes quas habent inter se. Hoc modo possunt deduci plus quam 300,000 composita quin ad mixturas attendatur. Unde hic elementa sunt priora quoad se, dum priora quoad nos sunt illa quae nos in experimentis sensibilibus observamus.

metaphysics.[24] Without a metaphysics, the real validity of any system cannot be certified.

Eunomius was the first to insist on the correspondence between words and reality in his attempt to show that there was no middle ground between the Nicene position of *homoousios* and his own extreme Arian position of *Anomoion*, arguing against the proposals of the Semi-Arians such as Acacius or Basil of Ancyra.[25]

The same totality can be ordered in different ways by equivalent systems. This potential multiplicity in ordering is most important. St Thomas distinguished between the ordering of things according to the priority they have among themselves, whence systems are formed, and their ordering according to their priority with regard to us, when we begin from the data of sense. Thus, for example, in the natural sciences we begin from the observation of the data of sense to construct hypotheses and formulate theories. But the textbooks of those sciences, whether mathematics or physics or chemistry, begin with the theories, such as Mendeleev's periodic table of the elements in chemistry, Newton's laws or Einstein's theories in physics, and so forth.

Empirical sciences are based upon belief and the possibility of continual correction. If any empirical law established over centuries is constantly verified and never challenged, its empirical verification is massive. Thus, in chemistry the elements in the periodic table are not defined by their relation to sense experience but by the relations they have to one another. In this way more than 300,000 compounds can be deduced, to say nothing of mixtures. These elements, therefore, are prior with respect to themselves, *priora quoad se*, whereas what we observe by our senses in our experiments are prior with respect to us, *priora quoad nos*.

24 Congar, 'Théologie,' DTC xv (29) 360–401. [*A History of Theology* 61–127.]
25 *Eunomii impii Apologia quam cofutavit Basilius Magnus*, MG 30, 835–68. ['He (Eunomius) was so insistent upon conceptualism that he taught (1) that whoever grasped the notion of "unbegotten" would know God as thoroughly as God knows himself, and (2) that names were either mere vocal sounds or else the very essences of things. Thus he went further than Arius, teaching that even the Son did not know the Father. The fundamental metaphysical principle affirming the correspondence between the true and the real he erroneously reduced to the conceptualistic disjunction that names either meant nothing at all or signified the very essences of things.' Lonergan, *The Triune God: Doctrines* 167. The Latin in 'De intellectu et methodo' has *anhomoiosianam*; but see *The Triune God: Doctrines* 166–67, where Eunomius is considered among the Anomoians.]

Eodem modo in theologia, secundum S. Thomam, aliquid primum constituitur articulis fidei. Ipsa sunt enim priora quoad nos quae ex fontibus revelationis immediate nobis patent. At in *Summa contra Gentiles*, v.gr., tantum in IV libro, et non semper, argumentatio incipit ab iis quae in Scriptura habentur. E contra, saepissime mentio Scripturae habetur tantum in fine capitum. Hoc accidit quia revera datur duplex via procedendi, alia inventionis (seu analytica, seu resolutionis in causas), qua proceditur ex iis quae sunt priora quoad nos ad ea quae sunt priora quoad se, ex iis quae habentur in fontibus fidei concluditur ad revelata et revelabilia; alia autem via doctrinae (seu synthetica, seu compositionis), quae incipit ab iis quae debent prius intelligi ut caetera intelligantur (sic enim debet fieri quando docetur). Sic in III libro *Summae contra Gentiles* ad visionem beatificam tamquam ad finem humanae vitae pervenitur tamquam ad conclusionem.

Diversa autem via non habetur diversa theologia: eadem enim totalitas propositionum dupliciter (saltem) ordinari potest.

Apud S. Thomam in *Contra Gentiles* duae viae adhibentur, at *Summa theologicae* tota invenitur in via synthetica: sic, v.gr., conferantur in Ia parte, quaestiones 27–43: in q. 27 agitur de processione divinarum personarum; in q. 28 de relationibus divinis; in qq. 29–32 de divinis personis in genere; in qq. 33–38 de divinis personis singulis; in q. 39 de nominibus communibus tribus personis; in q. 40 de nominibus propriis singulis personis; in q. 41 de actibus notionalibus; in q. 42 de divinis personis inter se; in q. 43 de divinis personis in relatione ad nos seu de divinis missionibus. Nunc autem id quod in scriptura maxima claritate habetur sunt divinae missiones (cfr. Gal. 4.4–6) et aliqua trinitas personarum. Quaestio autem de divinitate Filii maxime exagitata est saec. II-III-IV, quando theologia catholica pervenit ad notionem trium personarum consubstantialium quae sunt unus Deus; cum Patribus Cappadocibus orta est quaestio de proprietatibus personalibus, quae per relationes maxime determinatae sunt ab Augustino; metaphysica autem relationum habita est in Concilio Remensi (1148) contra Gilbertum Porretanum et in Concilio Lateranensi IV (1215) contra Ioachim a Flora. Unde via inventionis historicae modo opposito processit in re trinitaria ac via compositionis theologicae.

Id quod maximi est momenti est *punctum inflexionis*, quando scilicet ex inquisitione circa vera credenda (intellectus quaerens fidem) fit reditus ad eadem vera intelligenda (fides quaerens intellectum). Sic in capitibus

Similarly in the science of theology, according to St Thomas, the articles of faith constitute that which is first, or basic. For those things are prior with respect to us that are immediately known to us from the sources of revelation. But in the *Summa contra Gentiles*, for example, only in book 4 and not always there does he begin his argument from the data of scripture. On the other hand, scripture is most often brought in only at the end of a chapter. This occurs because there are actually two ways of proceeding: the way of discovery (or analytic way, or way of resolution into causes), which goes from what are prior with respect to us to what are prior with respect to themselves, that is, starting from what are contained in the sources of faith to conclude to what are revealed and revealable; second, the way of teaching (or synthetic way, or way of composition), beginning from what must be understood first in order that the rest may be understood, which is necessarily followed in teaching. Thus, book 3 of the *Summa contra Gentiles* ends with the beatific vision as the end of man.

But different ways of proceeding do not mean different theologies: the same totality of propositions can be ordered in (at least) two ways.

In the *Summa contra Gentiles* both ways are used, whereas in the *Summa theologiae* everything is found according to the synthetic way. Consider, for example, the order of questions 27 to 43 in part 1: q. 27, on the procession of the divine persons; q. 28, on the divine relations; qq. 29–32, on the divine persons in general; qq. 33–38, on the divine persons taken separately; q. 39, on the names common to the three persons; q. 40, on the names proper to each of the persons; q. 41, on notional acts; q. 42, on the divine persons in their mutuality; q. 43, on the divine persons in their relation to us, or the divine missions. Now, what is most clearly found in scripture are the divine missions (see Galatians 4.4–6) and a certain triad of persons. The question of the Son's divinity was most vigorously discussed in the second, third, and fourth centuries when Catholic theology was arriving at the notion of three consubstantial persons who are one God; with the Cappadocian Fathers the question arose concerning what was proper to the persons, which Augustine determined as being principally relations; and the metaphysics of relations is found in the Council of Rheims (1148) against Gilbert de la Porrée, and in the Fourth Lateran Council (1215) against Joachim of Fiore. In trinitarian theology, then, the way of historical discovery proceeded in the opposite direction to the way of theological synthesis.

Of supreme importance in all this is the *pivotal point*, that is, when from inquiry into the truths to be believed (*intellectus quaerens fidem*) one returns to an understanding of those same truths (*fides quaerens intellectum*). Thus,

Summae contra Gentiles punctum inflexionis habetur quando versus finem singulorum capitum saepe dicitur: 'Hinc est quod dicitur ...' cum citationibus scripturisticis. Ibi enim habetur non amplius merus locus biblicus sed eius intelligentia, non utique intelligentia historica neque exegetica, sed theologica. Theologia autem non eo magis est theologia quo magis ad id quod est revelatum attendit (hoc potius ad fidem pertinet), sed quo magis intelligentiam illius quod est revelatum excolit.

Si theologia concipitur et exponitur tamquam complexus conclusionum sive ex argumentis biblicis, sive patristicis, sive rationalibus desumptarum, nulla propria principia theologica possunt admitti. E contra principia proprie theologica sunt illa ad quae via analytica pervenit tamquam ad proprias conclusiones, et a quibus inflexio incipit a qua via synthetica proficiscitur. Principia theologica sunt ultima in via resolutionis et prima in via compositionis.

Sic in quaestione 27 Primae Partis, S. Thomas accipit notionem de Deo quam revelatio tradit, atque addita analogia psychologica iam ab Augustino pro divinis relationibus adhibita, obtinet aliquas a quibus redire potest ad intelligentiam dati revelati, et quae proinde principia proprie theologica constituunt, quales notiones processionum, relationum, personarum, nominum personalium et essentialium, proprietatum ...

Sic ratio, procedens ex revelatis et iis addendo veritates naturales, pervenit ad conclusiones theologicas, ex quibus reditus potest incipi ad intelligentiam revelatorum obtinendam.

Hic inveniuntur maximae disputationes circa naturam et notionem theologiae in schola thomistica. Nam apud plures classicos Thomistas theologia est tantum scientia de conclusionibus ad quas pervenitur ex datis revelatis, scilicet de iis quae generatim dicuntur veritates theologice certae, seu revelabilia, mediate vel virtualiter revelata: sic Capreolus, '(Theologia) non est scientia articulorum fidei, sed conclusionum quae sequuntur ex illis';[26] Caietanus;[27] Bañez, '... obiectum proprie et formaliter theologiae est virtualiter revelatum';[28] et praesertim Joannes a S. Thoma, et post illum

in the chapters in the *Summa contra Gentiles* the pivotal point occurs when towards the end of each chapter we frequently read: 'Hence it is said ...' followed by quotations from scripture. There is no longer here the mere biblical text but an understanding of it, not indeed a historical or exegetical understanding of the text, but a theological understanding. Theology is not all the more theological the more assiduously it ponders revelation – that is rather the role of faith – but the more it develops an understanding of what has been revealed.

If theology is conceived and explained as being a set of conclusions derived from arguments in scripture or the Fathers or from human reason, there can be no such thing as proper theological principles. On the contrary, principles that are properly theological are those to which the analytic way leads as to its proper conclusions and at which the pivoting begins which is the starting-point for the synthetic way. Theological principles are last in the way of resolution and first in the way of composition.

Thus, in q. 27 of the first part of the *Summa theologiae*, St Thomas accepts the idea of God as found in revelation, and having added to it the psychological analogy already used by Augustine with regard to the divine relations, arrives at some notions from which he can return to an understanding of the data of revelation and which accordingly constitute properly theological principles, such as the notions of processions, relations, persons, personal and essential names, properties ...

In this way human reason, proceeding from the revealed truths and adding to them natural truths, arrives at theological conclusions from which in turn it can begin its return journey to an understanding of revelation.

It is here that the main disagreements among Thomists regarding the nature and the idea of theology are to be found. For many classical Thomists theology is but a knowledge of conclusions arrived at from the data of revelation, that is, of those truths that are generally referred to as *theologically certain*, or revealable, mediately or virtually revealed. Thus Capreolus: '(Theology) is not knowledge of the articles of faith but of the conclusions that follow from them';[26] Cajetan;[27] Bañez: '... properly and formally the object of theology is that which is virtually revealed,'[28] and especially John

---

26 Quoted by Congar in 'Théologie,' DTC XV (29) 417. [Congar, *A History of Theology* 155.]

27 Ibid. 418. [Congar, *A History of Theology* 156.]

28 Ibid. 419. [Congar, *A History of Theology* 157–58; the quotation is found on p. 158.]

Gonet, Billuart.[29] Hic habetur conceptio opposita illi quam praebuimus supra.

1.4 De seriatione ordinationum responsionum

Soluta una seriatione quaestionum, oritur alia seriatio; multiplicatis seriationibus responsionum, ipsae debent ordinari.[30]

Concilium Vaticanum, verbis Vincentii Lirinensis, hortatur ut 'crescat ... et multum vehementerque proficiat, tam singulorum quam omnium, tam unius hominis quam totius Ecclesiae, aetatum ac saeculorum gradibus intelligentia, scientia, sapientia ...' (DB 1800). Hoc autem erit possibile tantum si semper novae oriantur quaestiones novaeque dentur responsiones, unde certe requiritur successiva et progressiva mutatio in ordinatione responsionum. Encyclica *Humani generis* (1950) docet quod '... uterque doctrinae divinitus revelatae fons tot tantosque continet thesauros veritatis ut numquam reapse exhauriatur. Quapropter sacrorum fontium studio sacrae disciplinae semper iuvenescunt ...'[31] Possibilis est ergo saltem aliquis progressus per ortum novarum quaestionum novarumque responsionum, et proinde novae seriationis ordinationum responsionum.

Haec novitas (seu progressus) potest consistere in eo quod:

(1) Subsequentia se habent ad praecedentia ad modum simplicis conclusionis ex priori ordinatione, quae totalitas quaedam virtualis erat. Unde novis quaestionibus nova responsa dantur facillime tantum applicata techica derivationis veteri ordinationi. Ad respondendum novis problematibus sufficit vetus ordinatio.

(2) Novis quaestionibus sufficienter non respondetur ex ordinatione iam exsistente, at potest responderi dummodo vetus ordinatio paululum evolvatur. Sic, dum antea tot erant propositiones primitivae quot erant termini primitivi, nunc facillime et modo latente introducuntur novae distinctiones impositae a novis problematibus. Haec evolutio seu mutatio prioris ordinationis non facile detegitur in theologia eo quod scholastici non faciunt

of St Thomas, and Gonet and Billuart after him.[29] This concept of theology is quite the opposite of that which we have given above.

1.4 The Serial Arrangement of the Orderings of Answers

Once one serial arrangement of questions has been solved, another serial arrangement arises; and with a proliferation of serial arrangements of answers, these themselves have to be arranged in order.[30]

The Vatican Council, adopting the words of Vincent of Lerins, urges that 'there be growth ... and all possible progress in understanding, science, and wisdom, in individuals and in everyone, in each person as well as in the whole church, according to the level of their development ...' (DB 1800, DS 3020, ND 136). This, however, can only come to pass if new questions continually arise and new answers are given to them, and for this a successive and progressive change in the ordering of the answers will most certainly be needed. The encyclical *Humani generis* teaches that 'both sources of divine revelation contain so many precious treasures of truth that they will never really be exhausted. Therefore through the study of these sacred sources the sacred disciplines are constantly being renewed ...'[31] Hence, at least some progress is possible as a result of the emergence of new questions and new answers, and therefore through a new serial arrangement of the orderings of answers.

This newness, or progress, can consist in the fact that:

(1) Subsequent answers are to their antecedents as simple conclusions from the prior ordering, which was a virtual totality. Hence, new answers are very easily given to new questions merely through applying to the older ordering a technique of derivation. To respond to new problems the old ordering is sufficient.

(2) An adequate response to new questions cannot be given from the existing ordering, but it can be given provided that the old ordering undergoes gradual development. And so while previously there were as many primitive propositions as there were primitive terms, now new distinctions made necessary by new problems are very easily and imperceptibly introduced. This development or change in the former ordering easily goes

---

29 Ibid. 419–20. [Congar, *A History of Theology* 158–61.]
30 See an example of this in the *Summa contra Gentiles*, 3, c. 48, ¶ 12, §2258.
31 *Acta Apostolicae Sedis* XLII (1950) 568 [DB 2314, DS 3886, ND 859].

completam enumerationem terminorum et propositionum primitivarum quas adhibent. Sic, v.gr., a S.Thoma ad Caietanum ad theologiam hodiernorum manualium historica inquisitio detegit veram evolutionem: alius est sensus aliquarum notionum aliquorumque vocabulorum in operibus Thomae et in scholastica hodierna, et hoc propter nova problemata orta et differentem intelligentiam quaestionum. Adest ergo intra priorem ordinationem nova ordinatio (utrum melior sit an peior est alia quaestio) quae tamen non apparet aperte.

(3) Ad nova solvenda problemata non sufficit praedicta evolutio praecedentis ordinationis. Quando huiusmodi exigentia oritur, tunc fiunt scholae de methodo. Novae quaestiones solvi possunt tantum mutando modum ordinandi responsiones secundum methodum novam quae simpliciter non invenitur in operibus iam exsistentibus.

V.gr., ordinatio quaestionum de sanctissima Trinitate potest concipi vel attendendo vel non attendendo ad prospectivam historicam. Si considerationem historicam praetermittimus, notio, v.gr., missionis systematica supponitur non differre a notione Paulina missionis, prout invenitur in Epistola ad Galatas; tunc 'missio' quae est ultima notio in seriatione synthetica perfecte aequivalet 'missioni' quae est prima notio in seriatione analytica, et eadem aequivalentia adest inter elementa correspondentia utriusque viae.

E contra, si attenditur ad prospectivam historicam, magna est differentia inter respectivas notiones prout in synthetica aut in analytica via accipiuntur, et eadem missio divina diversimode concipitur a Christianismo Paulino et a systematizatione theologica successiva.

Haec autem consideratio historica debet fieri ex eo quod causae cognoscendi differunt a causis essendi.

Sed de hac quaestione amplius agemus infra, tangentes problema historicitatis.

1.5 De criteriis novae ordinationis

Nova totalitas propositionum exigit novam ordinationem, et proinde novas propositiones primitivas et novam technicam derivationis seu novum principium evolutionis.

In omni actuali totalitate propositionum, adhibita technica derivationis distingui possunt termini derivati et non derivati, propositiones derivatae

unnoticed in theology because the Scholastic theologians do not make a complete enumeration of the primitive terms and propositions they use. So, for example, a historical investigation of the movement from St Thomas to Cajetan to the theology found in the present manuals reveals a true development: the meaning of some notions and some terminology is different in Aquinas and in modern Scholasticism, as a result of new problems and a different understanding of the questions. Within the prior ordering, therefore, a new ordering is present – whether better or worse is another question – which, however, is not clearly apparent.

(3) To solve new problems, the aforesaid evolution of the preceding ordering does not suffice. When this sort of need arises, courses on method appear. New questions can be solved only by changing the way of ordering responses according to a new method, which is simply not to be found in theological works at the present time.

The ordering of questions on the Trinity, for example, can be conceived either with or without the historical perspective being taken into account. If history is ignored, the systematic notion of mission, for instance, will not be thought of as different from the Pauline notion of mission, such as we find in the Epistle to the Galatians; in this case, the 'mission' that is the final notion in the synthetic serial arrangement is perfectly equivalent to the 'mission' that is the first notion in the analytic series; and the same equivalence holds for all the corresponding elements of each of the two ways.

On the other hand, if one takes historical perspective into account, there is a great difference between the respective notions as they occur in the analytic way and in the synthetic, and the same divine mission is understood differently in Pauline Christianity and in subsequent theological systematization.

However, because of the fact that the causes of knowing are not the same as the causes of being, such a historical consideration is necessary.

But we shall deal with this question a little later on, when we address the problem of historicity.

1.5 The Criteria for a New Ordering

A new totality of propositions calls for a new ordering, and hence for new primitive propositions and a new technique of derivation, that is, a new principle of development.

In every actual totality of propositions, by applying a technique of derivation one can distinguish derived and non-derived terms, and derived and

et non derivatae. Termini et propositiones non derivatae sunt primitivi. Si cum t indicantur termini primitivi, et cum Σ omnia derivata possibilia, Σt indicabit summam conclusionum quae possunt erui ex terminis primitivis (ex paucis terminis primitivis et propositionibus multa elementa derivata obtineri possunt). Tunc Σq indicabit summam omnium quaestionum possibilium intra systema, et Σr summam omnium responsionum in illo systemate.

Si $\Sigma q = \Sigma r$ systema est clausum: tot sunt responsiones quot quaestiones. Nullae aliae responsiones possunt derivari.

Si $\Sigma q > \Sigma r$ systema est apertum quando quaestiones superant responsiones. (Stultus semper magis potest quaerere quam sapiens respondere potest.) Tunc ut systema fiat clausum requiruntur tot termini et propositiones primitivae quot sufficiunt ad derivatas necessarias ad respondendum quaestionibus sese offerentibus.

Notandum est momentum technicae symbolicae, quae nunc est species quaedam scientiae mathematicae et quae ducit ad conclusiones sat miras. Momentum calculi functionalis secundi ordinis et quantificationis terminorum pro determinandis systematibus apertis vel clausis, differentiae inter definitiones per connotationem et per denotationem, inductionis transfinitae ...[32]

Huiusmodi methodum omnino differens est a scholastica methodo, quamvis aliquibus scholastica videatur nonnisi deductio ab aliquibus principiis. E contra, quam distent duae methodi ostenditur ex eo quod P. Bocheński putet reductionem *Summae theologiae* S. Thomae ad logicam symbolicam

non-derived propositions. Non-derived terms and propositions are primitive. If primitive terms are indicated by 't' and all possible derivatives by 'Σ,' then 'Σt' will indicate the sum total of conclusions that can be drawn from primitive terms (from a few primitive terms and propositions a large number of derived elements can be obtained). Then 'Σq' will indicate the sum total of all possible questions within the system, and 'Σr' will represent the sum total of responses within that system.

If $\Sigma q = \Sigma r$, the system is a closed system: there are as many answers as there are questions. No further answers can be derived.

If $\Sigma q > \Sigma r$, the system is open, since there are more questions than answers. (A fool can ask more questions than a wise man can answer.) In this case, in order that the system become closed, as many primitive terms and propositions are required as will be sufficient for the derived terms and propositions needed to answer the questions that arise.

Note the importance of the technique of symbols, which is now a branch of mathematics and which leads to some interesting conclusions. The importance of functional calculus of the second order and of the quantification of terms for determining open or closed systems, the differences between definitions by connotation and by denotation, of transfinite induction ...[32]

This sort of method is entirely different from the Scholastic method, although to some the Scholastic method appears to be but a deduction from some principles. On the contrary, the distance between the two methods can be seen from the fact that Fr Bocheński estimates that the reduction of the *Summa theologiae* of St Thomas to symbolic logic will require the col-

32 See Joseph M. Bocheński, *Formale Logik* (Freiburg: K. Alber, 1956 [2nd ed., 1962]); [in English, *A History of Formal Logic*, trans. and ed. Ivo Thomas (Notre Dame, IN: University of Notre Dame Press, 1961; 2nd ed., New York: Chelsea, 1970)]; A[rthur] N. Prior, *Formal Logic* (Oxford: Clarendon Press, 1955 [2nd ed., 1962]); Alonzo Church, *Introduction to Mathematical Logic*, vol. 1 (Princeton: Princeton University Press, 1956 [rev. and enlarged ed., 1996]); Jean Ladrière, *Les limitations internes des formalismes: Étude sur la signification du théorème de Gödel et des théorèmes apparentés dans la théorie des fondements des mathématiques* (Louvain: E. Nauwelaerts and Paris: Gauthiers-Villars, 1957 [repr. ed., Sceaux: Jacques Gabay, 1992]); Joseph M. Bocheński, *Nove lezioni di logica simbolica* (Roma: Angelicum, 1938).

requirere circiter tria vel quattuor saecula in quibus multi specialistae simul collaborent.[33]

Systema logicum scholasticum est quid potentiale implicitum quod explicitari posset, sed haec explicitatio numquam adhuc facta est. Nullus enim scholasticus enumerat suos terminos et propositiones primitivas. Saepe appellatur ad prima principia, at huiusmodi principia numquam enumerantur systematice. Unde neque accurata technica derivationis potest determinari neque nova systematizatio potest haberi.

Sic, relate ad principium medii exclusi (aut hoc aut non-hoc), quod aliqui mathematici acceptant, alii vero (intuitionistae) reiciunt simul cum mathematica classica, scholastici acceptant illud at saepe saepius introducunt aliquam distinctionem. Sic, v.gr., posita aliqua obiectione, 'Si A, ergo B; atqui A; ergo B,' respondent, 'Si A, in aliquo sensu, ergo B, concedo; Si A, in alio sensu, ergo B, nego.' Posita hac distinctione in maiori, contradistinguunt minorem et negant consequens et consequentiam. Ut talis tamen distinctio legitime introducatur, non exigitur quod praecontenta sit in terminis et propositionibus primitivis, saltem explicite, quae, ut diximus, numquam enumerantur, sed sufficit ut in tali momento inveniatur ad hoc problema particulare solvendum.

Haberi potest tamen utilis suggestio pro scholastica ex consideratione systematis aperti et incompleti. Tantum quia adest similitudo aliqua inter scholasticam et huiusmodi systema, possunt exsistere tot quaestiones disputatae per saecula a scholasticis quae saepe impediunt tractationem novae materiae, quia semper campum occupant. Si methodus scholastica adhiberet technicam logicae symbolicae, a priori omnibus pateret tales aeternas quaestiones solvi non posse, nemo dubitaret quin necessaria esset nova ordinatio et res fierent clariores. Unde ipsa exsistentia talium quaestionum innuit exsistentiam et necessitatem instituendi problema de methodo. Nam propter huiusmodi insolubiles quaestiones, apud multos discipulos dubia exsurgunt de validitate talis et talis, et deinde cuiuscumque, systematis; atque non raro talia dubia redundant in fidem, ad quae cavenda solida doctrina quaeritur extra omne systema, scholasticismo acriter resistitur atque contra illum inquisitiones et studia positiva et historica extolluntur.

laboration of many specialists working over a period of three or four centuries.[33]

The Scholastic system of logic is an implicit potential which can be explicitated, but this explicitation has never been made up to now. For Scholastics do not enumerate their primitive terms and propositions; they often appeal to first principles, but such principles have not been systematically enumerated. Hence, no accurate technique of derivation can be determined, and no new systematization can be devised.

Thus, the principle of the excluded middle (either this or not-this), which some mathematicians accept and others (intuitionists) reject along with classical mathematics, Scholastics accept, but they very often bring in a distinction. Thus, for example, suppose an objection is expressed as follows: 'If *A*, then *B*; but *A*; therefore *B*.' They answer: 'If *A* in some sense, therefore *B*, I concede; but if *A* in a different sense, therefore *B*, I deny.' Having made this distinction in the major premise, they contradistinguish the minor and deny the reasoning and the conclusion. To introduce such a distinction legitimately, it is not required that it be pre-contained, at least explicitly, in primitive terms and propositions, which, as we have said, are never enumerated; but it suffices that at a given moment it may be found in order to solve the problem at hand.

Scholasticism may find useful this suggestion that comes from a consideration of an open and incomplete system. It is only because there is a certain similarity between Scholasticism and this sort of system that there can exist so many questions disputed by Scholastics for centuries, which often get in the way of dealing with new material because they keep occupying the field. If the Scholastic method were to make use of the technique of symbolic logic, it would be obvious to all on a priori grounds that such eternal questions cannot be solved; no one would doubt that a new ordering is necessary, and the matter would be clarified. Hence, the very existence of such questions indicates the existence and the necessity of taking up the problem of method. For because of such insoluble questions, many students have doubts about the validity of this or that system and ultimately of any system. But doubts of this sort sometimes impact upon faith, and to avoid this they seek solid doctrine outside of all system, vehemently resist

---

33 [Lonergan gives no reference here, but he would seem to have in mind Bocheński's closing remarks in Appendix II of *Nove lezione di logica simbolica* 155.]

Sic tamen problema non solvitur, neque evitari potest nisi ad tempus, atque imminet periculum agnosticismi et proinde haeresis fideisticae.

1.6 De triplici problemate: fundamenti, historicitatis, chasmatis

1.6.1 Problema fundamenti

Problema fundamenti habetur quando intra aliquod systema oritur novum quoddam problema cuius solutio nequit inveniri intra ipsum systema. Unde exsurgit problema transitus ex aliqua ordinatione quae non solvit ad aliam quae forsan solutionem praebebit. Quomodo fiet iste transitus et quibusnam criteriis eligetur nova ordinatio?

Problema modo particulari ponitur quando quaeritur quodnam fuerit fundamentum alicuius particularis ordinationis factae ab hoc auctore, in tali ambienti, tali tempore, quando quaeritur si in diversis temporibus idem auctor diversas protulit opiniones. Sic, logice loquendo, multi Sancti Thomae debent distingui.

Problema modo generali ponitur quando agitur de transitu ex aliqua ordinatione in aliam ex eo quod novae quaestiones oriuntur (ita si verba Concilii Vaticani, DB 1800, aliquem sensum habent)[34] manentibus autem iisdem dogmatibus.

Tota historia philosophiae et theologiae potest concipi tamquam series et successio ordinationum et transituum ex una ordinatione in aliam. Hoc sensu loquuntur saepe de 'philosophia perenni,' de 'solida doctrina catholica' ... Attamen adsunt etiam multae aliae opiniones et theoriae quae sibi vindicant eadem nomina. Quale potest esse criterium selectionis?

Hic venit problema fundamenti. Nam quando agitur de saltu ex uno systemate ad aliud, istud nequit obtineri per meram deductionem a primo,

Scholasticism, and against it extol research and positive historical studies. Yet in this way the problem goes unsolved; but it cannot be avoided except for a time, and there remains hanging over us the danger of agnosticism and the heresy of fideism.

1.6 Triple Problem: of Foundation, of Historicity, and of the Chasm

1.6.1 The Problem of Foundation

The problem of foundation arises within any system when some new problem comes along whose solution cannot be found within that system. Hence, there emerges the problem of a transition from one ordering in which there is no solution to another that perhaps will provide a solution. How will that transition be made, and by what criteria will a new ordering be selected?

The problem comes up in a particular way when the question is asked regarding the foundation or basis for a particular ordering made by this particular author, in such a situation and at such a time, and when the question is asked whether at different times the same author expressed different opinions. In this way, logically speaking, we should have to distinguish several St Thomases.

The problem comes up in a general way when there is the question of a transition from one ordering to another as a result of the emergence of new questions while the dogmas remain the same – as happens, if the statement of Vatican I has any meaning.[34]

The entire history of philosophy and of theology can be conceived as a successive series of orderings and of transitions from one ordering to another. This is the meaning of the phrase 'perennial philosophy' and 'solid Catholic doctrine.' But there are many other opinions and theories which claim the same labels. What sort of criterion of selection can there be?

Here is where the problem of foundation comes in. For when there is question of a leap from one system to another, the latter system cannot be

---

34 ['Therefore let there be growth … and all possible progress in understanding, science, and wisdom …; but only within proper limits, that is, in the same doctrine, the same meaning, the same import' (DB 1800, DS 3020, ND 136). This is a quotation from the *Commonitorium* of Vincent of Lerins. See above, p. 29.]

secus non haberentur duo systemata, sed unicum; nam utriusque praemissae, termini propositionesque primitivae coinciderent.

1.6.2 Problema historicitatis

Aliae sunt causae essendi rerum, aliae causae cognoscendi res. Sic nos videmus phases lunares atque ex illis inducimus sphaericitatem in luna (phases sunt causae cognoscendi sphaericitatem); at revera sphaericitas lunae est causa essendi phasium lunarium: quia luna est sphaerica, ideo habet phases. Quapropter in syllogismo distinguendum est inter terminos medios explicativos qui assignant causam cognoscendi et illos qui assignant causam essendi.[35]

Causa cognoscendi est prior quoad nos, et proinde est prima in via inventionis; causa essendi est prior quoad se, et proinde est prior in via doctrinae. Ita est in scientiis naturalibus, ita etiam in theologia.[36]

Sic differente ordine utitur S. Thomas in re trinitaria, sive in commentario super *Sententias*, sive in *Summa contra Gentiles*, sive in *De potentia*, sive in *Summa theologiae*. In commentario sequitur ordinem Petri Lombardi. In *Contra Gentiles* sequitur partim ordinem inventionis (an sit) tractans, v.gr., utrum Filius sit Deus (IV, 3), sed post aliquot capita viam doctrinae sequitur (quid sit) quaerens de modo concipiendi Trinitatem (IV, 11, 13, 14). In *De potentia*, in q. 7 agit de divina essentia, in q. 8 de divinis relationibus, in q. 9 de divinis personis, in q. 10 de processione divinarum personarum. In *Summa theologiae* habetur purus ordo doctrinae, scilicet omnis gressus praesupponit gressum praecedentem, non secundum meram praesuppositionem facti, sed intelligentiae. Technica plene evoluta est (cfr. ordinem quaestionum, 1.3 supra). In hac via bene perspicitur theologiam non solum

obtained by a mere deduction from the former; otherwise there would not be two systems but only one, since the premises and the primitive terms and propositions of each would coincide.

1.6.2 The Problem of Historicity

The causes of the existence of things are not the same as the causes of our knowing those things. We see the phases of the moon and deduce from them that the moon is a sphere (the phases are the causes of our knowing its sphericity); but in reality the sphericity of the moon is the cause of the being of its phases: because the moon is spherical, therefore it has phases. For this reason we must distinguish in syllogisms between the explanatory middle terms that assign the cause of our knowledge and those that assign the cause of being.[35]

A cause of knowing is prior with respect to us, and so is first in the way of discovery; a cause of being is prior in itself, and so is first in the way of teaching. This is true for theology as well as for the natural sciences.[36]

Thus, in his trinitarian theology St Thomas uses different orders in his commentary on the *Sentences*, in the *Summa contra Gentiles*, in the *De potentia*, and in the *Summa theologiae*. In the commentary on the *Sentences* he follows the order of Peter Lombard. In the *Contra Gentiles* he follows partly the order of discovery ('is it so?'), when he discusses, for example, whether the Son is God (4, c. 3), but after several chapters he follows the way of exposition ('what is it?') when inquiring about how to understand the Trinity (4, cc. 11, 13, 14). In the *De potentia*, in q. 7 he discusses the divine essence, in q. 8 the divine relations, in q. 9 the divine persons, in q. 10 the procession of the divine persons. In the *Summa theologiae* there is the pure order of teaching; that is, each step presupposes the previous step, not, however, according to the mere supposition of fact, but of understanding. The technique is fully developed: see the ordering of questions in §1.3 above. In this way of teaching one can clearly see that theology not only begins from the

---

35 See Lonergan, *Insight* 272.

36 See §1.3 above, on the twofold way, and Bernard Lonergan, 'Theology and Understanding,' in *Gregorianum* 35 (1954) 630–48. [Available now in Bernard Lonergan, *Collection*, vol. 4 in Collected Works of Bernard Lonergan, ed. Frederick E. Crowe and Robert M. Doran (Toronto: University of Toronto Press, 1988) 114–32. Perhaps the most complete exposition of the two ways as they function in theology is found in *The Triune God: Systematics* 58–77.]

incipere ab articulis fidei (quae sunt causae cognoscendi pro theologo) sed
et terminare ad illa (procedentem ex causis essendi).

Si praetermittitur historia, uterque ordo est splendidus; at historia exsistit et ponit problema historicitatis. Conceptio quam habet S.Thomas de
divina missione tamquam termino ad extra divinae processionis requisito
ex praedicato contingenti divinae perfectioni attributo non est conceptio
quam de divina missione habent Sacra Scriptura necnon Patres. Hac simplici constatatione, quae posset extendi ad singulas notiones utriusque ordinis, tollit simplicem parallelismum inter illos. Idem problema non exsistit
eodem gradu in scientiis naturalibus, in quarum obiecto non intrat constitutive ipse homo, qui semper evolvitur in sua cogitatione.

Problema historicitatis est problema enorme, quod inde a Renascentia
perturbat theologos. Tunc nata et paulatim evoluta est sic dicta 'theologia
positiva,' sub cuius rubrica complectuntur tractationes sive de historia, sive
de religione, sive de exegesi, sive de literatura, sive de archaeologia, sive de
philologia, sive de geographia, sive de liturgia ... Secundum theologos po-
sitivos haec omnia tractantur modo non scholastico sed 'scientifico,' et hoc
secundum infinitas subdivisiones; studia fiunt de Vetere et de Novo Testa-
mento et de singulis libris et de singulis partibus uniuscuiusque libri utriusque Testamenti (theologia biblica); de singulis periodis Patristicis et de
unoquoque Patre et de diversis periodis productionis uniuscuiusque Patris
(theologia patristica); de singulis Conciliis sive oecumenicis sive non, deque
singulis sessionibus uniuscuiusque Concilii (theologia conciliaris); etc. Sic
bibliographiae enormes exstruuntur, ita ut ne specialista quidem alicuius
campi, quantumvis parvi, possit legere omnia ad suum campum pertinentia.

Haec enormis multiplicatio materiae, 'modo scientifico' excultae, ponit problemata gravissima quando attendatur ad problema historicitatis.
Si enim S. Paulus eodem modo missiones divinas concepit ac S. Thomas,
duae viae theologicae sunt mutuo correspondentes, respectivaeque notiones sunt aequivalentes, et sic progressus studiorum positivorum aequivalet progressui theologiae simpliciter. At, quia non eodem modo res concipiuntur systematice et historice, nullus processus logicus deductivus est
possibilis ut transeamus ex una ad aliam ordinationem. Datur enim quidam saltus.

At si inter varios modos historicos concipiendi dogmata non datur nisi
saltus simpliciter, simpliciter tollitur fundamentum theologiae speculativae
systematicae, tollitur omnis continuitas inter varias conceptiones de dogmatibus; non tantum diversimode eadem dogmata concepta sunt diversis
temporibus, sed simpliciter aliud conceptum est a scriptoribus biblicis,

articles of faith, which are the causes of knowing for a theologian, but also terminates at them, proceeding from the causes of being.

Leaving history aside, both orders are fine; history, however, does exist, and it poses for us the problem of historicity. St Thomas's concept of a divine mission as the extrinsic term of a divine procession required by a contingent predication attributed to the divine perfection is not the concept of a divine mission found in scripture or the Fathers. By itself, this statement, which could apply to each of the notions in both orders, denies any simple parallelism between these orders. The same problem does not exist to the same extent in the natural sciences, since human beings, whose thinking is in continual development, do not enter constitutively into their object.

The problem of historicity is an enormous problem, which has troubled theologians ever since the Renaissance. At that time what was called 'positive theology' came into being and gradually developed; under this rubric are grouped the disciplines of history, religion, exegesis, literature, archeology, philology, geography, liturgy ... According to positive theologians all of these are treated in a manner not Scholastic but 'scientific,' and this according to infinite subdivisions. The Old and the New Testaments are studied, and each book and every section of every book of both Testaments (biblical theology); each of the patristic periods, and each of the Fathers and each of the works of them all (patristics); each of the councils, both ecumenical and not, and each session of every council (conciliar theology); and so forth. Huge bibliographies are compiled, so that not even a specialist in any of these fields, however small, can possibly read everything pertaining to his field.

Such a massive proliferation of material, produced 'scientifically,' poses serious problems when one turns to the question of historicity. For if St Paul understood the divine missions in the same way as St Thomas, the two theological ways would mutually correspond, their respective notions would be equivalent, and so theological progress would simply be a matter of progress in positive theology. But since things are not understood systematically and historically in the same way, no deductive logical process can enable us to move from one ordering to another. There is a certain leap here.

But if among the various historical ways of conceiving dogmas there is just a leap, then the foundation of systematic speculative theology simply vanishes, as well as all continuity among the various conceptions regarding the dogmas. Not only are the same dogmas conceived differently at different times, but one thing is conceived by the biblical authors, something

aliud a Patribus, aliud a theologis mediaevalibus ... unde non remanet admittenda nisi evolutio transformistica dogmatum, prout a rationalistis et modernistis asseritur. Aliqua ergo continuitas est servanda, defendenda, at et intelligenda et explicanda.

Studia theologica positiva sunt separata inter se (hoc apparet etiam ex genere monographico); eorum conclusiones sunt 'scientificae' sensu moderno, hoc est, nonnisi probabiles et continuo reformabiles (exemplum revolutionis in campo positivo allatae ab inventionibus manuscriptorum Qumranicorum) etsi probabilissimae; unusquisque theologus positivus cognoscit tantum proprium campum, saepe valde restrictum. Problema historicitatis videtur tollere fundamentum theologiae speculativae, quae manere videtur sine directione, forma, fine, soliditate. Hoc problema, si schematice praesentatur, est gravissimum et actualissimum in hodierno statu theologiae.

Unde necessitas non tantum inveniendi integrationem inter theologiam positivam et speculativam, quae concrete et de facto in Ecclesia semper datur, sed inveniendi et declarandi eius fundamentum et iustificationem theoreticam, necessariam et sub aspectu methodi scientificae et ad haereses praecavendas et refellendas.

1.6.3 Problema chasmatis

Nomen 'chasma' desumitur a 'chaos' de quo sermo est in Lc 16.26 (parabola divitis et Lazari). Est problema notissimum. Quando S. Athanasius, ad divinitatem Filii vindicandam contra Arianas impugnationes, defendit introductionem in symbolis fidei alicuius verbi 'homoousios' quod in Sacra Scriptura non invenitur, hoc facit per modum exceptionis vix toleratae et lamentatae, agnoscens quod multo melior esset formulatio fidei tota verbis scripturisticis confecta.

> Decuisset igitur nihil de Domino et Salvatore nostro Iesu Christo dicere, nisi quae de illo in Scripturis habentur, non vero vocabula, quae in Scripturis non exstent, inducere. Ita sane oportuisse ego quoque consenserim: siquidem longe aptiora sunt veritatis argumenta quae ex Scripturis eruuntur, quam quae aliunde. Verum, uti iam dixi, perversitas astutiaque et versatilis Eusebianorum impietas

simply different by the Fathers, and something simply different again by medieval theologians, and so on. Hence, all that remains is to admit a transformative development of dogmas, as asserted by rationalists and modernists. Therefore, some continuity has to be maintained and defended, but it also has to be understood and explained.

The various fields of study in positive theology are mutually separate; this is evident from their respective monographs, among other things. Their conclusions are 'scientific' in the modern sense of the word, that is, only probable and continually reformable even though possessing a high degree of probability. A good example in a positive field is the revolution brought about by the discovery of the Qumrân scrolls. Each positive theologian knows only his own field, one that is often quite restricted. The problem of historicity seems to knock the foundation out from under speculative theology, leaving it without direction, form, purpose, or solidity. This problem, which we have presented schematically, is the most serious and real issue facing theology today.

Hence the necessity not only of finding integration between positive and speculative theology, an integration that concretely and in actual fact is always given in the church, but also of finding and clarifying its foundation and theoretic justification, which is necessary both from the point of view of scientific method and in order to forestall heresy and counteract it.

1.6.3 The Problem of the Chasm

We take the word 'chasm' (Greek, χάσμα, cognate with χάος, 'chaos') from Luke 16.26, the parable of the rich man and Lazarus. It is a very familiar problem. When St Athanasius, in vindicating the divinity of the Son against the attacks of the Arians, defended the introduction into the Creed of the word 'homoousios,' which is not found in scripture, he conceded that it was a barely tolerable and most regrettable exception, and agreed that it would be much better to have had a creedal formula using only biblical terminology.

> It would have been appropriate to say about our Lord and Savior Jesus Christ only what is in the scriptures and not to bring in terms that are not found there. I might also agree that such was indeed necessary, since the arguments on behalf of truth that are taken from scripture are far better than those from other sources. But, as I have said, the perversity, the cleverness, and the impious sophistry of

episcopos impulit, ut verba, quibus illorum impietas everteretur, liquidius exponerent …[37]

At si talis erat opinio initio saeculi IV, saepius eadem introductio terminorum technicorum repetita est temporibus sequentibus, et sine difficultate. Sic iam in Concilio Chalcedonensi (451) usurpatae sunt voces 'persona' et 'natura.' J. Lebon explicat Monophysitas Severianos non negasse revera aliam esse naturam humanam aliam divinam in Christo sed potius intelligere vocem 'naturae' non secundum evolutam conceptionem qua usus erat Chalcedonense, sed secundum archaicam conceptionem usurpatam a prioribus Patribus, qui naturam concipiebant ad modum illius quod nos vocamus 'subsistens.' Unde, ex usu patristico et ex incapacitate ostendendi continuitatem in evolutione notionum, Concilium impugnabatur.[38]

Theologia mediaevalis solutionem systematicam quaerebat; ipsa non verebatur uti terminis technicis, immo hoc non amplius per modum exceptionis faciebat, sed systematice. Sensus operis theologici mediaevalis erat ut solutio systematica haberetur pro qualibet quaestione. Hoc habitum est in inventione theorematis supernaturalis (circa a. 1230 cum Philippo Cancellario), in distinctione inter gratiam habitualem et actualem apud S. Thomam. Cfr. evolutionem relate ad conceptionem gratiae ut habitus ab epistola Innocentii III ad Ymbertum, a. 1201, ubi haec est secunda opinio,[39] ad decretum Concilii Viennensis, a. 1311–12, ubi haec est prima opinio.[40]

the Eusebian faction compelled the bishops to give clearer expression to the arguments they were using to refute the impiety of those men ...[37]

But if that was the opinion in the fourth century, afterwards the same introduction of technical terms was repeated often and without any trouble. Thus, already at the Council of Chalcedon (451) the terms 'person' and 'nature' were used. J. Lebon explains that the Severian Monophysites did not really deny the presence of a human nature and a divine nature in Christ, but rather that they understood the word 'nature' not according to the more developed meaning in which Chalcedon used it, but according to an older meaning used by the earlier Fathers who understood 'nature' as referring to what we call 'subsistent.' And so as a result of a patristic usage and an inability to show the continuity in the development of notions, the Council was attacked.[38]

Medieval theologians were seeking a systematic solution; they had no scruples about using technical terminology, and in fact they did so no longer by way of exception but quite systematically. They felt that for any question whatever there was a systematic solution. This can be seen in the introduction of the theorem on the supernatural with Philip the Chancellor, ca. 1230, and in the distinction between actual and habitual grace in St Thomas. See also the development of the concept of grace as a habit from the letter of Innocent III to Humbert, 1201,[39] in which this is a second opinion, to the decree of the Council of Vienne, 1311–12, where it is the first opinion.[40]

---

37 Athanasius, *Epistola de decretis Nicaenae synodi* 32; MG 25, 474 D – 475 A.
38 See Joseph Lebon, 'La christologie du monophysisme syrien,' in *Das Konzil von Chalkedon: Geschichte und Gegenwart*, vol. 1: *Der Glaube von Chalkedon*, ed. Aloys Grillmeier and Heinrich Bacht (Würzburg: Echter-Verlag, 1951) 425–580.
39 [See DB 410, DS 780, ND 1409 (abridged version of the letter).]
40 Joseph de Ghellinck, *Le mouvement théologique du XIIe siècle, sa préparation lointaine avant et autour de Pierre Lombard, ses rapports avec les initiatives des canonistes:études recherches et documents*, 2nd ed. (Paris: Desclée de Brouwer, 1948; [reprint ed., Bruxelles: Culture et civilisation, 1969]); Odon Lottin, *Psychologie et morale aux XIIe et XIIIe siècles*, tome I: *Problèmes de psychologie* 2nd ed. (Louvain: Abbaye du Mont César; Gembloux: J. Duculot, 1957). Artur Michael Landgraf, *Dogmengeschichte der Frühscholastik I/2: Die Gnadenlehre* (Regensburg: Verlag Friedrich Pustet, 1952). B. Lonergan, 'St. Thomas' Thought on Gratia Operans,' *Theological Studies* 2 (1941) 289-324 [available

Dum Patres agebant de quaestionibus particularibus, sive trinitariis vel Christologicis in Oriente sive de gratia et libero arbitrio in Occidente, magna controversia saeculi XIII inter Aristotelicos et Augustinianos erat radicalis: quamvis etiam tunc semper de particularibus disputabatur, revera quaestio erat utrum introducendae essent in theologia categoriae logicae et metaphysicae quas Aristoteles adhibuerat in scientiis naturalibus.

Rogerus Marston, OFM, magister in Oxford,[41] conatus est theologiam systematicam conficere categoriis non Aristotelicis (paganis) sed Augustinianis (Christianis). At difficultas erat in eo quod terminologia Augustiniana est saepe rhetorica; in ea termini non semper eodem sensu adhibentur; usus linguae est literarius nec fundamentum constans et solidum praebere potest theologiae systematicae. Tamen illa dualitas conceptionis et methodi usque hodie manet in oppositione exsistente inter scholam Thomisticam et Scotisticam.

Devotio moderna parum laudavit definitiones et disputationes: 'Quid prodest tibi alta de Trinitate disputare, si careas humilitate, unde displiceas Trinitati? ... Opto magis sentire compunctionem quam scire eius definitionem.'[42]

Haec reactio contra theologiam systematicam multo fuit apud Reformatores qui ad Evangelium contendebant redire, dum postea Baius et Jansenius in sua theologia purum Augustinum se sequi asserebant.

Nostris temporibus fortiter urgetur necessitas accessum permittendi omnibus fidelibus ad theologiam systematicam, positivam, moralem, asceticam, et multum loquuntur de theologia pastorali, de significatione theologica liturgiae, de theologia missae, da theologia kerygmatica, exsistentiali, etc.

Immo non agitur tantum de indigentiis fidelium sed de ipsis theologis, quomodo homines scientiae theologicae dediti synthesin faciant inter propriam cogitationem et propriam vitam spiritualem, inter theologiam

While the Fathers of the Church dealt with particular questions, trinitarian and Christological questions in the East and the problem of grace and free will in the West, the great controversy in the thirteenth century between the Aristotelians and the Augustinians was a radical one: although even at that time particular questions were disputed, the real question was whether or not the logical and metaphysical categories that Aristotle used in his studies of nature ought to be introduced into theology.

Roger Marston, OFM, Master at Oxford, [ob. 1303],[41] tried to construct a systematic theology using not Aristotelian (pagan) categories, but Augustinian (Christian) ones. The problem was that Augustinian terminology was often that of rhetoric, in which terms are not always used in the same sense; literary usage cannot provide a consistent and firm foundation for systematic theology. Yet this duality of concept and method continues today in the dispute between the Thomists and the Scotists.

Devotio moderna had little use for definitions and disputations: 'What good are your lofty disputations on the Trinity if you lack humility and so displease the Trinity? ... I would rather feel compunction than know its definition.'[42]

This reaction against systematic theology greatly influenced the Protestant reformers who strove to return to the Gospel, while later on Baius and Jansenius asserted that in their theology they were following pure Augustine.

In our days the necessity is being strongly urged of giving all the faithful access to systematic, positive, moral, and ascetical theology, and there is much talk about pastoral theology, about the theology of the liturgy, the theology of the Mass, kerygmatic theology, existential theology, and so on.

Indeed, at issue here are not only the needs of the faithful but also of theologians themselves – how those who are dedicated to theology might effect a synthesis between their thinking and their spiritual life, and between

---

now in Bernard Lonergan, *Grace and Freedom: Operative Grace in the Thought of St Thomas Aquinas*, vol. 1 in Collected Works of Bernard Lonergan, ed. Frederick E. Crowe and Robert M. Doran (Toronto: University of Toronto Press, 2000) 1–43.]

41 [Lonergan had in parentheses the dates 1270–92, which, presumably, refer to the years in which Marston was most active in constructing a systematic theology using Augustinian categories. See below, p. 617, note 40.]

42 Thomas à Kempis, *The Imitation of Christ*, I, 1.

systematicam et vitam; quo magis enim theologia fit systematica, quo plures complectit quaestiones, responsiones, ordinationes responsionum, eo longinquior fit a modo loquendi Evangelii et Scripturae in genere, necnon ab immediatis et concretis indigentiis humanitatis. Cfr. v.gr. doctrinam de Deo quam habet Concilium Vaticanum, DB 1782–84, cum notione de Deo quam praebent Vetus et Novum Testamentum. Undo reactio contra systematizationes, quia eo ipso quod theologia fit scientifica, ultra horizontem iacet simplicis fidelis.

Unde tria magna problemata quae non solvuntur applicando aliqua technica derivationis intra idem systema: (1) problema transitus ex una ad aliam ordinationem: *problema fundamenti*; (2) problema de continuituate ex una ad aliam ordinationem: *problema historicitatis*; (3) problema de progressiva multiplicatione et semper maiori systematizatione ordinationum, quae proinde semper remotiores fiunt a fontibus: *problema chasmatis*.

Solutio non obtinetur per deductionem, quia ordinatio successiva semper plus continet quam praecedens. Revera tria problemata non sunt nisi tres aspectus logice distincti unius realis problematis de methodo, quod profundiorem exigit tractationem.

1.6.4 De possibilitate solutionis

Agitur de inveniendo aliquo gradu initiali versus solutionem supradictorum problematum.
(a) Circa problema fundamenti
Solutio maxime pendet a genere in quo ponitur fundamentum. Utrum scilicet ponatur (1) in nominibus, propositionibus, terminis (fundamentum externum), (2) in conceptibus, iudiciis internis menti (fundamentum internum sese exterius manifestans), (3) in ipso intellectu, cum suis habitibus intellectualibus speculativis: scientia, intellectu, sapientia.

Scientia est aliquis habitus, seu dispositio difficile mobilis, unde non idem est ac conceptus et iudicium, nec ac declaratio facta per verba et propositiones. In fieri, scientia est processus ex principiis ad conclusiones. In facto esse, scientia vix distinguitur ab intellectu. Per eam conclusiones in principiis agnoscuntur, effectus in ipsa causa perspiciuntur.

Intellectus est habitus intelligentiae. Consequenter habetur quando posi-

systematic theology and life; for the more theology becomes systematic and the more complicated it gets with questions, answers, and orderings of answers, the farther it strays from the mode of speech of the gospels and of scripture generally, as well as from the urgent practical needs of humanity. Compare, for example, what Vatican I says about God (DB 1782–84, DS 3001–3003, ND 317, 412–13) with the notion of God in the Old and New Testaments. Hence the reaction against systematization, because by the very fact that theology becomes scientific, it goes beyond the horizon of the simple faithful.

There are therefore three major problems that are not solved by applying any technique of derivation within the same system. These are: (1) the problem of the transition from one ordering to another: *the problem of foundation*; (2) the problem of continuity from one ordering to another: *the problem of historicity*; (3) the problem of the increasing multiplication and ever greater systematization of these orderings, which thus become more and more remote from the sources of revelation: *the problem of the chasm*.

Their solution is not through deduction, because each successive ordering always contains more than the preceding one. In fact these three problems are but three logically distinct aspects of one real problem, that of *method*, which calls for a more profound and thorough treatment.

1.6.4 The Possibility of a Solution

Our concern here is to find some initial step towards a solution to the above-mentioned problems.

(a) Concerning the Problem of Foundation

The solution to this problem depends mainly on the category in which the foundation is placed; namely, whether it is placed (1) in nouns, propositions, terms (external foundation), (2) in concepts, judgments within the mind (internal foundation manifested externally), or (3) in the intellect itself with its speculative intellectual habits: science, understanding, and wisdom.

Science is a habit, that is, a relatively stable disposition, and so is not the same as a concept or judgment, nor as a declarative statement made in words and propositions. In its coming-to-be (*in fieri*), science is a process from principles to conclusions. As an accomplished fact (*in facto esse*), science differs little from understanding. Through science conclusions are recognized in their principles, effects are grasped in their cause.

Understanding is the habit of intelligence. It results when, as soon as the

tis terminis perspicitur statim nexus inter illos: sic cognoscuntur principia per se nota. Antecedenter, habetur ex eo quod in sensibilibus intelligentia perspicit aliquid intelligibile praeconceptuale ex quo pariter habentur et termini et nexus. Coram 1, 2, 3, 4 ..., intellectus, unico intelligendi actu, cognoscit infinitatem potentialem seriei numerorum, qui actus est praevius et ad numerationem numerorum et ad ipsos numeros, et ad eorum nexum. Si non devenitur ad hanc perspicientiam intelligibilis in sensibili, tollitur nexus inter intelligentiam et concreta, nexus quidem non necessarius, attamen verus, ut v.gr. habetur in legibus empiricis scientiarum naturalium (e.gr., de motu uniformiter accelerato). Intelligibilitas non necessaria, sed tamen vera, multo latius patet quam intelligibilitas stricte necessaria, ad quam ultimam si tantum attendatur, reici debet quaecumque scientia positiva, sicut facit theologia Scoti quae, cum valere praetendat de omni mundo possibili et non tantum de hoc concrete exsistenti, fere omnia dependere facit a libera Dei voluntate.

Hic habitus intellectus potest augeri, et hoc fit quando semper perfectiori modo intelliguntur termini eorumque nexus; sic crescente intelligentia, diversae exsurgunt seriationes conceptuum et nexuum, diversaeque ordinationes seriationum, etc.

Sapientia (1) est principium ordinis et iudicii de terminis et de principiis primis. Sic v.gr. multipliciter concipitur 'ens': diversimode a Parmenide, a Platone, ab Aristotele, ab Avicenna, a S. Thoma, a Scoto, ab Hegel. Quomodo poterimus iudicium ferre de omnibus his conceptionibus? Non certe secundum formulam iam praesuppositam et determinatam, quia agitur de termino primo qui ab omnibus aliis praesupponitur; sed tantum secundum sapientiam. Unde S. Thomas ait:

> ... cognoscere ... rationem entis et non entis, et totius et partis, et aliorum quae consequuntur ad ens, ex quibus sicut ex terminis constituuntur principia indemonstrabilia, pertinet ad sapientiam: quia ens commune est proprius effectus causae altissimae, scilicet Dei; et ideo sapientia non solum utitur principiis indemonstrabilibus, quorum est intellectus, concludendo ex eis, sicut etiam aliae

terms are stated, it immediately grasps the connection between them; this is how self-evident principles are known; antecedently, it occurs when intelligence grasps in sensible data something intelligible that is preconceptual, from which the terms and connections are likewise obtained. In considering the series 1, 2, 3, 4, ..., the intellect, in a single act of understanding, knows the potential infinity of the series of numbers, which act is prior both to the enumeration of the numbers and to the numbers themselves, and to the connection between them. If it does not arrive at this grasp of the intelligible in the sensible, there is no nexus between intelligence and concrete data, a nexus that is indeed not necessary but is nevertheless true – such as is had in the empirical laws of the natural sciences, in the uniform rate of acceleration, for example. Intelligibility that is not a necessary intelligibility, but still *true*, is much broader than intelligibility that is strictly necessary; if one attends only to the latter kind of intelligibility, all positive science must be denied. This is what the theology of Scotus does which, in professing to be valid for all possible worlds and not only for this concretely existing world, makes virtually everything dependent upon the free will of God.

This habit of understanding can be developed, and this happens when terms and the connections between them are ever more perfectly understood. With this sort of growth in intelligence there arise different serial arrangements of concepts and connections, different orderings of these serial arrangements, and so on.

Wisdom (1) is the principle of order and judgment with regard to terms and first principles. So, for example, 'being' is conceived in many different ways: by Parmenides, Plato, Aristotle, Avicenna, St Thomas, Scotus, Hegel ... How can we render judgment on all these concepts? Certainly not according to some presupposed and predetermined formula, because we are dealing here with a prime term that is presupposed by all others, but only in accordance with wisdom. Thus St Thomas:

> To know ... the meaning of being and non-being, and of a whole and of parts, and of all other things that are consequent upon being, from all of which undemonstrable principles are constituted as from their terms – this belongs to wisdom: because being, *ens commune*, is the proper effect of the highest cause, namely, God. Wisdom therefore not only uses undemonstrable principles, which belong to understanding, by drawing conclusions from them as other sciences do, but also by making judgments about them and arguing against

scientiae; sed etiam iudicando de eis et disputando contra negantes; unde sequitur quod sapientia sit maior virtus quam intellectus.[43]

(2) Est principium iudicii de intelligentia (de intelligibilitate nexus exsistentis inter terminos) utrum sit necessaria an empirica (contingens), et si contingens, utrum sit de facto vera.

(3) Est principium iudicii de ratiociniis, quae saepe sunt multa et ex diversis fontibus. Sic in *Summa contra Gentiles* habentur saepe plura argumenta: ... item ... praeterea ... adhuc ... amplius ... hinc est quod ... ulterius ... Sapientia iudicat utrum unumquodque solum probet, quomodo omnia inter se coalescant, atque utrum simul probabilitatem aut certitudinem attingant.

(4) Est principium iudicii de ordinatione totalitatis virtualis multipliciter ordinabilis; iudicat de fine ordinationis; utrum, quando, quomodo retinenda sit vetus ordinatio, an amplificanda, an nova sit instauranda.

Unde aliquis Deus ex machina est sapientia, principium ordinis et iudicii, de omnibus iudicans.

[a′] Conclusiones de problemate fundamenti

Primum genus fundamenti sufficit tantum quando quaestio est inter eos qui consentiunt de terminis et propositionibus primitivis, et tantum si non quaerunt *cur* consentiant; si non surgunt quaestiones quae intra systema non possunt solvi. Unde primum genus fundamenti est valde limitatum.

Secundum genus fundamenti sufficit tantum quando termini semper eodem modo concipiuntur. Sic usque ad saec. xix fuit de triangulo in geometria, cuius unica conceptio putabatur conceptio Euclidea. At non sufficit quando aliquis terminus multipliciter concipiatur. Ideo si ponatur problema de iudicandis diversis conceptionibus de ente quae in historia philosophiae habentur, hoc problema non poterit solvi intra hoc genus fundamenti. Nam nullum adest medium comparationis.

Hoc secundum fundamentum non sufficit quando ponuntur quaestio-

those who say otherwise. It follows, then, that wisdom is a higher virtue than understanding.[43]

Wisdom (2) is the principle of judgment about one's understanding (about the intelligibility of the connection between the terms), whether it is a necessary or empirical (contingent) intelligibility, and, if contingent, whether or not it is in fact true.

Wisdom (3) is the principle of judgment about processes of reasoning, which are often numerous and derived from various sources. Thus, in the *Summa contra Gentiles* many arguments are presented: '... likewise ... besides ... again ... furthermore ... hence ... moreover ...' Wisdom judges whether each one taken by itself proves, how all hang together, and whether all of them together arrive at probability or at certitude.

Wisdom (4) is the principle of judgment about the ordering of a virtual totality that can be ordered in many ways. It judges the purpose of the ordering; whether, when, and how the former ordering is to be kept, or to be extended, or whether a new ordering is to be introduced.

Thus, wisdom is a *deus ex machina*, a principle of order and of judgment, issuing judgments about everything.

[a'] We may indicate some conclusions about the problem of foundation.

The first type of foundation (external foundation) is sufficient when the question arises between those who agree on primitive terms and propositions, but only if they are not trying to find out *why* they agree, and if questions do not arise that cannot be solved within the system. Thus this first type of foundation is quite limited.

The second type of foundation (internal foundation manifested externally) suffices only when the terms are always conceived in the same way. Up to the nineteenth century this was the case in geometry regarding the triangle, whose only way of being conceived was thought to be the Euclidean. But this type does not suffice when any term is conceived in several ways. If therefore there arises the problem of judging the various conceptions of being that are found in the history of philosophy, this problem will not be able to be solved within this type of foundation. For there is no medium of comparison.

This second foundation does not suffice when questions arise concern-

43 Thomas Aquinas, *Summa theologiae*, 2-2, q. 66, a. 5, ad 4m.

nes respicientes nexum intelligibilem de iis quae sunt tantum empirice vera; quando iudicari debet de ipsis postulatis (v.gr., principium Euclideum quod duae rectae parallelae numquam inter se secantur est evidens nisi attendatur quod phantasma concretum extenditur ita ut fiat indefinite maius, extensione tamen facta – circulo vitioso – secundum principia Euclidea).

Sic in theologia quae apud S. Thomam reguntur ab argumentis convenientiae, apud Scotum reguntur a voluntarismo divino. In argumentis Thomisticis convenientiae agitur de intelligibilitate quando nexus inter terminos non est necessarius, sed est de facto verus; si contra haec argumenta dicatur continuo 'non probant,' ruit omnis scientia non necessaria, sive theologica, sive empirica … unde quaestio est revera de conceptione et notione scientiae.

Idem habetur in problemate de relatione inter naturam et gratiam: si nonnisi de nexu necessario sumus contenti, tunc: aut nexus inter naturam et gratiam adest, et tunc natura et gratia confunduntur et ruit gratuitas supernaturalis; aut non adest, et tunc natura et gratia sunt prorsus separatae et supernaturale modo pure extrinsecistico concipitur. Quaestio est potius methodologica: hic agitur de intelligibilitate convenientiae obtinenda, non necessitatis.

Omnis intelligibilitas historica est vera de facto (intelligibilitates necessariae sunt abstractae), sed conveniens. Sic, quando multa congeruntur ratiocinia et argumenta, logica quadam stricta possemus dicere: aut unum argumentum ex se vere probat aut non. Si probat, inutile est addere aliud argumentum; si non probat, inutile est illud addere argumento sequenti. Tamen, de facto, ex multis argumentis saepe efficitur aliquid unum, de quo iudicium aliquod mechanicum et automaticum nequit haberi. Unde secundum genus fundamenti non sufficit quando quaestiones excedunt systema, aut si solvit has quaestiones, hoc facit systema derelinquens.

Tertium genus fundamenti, seu intellectus, est principium terminorum et nexuum, et sufficit ubi deficiunt primum et secundum genus. Termini et nexus sunt principia verborum et propositionum: unde progrediente sapientia perficiuntur ordinationes. Intelligentia est de concretis, intelligibile perspicit in sensibilibus; intelligentia media est inter conceptus abstractos et data concreta, capax est tractandi utraque. Intelligentia est capax iudicandi de concretis per applicationem conceptionum abstractarum ad ipsa: sic possum statuere Petrum esse mortalem, ex eo quod est homo;

ing the intelligible nexus of those realities that are only empirically true, when a judgment has to be made about the postulates themselves. For example, the Euclidean principle that two straight parallel lines never meet is evident unless one notices that the concrete phantasm is given an ever greater extension – this extension, however, being made by a vicious circle, according to Euclidean principles.

Thus, in theology those judgments that for Aquinas are based upon arguments of fittingness, for Scotus are based upon divine voluntarism. In Thomist arguments from fittingness, there is intelligibility when the nexus between the terms is not necessary but is de facto true. If such arguments are immediately met with the objection 'They do not prove,' then all non-necessary science, whether theological or empirical, is undermined. Hence, the question really comes down to the concept and notion of science.

It is the same with the problem about the relation between nature and grace. If we are content only with a necessary nexus, then: either there is a nexus between nature and grace, and then nature and grace are intermingled and the gratuitousness of the supernatural vanishes; or there is no nexus, and then nature and grace are totally separate and the supernatural is conceived in a purely extrinsicist manner. The question is rather one of methodology: here it is a matter of obtaining the intelligibility of fittingness, not that of necessity.

All historical intelligibility is true de facto (necessary intelligibilities being abstract), but fitting. Thus, where there is an accumulation of many reasonings and arguments, in strict logic we could say: either one argument by itself truly proves, or it does not; if it does, there is no point in adding another argument; and if it does not prove, it is pointless to add it to the next argument. Nevertheless, in actual fact a multiplicity of arguments do often form one, about which no mechanical and automatic judgment can be made. Therefore, this second type of foundation is insufficient when questions go beyond a system, or if it does solve these questions, the system becomes outmoded.

The third type of foundation, understanding, is the principle of terms and nexuses, and it is sufficient when the first and second types are deficient. Terms and nexuses are principles of words and propositions; hence, with an advance in wisdom there will be a corresponding improvement in the orderings. Intelligence deals with what is concrete: it grasps the intelligible in sensible data. It mediates between abstract concepts and concrete data, and is capable of dealing with both. It is capable of making judgments about concrete data by applying abstract concepts to them: thus I can state

at intelligentia capax est stabiliendi etiam relationes circa concreta qua concreta.

Tamen tertium genus fundamenti habet duas difficultates. Nam sapientia revera sufficeret si homines essent sapientes. E contra, 'numerus stultorum infinitus.'[44] Ergo estne possibile hoc tertium genus fundamenti?

Non erit sine utilitate attendere ad difficultates quae possunt obici contra fundamentum positum in sapientia. Quod faciemus secundum technicam quaestionis quae invenitur apud S. Thomam.

[b'] Obiectiones contra fundamentum positum in sapientia

(1) Nos non nascimur sapientes, sed noster intellectus est quaedam 'tabula rasa,' unde habitu sapientiae privatus; neque naturali necessitate fimus sapientes, nam si ita esset, sapientia inveniretur vel in omnibus vel in pluribus, dum in paucioribus reperitur; immo ineptum videtur et nostrum consilium et nostra voluntas ad progrediendum versus sapientiam, nam si iam sapientes sumus haec sunt inutilia, si non sumus sapientes incapaces erimus sapienter utendi his mediis.

(2) Ex fundamento requiritur quod caeterum opus totum supra illud fundetur. At sapientia non praeiacet, quod patet ex prima obiectione, necnon ex ipsa analysi sapientiae et ordinis. Nam sapientia, quae omnia ordinat et iudicat, non fundatur in totali ignorantia omnium vel maioris partis hominum, sed praesupponit scientiam hominum. Est ergo non principium sed ultimus fructus qui post acquisitionem scientiae obtinetur. Sapientia, quae omnia ordinet, videtur potius tectum quam fundamentum aedificii.

(3) Similiter inutilis videtur recursus ad magni nominis auctoritates, nam, si non sumus sapientes nos ipsi, nec fimus sapientes naturali necessitate, et si sapientia non praehabetur, nec sufficiunt ad eam obtinendam nostrum consilium neque nostra voluntas, neque auctoritas aliorum nos reddet sapientes. Nam si sapientes fuissemus, superflueret auctoritas, si autem insipientes sumus, consilium aliorum interpretabimur secundum nostram insipientiam; quod confirmatur ex historico exemplo discipulorum magnorum philosophorum.

(4) Inutilis videtur etiam recursus ad hoc, quod etsi sapientes non simus, tamen ad sapientiam tendimus quia eam diligimus (quia 'philo-sophi' dicimur); nam si sapientes iam sumus, sapientia non indigemus, si autem

that Peter is mortal from the fact that he is a human being. But intelligence is also capable of establishing the relations of concrete realities as concrete.

There are two difficulties with this third type of foundation. Wisdom would really be sufficient if humans were truly wise. But alas, *numerus stultorum infinitus*.[44] Is this third type of foundation possible then?

It will be helpful to consider difficulties that can be raised concerning the foundation that is based on wisdom. We shall do this following the technique of the question as found in the works of St Thomas.

[b′] Objections against the foundation placed in wisdom

(1) We are not born wise, but rather our intellect is a *tabula rasa*, a clean slate, hence bereft of the habit of wisdom; nor are we under any natural necessity to become wise, for if that were the case, wisdom would be found in everyone or at least in many, whereas it is found in very few. In fact our decision and our determination to advance towards wisdom would seem rather pointless, for if we are already wise these means are otiose, and if we are unwise we shall be incapable of using them wisely.

(2) A foundation is that upon which all the rest of the work is built. But wisdom is not something already given, as is clear from the first objection, as well as from the analysis of wisdom and order. For wisdom, which orders and judges all things, is not founded upon the total ignorance of all or of most people, but presupposes the knowledge that people have. It is therefore not the beginning but the final flowering resulting from the acquisition of knowledge. Wisdom, then, seems to be the roof rather than the foundation of the edifice.

(3) It seems to be likewise useless to appeal to weighty authorities; for if we ourselves are not wise and do not become wise by some necessity of nature, and if wisdom is not a prior 'given,' neither our intention nor our willing will suffice to acquire it for us, nor will the authority of others render us wise. For if we were wise, authorities would not be needed, and if we are unwise, the advice of others will be interpreted in accordance with our lack of wisdom – a fact that is confirmed historically in the case of disciples of the great philosophers.

(4) It also seems useless to appeal to this argument, namely, that although we are not wise, yet we do have an inclination towards wisdom since we love it (after all, we are called philo-sophers, 'lovers of wisdom'); for if we are already wise, we do not need wisdom, and if we are not, what we love and

44 See below, p. 623, note 46.

non sumus, forsan falsam speciem sapientiae diligimus vel prosequimur, quae mala tendentia pergeret in corruptionem totius aedificii.

(5) Qui sapientiam invocat tamquam speciem pulchri nominis invocat, et de facto introducit relativismum; si fundamentum in sapientia ponitur, unusquisque suas personales opiniones nomine vestiet sapientiae, unde nonnisi multiplex habebitur relativismus, qui ab Ecclesia damnatur. Melius est confiteri adesse quaedam problemata insolubilia, atque contentos esse humili ignorantia quae a Scriptura commendatur: 'Altiora te ne quaesieris' (Ecclus. 3.22) vel ad orationem recurrere ('Domine, non superbit cor meum ... nec prosequor res grandes aut altiores meipso' (Ps 130 [131].1).

[c'] Gressus initialis solutionis problematis fundamenti

Problema quod ab obiectionibus proponitur est verum, non fictum, neque paucis potest absolvi plena solutio; unde tantum aliqua indicatio initialis dabitur, neque statim difficultates ulteriores solvemus. Si enim solutio esset facilis, non adesset problema methodi.

(1) Notemus modum quo augetur [scientia][45] humana. Ipsius augmentum non fit mera additione et ab extrinseco; e contra, illud quod paulatim scitur non erat antea totaliter ignotum, et ideo augmentum fit potius dividendo illud totum quod iam praeiacet. Id enim quod prius cadit in apprehensione intellectus est ens; ens autem est in se continens omnia; quae progressive paulatim semper magis cognoscuntur intra ens iacent, nam extra ens nihil est. Unde progressus intellectus movetur ab iis quae intus iam quodammodo cognita erant ad ea explicitius cognoscenda.

(2) Haec divisio entis, per quam progredimur ad sapientiam, semper completa esse potest, si fundetur in principio contradictionis. Sic, per dichotomiam, obtinetur arbor porphyriana, quae praebet completam divisionem, utique adhuc valde schematicam et abstractam, sed semper permanentem et talem ex qua possit fieri aliqua iudicia erunt possibilia.

(3) Augmentum sapientiae ulterius habebitur ex eo quod divisiones semper plures et aptiores fient. Cur enim puer septennis communiter aetatem rationalem attigisse censetur? Quia capax censetur divisionum intra ens sufficientium ut quaedam iudicia possit facere, distinguendo v.gr. inter

are pursuing is perhaps a false sort of wisdom, and this perverse inclination would lead to the undermining of the whole edifice.

(5) To appeal to wisdom as something beautiful and noble is in fact to leave the door open to relativism. For if the foundation is in wisdom, people will clothe their own personal opinions in the garb of wisdom, and this will lead to manifold relativism, which the church condemns. Better by far to admit that there are insoluble problems, and to be content with that humble ignorance recommended by scripture: 'Seek not the things that are too high for thee' (Sirach 3.22); or take to prayer: 'Lord, my heart is not proud ... nor do I occupy myself with things too weighty and too lofty for me' (Psalm 130 [131].1).

[c'] First step towards solving the problem of the foundation

The problem raised by these objections is a real, not an imaginary, problem, nor can it be fully solved in a few words. For this reason we shall give some initial indication of a solution, and we will not immediately solve further difficulties. If a solution were easy, there would be no problem about method.

(1) Notice how human knowledge grows.[45] It does not increase by purely adventitious accretions; on the contrary, that which gradually comes to be known was not totally unknown before, and therefore the increase in knowledge occurs rather by dividing that prior whole. For that which is first apprehended by the mind is being; but being contains all reality in itself; everything that progressively and by degrees becomes better known falls within being, since outside of being there is nothing. Hence, as it progresses, the mind moves from what are known in some way as within being towards a more explicit knowledge of these.

(2) This division of being by which we progress towards wisdom can always be a complete division, since it is based upon the principle of contradiction. Thus, through dichotomy we obtain the Porphyrian tree, which furnishes a complete division, still quite schematic and abstract but nonetheless permanent and such that upon it some judgments can be founded.

(3) Growth in wisdom will continue as more numerous and more apt divisions are made. Why, after all, are seven-year-olds generally regarded as having reached the age of reason? Simply because they are judged capable of a sufficient number of divisions within the field of being to enable them

---

45 [The Latin sentence has no noun. But see below, p. 626, where, in notes clearly related to the present text and context, Lonergan writes, 'Primum responsi elementum respicit modum quo augetur *scientia* humana.']

spontaneum et liberum, malum et bonum, voluntarium et involuntarium, ... quin tamen capax censeatur omnia iudicia possibilia faciendi, nec v.gr. statum eligendi. Immo Aristoteles adulescentes et iuvenes ineptos iudicavit scientiae ethicae. Unde in generali possumus dicere quod sapientia non stat in indivisibili, ita ut habeatur aut non habeatur simpliciter, sed potius semper augetur illa quae antea, aliquo gradu, habebatur. Sapientia augetur quatenus obtinentur pleniores ordinationes per omnes divisiones entis. Quando consulimus peritum in aliqua materia, hoc facimus fidentes sapientiae illius qui omnes divisiones entis in illa materia perfecit. Unde sapientia potest haberi plus vel minus, nam incipit a totalitate quadam, et progreditur per divisiones. Unde iam a parva aetate homo aliquomodo sapiens esse potest, atque, cum fit adultus, ad veram peritiam in aliqua arte et disciplina pervenire. Solus Deus est simpliciter sapiens, in sua sapientia omnes ordines complectens possibilium, atque perfectissime atque concrete cognoscens unumquodque possibile.

(4) Homo, hac in vita, talem sapientiam divinam participat tantum progrediendo ad sapientiam, et secundum quod habet aliquam mensuram sapientiae, bene cognoscit etiam limites suae sapientiae, unde de iis quae scit iudicat et non de aliis multis quae nescit, in quo est humilitas. Revera, 'scientia inflat' (1 Cor 8.1) non quatenus aliqua facit scire, sed quatenus facit ut, quaedam tantum cognoscentes, de omnibus iudicare praetendamus. At, ex alia parte, quando etiam nonnisi hoc unum sciam, me nihil scire, tamen aliquid scio. Unde bene distinguenda est sapientia absoluta (solius Dei), sapientia circa iudicia generalia, sapientia circa iudicia determinata ...

(5) Vidimus multas esse conceptiones entis ex qua multiplicitate ipsum fundamentum sapientiae vacillare videtur, ex eo quod multa genera sapientiae ex diversis conceptionibus deriventur. Attamen distinguere debemus notionem entis naturalem omnibus hominibus a notione entis reflexa, analytica, prout diversimode formulatur a diversis philosophis et theologis, unde diversae oriuntur philosophiae et theologiae.[46] Omnibus enim hom-

to make certain judgments, distinguishing, for example, between the spontaneous and the freely willed, between good and evil, between the voluntary and the involuntary, ... without, however, being considered capable of making all possible judgments, nor of choosing, for instance, a state of life. Aristotle, in fact, considered adolescents and young men unfit for learning ethics. Hence, we may say in general that wisdom is not an all-or-nothing proposition, so that either you simply have it or you do not, but rather, whatever degree it had at a certain point, it still continues ever to increase. Wisdom grows as fuller orderings are made through all the divisions of being. When we consult an expert in some field we do so trusting in the wisdom of one who has made all the divisions of being within that field. So wisdom can be had to a greater or lesser degree, for it begins with a certain totality or whole and progresses through divisions. Hence, from a very early age a person can be wise to some extent and when he or she has grown up can attain true expertise in some art or field of knowledge. God alone is simply wise without qualification, embracing in his wisdom all the orders of possible reality and knowing perfectly and in a concrete way each and every possible entity.

(4) In this present life, we share in this divine wisdom only by making progress in wisdom and, according to the measure of wisdom we have acquired, know very well the limits of our wisdom, so that we make judgments about what we know and not about the many things we do not know – and therein lies humility. In truth, 'knowledge puffs up' (1 Corinthians 8.1), not because by it we know certain things, but when our limited knowledge leads us to presume to make judgments about everything. But on the other hand, when I know only one thing, namely, that I know nothing, at least I do know something. And so we have to distinguish between absolute wisdom, which is God's alone, wisdom regarding general judgments, and wisdom regarding specific judgments ...

(5) We have seen that there are many conceptions about being, and because of this multitude the very foundation of wisdom would seem to be shaky, since many different kinds of wisdom are derived from various conceptions of being. But we must distinguish here between the notion of being natural to all and the reflex analytic notion of being as variously formulated by different philosophers and theologians, which gives rise to different philosophies and theologies.[46] We all have the same human na-

---

46 [See *Insight* 388–98.]

inibus eadem humana inest natura. Secundum S.Thomam nos naturaliter cognoscimus ens et ea quae per se sunt entis.[47]

(6) De hac naturali notione entis inquirimus utrum et qualis sit.

Si adest, est implicita et eadem sive in Johanne, sive in Paulo, sive in nobis, unde non habetur diversum genus fundamenti in Scriptura et in theologia scholastica, nec quaestiones scholasticae sunt totaliter extraneae Sacrae Scripturae.

Si non adest, nulla communis notio entis implicita est in cogitationibus auctorum sacrorum, unde legitime dubitatur de valore theologiae scholasticae, necnon definitionum Conciliorum, et recte Ariani recusabant loqui de 'ousia' et de 'homoousio.' E contra, S. Epiphanius,[48] ad demonstrandam legitimitatem introducendi notionem entis in definitionibus ecclesiasticis, conabatur illam invenire in Sacra Scriptura saltem in Ex 3.14 ('Ego sum qui sum') et in Io. 1.1 ('In principio erat Verbum'). Eratne haec introductio metaphysicae in Scriptura aliqua aberratio a mente biblica? Eratne quaedam Hellenizatio Semiticae mentis religiosae? Responsio fluit ex veritate assertionis S. Thomae quod nos naturaliter cognoscimus ens.

(7) Notio scientiae sese evolvit. Quia hodie plures sunt scientiae atque longe magis evolutae quam in medio aevo, atque exempla longe clariora praebentes, notio scientiae nobis magis quam mediaevalibus atque Graecis saec. IV-III innotescit. Apud Aristotelem diversa invenimus elementa ad scientiam pertinentia, v.gr. quod scientia est de necessariis et certissimis. At hodie ne mathematici quidem admittunt certitudines necessarias, unde multo minus periti in scientiis naturalibus. Unde fit obscuritas, notio Aristotelica scientiae evoluta est, quaedam clarificanda sunt in ea circa necessitatem et certitudinem, dum alia elementa in ea contenta etiam hodie verificantur.

(8) Nec tantum notio scientiae, sed ipsae scientiae evolvuntur. Per dichotomias dividitur ens, at dichotomiae non pendent tantum a principio

ture, and according to St Thomas we naturally know being and all that per se belong to being.[47]

(6) Does this natural notion of being exist, and if so, what is it like?

If it does exist, it is implicit and the same whether in John or in Paul or in us; hence, scripture and Scholastic theology do not have different kinds of foundations, and Scholastic questions are not totally foreign to sacred scripture.

If it does not exist, there is no common notion of being implicit in the thinking of the sacred writers, and so one may legitimately doubt the validity of Scholastic theology as well as conciliar definitions, and the Arians were right in refusing to speak about *ousia* and *homoousion*. Contrariwise, St Epiphanius,[48] in order to demonstrate the legitimacy of introducing the notion of being into ecclesiastical definitions, tried to find it in the Bible, at least in Exodus 3.14, 'I am who am,' and in John 1.1, 'In the beginning was the Word.' Was that introduction of metaphysics into scripture a deviation from the biblical mentality? Was it a hellenization of Semitic religious thought? The answer is to be found in the truth of St Thomas's assertion that we naturally know being.

(7) The notion of science is evolving. Because there are today many more and much more greatly developed sciences than there were in the Middle Ages, thus providing us with much clearer examples, the notion of science is more familiar to us than it was to the medievals or to the Greeks of the fourth and third centuries BC. We find in Aristotle various elements pertaining to science, such as, for example, that science is about the necessary and the certain. But today not even mathematicians admit necessary certitudes, and much less do those engaged in the natural sciences. As a result, there is a certain obscurity here; the Aristotelian notion of science has evolved, with certain features in it regarding necessity and certitude needing further clarification, while other elements in it are valid even today.

(8) Not only the notion of science, but sciences themselves, are evolving. Being is divided by dichotomy, but dichotomies do not depend solely on

---

47 [For Lonergan's earlier discussion of the natural knowledge of being in Aquinas, see *Verbum: Word and Idea in Aquinas*, vol. 2 in Collected Works of Bernard Lonergan, ed. Frederick E. Crowe and Robert M. Doran (Toronto: University of Toronto Press, 1997) 57–59, 69–70, 96–98.]

48 Epiphanius, *Adversus haereses*, lib. 3, tome 1, 73 'Adversus Semiarianos,' with the letter of the pseudo-synod of Ancyra (AD 358), MG 42, 399–474. [See below, p. 133.]

contradictionis, unde arbor porphyriana non est unica scientia. Dichotomiae pendent etiam a materia circa quam applicatur principium contradictionis, unde non amplius valent quam notiones quae fundant divisiones.
Sic divisio inter materiale et non-materiale pendet ab evolutione notionis
materiae, illa inter vivens et non-vivens pendet ab evolutione notionis vitae.
Unde quaestio exsurgit quid in evolutione scientiae maneat stabile et im-
mutatum.

His paucis habitis ad modum initialis solutionis, possumus respondere
ad obiectiones.

[d′] Solutio obiectionum

Ad primam: Quatenus inest omnibus naturalis notio entis et naturale desiderium cognoscendi et naturalis motus in sapientiam, habetur etiam gradus
initialis sapientiae sufficiens ad progrediendum. Obiectio enim implicite
admittit sapientiam esse aut perfectissimam aut nullam (= insipientiam).
Nos autem ponimus gradus in sapientia, et secundum gradum propriae
sapientiae homo iudicat de iis quae novit, nec iudicat de iis quae ignorat.

Ad secundam: Fundamentum utique praeiacere debet, at secundum modum fundamenti. Si fundamentum ponatur in propositionibus et iudiciis,
praeiacere debent propositiones et iudicia, si ponatur in intellectu, praeiacere debet intellectus. Et si ponatur in sapientia, praerequiritur utique
aliquis initialis gradus sapientiae ex quo progredi possimus. Hoc etiam
comprobatur. Quando enim invenimur in initio alicuius scientiae adest periodus obscuritatis, postea paulatim fit aliqua lux atque deinde fimus magistri in illa scientia. Hoc ostendit sapientiam evolvi.

Ad tertiam: Eadem respondenda contra obiectionem de inutilitate auctoritatis aliorum. Certe nullum datur remedium contra totalem insipientiam. Tamen hoc non tollit utilitatem auctoritatum. Non intelligitur mens
S.Thomae neque Aristotelis neque Augustini bene cognoscendo litteras
Graecas aut Latinas neque eorum opera, editiones, collectiones ... perle-
gendo, sed penetrando internam evolutionem eorum cogitationis, ita ut
perveniatur ad illorum sapientiam. Maximum adiutorium in legendis his
auctoribus habetur non tantum quatenus in illis invenimus ea in quibus
iam consentimus (periculum ne velimus videre nostras sententias in omnibus quae legimus), at potius quatenus invenimus quaedam quae non intelligimus (nam isti auctores superant normam communem intelligentiae),

the principle of contradiction, so that the Porphyrian tree is not the only science. Dichotomies depend also on the subject matter to which the principle of contradiction is applied, so that they are only as valid as the notions upon which the divisions are founded. Thus, the division between material and non-material depends on the development of the notion of matter, and the division between living and non-living depends on the development of the notion of life. Hence, there arises the question of what is stable and unchanging in the development of science.

With these brief observations by way of an initial solution, we can answer the objections stated above.

[d'] Solutions to the objections

To objection 1: Inasmuch as there is in all of us a natural notion of being and a natural desire to know and a natural drive towards wisdom, there is also in us an initial degree of wisdom sufficient to start us on our way. The objection implies that wisdom is either absolutely perfect or non-existent. But we put degrees in wisdom, and according to the measure of the wisdom one has, one makes judgments about what one knows and refrains from making them about things one does not know.

To objection 2: Certainly, a foundation has to be laid first, but in accord with the kind of foundation it is. If the foundation is located in propositions and judgments, then propositions and judgments must come first, and if it is located in understanding, then understanding must come first. And if it is located in wisdom, an initial degree of wisdom is indeed a prerequisite for further progress. We have confirmation of this in the fact that when we are beginners in some field of knowledge we go through a certain period of confusion, but after that we gradually get some light and eventually achieve mastery in that field. This shows clearly that wisdom develops.

To objection 3: The same answer can be given to the objection about the uselessness of the authority of others. There is certainly no remedy for a total lack of wisdom. Yet this does not mean that authorities are useless. The mind of St Thomas or Aristotle or Augustine is not understood simply by being well versed in Greek and Latin literature or by reading through the various editions and collections of their works, but by entering into the internal development of their thought and so arriving at their wisdom. What is most helpful in reading these authors is not so much finding in them ideas that we agree with (there is a danger of wanting to find our own ideas in everything we read), but rather finding things that we do not understand (those authors are, after all, somewhat above the general level

atque per investigationes ad difficultates superandas, discimus et progredimur in nostra sapientia.

Sic v.gr., per saecula locuti sunt de mente S. Thomae quasi S. Thomas legisset Bañez vel Molina. Revera mens S. Thomae, variis saeculis prior, est diversa. Opportunitas profectus in lectione auctorum habetur ex serie rerum in quibus auctor differt a nobis. Si colligimus loca in quibus S. Thomas pluries idem eodem modo repetit, parum proficimus, sed si idem dicit diverso modo, utilis est investigare materiam connexam cum his assertionibus: sic obtinetur quoddam rete referentiarum, atque talis vastitas visionis multum aufert libertatem errandi. Coram auctoritatibus attitudo initialis est fides, quae tamen componitur cum nostro initiali gradu sapientiae. Deinde addiscimus ulterius.

Ad quartam: Perfectissima sapientia tantum in Deo invenitur. Amor et desiderium sapientiae potest esse initium sapientiae quatenus, supposito gradu initiali, disponit hominem ad progressus ulteriores.

Ad quintam: Relativismus non consistit in affirmando quod homines carent divina sapientia. Praesupponit obiectio semper eandem dichotomiam inter sapientiam divinam et nullam sapientiam. Tunc homo aut est Deus aut totaliter insipiens. Verus relativismus excludit omnem certitudinem; ab illo differt gradualis sapientia quae de his quae bene novit iudicat atque certitudinem habet, at relate ad alia est sobria, modesta, humilis.

Difficultas nostri problematis est in eo quod problema de fundamento ponitur quando nos iam aliquid cognoscimus. Quaestio de possibilitate alicuius cognitionis semper valde difficilior est quam de actualitate illius cognitionis. Unde quaestio de possibilitate non potest esse prima quaestio. Ex factis ad posse est procedendum. Unde ante omnia debemus aliquid cognoscere, deinde cognoscere nos cognoscere, deinde quaerere de possibilitate nostra cognitionis. Unde quaestio de possibilitate est ultima et maxime fundamentalis.

(b) Circa problema chasmatis

Chasma considerabatur praesertim inter theologiam prout a scientia systematica excolitur et prout a simplicibus fidelibus cognoscitur. Nunc autem simplicibus fidelibus, quatenus sunt tales, competit simplex fides. Tamen

of intelligence); and by further investigation and inquiry in order to clear up our difficulties, we ourselves learn and make progress in wisdom.

A good illustration of this is that for centuries theologians spoke of the thought of St Thomas as if he had read Bañez or Molina. But in fact the thought of St Thomas, several centuries before them, was different. In reading a particular author, a series of points on which that author differs from us affords an opportunity for our own growth in understanding. If we make a collection of the various texts in which St Thomas repeats the same idea in the same way, we do not get very far ahead; but if he says the same thing in a different way, it will prove useful to investigate the subject matter with which those statements are connected. In this way one acquires a network of references, and such an extended field of vision greatly reduces the possibility of error. Our initial attitude towards authorities is one of belief, which, however, is combined with our initial degree of wisdom. From there we go on to increase our knowledge.

To objection 4: Absolutely perfect wisdom is found in God alone. A love of and desire for wisdom can be the beginning of wisdom inasmuch as, presupposing an initial degree of wisdom, they help a person make further progress.

To objection 5: Relativism does not consist in asserting that humans lack divine wisdom. This objection presupposes the same dichotomy between perfect wisdom and no wisdom at all. At that rate, we are either God or totally unwise. True relativism excludes all certitude; quite different from it is that graduated wisdom that makes judgments and has certitude in those areas in which it has competence, while in respect to other areas it conducts itself soberly, modestly, humbly.

The difficulty in this problem of foundation lies in the fact that it arises after we have already acquired some knowledge. The question of the possibility of some knowledge is always a much more difficult question that that of the actual possession of that knowledge. The question of possibility, therefore, cannot be the first question. We must proceed from what is to what is possible. Thus, the first thing we must do is to know, then to know that we know, and only then to inquire into our possibility of knowing. So, the question of possibility is last and the most fundamental.

(b) Concerning the Problem of the Chasm

The chasm used to be thought of mainly as the gap between theology as a systematically elaborated science and theology as known by the simple faithful. Now, however, there corresponds to the simple faithful, as such, simple faith. Nevertheless, even a believer is a human being and as such is naturally

etiam fidelis est homo, naturaliter intellectu praeditus atque quaestiones continuo ponens, non theologicas sed suas.

Quatenus simplex fidelis est homo intelligens, ei competit aliqua intelligentia fidei. 'Crede ut intelligas' differt certe a 'crede ut demonstres,' tamen etiam pro simplicibus fidelibus intelligentia fidei etsi analogica et imperfecta est revera fructuosissima (DB 1796). Novo modo nostris temporibus ponitur problema de intelligentia fidei apud fideles; nam datur hodie et educatio universalis obligatoria, et producitur instructio scholaris, et literatura scientifico-divulgativa multiplicatur ... Multi, etsi non omnes, de quadam cultura semper universaliori delectantur, atque apud plurimos oriuntur quaestiones et difficultates etiam religionem spectantes. Unde si volumus vitam fidelium non esse tantum materialem, biologicam, psychologicam debemus eis posse tradere etiam aliquam intelligentiam fidei. Ad hoc autem duo requiruntur:

– *ut theologi ipsi occupentur de fidei intelligentia.* De facto iam per tria ultima saecula theologi occupantur circa deductiones ex articulis fidei, practice omittentes illum punctum inflexionis ex quo reditus fit ad ipsam revelationem evangelicam ut intelligentiae fidei fructus colligatur.[49] Parum agnoscitur inter theologos exsistentia illorum duorum motuum de quibus supra sumus locuti, scilicet ex revelata ad revelabilia et ex revelabilibus ad revelata. Nec theologi poterunt fidelibus intelligentiam fidei communicare nisi eam habeant.

– *eliminari debet chasma inter intellectum et sensum.* Si continuo supponitur et repetitur – ut fit – quod intellectus versatur tantum circa universalia et necessaria, si praetermittitur quod intellectus intelligit in sensibilibus, si ignoratur cooperatio mutua intellectus et sensus in efformanda unica conscientia humana, hoc chasma permanebit. Notio talis intellectus, tamquam oculi cuiusdam interioris qui universalia contemplatur, debet et corrigi et compleri. Attendendum est ad id quod intellectus intrat in vitam sensitivam

endowed with an intellect and continually asks questions, not theological questions but his own.

Inasmuch as a simple believer is an intelligent human being, he or she has some understanding of the faith. 'Believe in order to understand' is certainly not the same as 'believe in order to prove,' yet even a believer's understanding of the faith, however analogical and imperfect, is truly fruitful (DB 1796, DS 3016, ND 132). In today's world the problem of the understanding of the faith among the faithful is posed in a new way. Today we have universal obligatory education, schooling is prolonged, and the *haute vulgarisation* of scientific knowledge is everywhere abundant. Many people, though not all, enjoy a culture that is ever more widespread, and in the minds of many there arise questions and difficulties even about religion. If therefore we want the faithful to live their lives not merely on the material, biological, and psychological levels, we shall have to give them some understanding of their faith. For this, two things are required.

The first requirement is *that theologians concern themselves with an understanding of the faith.* The fact of the matter is that for the last three centuries theologians have been taken up with making deductions from the articles of faith, ignoring in practice that pivotal point from which one returns to the sources of revelation in order to reap the fruit of an understanding of the faith.[49] The existence of the two movements that we referred to above, that is, the movement from what is revealed to the revealable and from the revealable to the revealed, is scarcely recognized by theologians. And theologians will not be able to communicate to the faithful an understanding of the faith unless they have that understanding themselves.

The second requirement is *that the chasm or split between intellect and the senses be bridged.* If – as happens – the supposition is continually repeated that the intellect has to do only with what is universal and necessary, if the fact that the intellect understands in sensible data is overlooked, if the mutual cooperation between intellect and the senses in developing a single unified human consciousness is ignored, this split will remain. The idea that the mind is like some sort of inner eye that contemplates universals has

---

49 For an example of the approach recommended, see Bernard Lonergan, *Divinarum personarum conceptionem analogicam* (Rome: Gregorian University Press, 1957). [This work was revised and published in 1964 as *De Deo Trino: Pars systematica*, which is available now in English as *The Triune God: Systematics* (see above, note 22). Appendix 4 presents material from *Divinarum personarum* that was omitted from *De Deo Trino*.]

et sensus in vitam intellectivam, ut theologus possit modo populari praebere et ea quae sunt credenda et eorum intelligentiam hominibus ordinariis.

Unde chasma impletur non reiciendo nec mutando intelligentiam fidei sed eam transferendo ex uno modo cogitationis ad alium modum, qui diversi modi cogitationis debent proinde a theologo cognosci, necnon eorum mutuae relationes.

Circa diversos hos modos cogitationis multae investigationes factae sunt nostris temporibus in omnibus campis scientiae humanae.

Sic, inde a saeculo XIX, Schelling studuit philosophiae mythologiae, Kierkegaard exsistentialismo, Nietzsche philosophiae artis. Nostris autem diebus studia multo exactiora facta sunt in multis disciplinis.

Aspectus philosophici problematis tractati sunt a E. Cassirer (neo-Kantiano scholae Marburgensis) in *Philosophie der symbolischen Formen,* I Teil (Die Sprache), Berlin, 1923; II Teil (Das Mythe), ibid. 1925; III Teil (Phänomenologie der Erkenntnis), ibid. 1929.[50] Quod Kant fecerat relate ad mechanicam newtonianam, Cassirer conatus est facere relate ad mentalitatem mythicam (Denkformen, Anschaungsformen, Lebensformen).[51]

Theoriam artis, sequens Cassirer, fecit S.K. Langer, *Feeling and Form, A Theory of Art Developed from* Philosophy in a New Key, New York, 1953.[52]

Aspectibus psychologicis studuit tota schola psychologiae profundae post Freud et Jung, quorum primus investigavit praesertim somnia et phaenomena neurotica, secundus connexionem inter scientiam et philosophiam et mythos antiquos conscientiae collectivae, etc.

to be both corrected and complemented. Theologians must pay attention to the role that the intellect plays in the life of the senses and the role of the senses in the life of the intellect, if they are to be able to present in a popular way to ordinary people both the truths of faith and an understanding of them.

And so this chasm is bridged not by rejecting or altering the understanding of the faith but by transferring it from one way of thinking to another; and these different ways of thinking must accordingly be recognized by theologians, along with their mutual relations.

In recent times there have been many different investigations into these various ways of thinking carried out in every field of human knowledge.

Thus, in the nineteenth century Schelling devoted himself to the philosophy of mythology, Kierkegaard to existentialism, and Nietzsche to the philosophy of art. In our own day much more exact studies have been done in many areas.

The philosophical aspects of the problem have been dealt with by Ernst Cassirer, a neo-Kantian of the Marburg school, in *Philosophie der symbolischen Formen*, I Teil: *Die Sprache* [Berlin: Bruno Cassirer, 1923]; II Teil: *Das mythische Denken* [Berlin: Bruno Cassirer, 1925]; III Teil: *Phänomenologie der Erkenntnis* [Berlin: Bruno Cassirer, 1929].[50] What Kant did with regard to Newtonian mechanics, Cassirer has tried to do with regard to the mythic mentality (*Denkformen, Anschauungsformen, Lebensformen*).[51]

Regarding the theory of art, Susanne K. Langer, following Cassirer, has written *Feeling and Form: A Theory of Art Developed from* Philosophy in a New Key (New York: Scribner; London: Routledge & Kegan Paul, 1953).[52]

The psychological aspects have been studied by the whole school of depth psychology following Freud and Jung. Freud investigated especially dreams and neurotic phenomena, while Jung explored the connection between science and philosophy and the archaic myths of the collective unconscious, etc.

50 [Available in English as *The Philosophy of Symbolic Forms*, trans. Ralph Manheim: vol. 1: *Language*; vol. 2: *Mythic Thought*; vol. 3: *The Phenomenology of Knowledge* (New Haven and London: Yale University Press, 1953–57).]

51 See also Hans Leisegang, *Denkformen*, 2nd ed. (Berlin: W. de Gruyter, 1951) on the various modes of thought (though he doesn't know his own).

52 [The title refers to Susanne K. Langer, *Philosophy in a New Key: A Study in the Symbolism of Reason, Rite, and Art* (Cambridge, MA: Harvard University Press, 1942; 3rd ed., 1957).]

In campo historiae religionis adsunt.opera R. Otto, *Das Heilige*, Gotha, 1926, qui tractavit de elementis irrationalibus in idea *tou* sacri;[53] M. Eliade, *Le Chamanisme et les tecniques de l'extase*, Paris, 1951, de technica archaica vitae mysticae; cfr. eiusdem, *Images et symboles. Essai sur le symbolisme magico-religieux*, Paris, 1952, et *Traité d'histoire des religions*, Paris, 1948, 1953.[54] Ipse psychologiam mechanisticam et chimicam reiciens, studuit formis primitivis expressionis transculturalibus, independentibus a lingua, concludendo effectum rationalismi in nostro mundo occidentali non fuisse quod mythi tollerentur, sed quod eius imago fundamentalis corrumperetur atque haec tamen degradatio mythi nullam diminutionem significaret illius influxus (cfr. imagines feminarum in reclames rerum quae venduntur, ideam paradisi amissi in 'South Pacific,' etc.)[55]

Studia phaenomenologica aggressi sunt Hegel, *Phänomenologie des Geistes*;[56] E. Husserl, *Die Krisis der europäischen Wissenschaften und die transzendentale Phänomenologie. Eine Einleitung in die phänomenologische Philosophie*, Haag 1954;[57] F.J.J. Buytendijk, *Wesen und Sinn des Spiels. Das Spielen des Menschen und der Tiere als Erscheinungsform der Lebenstriebe*, Berlin, 1934; cfr. eiusdem auctoris *Phénomenologie de la rencontre*, Paris-Bruges, 1952 (quid sig-

In the area of the history of religion we have the work of Rudolf Otto, *Das Heilige: Über das Irrationale in der Idee des Göttlichen und sein Verhältnis zum Rationalen* (Gotha: Leoplold Klotz, 1926), who treats of the non-rational elements in the idea of the 'holy';[53] also Mircea Eliade, *Le Chamanisme et les techniques archaïques de l'extase* (Paris: Payot, 1951) on the ancient techniques of mysticism; see also his *Images et symboles: Essais sur le symbolisme magico-religieux* (Paris: Gallimard, 1952), and *Traité d'histoire des religions* (Paris: Payot, 1948 and 1953).[54] Rejecting mechanistic and chemical psychology, he studied primitive transcultural forms of expression not dependent on language and came to the conclusion that the effect of rationalism in the Western world was not that myth was banished from it but that its fundamental image was corrupted and that this degradation of myth did not indicate any lessening of its influence – consider, for example, the images of women used in advertising, or the idea of a lost paradise in *South Pacific*, and so on.[55]

Phenomenological studies were undertaken by Hegel in *Phänomenologie des Geistes* [6th ed. (Hamburg: Meiner, 1952; first published in 1807)];[56] by E. Husserl, *Die Krisis der europäischen Wissenschaften und die transzendentale Phänomenologie: Eine Einleitung in die phänomenologische Philosophie* (Den Haag: Nijhoff, 1954);[57] by F.J.J. Buytendijk, *Wesen und Sinn des Spiels: Das Spielen des Menschen und der Tiere als Erscheinungsform der Lebenstriebe* (Berlin: K. Wolff Verlag, Der Neue Geist Verlag, 1933), and the same author's

---

53 [In English, *The Idea of the Holy: An Inquiry into the Non-Rational Factor in the Idea of the Divine and Its Relation to the Rational*, 2nd ed., trans. John W. Harvey (London: Oxford University Press, 1958). Lonergan retains a reference to Otto's book in the chapter on 'Religion' in *Method in Theology* (Toronto: University of Toronto Press, 1990) 106.]

54 [English translations for these three books: *Shamanism: Archaic Techniques of Ecstasy*, rev. and enl. ed., trans. Willard R.Trask (New York: Bollingen Foundation; distributed by Pantheon Books, 1964); *Images and Symbols: Studies in Religious Symbolism*, trans. Philip Mairet (London: Harvill Press, 1961; New York: Sheed & Ward, 1961); *Patterns in Comparative Religion: A Study of the Element of the Sacred in the History of Religious Phenomena*, trans. Rosemary Sheed (New York: Sheed & Ward, 1958). These three books are mentioned in *Understanding and Being* 216–17, and the last two titles are mentioned in *Insight* 572, note 7.]

55 [For a similar remark, see *Understanding and Being* 216.]

56 [English translation, *Phenomenology of Spirit*, trans. A.V. Miller, with analysis of the text and foreword by J.N. Findlay (Oxford: Clarendon Press, 1977).]

57 [English translation, *The Crisis of European Science and Transcendental Phenomenology: An Introduction to Phenomenological Philosophy*, trans., with an intro., David Carr (Evanston, IL: Northwestern University Press, 1970).]

nificet obviam fieri alicui).[58] Exsistentialismus phaenomenologicus est existentialismus M. Heidegger qui magnum influxum habuit: in R. Bultmann;
H. Jonas, *Gnosis und späntantiker Geist.* I Teil: Die mythologische Gnosis. Mit
einer Einleitung zur Geschichte und Methodologie der Forschung, Göttingen, 1934; II Teil, 1: Von der Mythologie zur systematischer Philosophie,
ibid. 1954;[59] L. Binswanger, *Le rêve et l'existence,* Paris-Bruges 1954.[60] Exsistentialismus moralis est philosophia G. Marcel dum exsistentialismus religiosus excolitur a N.A. Berdyaev.

Cogitatio liturgica maxime exculta est ab O. Casel in suis operibus, praesertim *Die Liturgie als Mysterienfeier,* Freiburg i.Br. 1923, *Das Christiche Kult-
mysterium,* Regensburg, 1932,[61] *Glaube, Gnosis, Mysterium,* Münster, 1941 (in
quibus apparet connexionem cum modo cogitandi mythico). Cfr. etiam
collectionem Jahrbuch Liturgiewissenschaft (Münster).

(c) Circa problema historicitatis

Ideae platonicae non evolvuntur sed aeternae sunt et fixae. Aliquid simile adest in cognitione humana. Conceptus dicuntur fixi et immutabiles.
Utique, idem conceptus semper eodem modo concipitur, nullus adest motus in conceptibus logice consideratis.

Phénoménologie de la rencontre (Paris: Desclée de Brouwer; Bruges: Impr. Saint-Augustin, 1952) on what it means to meet someone.[58] There is the phenomenological existentialism of Martin Heidegger, who had considerable influence on Rudolf Bultmann; on Hans Jonas, *Gnosis und spätantiker Geist.* I Teil: *Die mythologische Gnosis, mit einer Einleitung zur Geschichte und Methodologie der Forschung* (Göttingen: Vandenhoeck & Ruprecht, 1934 [2nd ed. 1954]); II Teil: *Von der Mythologie zur mystischen Philosophie* (Göttingen: Vandenhoeck & Ruprecht, 1954);[59] on Ludwig Binswanger, *Le rêve et l'existence*, with intro. and notes by Michel Foucault (Paris: Desclée de Brouwer; Bruges : Impr. les Presses Saint-Augustin, 1954).[60] Moral existentialism is found in Gabriel Marcel's philosophy, while religious existentialism is developed by Nikolai A. Berdyaev.

Liturgical thought was developed especially by Odo Casel; see especially his *Die Liturgie als Mysterienfeier* (Freiburg im Bresgau: Herder, 1923); *Das christliche Kult Mysterium* (Regensburg: F. Pustet, 1932 [4th ed., 1960]);[61] *Glaube, Gnosis, Mysterium* (Münster [Westf]: Aschendorff, 1941); in these writings he examines the connection with the mythic mentality. See also the collection *Jahrbuch für Liturgiewissenschaft* (Münster in Westf.: Verein zur Pflege der Liturgiewissenschaft).

(c) Concerning the Problem of Historicity

Platonic Ideas do not develop: they are eternal and fixed. There is something similar in human cognition: concepts are said to be fixed and immutable. True, the same concept is always conceived in the same way, and there is no movement in concepts considered logically.

---

58 [In one of a series of lectures Lonergan delivered in 1957, collected now in *Phenomenology and Logic*, he refers to both of these works (see p. 270), but says at that time (July 1957) that he has not yet seen *Wesen und Sinn des Spiels.*]

59 [English translation, *The Gnostic Religion: The Message of the Alien God and the Beginnings of Christianity* (Boston: Beacon Press, 1958; 2nd rev. ed., 1963).]

60 [English translation, 'Dream and Existence,' in *Being-in-the-World: Selected Papers of Ludwig Binswanger*, trans. Jacob Needleman (New York: Harper Torchbooks, 1963) 222–48. See also Lonergan's brief discussions in *Phenomenology and Logic* 273 and in *Topics in Education: The Cincinnati Lectures of 1959 on the Philosophy of Education*, vol. 10 in Collected Works of Bernard Lonergan, ed. Robert M. Doran and Frederick E. Crowe (Toronto: University of Toronto Press, 1993) 210.]

61 [English translation, *The Mystery of Christian Worship and Other Writings*, ed. Burkhard Neunheuser (Westminster, MD: Newman Press, 1962; New York: Crossroads Publications, 1999).]

Attamen, si concrete considerantur prout in mente humana exsistunt, adest continua variatio conceptuum, quia conceptus non sunt independentes ab intentione et intelligentia hominis concreti. Verbum mentale (conceptus) nonnisi expressio est illius quod intelligitur, seu actus intelligendi; quod haec sit sententia S. Thomae ostensum est in B. Lonergan, s.j. 'The Concept of Verbum in the Writings of St.Thomas Aquinas.'[62] Unde plus minusve progrediente intelligentia, plus minusve mutantur et evolvuntur conceptus. Hoc agnoscere est agnoscere punctum fundamentale ad inveniendam solutionem problematis historicitatis.

E contra, si conceptus concipiuntur tamquam inconsciae reproductiones rerum, sicut aliquid quod a rebus necessario et mechanice imprimitur in intellectu, et si actus intelligendi ponitur non ut praevium ad efformationem conceptuum sed tantum in comparatione conceptuum inter se (ut habetur in theologia Scoti), tunc negatur radicitus et evolutio conceptuum et problema historicitatis.

At actus intelligendi medium locum tenet inter sensum et conceptum, et quia actus intelligendi potest semper progredi et profundior fieri et magis comprehensivus, sic possibilis est progressus historicus scientiae. Tamen exsistit etiam possibilitas regressus. Auctores saec. XIV erant acutissimi logici, attamen parum colebant intelligentiam. Dexteritas logica intelligentiam non auxit, immo paulatim minuit. Magni scholastici saec. XII–XIII sunt antecessores scholasticorum saec. XIV–XV tantum per accidens, usquedum ad sceptiscismum perventum est cum Nicolao de Autrecourt (cfr. DB 553–70).

Systema logicum de se est abstractum, unde apud Scotum et Occam, praeter scientiam de solis necessariis, ad attingendam realitatem invenitur necessitas alicuius intuitionis rerum concrete exsistentium et praesentium. Tamen quia pro auctoribus illius temporis potest dari in aliquo mundo possibili intuitio alicuius rei quae praesens non sit, et quia scientia est de iis quae sunt necessaria in omni possibili mundo, etiam de nostro mundo de-

Nevertheless, if they are considered concretely as they exist in the human mind, they undergo continual modification because concepts do not exist independently of the intending and the understanding of a concrete human being. The inner word, or concept, is but the expression of what is understood, of the act of understanding or insight. That this is the opinion of St Thomas has been shown in 'The Concept of Verbum in the Writings of St Thomas Aquinas.'[62] Hence, with a greater or lesser advance in understanding, concepts undergo greater or lesser development and change. To recognize this fact is to recognize the fundamental point in solving the problem of historicity.

If concepts, on the other hand, are conceived as being like unconscious reproductions of things, as if mechanically and by necessity imprinted by things upon the intellect, and if the act of understanding is located not as prior to the formation of concepts but as consisting only in the comparison of concepts among themselves (as in the theology of Scotus), then both the development of concepts and the problem of historicity are radically denied.

But the act of understanding occupies the middle ground between sensation and the concept; and because the act of understanding is ever capable of further progress and of becoming more profound and more comprehensive, historical progress in knowledge is thus possible. Yet there is also the possibility of regression. The fourteenth-century writers were extremely sharp logicians, but they did very little to cultivate understanding. Dexterity in logic does not increase intelligence – in fact, it tends to diminish it somewhat. The great Scholastics of the twelfth and thirteenth centuries were only *per accidens* the predecessors of those of the fourteenth and fifteenth, all the way down to the skepticism of Nicholas of Autrecourt (DB 553–70, DS 1028–49).

A logical system is of its very nature abstract, and so for Scotus and Ockham, in addition to science, which regards only the necessary, there is also need of some sort of intuition of present and concretely existing beings in order to reach reality. Nevertheless, because for the authors of that period there can be in some possible world an intuition of a being that is not present, and because science concerns that which is necessary in every pos-

62 See *Theological Studies* 7 (1946) 349–92; 8 (1947) 35–79, 404–44; 10 (1949) 3–40, 359–93. [Available now as *Verbum: Word and Idea in Aquinas,* vol. 2 in Collected Works of Bernard Lonergan.]

bet negari quod necessario aliqua res debeat exsistere atque adesse tantum quia illam intuemur.[63]

Progressus potest dari in aliquo campo, dum fit regressus in alio. Inde a saec. XVI scientiae positivae et mechanicae maxime progrediuntur. Philosophia autem regreditur.

Distinguenda ergo sunt stadia fundamentalia in evolutione mentis humanae, attamen non tantum res historice considerantes, sed systematice. Sic R. Bultmann, in articulo 'Γινώσκω,'[64] enumerat et distinguit modum concipiendi Hebraicum, Iudaicum, Graecum, gnosticum, Christiano-primitivum atque subsequentem … Ita etiam multum loquuntur de Paulinismo, de Iohannismo, de mentalitate Hellenistica, Semitica … Hoc tamen non est nisi quaedam utilis enumeratio et nominatio phaenomenorum quin eorum causa assignetur.[65] Unde systematice distinguere diversa stadia evolutionis humanae significat statuere causas ex quibus derivant diversi modi humani concipiendi, iudicandi.

1.6.5 De unitate solutionis

Unitas solutionis consistit in intellectu humano potentiali.

In quantum intellectus humanus est potentialis, eius habitus scientiae et sapientiae possunt augeri, et ex intellectu humano proficienti initialem solutionem problematis fundamenti.

In quantum intellectus humanus est humanus, intime coniungitur cum parte hominis sensitiva, et ex hac connexione repetivimus initialem solutionem problematis chasmatis.

In quantum autem intellectus humanus et progreditur in scientia, intellectu, et sapientia, et ex altera parte intime coniungitur cum vita sensitiva, dantur diversae syntheses inter vitam intellectivam et sensitivam. Prout scientia, intellectus, sapientia sunt minus evoluta, praevalet vita sensitiva et modus concipiendi ad modum sensationis. Diversa evolutio scientiae, intellectus, et sapientiae inducit varias crises et transformationes, quae ducunt ad solutiones semper differentes. Hoc modo exsurgit problema et introducitur notio de methodo.

sible world, it must be denied that in our world also some being must necessarily exist and be present simply because we intuit it.[63]

Progress can take place in one area while regression takes place in another. From the sixteenth century on, the positive and mechanical sciences have made great progress; philosophy, however, has been regressing.

We must distinguish, therefore, the fundamental stages in the development of the human mind, considering matters not only historically but also systematically. Thus R. Bultmann, in his article 'γινώσκω,'[64] enumerates and distinguishes ways of thinking that are Hebraic, Judaic, Greek, Gnostic, Early Christian, and later ones ... So also people speak of Paulinism, Johannism, the Semitic mentality, the Hellenistic, and so forth. But all that is only a useful listing and labeling of phenomena without the cause of any of them being assigned.[65] Therefore, systematically distinguishing the various stages of human development means stating the causes that lead to different ways of conceiving and judging.

1.6.5 The Unity of the Solution

The unity of the solution is to be found in the potential human intellect.

Inasmuch as the human intellect is potential, its habits of science and of wisdom can increase, and this intellectual progress furnishes the initial solution to the problem of foundation.

The human intellect as human is intimately connected with the sentient element in humans, and upon this connection we have based the initial solution to the problem of the chasm.

Inasmuch, however, as the human intellect advances in science, understanding, and wisdom, and on the other hand is intimately connected with the life of the senses, different syntheses between the life of the intellect and that of the senses are formed. As science, understanding, and wisdom are less well developed, the life of the senses and a sensation-like mode of concept formation predominate. And as science, understanding, and wisdom develop in different ways, various crises and transformations result, leading to constantly different solutions. Thus a problem arises and we introduce the notion of method.

63 [See Lonergan, *Insight* 428–29.]
64 *Theologisches Wörterbuch zum Neuen Testament* (TWNT) I, 688–719 [*Theological Dictionary of the New Testament* (TDNT) I, 689–719].
65 For example, the Hebraic idea of knowing is such precisely because it lacks a clear-cut distinction between intellect, will, and appetite.

2   De Notione Scientiae

At etiam alio modo quaestio de methodo potest introduci.

Non tantum scientia evolvitur, sed ipsa notio scientiae. Aristoteles et S. Thomas loquebantur de scientia, moderni loquuntur de methodo. Unde philosophia (amor sapientiae) se habet ad sapientiam sicut methôdus se habet ad scientiam. Quod notio scientiae evolvatur non statim cognoscitur ab initio, quando practice nescitur quid scientia sit. Praxis autem scientifica celerius evolvitur quam cogitatio super illam, unde etiam celerius quam ipsa notio scientiae, unde oriri possunt conflictus semper graviores et periculosiores. Quia cogitatio manet eadem, notio scientiae eadem manet, dum progressus praxeos scientificae aliter non potest fieri quam talis quae de facto illam notionem non sequatur. Sic possumus pervenire ad problema de methodo.

2.1   Illustrationes ex diversis notionibus scientiae

2.1.1   Scientia potest concipi ut 'cognitio essentiae rei, qua cognita cognoscuntur rei proprietates'

Fundamentum huius notionis est logicum (suppones divisiones arboris porphyrianae: genus - species - differentia specifica - proprium - accidens). Haec definitio, quae partem habet veritatis, estne capax fundandi notionem adaequatam scientiae?

Ante omnia certe haec definitio nequit applicari scientiae quam Deus habet de seipso. Nam in Deo nulla realis distinctio inter essentiam et proprietates seu attributa. Ipse Deus se cognoscit unico simplicissimo intuitu.

Aliquomodo definitio posset applicari scientiae quam de Deo nos habemus dum sumus in via; inter notiones quas de Deo habemus distinguimus aliquomodo magis vel minus fundamentales. Tamen difficultas in eo est quod, dum sumus in via, nescimus quid sit Deus, essentiam eius ignorantes donec eam videbimus facie ad faciem.[66]

2   The Notion of Science

Here is another way of introducing the notion of method.

Not only science itself but also the very notion of science has been developing. Whereas Aristotle and St Thomas spoke about science, moderns speak of method. Thus, philosophy ('love of wisdom') is to wisdom as method is to science. That the notion of science itself develops is not known right from the very beginning, when practically speaking the nature of science is unknown. The practice of science develops more quickly than reflection upon it and hence more quickly also than the notion of science itself, and this can give rise to ever more serious and dangerous conflicts. Because the reflection remains the same, so also does the notion of science, while progress in scientific practice can only be such as departs in fact from that notion. In this way we can arrive at the problem of method.

2.1   Illustrative Examples Taken from Various Notions of Science

[2.1.1   Knowledge of Essence]

Science can be conceived as 'knowledge of the essence of a thing, by reason of which knowledge the properties of that thing may be known.' This notion is based upon logic: see the divisions of the Porphyrian tree: genus – species – specific difference – property – accident. Is this definition, which has some truth to it, capable of grounding an adequate notion of science?

First of all, this definition certainly cannot be applied to the knowledge that God has of himself, since in God there is no real distinction between his essence and his properties or attributes. God knows himself in one absolutely simple intuitive act.

This definition could in a way be applied to the knowledge which we in this life have of God; among the notions we have about God we do make some distinction between the more and the less fundamental ones. Yet the problem is that in this life we do not know what God is, for we shall remain ignorant of his essence until we see him face to face.[66]

---

66 Thomas Aquinas, *Summa contra Gentiles* 3, cc. 25–63; *Summa theologiae*, 1, q. 12, a. 1; 1-2, q. 3, a. 8.

Si autem universo ut toti haec scientiae definitio concrete rigide applicetur, devenitur logice ad determinismum Spinoza, qui duas series infinitas
attributorum universi deducebat ex unica substantia; vel etiam ad optimi-
smum moralem necessarium Leibniz.

Si e contra cognitio essentiae et proprietatum est consideratio rei abstractae, tunc valde limitata est scientia de rebus concretis, atque habetur positio
Scoti, secundum quem scientia non est de hoc mundo concrete exsistenti
sed de omni possibili mundo. Quare scientia de hoc concreto mundo habetur tantum ex consideratione liberae Dei voluntatis. Sic patet voluntari-
smum ex eo provenire non quod magis ametur voluntas, sed quod abest vel
deficit theoria scientiae et intelligentiae. Unde potius aliquid negativum est
quam positivum.

At quaerere demum possumus: cognoscimusne revera de facto essentias
rerum? Pueri generaliter non quaerunt essentias sed nomina rerum, seu
instrumenta conscientiae ad proprium mundum organizandum. Aliud autem est rerum cognitionem habere descriptivam et classificatoriam, qua res
nominamus et ordinamus logice per exteriora accidentia, aliud rerum habere scientiam explicativam. Unde forsan non tam saepe essentiam rerum
cognoscimus.

Unde, quamvis aliquam habeat applicationem, haec notio scientiae cum
limitatione accipienda est.

2.1.2 Scientia potest concipi tamquam 'certa rerum per causas cognitio'

Haec definitio fundat notionem scientiae Aristotelicam. Ubi res sunt aliquid in decem categoriis entis, et causae sunt vel finis, vel agens, vel materia,
vel forma. Scientia Aristotelica consistit in determinando quomodo categoriae se habeant ad res. Nec materia nec forma intrant in decem generibus
entis.

Praeterea datur motus, qui habet esse incompletum et quo multum utitur Aristoteles. Motus non est unum ex praedicamentis. Eius notio accepta
est a Bergson, pro quo omnis categoria intellectualis est fixa, aeterna, determinata, abstracta, et ideo inepta ad realitatem cognoscendam, quae eam
superat, quia fluens et nequit conceptibus contineri, sicut flumen nequit
contineri a rete quodam. Unde fere nihil cognoscitur per categorias intel-

This definition of science, if concretely and rigidly applied to the universe as a whole, leads logically to the determinism of Spinoza, who deduced two infinite series of attributes of the universe from a single substance; or again it would lead to the necessary moral optimism of Leibniz.

If, on the other hand, to know the essence and properties of a thing is to consider it in the abstract, then the science of concrete realities is extremely limited. This is Scotus's position, according to which science has to do not with this concrete existing world but with every possible world; and therefore knowledge of this concrete world is to be had only from a consideration of God's free will. From this it is evident that voluntarism stems not from a predilection for the will but rather from the absence or inadequacy of a theory of knowledge and of understanding; so it is something negative rather than positive.

Finally, we may ask, 'Do we in fact really understand the essences of things?' Children, as a general rule, do not ask about the essences of things but about their names, that is, the tools of consciousness for organizing their own world. It is one thing to have a knowledge of things that is descriptive and useful for classification, which enables us to label things and put them in some logical order according to their external accidents, and quite another to possess an explanatory knowledge of things. So perhaps we do not know the essence of things all that often.

Therefore, although this notion of science has some application, it is to be accepted only in a limited manner.

[2.1.2 Certain Knowledge of Things through Their Causes]

Science can be conceived as 'the certain knowledge of things through their causes.' This definition forms the basis of the Aristotelian notion of science. 'Thing' is anything that is found in the ten categories of being, and 'causes' are final, efficient, material, and formal. Aristotelian science consists in determining the relationship of the categories to things. Neither matter nor form enters into these ten kinds of being.

In addition there is motion, which has an incomplete act of existence; it is a concept that Aristotle uses a great deal. It is not one of the categories. His notion is accepted by Bergson, for whom every intellectual category is fixed, eternal, determinate, abstract, and hence not suitable for knowing reality, which is beyond it by reason of the fact that it is fluid and cannot be contained in concepts any more than a river can be contained in a net.

lectuales. Aristoteles movebatur in horizonte totaliter opposito quando asserebat motum esse quid nimis imperfectum ut possit in categoria quadam inveniri.[67]

Motus cum tribus categoriis connectitur: ubi, qualitas, quantitas. Sic motu locali movetur quod non est alicubi; motu qualitativo (= alteratione) movetur quod non habet quale; motu quantitative (= auctione vel diminutione) movetur quod non habet quantum. Non habetur alteratio quin praecedat motus localis alterantis ad alteratum, nec augmentatio habetur nisi praecedat alteratio, secus augmentatio esset mera adiunctio. Ex his omnibus habetur tota structura Aristotelica mundi. Quia motus in quantitate praesupponit motum in qualitate, alterans non alteratur, et sic corpora caelestia habent tantum motum localem, dum motores immoti nullum habent genus motus.

Ex caeteris categoriis, actio et passio definiuntur per motum: actio, motus alicuius ut ab hoc; passio, motus alicuius ut in hoc.

Tempus definitur ut mensura motus secundum prius et posterius spatiale, non temporale.

Situs et habitus sunt tantum descriptiones quae restringuntur animalibus.

Categoria 'quid' occasionem praebet investigandi in motum per generationem et corruptionem. Nec motus deest inter materiam et formam, quatenus actus entis in potentia huiusmodi.

Hic potest esse primus sensus illius definitionis scientiae, quam supra dedimus.

At eadem formula alio sensu accipi potest, scilicet quatenus supponit duplicem processum: analyticus, incipiens a rebus et, per resolutionem, perveniens ad causas, quae possunt esse sive logicae, sive physicae et metaphysicae; syntheticus, quo, cognitis causis, per compositionem fit reditus ad res. Prout, v.gr., haec conceptio scientiae adhibita est a S. Thoma in doctri-

Thus, virtually nothing is known through intellectual categories. But Aristotle moved in a totally opposite horizon in asserting that motion was something too imperfect to be found in any category.[67]

Motion is connected with three categories: location, quality, and quantity. Accordingly, that which is not in any place moves with local motion; that which has not a determinate quality moves with a qualitative motion (alteration); that which has not a determinate quantity moves with quantitative motion (increase or decrease). There is no alteration without a prior local motion of that which alters towards that which is altered, nor is there any increase without a prior alteration, for otherwise an increase would be simply an accretion. All of these together form the Aristotelian structure of the universe. Since quantitative motion presupposes qualitative change, that which changes something else is not itself changed; thus, the heavenly bodies have only local motion, while the unmoved movers have no motion of any kind.

Among the other categories, action and passion are defined in terms of motion: action is the motion of a thing with respect to that from which it originates, and passion is the motion of a thing with respect to that in which it is received.

Time is defined as the measure of motion according to a before and after that is spatial, not temporal.

Posture and dress are merely descriptive categories that are restricted to living creatures.

The category 'what' affords the opportunity to investigate motion by way of generation and corruption. There is also motion between matter and form, as the act of a being in this sort of potency.

This, then, can be the first meaning of the definition of science given above.

The same formulation, however, can be taken in another sense, namely, inasmuch as it supposes a twofold process: an analytic, beginning from things and proceeding by way of resolution, or analysis, into causes, which can be either logical or physical and metaphysical; and a synthetic process in which, when the causes are known, one returns to the things themselves

---

67 [It is useful to compare Lonergan's remark here on Bergson's position as contrasted with Aristotle's with a similar remark in *Verbum: Word and Idea in Aquinas* 113, note 33.]

na trinitaria exponenda, ea non praesupponit scientiam sensu Aristotelico. Nam, prout a S. Thoma adhibiti, duo processus neque perveniunt ex rebus stricte aliquibus categoriis pertinentibus ad aliquam veram causam, neque vice versa. Deus enim non est in ullo genere entis. Substantia et relatio de illo dicuntur non sensu univoco et stricto, nam in eo eadem sunt realitas. Neque fit stricta resolutio in causas, nam Deus non habet causas, sed tantum in aspectus qui diversificantur a nostro modo concipiendi res divinas.

E contra maxima structura analytico-synthetica habetur in chimia moderna, in tabula periodica elementorum (a Mendeleev): ubi elementa sunt conclusiones ad quas pervenitur per investigationes scientificas, et quae definiuntur per relationes quas habent inter se, dum composita definiuntur ex elementis.

Haec conceptio scientiae ut resolutio-compositio diversimode habetur, secundum diversos gradus evolutionis scientiae. Talis resolutio et compositio non habetur tamen inter praedicamenta et causas Aristotelicas.

2.1.3 Scientia potest concipi tamquam de legibus quae in aliquo systemate adhibentur

Ubi lex exprimitur per aliquam formulam mathematicam, v.gr., $s = \frac{1}{2}gt^2$. Talis lex est elementum fundamentale in notione moderna scientiae: cfr. Galileo, Kepler, qui potius leges particulares invenerunt tamen cum valore universali. Elementum systematicum introductum est a Newton, quando formulavit leges secundum quas planetae non tantum moventur (ut Kepler fecerat) sed debent moveri. Ita leges sunt conclusiones ex principiis primis mathematicis more Euclidiano deductae: sic systema mechanicum scientiae instituitur, quod postea applicatum est omni scientiae naturae, sive chimicae, sive physicae, biologicae, thermodynamicae … Sic habitum est splendidum exemplum systematizationis scientificae.

Nostris autem diebus ponitur totaliter alia notio scientiae secundum status et probabilitates. Leges classicae verificabantur in tempore et spatio imaginabilibus, quae eliminata sunt a theoria relativitatis. Theoria quanto-

by way of composition, or synthesis. As this conception of science is used by St Thomas, for example, in expounding the doctrine of the Trinity, it does not presuppose science in the Aristotelian sense. For as Thomas uses it, these two processes do not arrive at a true cause from things that strictly belong to some categories, nor vice versa. For God is not in any genus of being. Substance and relation are predicated of him not in a univocal and strict sense, since in God they are all the selfsame reality. Nor is there strictly speaking a resolution into causes, since God has no causes, but only a resolution into certain aspects that are differentiated by the way in which we conceive divine realities.

On the contrary, the most complex analytic-synthetic construct is to be found in modern chemistry, in Mendeleev's periodic table of the elements. In it the elements are arrived at through scientific investigation and are defined in terms of their mutual relationships, while compounds are defined in terms of their elements.

This concept of science as resolution-composition will be different according to the various degrees of scientific development. This sort of resolution and composition, however, is not found in the Aristotelian predicaments or causes.

[2.1.3 Laws and System]

Science can be conceived as dealing with laws that are used in some system. This is the case where a law is expressed in some mathematical formula: for example, $s = \frac{1}{2}gt^2$. Such laws are a fundamental element in the modern notion of science. Take for example Galileo and Kepler, whose discoveries were rather of particular laws that nevertheless had a universal value. Newton introduced a systematic element when he formulated laws according to which the planets not only moved (as Kepler had done), but according to which they had to move. In this way laws are conclusions deduced in a Euclidean manner from the first principles of mathematics, and this led to the introduction of a mechanical system of science that was subsequently applied to all the physical sciences, to chemistry, physics, biology, thermodynamics, and so on. Here we have a splendid example of scientific systematization.

In our time, however, there has been put forth a totally different notion of science according to states and probabilities. Classical laws used to be verified in imaginable time and space, which have been eliminated by the

rum et probabilismus infringunt[68] schemata deterministica. In quo ergo amplius consistit scientia?

2.1.4 Scientia potest concipi tamquam deductio ex principiis analyticis

Principium analyticum est illud in quo praedicatum est de ratione subiecti.

Sic ex dicto 'exsistens necessarium necessario exsistit' conati sunt deducere exsistentiam Dei a priori vel a simultaneo.

Quando autem dicimus 'ens contingens habet causam efficientem' adhuc praedicatum est de ratione subiecti.

Distinguendum tamen est inter principia analytica et propositiones analyticas. Propositio analytica habetur quando nos attingimus aliquod inconditionatum. Nos nequimus attingere inconditionatum simpliciter, qui est Deus solus, sed illud cuius conditiones sint impletae, quod vocabimus virtualiter inconditionatum. Aliquando ex solis definitionibus, regulis grammaticalibus et syntacticis debemus assentire alicui propositioni, v.gr., A habet relationem R ad B. Tunc habetur propositio analytica. Termini possunt sine fine multiplicari et fieri possunt deductiones ad omnes terminos. A cum suis relationibus ad omnes terminos B. Nullus tamen fit verus progressus cognitionis, immo fit tautologia, secundum positivistas linguisticos.[69]

E contra, principium analyticum habetur quando relatio inter A et B exsistit non tantum in propositione analytica, seu necessario debet poni ex regulis grammaticalibus et logicis, sed etiam in concreto iudicio exsistentiali, de realibus.[70]

Sic ex dicto 'ens contingens habet causam efficientem,' quia aliunde habetur transitus ad exsistentiam entium contingentium stabiliendam, potest concludi ad Dei exsistentiam. Sed ex dicto 'exsistens necessarium necessa-

theory of relativity. The quantum theory and probabilism discredit[68] deterministic systems. In what else, then, does science consist?

[2.1.4 Deduction from Analytic Principles]

Science can be conceived as a deduction from analytic principles. An analytic principle is one in which the predicate is contained in the definition of the subject.

Thus, from the statement 'a necessary existing being necessarily exists,' an attempt has been made to deduce the existence of God from what is logically prior or simultaneous.

When, however, we say 'a contingent being has an efficient cause,' the predicate is still contained in the definition of the subject.

Still, one must distinguish between analytic principles and analytic propositions. We have an analytic proposition when we arrive at something that is unconditioned. We cannot arrive at what is simply unconditioned, which is God alone, but we can arrive at that whose conditions are fulfilled; this is called the virtually unconditioned. Sometimes solely from definitions and rules of grammar and syntax we are led to assent to some proposition, for example, 'A has a relation R to B.' This is an analytic proposition. Terms can be multiplied indefinitely and deductions to all terms can be made. A with its relations to all terms B. Yet there is no progress in knowledge; in fact it is tautological, according to the linguistic positivists.[69]

On the other hand, an analytic principle is had when the relation between A and B exists not only in an analytic proposition, that is, one necessarily posited in accordance with the rules of grammar and logic, but exists also in a concrete existential judgment about real things.[70]

Thus, from the statement 'A contingent being has an efficient cause,' since on other grounds we may proceed to establish the existence of contingent beings, we can conclude to the existence of God. But from the statement 'A necessary existing being necessarily exists' no conclusion about the

---

68 [The word in the text is 'infangunt,' which is not found in Latin dictionaries. 'Infringunt' is an editorial alternative.]

69 See Lonergan, *Insight* 329–34. [Some editorial work is involved here.]

70 Ibid. 428. [See p. 331 for Lonergan's initial characterization of the difference between analytic propositions and analytic principles.]

rio exsistit' nequit fieri conclusio de necessitate exsistentiae Dei, nisi iam haec exsistentia praesupponatur.

Unde principium analyticum aliquid plus addit supra propositionem analyticam. Exinde necessitas sapientiae, quae eligit principia et terminos et iudicat de eorum actuali exsistentia. Dantur enim multa iudicia exsistentialia, at illa seligere quae scientiam fundent pertinet ad sapientiam.

Notio scientiae tempore perficitur quatenus semper melius determinantur termini primi et accuratiores relationes fundamentales inter illos.

2.1.5 Scientia potest concipi tamquam sit de necessariis

Haec conceptio est omnino vera si de scientia Aristotelica agatur, ubi mundus est aeternus, neque datur creatio in tempore, neque simpliciter, ubi exsistit determinismus in corporibus caelestibus, non autem in rebus terrestribus; quoad terrena, enim, determinismus frangitur ex causis per accidens, quae non sunt aliquid. Unusquisque eventus potest utique habere causam per se, at convenientia illorum saepe est per accidens (sic canis et currus qui simul obveniunt in via). Cur *tunc* fit ille effectus? Aristoteles respondit: quia antea subiecta non erant disposita, unde necessitas praemotionis aut in agente aut in patiente. Appropinquatio autem agentis ad patiens, vel eorum dispositio debetur saepe causae per accidens, non causae naturali. Causae per accidens inveniuntur in tota textura rerum terrestrium, unde totus mundus penetratur contingentia. Nunc autem nulla scientia est possibilis, pro Aristotele, de iis quae sunt per accidens.[71] Unde motus terrestris, quatenus aliquid totum, excluditur ab obiecto scientiae. Scientia est possibilis de generibus, de speciebus, ..., at non de individuis terrestribus exsistentibus.

S. Thomas, e contra, tenet dari scientiam illorum quae sunt per accidens, quia dantur non tantum agentia naturalia sed etiam agens per intellectum et voluntatem, seu Deus. Deus ab aeterno scit et vult coniunctiones effectuum, et est causa per se uniuscuisque effectus qui in mundo in tempore fit. Praemotio Aristotelica fit applicatio ex parte divinae providentiae, quam Aristoteles non cognoscebat. Nam pro illo primus motor movebat tam-

necessity of God's existence can be drawn, unless, of course, that existence is already presupposed.

An analytic principle, therefore, adds something to an analytic proposition. Hence the need for wisdom, which chooses principles and terms and makes judgments about their actual existence. There are many existential judgments, but it is the work of wisdom to choose those that would form the foundation of a science.

The notion of science develops over time to the extent that there is a continued improvement in the determination of primary terms and the fundamental relations among them are more accurately determined.

[2.1.5 Science and Necessity]

Science can be conceived as that which deals with necessary things. This concept is quite true in the case of Aristotelian science, where the world is eternal, where there is no creation in time, or no creation whatsoever, where determinism rules the celestial bodies, though not those of earth; as for earthly beings, their determinism is interrupted by causes *per accidens*, which are not anything. Each single event can have a cause *per se*, but their convergence often happens *per accidens*, such as a dog and a car that run into each other on the street. Why does that effect happen at this particular time? Aristotle's answer was: because previously the subjects were not disposed, whence the necessity of a premotion either in the agent or in the patient. The approach of the agent to the patient, or even their disposition, is often due to a cause *per accidens*, not to a natural cause. Causes *per accidens* are found in the total fabric of terrestrial reality, so that the whole world is shot through with contingency. Now for Aristotle there can be no science of things that exist *per accidens*.[71] Hence, terrestrial motion, insofar as it is a whole, is excluded from the object of science. There can be a science of genera, of species, etc., but not of individual terrestrial entities.

St Thomas, on the contrary, holds that there is a science of those realities that exist *per accidens*, because not only are there natural agents but also an agent that acts through intellect and will, namely God. God, from all eternity, knows and wills the conjunctions of effects and is the cause *per se* of each and every effect that takes place in the world in time. Aristotelian

---

71 Aristotle, *Metaphysics*, VI.

quam finis, non tamquam agens. Ille tamen ponebat aliquam causam per se continuitatis et perpetuitatis processus terrestris, id est corpora caelestia. Unde iste processus non relinquitur in mera contingentia.[72]

At pro Aristotele non datur ulla scientia de rebus historicis. Historia invenitur potius in poematibus. Hic saltus profundus habetur. Sic Toynbee quaerit categorias suae historicae cogitationis ex literatura, ex tragediis Graecis vel Shakespearianis. Revera hic habentur profundae categoriae ad intelligentiam obtinendam vitae humanae, tamen non aptae sunt quae ex illis scientia historica aedificetur.

Unde notio scientiae debet ampliari per determinationem illarum rerum quae in universo sunt necessariae et illarum quae non sunt tales. Secus impossibilis est, v.gr., scientia de Redemptione, de Ecclesia Corpore Christi Mystico, etc.

S. Thomas saepe eadem verba Aristotelica repetit: scientia est de necessariis, tamen aliud intelligit. Sic, v.gr., in *Summa contra Gentiles*, 2, cc. 28–30, multiplicem distinguit necessitatem absolutam et hypotheticam. Tantum Deus est simpliciter necessarius absolute, qui tamen nobis ut talis innotescit tantum ex contingentibus.

Dei voluntas non est concipienda independens a divino intellectu, sed necessario sequens ordinationem divinae sapientiae.[73]

Divina potentia non latius extenditur quam divina sapientia, nam realiter unum sunt. Distinctio inter potentiam absolutam et potentiam ordinatam non invenitur apud S. Thomam: nam potentia absoluta comprehenderet id quod Deus posset facere, si sapiens non esset! E contra, quidquid Deus

premotion becomes application on the part of divine providence, of which Aristotle knew nothing. For him the prime mover moved as a final, not an efficient, cause. Nevertheless, he did posit some cause *per se* of the continuity and perpetuity of the terrestrial process, namely, the celestial bodies, and so this process is not left in mere contingency.[72]

However, for Aristotle there was no such thing as a science of history. History was rather the stuff of poetry. There is a huge leap here. Toynbee goes to literature, to Greek and Shakespearian tragedy, for the categories of his thought on history. It is true that here one may find categories that furnish profound insights into human life, but they are not suitable as foundations on which to erect a science of history.

Hence, the notion of science needs to be enlarged by determining which realities are universally necessary and which are not. Otherwise it is impossible to have, for example, a science of the redemption, of the church as the Mystical Body of Christ, and so forth.

St Thomas often repeats Aristotle's dictum 'Science is of necessary things,' but he understands it differently. So, for example, in the *Summa contra Gentiles* 2, cc. 28–30, he makes a number of distinctions between absolute and hypothetical necessity. God alone is absolutely necessary without qualification, although he is known as such by us only through contingent beings.

The divine will is not to be understood as being independent of the divine mind, but as necessarily following the ordination of divine wisdom.[73]

Divine power does not extend more widely than divine wisdom, since they are the same reality. St Thomas does not distinguish between absolute and ordered power; for absolute power would cover whatever God could do if he were not wise. On the contrary, whatever God can do, he can do wisely.

---

72 Aristotle, *Physics*, VIII; *Metaphysics*, XII. On this question, see Bernard Lonergan, 'St Thomas' Thought on *Gratia Operans*,' Part 4: 'St Thomas' Theory of Operation,' *Theological Studies* 3 (1942) 375–402. [*Grace and Freedom* 66–93; see also Lonergan's remark on p. 375, note 146: 'To Aristotle the *per accidens*, that is, any coincidence of unrelated predicates, any unnecessary combination of causes or conjunction of effects, does not admit explanation: it is not considered by any science, even by metaphysics, which considers all reality. St Thomas agrees with Aristotle to the extent of admitting the *per accidens* to have no natural cause, but, as was shown in treating the significance of the doctrine of *applicatio*, he attributes all coincidence, conjunction, combination to providential design.' The doctrine of *applicatio* and its significance was discussed earlier on pp. 280–87; cf. pp. 75–82.]

73 Thomas Aquinas, *De veritate*, q. 23, a. 6; *Summa theologiae*, 1, q. 21, a. 1 ad 2m.

facere potest, illud potest sapienter facere. Unde non prius habentur in divina sapientia possibilia et dein eorum ordinatio per sapientiam: Deus videt in sua essentia omnes ordines possibiles, et in unoquoque singula possibilia sapienter ordinabilia.[74] Attamen non quia divina voluntas necessario sequitur ordinationem divinae sapientiae, ideo Deus necessario eligit; nam in Deo potentia et sapientia habent eandem extensionem, et omnis creaturarum ordo est de se imperfectus unde creatio est absolute libera.

Per comparationem ad Deum nihil fit per accidens. Saec. XVI, in controversia de auxiliis, quaerebatur reconciliatio inter libertatem humanam et divinam providentiam, id est duorum quae nulla indigent 're'-conciliatione, ex eo quod, pro S. Thoma, id quod est contingens intenditur a Deo sicut id quod est necessarium, non tamen eodem modo, quia Deus non imponit necessitatem entibus quae independentia a necessitate creavit. Thomas problema aggrediebatur terminis Aristotelicis relate ad contingentiam et necessitatem in mundo.

Unde conceptus necessitatis valde mutatus est, atque post illum possumus loqui de necessitate sive absoluta sive hypothetica (illa[75] a principio identitatis imposita), sive metaphysica, sive physica sive morali.

At fere nihil habemus apud S.Thomam de historia.

Patet ergo quod notio Aristotelica scientiae reducitur ad campum scientiarum naturalium, ad leges scientificas, ad theoriam probabilitatis … neque adaequate definit omnem scientiam.

2.2 Conclusio de notione scientiae

Evolvuntur scientiae et cum ipsis ipsa notio scientiae. Nullus ramus scientiae est simpliciter 'scientia.' Notio scientiae variat secundum subiectum. Unde clarior notio scientiae obtinetur tantum praxi scientifica amplius peracta, unde saepe notio quae hic et nunc de scientia habetur non valet de illa scientia quae exercetur.

Magnum meritum Thomae fuit systematizatio qua omnia conatus est reducere ad principia quaedam fundamentalia. Difficultas tamen illius operis

And so in the divine wisdom there are not first the possibles and then their ordination by wisdom: God sees in his essence all possible orders and sees in each one all the possibles that can be wisely ordered.[74] Yet, just because the divine will necessarily follows the ordination of divine wisdom, God is not therefore necessitated to choose; for in God power and wisdom are coextensive, and every created order is imperfect in itself, so that creation is absolutely free.

In relation to God, nothing happens *per accidens*. The sixteenth-century controversy *De auxiliis* was all about reconciling human freedom and divine providence, that is, about two things that need no *re*-conciling, because, according to St Thomas, both contingent and necessary beings are willed by God, although not in the same way, since God does not impose necessity upon beings that he created to be independent of necessity. Thomas addressed the problem using Aristotelian terminology regarding contingency and necessity in the world.

The concept of necessity, therefore, has greatly changed, and we can now speak of absolute and hypothetical necessity (the latter[75] being imposed by the principle of identity), and of metaphysical, physical, and moral necessity.

But there is virtually nothing about history in St Thomas.

It is clear, therefore, that the Aristotelian notion of science is restricted to the field of the physical sciences, to scientific laws, to the theory of probability, and so on, and does not adequately define all sciences.

2.2 The Notion of Science: Conclusion

Sciences develop, and the notion of science itself develops along with them. No branch of science is simply 'science.' The notion of science varies according to its subject. Hence, a clearer notion of science is to be had only with continued scientific work, and so the notion of science that is had at any given time often does not hold for the sciences that are actually being carried on.

St Thomas's great merit was systematization, by which he tried to reduce everything to certain fundamental principles. The difficulty with his work

---

74 Ibid. 1, q. 25, a. 5.
75 [*Illa* usually refers to the former; but see 'De Scientia atque Voluntate Dei,' §19, in *Early Latin Theology* (see below, note 102) 336–43.]

stat in eo quod Thomas numquam explicat quid faciat, at tantum facit: quod fecit, nos tantum ex analysi illius operis systematice detegimus. Obiectiones quae factae sunt et fiunt contra hoc opus saepe insistunt in punctis particularibus quin videant valorem methodi, et de methodo realiter quaestio erat implicita in controversia Thomistico-Augustinensi saec. XIII.

3   De Duplici Modo Humanae Cogitationis

Exsistit duplex modus quo homines experiuntur, concipiunt, iudicant, cogitant, cognoscunt: symbolicus scilicet et theoreticus.

(1) Modus symbolicus est naturalis, atque naturaliter maxime necessarius, universalis, tempore prior.

(2) Modus theoreticus consilio et voluntate paulatim invenitur et detegitur.

(3) Hi duo modi simul complentur inter se, quia ipsi soli sunt imperfecti, tamen de facto etiam vera dialectica opponuntur, ita ut ex hac oppositione tertium quid oriatur.

Modus symbolicus, quando solus exsistit et operatur, contendit implere totum munus cognoscendi, ideo facile errat, et habentur aberrationes mentalitatis mythicae, magicae, superstitiosae.

Suadentibus natura et praedictis erroribus incipit tunc secundus modus cogitandi theoreticus (cfr. historicam et classicam oppositionem inter mythum et logon). Oppositio tamen inter duos non statim percipitur. Id quod novus oritur non est modus theoreticus purus sed symbolico admixtus, et ideo in novos ducens errores.

Tantum subsequens evolutio generat tertium perfectiorem modum theoreticum qui opponitur non tantum modo symbolico sed etiam modo mixto. At etiam iste remanet diversimode mixtus, quatenus opponuntur non amplius purus mythus contra purum logon, at eorum diversae manifestationes.

3.1 Primus gressus: Symbolismus

Expressiones diversae quae habentur et assumuntur in vultu hominum habent determinatam significationem, sunt aliquid intentionale, non purae combinationes motuum muscularium; sic variae regulationes risus: risus – surrisus – irrisus – arrisus. Hoc intentionale est quid perceptibile

lies in the fact that he never explains what he is doing, but simply does it; and what he did we can only discern through a systematic analysis of his work. The objections that have been brought and are still being brought against it often fasten upon particular points and miss the value of the method; and it was really the question of method that was implicit in the thirteenth-century controversy between the Thomists and the Augustinians.

3   Two Modes of Human Thought

There are two modes or ways in which human beings experience, conceive, judge, think, and know: the symbolic and the theoretic.

(1) The symbolic way is natural, and it is naturally the most necessary, universal, and prior in time.

(2) The theoretic way is gradually discovered and further revealed through deliberate intellectual effort.

(3) These two ways are mutually complementary. Each by itself alone is imperfect. Yet in fact there is also a true dialectical opposition between them, so that from this opposition a third position results.

When the symbolic mode alone exists and is operative, it tends to take over the whole cognitive function and so it easily goes astray, with the resulting aberrations of the mythical, the magical, and the superstitious mentalities.

By a natural process and because of such aberrations, the second, theoretical way of thinking emerges; recall the historical and classical opposition between *mythos* and *logos*. However, the opposition between these two ways is not perceived immediately. The way that first emerges is not a purely theoretic way but is still mixed with the symbolic, and so leads to new errors.

Only subsequent development brings about a third, more perfect theoretic way that is opposed not only to the symbolic way but to the mixed way as well. But even it remains mixed in various ways, insofar as the opposition is no longer between pure *mythos* and pure *logos* but between their various manifestations.

3.1 First Step: Symbolism

Different facial expressions have definite meanings; they are intentional, in the sense that they are not merely certain combinations of muscular movements. See, for example, such variations as a laugh, a smile of joy, a smirk, or a smile of approval. This intentionality is something that is perceptible

praeter perceptionem motuum materialium. Haec materialis motus perceptio est perspectiva, secundum lucem, colorem … quibus variantibus variat, at semper eadem manet perceptio significationis motus, v.gr., risus. Hic actus percipiendi est activitas quae fit intra campum conscientiae psychologicae, ubi tantum intrant ea quae conscientia ipsa formare potest et vult.

Sensus horum motuum non tantum oculis videtur, at percipitur, seu habetur tota adaptatio psychologica ad ipsos.

Hoc elementum intentionale in his motibus contentum est naturale et spontaneum. Non addiscimus ridere, sicut non addiscimus manducare. Neque motus neque eorum sensus nobis per aliqua prius nota innotescit. Motus habet immanentem suum sensum, seipsum explicat. Utique, potest fieri analysis in eius causis, tamen ipsa significatio non ad aliud reducitur. Intentionale in visu est aliquid in suo ordine simplex et immediatum. Nec reducitur ad id quod per verba exprimi potest: verbis exprimitur intentionale alii ordinis (conceptus).

Dum sensus discursivus utitur unico signo pro unoquoque conceptu, sensus symbolicus utitur signis multivalentibus: sic risus potest exprimere delectationem, satisfactionem, omne genus amoris, tristitiam, ironiam, nec non statum aenigmaticum … hae diversae significationes variant secundum variationes situationum.

Dum sensus discursivus est ad unum determinatus, sensus symbolicus, praecise quia signis utitur plurivalentibus, est ambiguus, potest verum vel falsum celare, multo possibiliorem reddit simulationem, dissimulationem eodem signo, v.g risu.

Dum sensus discursivus accurate distinguit inter modum indicativum, optativum, imperativum, seu cognoscitivum aut voluntarium, sensus symbolicus neque distinguit neque separat id quod homo cognoscit ab illo quod appetit et vult; nam nullo signo abstracto utitur, et est de se rapidus, emotionalis; non tantum manifestare aliquid intendit, sed causare in aliis aliquid simile vel oppositum; non dictis sese exprimit sed factis.

Dum sensus discursivus est obiectivus, sensus symbolicus est intersubiectivus seu duo subiecta supponit inter quae causat mutuam adaptationem psychologicam (v.g. communicatio anxietatis matris ad infantem), et, quia intersubiectivus, simul revelat et creat situationem quam revelat (cfr. *Mit-*

besides the perception of the physical movements involved. The perception of the physical movements is perspectival, varying according to the conditions of light, color, etc.; but the perception of the meaning of the movement, say, a smile of joy, remains the same. This act of perception is an activity that takes place within the field of psychological consciousness, into which enter only those elements that consciousness itself can and wills to form.

The meaning of these movements is not merely seen by the eye but is perceived: there is a whole psychological adaptation to them.

The intentional element in such movements is natural and spontaneous. We do not learn to laugh any more than we learn to eat. Neither these movements nor their meaning become known to us through some prior knowledge. The movement has its own immanent meaning, it is self-explanatory. True, it can be analyzed as to its causes, but its meaning is not reducible to something else. The intentionality in seeing is something simple and immediate in its own order; nor is it reducible to what can be expressed in words, for words express the intentionality of another order, the conceptual.

While discursive meaning uses a single sign for each concept, symbolic meaning uses multivalent signs: thus, a smile can express delight, satisfaction, love, sadness, irony, puzzlement; these different meanings vary according to different situations.

While discursive meaning is single in its intention, symbolic meaning, precisely because it uses multivalent signs, is ambiguous, can conceal truth or falsity, and makes it much easier to pretend or to dissemble by the same sign – by a smile, for example.

While discursive meaning carefully distinguishes between the indicative, the optative, and the imperative mood, that is, between what is a matter of knowing and a matter of willing, symbolic meaning makes no distinction or separation between what one knows and what one desires or wills. For it does not use an abstract sign, and of itself is rapid and emotional; it aims at not only manifesting something but also at causing something similar or the opposite in others; it expresses itself not in words but in actions.

While discursive meaning is objective, symbolic meaning is intersubjective, supposing two subjects between whom it produces a mutual psychological adaptation – for example, the communication of a mother's anxiety to her child. And because it is intersubjective, it reveals and at the same time creates the situation that it reveals (compare *Mitsein* in the philosophy

sein in philosophia Heideggeriana), attentionem attrahit non ad se sed ad aliud quod evocat et in quo sibi complacet.

Dum sensus discursivus tendit ad synthesin tantum per analysin, sensus symbolicus, tamquam manifestatio spiritus incarnati, continet in se synthesin.

Magnum momentum symbolismi in vita infantili ex qua influit in reliquam vitam.[76]

Maximi momenti est determinare quid sit illa significatio quae implicite dicitur in symbolismo. Quando, v.gr., duo subiecta mutuo subrident, adest mutua cognitio sive in ordine sensitivo (inter animalia), sive in ordine humano intellectuali. Haec mutua cognitio inter homines ex agnitione sensibili oritur et completur per operationem intellectualem. At haec operatio est implicita, quia non clare et distincte cognoscitur.

Cognitio clara et distincta requireret analysin

(1) secundum unitatem numericam seu praedicamentalem, quae est principium et causa numeri secundum experientiam; eius ratio est in eo quod unitas intelligibilitatis potest multiplicari ratione materiae, neque haec multiplicatio addit novam intelligibilitatem, neque novam entitatem nisi numericam (hac unitate, v.gr., Christus est unus homo);

(2) secundum unitatem formalem seu naturalem (ubi distinguitur unum per se et unum per accidens) respondentem non principio identitatis sed primae intellectus operationi (quid sit) ex qua habentur conceptus rerum; agitur de illa unitate luminosa seu de unitate intelligibilitatis (secundum huiusmodi unitatem in Christo, v.gr., habetur duplex unitas per se ex intrinseca intelligibilitate sive naturae divinae sive humanae);

of Heidegger), and draws attention not to itself but to something else that it evokes and with which it is in sympathy.

While discursive meaning aims at synthesis only through analysis, symbolic meaning, as the manifestation of an enfleshed spirit, contains a synthesis within itself.

Symbolism has great importance in the life of the infant, from which it influences the rest of life.[76]

It is very important to determine just what that meaning is that is said to be implicit in symbolism. When, for example, two human subjects smile at each other, there is knowledge in both parties at the sense level (as among two animals), and at the intellectual level. This knowledge that both have originates in what they recognize through their senses, and it is completed through the operation of their intellects. This operation, however, is implicit, since it is not known clearly and distinctly.

Clear and distinct knowledge would require

(1) an analysis according to numerical or predicamental unity, the principle and cause of number as experienced, where the unity of intelligibility can be multiplied by reason of matter and where such multiplication adds no new intelligibility or new entity except numerically – by this unity, for example, Christ is one human being;

(2) an analysis according to formal or natural unity, where the distinction is made between one *per se* and one *per accidens*, and where the correspondence is not to the principle of identity but to the first intellectual operation, the question 'What is it?' giving rise to concepts of things; the unity in question here is a luminous unity of intelligibility in accord with which, for example, there is in Christ a double unity *per se* based on the intrinsic intelligibility of his human nature and his divine nature;

---

76 [For all of this] see Max Scheler, *Wesen und Formen der Sympathie,* (Bonn: Verlag von Friedrich Cohen, 1923); [published later as vol. 7 in Scheler's *Gesammelte Werke* (Bern: Francke, 1954–); English translation, *The Nature of Sympathy,* trans. Peter Heath, with a general introduction to Scheler's work by W. Stark (New Haven: Yale University Press, 1954)]. Martin Buber, *Je et tu* (Paris: F. Aubier, 1938); [English translation, *I and Thou,* 2nd ed., trans. Ronald Gregor Smith, with a postscript by the author (New York: Scribner, 1958)]. Paul Tillich, *Systematic Theology,* vol. 1: *Reason and Revelation,* [part 2] *Being and Good;* vol. 2: *Existence and the Christ* (Chicago: University of Chicago Press, 1951, 1957). Also, the works of C.G. Jung, and of O. Casel (on presence in liturgy; see above). [Buber's *Ich und Du* was first published in 1923 (Leipzig: Insel-Verlag).]

(3) secundum unitatem actualem seu transcendentalem (ubi distinguitur unum simpliciter et unum secundum quid) respondentem secundae
operationi intellectuali (an sit) ex qua habetur iudicium applicans principium identitatis et non-contradictionis; secundum hanc unitatem unum
(indivisum in se et divisum a quolibet alio) et ens convertuntur (et Christus,
v.gr., est una persona, unum suppositum, una res, unum ens).

Triplici unitati correspondet triplex identitas quae invenitur in triplici
operatione intellectuali: unitas numerica percipitur, unitas formalis intelligitur, unitas actualis iudicatur.

Haec omnia desunt in modo cognoscendi symbolico. Primitivi non clare
distinguunt inter hominem, eius partes, eius umbram et imaginem.

In cognitione clara et distincta habentur duo aspectus serierum elementorum et totalitatum. In singulis rebus apparet aspectus sensibilis, qui variat
variante perspectiva: id quod percipimus est res varios habens aspectus. At
secundum id quod revera est et non tantum apparet, res distinguimus ab
illarum aspectibus sensibilibus. E contra apud primitivos et parvulos non
clare distinguuntur varii aspectus, neque eorum linea demarcationis. Propterea nomina cum rebus identificantur et haec est ratio, potius quam aliquid solius Semiticae mentalitatis proprium, qua antiquis Hebraeis vetitus
est usus imaginum. Periculum idolatriae imminebat quia non clare distin-
guebant inter rem et rei repraesentionem.

Quare mythologia plena est personificationibus omnino differentibus a
personificationibus poeticis. In mentalitate mythica, ipsa prima perceptio
est intersubiectiva. Haec tendentia non est absurda, quare nec facile refutatur. Fundatur in vita sensitiva: animalia sentiunt ut nos, et etiam plantae vivunt ut nos, unde extenditur vitalismus universalis. Talis modus concipiendi praeest saepe societatibus erectis ad impediendam crudelitatem contra
animalia. Ita in artibus id quod repraesentatur ut vivens percipitur et non
ut pura repraesentatio, inde habetur apprehensio artistica intersubiectiva,
seu secundum modum subiecti.

Neque ignoratur ratio causalitatis, attamen non clare apprehensa. Causa-
litas est saepe metamorphosis; quia id quod videtur determinat notionem
causalitatis, causa est illud ex quo alia oriuntur.

(3) an analysis according to actual or transcendental unity, where the distinction is made between one absolutely speaking and one in a qualified sense, and where the correspondence is to the second intellectual operation, the question 'Is it so?' giving rise to a judgment applying the principle of identity or non-contradiction; according to this unity, being and one (i.e., that which is undivided in itself and divided from everything else) are convertible terms, and so, for example, Christ is one person, one supposit, one thing, one being.

To this threefold unity there corresponds that threefold identity found in the three intellectual operations: numerical unity is perceived, formal unity is understood, actual unity is judged.

These are all lacking in the symbolic mode of knowing. Primitive people do not clearly distinguish between a human being and his parts, his shadow, and his image.

In knowledge that is clear and distinct there are two aspects in the series [plural] of elements and totalities. In each thing there appears the sensible aspect, which varies according to the variation in perspective: that which we perceive is the thing having these variable aspects. But as to what really exists and not merely appears, we distinguish the thing itself from those sensible aspects. But primitive people and children do not clearly distinguish these various aspects or draw a sharp line of demarcation between them. Accordingly, names are identified with things, and this, rather than anything peculiar to the Semitic mentality, is the reason for the prohibition of images among the ancient Hebrews. There was a present danger of idolatry because a clear distinction between a thing and its representation was lacking.

For this reason mythology is full of personifications entirely different from the personifications in poetry. In the mythic mentality the primary perception is intersubjective. This tendency is not at all absurd, and for this reason it is difficult to refute. It is grounded in the life of the senses: animals have sensation as we do, and we even have a certain vital activity in common with plants, with the resulting extension of universal vitalism. This way of conceiving is the guiding principle of societies formed for the prevention of cruelty to animals. Thus, in artistic representations that which is depicted is perceived as being alive and not as being simply represented, whence we have artistic apprehension that is intersubjective, that is, according to the mode of the subject.

The notion of causality also is not unknown, albeit not clearly apprehended. Causality is often metamorphosis; since what is seen determines the notion of causality, a cause is that from which other things result.

Unde, in modo cognoscendi intersubiectivo, desunt plures distinctiones inter totum (unum) et partes, inter res et imagines rerum, inter naturas et earum qualitates, inter rem et causam rei, atque multa implicita sunt. Ex quo oritur magia, consistens in tribuenda causalitate omnibus rebus, immo causalitate voluntaria et personali.

Quod primus gressus humanae cognitionis est symbolicus non est sine consectariis etiam pro modo theoretico cognoscendi: hoc significat cognitionem humanam esse originarie realisticam, plenam vitae, dynamicam ... Si hoc negligatur adest periculum incidendi, in successiva evolutione, in conceptualismum atque intellectualismum rationalisticum.

In stadio symbolico ipsa intelligentia est pars constitutiva situationis humanae, quatenus adsunt operationes intellectuales quibus implicite agnoscitur et determinatur situatio. Homo intelligit, diligit, iudicat quin intelligat se intelligere, diligere, iudicare. Sic in artibus manifestatur id quod per conceptus abstractos exprimi nequit: nulla dissertatio de symphonia potest aequivalere ipsi symphoniae.

Spatium apprehenditur ab homine quatenus ipse spatialis, unde spatium cognoscitur kinesthetice, seu quatenus apprehenditur super et desuper, ante et post, dextera et sinistra, sive quatenus homo se movet. Sic homo primitivus in silvis semper iterum iter invenit ut redeat ad suum campum quin sciat neque possit explicare cur et unde et per relationem ad quae hoc sciat. Simpliciter scit. Talis notio spatii obiectivatur in statuis; in templis, ubi templum est centrum mundi, origo omnium coordinatarum vitae humanae capax orientandi totum populum in universo (cfr. homines orantes versus templum).[77]

Tempus non modo abstracto concipitur sed tamquam motionibus[78] plenum, et essentialiter tamquam expectatio; unde praesens apprehenditur tamquam anticipatio illius quod expectatur; memoria habetur quando obiectum expectationis est transactum. Talis apprehensio temporis obiectivatur in musica, in saltationibus praesertim bellicis, essentialibus pro vita communitatis.

Unde omnia quae sunt fundamentalia et vera et propria cognitionis humanae adsunt in hoc modo cogitandi symbolico, attamen modo implicito, et propterea tali ex quo sive errores sive veritates sequi possint; ex quibus erroribus multa sequuntur mala per aliquam dialecticam.

Accordingly, in the intersubjective way of knowing many distinctions between the whole (one) and its parts, between things and their representations, between natures and their qualities, between a thing and its cause, are lacking, and many are implicit. This gives rise to magic, which consists in attributing causality to everything, even causality that is willed and personal.

The fact that the first step in human knowing is symbolic is not without consequences for the theoretic way of knowing as well. It means that human knowledge is in the first instance realistic, full of vitality, dynamic. To neglect this is to run the risk of falling successively into conceptualism and rationalistic intellectualism.

At the symbolic stage, understanding is a constitutive part of the human situation, inasmuch as there are intellectual operations going on by which the situation is implicitly recognized and determined. One understands, loves, and judges without understanding that he or she understands, loves, and judges. Thus, the arts convey what cannot be expressed in abstract concepts: no disquisition upon a symphony can be equivalent to the symphony itself.

One apprehends space inasmuch as one is spatial oneself, and so one comes to know space kinesthetically, as one apprehends above and below, back and front, right and left, or as one moves. The primitive forest-dweller always finds the same road back to his camp without knowing or being able to explain why and wherefore or by what indication he knows it; he simply knows it. This notion of space is objectified in statues; in temples, where the temple is the center of the world, the origin of all coordinates of human life that is capable of orientating the whole people in the universe – people pray facing a temple, for example.[77]

Time is conceived not in an abstract manner but as full of movements[78] and essentially as expectation. Thus, the present is apprehended as the anticipation of what is awaited, while memory is had when the object of expectation has passed. Such an apprehension of time is objectified in music, especially in war dances so essential for the life of a community.

Accordingly, all that is fundamental and true and proper to human knowing is to be found in this symbolic mode of thinking, though in an implicit way, and therefore in a way that can lead both to truth and to error. And from those errors, by way of a dialectical process, many evils result.

77 [See Lonergan, *Topics in Education* 225–27.]
78 [Reading *motionibus* for *notionibus*.]

3.2 Secundus gressus: Usus linguae

Usus linguae pertinet ad modum cognoscendi symbolicum quatenus hunc modum et evolvit et extendit. Datur tamen distinctio. Hic operatio intellectualis, actus intellectualis recognitionis, qui non clare per symbola exprimebatur, exprimitur per linguam evolutam, per verba quae sunt symbola unice repraesentantia talem et talem operationem rationis. Unde usus linguae exsurgit ut melius attingatur symbolismus.

Sic oritur *logos*. Haec evolutio praesertim facta est in Graecia, tamen non gradu efficaci ad destruendam idolatriam, immo postea cum neo-Platonismo conati sunt ad *mythum* redire. Christianismus multum iuvavit evolutionem perficiendam.

In India habita est vera evolutio rationis, unde vera philosophia, at defuit tensio ad obiectum et fere tota ad subiectum directa est (cfr. Upanishad), unde defuit obiectivatio subiecti qua talis, quod cum Atman identificatum est.

Quando evolutio rationalis pervenit ad directionem non amplius versus id quod est traditionale in propria communitate sed versus id quod est verum, id est quando magis explicite principium contradictionis incipit adhiberi, fiunt conversiones religiosae.[79]

3.2.1 De nominibus propriis

Nomen proprium exprimit actum agnitionis intellectualis et pars ipsius agnitionis. Cognitio humana tres gradus comprehendit: experientia, intelligentia (quid sit), rationalis affirmatio (an sit). Quando fit agnitio intellectualis habetur et affirmatio unitatis et simul realitatis. Talis agnitio non constituit totum actum, nam totus homo agit, intellectus et sensus, spiritus incarnatus. Nomen dicit centrum istius affirmationis, quid determinatum ubi figi possunt et imagines. Per nomen etiam iterum evocatur transacta experientia intersubiectiva, unde nomen potest valere pro actuali experientia. Nomen praebet possibilitatem libere imaginandi, evocat sentimenta

3.2 Second Step: The Use of Language

The use of language pertains to the symbolic way of knowing, insofar as it develops and extends this way of knowing. There is, however, a distinction to be made. Here the intellectual operation, the act of intellectual recognition, which is not clearly expressed in symbols, is expressed in a developed language, in words that are symbols that stand for only such and such an operation of reason. Hence, the use of language emerges so that symbolism is better attained.

Such is the origin of *logos*. This development took place especially in ancient Greece, although not strongly enough to extirpate idolatry; later on in fact with Neoplatonism there was an attempt to return to *mythos*. But Christianity contributed greatly to the furthering of this development.

In India there occurred a genuine development of reason, hence a genuine philosophy, but the focus was almost entirely on the subject rather than the object, as in the Upanishads; as a result, there was no objectification of the subject as such, which was identified with Atman.

When the development of reason reaches the point at which it is no longer directed towards what is traditional in its own community but towards what is true – in other words, when it begins to use the principle of contradiction more explicitly – that is when religious conversions occur.[79]

3.2.1 Proper Nouns

A proper noun, or name, expresses an act of intellectual recognition, and is part of the recognition itself. There are three steps in human cognition: experience, understanding ('What is it?'), and rational affirmation ('Is it so?'). In intellectual recognition there is an affirmation of unity and at the same time of reality. Such recognition does not constitute the entire act, however, for the whole person acts, intellect and senses, an enfleshed spirit. A name indicates the center of that affirmation, something definite to which images can be attached. A name also summons up again a past intersubjective experience, so that the name itself can stand for the actual

---

79 [Lonergan may have had in mind here the story he tells in *Understanding and Being* 301 about the missionary in Japan convincing the bonze in the village of the principle of contradiction and the subsequent conversion of the bonze and the village to Christianity.]

et imagines; imaginatio autem est experientia non actualiter habita. Nomen non est tantum terminus agnitionis sed est quid sensibile, phantasma
quoddam ex quo intellectus ad ulteriores actus procedere potest. Unde
momentum nominis in antiquitate, praesertim nominis Dei. Tot numina
quot nomina.[80]

3.2.2 De nominibus communibus

Nomina communia non dicunt de se aliquam pluralitatem respectu nominum propriorum. Nomen proprium est instrumentum ad cuius usum
homo indiget intelligentia. Nomen commune signat aliquem progressum,
quia est quaedam generalizatio individuorum similium. Ita lingua evolvitur,
necnon organizatio ipsius intelligentiae. Maior est tamen evolutio ad nomina propria invenienda quam ad communia.

Lingua data est ad dicendam rerum universitatem indefinitam. Haec habitudo linguae ad res in mentem ducit notionem intellectus prout in Aristotele et Thoma habetur, seu id quod est omnia fieri,[81] et notionem mundi
ut totalitas obiectorum.

Unde pro homine linguam addiscere maternam significat quandam organizationem facere tum conscientiae, tum subiectorum, tum obiectorum,
mentis et mundi. Unusquisque vivit in proprio mundo (mundo sacerdo-
tum, medicorum ...) qui est illa pars universi iacens intra proprium horizontem. Intelligentia vulgaris[82] est praecise illa quae operatur intra aliquem
horizontem determinatum.

Centrum mundi huius vulgaris intelligentiae est subiectum, unde nova
habetur conceptio temporis, quod est tempus psychologicum praesens lo-

experience. A name renders possible the free exercise of the imagination, it evokes feelings and images; imagination, however, is of something not actually being experienced. A name is not only the term of recognition but is also something perceptible, a phantasm from which the intellect can proceed to further acts. This accounts for the importance of a name in the ancient world, especially the name of God. *Tot numina quot nomina* – as many deities as there are names.[80]

3.2.2 Common Nouns

Common nouns do not in themselves indicate any plurality as compared with proper nouns. A proper noun is a tool that requires intelligence to use it. A common noun is a sign of progress because it is a generalization of individuals that are alike. In this way language develops as well as the organization of intelligence itself. But there is a greater development in finding proper nouns than in finding common nouns.

Language exists for the purpose of indicating the indefinite totality of things. This relationship of language to things brings to mind Aristotle's and Aquinas's notion of intellect as being that which is open to all reality,[81] and the notion of the world as the totality of objects.

To learn one's mother tongue, therefore, means to carry out some organization of one's consciousness, of subjects, objects, mind, and world. One lives in a world of one's own (the world of priests, of doctors, etc.), which is that part of the universe that lies within one's own horizon. Ordinary intelligence[82] is precisely that which operates within a determinate horizon.

The center of the world of this ordinary intelligence is the subject, whence there is a new concept of time, the present psychological time of

---

80 See Hermann Usener, *Götternamen: Versuch einer Lehre von der reliogiösen Begriffsbildung* (Bonn: F. Cohen, 1896; [4th ed., Frankfurt am Main: Klostermann, 2000]), to which should be added other articles [by the same author]: 'Göttliche Synonyme,' *Rheinisches Museum für Philologie* 53 (1898) 329–79; 'Keraunos,' *Rheinisches Museum für Philologie* 60 (1905) 1–30; 'Mythologie, '*Archiv für Religionswissenschaft* 7 (1904) 6–32.

81 [Aristotle, *De Anima* III, 5, 430a 14; Thomas Aquinas, *In III De Anima*, lect. 10, §728.]

82 [Normally 'vulgaris' would be translated 'commonsense,' since it is Lonergan's usual Latin term for this familiar term. But here he is leading up to the expression 'common sense,' for which he uses the English word, so 'vulgaris' is rendered simply 'ordinary.']

quentis; inde desumuntur varii modi verborum. Res considerantur quoad nos, secundum exteriores apparentias relate ad subiectum. Remanet inter-subiectivitas. Lingua addit symbolismo, non tollit illum.

In arte poetica verba habent suam vim non tantum ex propria significatione sed ex illorum resonantia intra conscientiam. Figurae sermonis, de quibus grammatici loquuntur, pertinent ad modum hunc cogitandi.

Evolutio intelligentiae in intelligentia vulgari est sat magna: tamen non considerat principia generalia ex quibus fiant deductiones in omni campo, sed quaeritur utilitas generalis. Habitus intellectuales possunt evolvi secundum structuram scientificam, sed non necessario; ita de facto saepe talem structuram non habent.

Huiusmodi cogitatio non ordinatur ad dicendas veritates universales, sed potius ad genus proverbiorum, quae exprimunt non deductiones universales sed tantum id quod in pluribus communiter utile esse potest. Iudicia habentur non de qualibet re, sed illa quae cum parvis additamentis, secundum varios casus, praebere possint intelligentiam diversarum situationum concretarum. Haec intelligentia vulgaris maxime versatur circa particularia, ad cognoscenda et determinanda ut modus quo homo agat in his particularibus inveniatur.

Haec intelligentia non est individualistica sed communis; ita loquuntur de sensu communi ('common sense'). Utique, loquens est aliquis individuus, qui tamen semper inter alios invenitur, aliquis 'ego' inter 'nos.' Cogitatio habet munus publicum et fit secundum evolutionem intellectualem prout in communitate habetur.

Secundum hunc modum evolvuntur primae civilizationes collectivisticae, in Aegypto, Babylonia, India, Sinis; talis est etiam civilizatio Maya, Incas ... quae a stupenda evolutione artium practicarum et liberalium comitantur.

In his conditionibus, magnae felicitates et magnae miseriae stimulant reflexionem humanam et modum magis personalem cogitandi. Sic habetur ab anno 800 ad 200 a.C. evolutio philosophica secundum axem historicum in Sinis, India, Persia (cfr. Zoroastrismum). Apparatio locutionis et cogitationis magis individualis habetur inter Hebraeos apud prophetas, qui saepe sese contraponunt communitati et tamquam individui loquuntur pro Deo. Sic in Graecia apparent primi philosophi.[83]

the speaker; and from this, various verbal modes are derived. Things are considered in their relationship to us, *quoad nos*, according to what appears outwardly to the subject. Intersubjectivity remains. Language adds to symbolism, it does not do away with it.

In poetry words derive their force not from their proper meaning alone but from what resonates with them within one's consciousness. What grammarians call figures of speech belong to this mode of thinking.

Development within this ordinary intelligence is quite considerable. Nevertheless it does not take into account general principles from which deductions are made in all fields of knowledge, but rather seeks general usefulness. Intellectual habits can evolve according to a scientific structure, but not necessarily; in fact they often do not possess such a structure.

This sort of thinking is not such as to express universal truths, but is more suited to proverbial sayings that express not universal deductions but only what could for the most part be generally useful. The judgments it expresses are not about anything whatsoever, but those judgments that, with slight qualifications according to the case, might afford some understanding of various concrete situations. Such ordinary understanding has to do most of all with particular things, so as to learn and determine what a person should do in these particular circumstances.

This understanding is not individualistic but common. So we speak of 'common sense.' True, the speaker is some individual person, but he or she is always found among others, an 'I' among 'we.' Thinking has a public function and goes on according to the intellectual development that is to be found in a given community.

It was according to this mode that the first collectivist civilizations evolved, in Egypt, Babylonia, India, and China, as well as the Mayan and Incan civilizations, and along with their evolution there took place a remarkable development in both the practical and liberal arts.

In these situations, great prosperity and great misery stimulated reflection on the human condition and a more personal turn of thought. Thus, there took place between 800 and 200 BC the development of philosophy in this axial period of history in China, India, and Persia (Zoroastrianism). A more individualistic sort of thinking and speaking was prepared for by the Hebrew prophets, who often opposed the community and as individuals spoke on behalf of God. So also in Greece the first philosophers made their appearance.[83]

83 Karl Jaspers, *Vom Ursprung und Ziel der Geschichte* (Zurich: Artemis-Verlag,

3.3 Tertius gressus: Intelligentia scientifica methodica

Tunc oritur novus modus cogitandi et intelligendi. Husserl bene ostendit philosophos Graecos sumpsisse nomina ex modo cogitandi antiquo: *sophia, logos, alētheia, epistēmē* … tamen eis novum sensum tribuendo qui antea simpliciter ignorabatur. Sic crisis secundi modi cogitandi ita a M. Heidegger instituitur ut, non ad tertium scientifico-systematicum, sed ad primum symbolicum devenerit (quae est ratio forsan cur illius opera systematica incompleta maneant).

Momentum maximum Socratis est in incepta mutatione modi cogitationis. Aristoteles tribuit Socrati *logoi epaktikoi* – sermones inductivos vel conductivos.[84]

Agitur de inductione diversa a moderna scientifica, quae ex hypothesi incipit a puris sensibilibus sine ulla admixtione intelligentiae. Relate ad Socratem agitur potius de eo quod ipse explicitum fecit id quod antea iam implicite aderat. Athenienses sciebant quid esset fortitudo, ignorantia, iustitia, scientia … at Socrates novum introduxit ideale: utendo nominibus communibus (sic 'virtute' quae habita erat in Pericle, Solone …) introduxit ideale logicum, secundum quod ea quae per nomina communia designantur ita concipi debent ut possint sustinere totum pondus logicae deductionis (ita alius est sensus 'temperantiae' quando utimur hoc verbo ad praeceptum dandum puero, alia notio 'temperantiae' quae assumitur in constructione scientiae ethicae).

Sic anticipabatur structura logica in qua omnia connectuntur et singuli termini semper fixi manent. Ita, ut ex dialogis Platonicis apparet, lux progrediebatur inter difficultates quae insolubiles videbantur.

Socrates introduxit etiam modum magis individualem cogitandi, secundum quem nulla opinio sine scrutinio mentis privatae est toleranda, absque reverentia pro anteriori cogitatione. Quare Socrates subversivus visus est. Hic character etiam postea mansit proprius scholarum Socraticarum, sive Academiae sive Lycaei, quae in privato habebantur.

3.3   Third Step: Methodical Scientific Understanding

At this point in time a new mode of thinking and understanding appears. Husserl has shown quite well that the Greek philosophers took their terminology from the ancient mode of thinking – sophia, logos, alētheia, epistēmē – yet gave those words a new meaning that previously they did not have. Thus, Martin Heidegger has undertaken a critique of this second mode of thinking, but not in such a way as to proceed to the third, the scientific-systematic mode, but to revert to the first mode, the symbolic. (This is perhaps why his systematic works remain incomplete.)

The most important thing about Socrates was that he brought about this change in the mode of thinking. To him Aristotle attributed logoi epaktikoi, inductive or conductive arguments.[84]

The sort of induction referred to here is different from that of modern science, which ex hypothesi begins from purely sensible data without any admixture of understanding. In Socrates's case it referred rather to the fact that he made explicit what had hitherto been present implicitly. The Athenians knew what bravery, ignorance, justice, knowledge, etc., are, but Socrates brought in a new ideal: by using common nouns – 'virtue,' for example, as found in Pericles, in Solon, and others – he introduced the logical ideal according to which those realities designated by such common nouns had to be conceived in such a way as to be able to support the entire weight of logical deduction. So, for example, 'temperance' has one meaning when we are instructing a child and another when we are using it in constructing a theory of ethics.

Thus was anticipated the logical structure in which everything is interconnected and each term has a fixed meaning. In this way, as can be seen in the dialogues of Plato, more and more light is shed upon difficulties that had seemed insuperable.

Socrates also introduced a more individualistic mode of thinking according to which no opinion was to be admitted unless scrutinized by personal examination, without deference to any previous thinking. This is why Socrates was seen to be subversive. Even after his time this remained a special characteristic of the Socratic schools, both the Academy and the Lyceum, which were conducted in private.

1949). [English translation, The Origin and Goal of History, trans. Michael Bullock (New Haven: Yale University Press, 1953; 4th ed., 1968.]

84 Aristotle, Metaphysics, XIII, 1078b 17–31.

At, quid significat explicitum facere id quod intelligentia vulgari iam quodammodo cognoscitur?

Intelligentia vulgaris ea quae implicite cognoscit, non cognoscit qua implicita. Unde necessaria est argumentatio ut haec explicitentur. At, id quod argumentatione ex intelligentia vulgari obtinetur pugnat contra ipsam intelligentiam vulgarem; unde crises contra philosophos in Graecia et alibi.

Unde patet explicitationem involvere ulteriorem actuationem intellectus, qui antea non cognoscebat implicationes quae postea elucent. Per hanc novam actuationem intellectus manifestat et illa quae iam antea cognoscebat, et simul illa quae nesciebat se implicite cognoscere, et quae prima facie videntur opponi iis quae prius communiter cognoscebantur. Tamen manet dependentia cogitationis explicitae a praecedenti, et ita conclusiones Platonicae non alienae ab iis quae generaliter agnoscuntur se habent.

Attamen, processus explicitationis non clare et distincte cognoscit limites proprii valoris. Nam plus valet de logicis, ethicis, metaphysicis ... quam de iis quae pertinent ad scientias naturales (physicam, chimicam, biologicam ...) et humanas (sociologiam, historiam, oeconomiam, psychologiam ...). Hi limites ignorantur si unicus modus procedendi est tantum explicitum reddere id quod antea implicitum erat.

Inde ortum est problema temporum modernorum. In Renascentia, occasione renovationis scientiarum, posita est quaestio de methodo procedendi in scientiis. Occasio fuit status theologiae scholasticae saec. XIV–XV et exsistentia unici modi explicitatorii, quin resoluta esset quaestio de limitibus huius processus. Haec quaestio methodica semper magis intimius connexa est cum quaestione gnoseologica et epistemologica in tota philosophia moderna.[85]

Problema theologicum in eo est quod dogmata adsunt implicite in fontibus revelationis, et generatim a magisterio ecclesiastico proponuntur se-

But what does it mean to make explicit what is already known in some way by ordinary intelligence?

What ordinary intelligence knows implicitly, it does not know as implicit; hence, a process of reasoning is necessary in order to make it explicit. But what this reasoning process arrives at by ordinary intelligence goes against ordinary intelligence itself; hence the criticism leveled against philosophers in Greece and elsewhere.

Explicitation, therefore, obviously entails a further actuation of the intellect, which previously was not cognizant of those implications that subsequently became clear. Through this further actuation the intellect expresses both what it already knew before and at the same time what it did not know that it knew implicitly, and what at first glance seems to contradict what previously was common knowledge. Still, the dependence of this explicit thinking upon previous thinking remains, and so Plato's conclusions are not totally unrelated to commonly held opinions.

And yet, this process of explicitation does not have a clear and distinct knowledge of the limits of its own worth. For it is more valuable in systems of logic, ethics, and metaphysics than in the natural sciences (physics, chemistry, biology) or the human sciences (sociology, history, economics, psychology). These limits will be ignored if the sole way of proceeding is just to render explicit what had been implicit before.

It is this that has given rise to the problem of modernity. In the Renaissance, a time of renewal in the sciences, the question was raised about the method of proceeding in the sciences. This was occasioned by the state of Scholastic theology in the fourteenth and fifteenth centuries and the existence of a single way of explicitation, but the question of the limits of this procedure went unresolved. This question of method is always more closely connected with the gnoseological and epistemological question in the whole of modern philosophy.[85]

In theology the problem is that the dogmas are present implicitly in the sources of revelation and are generally taught by the ecclesiastical *magis-*

85 See Ernst Cassirer, *Das Erkenntnisproblem in der Philosophie und Wissenschaft der neueren Zeit*, 3 vols. (Berlin: B. Cassirer, 1922–23), especially about the problem of method in Descartes's *Regulae ad directionem ingenii* [vol. 1, pp. 439–505], in Spinoza (emendation of the intellect) [vol. 2, pp. 73–125], and in Leibniz (the characteristics of 'mathesis universalis') [vol. 2, pp. 126–90].

cundum modum cogitandi scientifico-systematicum alienum a modo cogitandi vulgari, quoad nos.[86]

4   De Methodo Eiusque Praeceptis[87]

Incipimus tractationem de methodo generali. Notio methodi est practica,
nam consistit methodus in praeceptis indicantibus quid faciendum et quid
non, quid omittendum, quid fieri non potest … quin rationes dentur quae
proprie in theoria cognitionis inveniuntur.

Propterea praeoccupatio in philosophia moderna est circa theoriam cognitionis, quia philosophi volunt determinare methodum efficacem perveni-
endi ad veritatem.

Methodus respicit futurum, quod, quando fit quaestio de methodo, non
cognoscitur, neque possumus scire utrum ad illud pervenire possimus
necne. Annuntiatio boni futuri movet dubitationes et quaestionem de
methodo.[88]

Dabimus quinque praecepta generalia respicientia omnem scientiam,
quae debebunt adaptari secundum diversitatem materiae uniuscuiusque.
Haec unitas methodi fundatur in eo quod mens humana est una; omnes
autem scientiae tendunt ad unitatem.

Quinque praecepta erunt:

1 Intellige.
2 Intellige modo systematico.
3 Inverte contrapositiones.

terium according to the scientific-systematic mode of thinking that is very different from the common, *quoad nos*, mode of thinking.[86]

4   Method and Its Precepts[87]

Here we begin our treatment of general method. Method is a practical notion, for method consists of precepts that indicate what is to be done or not done, what is to be omitted, what cannot be done, and so on, but without giving reasons, which properly belong in a theory of knowledge.

The reason why modern philosophy is preoccupied with the theory of knowledge is that philosophers want to determine an efficacious method for arriving at truth.

Method looks to the future, which, when the question of method is raised, is unknown, nor can we know whether or not it is attainable. An announcement of some future good raises doubts and brings up the question of method.[88]

We shall set forth five general precepts applicable to all branches of knowledge, which of course will have to be adapted to suit the subject matter of each particular science. This unity of method rests upon the fact that the human mind is one and the same; all branches of knowledge tend towards unity.

These five precepts are as follows:

1 Understand.
2 Understand systematically.
3 Reverse counterpositions.

---

86 [Lonergan will later speak of dogmatic development in terms of differentiations of consciousness rather than in terms of making explicit what was implicit in the sources. See below, p. 643, note 1.]

87 [In connection with this section, see Bernard Lonergan, 'Method in Catholic Theology,' in *Philosophical and Theological Papers 1958–1964*, vol. 6 in Collected Works of Bernard Lonergan, ed. Robert C. Croken, Frederick E. Crowe, and Robert M. Doran (Toronto: University of Toronto Press, 1996) 29–53, previously published in METHOD: *Journal of Lonergan Studies* 10:1 (Spring 1992) 3–26, and now available on www.loneganresource.com. Lonergan repeated these five precepts in the 1961 course on 'De Intellectu et Methodo.' See www.bernardlonergan.com, at 44100D0L060 and 44600D0L060–44900D0L060.]

88 See *Insight* [Index, s.v. 'Method'].

4 Positiones sunt evolvendae.
5 Responsabilitas iudicandi est acceptanda.

4.1 De primo praecepto: Intellige

Iudicia fiunt quatenus res reducimus in principia nostrae cognitionis, in intellectum et sensum.

Ex actu intelligendi procedunt conceptus, at intelligere verificatur ante conceptus et determinatur ex phantasmatibus, unde potest applicari sensibilibus. Quare actus intelligendi est medium inter abstractum et sensibile concretum.

(a) Dicimus 'intellige.' Non loquimur, ergo, ante omnia de verbis, neque de sententiis, neque de conceptibus, neque de iudiciis, neque de datis sensibilibus et conscientiae, sed de actu fundamentali, clavi omnium inventionum in quo aliquid novum vere invenitur, seu de actu intelligendi. Qui actus est praeconceptualis quo rerum cognoscimus propter quid, apprehendimus rationem, cognoscimus causas, videmus punctum. Hi actus possunt esse maximi momenti in historia, comitantur magna laetitia (cfr. 'eureka' Archimedis), fructus possunt esse absorptionis diuturnae (exemplum Newton).[89]

Quamvis, tamen, actus intelligendi tales possint esse, de se non sunt nisi actus ordinarii qui fere continuo occurrunt, normales, non difficiles, dummodo singularis evitetur stupiditas. Tamen sunt fundamentales: omnis magna inventio est intelligentia illius rei quae postea ab omnibus ut obvia cognoscitur et admittitur, et in scholis addiscetur.

Omnis scientia est accumulatio horum actuum. Munus methodi est tantum dirigere, ordinare, inspirare, laudare talem seriem actuum.

(b) Dicimus simpliciter 'intellige'; ergo non 'quaere actus intelligendi qui magnam habeant significationem.' Huiusmodi actus non constituunt aliquam peculiarem speciem. Sunt enim sicut caeteri, atque eorum mo-

4 Develop positions.

5 Accept responsibility for judging.

4.1 First Precept: Understand

Judgments are made inasmuch as we reduce things to the principles of our knowledge, to intellect and sense.

Concepts proceed from the act of understanding, but understanding is prior to concepts, and understanding is determined by phantasms, and so can be applied to data of sense. The act of understanding, therefore, is intermediate between the abstract concept and the concrete perceptible.

(a) 'Understand,' we say. We are, therefore, not talking primarily about words or statements or concepts or judgments or about the data of sense or data of consciousness, but about that fundamental act, the key to all discovery, through which anything new is truly discovered, namely, the act of understanding, or insight. It is a preconceptual act in which we come to know the 'why' of things, apprehend the reason, find out the cause, get the point. Such acts can be of momentous historical importance; they may occasion great joy, like Archimedes's *Eureka!*, for example, or can be the fruit of lengthy absorption of mind, as with Newton.[89]

Acts of understanding, however, although they can be like the above-mentioned examples, are nevertheless in themselves just ordinary acts that occur more or less continually, are normal and not difficult, apart from cases of egregious stupidity. Yet they are fundamental: every great discovery is an understanding of something that subsequently is recognized and admitted to be obvious, and is taught in school.

All knowledge is an accumulation of these acts. The function of method is merely to direct, to order, to foster, and to approve such a series of acts.

(b) We simply say 'Understand'; not, therefore, 'Try for an insight that will be tremendously significant.' Insights of this sort are not a breed apart; they are just like all the others, and their importance depends upon their

---

89 See *Insight* 27–31: 'A Dramatic Instance.' ['When Newton was working out his theory of universal gravitation, he lived in his room for weeks on end. A bit of food was brought to him now and then, but he had very little interest in it, and he slept only when necessary, but as soon as that was over he was back at work. He was totally absorbed in the enucleation, the unfolding, of his idea. Insofar as it is possible for a man, he was living totally in the intellectual pattern of experience.' Lonergan, *Topic in Education* 86.]

mentum pendet ex relatione quam habent cum aliis; actus inventionis claudit aliquam seriem actuum intelligendi praecedentium et aperit novam seriem. Quod aliquis actus intelligendi sit magni momenti non pendet a singulo actu sed potius ab eius loco in historia scientiae. Unde unusquisque actus intelligendi contributum affert ad magnum progressum.

(c) Nec dicimus 'fac actus intelligendi qui sunt veri.' Etiam huiusmodi actus non constituunt classem specialem. Veritas invenitur in iudiciis, non antea, et actus intelligendi possibilia reddunt iudicia. Unde actus intelligendi de se non dat veritatem, nam est aliquid prius; est sicut conceptus, qui de se nec verus est nec falsus. Ex actu intelligendi habentur hypotheses, definitiones, theoriae ... quae de se possunt esse verae vel falsae. Multi fere numquam ad intelligendum perveniunt quia nimis quaerunt verum, atque a praeoccupatione veritatis detinentur nimia. Si quis tantum verum quaerit, nihil intelligit, quia ad verum pervenitur praecise in fine, tantum postquam intellexerimus. Requiritur series quasi completa actuum intelligendi ut ad unum iudicium verum perveniamus.

Difficultates saeculi xiv in eo erant quod omnes nonnisi certitudinem quaerebant, probationes, intelligentiam oblivioni mandantes. Sic devenerunt ad scepticismum. Intelligentia ex probabilibus pervenit ad certa.

(d) Non dicimus 'vita omne praeiudicium, omnem prae-electionem.' Dubium enim universale est impossibile. Incipere debemus ex hoc quod hic et nunc sumus, nec possumus reverti ad conditionem primitivam in qua noster intellectus erat 'tabula rasa.' Ipse Descartes non habuit dubium universale: ipse mansit mathematicus atque homo renascimentalis; nam homo per dubium universale non mutatur; habitus intellectuales manent id quod sunt.[90]
Verum problema non est in deliberata partialitate, in mentalitate conscie clausa, in excessu voluntario certitudinis, sed in aberratione inconscia, in inconsciis praeiudiciis quae possunt derivari ex habitibus acquisitis. Huiusmodi praeconceptiones non corriguntur aliquid auferendo sed addendo aliquid in habitibus intellectualibus. Unde unica methodus ad hoc obtinendum est: 'intellige.'

relationship to other insights. An act of discovery brings to a close a series of preceding acts of understanding and opens up a new series. The importance of any given act of understanding does not come from that single act itself but rather from its place in the history of a science. Thus does each act of understanding make its contribution to great advancement in knowledge.

(c) Nor do we say, 'Have insights that are true'; even these do not constitute a special class of insights. Truth is reached only in judgments, not before, and it is acts of understanding, insights, that render judgments possible. The act of understanding, therefore, does not in itself express truth: it is something prior to truth, like the concept, which in itself is neither true nor false. Insights give rise to hypotheses, definitions, theories ..., which of themselves can be true or false. Many people hardly ever attain an understanding of something because they are too single-minded in their pursuit of truth and get unduly bogged down by their preoccupation with truth. If you concentrate only on what is true you will not understand anything, since we reach truth only at the end of the process, only after we have understood something. We need a more or less complete series of acts of understanding in order to arrive at one true judgment.

The problems in the fourteenth century stemmed from the fact that everyone was so concerned about certitude and proof as to forget about understanding altogether. This led to skepticism. Understanding proceeds from probabilities to what is certain.

(d) Nor do we say, 'Avoid all prejudging, all pre-deciding.' Universal doubt is impossible. We have to begin from where we are here and now; we cannot go back to some pristine state in which our intellect was a *tabula rasa*. Descartes himself did not have universal doubt: he continued to be a mathematician and a 'Renaissance man.' Universal doubt does not change a person, for intellectual habits remain what they are.[90]

The real problem is not with deliberate bias, with a consciously closed mind, or a willful excess of certitude, but rather with some unconscious aberration, with unconscious prejudices that can arise from acquired habits. Preconceptions of this sort are not corrected by subtracting anything but by adding something to one's intellectual habits. Hence, the only method for obtaining this result is: *Understand.*

90 [Lonergan discussed more fully the method of universal doubt in *Insight* 433–36.]

(e) Non dicimus 'observa, attende ad data prout revera sunt,' quia haec omnia ad materiam pertinent scientiae, et solum medium efficax ad huiusmodi observationem habendam est si intelligamus. Si quis revera quaerit intelligere, attendit ad data. Nequit inquisitio fieri nisi intelligatur id circa quod fit inquisitio, et actus intelligendi nequit haberi nisi in sensibilbus in quibus perspicitur intelligibile, ergo nisi in datis. Unde actus attendendi, inquirendi, observandi necessario praesupponitur ab actu intelligendi a quo perficitur. Campus attentionis non latius extenditur quam campus intelligentiae. Quo magis quis habet interesse et desiderium intelligendi, eo melior fit inquisitor et observator. Quo magis quis intelligit eo capacior fit in unum reducendi multa data et diversa. Distinctio accuratior inter inventa nonnisi ex ditioribus conceptibus habetur qui ex maiori intelligentia profluunt. Unde per augmentum intelligentiae augetur et capacitas observationis, necnon capacitas notandi differentias quae secus non observarentur.

Quid potest significare: attende ad ea quae pertinet ad tuam materiam, nisi mensura huius pertinentiae ex intelligentia desumatur? Quod magis quis intelligit, eo magis et melius videt quid pertineat ad suam materiam et quo sensu.

(f) Non dicimus 'concipe, cognosce id quod est necessarium, id quod est per se, id quod est universalis et abstractum ...' Si quis vellet describere actum videndi, uteretur utique vocibus et conceptibus; attamen actus videndi non consisteret in his elementis. Similiter de actu intelligendi, qui est aliquid primitivum. Describi potest in conceptibus universalibus, abstractis, necessariis (eum describendo loquimur de ratione, de causa, de puncto ...), at actus ipse non est neque universalis, neque abstractus, neque necessarius. Huiusmodi nomina et conceptus fere indicant rem, at minime cum ipsa re descripta sunt confundenda. Posset hic haberi vera fallacia psychologica describendi facta psychica per conceptus et verba, et dein identificare descriptionem factorum cum ipsis factis (cfr. psychologiam W. James).[91]

(e) Nor do we say, 'Observe and be attentive to what the data really are,' because they all belong to the matter of science, and the only efficacious means for acquiring this sort of observation is if we understand. If you really and truly seek to understand, you will pay attention to the data. Inquiry cannot take place unless you understand what you are to inquire into, and no act of understanding can occur except in the perceptible objects in which intelligibility is grasped, that is, only in the data. Hence, attention to the data, inquiry, and observation are necessarily prerequisite to the act of understanding by which they are completed. The field of attention is only as broad as the field of understanding. The more you have an interest and a desire to understand, the better inquirer and observer you will become. And the more you understand, the better able will you be to reduce a multiplicity and variety of data to unity. A more accurate distinction among your findings can be had only through richer concepts, which in turn arise from fuller understanding. Thus, as understanding increases, the capacity for observation increases along with it, as well as the capacity for noting differences that otherwise would go unnoticed.

What can 'attend to those things that pertain to your matter' mean if the measure of what are pertinent is not itself based on understanding? The better understanding one has, the more clearly will one see what pertains to one's matter, and in what sense.

(f) Nor do we way, 'Have a concept, know what is necessary, what is per se, what is universal and abstract ...' If you wanted to describe the act of seeing, you would surely use words and concepts; and yet the act of seeing does not consist in these elements. The same is true for the act of understanding, which is something fundamental. It can be described in universal, abstract, necessary concepts – in so doing we speak of the reason, the cause, the point – but the act itself is neither universal, abstract, nor necessary. Such nouns and concepts give a rough indication of a thing, but are in no way to be confused with the thing itself that they describe. Here is where there could occur the psychological fallacy of describing psychic facts in concepts and words and then identifying their description with the facts themselves. See the psychology of William James.[91]

91 [Lonergan does not give a more specific reference than this. In *The Principles of Psychology*, vol. 1 (London: Macmillan and Co., Ltd., 1891) 196–97, James speaks of the 'psychologist's fallacy,' namely, the psychologist's 'confusion of his own standpoint with that of the mental fact,' or again as 'the assumption

Et quoad necessitatem, intelligentia potest esse de necessariis et de iis quae necessaria non sunt, de universalibus et de iis quae non sunt universalia, de iis quae sunt per se et de iis quae non sunt per se ... Intelligibile est omne quod de facto est verum. Intelligibilitas potest dari etiam in theoria probabilitatis, in qua magnam partem habet id quod est per accidens. Intelligentia non impeditur ab eo quod non est intelligibile; tantum ad id attingendum et ad tractandum de eo requiritur technica specialis, ut in mathematica requiritur technica specialis ad tractandum de numeris irrationalibus et transcendentalibus.[92] Ita in saec. XVI ad hoc non bene attenderunt in disputationibus de gratia efficaci et sufficienti. Nam utraque refertur ad peccatum, quod est contra rationem, unde aliquid inintelligibile. Unde solutio huius quaestionis debet esse critica, atque procedi debet ut mathematici procedunt relate ad numeros irrationales.

Nos abstrahimus conceptus quia intelligimus, unde ubi abstractio ibi intelligendi actus; at non vice versa: non quotiescumque intelligimus, possumus abstrahere. In risu, v.gr., vel in aliqua symphonia attingit intelligibilitatem quin haec universaliter exprimi possit.

Conceptus abstracti se habent ad sensibilia tamquam universale ad particulare; at actus intelligendi non comparatur ad sensibilia tamquam universale ad particulare, qui perspicit intelligibilitatem in ipso concreto qua tali.

Sic concretum fit qua tale intelligibile quatenus eius partes inter se intelligibiliter connectuntur: hoc perspicitur quando intelligitur aliqua machina vel organismus. Ens sociale intelligitur per relationes quas habet ad alios; ecclesia non tota intelligitur quatenus de ea habetur conceptus abstractus alicuius societatis perfectae (per genus et speciem) sed quatenus perspicitur ut concreta multiplicitas spatio-temporalis, unde ad ha-

And as to necessity, understanding can be of what are necessary and of what are not necessary, of what are universal and of what are not universal, of those things that exist per se and of those that do not exist per se. The intelligible is everything that de facto is true. Intelligibility can be had even in a theory of probability, in which what exists *per accidens* plays a large part. Understanding is not hindered by that which is not intelligible; all that is required for attaining that and dealing with it is some special technique, as for example in mathematics for dealing with irrational and transcendental numbers.[92] Similarly, this point was largely overlooked in the sixteenth-century disputes concerning efficacious and sufficient grace. Both of these graces refer to sin, which is contrary to reason and hence something that is unintelligible; and so the solution to this problem has to be critical, and be approached in the way in which mathematicians proceed in dealing with irrational numbers.

We abstract concepts because we understand; hence, where there is an abstraction there is act of understanding. But not vice versa: sometimes we understand something and yet are unable to abstract. There is intelligibility in a smile, for example, or in a symphony, and yet it cannot be expressed in universal terms.

Abstract concepts are to sensible data as the universal to the particular; but acts of understanding, which grasp intelligibility in concrete data as such, are not related to sensible data as universal to the particular.

Thus, the concrete becomes intelligible in its concreteness to the extent that the connections between its various components become intelligible. This is what is grasped whenever a machine or an organism is understood, and a social being is understood through its relations with others. The total intelligibility of the church is not contained in the abstract concept of a 'perfect society' in terms of genus and species, but only in grasping it as a

---

that the mental state studied must be conscious of itself as the psychologist is conscious of it.' John Dewey in his article 'The Reflex Arc Concept in Psychology' (*Psychological Review* 3:4 (1896) 367) does speak of the 'the psychological or historical fallacy' and says it arises when 'a set of considerations which hold good only because of a completed process, is read into the content of the process which conditions this completed result' – in simpler language, reading back into a process what comes about only as a result of that process. An earlier discussion by Lonergan of the 'psychological fallacy,' but without any reference to either James or Dewey, can be found in *Understanding and Being* 41, 134, 283, 285–86.]

92 Think of Newton's first law of mechanics.

bendam completam theologiam de ea requiruntur purificatae categoriae historicae.

Intelligentia sese exprimit in conceptibus abstractis, at non limitatur ad eos. Intelligentia vulgaris, v.gr., non praeoccupatur in principiis universalibus sed tantum in concretis situationibus.

(g) Praeceptum 'intellige' respicit id quod est fundamentale in scientia. Scientia est habitus intellectualis (secundum S. Thomam), at non statim scientia ut habitus concipitur. Primo enim, scientia videtur esse id quod habetur in libro aliquo, in assertionibus, theorematibus, in terminis mediis. Sic, v.gr., in geometria primo apparet dependentia theorematum posteriorum a prioribus prout in libro habentur. At scientia progrediente, contrarium apparet verum, unde incipimus advertere scientiam esse in nobis et non in libro. Quando postea possumus sine difficultate et cum delectatione definitiones, theoremata, ... quin de memoria curemus, nos ipsi perficere, tunc pervenimus ad habitum intellectualem quo obiectionibus etiam per nos ipsos respondere possimus.

4.2 De secundo praecepto: Intellige systematice

Systematica intelligentia importat tria: (1) intentum versus scopum ideale intelligentiae; (2) fine intento uti ut medio ad finem attingendum; hoc fieri potest quia si ex una parte finis nondum adeptus est, ex alia finis est aliquomodo praecognitus et usurpari potest tamquam medium; (3) finem alicuius scientiae particularis attingere ita ut possint relationes haberi cum aliis scientiis.[93]

4.2.1 Ideale intelligentiae: Intelligentia vult esse completa

Ideale, seu bonum intelligentiae (finis) differt a bono sensus (sensibili) et a bono sensus communis seu intelligentiae vulgaris, quae operatur intra horizontem particularem, intra mundum proprium uniuscuiusque individui, intra sphaeram practicam utilitariam; nec sensus communis quaerit

concrete spatiotemporal manifold, and hence for a complete ecclesiology purified historical categories are needed.

Understanding expresses itself in abstract concepts but is not limited to them. Commonsense understanding, for example, is not concerned with universal principles but only with concrete situations.

(g) The precept 'understand' regards what is fundamental in science. According to St Thomas, science is an intellectual habit, but science is not immediately conceived of as a habit. For science first of all seems to be what is found in a book, in statements, theorems, and middle terms. Thus in geometry, for example, what appears first is the dependence of subsequent theorems upon previous ones as they are set forth in a book. But as science progresses, the contrary appears to be true, and so we begin to advert to the fact that science is in us and not in a book. Then later on, when we are able by ourselves to elaborate definitions, theorems, and so on, with ease and delight and without being concerned about memory, we have achieved that intellectual habit by which we can answer objections even on our own.

4.2 Second Precept: Understand Systematically

Systematic understanding involves three things: (1) aiming at or intending the ideal range of understanding; (2) using the end intended as a means to attain the end; this is possible because if on the one hand the end has not yet been attained, on the other hand it is in some sense already known and can be used as a means; (3) attaining the end of any particular science in such a way that it can be related to other sciences.[93]

4.2.1 The Ideal of Understanding: To Be Complete

The ideal, that is, the good, or end, of understanding, differs from the good of sensing (the perceptible), and also from the good of common sense or ordinary everyday understanding; these latter operate within a particular horizon, within each one's particular world, in the sphere of practical util-

---

93 [Lonergan devotes distinct subsections to the first two of these, but not to the third. However, the talk of metaphysics that bridges 4.2.2 and 4.2.3 below – these are editorial numberings, but the first two correspond to numbers in the text itself – has at least some bearing on the interrelations of the sciences.]

de omnibus, neque ultra hanc sphaeram particularem sese extendit, nisi deficiendo a sua natura intelligentiae vulgaris.

Intelligentia qua talis quaerit explicationem completam omnium phaenomenorum, intendit intelligere universa. Unde facit distinctiones sine fine ut distincta comprehendat secundum omnes aspectus. Finis intelligentiae est complexus relationum intelligibilium talis ut totum universum ut aliquid unum intelligatur.

Dicendo 'systematice' non connotamus systema abstractum constans propositionibus ex quibus omnia deducantur. Dicendo 'systematice' intendimus connotare intelligentiam totius universi concreti, distincti secundum omnes suos aspectus et relationes intelligibiles uniuscuiusque partis ad alias, unde totius universi ut aliquid unum est.

4.2.2 Finem adhibere tamquam medium ad finem

Huiusmodi ideale non tantum illuminat nostra iudicia iam peracta sed fit etiam medium ad finem ulterius et perfectius attingendum. Hoc enim ideale est implicitum in omni inquisitione. Ad methodum pertinet explicitare id quod antea implicitum erat.

Exemplum haberi potest ex mathematica. Si aliquod manuale algebrae accipiatur, observatur quod ad multa problemata solvenda primus gressus est nominare id quod actualiter est ignotum per aliquam x. Hoc, primo aspectu, potest videri vacuum et sensu carens, et sic videtur multis gnoseologis. Tamen, si bene attendatur, patet quod si id quod quaeritur tamquam x designatur, designatur tamquam numerus etsi indeterminatus, et implicite illi omnes proprietates numeri tribuuntur quae sunt bene determinatae. Sic nominando ignotum et addendo ea quae sunt implicita in illa nominatione, ponitur veluti praemissa maior syllogismi. Hoc posito, faciliter pervenitur ad numerum determinatum qui quaerebatur.[94] Hoc tamen non valet tantum pro scientiis a priori.

Aliud exemplum potest haberi ex physica. Physici sciunt id quod quaerunt, scilicet legem naturalem stabilire, nec indeterminatam tantum sed determinatam. Haec lex exprimitur ab aliqua functione, iterum determinata. Tunc assumunt generalissimam notionem functionis indeterminatae:

ity. Common sense does not ask questions about everything and does not venture beyond this particular sphere of interest without forsaking its nature as ordinary understanding.

Understanding, as such, seeks a complete explanation of all phenomena: it aims at understanding everything. Hence, it is constantly making distinctions in order to comprehend all these distinct realities in all their aspects. The end of understanding is the whole complex of intelligible relations such that the universe may be understood as a unity.

In saying 'systematic' we do not mean to connote some abstract system consisting of propositions from which everything can be deduced. 'Systematic,' as we are using it, is intended to connote an understanding of the whole concrete universe distinguished according to all its many aspects and the intelligible relations of each of its parts, hence an understanding of the entire universe as something that is one.

4.2.2 Using the End as a Means to the End

This kind of ideal not only throws light on judgments already made but also becomes a means for the further and better attainment of the end, for this ideal is implicit in every inquiry. Method's role is to explicitate what had previously been implicit.

Mathematics furnishes an example of this. Take any algebra textbook and you will observe that for the solution of many problems the first step is to name as x what is at present unknown. At first sight this may appear pointless and silly, as in fact it does seem to be for many gnoseologists. Yet closer attention will reveal that if what is being sought is designated as x, it is designated as a number, however indeterminate, and all the properties of number, which are determinate, are implicitly attributed to it. Thus, by naming the unknown and adding to it all that are implicit in that designation, it is posited just as would be the major premise of a syllogism. Once this is posited, it is easy to arrive at the determinate number that was being sought.[94] Nor is this valid only for a priori sciences.

Physics furnishes us with another example. Physicists know what they are looking for, namely, to establish a law of nature, not one that is just indeterminate, but determinate. This law is expressed in some function, which is also determinate. They then take the most general notion of an indetermi-

----

94 See Lonergan, *Insight* 60–70, 'Classical Heuristic Structures.'

$f(x,y,z,t) = 0.$[95] Functio seu lex, dein, determinatur per duplicem motum, sive ab infra (per considerationes particulares, mensurationes, praesentationes graphicas, formulas), sive a supra (quia omnis functio potest esse solutio aequationis differentialis, determinantur proprietates illius functionis ignotae quae quaeritur, per generaliores proprietates cuiuslibet functionis); inde ex solis aequationibus differentialibus absque legis cognitione multae quaestiones de facto solvuntur (cfr. exemplum motus undulatorii).

Hoc physici faciunt quia sciunt id quod volunt, seu legem; quae lex est aliqua functio; quae functio sit, nesciunt; at sciunt proprietates functionis in genere, et sic ex determinationibus generalibus possunt ad determinationes particulares pervenire.[96]

Sic ex intelligentia systematica non tantum habetur finis explicite cognitus, sed explicitatio procedens ex fine implicite cognito ad finem explicitius cognoscendum.

Hoc, quod exemplis et algebra et physica illustravimus, est verum de omni scientia. Ubicumque enim invenitur illa intentio intelligentiae completae et systematicae. Tantum sic intelligi possunt relationes evangelii ad theologiam et theologiae ad metaphysicam, quae omnia inter se facili levitate a pluribus opponuntur.

Breviter explicabimus quomodo, hac perspectiva, metaphysica concipiatur.

Initium omnis philosophiae est quaedam admiratio. Primo habetur ergo in homine intentio intendens quae non est nisi intellectus agens, cui correspondet categoria *ens*, sensu exsistentiali intellecta; nam ens ad quod intellectus humanus tendit non est quid abstractum sed universum concretum. Intellectus est quo omnia facere vel fieri, ubi omnia = ens. Sicut 'omnia' minime dicit aliquid abstractum, sic et 'ens', in quo omnia omnino concreta includuntur; possibile autem, sive ex agente sive ex patiente, nihil addit super potentiam activam vel passivam, et ideo continetur actu in ente.

nate function: $f(x,y,z,t) = 0.$[95] Next, the function or law is determined by two movements, one from below (by way of particular considerations, measurements, graphs, formulas) and one from above (for since every function can be the solution of a differential equation, the properties of that unknown function being sought are determined through the more general properties of any function). Hence, from differential equations alone without the knowledge of a law, many questions are in fact solved – the problem of wave motion, for example.

Physicists follow this procedure because they know what they want, that is, a law, and this law is a function; just what function it is they do not know, but they know the properties of functions in general and so are able to proceed from general to particular determinations.[96]

Thus, through systematic understanding we have not only the end known explicitly but also its explicitation, which proceeds from the end as implicitly known to the end that is to be known more explicitly.

What we have just illustrated from algebra and physics holds true for every branch of knowledge. For that drive towards complete and systematic understanding is everywhere to be found. Only thus can the relationship be properly understood between the gospel and theology, and between theology and metaphysics, which many with cavalier insouciance dismiss as being mutually contradictory.

With this perspective, let us now briefly explain how metaphysics may be conceived.

The beginning of all philosophy is wonder. First of all, then, in humans there is an intending intention, which is simply the agent intellect, to which corresponds the category *being*, understood in an existential sense; for being, to which the human intellect tends, is not something abstract but the concrete universe. The intellect is that which can make or become all things, where 'all things' = 'being.' Just as 'all things' does not in the least refer to anything abstract, neither does 'being,' in which all concrete realities whatsoever are included. Possible being, however, whether on the part of the doer or on the part of the receiver, adds nothing to active or passive potency, and so is contained actually in 'being.'

95 [See ibid. 784, notes f and i, for a brief discussion of a minor correction and clarification of Lonergan's terminology regarding the mathematical expression.]
96 Ibid. 62–64, 'Differential Equations.'

Haec intentio intellectualis primo illuminat phantasma quando quis vult intelligere aliquid, et ideo habetur effectus in phantasma (sicut in artifice ad artificiata). Phantasma, ope intellectus agentis, transit in speciem impressam et habetur actus intelligendi (= *eureka*). Si illa intelligentia quae habita est exprimatur, habentur definitiones et conceptus.

Deinde habetur aliqua verificatio utrum conceptus sint veri tantum de phantasmatibus an etiam de rebus sensibilibus ex quo proveniunt. Haec verificatio habetur per aliquod inconditionatum virtuale, et est iudicium.

Talis est structura nostrae cognitionis ut triplici elemento constituatur: actus iudicandi, seu elementum rationale; actus intelligendi, seu elementum intelligibile; quatenus id quod intelligitur est aliquid praesupponens aliud non intellectum habetur elementum experientiale.[97] Cui triplici elemento nostrae cognitionis correspondet in *ente* triplex contentum: potentia, quatenus ens experitur; forma, quatenus intelligitur; actus, quatenus affirmatur et actu cognoscitur.

Si intentio huiusmodi substat omni humanae inquisitioni atque omni loquelae, de omnibus prorsus valet.[98]

4.2.3 Exempla theologica

(a) Concilium Ancyranum (a. 358), ubi habita est unio homoiousianorum episcoporum qui turbati erant a doctrinis Eunomii et Arianorum qui dicebant Filium esse creaturam, Nicaenum accusantes de Sabellianismo. Cfr. apud Epiphanium expositionem factam a Georgio, episcopo Laodicaeae, pro quo etsi verbum *ousia* numquam appareat in Sacra Scriptura, tamen res ubique invenitur, et quaedam exempla ab illo allata (etsi vere pauca).[99]

(b) Saec. XIII S. Thomas invenit nostram categoriam 'gratiae actualis.'[100] Tamen in 1-2, q. 111, ubi agitur de divisionibus gratiae, loquitur de gratia

Whenever one wishes to understand something, this intellectual intention first illumines the phantasm, and so there is an effect produced upon the phantasm, as by a craftsman upon his artifacts. The phantasm, with the assistance of the agent intellect, becomes an impressed species, and there occurs an act of understanding or insight (*eureka*). If that understanding which has been obtained is expressed, you have definitions and concepts.

The next step is verification, determining whether the concepts are true only of the phantasms or also of the sensible data from which the phantasms originate. This verification is had through what is virtually unconditioned, and there occurs the judgment.

Such, then, is the structure of our knowledge, consisting as it does of three elements: the act of judging, the rational element; the act of understanding, the intellective element; insofar as that which is understood presupposes something else that is not understood, there is the experiential element.[97] To these three elements of our knowledge there correspond three elements in *being*: potency, being as experienced; form, being as understood; act, being as affirmed and actually known.

If such an intention underlies every human inquiry and every utterance, it is valid for absolutely everything.[98]

4.2.3 Some Theological Examples

(a) The Council of Ancyra (358) was a meeting of homoiousian bishops alarmed by the teachings of Eunomius and the Arians, who were maintaining that the Son was a creature and were accusing the Council of Nicea of Sabellianism. See Epiphanius's account of the explanation given by George, Bishop of Laodicea, pointing out that although the word *ousia* never occurs in the Bible, nevertheless the reality does, together with some examples, although very few.[99]

(b) St Thomas in the thirteenth century invented our category 'actual grace.'[100] And yet in the *Summa theologiae*, 1-2, q. 111, on the divisions of

---

97 [See Lonergan, *Insight* 299.]
98 See ibid. 456–60.
99 See above, p. 63, note 48.
100 [As Lonergan notes elsewhere, Thomas does not use the term 'actual grace,' but speaks of *divinum auxilium*, divine assistance, to mean the reality of what 'actual grace' was later used to mean. See Lonergan, *Grace and Freedom* 165.]

gratum faciente et gratia gratis data, de operante et cooperante, de praeveniente et subsequente, at nullibi invenitur division inter gratiam habitualem et actualem, quae tamen est divisio fundamentalis in cogitatione S.
Thomae. Saec. XII fiebat sermo de gratia, atque adhibebantur plurima adie-
ctiva ad illam designandam.[101] Saec. XIII, versus 1230, cum Philippo Cancellario habita est notio clara de gratia habituali supernaturali, atque factus
est nisus omnia explicandi per hanc notionem. S. Thomas autem perspexit
insufficientiam huius nisus et vidit necessitatem addendi notionem gratiae
actualis ad explicanda data revelata. Cf. 1-2, q. 6, introductio; qq. 1–5 (ubi
loquitur de fine); qq. 6–48 (ubi loquitur de actibus); inde a q. 48 incipit
tractationem de habitibus. Dum in prima parte inde a q. 77 tractaverat de
potentiis animae. Quando autem agitur de determinando quid sit haec
nova gratia (actualis), haec determinatio fit per exclusionem: non est forma (quia talis est gratia habitualis), non est potentia, seu facultas, ergo est
actus.[102] Unde etiam hic, structura heuristica utens notionibus heuristicis[103]
explicat introductionem categoriae gratiae actualis.

Sic ex eadem structura habentur divisiones in omni campo; ex.gr.:

actus = esse, visio, intellectio, velle, etc.;
forma = anima, visus, species, habitus, etc.;
potentia = corpus, oculus, intellectus, voluntas, etc.

Haec enim structura desumpta est ex ipsa structura cognitionis, unde
valida est pro qualibet scientia et pro quolibet problemate.

Quia intelligentia systematica non iacet intra limitatum aliquem horizontem, sicut vulgaris, capax est unumquemque progressum dirigendi usque
ad aliquid ultimum in unoquoque campo, quod constituat fundamentum

grace, he speaks about grace that is *gratum faciens* and grace that is *gratis data*, about operative and cooperative grace, and about prevenient and subsequent grace, but not a word about habitual and actual grace, which is nevertheless a fundamental distinction in his thought. In the twelfth- century discussions about grace, a number of adjectives had been used to describe it.[101] In the early thirteenth century, towards 1230, with Philip the Chancellor, a clear notion of habitual supernatural grace occurs, and an attempt is made to explain everything through this notion. St Thomas, however, realized the insufficiency of this attempt and saw the necessity of adding the notion of actual grace in order to explain the data of revelation. See *Summa theologiae*, 1-2, q. 6, introduction; qq. 1–5, where he speaks about the end; qq. 6–48, where he speaks about acts; with q. 49 he begins his treatment of habits; whereas in part 1, beginning with q. 77, he had talked about the powers of the soul. But when the question of determining the nature of this new (actual) grace came up, it was determined by way of exclusion: it is not a form – that is, habitual grace; it is not a potency, or faculty; therefore, it is an act.[102] Hence, even here a heuristic structure using heuristic notions[103] explains the introduction of the category of actual grace.

Thus, following this same structure we have these divisions in every field of knowledge:

act = being, seeing, understanding, willing, etc.;
form = soul, sight, *species*, habit, etc.;
potency = body, eye, intellect, will, etc.

Since this structure is taken from the very structure of cognition, it is valid for every field of knowledge and for every problem.

Because systematic understanding is not limited to any particular horizon, as is common sense, it is capable of directing progress towards what is ultimate in any field, which constitutes the foundation of that field. Thus,

101 See Landgraf, *Dogmengeschichte der Frühscholastik*, I:1: *Die Gnadenlehre*, 51–53, 'Die Erkenntnis der helfenden Gnade, Die Terminologie.'
102 [See Bernard Lonergan, 'The Supernatural Order,' in *Early Latin Theology*, vol. 19 in Collected Works of Bernard Lonergan, trans. Michael G. Shields, ed. Robert M. Doran and H. Daniel Monsour (Toronto: University of Toronto Press, 2011) 229. 'Interior actual grace essentially consists in vital, principal, and supernatural second acts of the intellect and the will.']
103 See Lonergan *Insight* 57–92, 718–25, 740–50.

Structura heuristica valida de omnibus scientiis

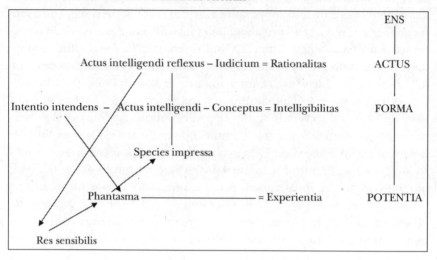

illius. Sic hoc ultimum vidimus in arithmetica numerum; in scientia physica functionem; in metaphysica ens.

Tale ens constat potentia, forma, et actu, quorum unumquodque potest haberi sive in ordine substantiali sive in accidentali.

Cum tali structura ultima intelligentia systematica potest procedere; sine illa semper manemus coram aliqua re ineffabili et indefinibili, quae ultimatim inexplicabilis est.

Ut patet, tota structura de quo locuti sumus reducitur ad actum intelligendi tamquam ad centrum. Quotiescumque inquirimus (= admiratio) ad intelligendum, volumus aliquid intelligere, unde praesuppoitur aliquod datum, nondum intellectum, circa quod fit inquisitio: hoc est elementum experientiale (cui correspondet categoria fundamentalis potentiae). Habito actu intelligendi (= intellectione), id quod intellectum est exprimitur per definitiones, seu conceptus. Multi putant vel dicunt se habere conceptum alicuius rei quin tamen possint definire vel hunc conceptum exprimere. Hoc falsum est ex eo quod conceptus non est nisi definitio. Hoc non significat omnem definitionem esse per genus et per speciem. Talis expressio actus intelligendi (= conceptus) de se non est neque vera neque falsa. Homo nondum potest nec debet recte iudicare (saltem non deberet) antequam intellexerit. Differentia inter astrologiam et astronomiam invenitur in tertio ordine (seu in ordine reflexionis iudicialis), non in secundo ordine intelligentiae. Postquam intellexerimus, ulterius progredimur. Nam nos volumus utique intelligere, sed non sumus contenti cum splendidis

Heuristic Structure Valid for All Fields of Knowledge

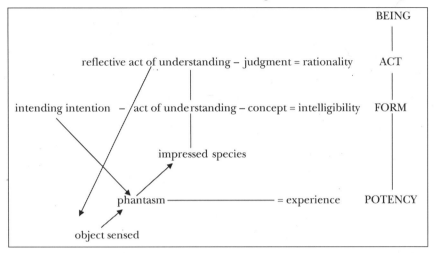

in arithmetic we have seen that this ultimate is number; in physics, function; in metaphysics, being.

Such being consists of potency, form, and act, each of which can be present in either the substantial or the accidental order.

With this sort of ultimate structure, systematic understanding can go forward; without it we are up against something that is inexpressible and indefinable, and ultimately inexplicable.

As is clear, the entire structure we are speaking of is centered upon the act of understanding. Whenever we inquire (wonder), we do so in order to understand; we want to understand something, and this presupposes something that is given but not yet understood, about which we inquire: this is the experiential element, to which corresponds the basic category of potency. When an act of understanding (intellection, insight) has occurred, that which is understood is expressed in definitions, or concepts. Many people think or say that they have a concept of something but cannot define it or express that concept. But this is wrong, because a concept is just a definition. This does not mean that every definition is by genus and specific difference. The expression of an act of understanding, that is, the concept, is in and of itself neither true nor false. One cannot make a correct judgment, nor ought one to do so (at least there would be no obligation to do so), until one has understood the matter. The difference between astrology and astronomy is to be found at this third level, that is, at the level of reflective judgment, not at the second level, that of understanding. Once we have

notionibus, unde post intelligentiam reflectimus ad stabiliendum utrum res revera ita se habeant ut eas intelleximus. Est momentum iudicii, quod praecise est ista reflexio.

Unde patet actum intelligendi esse illum ex quo homo transit ex statu experto ad statum intelligentiae, atque centrum esse totius retis humanae operationis.

4.3   De tertio et quarto praeceptis: Inverte contrapositiones; Positiones sunt evolvendae

Intelligentia systematica paulatim oritur in historia et in vita individuali. Tantum serius detegitur ideale intelligentiae. Sic quaestiones quae apud Parmenidem iam inveniebantur systematicam solutionem tantum apud Aristotelem habuerunt, et ultimatim in Aquinate.

Symbola interpersonalia obiectivantur in arte, at haec obiectivatio differt ab illa quae habetur per conceptus universales.

Intelligentia vulgaris evolvitur intra aliquem horizontem determinatum, pro situationibus concretis. In tali evolutione fit transitus ad universale. Hic transitus signat conversionem in subiecto, qui ex cura sui et ex proprio mundo sese orientat versus universum. Haec conversio requirit cognitionem multorum elementorum praeviorum et eorum limitationum. Homo non debet deponere omnem intelligentiam vulgarem et symbolicam sed tantum quatenus versatur in cognitione scientifica, eius modus cogitandi, iudicandi ... non debet determinari ex categoriis intersubiectivis. Vulgus quaerit utilitatem, propterea in utilitate videt scientiam, ex eo quod occupatur circa particularia et concreta. Tale criterium utilitaristicum debet deponi in cogitatione scientifica.

Hoc verum est non tantum de cognitione theoretica sed etiam de practica; agitur de mea cogitatione, de effectu transformationis ipsius subiecti, de evolutione eius versus cognoscendi modum scientificum. In statu vulgari subiectum est in potentia ad evolutionem; unde aequivalentia et ambiguitas: potest sese evolvere et potest non sese evolvere.

Ex.gr., apprehensio spatii kinesthetica (de qua supra) non est geometrice cognita sed experta in sensu proprii aequilibrii. Si autem tellus est ro-

understood something, we don't stop there. We want to understand, of course, but we are not content with just having bright ideas, and so after we have understood we reflect in order to determine whether the things really are the way we have understood them to be. This is the moment of judgment, which consists precisely in this reflective act.

From all of this it is clear that the act of understanding is that act by which one makes the transition from experiencing to understanding, and is the very hub and center of the whole network of human operation. [See figure p. 137.]

4.3   Third and Fourth Precepts: Reverse Counterpositions; Develop Positions

Systematic understanding arises gradually in human history and in the life of individuals. The ideal of understanding is discovered only later. Thus, questions that are to be found in Parmenides were systematically answered only in Aristotle, and ultimately in Aquinas.

Interpersonal symbols are objectified in art, but this objectification differs from that which is had through universal concepts.

Commonsense understanding develops within a determinate horizon, in accordance with concrete situations. In this development there is a transition to the universal. This transition indicates a conversion in the subject who, from being concerned for himself and his own world, is now orientated to the universe. This conversion requires a knowledge of many previous elements and of their limitations. One does not have to set aside all common sense and symbolic understanding, but only insofar as one is engaged in scientific thought must one's way of thinking, judging, and so on, not be determined by intersubjective categories. The average person, being absorbed with concrete particulars, looks for what is useful and sees science in terms of utility. Such a criterion of utility has to be set aside when engaged in scientific thinking.

This is true not only of theoretical but also of practical thinking; it is one's thinking, the effect of the transformation of the subject and the subject's development towards a scientific way of thinking, that is involved here. In the commonsense mode, the subject is in potency with regard to this development; hence, there is an ambivalence and ambiguity: one can both develop and not develop.

Take, for example, the apprehension of kinesthetic space, mentioned above. It is not known by geometry but experienced through one's sense

tunda, haec notio spatii debet purificari. Secundum revolutionem Coperni-
canam, secundum mathematicam et scientiam nihil refert utrum centrum
systematis sit in tellure an in sole. In mechanica Newoniana sunt multae
conceptiones quae hodie omittuntur (v.g., de vi tamquam causa efficienti
motus; hodie *ma* est functio temporis et spatii).

Tempus Aristotelicum definitur ut mensura motus secundum prius et
posterius. At quaestio fiebat a S. Thoma commentatore: multa sunt tempora quia multi motus? Unde necessitas unici motus primi motoris qui det
tempus normale pro toto universo. At post Copernicum poterant admitti
tempora diversa.[104] Similiter de determinismo: quia res per sensibilia cognoscuntur, leges putabant esse in sensibilibus, in atomis ...

Physici saec. XIX multos conatus fecerunt construendi typum aetheris im-
aginabile;[105] deinde venit aequatio electromagnetica Maxwell. Sic conversio
in scientiis habita est quatenus scientiae liberatae sunt a multis notionibus
quae fundamentum aliquod habebant, sed non erant generales.

In opere *Insight* potest inveniri completa tractatio de notionibus cognitionis, realitatis, obiectivitatis (cfr. speciatim cc. XI, XII, XIII, XIV).

Verum est medium in quo cognoscimus ens: ens et verum formaliter convertuntur. Et criterium cognitionis veritatis est evidentia. Attamen, secundum aliam conceptionem et realitatis et cognitionis, cognitio concipitur
tamquam contactus, praesentia. Sic habetur veluti duplex orientatio, versus
verum et ens et versus rem et obiectum, quae duplex orientatio potest haberi in uno eodemque subiecto. Sic in Cartesio, 'cogito' est orientatio versus
verum, dum conceptio substantiae tamquam rei extensae est orientatio versus rem. Prima evoluta est in rationalismo Kantiano, ex alia autem ortus est
empirismus.[106]

of equilibrium. However, if the earth is round, this notion of space needs to be refined. According to the Copernican revolution and according to mathematics and science, it does not matter whether the center of the system is located in the earth or in the sun. In Newtonian mechanics there are a number of conceptions that are discarded today – the concept of force, for example, as the efficient cause of motion; today *ma* is a function of space and time.

Aristotle defined time as the measure of motion with respect to 'before' and 'after.' But in commenting on this, St Thomas raised the question: Are there many times because there are many motions? Hence, the necessity of a single motion of a prime mover to provide a norm of time for the whole universe. Since Copernicus, however, many different times can be admitted.[104] The same can be said of determinism: because things are known through what is perceived by the senses, determinists thought that laws were in sense data, in atoms, and so on.

Nineteenth-century physicists made several attempts to discover an imaginable type of ether;[105] then Maxwell came along with his electromagnetic equations. Thus, in science conversion is had when sciences are freed from many notions that had some foundation, but were not general.

In *Insight* there can be found a thorough treatment of the notions of knowledge, reality, and objectivity; see especially chapters 11 to 14.

The true is the medium in which we know being: being and true are interchangeable terms; and the criterion for knowing truth is evidence. Yet, according to another way of conceiving both reality and knowledge, knowledge is conceived as a contact, a presence. Thus, there are as it were two orientations, towards the true and being, and towards thing and object, and these two orientations can coexist in the same subject. So Descartes's *cogito* is an orientation towards the true, while his concept of substance as extended being is an orientation towards 'thing.' The former orientation developed into Kantian rationalism, and the latter gave rise to empiricism.[106]

---

104 [See Lonergan, *Insight* 182.]
105 See E.T. Whittaker, *A History of the Theories of the Aether and Electricity from the Age of Descartes to the Close of the Nineteenth Century* (Dublin: Hodges Figgis; London: Longmans, Green and Co., 1910). [Lonergan refers to this book in *Insight* 115, note 7.]
106 [For slightly more on this, see Lonergan, *Insight* 363–65, 413–14. 'Thing' is not used here in the technical sense of chapter 8 of *Insight*, but as 'already out there now.']

Omnis vera intelligentia est retinenda, sive secundum orientationem versus rem sive versus verum. Tamen asserta quae fiunt ab inventoribus sunt discernenda: nam alia cohaerent cum intelligentia systematica (et sunt positiones), alia non cohaerent (et sunt contrapositiones). Pro recta methodo, ergo, a contrapositionibus debet fieri transitus ad positiones eliminando elementa non cohaerentia, dum positiones sunt ulterius evolvendae.

Sic egerunt Patres, spoliantes Aegyptios, seu assumendo vera ex auctoribus paganis, amissis autem eorum erroribus. Sic Newman, crisin instituens dubitationis universalis, asseruit quod si necesse esset eligere, eligisset potius credulitatem universalem. Tempore decurrente errores decident et veritas manebit, dum ex dubitatione universali nihil in intelligentia maneret.[107]

Haec vera sunt ex parte obiecti; at verum problema est in subiecto, quod debet converti ex mundo proprio ad mundum universalem. Unde quaestio non est in deducendis aliis elementis ex iis quae sunt cognita, sed in transformatione ipsius cognoscentis. Sic hodiernae laudes subiecti quaedam vera continent, et etiam quaedam falsa.

4.4 De quinto praecepto: Responsabilitas iudicandi est acceptanda

Quattuor praecepta praecedentia non tangunt rem quia non respiciunt iudicium. Antequam quis iudicet, enim, intelligat. Tamen, quando quis intelligit, nondum iudicat, et manet aes sonans donec affirmet: res ita est. In primis quattuor regulis habetur cogitatio, nondum cognitio. In iudicio e contra, pervenitur ad verum, ad id in quo cognoscitur ens, unde ad ens.

Quando quis intelligit aliquid quin sciat dicere quid est quod intelligit, habetur intelligentia non systematica (sicut in artistis) de qua in prima regula; quando quis aliquid intelligit et scit quid sit quod intelligit, habetur

Now, all true understanding must be retained, whether in the orientation towards 'thing' or towards the true. However, assertions that are made are to be discerned by those who make them: some of these assertions are coherent with systematic understanding (these are positions), while some are not (and these are counterpositions). The correct method, therefore, calls for the movement from counterpositions to positions by eliminating incongruous elements; positions are then to be further developed.

This is what the church Fathers did, 'despoiling the Egyptians,' adopting what was true in pagan writers and leaving their errors aside. This is how Newman, expressing his criticism of universal doubt, stated that if he had to make a choice, he would choose to believe everything rather than doubt everything. In the course of time errors fall by the wayside and truth remains, whereas from universal doubt there would be nothing left in one's understanding.[107]

All of this is true on the side of the object. But the real problem is in the subject, who must be turned from his own world to the universe. Hence there is no question here of deducing further elements from those that are known, but of transforming the knower himself. And so the present favorable attention being paid to the subject contains some truth, but also some things that are false.

4.4 Fifth Precept: Accept Responsibility for Judging.

The four preceding precepts do not touch upon reality, since they do not deal with judgment. Understanding must come before judgment. Yet, when we understand something, we have not yet made a judgment, and remain 'sounding brass' until we make the affirmation, 'This is so.' In the first four precepts there is thinking but not yet knowledge. In the judgment, however, we arrive at the true, that in which being is known, and so at being.

When we understand something without being able to say what it is that is understood, we have a nonsystematic understanding (as with artists), to which the first precept applies. When we understand something and know

---

107 [Lonergan is referring to Newman's remark, '... I would rather have to maintain that we ought to begin with believing everything that is offered to our acceptance, than that it is our duty to doubt of everything.' The remark occurs in Newman's *Grammar of Assent,* chapter 9, §3, part 2, no. 1.]

intelligentia systematica, de qua in secunda regula. Forma pertinet ad ens quatenus intelligitur, actus quatenus iudicatur, potentia quatenus et intelligitur aliquid et iudicatur de aliquo. Per iudicium fit reditus ad cognitionem concreti, nam concretum cognoscitur quando omnia cognoscenda et cognoscibilia de aliquo cognoscuntur. Tertia et quarta regulae, quatenus quaerunt cohaerentiam eorum quae cogitantur et dicuntur, postulant reflexionem subsequentis iudicii, unde praeparant viam ad iudicium et appropriquant ad illud.

Iudicium postulat plus quam intelligentiam; atque nos loquimur de responsabilitate iudicandi quia etiam voluntas tangitur. Etsi, enim, infantes septennes multa intelligant, tamen minorennes ante annum vigesimum primum reputantur. Certe plura ante hanc aetatem intelligunt, tamen eorum non censetur plena responsabilitas iudicandi. Post hanc aetatem exspectatur maior iudicandi capacitas. Ulterius fiunt variae specializationes, unde alii homines possunt credere experto.

Sapientia et ordinat omnia et bene intelligit et de omnibus iudicat. Capacitas iudicandi habetur quatenus pervenitur ad mensuram aliquam intelligentiae.

Transitus ex intelligibilitate ad iudicium fit per transformationem conscientiae intellectualis ex operatione qua quid sit res quaeritur ad operationem qua an res sit stabilitur. Prima operatio movetur a desiderio intelligendi, quod de se ducit tantum ad definitiones. Deinde exsurgit alia quaestio in eodem desiderio circa an sit: ita emergit conscientia rationalis qua quaeritur differentia inter astrologiam et astronomiam, alchimiam et chimiam, legendas et historiam ... Haec operatio peragitur per aliquam reflexionem super intelligentiam habitam, quae reflexio est critica qua intelligere volumus id quod revera est (reflexio ontica). Non agitur de maiori vel minori intelligibilitate. Saepe legendae sunt magis intelligibiles quam historia; agitur de reflexione critica, quae exigit quoddam inconditionatum. Possumus stabilire rem revera ita se habere si ..., si ..., si ... determinatae conditiones adimpleantur.

Habemus aliquem syllogismum:

si A, ergo B = conditio,

what it is that we understand, we have a systematic understanding, referred to by the second rule. Form belongs to being as understood, act belongs to being as affirmed in a judgment, and potency belongs to being insofar as *something* is understood and judgment is made about *something*. By means of judgment we return to knowledge of the concrete, for we know the concrete when we know everything that is to be known and is knowable about something. The third and fourth rules, in seeking the coherence of what we are thinking and saying, require the reflection of the judgment that is to follow, and so they prepare the way for judgment and bring us to it.

Judgment requires more than just understanding. We speak of the responsibility for judging, since the will also is involved. For, although seven-year-olds understand many things, they are still considered minors until they reach twenty-one. Certainly they understand many more things before they reach this age, and yet they are not deemed to have full responsibility in their judgments. After that age a greater capacity for judging is expected of them. Also, there is an increasing variety of specializations in knowledge, and we go to the respective experts for advice and help.

Wisdom orders all things, understands all things well, and judges all things. The capacity to judge comes as one progresses towards some measure of understanding.

The transition from understanding to judgment takes place through the change in intellectual consciousness from the operation in which it asks what a thing is to that operation by which it determines whether the thing is so. The first operation is set in motion by a desire for understanding, which in itself leads only to definitions. Thereupon another question arises in the same desire, to learn whether the thing is really so. Thus, rational consciousness emerges, in which we inquire into the difference between astronomy and astrology, between alchemy and chemistry, between legend and history, and so on. This operation is performed by reflecting upon the understanding we have, a critical reflection by which we wish to understand what really is (ontic reflection). There is no question here of a greater or lesser degree of intelligibility; legends often have a greater intelligibility than history. It is a matter rather of critical reflection, which requires something that is unconditioned. We can establish that a thing is so if ..., if ..., if ... certain conditions are fulfilled.

For this we have a syllogism:

If *A*, therefore *B* (condition),

atqui A = impletio conditionis (quae habetur ex experientia actuali vel ex memoria experientiae),

ergo B = inconditionatum.[108]

Huiusmodi intelligentia syllogismi opponitur intelligentiae Kantianae de syllogismo, quae exigit iterum novum syllogismum sive pro maiori sive pro minori et ita ad infinitum. Utrum id quod experientia actuali vel ex experientiae memoria habetur sit revera impletio conditionis positae pendet ab intelligentia.

Unum iudicium autem praesupponit conditiones; hae conditiones praesupponunt alia iudicia praecedentia, unde requiritur intelligentia evoluta. Sic diversi habentur typi iudiciorum: iudicia de experientia concreta, de veritate actus intelligendi, de scientiis, de mathematicis …[109]

Quando loquimur de inconditionato quod habetur in iudicio, non intelligimus inconditionatum absolutum, quod est tantum Deus, sed virtuale, secundum quid, id quod habet quidem conditiones quae de facto autem sunt impletae.

Conclusiones scientificae (sensu moderno) remanent semper tantummodo probabiles quia nunquam perveniunt ad inconditionatum; et ponere iudicium atque inconditionatum verum est et manet ab aeterno, etsi agatur de re contingenti, quae non habeat necessitatem nisi hypotheticam. Per verum cognoscitur ens.

Iudicium autem includit etiam aliquem aspectum et experientiam personalem. Sic La Rochefoucauld notat omnes facile queri se memoriam non habere (memoria est donum naturae), neminem autem queri se non habere iudicium, nam iudicium est totaliter in potestate hominis. Omne iudicium enim est aut verum aut non; praecluditur omnis excusatio; personalitas hominis intrat in omni suo iudicio.[110]

Saepe ex methodo expectatur quod tollat responsabilitatem iudicandi, atque methodus fingitur tamquam aliqua institutio publica succurens indigentes. Hoc methodus facere non potest: potest utique adiuvare homines

But *A* (fulfillment of the condition, which is arrived at through one's present experience or from the memory of past experience), Therefore *B* (the unconditioned).[108]

This way of understanding the syllogism differs from that of Kant, in which there is required a new syllogism whether for the major or for the minor, and so on *ad infinitum*. Whether the content of one's present experience or the memory of past experience truly fulfills the stated condition depends upon one's understanding.

A single judgment, however, presupposes conditions; these conditions presuppose other prior judgments, and hence a developed understanding is required. Thus, there are different types of judgment: judgments of concrete experience, of the truth of the act of understanding, of sciences, of mathematics, and so on.[109]

When we speak of the unconditioned that is had in judgment, we do not mean the absolutely unconditioned, which is God alone, but the virtually unconditioned, unconditioned in a qualified sense, namely, that which has conditions that, however, have in fact been fulfilled.

Conclusions that are scientific (in the modern sense) always remain only probable because they never arrive at the unconditioned; and the positing of a judgment and the unconditioned as true is and remains forever, even in the case of contingent being, which has only hypothetical necessity. Being is known through the true.

Judgment includes as well a personal aspect and personal experience. La Rochefoucauld observed that people readily complain about their poor memory – memory is a natural endowment – but they do not complain about their lack of judgment, for judgment is totally within one's power. Every judgment is either true or it is not; no excuses are allowed; one's personality enters into all of one's judgments.[110]

It is often expected of method that it would do away with one's responsibility in making judgments, and method is imagined to be like some public institution that helps the needy. But method cannot do this. It can, it is

---

108 [For more on this, see Lonergan, *Insight* 305–306, 'The General Form of Reflective Insight.']
109 See ibid. chapter 9, 'The Notion of Judgment' [pp. 296–303]; chapter 10, 'Reflective Understanding' [pp. 304–40].
110 [See ibid. 297.]

ad utendum proprio iudicio; at numquam potest praebere surrogatum iudicii.

Haec eliminatio responsabilitatis iudicandi non est chimerica. Responsabilitas iudicandi tollitur a rationalismo, quia pro eo verum est necessarium. Tollitur ab empirismo, pro quo verum non attingitur iudicando sed intuendo et experiendo. Tollitur a criticismo Kantiano, pro quo fides est actus voluntatis, et ratio (in qua iudicium peragitur) est tantum aliquod ideale; iudicium non est nisi aliqua copulatio inter universale (proveniens ex formis intelligibilibus) et particulare (proveniens ex formis sensibilibus); non consistit in affirmatione. Unde pro Kant habentur tantum experientia, intellectus, fides, dum pars rationis obscuratur. Tollitur ab idealismo, pro quo, quia veritas ontologice concipitur, ad veritatem pervenitur intelligendo; notio veritatis non est illa quae exigitur ab actu iudicii, atque a contingentia refugit. Tollitur a relativismo, qui iudicia simpliciter vera non admittit, sed tantum probabilia. Tollitur a scientiis naturalibus, in quibus iudicia de facto fiunt, sed quorum methodus de iudicio non curat. Ipsae progrediuntur criterio mathematico, et scientia concipitur tamquam praedictio. Cfr. etiam philosophiam Jaspers.[111]

In his omnibus praevalens conceptio est conceptio veritatis tamquam mentem cogentis omnium hominum. Unde etiam in re historica, si aliquid est verum, v.gr., tantum pro Catholicis, eo ipso non est veritas.

Haec explicantur per fugam a responsabilitate iudicandi. Nec res est propria tantum philosophiarum et scientiarum modernarum. Radices eius adsunt et in scholasticismo. Sic doctrina Scotistica fundatur in propositionibus necessariis et absolutis, universaliter validis pro omni possibili mundo. Ex hac conceptione orta est notio Wolffiana de possibilibus et notio rationis purae contra quam egit critica Kantiana. In Scotismo haec notio rationalistica coniungitur cum empirismo ex eo quod additur intuitio rei exsistentis et praesentis qua talis. Nulla manet possibilitas iudicii de contingenti de facto vero.

E contra iam S. Augustinus habet tamquam categoriam fundamentalem 'veritatem,' dum moderni loquuntur de 'realitate.' S. Thomas evolvit quam

true, help people to use their own judgment; but it can never provide a substitute for judging.

Such an elimination of the responsibility for judging is no mere figment of the imagination. Rationalism eliminates responsibility for judging, because it considers truth to be necessary. Empiricism eliminates it also, for according to it truth is not attained in the act of judging but in intuiting and experiencing. Kantian critique eliminates it, since for Kant faith is an act of the will, and reason, in which judgment occurs, is only something ideal; judging is simply a link between a universal, originating from intelligible forms, and the particular, originating from sensible forms; it does not consist in an affirmation. Hence, for Kant there is only experience, understanding, and faith; the role of reason is obscured. Idealism eliminates the responsibility for judging, since idealism conceives truth ontologically and so for it truth is arrived at by understanding; the notion of truth is not that which is required by an act of judgment, and it flees from contingency. Relativism eliminates it, because relativism does not admit of judgments that are simply true, but only probable judgments. The natural sciences eliminate it, for although they do in fact make judgments, their method pays no attention to judgment. They proceed according to a mathematical criterion, and science is conceived as prediction. See also the philosophy of Karl Jaspers.[111]

In all of the above, the predominant concept is the concept of truth as compelling the mind of everyone. Hence, even in historical matters, if anything is true, say, only for Catholics, by that very fact it is not truth.

These positions can all be explained as a flight from the responsibility for judging. And this is not found only in modern philosophies and sciences; it has roots also in Scholasticism. Scotus's teaching is based upon necessary and absolute propositions, universally valid for all possible worlds. From this conception there arose the Wolffian notion of possibles and the notion of pure reason against which the Kantian critique was a reaction. In Scotism this rationalistic notion is linked with an empiricism in that there is also an intuition of a thing existing and present as such. There is no room for the possibility of a judgment about contingent reality that is de facto true.

St Augustine, on the other hand, has 'truth' as a fundamental category, while modern thought speaks of 'reality.' St Thomas fully developed the

---

111 [In referring to Jaspers's philosophy so elliptically here, Lonergan leaves his meaning somewhat unclear. However, his remarks on p. 207 below on Jaspers's philosophy clarify what he intends.]

maxime categoriam *tou* esse, quam adiungit categoriis Aristotelis. Newman in opere *Grammar of Assent* insistit in charactere inconditionato actus quo assentimus. Maréchal, secundum principia Kantiana, insistit in charactere absoluto iudicii.

Quia iudicium involvit humanam personalitatem, reicimus notionem methodi quam habent logistici, secundum quam validitas methodi est quasi mechanica et necessaria.

At tunc exsurgit statim obiectio fundamentalis: si enim tota cognitio pendet a iudicio, et hoc implicat responsabilitatem individui qui illud facit, iudicium erit bonum si homines erunt responsabiles; quod de facto raro accidit. Unde methodus, prout a nobis proponitur, totum opus scientificum opinionibus singulorum relinquit.

Talis fuit revera critica quam E. Husserl fecit scientiae: data enim proliferatione indefinita camporum specializatorum, data autonomia uniuscuisque campi, et dato quod criteria quae praesunt singulis campis non fundantur in theoria generali sed potius in conventionibus, nullum remedium videtur possibile ad habendam unitatem et intelligentiam methodi. Nam si fieret nisus in directionem huius unitatis methodi, exsurgeret novus campus specializatus.

De facto tamen manet quod scientiae non possunt progredi sine usu iudicii personalis singulorum individuorum, quod iudicium est actus personalis. Hoc verum est etiam in re mathematica, ubi multi mathematici disputant inter se de natura ipsius matheseos. Pro aliquibus enim agitur tantum de deducendis iis quae continentur in axiomatibus quin explicetur unde axiomata habeantur; pro aliis (intuitionistis), maxima pars matheseos classicae non valet quia principia eius non accipiuntur. Attamen, si ex principiis intuitionisticis haberi possunt quaedam conclusiones quae coincidunt cum classicis, tunc libenter hae conclusiones acceptantur quia novum systema multo intelligibilius videtur; pro aliis mathematica debet connecti cum cultura generali et progressu scientifico generali (cfr. impulsum a mathesi receptum ex philosophia Descartes et Leibniz); pro aliis, demum, mathesis tota ex principiis logicis est deducenda (Russell).[112]

Similiter physici rigorem sic dictum scientificum servant dum novas inventiones non impediat. At de natura scientiae physicae infinitae fiunt disputationes.

category of *esse*, which he added to Aristotle's categories. Newman in his *Grammar of Assent* stresses the unconditioned character of the act by which we assent. Maréchal, following Kantian principles, insists upon the absolute character of a judgment.

Because judgment involves the human personality, we reject the logicians' notion of method according to which the validity of a method is, in a way, mechanical and inevitable.

But here is where the fundamental objection comes up: if all knowledge depends upon judgment and this involves responsibility on the part of the person judging, judgment will be good only if people are responsible – which rarely is the case. Method, therefore, as we propose it to be, leaves the whole of scientific endeavor to the opinions of individuals.

This, in fact, was Edmund Husserl's criticism of science: given the unlimited proliferation of specialized fields, the autonomy of each field, and the fact that the criteria governing each field are not grounded upon a general theory but rather on conventions, there seems to be no possible way to bring about the unity and the understanding of method. For if an attempt were made in the direction of this unity of method, a new specialized field would result.

But actually the fact remains that sciences cannot progress without the use of personal judgment on the part of individuals, and that judgment is a personal act. This is true even in mathematics, where many mathematicians argue about the nature of mathematics itself. For some it is simply a matter of deducing what are contained in axioms, without explaining where one gets those axioms; for others, intuitionists, most of classical mathematics is invalid because its principles are not accepted. And yet, if some conclusions that coincide with the classical can be derived from intuitionist principles, such conclusions can be gladly accepted, since the new system seems much more intelligible. For others, mathematics must be connected with the general culture and overall scientific progress – see the impetus given to mathematics by the philosophy of Descartes and of Leibniz – while still others (Russell) hold that the whole of mathematics is to be deduced from logical principles.[112]

In a similar way, physicists maintain so-called scientific rigor so long as it does not hinder new discoveries. But there is an infinite number of disputes about the nature of physics.

112 [See Lonergan, *Phenomenology and Logic* 40–49 for another brief discussion of different understandings of the 'nature of mathematics.']

Nostris temporibus loquuntur continuo de philosophia historiae, naturae, educationis, matheseos ... Ex alia parte philosophia videtur esse aliquid in se bene determinatum, ita ut non debeat esse philosophia ... de aliqua re.

Praeterea exsistit problema de philosophia Christiana quatenus philosophia involvit totalem reflexionem hominis super seipsum, et hominis non abstracte considerati sed actualiter exsistentis, ergo in se habentis effectus peccati originalis, gratiae, acceptationis vel reiectionis talium donorum ... quae omnia ad theologiam pertinent. Sed tunc quid remanet philosophiae?

Revera scientia est de obiectis: divisio scientiarum fit secundum earum obiecta formalia, quae obiecta sunt realia. Sic theologia est scientia de Deo et de universo prout ad Deum refertur (sic secundum S. Thomam; pro aliis est scientia de Christo toto); sic dantur scientiae de ordine subatomico, atomico, vitali, animali, humano ... Dantur etiam scientiae compositae: astronomia (physica + chimia), biophysica, biochimica, psychologia sensitiva, etc.

Aliae autem scientiae possunt haberi non tantum de obiectis sed potius de obiectificatione. Sic logica, mathesis non sunt de obiectis realibus sed potius omnia considerant quae ad realia applicare possunt, sive actualia sive possibilia. Hoc faciunt considerantes ea quae sunt similia, per processus generalizationis et idealizationis. Ita epistemologia quaerit de validitate obiectificationis; et metaphysica quaerit quid in genere ponatur quando fit obiectivatio, necnon de habitudine inter diversas scientias et de ordine rerum.

Unde aliae sunt scientiae de obiectis, aliae de obiectificatione; philosophia non est tantum scientia in seipsa sed etiam de aliis. Huiusmodo scientia est Christiana quatenus non excludit possibilitatem illius aperturae in qua theologia inseritur cum ordine revelationis supernaturalis; non est Christiana quatenus hanc possibilitatem excludit.

Regulae methodicae quas dedimus valent de omnibus scientiis, unde etiam de theologia. Regulae de intelligentia applicari possunt etiam categoriae 'mysterii'; nam id quod intellectum humanum excedit potest adhiberi tamquam praemissa quae tractatur secundum technicam specialem, modo analogo ac fit in mathesi pro numeris irrationalibus, quin realitas de qua agitur sit ipsa irrationalis. Regulae de iudicio modificationem peculiarem accipiunt in theologia quatenus tangunt sapientiam non humanam sed di-

In our days there is constant talk about a philosophy of history, of nature, of education, of mathematics, and the rest. On the other hand, philosophy would seem to be something that is well defined in itself, so that there ought not to be a 'philosophy of ...' about any particular thing.

Moreover, there is the problem of a Christian philosophy, in that philosophy involves man's unrestricted reflection upon himself, where 'man' is not considered in the abstract but as humans actually exist and therefore as affected by original sin, by grace, and by the acceptance or rejection of supernatural gifts, all of which lie within the domain of theology. What then remains for philosophy?

In actual fact, science is about objects. Sciences are divided according to their formal objects, and these objects are real. Thus, theology is the science of God and of the universe in relation to God (thus St Thomas; for others it is the science of the whole Christ). So also there are sciences of the subatomic order of being, of the atomic order, of plant life, animal life, human life ... There are also composite sciences, such as astronomy (physics + chemistry), biophysics, biochemistry, sentient psychology, etc.

There can be other sciences, however, that deal not so much with objects but rather with objectification. Logic and mathematics do not deal with real objects, but consider rather everything that can be applied to real things, whether actual or possible. This they do by considering those things that are similar, through the processes of generalization and idealization. Thus, epistemology inquires into the validity of objectification; metaphysics asks what in general is posited when there is objectification, and also about the relationship between different sciences and about the order of reality.

Hence, some sciences are about objects and others about objectification; philosophy is not only a science in itself, but also about other sciences. This sort of science is Christian insofar as it does not exclude the possibility of being open to theology along with the supernatural order of revelation; insofar as it excludes this possibility, it is not Christian.

The rules of method we have given are valid for all branches of knowledge, hence also for theology. The rules concerning understanding can be applied also to the category of 'mystery'; for that which exceeds our understanding can be used as a premise to be treated by way of a special technique, similarly to the way in which mathematics handles irrational numbers, without the reality in question being itself irrational. Rules concerning judgment are modified in a special way in theology, inasmuch as they touch upon divine, not human, wisdom, for the submission of faith is

vinam: iudiciis divinis revelatis submissio fidei debetur. At haec applicatio regularum ad theologiam ulterius manet evolvenda.

4.5 De applicatione regularum methodi theologiae

Generatim theologia dividitur in speculativam (potius in Medio Aevo excultam) et positivam (inde a Renascentia evolutam), in apologeticam et dogmaticam.

Distinctio inter theologiam dogmaticam et apologeticam nullo modo est methodica. Nam in dogmatica non desunt considerationes de obiectionibus, v.gr., rationalistarum contra Trinitatem, unde manet problema apologeticum. Ex altera parte, in theologia fundamentali occupamur in quaestionibus dogmaticis, ut sunt rationabilitas fidei et ipsa fides. Immo, ecclesia, de qua agitur in theologia fundamentali, non est tantum societas perfecta sed et Corpus Christi mysticum, realitas spatio-temporalis. Unde, sicut pro theologia trinitaria requiruntur conceptus technici, processionis, relationis, personae ... sine quibus nulla thesis systematica de SS. Trinitate haberetur, ita ad habendum tractatum de Corpore Christi Mystico requiritur conceptualizatio systematica de re historica. Nam aliquis tractatus theologicus non est nisi expressio veritatis Christianae secundum conceptualizationem systematicam. Sic in re trinitaria, pars logica exculta est ab Augustino, pars metaphysica in lucem venit in disputationibus provocatis a Gilberto Porrentano et Joachim a Flora ... Sine talibus conceptibus systematicis tollitur possibilitas habendi tractatum. Ita hodie non deest certe materia pro tractatu dogmatico de ecclesia, nec deest desiderium, nec investigationes positivae eximiae de Corpore Mystico ... attamen ex defectu systematicae conceptualizationis adhuc tractatus nequivit apparere. Revera nimiae sunt adhuc disputationes de conceptu historiae, nec aliqua theoria systematica de hac re definitive elaborata est.[113]

De nexu inter theolgiam speculativam et positivam, postea agemus.

owed to divinely revealed truths. But this application of the rules to theology remains to be further developed.

4.5 Application of the Rules of Method to Theology

Theology is generally divided into speculative theology, the main preoccupation of medieval theology, and positive theology, largely developed since the Renaissance, and into apologetic and dogmatic theology.

The distinction between dogmatic and apologetic theology is not at all methodical. For dealing with objections is not absent from dogmatic theology – rationalist objections against the Trinity, for example – hence, the problem of apologetics remains. On the other hand, in fundamental theology we are concerned with dogmatic questions such as the reasonableness of faith and the nature of faith itself. In fact, the church, which is treated in fundamental theology, is not just a 'perfect society' but the mystical body of Christ, a spatiotemporal reality. Thus, just as trinitarian theology requires the technical concepts of procession, relation, person, and so forth, without which there would be no systematic treatise on the Trinity, so a treatment of the mystical body of Christ requires a systematic conceptualization of history. Any theological treatise is simply an expression of Christian truth in terms of a systematic conceptualization. In trinitarian theology, Augustine developed the logical part, while the metaphysical part emerged in the discussions raised by Gilbert de la Porrée and Joachim of Fiore. Without such systematic concepts no treatise is possible. So today, although there is certainly plenty of material for a dogmatic treatise on the church and a desire to have such a treatise, and some excellent research has been done on the mystical body, nevertheless on account of the lack of systematic conceptualization no such treatise has yet been able to appear. In fact, there are still too many disputes about the concept of history, and no definitive systematic theory about it has been worked out.[113]

We shall deal with the connection between speculative and positive theology later.

---

113 See E. Troeltsch, *Der Historismus und seine Problem* (Tübingen: C.B. Mohr, 1922), where all the various theories about history are listed along with a critique of them and comparisons between them. [Although the available information is incomplete, there would seem to be a rare, partial English translation of this work, namely, *Historism and Its Problems. First book: The Logical Problem of the Philosophy of History* (Tübingen: Verlag von J.C.S. Mohr [Paul Siebeck], 1922).]

Ad applicandas regulas quas dedimus, iterum est insistendum in habitibus intellectualibus: primo aspectu theologia videtur esse id quod legitur
apud auctores theologicos; dein, facta aliqua purificatione, apparet esse
id quod intelligitur in illis operibus; principia acquiruntur ex quibus alia
deducuntur; ad structuram libri maxime attenditur, usque dum totus liber appareat exsistere propter ea quae in libro non tractantur. Tantum si
theologia pervenit ad habitus intellectuales theologi, nec ad internam re-
productionem singularum thesium consistit, sed in eo quod ipse theologus
potest ex seipso efformare definitiones sufficientes ad proprios fines, ipse
theologus poterit bene iudicare et etiam practice et kerygmatice id quod
intellexit communicare populo Christiano. Quando ad hanc versatilitatem
pervenitur, theologia fundamentalis et theologia dogmatica nonnisi ut duo
usus apparent eiusdem habitus.

Quinque regulae supra traditae pariter applicantur ad theologiam fundamentalem et dogmaticam, positivam et speculativam. Nam ipsae fundantur in natura intellectus humani, unde homines qui procedunt in scientiis
eas observant, etiam quando explicite de iis non cogitant. Methodus autem
non debet nisi explicitare id quod implicatur in structura processus intellectualis.

4.5.1 Theologica illustratio primae regulae: Intellige

Traditionalis est conceptio theologiae tamquam fidei quaerentis intellectum. Fides semper praesupponitur; non dicitur, 'Crede, postquam solutionem dederis difficultatibus,' sed 'Crede ut intelligas.' Talis fuit mens et
Augustini et Anselmi.

Theologia consistit in eo quod iam credidimus, et nunc volumus intelligere id quod credimus, nec tantum repetere quod credimus et ea quae
credimus. Hoc desiderium et huiusmodi exigentia intelligendi adest et
apud theologos et apud sacerdotes et apud omnem populum Christianum.

Tale desiderium intelligendi iam aderat in ecclesia primaeva et patristica. Illo tamen tempore quaestiones casu ponebantur, et proinde etiam
casu oriebantur haereses et quaerebantur solutiones, sive contra Gnosticos,
Montanistas, Arianos, Nestorianos, Monophysitas, Pelagianos ... Inquisitio
oriebatur non systematice sed tantum occasione haeresium.

Id autem quod casualiter factum est in ecclesia primaeva et patristica

For the application of the rules we have given, we must lay stress once again on intellectual habits. At first glance, theology would seem to be whatever one can read in theological books; next, a refinement of this notion suggests that it would seem to be what is understood in these works. Principles are drawn up from which other principles are deduced; close attention is paid to the makeup of the book, until the whole book seems to exist on account of things that are not treated in it. Only when theology permeates to the intellectual habits of the theologian and ceases to consist in inward-looking reproduction of particular theses, but consists rather in the fact that theologians themselves are quite capable of fashioning definitions sufficient for their own purposes, will theologians be able to make good judgments and even be able in a practical and kerygmatic way to communicate to the Christian people what they have understood. When this sort of versatility has been achieved, fundamental and dogmatic theology will be seen to be but two different uses of the same intellectual habit.

The five rules given above are equally applicable to fundamental, dogmatic, positive, and speculative theology. For they are grounded upon the nature of the human intellect; thus, those who make progress in their science observe them, even when they do not explicitly advert to them. Method need only make explicit what is implicit in the structure of the intellectual process.

4.5.1   Theological Illustration of the First Rule: Understand

The conception of theology as faith seeking understanding is a traditional one. Faith is always presupposed; we do not say, 'Believe, once you have solved all the difficulties,' but 'Believe so as to understand.' Such was the mind of Augustine and Anselm.

Theology consists in the fact that we already believe and now we want to understand what we believe and not simply repeat that we believe and what we believe. This desire, this need to understand, is to be found among theologians and priests and all the Christian faithful.

Such a desire to understand was present in the very early church and in the age of the Fathers. In those early times questions came up in random fashion and so also did heresies, and solutions were sought for countering Gnostics, Montanists, Arians, Nestorians, Monophysites, Pelagians, and others. Theological inquiry did not occur systematically but only as occasioned by some heresy or other.

Medieval theologians tried to do in a universal and systematic way what

modo universali et systematico conati sunt facere theologi mediaevales. Momentum operis *Sic et non* Petri Abaelardi fuit in eo quod, cum unaquaeque assertio ex auctoritatibus scripturisticis et patristicis possit et affirmari et negari, ostendit non sufficere semper citationem Patrum et Scripturae ad quaestionem determinandam, et proinde exsistere campum inquisitionis in quo homo mediaevalis ex seipso solutiones quaerere debebat.

Nec obliviscendum est momenti speculationis Anselmianae; cum valde acutum intellectum haberet, Anselmus fere de omnibus fundamentalibus problematibus theologicis egit, sive de processione Sancti Spiritus, sive de peccato originali, de redemptione, de incarnatione, de praedestinatione et libertate ... Attamen illi deerat labor eruditionis, collectio locorum Sacrae Scripturae et Patrum quae postea adfuit in saec. XII, ope praesertim Petri Lombardi. Unde Anselmus construebat domum fere sine lapidibus. Defectus elementi positivi maxime nocuit solutionibus quas Anselmus dederat quaestionibus illis ultimis, unde hae solutiones non habuerunt ullum valorem permanentem. Maximus tamen fit eius impulsus circa cogitationem subsequentem: sine Anselmo, forsan, scholasticismus non exsisteret. Maxima enim fuit eius auctoritas ex eo quod et sanctus erat. Eius sanctitas, aliter ac fuit pro Abaelardo, consacravit scholasticam et illam introduxit in scholis, sive cathedraticis sive monasticis.

Post Abaelardum notio quaestionis evoluta est praesertim a Gilberto Porretano, atque perfecta est praesertim a S. Thoma.[114]

Investigationes historicae et collectiones positivae curatae sunt praesertim a Petro Lombardo, qui usque ad saec. XVII legebatur in scholis. Tamen typicum est hoc commentariorum super *Sententias* Lombardi: in eo optime perspicitur ille processus conceptualizationis de quo supra locuti sumus; agitur in his commentariis saepissime de quaestionibus quae a Lombardo non positae erant neque intelligebantur; multiplicitas opinionum pendebat a multis diversis conceptionibus eiusdem materiae. Lombardus autem munere fungebatur quo hodie funguntur Denzinger aut Rouët de Journel.[115]

was done in a casual way in the time of the early church and of the Fathers. The importance of Peter Abelard's *Sic et non* lay in showing that since every statement based on the authority of scripture and the Fathers could be both affirmed and denied, quoting the Bible or the Fathers was not sufficient to settle a question, and that therefore there existed a field of inquiry wherein people in the Middle Ages would have to find the solutions by themselves.

Nor should the importance of Anselm's speculative work be overlooked. With great acumen he addressed virtually all the fundamental problems in theology – the procession of the Holy Spirit, original sin, redemption, the Incarnation, predestination and free will, and so on. But he did not have at his disposal the work of scholarship, the collections of scriptural and patristic texts that became available later on, in the twelfth century, especially through the labors of Peter Lombard. So Anselm was trying to build a house without very much in the way of bricks or stones. The lack of such basic materials greatly weakened the solutions Anselm gave to those questions, and so his solutions did not have any permanent validity. Nevertheless, he had an enormous influence upon subsequent thinking; without him, perhaps, there would be no Scholasticism. He enjoyed great authority also from the fact that he was a holy man. His sanctity – unlike as with Abelard – sanctified Scholasticism, so to speak, and won it entry into the cathedral and monastic schools.

After Abelard the notion of question was further developed especially by Gilbert de la Porrée and perfected above all by St Thomas.[114]

Historical research and collections of documentary materials were the careful work particularly of Peter Lombard, who was studied down to the seventeenth century. Yet it is typical of the various commentaries on the *Sentences* of Peter Lombard that whereas he clearly grasped that process of conceptualization which we mentioned above, the commentaries very often deal with questions that Peter did not raise or even understand, and a great variety of opinions resulted from the many different conceptions of the same material. Peter Lombard, however, performed in those days the function that Denzinger and Rouët de Journel do today.[115]

114 See above pp. 4–7.
115 [See Henricus Denzinger and Adolfus Schönmetzer, *Enchiridion Symbolorum: Definitionum et declarationum de rebus fidei et morum*, 32nd ed. (Freiburg im Breisgau: Herder, 1963); and M.J. Rouët de Journel, *Enchiridion Patristicum: Loci SS. Patrum, doctorum scriptorum ecclesiasticorum*, 21st ed. (Barcelona: Herder, 1959).]

Ita historice exhibetur sensus primae regulae: intellige! Quia conceptus proveniunt ex actibus intelligendi, novi semper conceptus oriuntur ex nova intellectione, unde sic explicatur processus conceptualizationis systematicae qui in scholastica habitus est. Unde tota scholastica est verificatio primae regulae.

4.5.2 Theologica illustratio secundae regulae: Intellige systematice

Quamvis possint esse et sint praeludia ad scientiam usquedum systema quaeritur, tamen, proprie loquendo, scientia exsistit tantum quando exsistit systema ex quo determinentur omnes relationes illi scientiae propriae.

In omni scientia alia est periodus praeparatoria et alia explicatoria. Multa de geometria habentur apud Pythagoram, tamen Euclides primus fuit qui aliquam systematizationem dedit geometriae. Multae leges mechanicae excogitatae sunt ante Newton a Galilaeo, Kepler … at systema habitum est tantum per Newton. Multa cognoscebantur de re chimica, at chimia incepit esse scientia tantum cum tabulis a Mendeleev statutis, quae praebuerunt elementum systematicum. Unde etiam in scientiis, ante formam datur motus ad formam: cum systematizatione scientia incipit habere formam, unde unitatem propriam, proprias leges et conceptus proprios, quibus omnibus ab aliis distingui potest, unde et methodum propriam.

Sic theologia nascitur tamquam scientia versus annum 1230.[116]

Saec. XII et initio saec. XIII multae inextricabiles quaestiones theologos cruciabant.

Non poterant recte concipere gratiam et libertatem. Nam duae dabantur definitiones libertatis, una philosophica (immunitas a necessitate), altera theologica (illa mediante qua homo bonum facit cum gratia, sine autem gratia malum facit). Gratia inserebatur in definitione libertatis, quia si exclusa fuisset, secutae essent haereses Pelagianae. Eadem difficultas pro gratia aderat. Gratia dicit gratuitum; at revera omnia sunt gratuita, etiam ordo creationis. Tunc distinguebantur gratuita minus proprie et gratuita magis proprie, usque ad praedestinationem, cuius gratuitatem volebant super omnia asserere. Eodem modo Augustinus rhetorice, at non realiter, sol-

So the meaning of the first rule, *Understand*, is illustrated from history. Because concepts flow from acts of understanding, further insights give rise to new concepts, and this explains the process of systematic conceptualization present in Scholasticism. Thus, the whole of Scholasticism is a verification of this first rule.

4.5.2 Theological Illustration of the Second Rule: Understand Systematically

Although there can be and are some preliminaries to a science prior to the move towards systematization, nevertheless, properly speaking, a science exists only when there is a system for determining all the relationships proper to that science.

In every science there is a preparatory period and an explanatory period. There is a good deal of geometry in Pythagoras, but it was Euclid who first systematized geometry. There were many laws of mechanics formulated before Newton's time by Galileo and Kepler and others, but no system until Newton. A lot was known about chemical reality, but chemistry as a science began only with Mendeleev's tables, which set forth the elements in a systematic way. Hence, in sciences also, before there is form there is movement towards form. It is with systematization that a science begins to have its form, hence its proper unity, laws, and concepts, which distinguish it from all other sciences, and which also give it its proper method.

The birth of theology as a science, therefore, occurred around the year 1230.[116]

In the twelfth century and around the beginning of the thirteenth there were many complicated questions that were vexing the theologians.

First, they were unable to arrive at a correct concept of grace and freedom. They had two definitions of freedom, one that was philosophical, 'freedom from necessity,' and the other theological, 'that by means of which man with grace does good and without grace does evil.' The notion of grace was introduced into the definition of freedom, since if it had been excluded, the heresy of Pelagianism would have been the logical consequence. There was the same difficulty with grace. Grace means that which is gratuitous, gratis. But in fact everything is gratuitous, even the created order. Then they began to distinguish between gratuitous in the strict sense and gratui-

---

116 See the references to Landgraf and Lottin, above.

vebat problema de libertate etiam sine gratia manente, dicens iustum esse
liberum a peccato, iniustum esse liberum a iustitia.[117] At quaestio insoluta
manebat usque dum gratia intraret in definitione libertatis.

Alia quaestio, minus apparens at latens in operibus primae scholasticae,
est problema de conceptu ipso theologiae. Distinctio inter theologiam et
philosophiam non clare (est minimum quod dici potest) concipitur ab
Anselmo. Ipse contendit probare necessitatem redemptionis, seu incarnationis et mortis Christi. Ergo de rationalismo improbandus est? Adsunt quidem in eius opere aliae expressiones quae hanc impressionem rationalismi
mitigant, distinguentes varios sensus necessitatis, unde etiam philologice
possibilis est illum sensu orthodoxo interpretari. At praesertim historice
attendendum est ad id quod est rationalismus ante cognitam naturam rationalismi et alius (v.gr. Hermes, Günther ...) ortus postquam cognita erat
distinctio inter theologiam et philosophiam. Unde certe potest admitti in
scriptoribus orthodoxis aliqua apparentia rationalismi inculpabilis ante
claram distinctionem inter fidem et rationem, theologiam et philosophiam.

Solutio, praeparata a Stephano Langton et a Praepostino, inventa est
praesertim a Philippo Cancellario Universitatis Parisiensis c. 1230 cum
distinctione entitativa inter ordinem naturalem et supernaturalem, quae
distinctio circa omnes divisiones facta est: fides est supra rationem, gratia
supra naturam, caritas supra amorem humanum, meritum supra debitum
naturae, etc. Facta hac distinctione fundamentali, statim controversia de
gratia et libertate solvitur, et nasci possunt tractatus de libertate et de gratia;
theologia clarius a scientiis naturalibus distinguitur, etc.

In tota hac quaestione vox fundamentalis est *ordo*. Ordo est aliqua relatio
vel complexus relationum multarum intelligibilium. Unde invento ordine
supernaturali, inventum obiectum theologiae proprium, seu complexus relationum intelligibilium intra se complectentes omnes res pertinentes ad
theologiam. Excogitatio huius notionis se habuit ad scientiam theologicam

tous in the broad sense, while wishing to maintain that predestination was gratuitous above all. In the same way Augustine gave a rhetorical, but not real, solution to the problem of freedom that remains even without grace, declaring the righteous to be free from sin, but the unrighteous to be free from righteousness.[117] But the question would remain unsolved so long as grace was part of the definition of freedom.

Another question, less obvious but one that is latent in early Scholasticism, is the problem of the concept of theology itself. The least that can be said is that Anselm did not clearly distinguish between theology and philosophy. He tried to prove the necessity of redemption, that is, of the Incarnation and death of Christ. Is he then to be accused of rationalism? In his writings there are other expressions, it is true, that lessen the impression of rationalism, distinguishing various meanings of necessity, so that it is philologically possible to interpret him in an orthodox sense. But especially from a historical perspective one must take into account what rationalism was before the nature of rationalism was understood, and what that other rationalism is, such as that of Hermes and Günther, that arose after the distinction between philosophy and theology became known. An inculpable appearance of rationalism, therefore, can certainly be admitted in orthodox authors before there was a clear distinction between faith and reason, theology and philosophy.

Stephen Langton and Praepositinus of Cremona [ca. 1150–1210] prepared the way for the solution that was hit upon by Philip the Chancellor of the University of Paris (ca. 1230) when he brought in the entitative distinction between the natural and supernatural orders, a distinction that applies to all divisions: faith above reason, grace above nature, charity above human love, merit above what is naturally due, and so forth. With this fundamental distinction, the controversy about grace and freedom was settled forthwith, and treatises on freedom and on grace could now appear. Theology becomes more clearly distinguished from natural branches of knowledge.

In this entire question the basic word is *order*. Order is a relation, or a complex of a number of intelligible relations. Hence, with the discovery of the supernatural order, the proper object of theology was also discovered, that is, the complex of intelligible relations comprising everything that pertains to theology. The elaboration of this notion was to the science of theol-

117 Augustine, *De gratia et libero arbitrio*, c. 15, n. 31; ML 44, 899–900.

sicut ea quae ab Euclide inventa sunt se habuerunt ad scientiam geometricam, inventa a Newton ad physicam, inventa a Mendeleev ad chimicam.

Quando dicitur ad theologiam pertinere ordinem supernaturalem, dicitur theologiam tractare de dono Dei, quatenus est non tantum aliqud a Deo acceptum, sed ipse Deus. Unde hoc prorsus transcendit quamlibet naturam creatam et creabilem, quodlibet ens finitum. Agitur ergo de ordine peculiari et proprio cuius elementa nequeunt ullo modo deduci vel concludi ex iis quae naturae humanae vel cuilibet naturae creatae, quatenus naturae illae sunt, pertinent. Haec notio est notio constitutiva illius quod est scientia theologica.

Saeculis XVI et XVII haec notio impugnata est a Baio et Jansenio, contra scholasticismum mediaevalem reagentes, ut reditus fieret ad purum Augustinum. At agebatur de reditu vere inepto. Mediaevales enim, etsi studia historica nequibant peragere, nonnisi de Augustino cogitabant, qui fuit maximus et fere unicus magister theologorum saeculi XII. Pro illis facere theologiam significabat dicere id quod dixerat Augustinus. Unde Augustinum cognoverunt et saepe aptissime citaverunt. Et tamen positiones Augustinianas sequentes et evolventes pervenerunt ad aliquam distinctionem quae clare non aderat in Augustino.

Unde melius perspicitur quid nostra secunda regula involvat.

(a) 'Intellige systematice' = intellige ita ut unico fluxu oriantur conceptus fundamentales proprii alicuius scientiae, atque determinentur per relationes reciprocas unius ad alium. Intelligentia systematica dicit conceptualizationem unitam totius campi alicuius scientiae, secundum quam possint haberi omnes propositiones de illa materia, fieri disputationes de illa re, atque ad difficultates contra illam disciplinam respondere possimus.

(b) At ipsa systematizatio est tantum unus aspectus intelligentiae systematicae. Nam, quia finis naturalis intellectus est intelligentia totius universi concreti, partialis systematizatio unius campi nondum respondet ad hunc finem. Unde necesse est extendere systematizationem ex uno campo ad caeteros. Unde S. Thomas voluit systematicam intelligentiam theologicam obtinere eam coniungendo cum aliis systematizationibus, eam integrando in intelligentia systematica reliqui universi. Dum autem S. Bonaventura in rebus naturalibus nonnisi signa et symbola videbat per quae mens humana elevaretur ad Deum, S. Thomas non attendit ad solam systematizationem theologicam sed suam systematizationem assumpsit in systematizatione universali, sive physica, sive psychologica, sive metaphysica, sive ethica, quam

ogy what Euclid's discoveries were to geometry, Newton's to physics, and Mendeleev's to chemistry.

When we say that what pertains to theology is the supernatural order, we are saying that theology deals with the free gift of God, not only as something received from God but as God himself. This is something that transcends any created and creatable order whatsoever, anything that is finite. Such an order is quite special and unique, and its elements can in no way be deduced or concluded to from the properties of human nature or any created nature, inasmuch as these are natures. This notion is constitutive of theology as a science.

In the sixteenth and seventeenth centuries this notion was attacked by Baius and Jansenius, who were reacting against medieval Scholasticism in favor of a return to pure Augustinian thought. But such a return was really quite wrong-headed. Even though the medieval theologians were unable to pursue historical studies, they were thoroughly steeped in Augustine, who was the supreme and virtually the only theological authority in the twelfth century. For them, to do theology meant to repeat what Augustine had said, and so they knew their Augustine and often quoted him very appositely. Yet in following and elaborating Augustinian positions they arrived at a distinction that was clearly not found in Augustine himself.

This helps us to understand what our second rule involves.

(a) 'Understand systematically' means to understand in such a way that in a single movement the fundamental concepts proper to any science may emerge and be determined by their mutual relations. Systematic understanding means a unified conceptualization of the entire field of a given science, according to which all the propositions concerning its subject matter can be arrived at, all the controverted points in that matter dealt with, and objections against that discipline answered.

(b) But this systematization by itself is but one aspect of systematic understanding. For since the intellect's natural goal is to understand the entire concrete universe, a partial systematization in one field of knowledge is not yet commensurate with that end, and therefore it was necessary to extend systematization from one field to all the others. Hence, St Thomas decided to achieve systematic understanding in theology by linking it with other systematizations, by integrating it with a systematic understanding of the rest of the universe. While St Bonaventure saw in natural realities only signs and symbols whereby the human mind might ascend to God, St Thomas attended not only to theological systematization but subsumed his systematization in a universal systematization, physical, psychological, metaphysical,

praesertim ex Aristotele desumpsit. Tunc tantum theologia potuit esse vere systematica. Quamvis enim theologia habeat suum proprium campum in ordine supernaturali, tamen hic campus exsistit in hoc concreto universo, unde cum relationibus ad alios campos.

Unde ad intelligentiam systematicam requiritur et systematizatio campi proprii illius scientiae de qua agitur, et integratio huius systematizationis cum systematizatione totius universi.

4.5.3 Illustratio theologica tertiae regulae: Inverte contrapositiones

Exemplum desumitur ex conflictu Thomistico-Augustinensi saec. XIII.

S. Thomas erat maximus innovator, unde acerrime reactio orta est in saec. XIII ex parte Fratrum Minorum et, in genere, anti-Aristotelicorum, contra Fratres Praedicatores et illos qui volebant uti scientia Aristotelica ad systematizationem theologicam perficiendam.

Iste conflictus ambiguus erat: nam, quatenus reactio reiciebat positiones Thomisticas quae assumebant scientiam, biologiam, physicam ... Aristotelicas, aequivalebat alicui contrapositioni. At, quatenus reactio intendebat reicere errores in Aristotelismo contentos, censenda est potius tamquam positio. Nisi enim fuisset acerrime resistentia in ecclesia contra Thomismum, Aristoteles habuisset ineluctabiliter auctoritatem exaggeratam et multo difficilius fuisset postea acceptare veriores conclusiones scientiarum naturalium in saeculis sequentibus.

Tamen reactio habuit etiam gravissimos defectus: Augustiniani volebant ex Aristotele accipere tantum id quod erat evidenter certum, seu logicam, non autem scientiam ab aliquo pagano excogitatam. Reicientes notiones fundamentales ad intelligentiam systematicam habendam, loco visionis plus minusve scientificae quam Aristoteles habebat de universo, intendebant meram systematizationem logicam abstractam.

E contra, pro S. Thoma scientia erat intelligentia rerum realium, universi concreti; parum vel nihil curabat de hypothesibus aliorum mundorum de quibus nihil scimus. Quare, etiam, nullibi de 'natura pura' loquitur.

Scotus autem concipiebat scientiam de omnibus rebus possibilibus. Unde, si hoc accipiatur, necessario poni debet notio 'naturae purae' ad

and ethical, which he took mainly from Aristotle. Only then could theology be truly systematic. For although theology has its proper field in the supernatural order, this field exists in this concrete universe and so is related to other fields.

Systematic understanding, therefore, requires both a systematization of the field that is proper to any given science and an integration of that systematization with that of the systematization of the universe as a whole.

4.5.3 Theological Illustration of the Third Rule: Reverse Counterpositions

The following example is taken from the conflict between the Thomists and the Augustinians in the thirteenth century.

St Thomas was a great innovator, and this stirred up a vehement reaction on the part of the Franciscans and the anti-Aristotelians in general against the Dominicans and all who wanted to use Aristotle to further the systematization of theology.

Now this conflict was ambivalent. Insofar as the reaction rejected Thomistic positions that adopted Aristotelian science, biology, physics, etc., it was equivalent to a counterposition; but insofar as this reaction aimed at rejecting errors in Aristotelianism, it should be considered rather as a position. For if there had not been this fierce resistance in the church against Thomism, the authority of Aristotle would inevitably have become greatly exaggerated, and it would have been much more difficult for the truer conclusions of the natural sciences to win acceptance in later centuries.

Nevertheless, the reaction did have very serious defects. The Augustinians wanted to take from Aristotle only what was evidently certain, namely logic, but not to accept any science that was elaborated by a pagan. Rejecting notions that were fundamental for acquiring systematic understanding, they opted for a merely logical and abstract systematization in place of the more or less scientific vision Aristotle had of the universe.

For St Thomas, on the contrary, science was an understanding of real things, of the concrete universe; he cared little or not at all about hypothetical worlds about which we know nothing. That is why he never mentions *natura pura,* 'pure nature.'

Scotus, however, conceived science as something that treats of all possible things. But if this notion is accepted, one must necessarily posit the notion of 'pure nature' in order to safeguard the gratuitousness of the su-

salvandum gratuitatem supernaturalis. Differentia erat potius in notione sapientiae et scientiae.

Scotus, cum actum intelligendi conceptibus priorem negasset, ipsos conceptus tamquam fundamentum scientiae habuit in quantum aut necessario inter se connecterentur aut mutuo sibi repugnarent; et ideo theologiam eatenus scientificam reputavit quatenus veritates determinaret quae, cum absolute necessariae atque universales essent, pro omni rerum ordine possibili valerent. Qua de causa, qui principiis Scoti imbuitur, theologum semper de ordinibus mere possibilibus loqui credit, vel si per accidens de ordine actuali fit sermo, hanc exceptionem qua exceptionem explicite notandam esse supponit.

At S. Thomas, cum actum intelligendi conceptibus priorem perspexisset, diversos scientiae gradus pro diversis intelligendi actibus distinxit. Unde secundum S. Thomam ipse Deus, cum divinam essentiam comprehendat, omnia prorsus possibilia perfecte cognoscit. Christus vero homo per scientiam suam beatam ita divinam essentiam videt ut eam non comprehendat; et ideo Christus omnia actualia cognoscit et omnia quae in potentia creaturae sunt, non autem omnia quae sunt in potentia creatoris, quia hoc praesupponeret comprehensionem essentiae divinae (*Sum. theol.*, III, q. 10, a. 2). Theologus denique, cum quid Deus sit nesciat (ibid. I, q. 1, a. 7, ad 2m), ad eam tantummodo scientiam pertingere potest quae scientiae Dei et beatorum subalternetur (ibid. a. 2). Qua de causa, theologia Deum per analogias deficientes cognoscit, res vero actuales ad Deum refert quatenus liberam Dei voluntatem manifestant et divinae sapientiae ordinationem supponunt (*C. Gent.*, II, 24; II, 26; III, 97, par. 13, 16), res denique mere possibiles per transennam tractabat et ubi de Dei omnipotentia agitur (v.g., *Sum. theol.*, I, q. 25). Quod quamvis principiis Scotisticis repugnet, mirum esse non potest cum theologus insanire videretur qui, quae Christum hominem nescire diceret, ipse se scire arbitraretur.

... Fieri enim non potuit ut Aquinas semper de actualibus fere tractans semper se de actualibus tractare dictitaret; quod tamen ii

pernatural. The difference is to be found rather in their respective notions of wisdom and science.

Scotus, denying the priority of the act of understanding over concepts, takes concepts themselves as the foundation of knowledge as they would be necessarily either connected to one another or opposed to one another. Hence, he considers theology to be scientific only insofar as it determines truths which, being absolutely necessary and universal, would be valid for every possible order of reality. Accordingly, anyone who is steeped in Scotistic principles thinks that theologians always talk about merely possible orders or, if they happen to be speaking about the actual order of things, supposes this to be an exception that should be noted as such.

St Thomas, on the other hand, having understood that the act of understanding is prior to concepts, distinguishes different degrees of knowledge according to different acts of understanding. Thus, according to him, God, in comprehending the divine essence, knows perfectly absolutely all things that are possible. But Christ as man, by reason of his beatific vision, beholds the divine essence but does not know it comprehensively; thus, he knows all actual reality and all that lies within the power of creatures, but not all that is within the power of the Creator, for this presupposes a comprehension of the divine essence (*Summa theologiae*, 3, q. 10, a. 2). Finally, a theologian, since he does not know what God is (ibid. 1, q. 1, a. 7, ad 2m), is capable of attaining only that knowledge which is subalternate to the knowledge possessed by God and the blessed (ibid. q. 1, a. 2). Hence, theology knows God through analogies that are imperfect. It relates actual beings to God inasmuch as they manifest God's free will and suppose an ordering on the part of his wisdom (*Summa contra Gentiles*, 2, cc. 24, 26; 3, c. 97, ¶13, §2735 and ¶16, §2738); but it treats of merely possible reality only incidentally in its discussion of God's omnipotence (see, for example, *Summa theologiae*, 1, q. 25). Contrary though this may be to Scotistic principles, it is surely not unreasonable to consider as mad any theologian who firmly believes that he knows things that he says Christ as man was ignorant of.

... It was out of the question that Aquinas, who practically always dealt with actual things, should have been continually declaring that what he was dealing with were actual things. Yet this is what is ex-

volunt quibus … videtur saepissime loqui Aquinas quasi ordo rerum actualium esse solus possibilis.[118]

Cum ergo Augustiniani vellent et solam systematizationem logicam ab Aristotele accipere et simul haberent notionem scientiae tamquam illius quae est de universalibus et necessariis – quae nota aprioristica quodammodo pertinent ad scientiam, quodammodo non[119] – aliquid vacuum construxerunt cuius fructus fuit subsequens scepticismus generalis nominalisticus. Tota cultura sequens, humanistica et Renascentiae, nisus aliquis fuit implendi vacuum notionis scientiae dominantis apud Augustinienses saec. XIV et XV.

Contrapositio est positio contradicens ipsi nisui scientifico. Contrapositio Scotistica valorem habuit quia Aristotelismus neque infallibilis erat, immo in pluribus erroneus. At, quatenus Scotismus reiecit systematizationem scientificam et intelligentiam systematicam et extruxit categorias vacuas mere logicas, abstractas, atque praetendit certitudini universali et absolutae, maximos defectus involvit. Qui nimis vult, nihil obtinet.

4.5.4 Illustratio theologica quartae regulae: Positiones sunt evolvendae

S. Thomas et tota theologia saec. XIII non constituit terminum systematizationis theologicae sed principium, unde perfectio in illis non est quaerenda. Praecipuus fuit apud illos defectus illius qui hodie dicitur 'sensus historicus.'

Ad tollendas contradictiones quae apparebant inter dicta Augustini vel aliorum Patrum vel Sacrae Scripturae, utebantur solutione logica quae, potius quam inquireret quid de facto, tempore decurrente, Scriptura vel Patres vel Augustinus dixissent, contenta erat seligendi, inter omnes possibiles sensus alicuius textus, illum qui cum aliis sensibus et caeteris veritatibus posset congruere, minime curantes utrum hic esset verus auctoris sensus necne.

pected by those who ... seem to think that Aquinas very often spoke as if this present order of reality were the only one possible.[118]

The Augustinians, therefore, being willing to accept from Aristotle only a logical systematization and at the same time entertaining the notion of science as that which regards only the universal and the necessary – aprioristic properties that in some ways do pertain to science but in other ways do not[119] – constructed a theology that was an empty shell, the fruits of which appeared later as general nominalist skepticism. All subsequent culture, that of the humanists and the Renaissance, was an attempt to fill in this empty notion of science that was predominant among the Augustinians in the fourteenth and fifteenth centuries.

A counterposition is a position that contradicts the scientific endeavor itself. The Scotist counterposition had some value inasmuch as Aristotelianism was not infallible, in fact was often wrong. But in rejecting scientific systematization and systematic understanding, in fashioning empty categories that were purely logical and abstract, and in pretending to universal and absolute certitude, Scotism was massively flawed. One who seeks too much ends up with nothing.

4.5.4 Theological Illustration of the Fourth Rule: Develop Positions

The theology of St Thomas and that of the thirteenth century did not mark the completion of theological systematization but was only its beginning, and so we must not look to it for the perfection of this systematization. Its chief defect was the lack of what is called today 'historical consciousness.'

In order to solve the contradictions found in the writings of Augustine or the other Fathers or of scripture, the theologians had recourse to logic. Rather than investigating what in the context of their own time the biblical writers or the Fathers or Augustine actually said, they were content to select from all the possible meanings of a text that meaning which could be squared with other meanings and all other truths, with little thought given to whether the author in question actually intended that meaning or not.

118 Bernard Lonergan, *De SS. Trinitate Supplementum* ... (mimeographed notes, Rome, 1955) 40–41. [Available now in Lonergan, *The Triune God: Systematics* 656–59.]
119 See above, pp. 82–95.

Sensus historicus supponit notitiam conceptus variari in tempore et, cum procedant ex actibus intelligendi, evolvi secundum maiorem evolutionem intellectus et depauperari secundum regressivam involutionem intelligentiae. Nam intelligentia et progreditur et regreditur; sicut datur augmentatio valoris conceptuum, sic et diminutio. Id quod ab aliquo homine geniali cogitatur et exprimitur in libro, non omnes lectores intelligunt eodem modo. Diversitas intelligentiae dat diversas series conceptuum in intellectu efformatorum; unde, lapsu temporis, quidam conceptus nullius momenti possunt fieri.

Hae tamen variationes, sive in melius sive in peius, non tantum possunt fieri sed sunt lege quadam determinatae. In qualibet schola inveniuntur tempora florescentiae et decadentiae. Schola floret quando ii qui ad illam pertinent intelligunt quod ipsi dicant. Decadentia habetur quando semper eadem in schola repetuntur, at cum minori intelligentia.

Dum autem sensus historicus deerat in theologia mediaevali, tota theologia subsequens magis et magis occupatur cum crisi originum doctrinae Christianae et cum quaestione de evolutione dogmatum. Unde id ad quod in mediaevo non attendebant, praecipuum est in theologia recentiori.

Reactio protestantica fuit aliquod tentamen redeundi ad ecclesiam primaevam, attamen spiritu revolutionario directa fuit potius quam historico. Luther modo absolute aprioristico determinavit canonem Sacrarum Scripturarum et authentiam librorum Novi Testamenti. Deinde gradualis evolutio notionis historiae permisit applicationem categoriarum historicarum ad scientias sacras et ecclesiasticas, praesertim theologiam biblicam, patristicam, mediaevalem …

Quando quaeritur quomodo nostra quarta regula methodi possit applicari ad hoc problema, dicendum est quod in actuali theologia positio evolvenda videtur praecise haec applicatio systematica categoriarum historicarum nostrae systematizationi theologicae. Loquentes de hac applicatione, distinguamus oportet inter applicationem ad historiam in genere et applicationem ad historiam particularem alicuius disciplinae, v.gr., theologiae. Et quia prima applicatio (ad hisoriam generalem) multo difficilior est, nihil nunc dicemus de ea, dum secunda (ad historiam particularem theologiae) longe facilior est, unde utiliora exempla praebet. De hac nunc est agendum. Aliquas applicationes nostrarum regularum ad historiam theologiae iam peregimus in illustrationibus theologicis primae, secundae, et tertiae regularum.

Historical consciousness supposes the awareness of the fact that concepts undergo modification in the course of time and, since they result from acts of understanding, develop with a growth in understanding, and are impoverished with a regressive decline in understanding. For understanding can both progress and regress. As there can be growth in the validity of concepts, so can there be a lessening of the same. Not all readers will understand to the same degree the ideas that a man of genius has put down in a book. Differences in understanding produce different sets of concepts in the intellect; hence, after a while certain concepts can lose their importance.

Yet these changes, whether for better or for worse, not only can happen but in so doing follow a certain law. Every school of thought has its heyday and its decline. A school flourishes when those who belong to it truly understand what they are saying. Decadence sets in when the same things are repeated over and over again with diminishing understanding.

Whereas historical consciousness was absent in medieval theology, all later theology has been increasingly taken up with examining the origins of Christian doctrine and the development of dogmas. Thus, what medieval theologians completely disregarded has become paramount in modern theology.

The Protestant reaction was an attempt to return to the early church, but it was motivated more by a revolutionary spirit than by a spirit of historical investigation. In an absolutely a priori fashion, Luther pronounced upon the canon of sacred scripture and the authenticity of the books of the New Testament. Subsequently the gradual development of the idea of history enabled historical categories to be applied to the ecclesiastical sciences, especially biblical theology, patristics, medieval studies, and so on.

When it is asked how our fourth rule of method can apply to this problem, our answer must be that in contemporary theology the position to be developed seems to be precisely this systematic application of historical categories to our work of systematizing theology. In speaking of this application, we must distinguish between application to history in general and application to the particular history of any given science, in this case, theology. And because the first application, to history in general, is much more difficult, we shall not speak about it at this point, whereas the second application, to the particular history of theology, is much easier and hence furnishes us with more useful examples. To this we shall now turn. We have already applied some of our rules to the history of theology in our theological illustrations of the first three rules.

[a] Quaedam puncta notanda circa historiam particularem alicuius disciplinae

(1) Mera competentia historica non sufficit ad componendam historiam specialem. Omnia quae faciunt hominem historicum requiruntur quidem (sic collectio datorum, critica textus, scientia de fontibus et manuscriptis ...), at non sufficiunt ad conscribendam historiam specialem, v.gr., matheseos, scientiae physicae, medicinae ... Si quis, bonus historicus, ignoret tamen has scientias, poterit quaedam colligere data, at ex hoc [non][120] sequitur quod in eius historia revera includantur omnia quae alicuius momenti sunt in historia illius disciplinae. Ad hoc requiritur enim scientia specialis de ipso subiecto, quam historicus qua talis non habet. Habebitur ergo opus compilatorium, at incompletum, nec vere historicum. Qui quaestiones non intelligit nequit historiam illarum scribere. Factum hoc videtur sat obvium.

(2) Possumus quaerere rationem istius facti (cur). Revera, historia alicuius disciplinae particularis est historia evolutionis istius subiecti. Evolutio autem quae in historia habita est non est aliquid simplificatum et compendiosum sed aliquid peractum per multos et diversos gressus, errores, deviationes, correctiones. Quatenus autem qui studet huic motui hunc processum evolutivum addiscit, iam in seipso exemplum habet istius evolutionis, quae per saecula forsan protracta est. Hoc tantum possibile est si iste homo intelligit et subiectum et suam addiscentiam subiecti: tunc tantum intelligit etiam quae elementa in historico processu evolutivo debuerint intelligi ante alia; quae fuerint causae progressus intelligentiae vel eius retardationis; quae elementa ad hanc scientiam pertineant et quae non; quae elementa erronea contineant; tunc tantum discernere poterit quando in historia ortae sint novae visiones totius; quando ortum sit primum verum systema; quando transitus habiti sint ex priori ad ulteriorem ordinationem systematicam; quae systematizatio fuerit tantum ampliatio prioris et quae radicaliter nova; quas transformationes progressivas tota materia passa sit; quomodo per novas systematizationes et omnia quae antea per veterem explicabantur etiam nunc explicentur, et multa alia quae non explicabantur (cfr. in re physica inventiones Einstein, Max Planck); tunc tantum intel-

[a] Some Observations on Writing the History of Any Particular Discipline

(1) Mere competence in history is not sufficient for producing a specialized history. Everything one needs to be a historian – collections of data, critical texts, knowledge of sources and manuscripts – all of these are certainly required but are not sufficient for one who wishes to write the special history of, say, mathematics, or physics, or medicine. Anyone, even a good historian, who is ignorant of these sciences can collect certain data, but it does [not][120] follow from this that their history will in fact include everything that is of importance in the history of that discipline. For this, one has to have a specialist's knowledge of that subject, which a historian as such does not possess. The result would be rather a work of compilation, but it would be incomplete and not truly a work of history. One who does not understand the questions will not be able to write their history. This fact seems obvious enough.

(2) We may ask why this is so. The history of any particular discipline is in fact the history of its development. But this development, which would be the theme of a history, is not something simple and straightforward but something that has occurred in a long series of various stages, errors, detours, and corrections. To the extent that the one studying this movement learns about this developmental process, one already possesses within oneself an instance of that development which took place perhaps over several centuries. This can happen only if one understands both the subject and the way in which he or she learned about it. Only then will one understand which elements in the historical developmental process had to be understood before the others, which were the causes of progress in understanding and what held it back, which elements really belong to that particular science and which do not, and which elements contained errors. Only then will one be able to tell at what point in the history of the subject there emerged new visions of the whole and when the first true system occurred, and when transitions took place from an earlier to a later systematic ordering; which systematization was simply an expansion of the former and which was radically new; what progressive transformations the whole subject matter underwent; how everything that was previously explained by the old systematization is now also explained by the new one, as well as many other things that the old one did not explain – as in the discoveries in physics, for example, by Einstein and

120 [It is obvious that the word *non* was inadvertently omitted here.]

ligere poterit quae faverint progressui et quae impediverint illum, et cur
faverint vel impediverint, etc., etc.

Sic patet historicum alicuius disciplinae penitus et cognoscere et intelligere debere totum subiectum. Nec sufficit ut subiectum quomodolibet
intelligat, at oportet ut illud intelligat systematice. Quando hoc praeceptum
dicitur de historia, hoc significat quod debent intelligi systemata successiva
quae progressive evoluta sunt in tempore. Haec systematica intelligentia
evolutionis uti debet analogia evolutionis quae habetur in mente investigatoris addiscentis rem, quae evolutio interna investigatoris debet comparari
cum processu historico quo scientia evoluta est.

Nam, quia illa quinque praecepta fundantur in ipsa natura intellectus
humani, ideo sunt generalia, atque facile intelligitur ea operari non tantum
nunc dum investigatio historica peragitur, sed etiam tunc quando res ita
sese evolvebant, quamvis hae regulae non explicite cognoscerentur. Prop-
tera potuimus illustrare secundum praeceptum ex historia theologiae saec.
xii et tertium ex historia theologiae saec. xiv.

Si res dictas ad theologiam applicamus, habemus quod theologia est fides
quaerens intelligentiam; nec qualemcumque intelligentiam sed systematicam; hoc significat quod id quod systematice intelligitur in theologia iam
intelligebatur aliquomodo etiam ante illam systematizationem. Diversitas
tamen adest inter modum intelligendi systematicum et illum alium modum
pertinentem potius ad modum intelligendi intersubiectivum, symbolicum,
vel proprium intelligentiae vulgaris.

Ulterius, theologus scribens historiam theologiae non ignorat has differentias inter modos cogitandi et intelligendi. Ipse enim, antequam esset theologus, erat Christianus non sine aliqua intelligentia suae fidei, etsi
initiali.

Praeterea, si theologus docet, debet facere ut alii, qui illam nondum
habent, intelligentiam systematicam acquirant. Unde ipse debet intelligere qualis intelligentia in suis discipulis praesupponenda sit. Ad bene docendum, enim, oportet ut cognoscamus et terminos et finem (terminum
ad quem: hic intelligentiam systematicam) et etiam terminum a quo procedendum sit. Unde cognoscenda est interactio exsistens inter intelligentiam systematicam et intelligentiam [vulgarem], ut ex ista discipuli adduci
possint ad illam.

Insuper, si theologus est praedicator, ministerium verbi exercens, trans-

Max Planck. Only then will one be able to understand what factors favored progress, what hindered it, why, and so forth.

Clearly, therefore, historians of any given discipline have to have a thorough knowledge and understanding of the whole subject. And it is not enough that they understand it any way at all, but they must have a systematic understanding of it. For that precept, when applied to history, means that they must understand the successive systems that have progressively developed over time. This systematic understanding of a development ought to make use of an analogy with the development that takes place in the mind of an investigator who is learning about the subject, and this interior development within the mind of the investigator ought to parallel the historical process by which the science itself developed.

Since our five precepts are based upon the very nature of the human intellect, they are general, and so it is easy to understand that they are operative not only now, during the course of a historical investigation, but also then, when the subject-matter itself was developing, even though these rules were not explicitly known. This is why we were able to illustrate the second precept from the history of theology in the twelfth century, and the third from the history of theology in the fourteenth.

If we apply all this to theology, we shall conclude that theology is faith seeking understanding – not any sort of understanding, but systematic understanding. This means that what is systematically understood in theology was already understood in some way even before that systematization. There is nevertheless a difference between the systematic mode of understanding and that other mode which pertains rather to a mode that is intersubjective, symbolic, and characteristic of commonsense or everyday understanding.

Furthermore, theologians writing a history of theology are not unaware of the differences between these modes of thinking and understanding. After all, before becoming theologians they were Christians who had some understanding, however rudimentary, of what they believed.

Again, a teacher of theology must see to it that those who have not yet acquired a systematic understanding do so. The teacher must know, therefore, what sort of understanding is to be presupposed in the students. Good teaching, then, requires us to know both *termini*, the *terminus ad quem*, the end, which in this case is systematic understanding, and also the *terminus a quo*, the point from which one must proceed. We must therefore be aware of the interaction that takes place between commonsense and systematic understanding if we are to bring the students from the first to the second.

Moreover, if a theologian is a preacher exercising the ministry of the

vertere debet suam intelligentiam systematicam in intelligentiam symbolicam, intersubiectivam, vulgarem. Christus enim, ad populum de incarnatione loquens, non locutus est de constitutivo formali incarnationis sed de
dimensionibus intersubiectivis ordinis illius. In opere kerygmatico eo modo
adhiberi debet systematica intelligentia revelationis ut ista sit quasi regula
inspiratrix eorum quae alio modo traduntur. Et quia si quis est verus et
bonus theologus debet cognoscere non tantum terminum ad quem (intelligentiam systematicam) sed et terminum a quo (intelligentiam symbolicam
et vulgarem), si quis est verus et bonus theologus non erit capax unico
munere 'specialistae' fungendi sed capax erit et ad populum loquendi et
ministerium verbi optime exercendi. Immo haec capacitas maior erit apud
theologum quam apud alios non-theologos. Et hoc patere deberet!

Unde si quis vult scribere historiam doctrinae Christianae et theologiae
debet esse non tantum historicus sed et theologus, et talis qui possit uti experientia personaliter habita et intelligentia systematica et non-systematica.
Unde falsum est quod saepius creditur, ad opus historicum conficiendum
minorem requiri intelligentiam speculativam quam ad theologiam speculativam excolendam, ita ut ad theologiam positivam confugiant qui vocatio-
nem speculativam non experiantur.

Modo magis concreto resumamus quae iam supra dicta sunt de comparatione inter intelligentiam systematicam et alias intelligentias ut melius theologiae applicentur.

Initialis apprehensio spatii, ut vidimus, est kinesthetica, ideo qualis implicite habetur in eo quod possumus stare pedibus quin cadamus, atque
ambulare et currere valeamus. Haec apprehensio est naturalis et necessaria. Sine hac apprehensione, etsi aliae multo magis scientificae habeantur,
vitam normalem conducere nequiremus, sensu gravitatis carente, unde graves difficultates psychologicae orirentur.

Tamen, si quis vult totum universum secundum hanc apprehensionem
concipere, in gravissimos incideret errores. Haec apprehensio est optima
ad fines particulares adipiscendos, at nequit legitime ad universum extendi.
Secundum illam, v.gr., homines in altero hemisphaero telluris deberent
extra tellurem cadere.[121]

word, he will have to transpose his systematic understanding to the symbolic, intersubjective, commonsense mode. Christ himself in speaking to the people about the Incarnation did not talk about the formal constitutive of the Incarnation but about the intersubjective dimensions of that order. The role of the systematic understanding of revelation in the work of preaching must be to serve as a formal norm of truth for what is being communicated in another mode. And one who is a true and good theologian must know both the *terminus ad quem*, systematic understanding, and the *terminus a quo*, the symbolic and everyday mode of understanding, and likewise will not be limited to operating narrowly within his own specialty, but will be capable of speaking to ordinary people and thus effectively exercising the ministry of the word. Theologians, in fact, will be better able to do this than non-theologians. That should be obvious.

So therefore, those who wish to write the history of Christian doctrine and theology will have to be not only historians but also theologians and be able to make use of their own personal experience and of both systematic and non-systematic understanding. The common belief, therefore, is false that holds that to write history requires a lesser degree of speculative intelligence than to do speculative theology, with the result that those who do not experience a call to speculative thinking take refuge in positive theology.

More concretely, let us go back now to what we said above comparing systematic understanding with other modes of understanding, so as the better to apply all this to theology.

As we have seen, our first apprehension of space is kinesthetic, implicit in the fact that we can stand without falling down, and walk and run. Such an apprehension is both natural and necessary. Without it, even with much more scientific knowledge, we should be unable to carry on a normal life, and lack a sense of gravity, with the serious psychological difficulties that would result.

Still, one who would want to understand the entire universe according to this apprehension would fall into many grave errors. Such an apprehension is excellent for certain particular purposes, but cannot be extended to the universe as a whole. According to it, for example, people in the southern hemisphere would fall off the earth.[121]

---

121 [Perhaps useful in connection with this issue are Lonergan's remarks in
    Insight 562–63.]

Eodem modo, quando modus intelligendi intersubiectivus generalizatur, habetur tendentia mythica ad omnia personificanda. Unde quamvis necessaria sit apprehensio intersubiectiva, secus ruina psychologica subiecti haberetur, tamen illa necessaria et utilis et valida est pro vita practica ordinaria; ultra vitam practicam autem univoce nequit extendi.

Similiter res in theologia procedunt. Saeculo IV enormis tumultus factus est ex unico vocabulo *homoousion* introducto in symbolis fidei. Sensus huius vocis non erat intersubiectivus neque symbolicus neque intelligentiae vulgaris proprius. Quare etiam hodie, qui necessitatem theologiae alicuius personalisticae praedicant, cogitant hunc vocem non posse esse valde utilem ad systematizationem theologicam.

Sensus huius vocis erat technicus. Haec vox signavit transitum ad modum cogitandi systematicum. Talis gressus prima vice fiebat in ecclesia, et quia prima vice fiebat, ideo maxima perturbatio eum comitata est. In toto saeculo IV habitum est quasi spectrum omnium possibilium opinionum circa hanc rem.

Etiam defendentes introductionem huius vocis non eam defendebant tamquam praetiossimam innovationem sed tamquam novitatem de se malam, at per accidens bonam et necessariam. Id tamen quod tunc, per quinquagenta annos post Concilium Nicaenum, animos turbavit, iam alio modo mentes perturbaverat saeculis praecedentibus, sive Iustini, sive Tertulliani, sive Hippolyti, sive Dionysii Alexandri, sive Dionysii Romani, sive Tatiani, etc.[122] Per hunc transitum ex modo intelligendi vulgari ad systematicum, per hunc terminum technicum, pax et unitas ecclesiae iterum servata est. Unde progressus habitus est cum introductione.

Hoc exemplum tamen non est unicum. Id quod factum est relate ad divinitatem Christi saeculo IV factum est relate ad unitatem inter divinitatem et humanitatem Christi saeculo V, quando Nestoriani, personam concipientes tamquam essentiam rei, ponebant in Christo duas naturas et ideo duas personas; dum Monophysitae, ex eodem praesupposito et ex ignorata distinctione inter essentiam et exsistentiam, asserebant quod si una persona, ideo una etiam natura erat admittenda. Cum distinctione inter *physin* et *hypostasin* factus est progressus et transitus ex modo intelligendi priori vulgari ad modum systematicum, atque solutum est problema logicum subiacens disputationi.

In the same way, when the intersubjective mode of understanding is generalized, there arises a mythic tendency to personify everything. Hence, although an intersubjective apprehension is necessary – without it a person would collapse psychologically – nevertheless, it is necessary and useful and valid for practical life only; it cannot be univocally extended beyond the realm of the practical.

The same holds for theology. In the fourth century there was quite an uproar about the introduction of a single word, *homoousion*, into the creed. This word did not have an intersubjective or symbolic or commonsense meaning. And so even today those who proclaim the need for a personalist sort of theology consider this word to be practically useless for theological systematization.

This word has a technical meaning. It signaled the transition to a systematic mode of thinking. That was the first time that step had been taken in the church, and because it was the first time it aroused a good deal of consternation. Throughout the fourth century one may find virtually the whole gamut of opinions about this one point.

Even those who defended the introduction of this word did not advocate it as a most valuable innovation, but rather as a novelty undesirable in itself, a necessary evil that was good *per accidens*. And what at that time, during the half-century after Nicea, upset people so much, had already during the previous centuries perturbed the minds of Justin, Tertullian, Hippolytus, Dionysius of Alexandria, Pope Dionysius, Tatian, and so on.[122] By reason of this transition from a commonsense mode of understanding to a systematic mode, and through the use of this technical term, the peace and unity of the church was restored. Thus, the result of its introduction was progress.

Nor is this example unique. What was done in the fourth century with regard to the divinity of Christ was done in the fifth century with regard to the unity between his divinity and humanity, when the Nestorians, taking 'person' as referring to essence, affirmed the existence in Christ of two natures and hence two persons; while the Monophysites, on the same premise, and unaware of the distinction between essence and existence, declared that if there is only one person to be admitted in Christ then there is only one nature also to be admitted. But introducing the distinction between *physis*, 'nature,' and *hypostasis*, 'person,' and a transition from a prior commonsense mode to a systematic mode of understanding, made for progress, and the logical problem underlying the dispute was solved.

122 See above, pp. 6–13.

Similiter saeculo VII processus extenditur ad quaestionem de duplici voluntate et duplici operatione in Christo.

Eodem modo, in Occidente saeculo V, cum disputationibuis contra Pelagianos, initium habuit systematizatio totius theologiae libertatis et gratiae quae per plura saecula producta est usque ad saeculum XII, quando clara notio gratiae habitualis obtenta est; et ad saeculum XIII, quando notio gratiae actualis introducta est a S. Thoma.

Similiter, tantum saeculo XII, obtenta clara notione gratiae, signi, et efficacitatis, primo inventa est definitio sacramenti, et prima vice septem sacramenta enumerata sunt.

Unde ex tota historia doctrinae habentur illustrationes horum transituum ex modo cogitandi non systematico ad systematicum.

Quatenus hoc factum intelligitur, eo ipso intelligitur et solvitur fundamentale problema subiacens in nostris tractatibus theologicis relate ad modum probandi varias theses, ex argumentis scripturisticis, patristicis, magisterii, theologicis ...

Postquam transitus ille detectus fuerit et circumscriptus, debet intelligi. In historia illius periodi in qua transitus factus est, invenietur pons inter duos modos intelligendi, priorem et posteriorem systematicum. Unde optime debet intelligi situatio quae habebatur ante transitum, cum omnibus suis antecedentibus scripturisticis, patristicis ... Ad hoc habendum, evidenter chronologia non sufficit.

Unde, si Filium esse consubstantialem Patri, vel unam esse personam in duabus naturis, est res omnino aliena a modo cogitandi et loquendi S. Scripturae, quomodo habebimus argumentum scripturisticum pro his thesibus dogmaticis? Tantum intelligendo transitum esse factum saec. IV et modum quo factum sit; bene intelligendo valorem omnium disputationum habitarum sive pro sive contra *homoousion*, sive orthodoxarum sive heterodoxarum, quae ultimae manifestant quae essent difficultates contra acceptationem huius notionis. In intelligentia transitus habetur basis ad intelligendum initium evolutionis subsequentis et ad investigationem faciendam temporis praecedentis, ut in lucem ponatur utrum et quando et quomodo in tempore praeterito lateret problema quod postea explicite positum est.[123]

In the seventh century this process was in a similar way extended to the question of the two wills and two sets of operations in Christ.

Likewise, in the West during the fifth century in the controversies with the Pelagians, the systematization of the whole theology of grace and freedom was begun. It continued down to the twelfth century, when a clear notion of habitual grace was arrived at, and into the next century with St Thomas's introduction of the notion of actual grace.

Also, it was only in the twelfth century, with the clear notions of grace, of sign, and of efficaciousness that the definition of sacrament was hit upon, and for the first time the number of sacraments was set at seven.

From this one can see that the whole history of church teaching provides us with examples of these transitions from a nonsystematic to a systematic way of thinking.

Understanding this fact, one will also understand and solve the fundamental problem underlying the treatment of theology in our treatises today regarding the method of proving various theses by arguments taken from scripture, the Fathers, the *magisterium*, and theologians.

Once a transition is adverted to and delineated, it needs to be understood. Somewhere in the history of the period in which the transition took place, the bridge between the two modes of understanding, the earlier one and the later systematic one, will be found. This requires a thorough understanding of the situation that existed prior to the transition itself, with all its scriptural and patristic premises. For this, obviously, chronology is not enough.

If, then, it is utterly foreign to the biblical way of thinking and speaking to say that the Son is consubstantial with the Father, or that there is one person in two natures, how shall we ever find a scriptural argument for these dogmatic theses? Only by realizing that a transition took place in the fourth century and understanding how it took place, by appreciating the value of all the disputations that took place, both for and against *homoousion*, whether orthodox or heterodox, the latter clearly indicating what the difficulties were against the acceptance of that notion. An understanding of that transition is the basis for understanding the beginning of all subsequent development and also for investigating earlier centuries in order to determine clearly whether and when and how the problem that later became overtly explicit had previously been latent.[123]

123 [See also Lonergan, *The Triune God: Doctrines* 254–55.]

Praesens systematizatio theologiae catholicae est quidem vera; tamen, ita debet extendi et evolvi ut motum historicum includat. Tamen, quamvis in Medio Aevo reconciliatio inter auctoritates traditionis fieret praesertim grammatice vel dialectice vel systematice potius quam historice, initia quaedam methodi historicae non absolute desunt, v.gr., quando S. Thomas comparationes instituit inter ea quae ex Aristotrele exponuntur in *Libro de causis* (qui alicui auctori Arabico tribuebatur) et in operibus Procli.[124] Ex altera parte, etiam hodie historici viri, qui methodum historicam sequi profitentur in factis exponendis, saepissime disputationes, valuationes, conclusiones, divisiones ... desumunt ex praefixis categoriis extrahistoricis.

[b] Ulteriores notiones de investigatione ipsius transitus

Exemplum circa huiusmodi investigationem desumi potest ex alia scientia, magis evoluta, quia minus difficile.

In sua systematizatione de re mechanica, Newton quam saepissime repetebat, 'Hypotheses non fingo.'[125] Hoc effatum est maximi momenti ad intelligendam historiam scientiae. Revera, res attentius considerando, aliquo sensu possumus dicere theoriam, v.gr., gravitationis universalis esse de facto aliquam hypothesin. At alio sensu hoc non dici potest, et hic sensus nunc nostra interest.

Sensus quo theoria gravitationis universalis non est hypothesis, et quo Newton contendebat se non fingere hypotheses, tribus gressibus explicatur:

(1) *Non quaerere de causa efficiente* (in casu, quid faciat ut corpus cadat). Utilissima quidem est ad scientiam habendam de aliqua re investigatio de influxu qui super illam exercetur, qualis et unde sit, etc. Tamen initio praescindi debet ab hac consideratione. Antequam examinetur influxus causae in effectum, debent in seipsis intelligi et effectus et causa, neque possibilis est investigatio circa influxum nisi antea constet quid sit id ex quo et quid

The present systematization of Catholic theology is a reality, of course, but it needs to be extended and developed to include the movement of history. Nevertheless, even though in the Middle Ages the various traditional authorities were reconciled with one another, especially in a grammatical or dialectical or systematic rather than in a historical way, the beginnings of historical method are not entirely lacking – for example, when St Thomas compared statements once thought to be from Aristotle in the *Liber de causis* (which is attributed to an Arabic author) with statements in the writings of Proclus.[124] On the other hand, even today, historians who profess to follow the historical method in presenting their findings often derive their arguments, evaluations, conclusions, divisions, and so forth, from predetermined extra-historical categories.

[b] Some Further Points Regarding the Investigation of This Transition [to a Systematic Way of Thinking]

A less difficult example can be taken from another science, one that is more developed.

In systematizing mechanics Newton often used to say, '*Hypotheses non fingo,*' 'I form no hypotheses.'[125] This dictum is most important for understanding the history of science. But in fact, if we look at the matter more closely, there is a sense in which we can say that a theory, for example, of universal gravitation, is actually a hypothesis. Yet in another sense it is not, and it is this that we are concerned with here.

The sense in which the theory of universal gravitation is not a hypothesis and in which Newton insisted that he did not 'form hypotheses' can be explained in three steps.

(1) *Not to inquire about an efficient cause* (in this case, what makes a body fall). While it is certainly true that in order to acquire knowledge about some reality an investigation into the nature and source of the influences upon it is very useful, nevertheless at the beginning one ought to prescind from this consideration. Before the influence of a cause upon an effect is examined, the effect and the cause ought to be understood in themselves;

124 [Lonergan is referring to Thomas's remarks towards the end of the *Prooemium* to his commentary on the *Liber de causis.*]
125 [Sir Isaac Newton, *Mathematical Principles of Natural Philosophy*, vol. 2, book 3, 'General Scholium'; in Motte's translation, as revised by Florian Cajori (Berkeley: University of California Press, 1934) 547. On the ancient Greek meaning of *hypothesis* that Newton used, see Philip Wheelwright, ed., *The Presocratics* (New York: Odyssey Press, 1966) 315.]

sit id in quo hic influxus habetur. Secus nihil solidum invenire poterimus nec vitare processum in infinitum. Unde, in re historica quaerenda est ante omnia intrinseca intelligibilitas ipsius textus de quo agitur.

(2) *Non loqui de causis occultis.* Sic Descartes problema de motu planetarum solverat supponendo materiam aliquam invisibilem et imponderabilem quae volvebatur exacte prouti planetae videbantur se moveri. Haec solutio erat quidem valde secura, quia erat impossibilis eius confutatio.

Eadem res habetur in re historica quando appellamus ad conceptus obscuros et globales, ut capitalismum, democraticismum, romanticismum, classicismum, humanismum ... Agitur revera de notionibus valde complexis, atque eorum sensus est plus minusve determinatus, neque historicus potest aut vult eas magis determinare ex eo quod aliis scientiis hoc pertineat. Unde in usu historico huiusmodi conceptus ita indeterminati esse possunt ut nullum sensum habeant vel valde vagum.

Hoc accidit in materia theologica quando maxima facilitate et levitate appellant ad mentem Hebraicam, biblicam, mediaevalem, Palestinensem, Renascentiae ... Non asserimus omnes has notiones carere sensu, attamen aliter esse procedendum ut sensum habeant. Si, potius quam appellare ad has notiones tamquam ad aliquem deum ex machina, conamur intelligentiam intrinsecam obtinere circa ipsa documenta, quam intelligentiam coniungimus cum evolutione totali humanae intelligentiae, tunc, v.gr., loco loquendi de mente Hebraica modo vago et obscuro, loquemur de evolutione mentis et culturae humanae quae, cum consistat in progressiva distinctione et specializatione singulorum elementorum constitutivorum vitae proprio sensu humanae, apud Graecos magis perfecta erat quam apud Hebraeos, ex eo quod apud illos distinguebantur et intelligentia et volitiones, et affectus et praxis ... quae, e contra, apud istos nondum distinguebantur, quam ob rem nec vocabula nec notiones nec ipsa vita aliquam specializationem denotant.

Tunc appellando ad has notiones, non tantum merum factum describitur sed aliquid intelligitur.

(3) *Non quaerere de causa finali neque de valore.* In hoc Newton quam maxime Aristoteli opponebatur. Nam pro Aristotele motus ultimatim produ-

no investigation of causal influence itself is possible unless one has previously determined the nature both of the source of this influence and of that upon which it is exerted. Otherwise it will be impossible to reach any solid conclusions or to avoid proceeding *ad infinitum*. Hence, in historical studies the first thing to inquire into is the intrinsic intelligibility of the text in question.

(2) *Not to speak of hidden causes.* This was how Descartes had solved the problem of the planetary motions, by supposing some invisible and weightless matter that turned in precisely the same way in which the planets were seen to move. This solution was, of course, quite secure since it was impossible to refute.

The same thing happens in historical studies when we appeal to vague generalizations such as capitalism, democracy, romanticism, classicism, humanism, and so forth. In fact these are quite complex notions whose meaning is only more or less fixed, and historians neither can nor want to define them more clearly, because this is something that belongs to other sciences. Thus it happens that in historical works such concepts can be so indeterminate as to be meaningless, or at least extremely vague.

Now in theological matters this occurs when in a quite facile and offhand manner an appeal is made to the Hebrew mentality, or the biblical or medieval or Palestinian or Renaissance mentality, and so on. We are not saying that these notions are meaningless; but they must be approached differently if they are to have a meaning. If, rather than appealing to such notions as to a *deus ex machina*, we try instead to get some intrinsic understanding of the documents under consideration and relate that understanding to the overall development in human understanding, then instead of speaking of, say, the Hebrew mentality in some vague and obscure way, we shall speak about the development of the human mind and human culture that, since it consists of the progressive distinction and specialization of all those elements that constitute life that is properly human, reached a higher degree of development among the Greeks than among the Hebrews because the former distinguished between understanding and willing, and between feelings and action. These distinctions were not yet made by the Hebrews, and this is why neither their vocabulary nor their ideas nor their life itself gives any indication of such specialization.

Then if we appeal to such notions, we are not just describing a mere fact but understanding something.

(3) *Not to inquire about final cause or value.* On this point Newton is totally opposed to Aristotle. For Aristotle, motion is ultimately produced by a final

citur a causa finali, quia unaquaeque res movetur versum suum locum naturalem qui fungitur munere finis. E contra Newton suam investigationem primo limitavit ad ea quae praesentantur, ut in illis inveniret intelligibilitatem, immanentes relationes intelligibiles inter ea quae apparent ut – modo loquendi Aristotelico – forma rerum innotesceret. Nam iam ante Aristotelem multi locuti erant de causa finali, efficiente, materiali, sed originalis in consideratione Aristotelica fuit notio formae. Ante Newton quidem, multi disputabantur de formis quin autem intelligerent rem de qua disputarent, quod non raro apud scholasticos accidit. Ope Newton iterum surrexit notio formae Aristotelica seu intelligibilitatis quaerendae in iis quae sensibiliter dantur.

Similiter intelligentia historica eius quod factum est in Concilio Nicaeno, Chalcedonensi, Constantinopolitano I et III[126] non habetur considerando et extollendo veritatem illius quod in his conciliis definitum est (quod pertinet ad inquisitionem dogmaticam), sed quaerendo intelligentiam illius quod factum est, qua ratione factum sit, quibus contradicentibus ... Si hoc praevie fit, multo facilius erit iudicium circa veritatem et utilitatem definitionum illarum, quod est iudicium subsequens. Intelligentia horum transituum facilius habetur ex eo quod, quando nos theologiam discimus, hic transitus ex modo cognoscendi vulgari ad systematicum in nobis fit.

Ad modum exempli consideretur ingens illa oppositio quae per diuturnum tempus orta est cum magno tumultu post Concilium Nicaenum saeculo IV. Aliqua intelligentia illius quod in Ecclesia factum est illo tempore habetur si tantum attendatur ad oppositiones exsistentes inter varias positiones. Habita oppositionum harum intelligentia, habetur intelligentia ex ipsis datis.

[a′] Oppositio inter Arium et Alexandrum Alexandrinum

Doctrina Arii clare perspicitur ex anathematibus Nicaenis (DB 54, in fine): Verbum est creatura ut aliae, ex nihilo creatum, vel saltem non factum ex substantia primi entis; unde non est aeternum, sed convertibile et mutabile. Vox qua Arius usus est ad Verbum designandum est *ktisma*. Haec vox non erat magni momenti in philosophia Graeca, ubi notio deerat creationis. In terminologia Ariana autem haec vox exhibet mentem et categoriam

cause, because each and every thing moves towards its natural place, which functions as its end. Newton, by contrast, first of all limited his investigation of the data before him to discover their inherent intelligibility, the immanent intelligible relations among the data, so as – in Aristotelian terms – to come to a knowledge of their form. Before Aristotle's time many philosophers had spoken about final, efficient, and material causes, but what was original in Aristotle was the notion of form, formal cause. And indeed before Newton's time many argued about forms without understanding what they were arguing about – something that happens not infrequently among Scholastics. Thanks to Newton's work the Aristotelian notion of form was revived, that is, form as the intelligibility to be sought in the data presented to the senses.

Similarly, a historical understanding of what went on at Nicea, Chalcedon, and Constantinople I and III[126] is not obtained by considering and praising the truth of those conciliar definitions (that is a matter for the study of dogmas), but rather by seeking an understanding of what went on, how it came about, who opposed it and why, and so forth. If this is done first, it will be much easier to make a judgment on the truth and usefulness of those definitions, which is a consequent judgment. An understanding of these transitions will be made easier if, when we are learning theology, the transition from the commonsense to the systematic mode of knowing takes place in us as well.

As an example, let us consider the huge controversies that raged for quite a long time after the Council of Nicea in AD 325. We can get some understanding of what was going on in the church at that time if we limit our attention to the opposing positions that were espoused. From an understanding of these opposing views, an understanding of the data themselves is obtained.

[a'] Arius vs. Alexander of Alexandria

What Arius taught is clear from the anathemas of Nicea (DB 54, DS 125–26, ND 7–8, towards the end): the Word is a creature like other creatures, created out of nothing, or at least not made out of the substance of the First Being; hence he is not eternal, but changeable and alterable. Arius's term for designating the Word is *ktisma*, 'creature.' In Greek philosophy this term had little importance, since the Greeks lacked the notion of crea-

126 [The Latin text has 'Constantinopolitano II et III.' It was an editorial decision to change 'II' to 'I.']

religiosam Hebraicam sese exprimentem in lingua Graeca atque sese imponentem culturae Hellenisticae. Haec translatio fructus novae exegeseos Antiochenae fuit, a Luciano inceptae, cuius Arius discipulus erat. Unde pro Ario Filius est *Ktisma*. Quae positio Arii damnata est ab eius episcopo Alexandro Alexandrino, qui cum Athanasio et omnibus orthodoxis Homoousianis tenebat 'consubstantialitatem' fidei Nicaenae, sub influxu theologiae occidentalis elaboratam.[127]

[b'] Oppositio inter Eusebium Caesariensem et Marcellum Ancyranum

Eusebius sequebatur potius aliquem lineam traditionalem quae simul accipere volebat omnia et sola quae habebantur in sacra scriptura et traditione, et ea exprimere in categoriis culturae Hellenisticae, exemplum Origenis sequens, pro quo tantum Pater erat *ho Theos*, dum Filius erat *theos* participative.[128] Origenes, enim, saltem in suo modo loquendi et in suis interpretationibus nimis litteralibus sacrae scripturae, subordinationismo indulserat. Hanc positionem intermediam inter alam sinistram Arianam (anhomoianam)[129] et alam dexteram semi-Arianam (homoiousianam) amplexi sunt dein Acacius Caesariensis et Eusebius Nicomediae. Haec tendentia praevaluit in Concilio Antiocheno (in incaeniis, a. 341), ubi relictus est purus Arianismus, quin tamen mentio fieret de *homoousio* Nicaeno, quem immo conati sunt identificare cum positionibus Marcelli Ancyrani, quem in Oriente suspicabantur de Sabellianismo. Cum Marcello, tamen, ipse Athanasius impugnabatur plus vel minus explicite.

Pro Antiochenis, Filius est uti *ktisma*, sed non unum ex multis, ut Arius volebat. Haec positio occasionem praebuit Arianisimo qui Nicaeae victus erat, iterum resurgendi sub aliis formis.

Marcellus Ancyranus, quamvis esset inter ardentiores adversarios Arii et defensores Concilii Nicaeni, lineam aliquatenus diversam sequebatur quam eius amicus Athanasius. Eius positio ostendit problema exegeticum subiacens toti huic disputationi. Secundum novam scholam exegeticam Marcelli, omnia quae in sacra scriptura de Christo dicuntur de solo Christo homine dicuntur, praeter ea quae habentur de *Logo* in capite primo Iohannaeo.

tion. In Arian terminology, however, this term represents a transposing of the Hebraic mentality and religious categories into Greek terminology and their importation into Hellenistic culture. This transference was the fruit of the new Antiochene exegetics instituted by Lucian, of whom Arius was a pupil. Hence, for Arius the Son was a *ktisma*. This position was condemned by his bishop, Alexander of Alexandria, who along with Athanasius and all the orthodox 'homoousians' adhered to the 'consubstantiality' of the creed of Nicea that had been elaborated through the influence of Western theology.[127]

[b'] Eusebius of Caesarea vs. Marcellus of Ancyra

Eusebius for his part followed the rather traditional line that wanted to accept all things and only those things found in scripture and tradition and at the same time to express them in the categories of the Hellenistic culture; in this he was following the example of Origen, for whom the Father alone was *ho theos*, 'The God,' whereas the Son is *theos*, 'God,' by participation.[128] For Origen in his terminology and his too literal interpretation of scripture had indulged in subordinationism. Subsequently, Acacius of Caesarea and Eusebius of Nicomedia embraced this position, which is intermediate between the left wing of Arianism, the Anomoians,[129] and the right wing of semi-Arianism, the Homoiousians. This tendency prevailed in the Dedication Council of Antioch (AD 341), which abandoned pure Arianism without, however, mentioning Nicea's *homoousion*, which in fact they tried to identify with the position of Marcellus of Ancyra, whom those in the East suspected of Sabellianism. Nevertheless, along with Marcellus, Athanasius himself was more or less explicitly attacked.

The Antiochenes held that the Son was indeed a *ktisma*, but not one of many, as the Arians would have it. This position allowed Arianism, which had been routed at Nicea, to rise again in another guise.

Although he had been among the more vehement opponents of Arius and defenders of the Council of Nicea, Marcellus of Ancyra followed a line of thought that was somewhat different from that of his friend Athanasius. His position reveals the exegetical problem that underlay this whole controversy. According to Marcellus's new school of exegetics, all biblical statements about Christ are predicated of Christ as man only, except for state-

127 [See also Lonergan, *The Triune God: Doctrines* 136–47, 340–45.]
128 See above, pp. 10–13.
129 [The Latin text has *anhomoiosianam*, but see above, n. 25.]

Casus Marcelli est valde obscurus. Ipse defendebatur a Concilio Sardicensi
(a. 343), a Papa Iulio I et ab Athanasio; multis (inter quos Basilio, Hilario,
Iohanni Chrysostomo, et Sulpitio Severo) visus est implicatus in ideis haereticis eius discipuli Photini, qui postea damnatus fuit a Concilio Mediola-
nensi (a. 344–45) ob non factam distinctionem inter Verbum et Patrem.
Certe acerrime improbatus erat de Sabellianismo et de adoptionismo ab
omni Semi-Arianis, praesertim ab Eusebio Caesariensi, atque circa illum
interminabiles discussiones factae sunt.[130]

[c′] Oppositio inter *mian hypostasin* Nicaenam et Sardicensem et *treis
hypostaseis* Chalcedonenses
    Antea vox *hypostasis* sumebatur generatim pro *ousia*, seu pro essentia, na-
tura, substantia, ut apparet ex anathemate Nicaeno (DB 54) et ex Concilio
Sardicensi (a. 343):

> Nos autem hanc percepimus et didicimus et hanc habemus catholi-
> cam traditionem et fidem atque confessionem unam esse *hypostasin*,
> quam ipsi haeretici *ousian* vocant, Patris et Filii et Spiritus Sancti.
> Et si quaerant quae sit Filii *hypostasis*, profitemur eam esse quam et
> Patris solam esse in confesso est.[131]

Ab adversariis tamen Concilii Nicaeni haec expressio sumebatur
tamquam plena suspicionibus Marcellianis, atque tamquam confirmatio
circa Sabellianismum doctrinae Nicaenae. *Mia hypostasis* erat vox quam
praeferebant qui, tendentiae occidentali magis faventes, in unitate divina
potius insistebant.
    E contra, tota traditio orientalis tendentiam oppositam habebat insisten-
di in trinitate. Pro hac tendentia, iam in Clemente Alexandrino et Origine
hypostasis, quamvis etymologice significet substantiam, stabat pro eo quod
Latini, post Tertullianum, vocabant 'personam.' Inde tendentia ad affir-
mandas tres hypostases in Deo, quae habita iam erat apud anti-Sabellia-
nismum Dionysii Alexandrini (cfr. DB 48–51; epistolam Dionysii Romani
Papae.)

ments about the *Logos* in the first chapter of John's Gospel. Marcellus's case is quite unclear. He was defended by the Council of Sardica (343), by Pope Julius I, and by Athanasius; but many, including Basil, Hilary, John Chrysostom, and Sulpicius Severus, thought him to have shared the heretical notions of his pupil Photinus, who was condemned in the Council of Milan (344–45) for not distinguishing between the Word and the Father. It is certain, however, that he was bitterly accused of Sabellianism and adoptionism by all the semi-Arians, especially by Eusebius of Caesarea, and his case has been discussed interminably.[130]

[c'] The *mia hypostasis* of Nicea and Sardica vs. the *treis hypostaseis* of Chalcedon

The word *hypostasis* was earlier taken to refer to *ousia* in a general sense, that is, essence, nature, substance, as is clear from the Nicene anathema (DB 54, DS 126, ND 8), and also from the following statement of the Council of Sardica:

> We have accepted and learned and hold the following catholic tradition and faith and confession, that the Father and the Son and the Holy Spirit have one hypostasis, which the heretics call *ousia*. And if they should ask what is the hypostasis of the Son, we affirm that it is the same and the only one that is affirmed also of the Father.[131]

However, the opponents of the Council of Nicea found this expression to be full of hints of Marcellianism and saw in it a confirmation of Sabellianism in Nicea's teaching. *Mia hypostasis* was the expression preferred by those who leaned towards the Western emphasis upon the oneness of God.

The whole Eastern tradition, on the other hand, tended to emphasize the threeness in God. On this side, as early as in Clement of Alexandria and Origen, the word *hypostasis*, although etymologically the equivalent of the Latin *substantia*, 'substance,' stood for what the Latin Fathers, after Tertullian, called *persona*, 'person.' Hence the tendency to affirm three *hypostases* in God, which is already present in the anti-Sabellianism of Dionysius of Alexandria; see the Letter of Pope Dionysius (DB 48–51, DS 112–15, ND 301–303).

---

130 [See also Lonergan, *The Triune God: Doctrines* 114–17, 138–39, 152–55, 160–61, 180–81, 444–45.]

131 Theodoret, *Historia Ecclesiae* 2, 6; MG 82, 1011.

Athanasius, quamquam cognovit alios usurpare vocem *hypostasin* sensu 'personae,' atque hunc usum approbavit, tamen ipse non adhibuit tali sensu.

Similiter vox *hypostasis* sumitur adhuc pro *ousia* in Concilio Romano sub Damaso (a. 382), apud Epiphanium, Cyrillum Hierosolymitatum, Hieronymum, et adhuc in v saeculo apud Cyrillum Alexandrinum.

Mutatio significationis huius vocis facta est in Oriente in secunda mediaetate saeculi iv a Patribus Cappadocibus Basilio, Gregorio Nazianzeno, et Gregorio Nysseno, qui utuntur hac voce ad designanda elementa distinctiva in Deo, scilicet proprietates sive Patris, sive Filii, sive Spiritus. Inde vox invenitur hoc sensu in Synodica Concilii Constantinopolitano i,[132] in Concilio Chalcedonense (DB 148), in Constantinopolitano ii (DB 213), etc.[133]

[d'] Oppositio inter Eunomium (et Aëtium) et Basilium Ancyranum

Positio Eunomiana erat pure Ariana, seu anhomoiana seu heteroousiana. Eius fundamentum erat philosophicum, atque Eunomius est quasi introductor metaphysicae in theologia. Pro illo, quando aliquid 'dicitur,' debet 'poni' realitas correspondens. Unde, dictis scripturisticis ostendentibus veram distinctionem inter Patrem et Filium debet correspondere dissimilitudo in illorum natura. Unde reiciebat et positionem homoianam[134] traditionalistarum, et semi-Arianam homoiousianam et orthodoxam homoousianam.

Contra Eunomium egit Concilium Ancyranum (a. 358) et Sirmianum (a. 358), ubi episcopi, atque ipse Papa Liberius, potius turbati ab innumeris divisionibus ex enormibus disputationibus quae fiebant in ecclesia quam rem intelligentes, adhaeserunt expressionibus non heterodoxis, attamen a Semi-Arianis propositis, spiritu quodam anti-Nicaeno. Praecipui fautores semi-arianismi erant tunc Basilius Ancyranus et Georgius Laodicensis. Eorum positio contraria et *homoousio* Nicaeno et positioni anhomoianae Eunonomii.[135]

Athanasius knew that others were using the word *hypostasis* in the sense of 'person' and approved of this usage, although he himself did not use it in this sense.

Hypostasis was still used for *ousia* in the Council of Rome under Pope Damasus in 382, in the writings of Epiphanius, of Cyril of Jerusalem, of Jerome, and even of Cyril of Alexandria in the fifth century.

It was the Cappadocian Fathers Basil, Gregory Nazianzus, and Gregory of Nyssa who in the second half of the fourth century were instrumental in changing the meaning of this word in the East. They used *hypostasis* to designate the distinct elements in God, those that are proper to the Father and to the Son and to the Spirit. Hence, this word is found with this meaning in Constantinople I,[132] Chalcedon (DB 148, DS 301–303, ND 614–16), Constantinople II (DB 213, DS 421, ND 620/1), and so on.[133]

[d'] Eunomius (and Aëtius) vs. Basil of Ancyra

Eunomius's position was pure Arianism, that is, Anomoian or heteroousian. It had a philosophical basis, and in fact Eunomius was the first one to bring metaphysics into theology. For him, whenever something is 'said,' a corresponding reality must be 'posited.' Accordingly, since the scriptures manifest a true distinction between the Father and the Son, there must be a corresponding dissimilitude in their natures. Hence, he rejected both the homoian[134] position of the traditionalists on the one hand and the semi- Arian homoiousian and orthodox homoousian positions on the other.

The Councils of Ancyra in 358 and of Sirmium in the same year condemned Eunomius. These bishops and Pope Liberius himself, who were more upset by the many factions and vehement controversies in the church than knowledgeable about the question at issue, clung to expressions that, while not heterodox, had nevertheless been suggested by the semi-Arians in a rather anti-Nicene spirit. The chief advocates of semi-Arianism at that time were Basil of Ancyra and George of Laodicea, whose position was contrary to both Nicea's *homoousion* and the Anomoian position of Eunomius.[135]

---

132 See Konrad Kirch and Leo Ueding, *Enchiridion fontium historiae ecclesiasticae antiquae*, 5th ed. (Friburgi Birsgoviae: Herder, 1941) no. 652 [pp. 374–76].
133 [See also Lonergan, *The Triune God: Doctrines* 114–17, 164–71, 182–83, 198–99, 442–51.]
134 [Reading *homoianam* for *homoiosianam*.]
135 [See also Lonergan, *The Triune God: Doctrines* 138–39, 166–69, 420–21, 446–47, 456–57, 464–65, 498–99, 560–61.]

Exemplum habetur hic alicuius transitus magno cum tumulto effecti in ecclesia. Circa hunc transitum historicus theologiae duo praesertim debet facere: intelligibilitatem diversarum positionum et transitus ab una ad aliam obtinere, atque deinde iudicium ferre atque rationem reddere harum diversarum tendentiarum.

Interna intelligibilitatis transitus habetur quatenus exponuntur omnia data historica in eorum successione atque omnes diversae positiones quarum unaquaeque illuminatur a positione opposita. Iudicium et rationes diversarum tendentiarum habentur multo facilius postquam haec intelligibilitas obtenta sit. Sic multiplicitas positionum explicatur ex complexitate quaestionis, quae revera non erat tantum speculativa (quomodo Filius sit realiter a se et realiter ab alio), sed et exegetica (difficilis erat selectio textuum scripturisticorum atque eorum interpretatio ad probandam divinitatem Christi), et terminologica (varii sensus vocum adhibitarum, *hypostasis, ousia* ...), et methodologica (utrum legitimum esset in Symbolum introducere vocem quae in scriptura non inveniebatur), et dogmatico-disciplinaris (agebatur de primo concilio oecumenico, atque nondum clara doctrina habebatur in ecclesia de valore huiusmodi concilii) ...

His rationibus intrinsecis quaestioni accedebant aliae quae desumuntur ex consideratione ambientis, sive interferentia imperialis in quaestionibus theologicis et rebus ecclesiasticis, cum suo nefasto influxu etiam in viros ecclesiasticos; ipsa organizatio ecclesiae (episcopi unius regionis connectabantur cum Sede Romana quatenus ipsi inter se directe uniti erant; dum hodie episcopi inter se uniuntur quatenus communionem habent cum Sede Romana) ...

[e' The Historian's A Priori and Dialectical Argument]

Huiusmodi attentio ad intelligibilitatem ipsorum datorum et iudicium de causis illis intrinsecis est unicum medium crisis instituendi diversarum interpretationum quae circa eadem facta historica dantur a diversis historicis, sive idealistis, sive empiristis, sive exsistentialistis, sive Catholicis ... Haec interpretationis diversitas certe non provenit ex factis sed ex aliis capitibus. Crisis harum diversarum interpretationum historiae facilius habebitur quatenus et ad documenta bene attendimus et ad intelligentiam pervenimus elementi aprioristici proprii mentis illius viri historici. Sic clare distinguetur aliqua interpretatio quae cum datis optime congruit et semper eadem manet, et aliae interpretationes quae continuo mutantur quia ad intelli-

In all this we have an example of a transition that caused great turmoil in the church. In dealing with this transition, a historian of theology must do two things above all: first, grasp the intelligibility of these different opinions and of the transition from one to the other, and then render judgment upon these divergent tendencies and the reasons for them.

The immanent intelligibility of the transition is arrived at when all the historical data are set forth in their order of occurrence, along with all the various positions, each of which throws light upon its opposite. Once this intelligibility is grasped, a judgment upon and reasons for the divergent tendencies are much more easily arrived at. The large number of opinions is explained by the complexity of the question, which is actually not only a speculative question (how the Son is really *a se* and also really *ab alio*), but an exegetical question (the difficulty of selecting biblical texts and interpreting them to prove the divinity of Christ), a terminological question (the various meanings of the words used, such as *hypostasis, ousia,* etc.), a methodological question (whether it was legitimate to insert into the creed a non-scriptural term), and a dogmatic-disciplinary question (since it deals with the first ecumenical council when there was not yet a clear position in the church regarding the force of this sort of council).

In addition to these considerations, which are intrinsic to the question, there are others that regard external circumstances. Such would be the interference of the imperial authorities in theological matters and the affairs of the church, with the baneful influence this had on churchmen; also, the way the church was organized at that time, when the bishops of one region were in communion with the See of Rome inasmuch as they were in communion with one another, whereas today bishops are in communion with one another inasmuch as they are in direct communion with Rome.

[e′ The Historian's A Priori and Dialectical Argument]

Such attention to the intelligibility in the data themselves and judgment upon the causes intrinsic to them is the only way to examine critically the divergent interpretations of the same historical facts given by various historians – by idealists, empiricists, existentialists, Catholics, and others. This diversity of interpretation certainly does not arise from the facts themselves, but from other sources. This sort of critical examination of these various interpretations of history will be all the easier to the extent that we pay close attention to the documents and come to understand the a priori element to be found in the mindset of each historian. In this way we shall be able to distinguish clearly between an interpretation that fits the data extremely

gentiam rerum simpliciter numquam pervenerunt. Viri historici enim non tantum factorum sed et aliorum historicorum crisim instituere.

· Hanc crisim aliorum historicorum possumus facile instituere mediante argumento dialectico, quod differt ab argumento logico quia, dum argumentum logicum praesupponit notiones et propositiones communes, argumentum dialecticum pervenit ad transformationem alicuius originalis asserti falsi procedendo ab ipso asserto.

Sit aliquod exemplum alicuius argumenti dialectici:

Stet quaestio: 'Utrum substantia prima per conscientiam immediate percipiatur.'

Qui hanc ponit quaestionem, rem nullatenus videtur intelligere. Nam subest huic problemati et falsa notio conscientiae et falsa gnoseologia.

Ad ostendendam hanc falsitatem procedimus per quaestiones et responsiones obvias:

Primus gressus: aut substantia prima immediate percipitur a nullo aut ab aliquo; et si ab aliquo aut inconscio aut conscio. Si affirmative respondatur, certe ab aliquo conscio haec perceptio habetur.

Secundus gressus: is qui est conscius talis est sive quando seipsum percipit sive quando percipit alia a se, quia conscientia habetur sive ipse percipiens sive aliquid aliud percipiatur.

Tertius gressus: quid potest significare 'immediate'? Sine medio; sic loquimur de principiis immediatis. Mediatio tamen duplex distingui potest: sive psychologica, quando subiectum reflectitur in seipsum, cum qua mediatione connectitur mediatio cognoscitiva, quando subiectum reflectitur in seipsum ut data conscientiae consulat. Unde 'immediate' excludit sive mediationem psychologicam sive cognoscitivam. Unde, conscientia immediata habebitur in percipiente in quantum percipit et non in quantum percipitur.

Quartus gressus: at id quod percipitur sunt plantae, animalia, homines ... Certe id quod per data conscientiae habetur non est substantia prima praecisive sumpta.

Substantia prima aliquomodo opponitur subiecto. Subiectum est id quod est sui conscium: percipiens qua percipiens, ut sui conscius. Substantia prima est subiectum non actu sed potentia tantum; nam homo est semper substantia prima, sive sit conscius sive non.

well and remains constant, and other interpretations that are continually changing because they simply have not arrived at an understanding of the matter. Historians, of course, critically examine not only the facts but also other historians.

We can easily do this critique by means of a dialectical argument, which is different from a logical argument in that, while a logical argument presupposes common notions and propositions, a dialectical argument arrives at the transformation of an original false assertion by proceeding from that assertion itself.

Here is an example of a dialectical argument:

Let this question be posed: 'Is a primary substance immediately perceived through consciousness?'

One who would pose this question would seem to have no understanding of the matter at all. For underlying this problem are a false notion of consciousness and a false gnoseology.

To demonstrate this falsity, we shall proceed by way of a series of questions and their obvious answers:

First step: Primary substance is either perceived by no one or by someone; and if by someone, then by one who is either unconscious or conscious. If the reply is affirmative, then certainly this perception is had by someone who is conscious.

Second step: One who is conscious is so both when he perceives himself and when he perceives things apart from himself, because consciousness is had whether either the perceiver or anything else is perceived.

Third step: What can 'immediate' mean? It means 'without an intermediary'; thus, we speak of immediate principles. But there are two kinds of mediation: psychological, when the subject reflects upon himself; and, connected with this mediation, cognitive mediation, when the subject reflects upon himself in order to consult the data of consciousness. Hence, 'immediate' excludes both psychological and cognitive mediation. There is, therefore, immediate consciousness in a perceiver inasmuch as one is perceiving and not inasmuch as one is being perceived.

Fourth step: Objects of perception are plants, animals, human beings, and so on. That which is had through the data of consciousness is certainly not primary substance as such.

Primary substance is in some way opposed to subject. A subject is that which is conscious of self: a perceiver precisely as perceiver, as conscious of self. Primary substance is a subject in potency only, not in act; one is always a primary substance whether actually conscious or not.

Attamen, ut Aristoteles ait, substantia prima est id quod alteri non inest neque de altero praedicatur.[136] At subiectum praecise nec alteri inest nec de altero praedicatur. Ergo subiectum est substantia prima.

Tamen haec ultima propositio nisi per ratiocinium non cognoscitur, ad quod requiritur definitio substantiae primae, quae habetur non ex conscientia sed ex categoriis Aristotelicis. Ratiocinium importat autem mediationem.

Sic apparet processum dialecticum vim suam obtinere ex eo quod adversarius implicite admittit positionem nostram (= veram), quamvis explicite cogitet de re diversa.

Simili modo possumus procedere ad ostendenda elementa aprioristica diversarum theoriarum historicarum. Quando obtinetur intelligentia intrinseca ipsis datis, habetur basis ut fiant argumenta dialectica contra interpretationes aprioristicas, in quibus manifestetur oppositio latens inter a priori viri historici et data quae ipse quaerit intelligere. Hoc autem non est possibile si quaerimus de causis efficientibus, vel finalibus, vel occultis, ved de dando iudicio valoris ...

Exemplum optimum dedit huius operis, v.gr., G. Boissier, in suo libro *Cicéron et ses amis*,[137] qui, etsi multa opera conscripta sunt tempore elapso post suam apparitionem, tamen remanet maximi valoris in hac materia, non quia auctor potuit legere omnia quae post ipsum scripta sunt, sed quia simpliciter intellexit suam materiam.

[c] Comparatio inter theologiam historicam et speculativam

Non agitur de duabus theologiis, nam theologia historica est theologia speculativa in fieri, dum theologia speculativa est theologia historica in facto esse.

Termini et categoriae propriae theologiae speculativae (ut ecclesia, supernaturale, sacramenta, *homoousion*, personae ...) orta sunt intra theologicum motum historicum, atque allata sunt ab ipso motu quando perventum est ad illa puncta transitionis quae sunt clavis totius motus theologici atque maxime connectuntur cum magnis haeresibus et cum celeberrimis disputationibus.

However, as Aristotle says, primary substance is that which neither exists in nor is predicated of anything else.[136] But a subject is precisely something that neither exists in nor is predicated of anything else. Therefore, a subject is a primary substance.

Now, this last proposition is known only through a process of reasoning, and for this there is required a definition of primary substance, which is not obtained from consciousness but from Aristotle's categories. Reasoning, however, involves mediation.

Thus, it is apparent that the dialectical process gets its cogency from the fact that our opponent implicitly admits our position, the correct one, even though explicitly he thinks otherwise.

In a similar way, we can proceed to lay bare the a priori elements of various historical theories. When you have obtained an intrinsic understanding of the data themselves you have a basis for constructing dialectical arguments against a priori interpretations in order to bring to light the hidden discrepancy between the historians' a priori and the data that they seek to understand. This cannot be done, however, if you ask about efficient causes or final causes or hidden causes, or about making value judgments.

An excellent example of this is the work of G. Boissier in his book *Cicéron et ses amis*.[137] Even though much has been written since it first appeared, it is still a most valuable book in this area, not because its author was able to read everything that was written after it, but simply because he really understood his material.

[c] The Comparison between Historical and Speculative Theology

These are not two theologies. Historical theology is speculative theology-in-process (*in fieri*), while speculative theology is the end product (*in facto esse*) of historical theology.

The terminology and categories of speculative theology, such as church, supernatural, sacraments, *homoousion*, person, and the like, came into existence within the historical movement of theology and were introduced by that very movement when it reached those pivotal points that are the key to the entire movement of theology and are very closely connected with the major heresies and the more important controversies.

---

136 Aristotle, *Categories*, v, 2a 11–13.
137 Gaston Boissier, *Cicéron et ses amis: Étude sur la société romaine du temps de César* (Paris: Hachette et Cie, 1865, [1941]); [English translation, *Cicero and His Friends: A Study of Roman Society in the Time of Caesar*, trans. Adnah David Jones (London: Wark, Lock, 1897; New York: G.P. Putnam's Sons, 1925).]

Unde qui cognoscere vult theologiam speculativam debet cognoscere etiam motum historicum, et qui vult cognoscere motum hunc opportet ut cognoscat theologiam speculativam (cfr. exemplum de stadiis evolutionis, v.gr., oculorum in foetu).[138]

Diximus antea historiam specialem alicuius scientiae posse fieri tantum ab illo qui peritissimus sit in illa scientia; sic historia theologiae potest scribi tantum a peritissimo in re theologica, unde a theologo speculativo.

Si theologia speculativa et historica separantur, maxima inconvenientia exsurgunt pro utraque disciplina.

Nam theologia positiva amittit propriam methodum. Historia enim cogitationis theologicae non est tantum aliquod elementum indistinctum in historia philosophiae, litteraria, religiosa … sed debet seligi ut motus aliquis determinatus. Omissa theologia speculativa, omittitur autem determinatio illius campi cognitionis. Similiter, qui vult facere historiam scientiae physicae in stadiis praecedentibus systematizationem scientificam, criterium ad seligendum id quod in illis stadiis pertinet ad obiectum scientiae physicae repetit ex iis quae ex stadiis posterioribus scit ad scientiam physicam pertinere.

Ipsa natura theologiae speculativae corrumpitur. Nam theologia non est intelligentia quaecumque, sed fidei; si contactus cum datis revelatis amittitur, poterit dari aliqua intelligentia, non autem intelligentia fidei; sic habebitur aliquis esoterismus, absque connexione cum realitate. Omissa theologia positiva, theologia speculativa separatur a propriis originibus, et, si hoc non fit, saepe origines falsificantur per anachronismum qui categorias posteriores in stadiis prioribus proicit.

Utique, sine theologia positiva theologia speculativa poterit inniti super magisterium ecclesisaticum. Sic demonstare poterit quid sit de fide, quid non, quid sit theologice certum, quid probabile aut tutum, quid non, quid temerarium … At hoc modo iudicium dabitur de fide, seu de eo quod est credendum, non illius intelligentia obtinebitur. Haec theologia 'inquisitoria' potius utilis est ad haereses discernendas et ad errores vitandos.

It follows, then, that anyone who wants to learn speculative theology must also have a knowledge of the movement of history, and conversely one who wants to learn about this movement needs to know speculative theology. As an example of stages in development, compare that of the eye in a fetus.[138]

We stated above that one who would write the special history of any science must necessarily be thoroughly versed in that science. Thus, the history of theology can be written only by one who is very knowledgeable in theology, hence by a speculative theologian.

Separating speculative and historical theology would have unfortunate consequences upon both disciplines.

First, positive theology would lose its proper method. For the history of theological thought is not just an indistinguishable element in the history of philosophy, literature, religion, and so forth, but also needs to be separated out as a determinate movement. If speculative theology is disregarded, there will be no determining that field of knowledge. Similarly, one who would write the history of physics as it was before being systematized as a science will obtain the criterion for selecting what pertained to its object in those earlier stages from what he knows to be part of physics in its later stages.

Second, speculative theology would be corrupted. For theology is not just any understanding, but an understanding of the faith. If contact with the data of revelation is lost, some understanding can be had, but it will not be an understanding of the faith; the result would be some sort of esoteric doctrine without any connection with reality. Divorced from positive theology, speculative theology would be severed from its roots; and even if this were not the case, those very roots would be falsified by an anachronistic retrojection of later categories into the earlier stages.

Of course, without positive theology speculative theology could rely upon the teaching authority of the church. It could accordingly point out what are matters of faith and what are not, what are theologically certain or probable or safe opinions and what are not, what are rash and temerarious, and so on. But this would only be rendering judgments about faith, that is, about what is to be believed, but no understanding would be obtained. This sort of 'inquisitorial' theology is better suited to detecting heresy or guarding against error.

138 [See Lonergan's reference to the fetal eye in *Insight* 507.]

Ex his observationibus notio quaedam initialis potest desumi circa quaestionem, hodie multum agitata, de theologia biblica et patristica, de eiusque methodo.[139]

Quid intelligimus quando loquimur de theologia biblica vel patristica? Non agitur de philologia, neque de historia generum litterariorum cogitationis humanae, sed de scriptura et Patribus quatenus praebent aliquam theologiam. Theologus biblicus vult facere transitum a studio historiae, philologiae, culturae, litterarum ... ad aliud genus quod nominatur theologia.

Nunc autem, theologia, quatenus scientia, incepit tantum saeculo XIII (ut vidimus in exemplis supra propositis). Tunc temporis facta est systematizatio totius materiae theologicae adhibito theoremate (non amplius singulis hypothesibus) de supernaturali.

Tantum nostris diebus, et in nostro saeculo, theologi explicite agnoscunt stadium praescientificum theologiae exsistere. Ut clare fiat distinctio inter stadium theologiae praescientificum et stadium scientificum, requiritur inter theologos clara et distincta agnitio differentiae inter modum cogitandi systematicum et modum symbolicum-vulgarem. Haec autem distinctio est tantum recentior. In nostris manualibus theologicis adhuc non attenditur ad hanc differentiam.

Stadia praescientifica alicuius scientiae describuntur et circa ea investigatio fit scientifica tantum secundum intelligentiam posterioris stadii scientifici (solus medicus potest investigationem peragere circa historiam medicinae). Unde, qui non intelligit theologiam systematicam atque scribere vult de theologia in stadio praescientifico agit de re quam non intelligit, multa essentialia omittet, et multa quae ad rem non pertinent extollet ...

Magis quam aliae, scientia theologica tenetur investigare suum stadium praescientificum. Hoc revera non est essentiale pro scientia mathematica,

From the above observations we can get some initial notion about the question, much discussed these days, concerning biblical and patristic theology and its method.[139]

What do we understand by biblical or patristic theology? Not philology, nor a history of the literary genres in human thought, but the Bible and the Fathers inasmuch as they contain a theology. The biblical theologian's aim is to make the transition from the study of history, philology, culture, literature, and the rest to another genre that we call theology.

Theology as a science began only in the thirteenth century, as we have seen from the examples given above. It was at that time that the systematization of the whole field of theology occurred through the introduction of the theorem of the supernatural in place of particular hypotheses.

It is only in our own day, in this century, that theologians have come to explicitly recognize the existence of the prescientific stage of theology. In order to establish a clear distinction between the prescientific and the scientific stages of theology, theologians need to have a clear and distinct recognition of the difference between the systematic mode and the symbolic and commonsense mode of thought. This distinction, however, is relatively recent, and so far the theological manuals have not adverted to this difference.

The description of the prescientific stages of any science and the investigation of them are done scientifically only in accordance with an understanding of the later stages of that science: only a medical doctor is equipped to conduct an investigation into the history of medicine. Anyone, therefore, who does not have a grasp of systematic theology and yet wants to write about theology in the prescientific stage of its history is attempting to work at something he doesn't understand; he will leave out many essential points, and will give undue importance to things that are not germane to the matter.

The science of theology has a greater obligation than any other science has to investigate its prescientific stage. It is really not essential for math-

---

139 See Luis Alonso-Schökel, 'Argument d'Écriture et théologie biblique dans l'enseignement théologique,' *Nouvelle Revue Théologique* 81 (1959) 337–54, and the appended bibliography. [Lonergan would soon appeal regularly in this context to Albert Descamps, 'Réflexions sur la méthode en théologie biblique,' in *Sacra Pagina: Miscellanea Biblica Congressus Internationalis Catholici de Re Biblica*, vol. 1, ed. J. Coppens, A. Descamps, and E. Massaux (Gembloux: Éditions J. Duculot, 1959) 132–57.]

neque physica, neque chimica, quamvis utile possit esse ad paedagogiam istarum scientiarum. At theologia est intelligentia fidei; fides autem obiectiva, quae creditur, primo proposita est in Sacra Scriptura, apud Patres primaque concilia ... Unde expositio revelationis facta est potius in stadio praescientifico scientiae theologicae.

Theologia categorias suas evolvere debet ad investiganda sua stadia praescientifica; nam non tantum debemus intelligere, sed intelligere systematice. Qualia sunt autem elementa systematica assumenda in intelligentia stadiorum praescientificorum? Hoc est fortasse maximum problema scientiae theologicae nostri temporis, cuius solutio nondum exsistit. Aliqua indicatio potest haberi quatenus stadia praescientifica concipiantur tamquam motus ad theologiam speculativam. Quomodo intelligere possumus fidem, revelationem, inspirationem ... quae habebantur antequam transitus fieret, post quem explicite has notiones habuimus? Hoc est fundamentale problema metholologicum, ad cuius solutionem quaerenda est cooperatio intima inter theologos biblicos, dogmaticos, patristicos, conciliares ...

Actualis habitudo inter theologiam systematicam et theologiam biblico-patristicam est fere opus transitionis ad novam synthesin theologicam obtinendam in futurum tempus.[140]

4.5.5   Illustratio theologica quintae regulae: Responsabilitas iudicandi est acceptanda

Omnis inquisitio scientifica duplici perficitur motu, ascensivo (ex elemento aposteriori) et descensivo (elemento aprioristico). Nostrae quinque regulae comprehendere intendunt illud quod est elementum aprioristicum in qualibet scientia.

Nostra quinta regula est regula suprema in omni scientia. Ipsa directe agit contra conceptionem methodi mechanicam atque scientiae, prouti a Jaspers concipitur, tamquam cognitio quae ita obiective stabiliatur ut nemo ei resistere possit. Huiusmodi scientia esset revera infrahumana, pragmati-

ematics to do this, or physics, or chemistry, although it could be useful from a pedagogical point of view. But theology is an understanding of the faith; objective faith, however, that which is the object of belief, was first set forth in sacred scripture, the Fathers, and the early councils, and that is why the exposition of revelation was done more at the prescientific stage of theology.

Theology has to develop its own categories for investigating its prescientific stages; for we must not only understand, we must understand systematically. But what kind of systematic elements should it adopt for an understanding of its prescientific stages? This is perhaps the biggest problem facing the science of theology today, and no solution for it has yet appeared. Some indication of it may be seen inasmuch as the prescientific stages are conceived as movements towards speculative theology. How can we understand faith, revelation, inspiration, etc., as they were before the transition [to systematic theology] took place, since these notions were only worked out explicitly after that transition? This is a fundamental methodological problem, which can only be solved through close cooperation among biblical, patristic, dogmatic, conciliar theologians, and theologians generally.

The present relationship between systematic theology and biblical and patristic theology is largely a transitional movement towards a new theological synthesis to be achieved at some future time.[140]

4.5.5 Theological Illustration of the Fifth Rule: Accept Responsibility for Judging

All scientific investigation takes place in two movements: a movement from below (from the a posteriori element), and a movement from above (from the a priori). It is our intent in these five rules to encompass the entire a priori element in any and every science.

This fifth rule of ours is the supreme rule of every science. It is the exact opposite of a mechanical concept of method and of science, such as conceived by Jaspers, as knowledge that is so well established objectively as to be unassailable. A science of this sort would really be sub-human, pragmatist,

---

140 [See material to this effect in 1957 and 1959 texts in *Divinarum personarum* that Lonergan omitted from the 1964 revision in *De Deo Trino: Pars systematica*. This material can now be found in appendix 4 in Lonergan, *The Triune God: Systematics*, esp. pp. 755–61.]

stica, nec longinquam a radicali subiectivismo, quo de facto imbuitur philosophia Jasperiana.[141]

Regula de responsabilitate iudicandi est fundamentalis in theologia. Ipsa
enim praesupponit et fidem et intelligentiam fidei. Fides autem est assensus intellectualis, seu iudicium, quo verum attingitur non ex perspecta evidentia terminorum sed ex imperio voluntatis, quod tamen sit rationabile.
Aliqua perspicientia terminorum requiritur ut fundentur iudicia credibilitatis et credenditatis, quae iterum fundent rationabilitatem imperii voluntatis.[142]

Quoad fidem, amplianda est notio veritatis, ita ut verum sit non tantum
id quod nos intelligere possumus sed id quod Deus intelligit. Si verum est
tantum id quod ex intrinsecis procedit in humano intellectu, tunc ad fidem
non accedimus. Unde analogia veri est acceptanda.

Scientiae naturales fundantur in fide humana. Nullus enim vir scientificus verificat nec verificare potest omnes propositiones et leges scientificas,
sed libris et magistris utitur. Talis fides scientifica, tamen, non exigit analogiam veri. Etiamsi unusquisque vir scientificus non cognoscit ex intrinsecis
omnes propositiones scientificas, tamen sunt alii qui sciunt, unde obiectum
totale scientiae illius iacet intra campum veri humani. Lumen fidei, e contra, in eo est ut homo per suum lumen naturale lumine divino ocületur ita
ut verum esse affirmet id quod Deus pro vero habet.

Radicalis oppositio contra fidem est rationalismus, pro quo verum est
tantum id quod per intelligentiam et reflexionem humanam easque solas
producitur.

Et quia quaestio est de vero, veritas autem formaliter in iudicio invenitur,
quaestio tangit directe iudicium.

Quia theologia est intelligentia veri divini revelati excedentis vires intellectus humani, transformatio radicalis requiritur omnium regularum nostrarum.

and not far removed from radical subjectivism, with which, in fact, Jaspers's philosophy is imbued.[141]

The rule about responsibility for judging is fundamental in theology. It presupposes both faith and an understanding of the faith. Faith, however, is an intellectual assent, a judgment in which truth is attained, not through a grasp of the evidence of the terms but by a dictate of the will, one that nevertheless is reasonable. Some grasp of the terms is required to ground judgments of credibility and credendity, which in turn ground the reasonableness of the dictate of the will.[142]

In the case of faith, the notion of truth has to be broadened, so that truth is not only that which we can understand but also that which God understands. If truth is only that which arises from factors immanent in the human intellect, then we do not reach faith. We must accept, therefore, the analogy of truth.

The natural sciences rest upon human belief. No scientist verifies or is able to verify all scientific propositions and laws, but takes them from books and teachers. Yet this scientific belief does not require the analogy of truth. Even if no scientist knows all scientific propositions from his or her own immanently generated knowledge, still there are other scientists who do know them in this way, so that the totality of that particular science lies within the ambit of human truth. The light of faith, by contrast, is that by which one's natural light of reason is divinely enlightened so that one can affirm as true what God knows to be true.

Radically opposed to faith is rationalism, according to which only that is true which arises from human understanding and reflection and from them alone.

And since the question we are dealing with has to do with truth, and truth is found formally in judgment, the question touches directly upon judgment

In view of the fact that theology is an understanding of divinely revealed truths that exceed the scope of the human intellect, it will call for a radical transformation of all our rules.

141 [For some examples of Lonergan's other brief discussions of Jaspers's philosophy, see *Phenomenology and Logic* 225–27, 231–32, 294.]
142 [For a fuller account, see Bernard Lonergan, 'Analysis of Faith,' in *Early Latin Theology*, vol 19 of Collected Works of Bernard Lonergan, trans. Michael G. Shields, ed. Robert M. Doran and H. Daniel Monsour (Toronto: University of Toronto Press, 2011) 413–81. On the judgment of credibility and credendity, see below, pp. 514–17 and note 160.]

In caeteris scientiis enim scientia incipit non ex vero sed ex dato empiri-
co, seu ex materia intentionali circa quam fit inquisitio, cui accedit forma
intelligibilis per actum intelligendi, quae forma pedetentim evolvitur, et
tantum in fine, quando omnia data sint intellecta, potest haberi iudicium
verum de obiecto scientiae. Unde in caeteris scientiis data per intelligentiam promoventur ad verum, quia ex datis incipitur atque ad verum proceditur.

Theologia autem ex veris revelatis incipit, nec ad verum accedit per intelligentiam datorum. Verum habetur iam inde ab initio. Id quod quaeritur non est verum sed intelligentia huius veri. Dum verum in aliis scientiis
est ideale ad quod tendimus, in theologia est aliqua praesentia permanens
atque dirigens totam evolutionem intelligentiae inde ab initio. In aliis
scientiis intelligentia praecedit et determinat verum; in theologia intelligentia praeceditur et dirigitur a vero.[143]

Haec differentia fundat modos procedendi speciales in theologia. Maxime occupantur theologi circa propositiones veras, unde maximi momenti
est logica, qua ostendere possimus quid implicite in propositionibus veris
contineatur. At maximi momenti est etiam semantica (seu metaphysica)
considerans habitudinem inter propositiones veras qua tales et realitatem
per illas propositiones significatam. Semanticae est inquirere in constitutivo formali.

Tamen, omnes hae technicae non pertinent ad ipsam medullam theologiae, sed sunt tantum media ad finem; sunt non ipsum aedificium sed
structurae circa aedificium; utilissimae sunt ad delimitandas quaestiones,
ad designandas res quarum intelligentia quaeritur, quid exacte intelligi
possit et quid non ... at nondum sunt intelligentia fidei.

Intelligentia fidei (seu theologia) est imperfecta perspicientia mysteriorum analogica, sive ex analogia eorum quae naturaliter cognoscuntur
sive ex analogia nexus mysteriorum inter se et cum fine ultimo hominis
(DB 1796).

The other sciences begin not from truth but from empirical data, that is, from intentional matter about which inquiry is made, followed by the intelligible form had through an act of understanding; this form gradually develops until finally, when all the data have been understood, a true and certain judgment can be made upon the object of the science. Hence, in the other sciences the data are promoted through understanding to the level of truth, because the process begins from data and progresses to truth.

Theology, on the other hand, begins from revealed truths: it does not move towards truth through an understanding of the data. The truth is had right from the beginning. What is sought is not a truth but an understanding of this truth. Whereas in other sciences truth is the ideal towards which we strive, in theology it is a certain permanent presence that from the outset directs the entire development of our understanding of it. In the other sciences understanding precedes and determines truth; in theology understanding is preceded and directed by truth.[143]

This difference grounds the special ways of proceeding in theology. Theologians are most of all engaged in dealing with true propositions, whence the paramount importance of logic, by which we are able to show what is implicitly contained in the true propositions. But also of the utmost importance is semantics, or metaphysics, which regards the relationship between true propositions as such and the reality signified by those propositions. It is the task of semantics to inquire into the formal constitutive.

However, these techniques do not pertain to the central core of theology, but are only means to the end; they are not the building itself but only the scaffolding around it. They are very useful for carefully defining questions, for indicating what things are to be understood through inquiry, what exactly can be understood and what cannot, and so forth, but they are not yet themselves an understanding of the faith.

The understanding of the faith, theology, is an imperfect and analogical grasp of the mysteries, either by analogy with what can be known by natural human reason, or by analogy with the mysteries of faith as connected with one another or with the final end of man (DB 1796, DS 3016, ND 132).

---

143 [By the time of *Method in Theology*, what Lonergan says here about 'theology' pertains to the functional specialty 'systematics.' The whole of a theology structured by functional specialties *does* begin from data (research) to reach truth. The truth of doctrines becomes the data for systematic understanding.]

Huiusmodi intelligentia est imperfecta quia centrum mysterii numquam penetratur, nam est Ipsum Esse, Ipsum Intelligere. Per intelligentiam theologicam perspicimus multas lineas convergentes, non tamen centrum in quo convergunt, unde mysteria manent incomprehensa in sua radice, atque 'quid sit Deus nescimus.'

Huiusmodi effatum, a traditione patristica atque a S. Thoma saepissime usurpatum, difficultatem facit tantum illis qui obliviscuntur sensus historici illius. 'Quid sit' aliqua res cognoscitur non per quemlibet conceptum, neque per definitionem per genus et differentiam, sed per ipsam rei intelligentiam. Ne Christus quidem videt omnia possibilia in potentia Creatoris, quia secus ipse intellectus humanus Christi esset Deus! Scientia ipsius divini pertinet ad Deum et tantum per visionem beatam participatur.

Nec inutilis est conatus intelligendi verum revelatum, etsi imperfecte, analogice ... immo fructuossimus dicitur a Concilio Vaticano (ibid.). Permanens fundamentum huius investigationis, in qua theologia consistit, est ipsa fides. Si enim theologia fit intelligentia, non fidei, sed alicuius alterius rei, eo ipso a suo munere cessat.

Theologus credit Deum revelasse, atque modo providentiali conservare verum revelatum per ecclesiam suam. Quivis theologus ipsam fidem ex Deo habet atque directionem circa fidem ex magisterio Ecclesiae; tamen debet et ipse propria facere iudicia. Theologia enim non est aliquod exercitium repetitionis, sed intelligentia augetur per saecula, atque illicitum est affirmare superfluitatem orationis Concilii Vaticani (cfr. DB 1800).[144] Unde quando theologus habuit novam aliquam intelligentiam veri revelati, iudicare debet utrum huiusmodi intelligentia vera sit necne. Quatenus autem aliquis theologus profundius intelligit, est quodammodo initiator; nam generatim multo postea eius doctrina acceptabitur communiter inter theologos, tardius autem fiet doctrina ecclesiae atque rarissime definietur.

Circa huiusmodi iudicia propria acceptanda est responsabilitas iudicandi. Etiam in theologia non dantur iudicia mechanica. Quando iudicandi responsabilitas non acceptatur (1) omne novum occurrens in intelligentia

This sort of understanding is imperfect because the core of the mystery can never be penetrated, for that core is Being Itself, Intelligence Itself. Theological understanding gives us a grasp of many lines of convergence, but not of the core upon which they converge, and so the mysteries remain radically uncomprehended, and 'what God is we do not know.'

This saying, often quoted by the Fathers and St Thomas, presents a difficulty only for those who are unmindful of its historical meaning. The 'whatness' (*quid sit*) of anything is known not through any concept or through a definition by genus and specific difference, but through an understanding of the thing itself. Not even Christ himself sees all the possible beings within the Creator's power, because otherwise his human intellect would be God. Knowledge of the divine is God's alone, and is communicated only through the beatific vision.

But it is not a useless endeavor to try to understand revealed truth, imperfect and analogical though that understanding may be; indeed, such an understanding has been declared to be most fruitful by the Vatican Council. The unchanging foundation of this investigation, which is what theology is all about, is the faith itself. If theology becomes an understanding, not of the faith but of something else, it ceases to perform its proper and essential function.

Theologians believe that God has revealed truth and in a providential way safeguards revealed truth through his church. They derive their faith from God and get direction concerning faith from the teaching authority of the church; nevertheless, they must form their own judgments. Theology is not an exercise in repetition; it is an understanding that grows with the passage of time, and it is wrong to dismiss as otiose the prayer of Vatican I in this regard (DB 1800, DS 3020, ND 136).[144] Accordingly, when theologians have some new insight into a revealed truth, they must judge whether their idea is true or not. Depending upon the depth of their understanding, theologians are, in a way, trail-blazers; it is usually only much later that their findings will be accepted by theologians generally, more slowly still will they become the teaching of the church, and only very rarely will they achieve dogmatic definition.

It is in this matter of making one's own judgments that there is the obligation of accepting responsibility for judging. Even in theology judgments are not the result of a mechanical process. When responsibility for judging

---

144 See above, pp. 28–29, and the reference there to *Humani generis*.

fidei hypothesis reputatur, (b) si eodem modo circa theologiam anteriorem proceditur, etiam ipsa, in maiori parte, hypothesis dicetur, (3) unde si tota theologia praecipue in hypothesibus consistit, auditores et discipuli non vident cur eam addiscant; et (4) quia systemata ad hypotheses reducuntur, dogmata autem sint expressiones fidei secundum modum apprehendendi systematicum (non enim sunt pura repetitio propositionum revelatarum in fontibus), ipsa dogmata videntur hypotheses, et consequentiae patent.

Plenior atque nova apprehensio veri revelati non eo ipso fit per deductionem necessariam ex conceptibus iam habitis. Extensionem enim requirit in principiis atque ampliationem conceptuum. Unde invalida est simplex deductio. Nam, quando deductio rigide et stricte peragitur, nullam dicit pleniorem intelligentiam. Unde, potius quam deducamus, aliquid novum intellectu perspicimus, atque responsabiliter iudicamus utrum haec plenior intelligentia sit vera necne. Iudicium est unicum medium quo illa plenior intelligentia transire possit prima vice in verum.

Iudicium autem fit secundum aliquam sapientiam. Sed sapientia proportionata ad iudicandum de intelligentia fidei est sola divina sapientia, quam theologus non habet. Quare ipse iudicat secundum suam sententiam, opinionem, atque promptus est, cum insufficientiam suae sapientiae cognoscat, ad submittendum suum iudicium iudicio ecclesiae, quia novit magisterium ecclesiasticum per Spiritum Sanctum dirigi ad doctrinam dominicam custodiendam et declarandam. Unde theologus non definitive iudicat de valore suae intelligentiae, at humiliter proponit suam sententiam et acceptat iudicium ecclesiae.

Momentum huiusmodi iudiciorum apparet ex historico exemplo.

Vehemens oppositio contra doctrinam S. Thomae, ipso vivo, facta, post eius mortem acrior effecta, duxit ad condemnationem multarum thesium Thomisticarum simul cum thesibus Averroisticis (a. 1277; ex parte Stephani Tempier, Archiepiscopi Parisiensis). Eodem anno Thomas damnatus est etiam a Roberto Kilwardby, Episcopo Cantuarensi, atque ab eius successsore Ioanne Peckham (a. 1284 et iterum 1286). Nec defuerunt 'Correctoria' Fratris Thomae (praesertim a Gulielmo de la Mare). In Universitate autem Parisiensi, ubi Thomas docuerat, dubium erat utrum legens opera Thomae esset excommunicatus necne. Post canonizationem autem S. Thomae a. 1323 factam, oppositio minus vehemens fiebat, atque a. 1325 Episcopus

is refused, (1) everything new that emerges in the understanding of the faith is regarded as a hypothesis; (2) if an earlier theology is approached in the same way, even it will be said to be mostly hypothetical; (3) hence, if the whole of theology consists mainly of hypotheses, students will not see why they should learn it; and (4) because systems are reduced to hypotheses while dogmas are expressions of the faith according to the systematic mode of apprehension, for they are not mere repetitions of propositions found in the sources of revelation, it follows that dogmas themselves will be seen as hypotheses, and the consequences of this are obvious.

A new and fuller apprehension of revealed truth does not occur automatically by necessary deduction from pre-existing concepts; it requires an extension in principles and a broadening of concepts. Hence, mere deduction is invalid. For when a deduction is made strictly and rigorously, it does not issue in fuller understanding. Rather than deducing, therefore, we grasp something new by our intellect and we judge responsibly whether this fuller understanding is true or not. Judgment is the only way by which a fuller understanding can for the first time pass into the realm of truth.

A judgment is made in accordance with a certain wisdom. But the only wisdom adequate for judging about an understanding of the faith is the wisdom of God, which theologians do not possess. For that reason they make a judgment according to their own considered opinion and, when they realize the insufficiency of their own wisdom, readily submit their judgment to that of the church, because they know that the church's teaching authority is guided by the Holy Spirit in its task of guarding and declaring the teaching of the Lord. Accordingly, theologians will refrain from rendering a definitive value judgment upon their understanding, but will humbly state their opinion and accept the judgment of the church.

The importance of such judgments is illustrated by the following historical example.

The vehement opposition to the teaching of St Thomas during his lifetime became even more fierce after his death in 1274 and led to the condemnation of many Thomist theses along with those of Averroes in 1277 by the authority of Étienne Tempier, Archbishop of Paris. Thomas was condemned in the same year by Robert Kilwardby, Archbishop of Canterbury, and by his successor John Peckham in 1284 and again in 1286. There were plenty of *Correctoria Fratris Thomae* around, notably the one by William de la Mare. At the University of Paris, in fact, where Thomas had taught, there was considerable doubt as to whether those who read his works were excommunicated or not. After his canonization in 1323 the opposition abated

Parisiensis abstulit censuras, quas successor Episcopi Peckham non iteravit. Saeculo XIV incipiente, iam Thomas Sutton loquitur de S. Thoma tamquam de eo qui 'in ore omnium communis doctor dicitur.'

Ut faceret suum opus, S. Thoma plene excoluit categoriam supernaturalis, ante ipsum inventam, invenit categoriam gratiae actualis, atque investigavit in relationes quas theologia habet cum caeteris campis omnium scientiarum atque totius universi. Unde eius opus est vera quaedam magna cathedralis mediaevalis. Hoc autem non fecit sine maxima audacia in intelligendo atque sine acceptatione responsabilitatis in iudicando. Maxima fuit eius prudentia et sapientia, quia non tantum ausus est intelligere quae ...[145] sed ea responsabiliter proposuit. Quod fecit etsi huiusmodi nova iudicia non acceptabantur ab ipsis suis successoribus in Parisiensi domo S. Iacobi, ut fuerunt Iacobus a Metz atque Durandus a S. Porciano.

Probabiliter nos iudicia talia ut S. Thomas habuit non habebimus, sed unusquisque, quatenus aliquid intelligit, responsabilitatem iudicandi acceptare debet, scilicet accurate evolvere illam[146] atque humiliter eam proponere.

Conclusio

[1] Vidimus unicuique quaestioni correspondere aliqua responsio, quam aliqua quaestio consequitur, etc. Sic exsurgunt ordinationes responsionum, atque oritur successio diversarum ordinationum responsionum; quia autem datur haec successio, ultima ordinatio responsionum differt a paenultima, paenultima ab antepaenultima ... usque ad primam ordinationem, quae valde differt ab ultima. Sic progressus factus est ab ordinatione biblica responsionum ad ultimam ordinationem theologicam. Unde oritur problema historicitatis.

Idem effectus sub alio aspectu potest considerari. Quo magis differt modus concipiendi ultimus a modo concipiendi anteriori, eo magis augetur

somewhat, and in 1325 the archbishop of Paris removed the censures, and these were not repeated by Archbishop Peckham's successor. At the beginning of the fourteenth century, Thomas Sutton was already speaking of Aquinas as 'the one whom all proclaim to be *Doctor Communis.*'

In order to do his theology, Thomas fully elaborated the category of the supernatural that had originated before his time, introduced the category of actual grace, and studied the relationship of theology to all other sciences and to the universe as a whole. Hence, his work is like a great medieval cathedral of truth. He did not achieve all this without considerable intellectual audacity and an acceptance of responsibility in making his judgments. Great indeed was his wisdom and prudence in not only daring to understand what were …,[145] but also in presenting them in a responsible way. This he did despite the fact that such new judgments were not being accepted by some who succeeded him at the [College of] St-Jacques in Paris, such as James of Metz and Durandus of St Porcianus.

We shall probably not have to make the sort of judgments that St Thomas made; but everyone who understands something must accept the responsibility for making a judgment, namely, to form it[146] carefully and propose it humbly.

Conclusion

[1] We have seen that to every question there is a corresponding answer, which gives rise in turn to another question, and so on. In this way there emerge orderings of answers and a succession of different orderings of answers. Because there is this succession, however, the last ordering of answers will be different from the penultimate, the penultimate will be different from the one before it, and so on right up to the first ordering, which will be very different from the last. Such has been the progression from the biblical ordering of answers down to the latest theological ordering. Hence the problem of historicity.

This same movement can be considered from another viewpoint. The more the latest mode of conception differs from a previous one, the wider

145 [Three or four words have been obliterated here in the Latin typescript.]
146 [The Latin has *illam* and *eam*, which grammatically can only refer to *responsabilitatem*; but it is surely the judgment itself that is to be carefully formed and modestly proposed.]

chasma inter doctrinam theologicam et simplicem fidem, atque habetur problema chasmatis.

Si dein quaeratur quomodo modus concipiendi theologicus, seu dogmata, fundentur in fide atque in revelatione divina, respondetur: 'implicite!' At remanet problema quid significet hoc 'implicite.'

Si demum inter multas scholas theologicas quaeritur criterium iudicii et discretionis, alius aspectus habetur problematis fundamenti.

[2] Egimus de notione scientiae, praebendo aliquos conceptus initiales. Primitivi non faciunt scientiam: ita civilizatio Cretensis, Babylonica, Aegyptia, Maya, Incas ..., quamvis essent excultae atque scripturam novissent, cogitationem scientificam definitam non cognoverunt. Eorum libri, etiam artithmetici vel astronomiae, aliqua continebant utilia ad tempus mensurandum, at non elementa scientifica de illis materiis. Civilizationes huiusmodi potius sub mytho erant.

Tantum apud Graecos incepit scientia. Ad hoc initium requiritur iam aliquis conceptus scientiae, seu prima organizatio conceptualis notionis scientiae non supponit neque fundatur in praxi scientifica. Transitus ad conceptum scientiae habitus est apud Graecos quatenus ipsi acceperunt vocabula iam praeexsistentia, illisque novum sensum technicum tribuerunt: sic *epistēmē* valuit pro scientia; *sophia* pro sapientia; *nous* pro intellectu; *alētheia* pro veritate; *logos* pro ratione. Per aliquam *Umdeutung* sensus harum vocum mutatus est ut technicus fieret.

Sic devenimus ad notionem Aristotelicam scientiae quam vidimus tamen ita differre a conceptione moderna.

Remanet quod aliqua initialis notio scientiae, seu aliqua initialis expressio purae finalitatis mentis est necessaria ut habeatur initium operationis scientificae. Quo magis, dein, adduntur cognitiones determinatiores circa id quod scientia est, eo maior influxus habetur in conceptione scientiae; maiores tamen etiam confusiones oriuntur.

Problema de notione scientiae, prout hodie ponitur, ita videtur ortum habuisse in decursu saeculorum. Prima systematizatio scientifica moderna excogitata est a Newton in sua theoria mechanica. Huiusmodi scientia concrete concepta et empirice stabilita maxime influit in criticam Kantianam. Ratio pura Kantiana est ideale scientificum ex Aristotele acceptum, tamen conceptum prout apud Scotum concipitur et ab Occam divulgatum est (scientia de universalibus et necessariis: notio conceptualis scientiae facile efformata ex aliqua superficiali notitia scientiae logicae). Haec fuit vera

becomes the gap between what theologians are teaching and simple faith. Hence the problem of the chasm.

Next, if one asks how the theological mode of conception, or dogmas, are based upon faith and divine revelation, the answer is, 'Implicitly.' But the question remains, what does 'implicitly' mean?

Finally, if one asks for a criterion for judging between the many schools of theology, we have another aspect of the problem of foundation.

[2] We have discussed the notion of science, providing some elementary concepts. Primitive peoples do not do science; thus, civilizations such as the Minoan, Babylonian, Egyptian, Mayan, Incan, and the like, although they had a culture and knew the art of writing, never acquired a definite scientific mentality. Their books, even those on arithmetic or astronomy, contained things that were useful for measuring time, but not the scientific elements of those matters. Civilizations of this sort were very much under the influence of myth.

It was only with the Greeks that science began. For this beginning there had to be already some concept of science, some conceptual organization of a notion of science that does not presuppose and is not based on scientific practice. The transition to the concept of science occurred among the Greeks, who took already existing words and gave them a new technical sense. Thus, *epistēmē* stood for science, *sophia* for wisdom, *nous* for intellect, *alētheia* for truth, *logos* for reason. Through a certain *Umdeutung*, the meaning of these words was modified to give them a technical meaning.

Thus, we come to the Aristotelian notion of science, which, as we have seen, is rather different from the modern concept.

The fact remains that some initial notion of science, that is, some initial expression of the pure finality of the mind, is necessary to initiate scientific work. Next, the addition of further and more precise ideas about the nature of science influences the development of the concept of science, although more confused notions also emerge.

The problem of the notion of science as it is expressed today seems to have arisen in the following way over the centuries. Newton in his theory of mechanics was the first to conceive the modern systematization of science. This sort of science, as concretely conceived and empirically established, had a very great influence upon the Kantian critique. Kant's 'pure reason' is the ideal of science taken from Aristotle, but as conceived by Scotus and given currency by Ockham – science as being about the necessary and the universal, a conceptual notion of science easily elaborated from a super-

'ratio pura' quam Kant reiecit, insufficientiam agnoscens illius ad aliquam realitatem cognoscendam. Nam, ex processu logico, ex puris notionibus, ex coniunctione notionum et deductione ex notionbibus ... impossibilis fit transitus ad mundum exsistentem. Applicatio huiusmodi scientiae ad mundum realem requirit Scotisticam intuitionem mundi exsistentis et praesentis, qua exsistentis et qua praesentis.

Pro Aristotele, intellectus videt formam intelligibilem (*eidos*) in sensibilibus. Scotus reicit hanc conceptionem, dicens: aut forma intelligibilis iam adest in sensibilibus aut non. Si adest, est forma sensibilis, non intelligibilis; si non adest, intellectus videt in sensibilibus illud quod non adest; unde cognitio intellectualis est falsa.

Praeterquam excludat intelligentiam in phantasmatibus, Scotus praetermittit etiam alium actum intelligendi reflexum, seu affirmationem per verbum 'est.' Intuitio Scotistica vult surrogatum esse sive pro iudicio sive pro intelligentia in sensibili. Sic intelligentia duplici via separata a realitate, oritur essentialismus intermedius quem Kant optimo reicit iure.

Ut mundum realem possit cognoscere, Kant ponit sive impressiones (quas a Locke et Hume acceperat), sive formas sensibilitatis, sive categorias intellectus. Ex his tribus construit intelligentiam atque cognitionem scientifico-obiectivam mundi secundum typum Newtonianum, vere scientificam quamvis in campo pure phaenomenali. Omnia illa autem quae ex philosophia traditionali habebantur sive de Deo sive de alio assignantur a Kant ad rationem practicam, quae plus minusve correspondet voluntarismo Scotistico.

Id tamen quod facit differentiam nostrae aetatis a saeculo xix est cogitatio ad modum Bergson, quae reicit cognitionem intellectualem Kantianam. Pro Bergson, scientiae empiricae non pertinent ad intellectum purum; nec sunt vere cognoscitivae, sed pertinent ad rationem practicam; non cognoscunt aliquam sectionem illegitimam realitatis, quae de se est fluens, nec potest categoriis scientificis secari. Utilitarismus scientiae opponitur veritati vitae. Reiecto tamen eo quod apud Kant ad scientiam pertinebat, id quod apud illum pertinebat ad hominem confunditur cum fide et voluntate, unde mundo obiectivo relicto relinquimur et claudimur in subiecto. Inde influxus phaenomenologiae Husserlianae, atque philosophiae Max Scheler et variorum existentialistarum. Bene perspicitur, hoc modo, quantus sit influxus evolutionis notionis scientiae in philosophia.

Ex altera autem parte, inter scholasticos philosophi et theologi generatim

ficial knowledge of the science of logic. This was the true 'pure reason' rejected by Kant, who recognized that it was insufficient for attaining any knowledge of reality. For through a logical process, from pure notions, from the linking of notions and deduction from notions it is quite impossible to get to the world as existing. To apply this sort of science to the real world requires the Scotist intuition of the existing and present world as existing and as present.

For Aristotle, the intellect sees the intelligible form, *eidos*, in the data of sense. But Scotus rejects this conception, as follows: intelligible form is either already present in sensible data or it is not; if it is, it is a sensible, not an intelligible, form; if it is not, then the intellect sees in sensible data that which is not present in them; therefore, intellectual knowledge is false.

Besides rejecting insight into phantasms, Scotus also overlooks another act of understanding, the reflective, and so affirmation by the word *is*. Scotist intuition purports to be a substitute both for judgment and for insight into sensible data. Understanding is thus twice removed from reality; essentialism arises to fill the gap and is very properly rejected by Kant.

To be able to know the real world, Kant posits impressions (accepted also by Locke and Hume), forms of sensibility, and intellectual categories. Out of these three elements he constructs a Newtonian type of scientific-objective understanding and knowledge of the world, one that is truly scientific although limited to the field of the purely phenomenal. Everything else that used to be found in traditional philosophy, whether about God or about anything else, Kant assigns to practical reason, which roughly corresponds to Scotist voluntarism.

What differentiates our age from the nineteenth century is Bergsonian thought, which rejects the Kantian concept of intellectual knowledge. For Bergson, the empirical sciences do not belong to pure intellect, nor are they truly cognitive, but they belong rather to practical reason; they afford a knowledge of only a certain illegitimate sector of reality, which by its very nature is in a state of flux and cannot be parceled into scientific categories. Utilitarianism in science is opposed to truth in life. With the rejection of Kant's philosophy regarding science, his philosophy regarding man is confused with faith and will, so that, having forsaken the objective world, we remain imprisoned in the subject. Hence, the influence of Husserl's phenomenology, the philosophy of Max Scheler, and various existentialists. Thus, we can clearly see how influential in philosophy has been the evolving notion of science.

On the other hand, Scholastic philosophers and theologians, generally

nullam aliam scientiam cognoscunt nisi philosophiam et theologiam, unde non directe subsunt influxui evolutionis notionis scientiae. Datur tamen conflictus inter philosophiam perennem et scientias naturales; maior etiam inter philosophiam perennem et scientias humanas, praesertim historiam religionum, litterariam ... quae etiam libros sacros comprehendunt. Unde oritur problema conciliandi studium scientificum sacrae scripturae et notionem scientiae.

Haec est forma concreta sub qua, hodie, urgetur problema methodologicum. Agitur de problemate chasmatis inter investigationem historicam et litterariam circa litteras sacras, ex una parte secundum evolutam notionem scientiae peragendam et ex alia parte illam notionem scientiae quae habetur apud philosophos et theologos scholasticos, quae efformata est potius secundum initiale ideale quam ex concreta evolutione praxis scientificae.

[3] Dedimus, deinde, quasdam regulas methodicas, scientiam in genere spectantes. Non theoretice locuti sumus de theologia ut scientia. Analogiam secundum quam theologia est scientia potius determinavimus ex adaptatione regularum generalium ad materiam theologicam. Si abstracte scientia consideretur, possunt dari de ea variae definitiones. Concrete autem dari possunt regulae quae diversis temporibus sensum pleniorem acquirere possunt quin tamen amittant sensum fundamentalem.

Nam actus intelligendi est aliquid homini naturale (prima regula), atque modus intelligendi dicit differentiam inter cognitionem scientificam et alios modos cognoscendi (secunda regula). Praeterea homo non est aliquid ad unum determinatum. Sicut adest philosophia perennis, ita adsunt perennes philosophiae contradictoriae: perennis materialismus, positivismus, pragmatismus, phaenomenalismus. Inter has duas positiones habetur etiam intermedia positio idealistica. Quia homo est polymorphicus, potest se formare atque vivere modis diversis et sese exprimere diversis temporibus, modo diverso, ex his philosophicis tendentiis fundamentalibus quae semper eaedem manent.

Contrapositiones habentur quatenus id quod scientifice intellligitur proponitur sub aliqua ex his tendentiis sat perennibus, at erronea. Etiam qui nullo modo intelligit Aristotelem et S. Thomam potest mira inventa scientifica invenire; at quando exprimit illud quod invenit, magis apparet fundamentale elementum non scientificum sed philosophicum suae mentalitati

speaking, know no other science except philosophy and theology, and so are not directly influenced by the evolving notion of science. Nevertheless, there is a conflict between perennial philosophy and the natural sciences, and an even greater conflict between perennial philosophy and the human sciences, especially the history of religions and literary criticism, which also include the biblical writings in their subject matter. Hence, there arises the problem of reconciling the study of sacred scripture with the notion of science.

It is in this concrete form that the methodological problem is so pressing today. It involves the problem of the gap, the chasm between, on the one hand, the historical and literary investigation of the bible in accordance with the ongoing development of the notion of science and, on the other hand, the notion of science had by Scholastic philosophers and theologians, which owes more to the initial ideal of science than to the concrete development of scientific practice.

[3] Next, we have given some rules of method regarding science in general. We have not spoken about theology as a science in a merely theoretical way; rather, we have determined the analogy by which theology is a science by adapting these general rules to the subject matter of theology. If science is considered abstractly, it can be given a variety of definitions. Concretely, however, there are rules that at different times can become more meaningful, yet without losing their basic meaning.

The act of understanding is something natural to man (first rule), and the mode of understanding refers to the difference between scientific thinking and other modes of knowing (second rule). Furthermore, we are not beings that are already programmed. Just as there is a 'perennial philosophy,' so there are contradictory perennial philosophies: a perennial materialism, a perennial positivism, a perennial pragmatism, a perennial phenomenology. Between these two positions there is also the intermediate position of idealism. Since humans are polymorphic, they can shape themselves and their life in different ways, and can express themselves in various ways at different times by way of these basic philosophical tendencies, which themselves remain the same.

Counterpositions are had when that which is understood scientifically is proposed under one of these perennial tendencies, but an erroneous one. Even those who do not know anything of Aristotle or St Thomas can make many wonderful scientific discoveries; but when they express what they have discovered, a fundamental element, not scientific but philosophical,

subiacens, unde habetur mixtio veritatis et falsitatis. Unde necessitas inver-
tendi contrapositiones (tertia regula).

Homo est in genere intelligibilium non ut actus sed ut potentia. Unde
tempore augetur intelligentia humana et semper meliora inventa scientifica sunt possibilia; quare positiones sunt evolvendae (quarta regula), atque
in theologia oritur necessitas considerationis historicae.

Quia demum mens humana est spiritualis, nulla methodus mechanica
nec collectio regularum et praeceptorum poterit esse surrogatum pro usu
boni iudicii. Quatenus hic usus negatur, habentur fundamentales aberrationes.

Quoad historiam specialem, vidimus tantum eum qui peritus sit in scientia speciali posse illius historiam conficere. In historia theologiae attendimus praesertim ad puncta transitionis, quae eminent propter controversias diuturnas et acerrimas. Illis attendendum est quia ibi habetur
nexus concretus historicus inter modum cogitandi systematicum et priores
symbolicum, intersubiectivum, vulgarem. In his punctis habetur, atque ad
illa attendendo possumus empirice determinare, quid significet illud 'implicite' quod invenimus in problemate fundamenti.

Notiones quibus utitur Symbolum Athanasianum (saec. v: persona, substantia, subsistens, conversio, assumptio, confusio, anima rationalis) non
inveniuntur in Symbolo Constantinopolitano (a. 381), in quo explicite non
dicitur Spiritum Sanctum esse Deum sed tantum illum esse Dominum, vivi-
ficantem, ex Patre procedentem, cum Patre et Filio adorandum et conglo-
rificandum, locutum per Prophetas. In Symbolo autem Nicaeno (a. 325)
ne haec quidem habentur de Spiritu. Clare exprimitur divinitas Filii, sed
de Spiritu non dicitur quid credamus. Quae demum non inveniuntur in
Symbolo Apostolico, quod modum loquendi adhibet Evangeliorum.

Quid significat ergo illud 'implicite'?
Si determinationem empiricam quaerimus, investigandus est transitus
factus, v.gr., in IV saecula, qui inde a II et a III praeparabatur. Similiter de
transitu circa unitatem Christi Dei et hominis, facto saec. V, et de aliis.

Si determinationem theoreticam quaerimus, explicite cognoscere id
quod antea implicitum erat significat exprimere, cogitare, et apprehende-
re modo magis systematico id quod antea modo non systematico cogno-

underlying their mentality comes to light, giving rise to a mixture of truth and falsity. Hence the necessity of reversing counterpositions (third rule).

In the genus of the intelligible, man is in potency, not in act. This is why human understanding grows, and why ever greater scientific discoveries are possible. Positions, therefore, must be developed (fourth rule), and in theology there arises the need for considering its subject matter historically.

Finally, since the human mind is spiritual, no mechanical method or set of rules and precepts can take the place of using one's good judgment. Denial of its use results in some fundamental aberrations.

In the case of a specialized history, we have seen that only one who is an expert in that special field is capable of writing its history. In the case of the history of theology, we paid special attention to the turning points that stand out by reason of the long and bitter controversies that have occurred. These junctures deserve most careful attention, for there one will find the concrete historical link between the systematic mode of thinking and earlier symbolic, intersubjective, and commonsense modes. By attending to them we can empirically determine the meaning of the word 'implicitly' that we noted in the problem of foundation.

Notions used in the fifth-century Athanasian Creed – person, substance, subsistent, conversion, assumption, confusion, rational soul – are not found in the Constantinopolitan Creed of 381, in which there is no explicit statement that the Holy Spirit is God but only that he is Lord, is Life-Giver, proceeds from the Father, is to be adored along with the Father and the Son, and has spoken through the prophets. And in the Nicene Creed, in 325, not even these statements are made about the Spirit; it clearly states the divinity of the Son, but does not say what we are to believe about the Spirit. And these are not mentioned at all in the Apostles' Creed, which uses the terminology of the Gospels.

What, then, does 'implicitly' mean?

If we are looking for an empirical determination of its meaning, we must investigate the transition that occurred, for example, in the fourth century, whose way was prepared during the two previous centuries; or again, the transition concerning the unity of Christ, God and man, that occurred in the fifth century, and similarly for other transitions.

If we are looking for a theoretical determination of its meaning, we say that to know explicitly what was previously implicit means to express, to think about, and to apprehend in a more systematic way that which was

scebatur et apprehendebatur, sed symbolico, intersubiectivo, intelligentiae vulgaris proprio.

Unde punctum centrale problematis historicitatis invenitur empirice in punctis crucialibus horum transituum; theoretice autem in motu ex modo cogitandi non systematico ad modum cogitandi systematicum.

De theologia positiva atque speculativa tractantes, vidimus theologiam positivam esse theologiam speculativam in fieri, speculativam esse theologiam positivam in facto esse.

Tamen difficultas adest ex modo proponendi theologiam in manualibus. Finis manualium simul est scientificum et paedagogicum, qui fines conflictum admittunt inter se. Caeterum huiusmodi modus manualia conficiendi ortus est in ecclesia tantum a saec. XVIII. Difficultas est in tractando systematice de diversis ordinationibus responsionum sive scripturisticis, sive patristicis, sive conciliaribus, sive theologicis … simul in unaquaque thesi, secundum divisionem illarum thesium. Unde problema practicum, quomodo docendum, quomodo examinandum …, et problema scientificum, quomodo coniungenda cognitio systematica et historica. Quibus problematibus nondum inventa est solutio.

Sic problemati chasmatis nulla solutio datur si, facto transitu ex uno modo apprehendendi ad alium, iam non fit reditus ad primum; aliter, si modus apprehendendi systematicus intime connectitur cum modo intersubiectivo.

Fundamentum autem nullum aliud est nisi fides in Deo revelante, fides in Deo ecclesiam conservante. Tamen, quatenus theologus ultra procedit in intelligentia fidei, quaerere non debet mechanismum aliquem in quo fiduciam reponat, sed et divinae gratiae lumen implorare atque iudicii proprii responsabilitatem assumere.[147]

227 Understanding and Method

previously known and apprehended not in the systematic way but in the symbolic, intersubjective, commonsense way.

Hence, the crux of the problem of historicity is to be found empirically in the crucial points and theoretically in the movement from a non-systematic to a systematic way of thinking.

As to the question about positive theology and speculative theology, we have seen that positive theology is speculative theology-in-process, and speculative theology is positive theology reaching its end product.

Still, there is a problem with the way the manuals present theology. The aim of the manuals is at one and the same time scientific and pedagogical, and there can be a conflict between these two. Besides, the way in which these manuals were composed in the church dates only from the eighteenth century. The difficulty lies in systematically treating different orderings of answers, the scriptural, patristic, conciliar, and theological, all together in each thesis, according to the way in which these theses are divided. Hence, we have a practical problem, how to teach, how to examine, and so on, and a scientific problem, how to bring together systematic and historical knowledge. So far no solution to these problems has been found.

Thus, there is no solution either to the problem of the chasm if, having made the transition from one mode of apprehension to the other, one no longer returns to the first one; but there is if one sees the close connection between the systematic and the intersubjective modes of apprehension.

There is, however, no other foundation save that of faith in God as revealer and as the preserver of the church. Nevertheless, as theologians make further progress in their understanding of the faith, they must not seek any sort of mechanical method to rely upon, but rather beg for the light of God's grace and accept responsibility for making their own judgments.[147]

147 [Lonergan taught 'De intellectu et methodo' again two years later, in the spring semester of 1961. His handwritten notes for the 1961 course may be found on the website www.bernardlonergan.com, beginning (probably) at 43300DOL060 and extending to 44900DOL060. Transcriptions by Robert M. Doran are also available on the site, accompanying Lonergan's notes. Chapter 4 of the current volume contains a brief report on, or synopsis of, new material in these notes. It would seem from an indication in 44900DOL060 that Lonergan may have distributed the 1959 notes to the 1961 students, or at least that he worked from them in his lectures, as his handwritten notes for 1961 refer to 'page 18,' and it is on p. 18 of the original version of the present notes that the material that he was treating at that point in 1961 was first handled in 1959. The same tripartite division that is indicated in the 'Conclusion' of the present document seems to have been followed in

1961. (Actually, the notes drawn up by Lonergan's students have four main divisions: the notion of question, the notion of science, the two modes of thought, and the precepts of method.) One development is the influence that came from Lonergan's reading of a book published in 1960 and later reviewed by Lonergan in *Gregorianum* in 1963, *La crise de la raison dans la pensée contemporaine*, with essays by Edmond Barbotin, Jean Trouillard, Roger Verneaux, Dominique Dubarle, and Stanislas Breton (Bruges: Desclée de Brouwer, 1960). Lonergan's review of the book, first published in *Gregorianum* 44 (1963) 372–73, may be found in Bernard Lonergan, *Shorter Papers*, vol. 20 in Collected Works of Bernard Lonergan, ed. Robert C. Croken, Robert M. Doran, and H. Daniel Monsour (Toronto: University of Toronto Press, 2007) 234–36. Lonergan mentioned the book again in the lectures on method at Georgetown in 1964, as is evident from p. 390 in Lonergan, *Early Works on Theological Method 1*, vol. 22 in Collected Works of Bernard Lonergan, ed. Robert M. Doran and Robert C. Croken (Toronto: University of Toronto Press, 2010) 390. There are also references in the 1963 courses 'De methodo theologiae' reconstructed in volume 24, *Early Works on Theological Method 3*. The influence of this book seems clearly related to the emphasis on the 'Ideal of Reason' in the 1961 notes. However, that emphasis is also prefigured in earlier lectures, such as the 1957 lectures on mathematical logic and the 1958 lectures that became *Understanding and Being*. This emphasis on the ideal of reason in terms of functionally operative and related tendencies immanent in the subject appeals to a language that is not to the fore in the 1959 notes, though the ideas are certainly prefigured in the discussion of wisdom (to say nothing of *Insight*). The language itself perhaps emerges in the emphasis on the fundamental circle of operations in the notes on 'System and History.' See below, chapters 2 and 3.]

De Systemate et Historia[1]

1 Introducitur quaestio

1 S. Thomas, *Sum. theol.*, 1, 1, 2, quaerit utrum sacra doctrina sit scientia.

Et videtur quod non, secundo loco, quia scientia non est singularium, sed sacra doctrina est singularium, puta, rerum gestarum ab Abraham, Isaac, et Iacob.

Respondet tamen sacram doctrinam esse scientiam sed subalternatam quae principia ab alia scientia accipit, nempe, a Deo revelante.

Ad secundum dicit sacram doctrinam tractare de singularibus quidem sed non quasi de principali. Adducit Abraham, Isaac, Iacob (1) per modum exemplorum uti in moralibus, (2) ad confirmandam auctoritatem eorum per quos nobis divina revelatio facta est.

System and History[1]

1   Introducing the Question

1 St Thomas Aquinas, *Summa theologiae*, 1, q. 1, a. 2, asks whether theology is a science.

Proceeding in his usual manner, he states two arguments for the negative reply to this question, the second of which is that science is not about singular instances, whereas theology is, such as, for example, the deeds done by Abraham, Isaac, and Jacob.

Next, to the question itself, he first responds affirmatively that theology is truly a science, though subalternate, or derivative, that is, one whose principles are taken from another knowledge, namely, from God who reveals.

Then to the above negative argument he replies that theology does deal with singular instances, but not as its principal concern, and that Abraham, Isaac, and Jacob are mentioned (1) as providing examples, as in matters of conduct, and (2) as confirming the authority of those persons through whom God's revelation has been communicated to us.

---

1 [This material is found in the Lonergan Archive, A 485 – A 488, and on the website www.bernardlonergan.com at 48500DTL050 – 48800DTL050. Lonergan's course 'De Systemate et Historia' was offered in the fall semester of 1959, and so in the semester following the first offering of 'De Intellectu et Methodo.' This course also followed the summer lectures on education now available in vol. 10 of the Collected Works (see below, note 34). In those lectures extensive reference was made to Piaget, and Piaget influences what

2 Contra hoc responsum obicitur quod mentalitati graecae inhaeret et menti modernae alienum est. Constat enim in VT Deum concipi, non systematice, metaphysice, sed historice.[2] Deus est *is qui* est Deus Abraham, Isaac, et Iacob et patrum nostrorum, *is qui* brachio extento nos eduxit de Aegypto, *is qui* in monte Sinae foedus cum populo inivit, *is qui* dedit terram Chanaan, constituit iudices et reges, misit prophetas, promisit venturum messiam. Constat in NT Iesum Christum esse hominem singularem, passum, mortuum pro peccatis nostris, resurrectum, qui misit Spiritum sanctum in apostolos singulares homines, qui iterum venturus est iudicare vivos et mortuos. Constat ecclesiam esse coetum quendam singularem, apostolicum, traditionalem, historicum, qui docet et sanctificat homines singulares et historicos.

3 Quod si quaeritur cur haec a S. Thoma praetermitti videantur, etiam

2 To this reply by St Thomas the objection is made that it reflects a classical Greek mentality that is foreign to the modern mind. There is general agreement that in the Old Testament God is conceived not in a systematic or metaphysical way, but historically.[2] God is *he who* is the God of Abraham, Isaac, and Jacob, the God of our fathers, *he who* with his outstretched arm brought us out of the land of Egypt, *he who* entered into a covenant with his people on Mount Sinai, *he who* gave them the land of Canaan, set up judges and kings, sent the prophets, and promised a coming Messiah. It is likewise clear that in the New Testament Jesus is an individual man who suffered and died for our sins, was raised up, sent the Holy Spirit upon the Apostles, who also are individuals, and who will come again to judge the living and the dead. Finally, it is clear that the church is a singular group or community, apostolic in its origin, traditional and historical, whose mission it is to teach and sanctify individual historical persons.

3 If one asks why St Thomas seems to ignore all these singular instances,

is possibly the central notion of the present notes, namely, the notion of the circle of operations.

The notes contained here reproduce typed pages prepared for or related to the course. These pages appear in the midst of a number of additional handwritten notes relevant to this course found on the same website beginning at 47600DOE050 and ending at 50200DOE050. The typed notes for the first four sections, all of which constitute 48500DTL050, represent the introductory material in the course: handwritten notes of a student in the course, Francisco Rossi de Gasperis, s.j. (notes available at the Lonergan Research Institute, Toronto), confirm this. The other sections contained in this chapter did not follow immediately and in order; some of the materials that did follow those four sections are found in the handwritten notes; nonetheless, the decision has been made to reproduce the typed notes in one chapter with Latin and English facing pagers, and to provide reports and partial translations on the handwritten notes (some of which are in English and some in Latin, and all of which are schematic) in the next chapter. It remains for some future researcher to reconstruct the course from the notes that are provided in these two chapters.

Some of the topics discussed in this document are also mentioned in a lecture Lonergan gave at the Thomas More Institute, Montreal, a few months later, on 23 September 1960, in the course 'The Philosophy of History.' The lecture is now published as 'The Philosophy of History,' in Bernard Lonergan, *Philosophical and Theological Papers 1958–1964* 53–79. As with the chapter 1 notes, so here, material that appears without brackets is found in the text, whereas bracketed material is editorial.]

2 See the writings of Gerhard von Rad and G.E. Wright. [Lonergan adds their names by hand.]

sat prompte responderi solet: notionem de scientia quam elaboraverunt philosophi et mathematici graeci ulteriori quadam evolutione indigere ut non solum abstracta, statica, generalia tractentur sed etiam concreta, dynamica, individualia; ad normam mentis graecae S. Thomam concepisse theologiam uti scientiam; iam vero mens graeca, quamvis suo tempore magnum quoddam atque eximium opus fecerit, hodie tamen obsoleta est. Sicut dicit Apostolus (1 Cor 13.11) 'cum essem parvulus, loquebar ut parvulus, sapiebam ut parvulus, cogitabam ut parvulus, quando autem factus sum vir, evacuavi quae erant parvuli.'

4 Quibus positis, ad generalem nostram quaestionem propius accedimus. Non enim hoc in cursu investigamus articulum quendam a S Thoma conscriptum de theologia uti scientia, sed generalem quaestionem movemus quae in illa oppositione conspicitur quae inter mentem graecam et modernam, scientiam graecam et modernam, saepius exprimitur. Quae quidem quaestio pro theologo vel philosopho catholico momentum quoddam speciale habet. Qui enim extra ecclesiam versantur, mentem et scientiam graecam esse obsoletam facillime concedunt; sed quod ita ab iis conceditur, non ita a nobis concedi potest. Quamvis enim ecclesia laudet studia scientiasque modernas, quamvis facultatem historiae, institutum sociale, institutum biblicum habeamus, quamvis ipsae facultates philosophica et theologica disciplinis auxiliaribus iisque permultis ornentur, manent tamen dogmata trinitaria et christologica mentalitate graeca exarata, et manent in ipsis disciplinis principalibus secundum praeceptum iuris canonici doctrina, principia, ratio docendi a S. Thoma olim adhibita.[3] Non ergo possumus ita accipere moderna ut antiqua habeamus ut penitus obsoleta. Neque ita antiqua possumus retinere ut disciplinas auxiliares et instituta specialia ab ecclesia approbatas spernamus.

5 Si tamen omnino clarum est nobis laudanda atque retinenda esse tam antiqua quam moderna, longe minus clarum est quemadmodum hoc fieri possit. Nullo sane negotio in catalogo eiusdem universitatis enumerantur atque praescribuntur et aliae scientiae modo antiquo conceptae et aliae

the ready answer generally given is that the concept of science developed by Greek philosophers and mathematicians needs further development in order to handle not only what is abstract, static, and general, but also what is concrete, dynamic, and individual. St Thomas conceived of theology as a science according to the Greek way of thinking. Greek thought, however, although in its day a magnificent piece of work, is now obsolete. As St Paul put it, 'When I was a child I spoke like a child, I thought like a child, I reasoned like a child; when I became an adult, I put an end to childish ways' (1 Corinthians 13.11).

4 Accordingly, we can now examine more closely the general question before us. In this course we are not investigating a particular article by St Thomas on theology as a science; rather, we are addressing the general question that arises out of the opposition so often noted between the classical Greek and the modern mentality, between Greek science and modern science. This question is of special importance for the Catholic philosopher or theologian; for whereas non-Catholics can readily grant that the Greek mentality and Greek science are *passé*, we cannot so easily do so. Although the church commends modern studies and modern sciences, although we have a department of history, a social institute, and a biblical institute, and although our faculties of philosophy and theology are enriched by a variety of auxiliary disciplines, nevertheless we still have the trinitarian and Christological dogmas that have been shaped by the Greek mentality, and in accordance with Canon Law we still follow the teaching, the principles, and the method used long ago by St Thomas.[3] In accepting the modern, therefore, we cannot reject the classical mind as totally out of date; nor on the other hand can we so cling to the classical as to discount those auxiliary disciplines and special institutes approved by the church.

5 If it is quite clear, then, that we must appreciate and retain both the classical and the modern, it is much less clear how this is to be done. It is certainly quite easy for the same university to list in its calendar and offer courses in sciences conceived along classical lines together with those that

---

3 [Lonergan has in mind canon 1366, §2 of the 1917 revision of the *Code of Canon Law*. Canon 252, §3 of the most recent revision of the *Codex Iuris Canonici* has the following, comparatively weaker admonition: 'There are to be classes in dogmatic theology, always grounded in the written word of God together with sacred tradition; through these, students are to learn to penetrate more intimately the mysteries of salvation, especially with St Thomas as a teacher.']

spiritu moderno imbutae. Sed difficilius multi et diversi professores cohaerenter et consentanee docent; et longe difficilius ipsi alumni illam synthesin perficiunt quam neque ipsa universitas neque eiusdem professores
perfecerunt.

6 Quibus dictis, quale sit consilium nostrum forte videtis. Ideo enim de
systemate et historia quaerimus, ut oppositio illa dialectica inter mentem
graecam et modernam superetur. In multis sane inter se differunt parvulus
et vir; tamen idem qui erat parvulus iam est vir. Et similiter ideale illud scientificum quod a graecis formatum est et a modernis ulterius elaboratum,
propriam quandam unitatem habet quae qualis sit inquirendum est.

Generaliora sunt quae dixi; ut clarius et exactius problema perspiciatur,
quaedam addenda sunt de mente graeca, de moderna, de historicismo.[4]

2   Mentalitas Graeca

1 Obiectum scientiae est aeternum, necessarium (Aristoteles), abstractum.
   Primo aspectu Euclides in rebus practicis versari videtur: puncta coniungit, lineas producit, circulos describit. Sed re vera exemplis sensibilibus
aeternas veritates atque necessarias exponere intendit. Quod etiam hodie
a Husserl propositum est: 'Philosophie als strenge Wissenschaft.'[5] Scientia
est de essentiis; subiectum est ab omni elemento contingenti purificandum.

2 Motus sicut a realitate ita a cognoscibilitate deficit. Unumquodque cognoscitur secundum quod est actu. Motus est actus exsistentis in potentia
inquantum huiusmodi; est via ad ens, esse incompletum, in categoriis ubi,

are inspired by modern thought. But it is more difficult for professors of these different subjects to be consistent in their teaching and for many different professors to agree among themselves as to what to teach. And it is far more difficult still for the students themselves to arrive at a synthesis when neither the university nor its professors have been able to do so.

6 From the foregoing you may perhaps have gathered how we plan to proceed. We shall inquire into the nature of system and history so that the dialectical opposition between the classical and the modern mind may be transcended. A child and an adult are certainly different in many respects; yet the adult is the same person who was once a child. In similar fashion, the scientific ideal instituted by the Greeks and further elaborated by the moderns has its own proper unity; our task is to investigate the nature of that unity.

So far we have been speaking in general terms. Now we must add something about the Greek mentality, the modern mentality, and historicism, so as to have a clearer and more accurate grasp of the problem.[4]

2   The Greek Mentality

1 The object of science is the eternal, the necessary (Aristotle), the abstract.

At first glance Euclid seems to be dealing with practical matters: he joins points, draws lines, describes circles. But in fact he intended to demonstrate eternal and necessary verities through visible examples. This view of science has also been proposed in our own day by Husserl in 'Philosophie als strenge Wissenschaft.'[5] Science is of essences; its subject-matter is to be purged of every contingent element.

2 Motion or change falls short of full reality and therefore also of intelligibility. Everything is known inasmuch as it is in act. Motion is an act of a being in potency insofar as it is in potency; it is on the way to being, an

---

4 [This paragraph was written in hand in the manuscript by Lonergan.]
5 Edmund Husserl, 'Philosophie als strenge Wissenschaft,' *Logos: International Zeitschrift für Philosophie der Kultur* 1:3 (1910–11) 289–341. French translation, *La philosophie comme science rigoureuse*, trans. Quentin Lauer (Paris: Presses universitaires de France, 1955). English translation, also by Quentin Lauer, 'Philosophy as a Strict Science,' *Cross Currents* 6:3 (1956) 227–46 and 6:4 (1956) 325–44; [more recently, 'Philosophy as Rigorous Science,' in Edmund Husserl, *Phenomenology and the Crisis of Philosophy*, trans. with notes and an intro. by Quentin Lauer (New York: Harper & Row, 1965) 71–147.]

quale, quantum. Quod modo inverso a Bergson docetur: scilicet intellectum humanum esse incapacem cognoscendi realitatem; reale enim esse fluens; intellectum esse schematicum.[6]

3 Graeci et Romani historias composuerunt; Thucydides et Polybius explicant methodum a se adhibitam; caeteri indicationes methodologicas introducunt et supposita philosophica et moralia. Deest tamen apud eos logica seu methodologia historiae quae comparari potest cum *Post. Anal.* circa scientiam, philosophia historiae quae comparari potest cum philosophia naturae, philosophia hominis, philosophia societatis quas elaboraverunt.[7]

At Cartesius explicite exclusit methodum historiae quando conscripsit *Discours sur la méthode.* Kant non inclusit possibilitatem historiae in theoria sua transcendentali de possibilitate scientiae.[8] Usque ad Leibniz per auctores innumeros inculcatur historiam esse principaliter ad docendam prudentiam et virtutem et ad vitia eo modo exponenda ut homines ab eis verterentur et retraherentur.[9]

Similiter, scientiae humanae erant, non empiricae, sicut oeconomia, sociologia, psychologia moderna, sed philosophicae et normativae, non de hominibus qui sunt, sed de eo quod vel est vel esse debet ex ipsa rei natura. Similiter, artes liberales et litterae humaniores exemplis classicis regebantur, quasi in iis semel pro semper aeterna exemplaria locum et tempus et incarnationem acceperunt.

incomplete act of existence in the categories of place, quality, or quantity. This is also what Bergson holds, but in the opposite way, namely, that the human intellect is incapable of knowing reality, since the real is in constant flux, and understanding is schematic.[6]

3 The Greeks and the Romans wrote histories. Thucydides and Polybius explain the method they use, and the other historians give indications of their methodology and state their philosophic and moral presuppositions. Nevertheless, they lack a logic or methodology of history comparable to the *Posterior Analytics* with respect to science, and a philosophy of history comparable to the philosophy of nature, of man, and of society that the ancients worked out.[7]

But Descartes explicitly excluded a method of history when he wrote *Discours sur la méthode*. Nor did Kant include the possibility of history in his transcendental theory of the possibility of science.[8] Down to the time of Leibniz [1646–1716] countless writers taught that the function of history was principally to inculcate practical wisdom and virtue, and to treat of vices in such a way as to deter and dissuade people from them.[9]

Similarly, the human sciences were not empirical like economics, sociology, and modern psychology, but were philosophical and normative, concerned not with human beings as they actually are, but with what either is or ought to be from their very nature. In the same way, classical examples were the supreme norm governing the liberal arts and humanities, as if in them eternal exemplars were once for all incarnated in place and time.

6 [See above, p. 85 and note 67, and p. 221.]
7 [The comparison between the reflections of Thucydides and Polybius on historical method and the worked-out methodology of Aristotle's *Posterior Analytics* can also be found near the beginning of the section on Historicism below. The source of the comparison is indicated there. See p. 275.]
8 [Lonergan may be drawing here on R.G. Collingwood, *The Idea of History* (Oxford: Oxford University Press, paperback ed., 1956). Collingwood discusses Descartes's attitude to history on pp. 59–61, and Kant's on pp. 93–104.]
9 Gottfried Wilhelm Leibniz, *Theodicy: Essays on the Goodness of God, the Freedom of Man and the Origin of Evil*, ed. Austin Farrer, trans. E.M. Huggard (London: Routledge & Kegan Paul, 1951) 217: ['The chief end of history, as also of poetry, should be to teach prudence and virtue by examples, and then to display vice in such a way as to create aversion to it and to prompt men to avoid it, or serve towards that end.']

3   Mentalitas Moderna

1 Obiectum scientiae esse videtur mobile qua mobile, ut scilicet rerum intelligibilitas non in statico motus termino sed intra ipsum motum quaeratur et inveniatur: (a) mathematica: calculus, series infinita, numeri transfiniti, inductiones transfinitae; (b) physica: isomorphica cum mathematica; (c) biologia: evolutio, non per modum particularis cuiusdam hypotheseos, sed per modum principii classificationis et explicationis; (d) scientiae humanae empiricae: non de homine prout est vel esse debet ex ipsa natura rei, puta in statu naturae purae, sed de hominibus prout de facto revelantur observatione, experimento, investigatione statistica, narratione historica. Qui homo concretus in omnibus evolvi invenitur: religio, familia, artes techicae et liberales, linguae, litterae humaniores, status, gubernia, leges, iura, oeconomia, doctrinae, opiniones, scientiae, philosophiae, theologiae, dogmata.

2 Mobilitas obiecti in ipsam cognitionem transire videtur: (a) mathematica, hypothetico-deductiva, et novae hypotheses eaeque generaliores semper fieri possunt; (b) scientiae naturales non certa rerum cognitio sed successio theoriarum semper magis probabilium; (c) scientiae humanae, loco definitionis ponitur historia evolutionis. Quid capitalismus? Aliud et aliud diversis locis et temporibus; neque utiliter de abstracta quadam ratione, quae omni et soli convenit, disputatur; ipsa res in concreta sua evolutione perspicienda est. Et similiter de caeteris omnibus. Loco consultationis rationum aeternarum, vel ipsius rei naturae, iudicatur secundum ipsam rei evolutionem intime cognitam utrum in bonum semper maius procedat an in sui ipsius destructionem pergat.

(d) Quod si urgetur tales scientias relativismum sapere, ipsi scientifici vel quaestionem philosophis relinquunt, vel responsum ex ulteriori progressu scientifico sperant; ipsi autem philosophi in multas et diversas partes abeunt, quae quales sint haud dicitur nisi evolutionem philosophicam describendo.[10]

3   The Modern Mentality

1 The object of science seems to be the changeable as such, so that the intelligibility of things is to be sought and found not in the static term of a movement but within that movement itself: (a) in mathematics: calculus, infinite series, transfinite numbers, transfinite inductions; (b) in physics, isomorphic with mathematics; (c) in biology: evolution, not as a particular hypothesis but as a principle of classification and explanation; (d) in the empirical human sciences, which are not about humanity as it is or ought to be by nature, such as would be in a state of 'pure nature,' but about people as they in fact come to be known through observation, experimentation, statistical investigation, and historical narration. Human beings in their concreteness are found to be undergoing development in every respect: in their religion, family life, technical and liberal arts, language, literature, polity, government, laws, juridical systems, economic structures, doctrines, opinions, sciences, philosophies, theologies, dogmas.

2 This mobility or changeableness of the object seems to have entered into knowledge itself: (a) mathematics is hypothetico-deductive, and new and more general hypotheses can always be formed; (b) the natural sciences give not the certain knowledge of things but a succession of increasingly probable theories; (c) in the human sciences, instead of a statement of their definition, the history of their development is given. For example, What is capitalism? It is different in different times and places. Nor is it helpful to discuss it in terms of some abstract essential meaning that applies to all capitalism and only to capitalism; rather, the thing itself is to be grasped in its concrete development. And the same holds for everything else. It is on the basis of a thorough knowledge of something's development, rather than by consulting eternal reasons or the nature of a thing itself, that a judgment is made whether that development is for its betterment or tends rather towards its destruction.

(d) Now if the charge is made that such sciences smack of relativism, scientists either refer the question to philosophers or hope for further progress in science to answer it; but philosophers themselves are divided into different camps, the nature of which can be determined only by describing philosophic development.[10]

10 [The material from 'quae quales sint' on was added by hand.]

4   Conceptio Historiae[11]

4.1 Evidentia directa et circumstantialis

1 Directa. Adhibentur testes. Circa singulos determinatur quinam sint (authenticitas), utrum rem quam attestantur sciant (scientia), utrum sint veraces. Quibus stabilitis, testimonio eorum creditur.

2 Circumstantialis. Per modum exempli ponimus fabulam a Collingwood inventam. Omnes testes mentiuntur. Omnes indicia materialia sunt fabricata. Nihilominus detectivus determinat (a) quaenam sint mendacia, (b) curnam singuli testes sint mentiti, (c) cur et quando indicia sint fabricata, (d) quid re vera factum fuerit.[12]

3 In evidentia directa, criteria sunt extrinseca, et obiectum est creditum. Criteria [sunt] extrinsica: authenticitas, scientia, veracitas. Obiectum [est creditum] non propter intrinsecam rei evidentiam, sed propter auctoritatem testium credibilium et credendorum.

4 In evidentia circumstantiali, criteria sunt interna et obiectum non est creditum. Criteria sunt interna: ex quibus concluditur testes non esse credibiles, et quid re vera factum fuerit. Obiectum non est creditum: negatur

4   The Conception of History[11]

4.1 Direct and Circumstantial Evidence

1 Direct evidence entails the use of witnesses; concerning each of them, it is determined who they are (their authenticity), whether they know the matter about which they are testifying (their knowledge), and whether they are truthful (their veracity). Once these points have been established, their testimony is given credence.

2 An example of circumstantial evidence is found in Collingwood's story in which all the witnesses are lying, all the material clues have been fabricated, and nevertheless the detective is able to determine (a) which statements are lies, (b) why each of the witnesses lied, (c) why and when the clues were fabricated, and (d) what actually did happen.[12]

3 In the case of direct evidence the criteria are extrinsic, and the object [of the inquiry] is believed. The criteria are extrinsic: authenticity, knowledge, veracity. The object [is believed], not on account of evidence intrinsic to the case, but because of the authority of witnesses who are believable and ought to be believed.

4 In circumstantial evidence the criteria are internal, and the object is not believed. The criteria are internal, from which one can conclude that the witnesses are not credible, and one can determine what actually hap-

11 [Lonergan inserted by hand at the top of the page immediately above the heading references to the following two works. (The editors have augmented the bibliographic information he provided.) Eduard Fueter, *Geschichte der neueren Historiographie* (München; Berlin: R. Oldenbourg, 1911; New York: Johnson Reprint Corp., 1936; Zurich: O. Füssli, 1936, 1985). G.P. Gooch, *History and Historians in the Nineteenth Century*, 1st and 2nd eds. (London: Longmans, Green, and Co., 1913; the second edition adds only 'a few trifling corrections and additions' and an 'enlarged' index); 2nd rev. ed., 1952.
    This section may fairly be regarded as an early attempt to discuss the varieties of oral and written history that are given greater precision in chapter 8 of *Method in Theology*.]
12 [See Collingwood, *The Idea of History* 266–74. For an earlier reference to Collingwood's detective story, see Bernard Lonergan, *Understanding and Being: The Halifax Lectures on* Insight, vol. 5 in Collected Works of Bernard Lonergan, ed. Elizabeth A. Morelli and Mark D. Morelli (Toronto: University of Toronto Press, 1990) 384. A later reference can be found in Lonergan, 'The Philosophy of History,' in *Philosophical and Theological Papers 1958–1964* 55–56.]

auctoritas testium; perspicitur in ipsis indiciis fabricatis et testimoniis inco-
haerentibus rei veritas.

4.2 *Historia concepta secundum evidentiam directam*

1 Materia historiae est collectio quaedam testimoniorum.

2 Critica historia est ut haec testimonia examinentur secundum authenticitatem, scientiam, veracitatem.

3 Obiectum historiae: principale: id ipsum quod per testimonia credibilia stabilitur; secundarium: certum, id quod certo ex principali deducitur;
probabile, id quod certis per coniecturas addi potest.

4 Ubi unica criteria sunt extrinseca, et obiectum principale est obiectum
non scientiae sed fidei.

5 Meritum huius conceptionis est ut clare videatur quemadmodum historia possit esse certa.

6 Dupliciter tamen ad aliam historiae conceptionem conducit. Primo
modo, haec methodus apta est ad facta quaedam particularia determinanda. Sed ipsa facta relinquit isolata, sine contextu, in multis parum explicata. Unde adest grave periculum malae interpretationis, falsae deductionis,
anachronismi, etc. [Secundo modo,] quo remotiores sunt testes, eo difficilius determinatur de eorum authenticitate, scientia, veracitate. Ut sciamus
haec de teste *A*, requiritur alius testis *B*, de cuius authenticitate, scientia,
veracitate non constat nisi per tertium testem, *C*, et ita deinceps donec lon-
gissima astruatur series. Praeterea, cum fortior esse non possit catena quam
anulus debilissimus, non magis valet tota series quam ille testis qui inter
omnes minus fidem nostram conciliat.

7 Quibus non obstantibus, agnosci oportet casus particulares. Primus casus particularis est traditio popularis, de qua postea perpauca erunt dicenda.[13] Alter casus particularis est traditio ecclesiastica, ubi initium traditionis

pened. The object is not believed: the authority of the witnesses is denied, and in the fabricated clues themselves and the incoherent testimonies the truth of the matter comes to light.

4.2 History Conceived according to Direct Evidence

1 The material of history consists of a collection of testimonies.

2 Critical history consists in examining these testimonies as to authenticity, knowledge, and veracity.

3 As for the object of history, the principal object is that which is established through credible testimonies; the secondary object is either certain, as that which is deduced with certitude from the principal object, or probable, as that which can by conjecture be added to that which is certain.

4 The only criteria are extrinsic, and the principal object is an object not of knowledge but of belief.

5 The merit of this conception lies in this, that it clearly shows how history can be certain.

6 But in two ways it leads to another conception of history. First, this method is well suited for determining particular facts, but it leaves the facts themselves isolated, without a context, and in many cases insufficiently explained. Hence, there is serious danger of a wrong interpretation, faulty deduction, anachronism, and so on. Second, the more remote in time the witnesses are, the more difficult it is to determine their authenticity, knowledge, and veracity. In order to know these things about witness *A* we need to have the testimony of *B*, whose authenticity, knowledge, and veracity can only be established by a third witness, *C*, and so forth, through quite a lengthy series. Besides, since a chain is only as strong as its weakest link, this whole line of witnesses has no more credibility than that witness to whom we can give the least credence.

7 Despite what we have said, however, we must recognize a couple of special cases. The first particular case is popular tradition, about which we shall have a few remarks to make further on.[13] The second particular case is the

---

13 [It is not clear where, if anywhere, in the document these remarks about popular tradition are to be found. Perhaps Lonergan has in mind what in *Method in Theology* (New York: Herder and Herder, 1972; repr. ed., Toronto: University of Toronto Press, 1999) 185, he calls 'precritical history,' namely, the narrative of one's community that is at once artistic, ethical, explanatory, apologetic, and prophetic.]

in divina revelatione et inspiratione ponitur et ipsa traditio divina providentia protegitur et salvatur.[14]

4.3   Historia concepta secundum evidentiam circumstantialem

1 Materia historiae non restringitur ad testimonia sed omnia et quaelibet includit vestigia anteacti temporis; includit ergo scripta historica et alia quaelibet, etiam pseudepigrapha, noti vel etiam ignoti, imo falsarii, auctoris, inscriptiones, numismata; includit ruinas urbium: domicilia, palatia, aedificia publica, templa; includit vestimenta, instrumenta, architecturam, statuas, picturas, musicam, canticos, poemata, legendas, mythos, ritus, etc.[15]

2 Critica historia non est ut seligantur testimonia credibilia. Ipsa vestigia iam nunc exsistunt et iam nunc actu inspiciuntur, non minus quam phaenomena physica, chimica, biologica. Praeterea, non supponuntur testes re vera scientes et re vera veraces, sed id supponitur quod communiter fit, nempe mira illa et parum determinata mixtura scientiae et ignorantiae, sinceritatis et plus minus larvatae debilitatis.[16] Proceditur sicut et detectivus ex evidentia circumstantiali. Niebuhr loquebatur de divininatione quadam.[17]

Exsistentia vestigia, si singula considerantur, multis et diversis modis oriri potuissent; sed ubi ingens est multitudo possibilium, longe parvior est numerus compossibilium, et ita historicus pedetentim procedit, et quo magis

tradition of the church, whose origin is to be found in divine revelation and inspiration, and which is protected and safeguarded by divine providence.[14]

4.3 History Conceived according to Circumstantial Evidence

1 Historical material is not limited to testimonies, but includes anything and everything that is a vestige or relic of the past. Hence, it includes the historical writings and anything else, including pseudepigrapha, of any writer, known or unknown, and even forgeries; inscriptions and coins, ruins of houses, palaces, public buildings, temples, clothing, tools, architecture, statues, paintings, music, songs, poems, legends, myths, rituals, etc.[15]

2 Critical history is not a matter of selecting testimonies that are credible. The traces of the past are still extant, still actually available for examination just like physical or chemical or biological phenomena. Besides, there is no presupposition that witnesses really are knowledgeable and truthful, but rather that as a general rule they exhibit a remarkable but largely undetermined mixture of knowledge and ignorance, of sincerity and a certain amount of disingenuousness.[16] The procedure it follows is like that of a detective with circumstantial evidence. Niebuhr speaks about a kind of divination.[17]

Extant traces of the past, if examined individually, could have come about in many different ways. But when there is a large number of possibilities, there is a much smaller number of mutually compatible possibilities,

14 [At the end of this section, Lonergan will mention the *sensus fidelium*, the mind or sense of the faithful.]
15 [The Latin for 'including pseudepigrapha,' 'even forgeries,' 'temples,' and 'rituals, etc.' was added by hand.]
16 ['Disingenuousness': literally, 'a more or less concealed weakness.']
17 [This sentence was added by hand. Lonergan is referring to Barthold Georg Niebuhr (1776–1831), the author of *Römische Geschichte*, whom Gooch, in *History and Historians in the Nineteenth Century* (p. 14), describes as 'the first commanding figure in modern historiography.' Peter Hanns Reill, in his article 'Barthold Georg Niebuhr and the Enlightenment Tradition,' *German Studies Review* 3:1 (1980) 9–26, at 18, with supporting references to Niebuhr's writings provided in notes 28 and 29 at the bottom of the page, writes that Niebuhr, when talking about his own conclusions, 'employed terms such as divinations, dream-like hypotheses, poetical fantasies, and intuitions,' and even 'characterized himself as an "autodidact," one who approached his goal "like a sleepwalker groping his way along the edge of a precipice."']

compossibilitatem plurium vestigiorum considerat, eo magis ad solutionem determinatam pervenit.

3 Ubi criteria adhibita sunt non externa sed interna: non enim agitur de authenticitate, scientia, et veracitate testium, sed de interna vestigiorum intelligibilitate.

Ubi obiectum historiae non restringitur ad id quod testes credibiles affirmant. Sed quam latissime patet, ut nunc melius intelligi et exactius cognosci possit historia anteacti temporis quam olim ab ipsis viris agentibus et historiam, ut ita dicam, facientibus. Quam ob causam, saepius auditur illud, componi et conscribi historiam veriorem non a contemporaneis sed a posteris.

4.4 Quo sensu haec historia moderna sit scientia sensu antiquo[18]

1 Genetice, est scientia ex effectibus, nempe, ex vestigiis; sed concludit ad cognitionem causarum; vult enim determinare quis, quid, ubi, quibus auxiliis, cur, quomodo, quando. Quia est cognitio per causas, quia attingit intelligibilitatem rerum humanarum, habet essentiale elementum scientiae, etiam prout antiquitus concipiebatur. Non tamen potest statim dici cognitio certa: est cognitio quaedam probabilis quae decursu temporum magis semper ad certitudinem approprinquare potest.

2 Qui quidem profectus multipliciter oriri potest: (a) ex novis vestigiis inventis: Qumrân, Nag Hammadi, archaeologia, diluvium, Wooley;[19] (b) ex novis investigatoribus: alius enim aliter de compossibilibus iudicare potest; quod quidem inde provenire potest quod placitis nimis indulget quae proprio tempori, propriae nationi, proprio statui sociali quodammodo conveniunt et quasi veritates per se notae habentur; quod quidem corrigitur quatenus alii adveniunt et eandem investigationem repetunt qui tamen alio statu sociali, alia natione, alio saeculo vivunt; unde multae et diversae perspectivae de eadem re proponuntur, quae quidem inquantum mutuo sibi contradicunt, ulteriori investigatione corrigenda sunt, et inquantum

and so the historian proceeds one step at a time, and the more he considers the compossibility of the various traces, the closer he comes to a definitive solution.

3 Here the criteria used are not external but internal. For it is not a matter of the authenticity, knowledge, and veracity of witnesses, but of the internal intelligibility of the traces.

Here the object of history is not restricted to the testimony of credible witnesses, but extends as broadly as possible, so that the history of a bygone era can be better understood and more accurately known today than it was long ago by people who were living at that time and who were, so to speak, its history-makers. Hence, one often hears it said that a truer history of a period is written by posterity than by those living at that time.

4.4 How Is This Modern History a Science in the Classical Sense?[18]

1 Genetically, it is a science that arises from certain effects, in this case, from traces or remnants of the past. But it arrives at a knowledge of causes; for it seeks to determine who, what, where, by what means, why, in what way, when. Since it is knowledge through causes, since it arrives at an intelligibility in human affairs, it possesses an essential element of science, even as science was conceived in classical antiquity. Still, it cannot immediately be called knowledge that is certain; rather, it is probable knowledge that with the passage of time more and more closely approximates certitude.

2 This progress towards certitude can result from a number of things: (a) from new discoveries: Qumrân scrolls, Nag Hammadi, archaeology, a flood, Wooley;[19] (b) from new researchers: different researchers may come to different conclusions about what possibilities are compatible; such differences may result from one's bias towards ideas and ways that are more in keeping with one's own times or nation or social class and are virtually taken for granted; as a corrective for this, others come along and repeat the research, but they in turn belong to a different social class or nation or age; hence, several different perspectives on the same subject are proposed; inasmuch as they are mutually contradictory they call for further investigation, and

---

18 [The Latin for 'in the Classical Sense' was added by hand.]
19 [Sir Charles Leonard Wooley (1880–1960), a British archaeologist, known especially for the information he gathered about the Sumerians from the excavations at Ur of the Chaldees.]

non sunt contradictoria ad pleniorum cognitionem unius realitatis confe-
runt; (c) ex profectu scientiarum naturalium: temporis determinatio per
elementum carbonium quattuordecim; (d) ex profectu scientiarum humanarum: Rostovtzeff, *The Social and Economic History of the Roman Empire*; M.
Eliade, *Le chamanisme, Histoire des religions.*[20]

4.5   *Quo sensu historia moderna sit scientia sensu moderno*[21]

1 Perpauca accuratius de scientia sensu moderno sunt dicenda. (a) Scientia
moderna duo praecipue exhibet stadia: (a′) stadium praeparatorium: col-
lectionis 'factorum': per observationes, experimenta, enumerationes statis-
ticas; comparationis et classificationis secundum similitudines: ubi oriuntur
novi termini technici, uti in botania, ad ea denotanda quae antea defectu
intelligentiae innominata manserunt; determinationis legum empiricarum:
Galileo, Kepler, Priestley, Boyle, Lavoisier, Volta, Ampère, Harvey, Pasteur; (b′) stadium explicativum: ex ipsis legibus empiricis formantur conceptus fundamentales; unde habentur termini technici ad ea designanda
quae antea, non defectu attentionis sed defectu intelligentiae innominata
manserunt: massa, pondus; temperatura, calor; intensitas campi electrici, E,
et magnetici, H, lumen, motus; hydrogenium, helium, oxigenium, &c. Qui
conceptus systemate quodam legum empiricarum inter se uniuntur: systema mechanicum Newtonii, Einsteinianum, quantorum; tabula periodica;
evolutio ut systema probabilitatum conditionatarum.

(b) Scientia moderna duplici procedit motivo, alio insuper[22] ex sensibilibus, et alio desuper ex intentione recte intelligendi. (a′) Motivum quod

inasmuch as they are not contradictory they lead to a fuller knowledge of the same reality; (c) from progress in the physical sciences: dating material by the carbon-14 method, for example; (d) from progress in the human sciences: Rostovtzeff, *The Social and Economic History of the Roman Empire*; Eliade, *Le Chamanisme et les techniques archaïques de l'extase* and *Traité d'histoire des religions.*[20]

4.5 How This Modern History Is a Science in the Modern Sense[21]

1 First, let us state more precisely what moderns mean by science. (a) There are two principal stages in modern science: (a′) a preparatory stage: collecting the 'facts' through observation, experimentation, tabulation of statistical data; comparing and classifying according to similarities: when new technical terms are coined, as in botany, to denote what had previously remained unnamed simply because they were not understood; determining empirical laws: Galileo, Kepler, Priestly, Boyle, Lavoisier, Volta, Ampère, Harvey, Pasteur; (b′) an explanatory stage: from these empirical laws fundamental concepts are formed; hence, technical terms are coined to designate what had previously remained unnamed, not because they were not noticed, but because they were not understood: mass/weight; temperature/heat; the intensity of the electrical field, E, and of the magnetic field, H; light, motion; hydrogen, helium, oxygen, etc. These concepts are brought together in a system of empirical laws: the system of Newtonian and Einsteinian mechanics, and of quantum theory; the periodic table of the chemical elements; evolution as a system of conditioned probabilities.

(b) There are two movements operative in modern science, a movement from below,[22] from sense data, and another movement from above, from

20 [Michael Ivanovitch Rostovtzeff, *The Social and Economic History of the Roman Empire* (Oxford: Clarendon Press, 1926; 2nd rev. ed. in 2 vols by P.M. Fraser, 1957); Mircea Eliade, *Le chamanisme et les techniques archaïques de l'extase* (Paris: Payot, 1951) and *Traité d'histoire des religions* (Paris: Payot, 1948 and 1953); in English: *Shamanism: Archaic Techniques of Ecstasy*, rev. and enl. ed., trans. Willard R. Trask (New York: Bollingen Foundation; distributed by Pantheon Books, 1964); *Patterns in Comparative Religion: A Study of the Element of the Sacred in the History of Religious Phenomena*, trans. Rosemary Sheed (New York: Sheed & Ward, 1958).]
21 [See also Lonergan's discussion in 'The Philosophy of History,' in *Philosophical and Theological Papers 1958–1964* (CWL 6) 60–66.]
22 [This is the first occurrence in this document of *insuper*, translated here and throughout as 'from below.' *Insuper*, however, literally means 'on top of,'

insuper operatur maxime manifestum est: ipsa enim data sensibilia sunt (1) de quibus quaeritur, (2) in quibus inspicitur intelligibile, unde formantur leges, hypotheses, theoriae, (3) per quae fit verificatio. (b′) Motivum quod desuper operatur tripliciter manifestatur: (a″) inde ab ipsis initiis, est lumen intellectus agentis, unde habentur quaestiones, quid, cur, quomodo, quoties, an sit; (b″) in stadio explicativo, ubi iam determinatum est aliquod systema; ipsum systema praesupponitur, non quia certum esse creditur, sed pragmatice; scilicet, si falsum est, hoc ipsum ex sequelis assumptionis et praesuppositionis quam celerrime manifestabitur; ita physicus inquirens minime dubitat se quaerere functionem quandam in qua apparebunt notissima iam variabilia, quae solutio quaedam erit aequationum differentialium; similiter, chimicus inquirens minime dubitat se inventurum formulam quandam quae compositionem denotabit ex elementis vel iam notis vel locum inoccupatum in tabula periodica occupaturis; (c″) in stadio praeparatorio adest quaedam systematis anticipatio, sed imperfecta: Galileo, geometria euclidiana; chimici, de substantiis et transmutationibus; &c.

2 Quibus positis, exactius quaeri potest de historia moderna utrum sit scientia ad modum scientiae modernae. Quam quaestionem considerabimus, non de omni historia, sed de typis quibusdam generalibus,[23] puta, de historia scientiae, de historia philosophiae, de historia artis, &c.

3 Utrum scientia (sensu moderno) possit esse historia cuiusdam scientiae sive purae sive applicatae vel historia cuiusdam artis technicae – puta historiam matheseos, physicae, chimicae, biologiae, medicinae, navigationis, &c.

(a) Habetur motivum quod insuper operatur ex ipsis datis historicis.

the intellectual drive towards a correct understanding of the data. (a′) The movement that operates from below is very obvious. The sensible data themselves are that (1) about which questions are raised, (2) in which intelligibility is grasped, leading to the formulation of laws, hypotheses, and theories, and (3) through which verification is made. (b′) The movement that operates from above appears in three ways: (a″) from the very beginning of the process it is the light of agent intellect giving rise to the questions what? why? how? how often? is it so? (b″) in the explanatory stage, when some system has already been determined, this system is itself presupposed, not because it is held to be certain, but as a working hypothesis; that is to say, if it is wrong, that fact will very soon come to light from the consequences of the assumption and presupposition; thus, a physicist in doing research has not the slightest doubt that he is seeking a certain function in which the most obvious variables will now appear, a solution expressed in differential equations; similarly, a chemist in his research is sure that he will discover some formula that will denote a compound resulting from elements that either are already known or will occupy a hitherto empty place in the periodic table; (c″) in the preparatory stage there is already an anticipation, however imperfect, of a system: for Galileo, there was Euclidean geometry; for chemists, there were substances and substantial change; etc.

2 With this in mind we may go on to investigate more exactly whether modern history is a science in the modern sense. In doing so we shall consider not all history but certain general types of history,[23] such as the history of science, the history of philosophy, the history of art, and so forth.

3 Can the history of some science, pure or applied, or the history of some technical art be a science (in the modern sense) – a history of mathematics, for example, or of physics, chemistry, biology, medicine, navigation, and the like?

(a) There is the movement that operates from below, from the historical data themselves.

'over,' and is often used in the sense of 'moreover,' 'besides,' as Lonergan himself uses it below, p. 272. In classical Latin it can also mean 'from above,' exactly like *desuper* with which it is contrasted here. The reference is to Lonergan's familiar notion of the 'scissors-action' of scientific method with its two blades, upper and lower; see the index to Lonergan, *Insight*, under 'Heuristic method.']

23 ['General types of history' (*typis quibusdam generalibus*) may be a slip for 'special types of history.' For in (3h) Lonergan will say 'The history of a science or art that we have been considering is a special type of history.']

(b) Habetur motivum quod desuper operatur in ipsa scientia vel arte actuali.

(c) Aliud motivum sine alio non sufficit: qui motivum insuper operans negligit fingere potest quid accidere potuisset, sed scire non potest; qui motivum desuper operans negligit nescit ipsam materiam quam tractat.

(d) Utrumque motivum simul adhibitum ad scientiam conducit. Ex datis plene cognitis et ex scientia vel arte plene intellecta, modo valde intelligibili exhiberi possunt stadia scientiae, felices progressus, infelices retardationes, nexus subtiliores, evolutionem conceptuum et methodorum, &c.

(e) Attamen, status actualis scientiae vel artis non excludit ulteriorem progressum, et progrediente ipsa scientia vel arte, pro magnitudine ipsius progressus, accidentaliter vel substantialiter reficienda erit historia. Status enim actualis erat principium intelligendi et iudicandi de datis historicis; quo principio mutato, plus minus mutantur et intelligentia praeteriti et iudicium de praeteritis. Status etiam actualis erat principium iudicandi quaenam ex datis revera ad historiam scientiae vel artis pertinebant; unde ex nova perspectiva vel ampliora vel pauciora data ad historiam re vera pertinere iudicantur.

(f) Unde concludendum est historiam scientiae vel artis esse scientiam sensu moderno si quidem intelligentiam rei satis profundam parat, ad plenam certitudinem non pertingit, sed potius seriem quandam historiarum offert, quae ad maiorem perfectionem semper accedunt ex novis vestigiis inventis et ex novo principio intelligendi et iudicandi ex ipsa scientia vel arte adepto.

(g) Quod si quaeritur utrum priores historiae sint falsae, vel relativae, respondendum esse videtur secundum analogiam spatialem et visivam. Idem aedificium ex diversis locis inspectum diversimode apparet. Quaeretur ergo quaenam sit vera visio aedificii. Respondetur sane omnes visiones esse veras, modo quis (1) non credat unam quandam esse unice veram, (2) non ignoret eas multas certa quadam lege componi in unam eandemque rem manifestandam.

Similiter, si quis credit quandam historiam priorem esse unice veram, si quis ignorat multas fieri historias eiusdem scientiae pro profectu ipsius scientiae, sane errat. E contra, si quis credit omnes historias successivas ve-

(b) There is the movement that operates from above in that science or art as it is at present.

(c) Either one of these movements by itself is not enough. One who ignores the movement from below can imagine what possibly could have happened, but cannot know what did happen; and one who ignores the movement from above will not really know what he is dealing with.

(d) Both movements operating together lead to scientific knowledge. From a thorough knowledge of the relevant data and a thorough understanding of a science or an art, one can set forth in a quite intelligible manner the various stages of the science, its successes, its setbacks, its more subtle interconnections, the development of its concepts and methods, and so on.

(e) The current state of a science or an art, however, does not preclude further development; and as a science or art progresses, its history will have to be revised accordingly, either in its details or substantially, depending upon the magnitude of the development. For it is the state of a science as it currently is that was the basis for understanding and judging the historical data; when this basis changes, there will be a greater or lesser change in both the understanding of and the judgment upon the past. The current state of a science or art is also the basis for judging which data really did belong to the history of that science or art; hence, a new perspective will lead one to judge whether additional data or fewer data do in fact belong to its history.

(f) From all this we conclude that the history of a science or art is itself a science in the modern sense, if indeed it prepares the way for a satisfactory understanding of the matter, and does not attain complete certitude but presents rather a series of histories that are continually improved upon as new discoveries of the past are made and a new basis for understanding and judging is obtained from that science or art itself.

(g) If one asks whether those earlier histories are false or relative, we may answer by means of a spatial and visual analogy. The same building looks different when viewed from different standpoints. Which, then, is the true appearance of the building? The answer surely is that all the appearances are true, so long as (1) you do not believe that any one is the only true one, and (2) you are aware of the fact that by a definite law those several appearances combine to manifest one and the same object.

Similarly, if you believe an earlier history to be the only true one, unaware that there have been several histories of the same science done at different stages of its development, you are certainly in error. On the other

ritatem quodammodo attingere, nullam ex iis ita esse perfectam ut pleniorem intelligentiam vel nova et invenienda vestigia excludat, non errat.

Ubi dupliciter claudicare analogiam confitendum est; [1] nova perspectiva visiva ab aliis praescindit, sed subsequens historia in se includit veritatem
prioris; [2] iam hic et nunc possumus intelligere quemadmodum omnes
perspectivae eiusdem rei in unam rem manifestandam conveniant, sed hic
et nunc non possumus futuras historias praevidere et per eas praesentem
historiam corrigere.

Quae dicta sunt, ut differentia inter relativismum et perspectivismum
quodammodo illustretur. Plenius, postea, de perspectivismo dicendum
erit: nostra enim quaestio de systemate et historia etiam illam quaestiun-
culam includit, utrum scilicet systema quoddam perspectivarum cogitari et
determinari possit.[24]

(h) Quam consideravimus historiam scientiae vel artis technicae, ea specialis est. (a') Nam motivum quod desuper operatur est speciale, nempe,
ipsa scientia vel ars in statu actuali una cum analogia inter praesentem addiscendi experientiam et illud addiscere quod erat scientiam vel artem invenire. (b') Unde nexus qui tali historia exhibentur non proprie historici
sunt sed iterum speciales; nexus enim sunt eiusmodi qui in addiscendo il-
lustrantur, sed processus vel evolutio rerum historica non est tantummodo
addiscere. (c') Quare etiam peracta historia speciali, remanet alia historia
conscribenda: puta, actionem et reactionem inter hanc scientiam vel artem
et alias scientias vel artes, inter has et vitam hominum concretam, etc.

4 Utrum historia philosophiae sit scientia sensu moderno.

(a) Est historia specialis: agitur de uno quodam genere sat restricto ac-
tivitatis humanae.

(b) Est quodammodo similis ad historiam scientiae vel artis technicae:
agitur enim de activitate quadam conceptualizata.

(c) Attamen differt a casu praecedente: (a') tum quia non unica est
philosophia, sicut unica est mathematica, physica, chimica, medicina, sed
inde ab ipso initio philosophandi multae et diversae exstant philosophiae inter se oppositae; (b') tum quia maxima quadam universalitate gaudet philosophia; tractat enim de ipsa natura cognitionis et cogniti; unde

hand, if you hold that all the successive histories have attained the truth in some way and that none of them is so perfect as to leave no room for a fuller understanding or for new discoveries, you are quite correct.

We must confess, however, that our analogy limps in two ways: [1] a new visual perspective prescinds from the others, but subsequent history includes within itself the truth of earlier ones; [2] we are able here and now to understand how all the perspectives of a particular object come together to manifest this same object, whereas we cannot here and now foresee future histories and by means of them correct the current history.

Our point has simply been to illustrate in some way the difference between relativism and perspectivism. Later we shall have something more to say about perspectivism; for our question about system and history involves this particular question, whether a system of perspectives can be devised and delineated.[24]

(h) The history of a science or art that we have been considering is a special type of history. (a′) For the movement that operates from above is special, namely, it is the science or art itself in its current state together with the analogy between the ongoing experience of learning and that process of learning that led to the discovery of that science or art. (b′) Hence, the connections found in such histories are not properly speaking part of the history, but are also special; for the connections are of the sort that come to light in the learning process, whereas the historical process or development of things is not just a matter of learning. (c′) Therefore, even after that special history is done there remains another history to be written, such as the interaction between this science or art and other sciences and arts, between them and concrete human living, and so on.

4 Is the history of philosophy a science in the modern sense?

(a) It is a special history: it deals with one quite restricted kind of human activity.

(b) It is similar, in a way, to the history of a science or a technical art, for it deals with a certain conceptualized activity.

(c) Yet it is different from the above. (a′) There is not just one philosophy, as there is only one mathematics, one physics, one chemistry, or one medical science; instead, from the very beginnings of philosophical speculation there have been many diverse and mutually opposed philosophies. (b′) Philosophy enjoys a certain maximum universality, for it deals with the

24 [See below, pp. 318–19.]

qui historiam scribit et determinatam methodum adhibet, eo ipso praesupponit determinatam quandam philosophiam esse veram; (c′) quibus
positis, videtur omnes maximeque radicales differentias quae philosophos
dividunt, etiam historicos philosophiae dividere, si quidem (a″) conscrip-
tio historiae philosophiae supponit: selectionem: non enim agitur de omnibus operibus omnium philosophorum edendis; interpretationem: non
enim agitur de quaestione, quid quis dixerit, sed potius quid quis senserit
et cur ita senserit; intelligentiam et sapientiam in seligendo, interpretando,
ordinando, iudicando; (b″) sed pro diversitate philosophiae praesupposi-
tae alia erit praesupposita sapientia, notio intelligentiae, aestimatio rectae
interpretationis, iudicium de adaequata selectione;[25] (d′) unde tot diversae sententiae de Platone, Aristotele, Augustino, Aquinate, Cartesio, Kant,
Hegel, etc.; ne credatis hoc fieri solummodo de Aquinate: professor in
Universitate McGill, qui olim in universitate Berolinensi studuit, mihi nar-
ravit suo tempore quindecim professores exponere mentem Kant: quorum
quattuourdecim suas theorias propugnaverunt et decimus quintus caeteros
refutavit.[26]

(d) Quae cum ita sint, omnino quaerendum est utrum historia philosophiae possit esse scientia. Si enim non potest, sat clare sequitur reliquam
historiam eatenus esse impossibilem quatenus quaestiones fundamentales
philosophiae, moralitatis, religionis tangit.

nature of knowing and the known; hence, one who would write its history and follow a definite method by that very fact presupposes that a certain determinate philosophy is true. (c′) Accordingly, it appears that all the very radical differences among philosophers also divide the historians of philosophy, since (a″)writing a history of philosophy supposes: selectivity, in that it is not a question of treating all the books that all philosophers have ever written; interpretation, in that the question is not what so-and-so said, but what he meant and why; intelligence and wisdom in selecting, interpreting, ordering, and judging; (b″) but according to the diversity of philosophical presuppositions, there will also be presupposed different wisdoms, different theories about understanding, different criteria for correct interpretation, and different judgments about satisfactory selection.[25] (d′) This is why there are so many different opinions about the philosophy of Plato, Aristotle, Augustine, Aquinas, Descartes, Kant, Hegel, etc. Do not imagine that this is true only of Aquinas: a professor at McGill University who had previously studied at the University of Berlin told me that at that time there were fifteen professors expounding the philosophy of Kant; fourteen of them were expounding their own theories and the fifteenth was busy refuting all the others![26]

(d) This being the case, we must surely ask whether the history of philosophy can possibly be a science. For if it cannot, the fairly obvious consequence is that all other history is impossible to the extent that it touches upon fundamental questions of philosophy, morality, or religion.

25 ['A philosopher from the viewpoint of *his* philosophy can write an explanatory history of philosophy ... But another philosopher with a different philosophy can do the same thing, and you get different results, because any philosophy will supply an upper blade if it is sufficiently developed, and it can take on the form of a philosophy of philosophies. Also, it can take on the task of fulfilling the function of an upper blade in the history of philosophy. The trouble is that there are many philosophies, and the debate here obviously shifts. It is not to be settled so much by historical criteria as by the debate between the philosophers themselves.' Lonergan, 'The Philosophy of History,' in *Philosophical and Theological Papers 1958–1964* 62. See also Lonergan, *Topics in Education* 238–40.]
26 [Lonergan mentions this also in his third lecture on mathematical logic, given at Boston College on 10 July 1957. See Lonergan, *Phenomenology and Logic* 94. Unfortunately, neither here nor in the lecture does he identify the professor, though in the lecture Lonergan describes him as 'a friend of mine.']

(e) Methodus quae sponte sua usurpari semperque redire solet est con-troversialistarum, nam, quo magis quisque imaginatione caret, ut possibilia ne in mentem quidem ei venire possint, quo magis quisque est incapax criticae reflectionis ut, quod in mente sua tenet undenam provenerit, in-quirere neque audeat neque forte possit, eo magis in omnibus omnium cer-tissimus invenitur. Quippe quem fugit non solum illud, quidquid recipitur ad modum recipientis recipi, sed praecipue hoc, quod tale principium uni-versale in se ipso veritatem habere suamque recipiendi capacitatem quam maxime esse augendam.

Porro, defectus imaginationis et incapacitas criticae reflectionis ad mem-bra unius scholae vel doctrinae non restringitur; oriuntur ergo controver-siae in quibus disputantes summa certitudine veritates maxime obvias ore rotundo proclamant, summa certitudine pro veritate ipsa sese dimicare au-tumant, suasque opiniones non solum ore rotundo proclamant sed etiam omnes homines alterius sententiae tamquam improbos, perditos, turpis-simos impugnant. Quae controversiae sine fructu non per annos vel de-cennia sed per integra saecula protrahi solent, donec communi hominum consensu oblivioni consignantur.

(f) Alia via seu methodus est 'historicae technicae.'[27] Quae quidem tech-nica imitatur scientias empiricas naturales in quibus quaestiones in duas classes dividuntur. Aliae enim quaestiones consectaria concreta et sensibi-lia non habent, et hae metaphysicis relinquuntur. Aliae autem consectaria concreta et sensibilia habent, et in his occupatur scientificus.

Historicus ergo technicus non omnes quaestiones de anteactis tempo-ribus a se resolvendas assumit sed eas tantummodo quae ex vestigiis re-lictis determinationem admittunt per evidentiam circumstantialem atque cumulativam; quae quidem determinatio eo magis erit probabilior quo

(e) The method that is spontaneously followed and comes back again and again is that of the controversialists. This is because the more a person lacks imagination, so that other possibilities never even occur to him, and the more one is incapable of critical reflection and so never dares to and perhaps cannot ask himself where the opinions that he holds came from, the more will he be supremely certain about everything. For what he is quite oblivious to is not only the familiar axiom that whatever is received is received according to the capacity of the receiver, but also and especially this, that this universal principle is true in his own case and that his capacity for receiving should be enlarged as much as possible.

Moreover, lack of imagination and lack of ability for critical reflection are not restricted to the adherents of one school of thought or doctrine. Controversies arise, therefore, in which the disputants with utmost certitude grandiloquently proclaim obvious truisms, protesting that they are fighting for truth itself; and not only do they pompously propound their own opinions, but they go so far as to attack as wicked, perverse, and vile all who have an opinion that differs from theirs. Controversies of this sort generally go on fruitlessly not for years or decades but for centuries, until the common consent of humankind finally consigns them to oblivion.

(f) Another way or method is that of 'technical history.'[27] This technique is patterned after the empirical physical sciences in which questions are divided into two sets. One set of questions has no concrete sensible consequences, and so these questions are left to the metaphysicians. The second set does have such implications, and these are the questions for the physical scientists.

The technical historian, therefore, does not presume to solve all questions about the past, but only those which on the basis of the traces that remain admit of being progressively determined thorough the accumulation of circumstantial evidence. This determination will become more probable

---

27 ['... the historical interpretation of a period, of all the particular cases in a given section of space-time, has to present something of a coherent picture; an interpretation of one set of events has to be able to fit in with another closely related set of events; so there is a fair analogy between the understanding the historian seeks of the traces of the past and the procedure of the empirical scientist. That type of historical work I venture to call technical history.' Lonergan, 'The Philosophy of History,' in *Philosophical and Theological Papers 1958–1964* 57; the entire discussion of 'technical history' begins on p. 55 and goes to p. 60.]

magis evidentia ex multis et diversis fontibus in unam conclusionem conducit.

Qualis praecise sit haec technica addiscitur (1) in lineamentis fundamentalibus ex manualibus uti Bernheim, Langlois,[28] (2) ex studio tum magnorum historiographorum tum animadversionum in eorum opera, (3) ex praxi seu seminariis quae conducunt viri eminentes.

Illustratio, quam amant historici britannici, ex fabulis detectivis desumitur, et praecipue ex iis in quibus primus advenit custos ordinis publici qui omnia clare et exacte explicare videtur et deinde accedit detectivus privatus qui totam rem profundius scrutatur, nova invenit vestigia, et ad veram prorsusque aliam conclusionem pervenit.

Exemplum quod ex propria experientia proferre possum in articulis meis de gratia operante apud S. Thomam exstat.[29] Ibi enim [1] exhibetur S. Thomas tres successive sententias de gratia operante emissise, [2] causae cur sententiam mutaverit inveniuntur, [3] similes adesse variationes in materiis connexis de Deo operante in omni operatione, de voluntate, de libertate, [4] causae cur hae mutationes sunt factae etiam exhibentur. E quibus omnibus simul sumptis (1) tota quaestio liberatur a contextu saeculi decimi sexti, (2) ipsa multiplicitas et convergentia evidentiae tales sunt ut ipse S. Thomas quasi publice cogitans perspiciatur, (3) id quod determinatur est potius ipse motus mentis Divi Thomae quam sententia ad quam ultimo pervenerit.

(g) Circa historiam technicam haec notanda videntur.

Primo, non omnes quaestiones assumit solvendas. Secundum Butterfield, si ipse affirmaret se esse Beethoven, recte eum insanire dices, quod tamen

as the evidence derived from many different sources progressively points towards one conclusion.

We can learn more about the precise nature of this technique (1) in the basic outlines found in the manuals, such as those of Bernheim or Langlois;[28] (2) from studying the major historiographers and the critical comments made about their writings; and (3) from the practice of such eminent persons or from their seminars.

An illustration of this, one that British historians are fond of, is taken from detective stories, especially those in which the policeman who is first on the scene gives a clear and precise explanation of what happened, and then the private detective comes along who scrutinizes the situation more closely, finds new clues, and reaches the true and quite different conclusion.

The example that I am able to give from my own experience will be found in my articles on *gratia operans* in the works of St Thomas.[29] In these articles I have shown [1] that St Thomas expressed three successive opinions on operative grace, [2] why he changed his mind, [3] that there were similar changes in related matters about God as operating in every operation, about the will, and about freedom, and [4] the reasons why these changes were made. From all these taken together, (1) the whole question [of grace and free will] was freed from its sixteenth-century context, (2) the multiplicity and convergence of evidence are such that St Thomas could seem to be thinking aloud, so to speak, and (3) the main point was to chart the movement in St Thomas's thinking rather than to determine what his final opinion was.

(g) Some points to be noted about technical history.

First, it does not presume to answer all questions. As Butterfield has put it, if he were to declare that he was Beethoven, you would rightly say he was

28 [Ernst Berheim, *Lehrbuch der historischen Methode und der Geschichtsphilosophie: Mit Nachweis der wichtigsten Quellen und Hülfsmittel zum Studium der Geschichte* (Leipzig: Duncker & Humblot, 1889; 5th and 6th ed., 1908). Charles-Victor Langlois and Charles Seignobos, *Introduction aux études historiques* (Paris: Hachette, 1898); in English, *Introduction to the Study of History*, trans. G.G. Berry (London: Duckworth; New York: H. Holt & Co., 1912).]

29 [The articles, originally published in *Theological Studies* 2 (1941) 289–324 and 3 (1942) 69–88, 375–402, 533–78, are available now in *Grace and Freedom* 1–149. Lonergan's doctoral dissertation on *Gratia operans* in St Thomas, which provides the basis for the articles, is also available in the same volume. Lonergan used the same example in 'The Philosophy of History' 57–58.]

per media et apparatum historiae technicae demonstrare non poteris.[30] Aliis verbis, ipsa methodus technica determinat suum obiectum formale: id pertinet ad historiam technicam quae methodis technicis determinari potest.

Deinde, ad proprias quaestiones solvendas methodus technica modo scientifico procedit, scilicet, non attingit omnimodam certitudinem, sed conclusio quae methodo technica stabilita est non refutatur nisi alia conclusio per eandem methodum stabilitur; et ubi prima vice omnibus vestigiis perspectis atque scrutatis tam acute quam prudenter concluditur, haud facile[31] fieri potest ut secunda vice per eandem methodum ad aliam conclusionem terminetur. Exsistit ergo 'acquisitum' quoddam, seu difficile mobile, quod ex obiectivis vestigiorum nexibus oritur neque ex opinionibus investigantis dependet.

Tertio, qualis sit vis huius methodi, ex comparatione cum determinatione legis empiricae elucet.

Sumamus legem empiricam, $s = gt^2/2$. Ad cuius determinationem, confluunt: clarae definitiones *tou* 's' et *tou* 't', quae sunt notiones satis manifestae; permultae mensurationes tum 's' tum correspondentis 't'; mensurationum repraesentatio graphica; selectio curvae simplicissimae; defectus consequentis difficultatis quandocumque in aliis legibus determinandis assumitur tamquam verum illud $s = gt^2/2$.

In re historica, loco multarum mensurationum habentur multa vestigia seu indicia unius rei, loco inventionis curvae simplicissimae habetur conclusio, loco verificationis indirectae ex aliis experimentis habetur verificatio indirecta in cohaerentia huius conclusionis cum reliquis omnibus eadem methodo determinatis.

Quibus perspectis, elucent differentiae. Varia indicia eiusdem conclusionis non tam clare et distincte ad conclusionem referunt ac variae mensurationes ad functionem. Ipsa varia indicia non inter se tam clare et distincte coniunguntur ac variae mensurationes eorundem variabilium, s, t. Ipsa conclusio ex indiciis non tam clare est simplicissima ac est functio. Verifica-

insane, but you will not be able to prove this through the means and apparatus of technical history.[30] In other words, the method of technical history determines its own formal object: to technical history belongs whatever can be determined by technical methods.

Next, in order to answer questions that are proper to it, the technical method of history proceeds scientifically; that is, it does not attain certitude in every aspect of the matter, but the conclusion it has established is not to be rejected except by another conclusion arrived at through the same method; and when the first conclusion was both intelligently and prudently arrived at through a careful examination of all the evidence, it is not easy[31] subsequently to reach a different conclusion through the same method. There exists, therefore, something 'acquired,' not easily changed, that results from the objective connections among the traces and is independent of the opinions of researchers.

Third, the effectiveness of this method can be seen by comparing it to the procedure for determining an empirical law.

Let us take the empirical law, $s = gt^2/2$. To determine it, these elements all contribute: clear definitions of s and t, which are sufficiently clear notions; a large number of measurements of s and of its corresponding t; the representation of these measurements on a graph of some sort; the selection of the simplest curve; the absence of any consequent difficulty whenever in determining other laws $s = gt^2/2$ is assumed as true.

In history, instead of a large number of measurements we have many traces or indications of one thing; instead of the simplest curve we have a conclusion; instead of indirect verification through further experiments we have indirect verification in the coherence of this conclusion with all the others arrived at in the same way.

But in this there are differences. The various indications pointing to the same conclusion are not so clearly and distinctly related to that conclusion as the many measurements are to the function. These various indications are not so clearly and distinctly linked together as are the various measurements of the same variables s and t. The conclusion drawn from the

---

30 ['If I claimed to be the incarnation of Beethoven, any man would have as much right as any other to put me down as a lunatic, but it is not by the apparatus of the historian that I could be proved to be actually wrong.' Herbert Butterfield, *Christianity and History* (New York: Charles Scribner's Sons, 1950) 18.]

31 [The Latin word 'facile' is added by hand.]

tio indirecta in scientiis naturalibus et empiricis longe clarior et certior est
quam cohaerentia cum reliquis conclusionibus historicis.

In utroque casu habetur 'inspicere in phantasmate' Aristotelicum et
Thomisticum. Sed in scientia habetur hoc inspicere evolutum et expressum ad modum mathematicum vel saltem systematicum; in historia autem
habetur inspicere evolutum et expressum ad modum intelligentiae vulgaris
seu 'common sense.' Aliis verbis, sicut omnes homines ad eam intelligentiam vulgarem perveniunt quae ad usum cotidianum sufficit, ita historicus
ad intelligentiam vulgarem alterius aetatis, alterius populi, alterius mentis
pervenit.

Quarto, sequitur historiam technicam esse potius fragmentariam quam
completam, nam non omnes quaestiones solvendas assumere potest; et ipsas quas solvit non ad perfectionem scientiae adducit sed in statu incomple-
to relinquere debet, sicut et scientificus deberet si leges quidem empiricas
et particulares determinaret sed quemadmodum multae hae leges in unum
quoddam systema coalescant simpliciter ignoraret.

(h) Quibus perspectis, dicendum videtur historiam technicam (a′) bene
uti motivo quod insuper ex datis operatur; (b′) insolutas relinquere quaestiones quae magis ex motivo desuper operante pendent, quasi quis scrib-
eret historiam mathematicae vel medicinae ut per ipsam hanc investigationem historicam ipsas has scientias primo addisceret; (c′) et ideo intra
limites historiae technicae magis articuli et notae conscribuntur quam libri,
magis fiunt editiones, construuntur indices, describuntur collectiones in-
scriptionum, numismatum, etc., quam quaestiones historicae investigentur.

(i) Unde oritur quaestio utrum ad complementum historiae technicae
efformari non posset systema quoddam quae se haberet ad historiam sicut
mathematica ad omnes hypotheses et theorias physicas, sicut status scientiae actualis ad historiam mathematicae, physicae, etc. Ex quo sequeretur
historiam operari non solum ex motivo insuper per technicam sed etiam ex
motivo quodam desuper, nempe, systemate desiderato.

Quae quaestio, si generaliter ponitur, historicismum inducit, de quo
postea aliquid;[32] sed facilius ponitur relate ad historiam philosophiae, et
quidem duplici de causa; primo, cum philosophia sit in se conceptualizata,

indications is not so obviously the simplest, as the function is. And indirect verification in the physical empirical sciences is far clearer and more certain than coherence with all the other conclusions arrived at in a history.

In both cases you have the Aristotelian and Thomist 'insight into phantasm.' In the sciences, however, this insight is developed and expressed in a mathematical or at least systematic manner, while in history the insight is developed and expressed in the manner of ordinary understanding or common sense. In other words, just as everyone attains the ordinary sort of understanding that suffices for everyday living, so does the historian attain the ordinary everyday understanding of another era, another people, another mentality.

Fourth, it follows from this that technical history is fragmentary rather than complete. It cannot presume to answer all questions, and those that it does solve it does not bring to the state of scientific perfection; it has to leave them in a state of incompleteness, just as a scientist would have to do if he were trying to determine particular empirical laws and yet simply did not know how these laws come together to form a coherent unified system.

(h) From all of this, it seems we must say that technical history (a') makes good use of the movement that operates from below from data; (b') leaves unresolved questions that depend more upon the movement from above, like someone who in writing a history of mathematics or medicine as a result of his historical research is first learning these sciences themselves; (c') and therefore within the field of technical history there are more articles and notes than books written, and more publications, more indices compiled, more collections of inscriptions, coins, etc., than historical questions that are investigated.

(i) Here the question arises whether or not some system can be constructed as a complement to technical history that would be related to history as mathematics is to all the hypotheses and theories of physics, and as the current state of mathematics, physics, etc., is to the history of those sciences. It would follow from this that history operates not only from the movement from below through its technique, but also from the movement from above, namely, the desire for system.

If stated in general terms, this question leads to historicism, about which we shall say something later.[32] But it is more easily stated in relation to the history of philosophy, and that for two reasons: first, since philosophy

---

32 [See the section 'Historicism' below, pp. 272–81, and again pp. 282–87.]

altiorem quandam systematizationem non sponte et natura respuit, deinde, quia conceptus philosophici sunt difficiliores et captum intelligentiae vulgaris effugere solent, minus efficax in historia philosophiae est ipsa technica historia.

(a′) Notamus tale systema esse debere non philosophiam quandam sed potius philosophiarum philosophiam; scilicet, debet se habere ad omnes philosophias sicut mathematica ad omnes theorias et hypotheses physicas, unde ex tali systemate construi possunt tum omnes conceptus singularum philosophiarum tum relationes et oppositiones quae inter diveras philosophias obtinent.[33]

(b′) Notamus ulterius non esse aestimandum tale systema unico quodam modo construi posse sed multipliciter, ut totum inde ab initio sit in actu, uti dialectica Hegeliana quae autumant se gressibus semper necessariis ex conceptu entis usque ad spiritum absolutum procedure; ut ab initio non habeatur nisi potentiale quid, quod evolvitur, perficitur, determinatur per ipsam investigationem historicam; ut hoc potentiale consistat in potentia conceptuali, ut systema sit conceptuum systema; vel ut sit in potentia non conceptuali sed alia, puta, operationali, ut systema sit non conceptuum sed aliorum.

(c′) Satis inutiliter ponitur quaestio abstracta de possibilitate systematis eiusmodi; si quis perspicit possibilitatem systematis, ipsum iam systema habet; si quis non perspicit talem possibilitatem, argumenta sua procedere possunt non solum ex obiectiva impossibilitate sed etiam ex subiectivo defectu ingenii et acuminis.

(d′) Negatio vel negligentia systematis minime systema excludit; imo, potius favet subreptioni systematis latentis atque incohaerentis. Ita valde communiter dicitur illud esse scientificum quod omnium assensum sibi vindicat; scilicet, si aliquid bene determinatur vel demonstratur, pariter atheos et theistas, capitalistas et communistas, Christianos et Mohammeda-

in itself is conceptualized, it does not automatically and naturally reject a higher systematization; second, since philosophical concepts are rather difficult to grasp and are generally over the head of the ordinary person, technical history is less useful in a history of philosophy.

(a') We note that such a system must be not a certain philosophy but rather a philosophy of philosophies. That is, it must be related to all philosophies as mathematics is to all the hypotheses and theories of physics. Such a system, therefore, can bring together all the concepts of every kind of philosophy along with all the relations and contradictions that exist between these different philosophies.[33]

(b') We note further that it must not be thought that such a system can be constructed in only one way; it could be done in several ways, so that the whole system would be in act from the very beginning, like Hegelian dialectic, which claims to proceed in a series of necessary steps from the concept of being to absolute spirit; or at the outset it could only be something potential, to be developed, perfected, and determined through historical research; this potential system could consist in conceptual potency, so that the system would be a system of concepts; or it could be not in conceptual potency but in some other potency, such as operational, so that the system would not be a system of concepts but of something else.

(c') It is quite useless to pose the abstract question of the possibility of this sort of system; for to grasp the possibility of a system is to already possess a system; but if one does not grasp such a possibility, one's arguments can proceed from an objective impossibility but also from a subjective lack of intellectual acumen.

(d') Denying or ignoring a system does not mean there is no system; rather, it actually facilitates the surreptitious introduction of a hidden system that lacks coherence. Thus, one quite commonly hears that if something wins universal acceptance it is a scientific fact; that is to say, if something is thoroughly determined or demonstrated to be true, it will convince atheists

---

33 ['... any philosophy will supply an upper blade if it is sufficiently developed, and it can take on the form of a philosophy of philosophies.' Lonergan 'The Philosophy of History' 62; '... it is the failure to reach the full critical position that accounts for the endless variety of philosophic positions so rightly lamented by Kant; and it is by a dialectical analysis, based on the full critical position, that one can hope to set up a philosophy of philosophies in the fully reflective manner that at least imperfectly was initiated by Hegel and still is demanded by modern needs.' Lonergan, *Insight* 293.]

nos, convincit, europaeos et asiaticos. Sed quidquid recipitur, ad modum recipientis recipitur; minime requiritur a determinatione scientifica ut errores subiectivos corrigat; quod si falso supponitur hoc requiri, a scientifica inquisitione expellitur omnis quaestio maioris momenti, et quidem systematice expellitur.

Iterum, quamdiu deest tale quoddam systema, deest unum de duobus motivis scientiae modernae propriis, qui tamen defectus non communiter agnoscitur ut defectus; imo, supponitur pars methodi esse tota methodus, unde illud concluditur esse non-scientificum, mythicum, obiectum credulitatis, quod forte tale non est sed potius obiectum quod attingi non potest per methodum dimidiatam.[34]

5 Utrum historia theologiae sit scientia sensu moderno.

(a) In ipsa theologia Christiana clare apparent duo stadia scientiae sensu moderno: stadium enim explicativum incipit saeculo XIIIo cum positum fuerit theorema supernaturalitatis, quod se habet ad theologiam sicut theoremata Newtoniana ad scientiam mechanicam, theorema Einsteinianum ad scientiam electro-magneticam, tabula periodica ad scientiam chimicam, theoria evolutionis (non Darwiniana sed generalizata de probabilitatibus conditionatis) ad scientiam biologicam.

Cuius stadii explicativi elementa anticipatoria inveniuntur in definitione Filii tamquam consubstantialis Patri, in definitione unius personae Filii in duabus naturis, in definitione et enumeratione sacramentorum, in conceptione gratiae per modum habitus et actuum.

(b) Inquantum inceptum est stadium explicativum, sive in sua radice totali, sive in aspectibus particularibus, assimilatur historia theologiae ad historiam mathematicae, physicae, medicinae. Scilicet, ex statu actuali

and theists, capitalists and communists, Christians and Muslims, Europeans and Asians alike. But whatever is received is received in accordance with the disposition of the receiver. It is by no means required of a scientific determination that it correct subjective errors; but if it is mistakenly supposed that this is required of it, then all questions of greater importance are excluded, and indeed systematically excluded, from scientific inquiry.

Again, as long as such a system is lacking, one of the two movements proper to modern science [from below and from above] will also be lacking. This defect is not generally recognized as a defect; in fact, however, a partial method is taken to be the whole method. Hence, the conclusion is drawn that something is unscientific, a myth, or an object of credulity, which is perhaps not so at all but rather an object that cannot be apprehended through what is only a partial method.[34]

5 Is the history of theology a science in the modern sense?

(a) In Christian theology there clearly appear the two stages of a science in the modern sense. The explanatory stage begins in the thirteenth century with the introduction of the theorem of the supernatural order. This theorem is to theology what Newton's theorems are to mechanics, the periodic table to chemistry, Einstein's theorems to the science of electromagnetics, the theory of evolution (not Darwinism, but a generalized theory of conditioned probability) to biology.

There were certain events that anticipated this explanatory stage of theology: the definition of the Son as consubstantial with the Father, the definition of the one person of the Son in two natures, the definition and enumeration of the sacraments, the conception of grace as a habit and as acts.

(b) With the entry into its explanatory stage, whether with regard to its entire basis or with regard to particular aspects, the history of theology comes to resemble the history of mathematics or physics or medicine; that

---

34 [Of some relevance to the issue of whether some system can be constructed as a complement to technical history, which would be related to history as mathematics is to the hypotheses and theories of physics, is Lonergan's discussion of the problem of general history in Lonergan, *Topics in Education* 250–57, and also his discussion of the notion of a 'universal viewpoint' in *Insight* 587–91. Note, however, that in *Method in Theology* 153, note 1, Lonergan remarks that what in *Insight* is termed a universal viewpoint, in methodical theology is realized 'by advocating a distinct functional specialty named dialectic.' In 'The Philosophy of History' 63–66, Lonergan discusses several 'contenders' for 'an upper blade for *general* history,' that is, 'history in the ordinary sense as contrasted with, say, a history of capitalism.']

scientiae habetur motivum desuper operans per quod dirigitur selectio, ordinatio, explicatio materiae historicae.

(c) Inquantum status actualis theologiae subest divisionibus vel secundum fidem (inter catholicos et acatholicos) vel secundum supposita philosophica, redit totum problema historiae philosophiae et insuper aliud problema quod ex fide habetur.

Quam ob causam, si catholicus quaerit systema ad solutionem problematis historiae philosophiae, etiam debet quaerere systema quod non solum differentias philosophiarum respicit sed etiam differentias fidei. Cui problemati subest tota quaestio de relatione inter philosophiam et theologiam, de philosophia Christiana, etc.

(d) Inquantum historia theologiae debet nexum exhibere inter theologiam doctam et explicativam et, alia ex parte, illam fidem quae magna concilia et inventiones scholasticas praecessit, iam ad aliud genus problematis historici progredimur; non enim agitur de cognitione systematice ordinata uti in scientiis, in philosophiis, in theologiis, sed agitur de mente seu sensu fidelium; quam mentem et sensum exsistere nemo dubitat, sed quid praecise sit et quemadmodum ex ea ad theologiam doctam procedatur, non valde clarum videtur.

5   De Historicismo[35] (maxime ex H. Meyerdorff, PB)[36]

1 F. Meinecke comparavit reformationi, affirmavit eum esse maximum quendam eventum in cultura occidentali; Lord Acton comparat revolutioni copernicanae.[37] Sane maxime influit in omne quod dicimus, cogitamus.

is, the present state of the science provides the movement that operates from above, directing the selection, ordering, and explanation of the historical materials.

(c) Inasmuch as in its present state theology is divided either according to matters of faith (Catholics and non-Catholics) or according to philosophical presuppositions, the whole problem of the history of philosophy returns and, moreover, another problem that is a consequence of faith.

Because of this, if a Catholic seeks a system to solve the problem of the history of philosophy, he ought also to seek a system that regards not only philosophical differences but also differences in matters of faith. Underlying this problem is the whole question of the relation between philosophy and theology, the question of Christian philosophy, and so forth.

(d) Inasmuch as the history of theology ought to show the connection between theology that is taught and explained and, on the other hand, the faith that preceded the great councils and the work of the Schoolmen, we now come upon another kind of historical problem; for it is not a question of systematically ordered knowledge such as is had in the sciences, in philosophy, and in theology, but of the mind or 'sense' of the faithful (*sensus fidelium*). No one denies that this mind or sense exists; but precisely what it is and how the transition is made from it to theology as taught is not yet clear.

5   **Historicism[35] (taken mostly from Hans Meyerhoff, paperback)[36]**

1 Friedrich Meinecke [1862–1954] compared historicism to the Reformation, declaring it to be a most important event in Western culture. Lord Acton [1834–1902] compares it to the Copernican revolution.[37] Certainly

---

35 [Lonergan Archive A 486 (www.bernardlonergan.com 48600DTL050). This section consists of six pages, typewritten in the same way as the preceding section, 'De systemate et historia.' Only pages 2 and 3 are numbered, but at the top of the last three pages there is the typewritten notation 'S&H,' an indication that this section belongs with the previous one. It appears to be incomplete.]

36 [Lonergan is referring to Hans Meyerhoff, ed., *The Philosophy of History in Our Time: An Anthology Selected, with an Introduction and Commentary* (New York: Doubleday Anchor Books, 1959). This section would seem to consist mostly of Lonergan's typewritten notes on Meyerhoff's introductory essay, 'History and Philosophy: An Introductory Survey' (1–25).]

37 [See ibid. 9.]

Karl Mannheim asserit eum esse ipsam mundi visionem actu dominantem omniaque ...[38]

2 *Primum elementum*: liberatio historiae a theologia, religione.

(a) Saepius dicitur populum Israeliticum historicitatem invenisse, in culturam occidentalem invehisse.

(b) Iam vero Graeci et deinde Romani sensum quendam historicum habuerunt et historias composuerunt: Herodotus, Thucydides, Polybius, Sallustius, Livius, Tacitus, Josephus. Thucydides et Polybius propriam methodum explicant; Thucydides *to ktēma eis aiei perfecit*, eo sensu quo Sophocles.[39] Omnes indicationes methodologicas dant et supposita philosophica et moralia habent. Herodotus: theoria cyclica compensationis.

(c) Eis tamen defuit philosophia historiae: sensu speculativo, sicut

it does have an enormous influence upon everything we say or think. Karl Mannheim [1893–1947] states that it is the actually dominating world-view … everything.[38]

2 *First element*: the freeing of history from theology and religion.

(a) It is often said that the Israelites discovered historicity and introduced it into Western culture.

(b) But the Greeks and later the Romans had a certain historical sense, and Herodotus, Thucydides, Polybius, Sallust, Livy, Tacitus, and Josephus wrote histories. Thucydides and Polybius explained their method; Thucydides composed his history to be *to ktēma eis aiei*, 'a possession for all time,' like the plays of Sophocles.[39] They all give indications of their method, and have certain philosophical and moral presuppositions. Herodotus: cyclical theory of compensation.

(c) But they did not have a philosophy of history, either in a speculative

38 [The last word in this handwritten sentence is not clear. Mannheim published an article on historicism in *Archiv für Sozialwissenschaft und Sozialpolitik* in 1924, a translation of which appears in his *Essays on the Sociology of Knowledge* (London: Routledge & Kegan Paul Ltd, 1952) 84–133. In the essay, Mannheim characterizes historicism as 'an intellectual force' that is 'the very basis on which we construct our observations of the socio-cultural reality' (84–85), as a *Weltanschauung* that 'not only dominate[s] our inner reactions and our external responses, but also determine[s] our forms of thought' (ibid.; this could well be the source of Lonergan's insertion). It 'reaches into the most remote corners and the most specialized problems of philosophy and methodology …' and indeed is 'a principle which pervades every phase of our world experience' (126). It is 'a kind of philosophy which goes beyond epistemology and tries to secure a basis of it,' and its 'systematic place corresponds to that of the "metaphysics" of earlier times' (127). And it completes its philosophical step by 'attempting to grasp the overall inner meaning of the historical transformation process with the help of the category of "totality"' (ibid.). Finally, historicism is 'the only solution of the general problem of how to find *material* and concretely exemplified standards and norms of a world outlook which has become dynamic' (132). It is 'a world-view which does not try to do violence to the new element which moves us – the dynamic, … but attempts to place it right in the centre and to make it the Archimedean lever by which our whole world-view is unhinged' (133). It is possible that Lonergan's written insertion reports one or more of these claims by Mannheim.]

39 [The Greek expression occurs in Thucydides, *History of the Peloponnesian War*, book I, chap. 22.]

habuerunt philosophiam naturae, hominis, societatis; sensu logico: nihil de historia sicut *Post. Anal.* de scientia.[40]

(d) Quod additum est ab Hebraeis et Christianis erat historiam habere sensum, directionem, finem uti in Exodo, in populo proprio Dei, in die Dominica expectata, in Incarnatione, Redemptione, praedicatione evangelii, parousia; unde historiam manifestare Dei intentionem, providentiam, tum in singulis eventibus, tum in quantum ipsa historia non meram eventuum congeriem sed unam intelligibilitatem universalem exhibet.[41]

(e) Tota historia sensu religioso imbuta atque interpretata in opere Augustini, *De civitate Dei.*[42]

(f) Quam conceptionem indirecte et directe impugnaverunt (a′) Machiavelli, Guicciardini; (b′) Voltaire, contra Bossuet, *Histoire universelle*, 1681; (c′) Gibbon: destructio imperii Romani opus, triumphus religionis et barbarismi; (d′) Vico: loquitur de providentia inquantum est ordo divinae gubernationis rebus immanens et ipsis rebus manifestata; non de providentia transcendenti, miracula patrante; similiter lex naturalis non est collectio statutorum a moralistis compilata sed principium immanens iuri positivo idque crisi subiciens atque perficiens; (e′) Herder, quamvis totus contra rationalismum, illuminismum Voltaire, tamen ei etiam historia est processus quidam mundo immanens, autonomus; (f′) Hegel et Marx: tempus fit categoria quaedam ultima; apud Hegel, Deus quodammodo historiae involvitur et per eam evolvitur; apud Marx, tollitur Deus de medio.[43]

(g) Unde philosophiae historiae doctrinas religiosas et Christianas quodammodo imitantur; constituunt saecularizationem historiae; et tamen quod per religionem habebatur, etiam per eas haberi posse voluerunt:

(a′) Dialectica Hegeliana – divina sapientia; spiritus obiectivus – *Logos* Ioannaeus; magni homines – incarnationes spiritus obiectivi (Napoleon); stadia historica: tyranni Asiatici, ars Graeca, ius Romanum, libertas Ger-

sense, as they had a philosophy of nature, of man, of society; or in a logical sense, for they had nothing concerning history comparable to the *Posterior Analytics* concerning science.[40]

(d) What Judaism and Christianity added was that history had a meaning, a direction, a purpose, as in Exodus, in the People of God, in waiting for the Day of the Lord, in the Incarnation, the redemption, the preaching of the gospel, the parousia; hence, the idea that history manifests God's intention and providence, both in particular events and in the sense that history itself is not a mere series of events but exhibits a single overall intelligibility.[41]

(e) In St Augustine's *De civitate Dei*, the whole of history is infused with a religious meaning and interpreted accordingly.[42]

(f) The following have attacked this approach, directly or indirectly: Machiavelli and Guicciardini; Voltaire, against Bossuet's *Histoire universelle* (1681); Gibbon: the ruin of the Roman empire was the work, the triumph, of religion and barbarism; Vico speaks of providence in terms of the order of divine governance immanent in things and manifested by those things themselves, but with no mention of a transcendent providence, producing miracles; likewise, the natural law is not a collection of statutes compiled by moralists, but rather a principle immanent in positive law and so subject to critical evaluation and open to further development; Herder: although he was totally opposed to rationalism and the illuminism of Voltaire, nevertheless for him history is a process immanent in the world and autonomous; Hegel and Marx: time becomes an ultimate category; for Hegel, God is in some way involved in history and evolves through it; Marx does away with God entirely.[43]

(g) Thus, philosophies of history imitate in a way the religious doctrines of Christianity. They constitute the secularization of history, yet what used to be had through religion they wanted to have through the philosophies.

(a') Hegelian dialectic – divine wisdom; objective spirit – the Johannine *Logos*; great men – incarnations of the objective spirit (Napoleon); the stages of history: Asiatic tyrannies, Greek culture, Roman law, Germanic liberty

---

40 [See Meyerhoff, 'History and Philosophy,' in *The Philosophy of History in Our Time* 1–2.]

41 [See ibid. 2.]

42 [On Augustine's *De civitate Dei* and its significance, see ibid. 2–4.]

43 [On all of the writers that Lonergan mentions here, from Machiavelli and Guicciardini to Hegel and Marx, see ibid. 4–6. See also below, pp. 284–87.]

manica – quasi eschatologia; cf. societas sine classibus, reditus ad naturam (Rousseau), triumphus rationis (revolutio Gallica), *Übermensch.*[44]

(b′) Motus magni recentiores ideologiam historicam prae se ferunt: liberalismus – progressus; Hegelianismus – maximus influxus in theologiam Germanicam, exegesin; Marxismus – interpretatio materialistica historiae; Fascismus, Nazismus.

(c′) Ubi deficiunt hi motus, opiniones, realitas humana sensu, fine, veritate carere videtur.[45]

3 *Alterum elementum:* romanticismus.[46]

(a) Sensus historiae residet, non in structura quadam universali, sive necessaria, sive teleologica, sed in ipsa rerum multiplicitate, individualitate, valore proprio (Ranke: omnia aeque immediata ad Deum).[47]

(b) Subiectum historiae est ipsa vita humana, tota, multiformis, non systematica. Est processus continuus crescendi, transformationes subeundi, in populis, nationibus, culturis, moribus, institutis, cantibus, mythis, opinionibus. Fugit categorias philosophicas, staticas, abstractas, generales; est dynamicum, concretum, individuale. Forte est ars; sed certo non est philosophia.[48]

(c) Munus est praeteritum re-creare, per sympathiam, empathiam: induere sentimenta, opiniones, etc., ut praeteritum contemplare possimus prout erat.[49]

4 *Tertium elementum:* historia ut scientia.[50]

(a) Primum stadium: historia quamvis non sit philosophia, tamen non est ars; quaerit verum, et quidem methodologice atque proprie scientifice (Ranke: 'wie est eigentlich gewesen').[51]

– quasi eschatological; see also the 'classless society,' Rousseau's 'return to nature,' the triumph of reason (French Revolution), the *Übermensch*.[44]

(b′) The major movements of more recent times exhibit a historical ideology: liberalism – progress; Hegelianism – immense influence on German theology and exegesis; Marxism – materialistic interpretation of history; Fascism, Nazism.

(c′) The defect in these movements and opinions is that in them the reality of human existence appears to be without meaning, purpose, or truth.[45]

3 *Second element*: Romanticism.[46]

(a) The meaning of history is to be found not in some universal structure, whether necessary or teleological, but in the very multiplicity, individuality, and proper value of things. (Ranke: all things are equally immediate to God.)[47]

(b) The subject of history is human life itself in its entirety, its great variety, and its unsystematic character. It is an ongoing process of growth, of transformation, in peoples, nations, cultures, customs, institutions, songs, myths, opinions. It shuns categories that are philosophical, static, abstract, and general; it is dynamic, concrete, individual. It may be an art; it is certainly not philosophy.[48]

(c) Its task is to re-create the past, through sympathy, empathy: to appropriate the sensibility, the opinions, etc., of the past in order to be able to contemplate it as it was.[49]

4 *Third element*: history as a science.[50]

(a) First stage: although history is not philosophy, it is not an art either; it seeks what is true, and indeed does so methodically and in a properly scientific way (Ranke: *wie est eigentlich gewesen*.)[51]

---

44 ['Despite ... radical differences, ... there are distinct formal analogies between philosophical and religious historiographies which indicate that both express the same type of historical consciousness.' Ibid. 6. Meyerhoff then proceeds to outline these analogies on pp. 6–8. Lonergan's discussion above draws, in part, from Meyerhoff's outline.]
45 [See ibid. 8–9.]
46 ['Historicism is a by-product of the romantic revolt against enlightenment and rationalism.' Ibid. 9.]
47 [See ibid. 10.]
48 [See ibid.]
49 [See ibid. 11.]
50 ['... during the nineteenth century, historicism itself passed through two distinct phases, one predominately scientific and positivistic, the other "pure and complete," in Croce's words.' Ibid. 12.]
51 ['how it really happened'; see ibid. 12–13.]

Evolvebantur technicae criticae investigationis Bernheim, Langlois-Seignobos, Niebuhr, Ranke, Droysen, Mommsen, Taine, Fustel de Coulanges, Acton, Bury, eorumque sequaces usque hodie.[52]

(b) Alterum stadium: Burckhardt: historia inter omnes disciplinas minime scientifica est, quae tamen multa continet quae scire prodest.[53]

Motus, qui primatum intellectus in dubium revocabant, historicos intra ipsum cursum historiae versari demonstravit: Kierkegaard, Schopenhauer, Nietzsche, William James, Bergson, Marx, Comte, Pareto, Sorel, Freud.[54]

(c) Tertium stadium: W. Dilthey agnovit relativitatem cuiusvis doctrinae metaphysicae vel religiosae: caetera in *Weltanschauung* reduci, quae irrationalis est.[55] Voluit (non perfecit) criticam rationis historicae (quae se haberet ad scientiam historicam, sicut critica Kantiana ad scientiam mechanicam).[56] Laboravit ut fieret logica scientiarum humanarum, *Geiesteswissenschaften*, quae quidem neque philosophica neque scientifica esset sed rei humanae, historicae, propria. Initium non parvum[57] dedit studiis quae hodie 'phaenomenologica' nominantur, quae occupantur circa realitates vitae psychicae.[58]

Cf. Díaz de Cerio.[59]

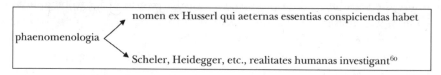

phaenomenologia

nomen ex Husserl qui aeternas essentias conspiciendas habet

Scheler, Heidegger, etc., realitates humanas investigant[60]

The following developed the techniques of critical historical research: Bernheim, Langlois-Seignobos; Niebuhr, Ranke, Droysen, Mommsen; Taine, Fustel de Coulanges; Acton, Bury; and their followers down to the present time.[52]

(b) Second stage: Burckhardt: of all the disciplines, history is the least scientific, yet it contains many things that are helpful to know.[53]

The following have shown that the historical movements that called into question the primacy of the intellect are present within the course of history itself: Kierkegaard, Schopenhauer, Nietzsche, William James, Bergson, Marx, Comte, Pareto, Sorel, Freud.[54]

(c) Third stage: Wilhelm Dilthey [1833–1911] recognized the relativity of any metaphysical or religious doctrine; everything else is reducible to the *Weltanschauung*, which is irrational.[55] He wanted (but did not achieve) a critique of the rational basis of history (which would stand to historical science as the Kantian critique to the science of mechanics).[56] He strove to construct a logic of the human sciences, the *Geisteswissenschaften*, which, in fact, would be neither philosophic nor scientific but proper to human reality and human history. He initiated to a great extent[57] those studies that are now called 'phenomenology' and deal with the realities of psychic life.[58] See Díaz de Cerio.[59]

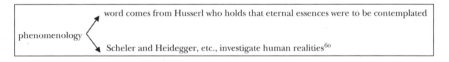

phenomenology: word comes from Husserl who holds that eternal essences were to be contemplated / Scheler and Heidegger, etc., investigate human realities[60]

52 [See ibid. 13–14. The semicolons here represent line breaks in Lonergan's schematic text.]
53 [See ibid. 14.]
54 [Some handwritten words appear at this point; the translation is an interpretation of their connection with the typed words. See ibid. 15, where all the names Lonergan mentions here appear.]
55 [See ibid. The last part of this sentence was added by hand.]
56 [See ibid. 17.]
57 [The words 'non parvum' were entered by hand.]
58 [See ibid. 17–18.]
59 [Lonergan gives no more information here. He has in mind the Jesuit Franco Díaz de Cerio Ruiz (1921–2005), the author of *W. Dilthey y el problema del mundo histórico: Estudio genético-evolutivo, con una bibliografía general* (Barcelona: J. Flors, 1959) and of other writings on Dilthey. For more on Díaz de Cerio Ruiz, see S. Pagano, 'In memoriam R.P. Franco Díaz de Cerio, s.i.,' *Archivum Historiae Pontificiae* 43 (2005) 9–11.]
60 [This diagram was added by hand.]

[6   De Historicismo (bis)][61]

1 Historicismus ut saecularismus

(a) Quod saepius auditur, Hebraeos atque Christianos sensum historicitatis invexisse, non verum est eo sensu quod alii populi et, in specie, Graeci et Romani, neque sensum historiae habuerunt neque historias conscripserunt, sed verum est hoc sensu quod Hebraei et Christiani tum omnes et singulos eventus tum totum historiae cursum sensu religioso auxerunt, nempe, populus Israeliticus initium sumpsit ex vocatione Abrahae, ex miraculosa conceptione Isaac, ex duodecim filiis Iacob, qui in Aegyptum abierunt et post quadringentos annos duce nube et ignis columna ex Aegypto exierunt. Qui populus electus foedus cum Deo suo inivit, qui propter peccata punitur et iterum iterumque Deo placato salvatur, qui diem Domini magnum et ducem a Domino constitutum exspectat atque desiderat.

Quae conceptiones, forma narrativa expressae, non solum totam religionem Hebraicam penetrant atque informant, sed etiam eandem religionem tamquam historicam a cultu sive Aegyptiaco sive Babylonico sive Graeco-Romano penitus distinguunt.

Et pariter religio Christiana est essentialiter historica, cum Iesus Nazarenus fuerit exspectatus Christus, cuius passio, mors, et resurrectio redemptionem universalem perfecerint, quod factum praeconio evangelico omnibus hominibus ab apostolis annuntiatur, ut omnes iterum adventurum Dominum Iesum expectarent. Neque tantum totus historiae cursus sensum habet, initium nempe in peccato originali, et restitutionem in Christo Iesu, et finem in secundo Christi adventu, sed etiam omnes et singuli eventus secundum beneplacitum Dei Patris occurrunt, qui vel capillos capitis in unoquoque enumerat, neque praeter eius voluntatem passer in terram cadit (Mt 10.30).

(b) Unde mentem biblicam expressit Augustinus qui in opere *De civitate Dei* totam humanam historiam et singula magna imperia secundum significationem religiosam interpretatus est atque iudicavit.

6 Historicism [bis][61]

1 Historicism as Secularism

(a) One often hears that the Hebrews and Christians introduced the meaning of historicity. This is not true in the sense that other peoples, particularly the Greeks and Romans, had no sense of history and wrote no histories, but it is true in the sense that the Hebrews and Christians added a religious dimension both to all particular historical events and to the course of history as a whole; that is to say, the people of Israel took their origin from the call of Abraham, the miraculous conception of Isaac, and the twelve sons of Jacob who went into Egypt and four hundred years later came out of Egypt guided by a cloud and a pillar of fire. This chosen people entered into a covenant with God. They are punished for their sins and time after time are saved by a placated God; they await and long for the great Day of the Lord and a leader ordained by the Lord.

These notions, expressed in narrative form, not only penetrate and inform the whole Hebrew religion, but also characterize that religion as historical and thus totally different from Egyptian or Babylonian or Greco-Roman worship.

But Christianity is also an essentially historical religion, since Jesus Christ was the expected Messiah whose passion, death, and resurrection effected universal redemption, a fact proclaimed to all humankind by the apostolic preaching of the gospel, so that all once again await the coming of the Lord Jesus. Again, not only does the whole course of history have its meaning, that is, its beginning in original sin, its restoration in Christ Jesus, and its end in the second coming of Christ, but each and every event occurs by the good pleasure of God the Father, who numbers the hairs of each one's head and apart from whose will no sparrow falls to the ground (Matthew 10.30).

(b) Hence, Augustine expressed the biblical mentality in his work *De civitate Dei*, in which he interpreted and judged the whole of human history and all its great empires in accordance with a religious meaning.

---

61 [Here begins page 4 of this section, bearing the notation 'S&H' at the top of the page. It could be a revision of the first three pages – or perhaps the first three pages are a revision of these last three. In either case, like the prior pages under the same title, these pages draw upon the previously mentioned introductory essay by Meyerhoff. Few as they are, these pages seem to contain slightly more of Lonergan's own phrasing.]

(c) Quam Christianam historiae interpretationem impugnaverunt (a′) implicite, exhibendo quemadmodum de facto res procedant, Machiavelli, Guicciardini; (b′) explicite, Voltaire qui opus a Bossuet confectum, *Histoire universelle*, 1681, innumeris arguments sat simplicibus ridiculum reddidit; iterum explicite Gibbon, *The Decline and Fall of the Roman Empire*. contra Romanum imperium victoriam atque triumphum reportaverunt barbaries et religio.

(d) Cum parum sit doctrinam refutare nisi quis etiam aliam habeat doctrinam quae in locum succedere possit, novam historiae interpretationem diversis modis introduxerunt:

(a′) G.B. Vico, qui de divina providentia sane loquitur, sed de ea inquantum est ordo divinae gubernationis ipsis rebus humanis immanens iisdemque manifestata. Non ergo cogitat Vico de providentia modo populari quae in cursu rerum naturali intervenit et miracula patrat. Similiter loquitur Vico de lege naturali, quam tamen non cogitat per modum statutorum legumque quae a moralistis promulgantur, sed de vi quadam naturali rationi insita quae sese manifestat in evolutione legis positivae humanae.

(b′) Herder, 1784, *Ideas for a Philosophical History of Mankind*, tendentiam romanticam fovit de qua aliquid plenius erit postea dicendum.[62]

(c′) Hegel, cuius philosophia idealistica ulterius processit quam deismus saeculi XVIII, ut scilicet ipse Deus quodammodo intra processum historicum includatur. Imo in doctrina Hegeliana detegi potest quemadmodum mentalitati olim Christianae satisfacere possit haec nova doctrina historica, si quidem loco divinae sapientiae habetur ipsa dialectica, loco tou *Logou* Ioannaei habetur spiritus obiectivus, loco incarnationis Verbi habentur incarnationes spiritus obiectivi in magnis viris historicis, uti in Napoleone, loco stadiorum vocationis populi Israelitici, redemptionis, praedicationis evangelicae, secundi adventus, habentur stadia evolutionis historicae per tyrannos Asiaticos, artem Graecam, ius Romanum, usque ad libertatem Germanicam.

Aspectus eschatologicus saepius recurrit: reditus ad naturam (Rousseau), triumphus Rationis (revolutio gallica), societas sine classibus (Marx), *Übermensch* (Nietszche).

(c) This Christian interpretation of history was attacked (a′) implicitly by Machiavelli and Guicciardini by pointing out how in fact events happen, and (b′) explicitly by Voltaire, who by many quite simple arguments ridiculed Bossuet's work, *Histoire universelle* (1681). Edward Gibbon also attacked this interpretation explicitly in *The Decline and Fall of the Roman Empire*, declaring that decline and fall to be the victorious triumph of barbarism and religion over the Roman Empire.

(d) Since it is largely ineffective to refute a doctrine unless one has another one to replace it with, several writers came up with various novel ways of interpreting history.

(a′) G.B. Vico did speak about divine providence, but as being the order of divine governance immanent in human affairs themselves and manifested by them. Vico, therefore, did not think of providence in the way ordinary people do, as intervening in the course of events and performing miracles. In a similar vein, Vico spoke about the natural law, but thought of it not as statutes and laws promulgated by moralists, but rather as a certain natural force innate in human reason and manifested in the development of human positive law.

(b′) Herder, in his *Ideas for a Philosophical History of Mankind* (1784), tended towards Romanticism, about which we shall speak more fully later.[62]

(c′) Hegel's idealistic philosophy went beyond eighteenth-century deism to include God himself in some way within the historical process. As a matter of fact, in Hegel one can detect how this new notion of history could satisfy the former Christian mentality, since his dialectic replaces divine wisdom, the objective Spirit replaces the Johannine *Logos*, the incarnations of the objective spirit in the great men of history (in Napoleon, for example) replace the incarnation of the Word, and instead of the historical stages of the vocation of Israel, the Redemption, the preaching of the gospel, and the second coming, there are the stages of historical progress through the Asiatic tyrants, Greek art, Roman law, right down to Germanic liberty.

An eschatological outlook often recurs: the return to nature (Rousseau), the triumph of Reason (French Revolution), the classless society (Marx), the *Übermensch* (Nietzsche).

---

62 [This discussion in fact breaks off before Romanticism comes up for discussion. See, however, the brief discussion of Romanticism in the preceding section, also on historicism. See also below, pp. 328, 330–31, 336–37.]

(d′) Completam saecularizationem effecit Marx: Deus non exsistit; intelligibilitas historica in mediis productionis cernitur; finis historicus est per proletariatum dictatorem ad perfectum communismum.

2 Historicismus uti negatio naturalismi

(a) Naturalismus in eo est quod res humanae ad ordinem rerum naturalium reducuntur et secundum methodos scientiarum naturalium investigantur. Qui modus cogitandi maxime in Gallia et Anglia praevaluit. E contra, historicismus spiritum a natura distinguit, et campum ut ita dicam intentionalem sui generis agnoscit. Scilicet, id quod proxime influit in actiones humanas modumque vivendi non in ipsis rebus materialibus invenitur sed in rerum apparentiis, in modo cogitandi atque iudicandi.

(b) Quem historicismi aspectum in primis apud Vico invenimus qui prioritatem artis poeticae affirmavit, ut non prior sit status rationaliter conceptus et contractus quidem inter homines initus, quibus postea accesserunt ornamenta artis litterarumque humaniorum, sed ut initia in mythis, in poematibus, etc., exquirantur.[63]

7   De Arte[64]

Problematis historiae alium aggredimur aspectum.

Hactenus iam de duplici scientiae notione locuti sumus, alia antiquiori et alia recentiori, unde duplicem evidentiae notionem hausimus, aliam directam ad fidem faciendam, aliam indirectam et circumstantialem ad rerum praeteritarum intelligentiam gignendam, quae intelligentia utrum scientifica esse possit in duobus casibus iisque facillimis consideravimus, nempe, utrum historia cuiusdam scientiae vel artis technicae scientifica esse possit, et utrum historia philosophiae scientifica esse possit.

Et primo in casu non ad historiam sed ad seriem historiarum pervenimus; ut relicta sit quaestio utrum systema quoddam inveniri possit quod manifestaret qualis sit illa series, seu quid in prioribus membris mutabile,

Marx produced a total secularization: God does not exist; the intelligibility of history is to be discerned in the means of production; and the end of history is the perfect communism to be attained through the dictatorship of the proletariat.

2 Historicism as the Negation of Naturalism

(a) Naturalism consists in the reduction of human affairs to the order of things in nature and in studying them according to the methods of the natural sciences. This type of thinking has been especially prevalent in France and England. Historicism, by contrast, makes a distinction between spirit and nature, and recognizes what I might call the 'field of intentionality' as something unique and distinct. This means that what has the most direct influence upon human affairs and manner of living is not to be found in material things but in the appearances of things, in the ways of thinking and judging.

(b) This aspect of historicism we find especially in Vico, who affirmed the priority of poetry; that is, it was not the state as conceived by reason or as some contract entered into by human beings that came first and was subsequently embellished by art and literature, but rather the beginnings are to be found in myths, in poems, and the like.[63]

7   Art[64]

Here we move on to another aspect of the problem of history.

We have already spoken about the two notions of science, the ancient and the modern. From them we derived two notions of evidence, one that is direct and aimed at winning credence, and the other that is indirect and circumstantial aimed at generating an understanding of the past. By looking at two quite simple cases, we inquired whether this understanding could be considered scientific, that is, whether the history of a particular science or technical art can be scientific, and whether the history of philosophy can be scientific.

In the first case we arrived not at a history but at a series of histories, thus leaving aside the question whether a system could be found that would reveal the nature of that series, that is, what would be changeable and what

63 [In the autograph, the discussion breaks off abruptly at this point with a section (c) indicated that contains nothing.]
64 [A 487, www.bernardlonergan.com 48700DTL060).]

quid immutabile; altero autem in casu, confessi sumus exsistere historiam quandam technicam quae quidem bene facit opus motivi insuper ex datis operantis, caret tamen motivo clare definito et desuper ex principiis operantis, neque tale motivum acquirere potest nisi mira quaedam philosophia philosophiarum inveniatur.

Nemo tamen non videt quam longe hi casus particulares a communi cursu rerum humanarum distent; quidquid enim sit hic communis rerum cursus, certo certius non consistit in solis artibus practicis, in scientiis, in philosophiis; ideoque omnino aggredi oportet principalem illum vitae humanae aspectum atque modum qui sine reflexa conceptualizatione sui procedit. Quam ob causam, tamquam gressum praeparatorium instituentes, non nulla de arte veniunt iam dicenda.[65]

In arte enim invenitur (1) activitas quaedam proprie humana, (2) etiam a primitivis antiquissimis exercita, et (3) adeo expers reflexae sui conceptualizationis ut etiam ipsa theoria artis esssentialiter quodammodo ab arte differre cernatur.

7.1 De notione artis

Ars dici potest 'formarum sensibilium et purarum compositio quaedam expressiva atque symbolica.'[66] Quae definitio quid sibi velit per singula verba discurrendo aperire oportet.

unchangeable in its prior elements. In the second case we maintained that there exists a technical history that, while ably fulfilling the function of the movement that operates upwards from the data, nevertheless lacks a clearly defined movement operating from above, from general principles, and cannot acquire such a dynamic unless some marvelous philosophy of philosophies should be found.

It is quite obvious how remote these cases are from the ordinary course of human life. For whatever this ordinary course may be, it most certainly does not consist solely in the practical arts, in the sciences, and in philosophies. Therefore, we must by all means turn to consider the principal aspect and feature of human activity that is carried on without any reflective conceptualization of itself. Accordingly, by way of an introductory step, we have a few observations to make concerning art.[65]

In art we find: (1) an activity that is properly human, (2) that was practiced by even the most ancient and primitive people, and (3) that is so lacking in a reflective conceptualization of itself that even the theory of art is seen to be somehow essentially different from art itself.

7.1 The Notion of Art

Art can be defined as 'an expressive symbolic composition of pure sensible forms.'[66] Let us now see what this definition means by considering each word.

---

65 [Perhaps an indication of the connection between art and history, as Lonergan understands it, can be found near the beginning of his discussion of history in *Topics in Education*: 'With regard to the problem of history, we may start from our discussion of human life as basically artistic, creative' (p. 235). For a further elaboration of this remark, see ibid. 251–54, where Lonergan discusses briefly regional culture as a realization of a way of life, artistic living as simply living, but not a purely individual affair, and the 'style' of the regional group that comes about more by artistic communication than through the communication of concepts.]

66 [This definition of art raises some interesting questions. In the lectures on education at Xavier University, Cincinnati, in the ninth lecture, whose topic was art, Lonergan presented what would subsequently become his standard definition of art: 'I propose to reflect on a definition of art that I thought was helpful. It was worked out by Susanne Langer in her book, *Feeling and Form: A Theory of Art Developed from* Philosophy in a New Key (New York: Charles Scribner's Sons, 1953). She conceives art as an objectification of a purely experiential pattern.' (See Lonergan, *Topics in Education* 211; an editorial footnote adds the following: '... this definition does not appear in

(1) Forma sensibilis: id quod apparet visioni, auditui, kinaesthesiae. Iterum: obiectum materiale phaenomenologiae. Iterum: eadem compositio habetur tum in notis musicis exscriptis tum in iisdem notis sonatis; sed in illis deest, in his adest forma sensibilis, nempe, sonus.

(2) Purae formae sensibiles: scilicet, non instrumentalizatae, sed quodammodo propter se.

Communiter in vita humana formae sensibiles subsunt fini, ordinationi, attentioni, structurationi, dynamismo non propriis sed alienis, puta vitae intellectualis, uti in Thale philosopho qui totus in stellis observandis puteum prae oculis non percepit; vel vitae intersubiectivae, interpersonalis, ubi sensibiles formae apprehenduntur quatenus mentem, sensum, sentimenta alterius manifestant; vel vitae practicae, ubi iterum formae sensibiles apprehenduntur, sed per modum signorum quae actionem faciendam indicant et quodammodo inducunt (lux rubra apparet, et frenum automobilis constringitur; lux viridis apparet, et premitur accelerator).

(3) Compositio est quaedam forma, ordinatio, sed sui generis. Exclusa enim instrumentalitate vitae sensitivae, non habetur vacuum seu status quidam iners, sed efficitur quaedam liberatio ut ipsa vita psychica secundum

(1) 'Sensible form': that which is perceptible to one's vision, hearing, or sense of motion; or again, the material object of phenomenology. Still again, the same musical composition is present both in the notes in the written score and in those same notes when played; but the sensible form, namely sound, is lacking in the first while present in the second.

(2) 'Pure sensible forms': that is to say, not instrumentalized, but existing for their own sake in some way.

Very frequently in human life sensible forms are subordinated to some purpose, ordering, attention, structuring, or dynamism that is not proper to them but alien – in the intellectual life, for example, as in the case of the philosopher Thales who while gazing up at the stars failed to notice the well at his feet; in intersubjective or interpersonal life, where sensible forms are apprehended as manifesting the thoughts or meaning or feelings of another; or in practical day-to-day living, where sensible forms are apprehended but only as signs indicating some action to be performed and even somehow inducing it (e.g., the traffic light is red, and the brakes are applied; it turns green, and the accelerator is pressed).

(3) 'Composition' means a form, an ordering or arrangement, but unique. The exclusion of the instrumentalization of the life of the senses does not leave a vacuum or inert state; rather, there results a certain libera-

---

Langer's book; it seems to be a definition that Lonergan worked out from reading Langer.' The note adds that Langer defines art as 'the creation of forms symbolic of human feeling.') The definition offered in the education lectures is maintained all the way to *Method in Theology*, where it appears in the discussion of art as a carrier of meaning (p. 61). Now the course 'De systemate et historia' was first given in the fall semester of 1959, which would place it after the Cincinnati lectures on education. The definition of art given in these notes, which presumably were part of the material prepared for 'De systemate et historia,' differs at least verbally from that given in the Cincinnati lecture. And it includes no mention of Langer's book, even though that book was cited in another connection in the course 'De intellectu et methodo,' which was first given in the spring semester of 1959, and so before the Cincinnati lectures. The treatment of art is very similar, no matter which definition is employed. The question, then, is: if Lonergan had worked out by mid-August of 1959 what was to become his standard definition of art, why does it not appear in his notes on art for 'De systemate et historia'? Did he perhaps prepare these notes earlier than mid-August of 1959 and simply not change the definition of art in them, and perhaps also in his course presentation, to agree verbally with the definition he gave in the Cincinnati lecture? No matter what the answer to this question, the basic notion of art remains constant.]

proprias leges in actum prorumpatur. Quae quidem vita non informis sed suo modo ordinata est, unde artistae loqui solent de quadam inevitabilitate formae. Puta, si sonatur 'Do,' quilibet alius sonus sequi potest; sed si sonatur series quaedam vel brevissima[67] notarum, ipsa incepta series suam continuationem quodammodo determinat atque exigit; et magnorum compositorum virtus in eo conspicitur quod hanc exigentiam ita implent ut tamen modo inopinato, locupletiori, pleniori faciant.

Quamvis compositio in re musica magis obvia est, pariter tamen adest in reliquis artibus, in coloribus, lineis, lucis et umbrae successionibus, voluminibus, saltantium motibus, etc., componendis.

Quae quidem compositio intellectu conspici potest et conceptibus verbisque exprimi. Ita critici ad compositionem operis advertunt, elementa distinguunt, ipsam compositionem describunt, aliam et aliam inter se comparant; imo, quaedam educatio artistica requiritur et quaedam notitia evolutionis artisticae, ut quis perveniat ad illum gustum cui complacet non tantum ars simplicior sed etiam subtilior et evolutior.

Attamen, quamvis compositio artistica intelligibilitatem habeat, nihilominus haec intelligibilitas totam compositionis rationem neque totam neque principalem compositionis rationem dicit. Propria enim et principalis compositionis ratio potius in ordine sensibili quam intelligibili invenitur; nam sicut res inorganicae et multo magis res organicae proprias formas habent, ita etiam ipsa vita psychica et humana; et propria compositionis ratio non in eo est quod concipi et describi potest sed in eo quod vitam humanam psychicam secundum proprias leges, secundum proprias exigentias, secundum propriam connaturalitatem actuat.

Connectitur ergo hoc quod de compositione diximus cum eo quod antea de puris formis sensibilibus dixeramus: ideo ars vult formas sensibiles puras, ab omni instrumentalitate liberatas, ut eas componat secundum connaturalitatem, exigentias, leges ipsius sensibilitatis.

(4) Artem diximus purarum formarum sensibilium compositionem *expressivam*, et iam de illa voce 'expressiva' loquendum est.[68]

tion so that one's psychic life might break forth into activity in accordance with the laws proper to it. This life is not formless, but is ordered in its own way, so that artists often speak of a certain inevitability of form. For example, if one plays the note *Do*, any other sound can follow it; but if one plays a series of notes, even a very short series,[67] that initial series somehow determines and demands its continuation. The genius of the great composers lies in their ability to fulfill that demand in an unexpected yet in a richer, fuller manner.

Although musical composition is the most obvious instance, the same obtains in the other arts, in color, line, the interplay of light and darkness, the composition of volumes in space, of movements in a dance, and so on.

This sort of composition can be grasped intellectually and expressed in concepts and words. Thus, critics comment upon the composition of a work, distinguish its elements, describe the composition itself and compare it to other compositions. Indeed, a certain artistic education and some knowledge of the development of the art are required in order to acquire that taste that would find pleasure not only in the simpler sort of art but also in subtler and more highly developed artistic forms.

However, even though artistic composition has intelligibility, still this intelligibility expresses neither the overall nor the fundamental idea of the composition. The fundamental idea of a composition is to be found in the sensible rather than in the intelligible order. For just as inorganic matter, and even more so organic matter, have their proper forms, so also does the psychic human life; and the proper meaning of [an artistic] composition is to be found not in the fact that it can be conceived and described but in the fact that it actuates the human psyche in accordance with its proper laws, its proper exigencies, and its proper connaturality.

What we have said here about composition is connected with what we said previously about pure sensible forms. Art, therefore, needs pure sensible forms, freed from all instrumentalization, in order to compose them according to the connaturality, the exigencies, and the laws of human sensibility.

(4) We defined art as the *expressive* composition of pure sensible forms, and so now we must explain what we mean by 'expressive.'[68]

---

67 [The Latin words 'vel brevissima' were added by hand.]
68 [See below, pp. 294–97. See also 'De expressione, Expression' the first item in appendix 2 below.]

Iam vero ars potest esse etiam representativa: ita pictura occidentalis per saecula res, plantas, animalia, homines repraesentabat; ita ipsa musica, quae dicitur programmatica, cantus avium vel sonos naturales sive fluminum sive tonitruum, etc., imitari et repraesentare potest. Sed hic aspectus repraesentativus est superadditus; non tam ad ipsam artis essentiam pertinet quam ad complementum quod adesse vel abesse absolute potest.

E contra, compositio artistica debet esse expressiva, hoc est, debet habere aliquem sensum; non quidem sensum conceptualem sicut in nominibus et verbis invenitur, sed sensum ipsius vitae psychicae praeconceptualem, qui non per conceptus sed tantummodo per artes communicatur.

Qualis sit ille sensus praeconceptualis, psychicus? Nisi analogiis non exprimitur; et ipsa expressio analogica non est nisi quaedam indigitatio, quasi quis responderet ad quaestionem, quid sit homo, per interiectionem, ecce! hic est homo.

Iamvero in ipso ordine intellectuali, duplex est sensus: alius externus, denotativus; et alius internus in intrinseca rationum cohaerentia fundatus. Ita hoc nomen, vectis (lever, ital. leva, gall. levier) denotat instrumentum quo pondera magna facilius elevantur. Sed ulterius mechanici agnoscunt legem quandam vectis, nempe, $aF' = bF''$,[69] et quia ipsa haec lex in se est intelligibilis, ita eam sensum habere, facere, dicimus.

Similiter in vita sensitiva, quae ad ordinem intentionalem pertingit, ipsa interna elementorum cohaerentia, ordinatio, compositio est sensus quidam, qui sensus ipsi vitae psychicae immanens exprimitur per compositionem artisticam purarum formarum sensibilium. Dicitur ergo compositio sensum habere quatenus ipse compositionis ordo quodammodo correspondet ad sensum vitae psychicae immanentem, quae quidem correspondentia non est materialis sed formalis; non materialis quia interior vitae psychicae sensus non inest coloribus, sonis, figuris, saltantium motibus, sed formalis quia qualis est compositio in coloribus, sonis, figuris, motibus, talis est compositio in ipsa vita psychica.

Iterum, dicitur opus artisticum exprimere, vel esse compositionem expressivam, quatenus compositioni, ordinationi operis correspondet similis quaedam compositio vel ordinatio in ipsa experientia vitae. Notate tamen artistam exprimere non experientiam personalem et actualem. Alia est ars et alia est autobiographia: quo maior est artista, eo plenius sensum vitae non suum sed alienum exprimere potest. Et multo minus actualis experien-

Art can also be representational. For centuries Western art depicted material objects, plants, animals, people; and music that is called programmatic imitates and represents the singing of birds or the sounds of nature such as flowing water, thunder, and the like. But this representational aspect is something superadded; it pertains not so much to the essence of an art as to a complementary feature that absolutely speaking can be present or absent.

On the other hand, artistic composition has to be expressive, has to have some meaning, not a conceptual meaning as found in nouns and verbs, but a preconceptual meaning of the psyche itself that is communicated not through concepts but only through art.

What is the nature of this preconceptual psychic meaning? It can only be expressed by analogies. And this analogical expression can only point at something, like someone answering the question, 'What do you mean by a man?' by saying, 'Look! that is a man.'

In the intellectual order there are two kinds of meaning, one that is external and denotative, the other internal and based upon the intrinsic coherence of ideas. For example, the word 'lever' denotes an instrument for more easily moving heavy objects; but those who know mechanics are aware of the law of the lever, namely, $aF' = bF''$,[69] and since this law is intelligible in itself, we say that it has meaning, it makes sense.

Similarly in the life of the senses, which belongs to the intentional order, the very internal coherence, arrangement, and composition of the elements is a certain meaning, a meaning immanent in the psyche and expressed through the artistic composition of pure sensible forms. Such a composition, therefore, is said to have meaning inasmuch as the order of the composition itself corresponds to the meaning immanent in the psyche. This correspondence is not material, but formal: it is not material, because the interior life of the psyche does not consist of colors or sounds or shapes or the movements of dancers; it is formal because as the composition in colors, sounds, shapes, or movements is, so is the composition in psychic life itself.

Again, a work of art is said to express, to be an expressive composition, inasmuch as to its composition, its arrangement, there corresponds a similar composition or arrangement in lived experience. Note, however, that the artist does not express his actual personal experience. Art is not autobiography; the greater the artist, the more fully he can express the meaning not of his own life but that of others. Much less is actual experience expressed

---

69 [The editors thank Terrance Quinn for his help in identifying this formula.]

tia per artem exprimitur: actualis enim experientia ab instrumentalizatione raro liberatur; idealizatio requiritur ut a multis et confusis vitae accidentibus et perturbationibus liberatur quasi essentia cuiusdam experientiae; et quamvis artista sive ex experientia sua sive ex sympathia inspirationem hauserit, tamen opus artisticum hanc inspirationem tamquam thema elaboratum atque complendum adsumit. Unde Wordsworth dixit poemata exprimere non ipsas emotiones actu expertas sed emotiones quae in tranquillitate recoluntur; et lamentatus est Mozart vitam suam tot aerumnis deprimi ut componere non possit, scilicet quia defuit necessaria tranquillitas.

(5) Illustratur hic sensus haecque expressio ex diversis artis generibus.

(a) Ars decorativa facit superficiem visibilem. An vidistis muros huius aulae? Ita vidistis ut certo sciatis nihil adesse videndum. Nihil enim adest quod attentionem moveat, nihil quod interesse excitet, nihil in quo vita vel psychica sustentetur.

Unde duplex distingui potest visibilitas. Alia est visibilitas quae eo ipso habetur quod oculi non sunt caeci et spatium tenebris non obruitur. Alia autem est visibilitas quae non solum actum videndi reddit possibilem sed eum invitat, sustentat, et ab alia activitate hominem revocat.

Quid facit differentiam inter duplicem visibilitatem? Bene, conscientia humana non est automatica quaedam functio datorum externorum. In datis externis quoddam initium invenit vel potius invenire potest; sed utrum inveniat necne dependet ex orientatione ipsius conscientiae, quae inde ab ipsa sensibilitate est quid liberum, quid sui dominus, quid in suos fines propter suam curam, suam *Sorge*, intentum.

Ulterius, nisi ordinatum intra conscientiam non assumitur. Transimus per vias publicas et colloquimur. Strepitus fere continuus vix auditur. Sed soni ex voce colloquentis audiuntur. Audiuntur quia habent sensum; et strepitus non auditur quia sensu caret. Facillime audimus et repetimus melodiam; sed difficillime diceremus quo ordine quos strepitus in viis publicis ultimo quodam momento audiverimus.

Decoratio ergo facit superficiem visibilem quia ponit ordinem visibilem, et ipse ordo visibilis attentionem percellit quia ordo in decoratione posita est, generatim, ordo quidam organicus, ordo ramorum ex trunco, ordo fo-

through art; for actual experience is rarely freed from instrumentalization. Idealization is required to free the essence, as it were, of an experience from the jumble of the multitude of incidents and upheavals in one's life; and although an artist may have drawn inspiration from his own experience or his sympathetic feeling, his artistic work takes this inspiration as a theme to be developed and brought to completion. Thus it is that Wordsworth wrote that poetry does not express emotions that are actually being experienced but 'emotion recollected in tranquillity.' And Mozart complained that his life was encumbered with so many troubles that he was unable to compose; in other words, he lacked the peace and quiet necessary for his work.

(5) This meaning and expression is illustrated by examples in various forms of art.

(a) Decorative art renders a surface visible. Do you see the walls in this room? In seeing them you realize that there is nothing there to be looked at. There is nothing to attract your attention to them, nothing to arouse your interest, nothing to contribute to your psychic life.

Hence, we may distinguish two kinds of visibility. There is the visibility that occurs automatically when your eyes are open and not blind and you are not in the dark. But there is also the visibility that not only renders the act of seeing possible but also invites it, fosters it, and diverts one's attention away from what one is doing.

What makes the difference between these two? Well, human consciousness is not an automatic function of external data. It begins, or rather, can begin, in external data; but whether it succeeds or not depends on the orientation of one's consciousness, which, beginning with its sensibility, is something free and autonomous, and intent upon its own ends because of its concern, its *Sorge*.

Furthermore, nothing is absorbed unless it is ordered within one's consciousness. For example, we are walking down the street engaged in conversation. We hardly hear the continuous noise. But we do hear the sounds of the voice of our companion. They are heard because they carry a meaning. The street sounds are not heard because they have no meaning. We can easily hear and repeat a melody, but it would be very hard for us to say in what order the street sounds came to us even a moment ago.

In this way decoration renders a surface visible because it produces a visible order. And that visible order strikes our attention because the order produced in a decoration is, generally speaking, an organic order, the order of branches from the trunk of a tree, the order of leaves on the branch-

liorum ex ramis, non ipsa complexitate naturae, sed modo quodam faciliori et idealizato et saepius repetito.[70]

8 De Circulo Operationum[71]

8.1 Operabile, operatio, operatum

Declarari possunt per relationes praesuppositionis, resultantiae, transitionis.

Praesupponitur operabile ab operatione (finita). Resultat operatum ex operatione. Transitur per operationem ex operabili in operatum.[72]

8.2 Operatio identica (seu nulla)

Identica dicitur operatio ubi inter se non differunt operabile et operatum. V.g., additur vel subtrahitur zero; multiplicatur vel dividitur per unum; differentiatur e^x. Ubi exsistit operatio identica, (1) omne operabile statim ut operatum considerari potest, ut sermo sit solummodo de operationibus et operatis; (2) determinata operatione, etiam determinatur aliquod operabile, puta, zero, unum, e^x.

es – not, however, with the complexity found in nature, but in a manner that is easier and idealized and often repeated ...[70]

8   The Circle of Operations[71]

8.1 Operable, Operation, Result (Operated)

These terms can be clarified by reference to relations of presupposition, resultance, and transition.

An operable, something that can be operated on, is presupposed by a (finite) operation. An operation results in something 'operated.' There is a transition through an operation from an operable to something operated.[72]

8.2 Identical Operation (or None)

An operation is said to be identical where there is no difference between the operable and the result; for example, when zero is added or subtracted, or when a sum is multiplied or divided by one, or when there is the differential e^x. When there is an identical operation, (a) every operable can immediately be considered as what is operated, so that there is mention only of operations and what is operated; (b) once the operation is determined, any operable such as zero, one, or e^x is also determined.

70 [Here the typescript breaks off.]
71 [A 488 in the Lonergan Archive, 48800DTL050 on the website www.bernard lonergan.com. The handwritten notes reported on in the following chapter in this volume will confirm the view that the circle of operations is probably the most significant notion in the material on system and history. 48200DTE050 begins with the handwritten heading 'History and System,' under which the first item reads: '(A) There is a systematic component to human living: (1) Assimilation; (2) Accommodation → circ. op.' See below, p. 326.]
72 [See below, p. 313, item 47600DTE050. In this item, under an underlined subhead 'A group of operations carries and reveals a set of immanent meanings,' Lonergan writes the following:
carries[:]   operabilia   operationes   operata are all interrelated
materials : means : ends.
It is difficult to align the translation of 'operatum' and 'operata' with that of 'operabilia' and 'operationes,' so that the same root appears in each English word. 'Operated' is not a noun in English, so it will be used sparingly here. 'Result' or 'resultant' has been chosen, rather than 'work,' which has a connotation of production; the relevant relation is called 'resultantia' rather than 'productio,' and hence 'result' or 'resultant' would seem to translate 'operatum' accurately.]

8.3 Operationum coniunctio; series cyclica; operatio directa et inversa

Coniungi dicuntur operationes successivae, ubi operatum, ex priori operatione resultans, tamquam operabile a subsequente operatione praesuppositum adsumitur.

Series operationum coniunctarum dicitur cyclica ubi tota series operationi identicae aequivalet, seu ubi inter se non differunt primum operabile et ultimum operatum.[73] Ubi duae operationes coniunctae aequivalent operationi identicae, prior dicitur directa et altera inversa.

Diversimode coniunguntur simultaneae – cf. chorda in musica.[74]

8.4 Operationum compositio; isomorphismus

Non solum coniungi sed et componi dicuntur operationes et operata ubi in singulis operationibus nulla invenitur identica et in pluribus simul sumptis deest series cyclica.

Compositis operationibus correspondent operata similiter composita. Scilicet, aliud est elementum materiale (operatio, operatum) et aliud est elementum structurale (ipsa compositio); et quamvis inter se dissimilia sint operationes et operata, similis tamen est ipsa compositio seu structura qua inter se uniuntur tam operationes quam operata.

Quae similitudo, quam isomorphismum nominamus, inveniri potest (1) si inter se comparantur duae operationum series, (2) si inter se comparantur duae operatorum series, (3) si inter se comparantur tum operationum series tum operatorum series.

Qui ad talem similitudinem attendit, gradum quendam specificum abstractionis attingit, quem vocari licet 'abstractionem operatoriam.'[75]

8.3   The Linking of Operations; Cyclical Series, Direct and Inverse Operations

Successive operations are said to be linked where something resulting from a previous operation is taken as an operable presupposed by a subsequent operation.

A series of linked operations is said to be cyclical where the series as a whole is equivalent to an identical operation, that is, where there is no difference between the first operable and the last 'operated.'[73] When two linked operations are equivalent to an identical operation, the former is called direct, the latter inverse.

Simultaneous operations are conjoined in different ways – compare musical chords, for example.[74]

8.4   The Composition of Operations; Isomorphism

Operations and resultants are said to be not only linked but also composite where none of the operations is found to be identical and several taken together do not make up a cyclical series.

To composite operations correspond results that are similarly composite. Thus, the material element (the operation, the result) and the structural element (the composition) are different; and although the operations and the results are dissimilar, yet the composition or structure uniting the operations is similar to the composition or structure uniting the results.

This similarity, which we call isomorphism, is to be found (a) if two series of operations are compared to each other, (b) if two series of results are compared to each other, (c) if both a series of operations and a series of works are compared to each other.

One who attends to this similarity reaches a specific degree of abstraction, which may be termed 'operatory abstraction.'[75]

---

73 [Compare the distinct notion of schemes of recurrence in *Insight*.]

74 [A handwritten marginal remark by Lonergan.]

75 [The words 'operatoria' and 'operatorius' are difficult to translate. 'Operatory' was chosen, since (1) Lonergan explicitly distinguishes what he is talking about from 'operative' as in the Scholastic 'operative habit,' and (2) 'operational' denotes only one aspect of what is included in 'operatoria' or 'operatorius.' He is proposing something that 'abstracts from operables, operations, and *operata* to attend solely to their structural composition.' In fact, it may be that the related 'habitus operatorius' is a very important notion,

Unde provisorie[76] definitur: operatoria est abstractio quae ab operabilibus, operationibus, et operatis ita abstrahit ut ad solam earum compositionem structuralem attendat.

Momentum abstractionis operatoriae in eo est ut quis uno quasi intuitu simul dynamicum et staticum, schematica maximeque concreta considerare possit. Ipsae enim operationes sunt dynamicae; operata autem statica esse possunt. Ipsa structura est schematica, quae tamen in maxime concretis operationibus et operatis discernitur. Praeterea, per modum unius coniunguntur methodus (compositio operationum) et obiectum structurale (quasi formale) [compositio operatorum].[77]

8.5 Operationum circuli

Sicut operationes coniungi et componi possunt, ita etiam mutuo se indigent seque complent. Quae enim operatio tamquam operabile adsumit quod alia operatione operatum est, et prioribus indigentiis subvenit eiusdemque opus perficit. Circulum operationum dicimus totalitatem quandam atque quasi synthesin operationum quae coniungi et componi possunt, mutuo se indigent seque complent.

Criterion ergo circuli ex ratione syntheseos peti potest: ut adsit circulus, ubi subtracta operatione quadam caeterae quodammodo incompletae et mancae manent, sed addita ulteriori quadam operatione etiam aliae addendae sunt; e contra, ut desit circulus, ubi addita vel subtracta operatione quadam, vel parva omnino efficitur differentia (quia nondum ad circulum acceditur) vel maxima efficitur (quia iam habetur circulus completus).

Secundum mathematicos, est operationum circulus ubi (1) exsistit operatio identica, (2) singulis operationibus directis adsunt correspondentes inversae, (3) si operatio A, et operatio B, ad circulum pertinet, etiam coniuncta operatio, AB, ad circulum pertinet.

Latius quodammodo magisque dynamice concipitur circulus quasi equi-

Hence, we have a provisional[76] definition: operatory abstraction is abstraction from operables, operations, and results (*operata*) to attend solely to their structural composition.

The importance of operatory abstraction lies in this, that a person in one insight can consider simultaneously what is dynamic and what is static, what are schematic and what are most concrete. For the operations themselves are dynamic, while the results may be static. The structure itself is schematic, yet it is nevertheless discernible in the most concrete operations and results. Besides, a method (the composition of the operations) and a structural (quasi-formal) object [the composition of the results] are linked together as one.[77]

8.5   Circles of Operations

As operations can be linked and composed, so also they need and complement one another. One operation undertakes as its operable the results of another operation, and so assists and perfects the prior operation. A totality and quasi synthesis of operations that can be linked and composed and that need and complement one another is called a 'circle of operations.'

Hence, the criterion of such a circle can be found in the very nature of a synthesis: there is a circle when with the removal of an operation all the others remain in some way or other incomplete and defective, but with the addition of some further operation others also are to be added; on the contrary, there is no circle when the addition or removal of an operation makes either the very slightest difference (because there is no circle yet) or the very greatest difference (because there is already a complete circle).

According to mathematicians, there is a circle of operations where (1) there exists an identical operation, (2) for each direct operation there is a corresponding inverse operation, or (3) where operation A and operation B belong to the circle, their compound operation AB also belongs to that circle.

A circle can be conceived in a broader and more dynamic way as a sort

---

original with Lonergan; it should be given a term that distinguishes it from operables, operations, and *operata*, and at least partly for this reason 'operatory' was chosen.]

76 [The Latin word *provisorie* was added by hand.]

77 [This sentence was added by hand in Latin.]

librium quoddam operatorium, in quod tendit evolutio praevia, et in quo fundatur evolutio subsequens. Quare, [1] *fit* circulus inquantum operatio operationi accidit, donec circulus compleatur; [2] *perficitur* circulus iam exsistens inquantum operationes iam exercitae paulo mutantur ut novis operabilibus paulo diversis adaptentur; [3] *integrantur* circuli quatenus iam exsistentes et diversi quodammodo coalescunt ut unus oriatur circulus maior, efficacior, perfectior;[78] [4] *specializantur* circuli quatenus circulus operationum maior in duos, vel plures, quasi sub-circulos dividitur.[79]

8.6 Habitus operatorius

Cum de ratione compositionis est ut operatio operationi succedat, totus quidam operationum circulus non simul exercetur actu. Quare, ne abstracta sit cogitatio de circulis, ex actu ad potentiam transeundum est.

Et passive quidem potentia ad circulum operationum in operabilibus invenitur; active autem in principiis vel quae operantur vel quibus fiunt operationes, et quidem prompte, facile, delectabiliter, opportune, et similia pro rerum diversitate et natura.

Notate non idem prorsus hunc habitum operatorium et quem Scholastici nominant habitum operativum. Operativus enim habitus in una quadem et determinata potentia subiectatur, puta, in intellectu, in voluntate, in irascibili vel concupiscibili. Operatorius autem habitus in multis simul potentiis subiectari potest, uti in artibus conspicitur quibus totus homo occupatur tam secundum corpus quam secundum animam, vel etiam in multis simul hominibus subiectatur, uti in operationibus manifestum est quae instituta socialia et culturalia supponunt atque actuant.[80]

Exercentur habitus operatorii, alii quidem sine ulla cognitione, et alii cum cognitione et quodammodo per cognitionem. Hi ulterius dividuntur prout tantummodo in actu exercito cognoscuntur vel etiam in actu signato

of operatory equilibrium to which the previous development tends and on which subsequent development is based. Therefore, [1] a circle is *created* as one operation follows upon another, until the circle is complete; [2] an already existing circle is *perfected* inasmuch as operations already being performed are slightly changed so as to be adapted to new and slightly different operables; [3] circles are *integrated* insofar as, being already existing and diverse, they in some way coalesce to form one larger, more effective, and more perfect circle;[78] [4] circles are *specialized* insofar as a circle of operations is divided into two or more 'sub-circles.'[79]

8.6 Operatory Habit

Since it is of the nature of composition that one operation follows another, an entire circle of operations is not actually in operation at the same time. Hence, lest our thinking about circles be abstract, we must now turn from act to potency.

Potency to a circle of operations is passively in the operables; actively, potency is in either the principles that operate or those by which operations are carried out, and indeed done so promptly, easily, pleasurably, opportunely, and in keeping with the nature of the various things in question.

Note that this operatory habit is quite different from what the Scholastics call 'operative habit.' An operative habit is in one determinate potency as its subject, such as in the intellect, the will, or the irascible or concupiscible appetite. An operatory habit, however, can have as its subject a number of potencies at the same time, as in the case of the arts, for example, in which the whole person is involved, body and soul. It can even reside in a multitude of persons at the same time as its subject, as can be clearly seen in the operations that social and cultural institutions support and carry out.[80]

Some operatory habits are exercised apart from any cognition, others with cognition and in a certain way through cognition. The latter are divided according as to whether they are known only in their actual exercise

---

78 [Lonergan has the following, partially undecipherable handwritten insertion at this point: 'Psychological development in children: Piaget. Culture ...: Olympians and Dionysians.' The Latin word 'integrantur' is added by hand in this sentence, replacing 'evolvuntur.']

79 [The material in [4] was added by hand.]

80 [The Latin words from 'instituta' were added by hand, replacing 'ad rem culturalem et socialem pertinet.']

per reflexionem quandam innotescunt. Qui sine cognitione exercentur, naturales dici possunt. Qui per cognitionem sed tantummodo in actu exercito fiunt, impliciti seu latentes seu inconscii dicuntur. Quorum cognitio ad actum signatum pervenit, iam expliciti vel conscii sunt.[81]

Sicut ipse operationum circulus fieri, perfici, integrari, specializari dicitur, ita etiam habitus operatorius acquiritur, perficitur, integratur, specializatur. Habitus enim operatorius est principium activum relate ad circulum operationum. Praeterea, sicut ipse habitus potest esse naturalis vel implicitus vel explicitus, ita etiam habitus acquisitio, perfectio, integratio, specializatio.[82]

8.7 Operatorum systema

Operationum circulus, sicut ad habitum operatorium tamquam ad principium respicit, ita ad systema operatorum tamquam terminus vel etiam finem comparatur.

Tot enim diversa operata ex uno eodemque operationum circulo oriri possunt quot sunt diversae combinationes quibus operationes diversae componi possunt, quot sunt diversae permutationes quibus ipsae combinationes variantur, quot ulterius diversa fiunt operata ex repetitione eiusdem vel operationis vel combinationis vel permutationis, etc.

Quae tamen quantumvis magna operatorum possibilium multitudo ita sibi cohaeret ut systema recte nominetur. Supposito enim habitu operatorio[83] vel naturali vel implicito, statim effici potest quodlibet ex operatis possibilibus. Supposito autem habitu explicito, (1) statim reduci potest quodlibet operatum in operationes quibus efficitur, et (2) mediante ipso

or whether they are also known objectively through conscious reflection upon them. Those habits that are exercised apart from any cognition may be called natural habits. Those that involve cognition but only in their exercise are said to be implicit or latent or unconscious, while those whose cognition has reached the level of reflective knowledge are now explicit or conscious.[81]

Just as the circle of operations itself is said to be created, perfected, integrated, and specialized, so also are operatory habits acquired, perfected, integrated, and specialized; for an operatory habit is the active principle with regard to a circle of operations. Moreover, just as a habit itself can be natural or implicit or explicit, so are the acquisition, the perfection, the integration, and the specialization of the habit similarly divided.[82]

8.7   The System of the Results

As a circle of operations regards an operatory habit as its principle, so also is it related to a system of results as to its term or even its purpose.

There are as many different results that can emerge from one and the same circle of operations (1) as there are different combinations in which different operations can be composed, (2) as there are different permutations by which these combinations themselves can vary, and (3), still further, as there are various results from the repetition of the same operation or combination or permutation, etc.

Yet, however great the number of possible results may be, they are so cohesive that they may rightly be said to be a 'system.' For presupposing a natural or an implicit operatory[83] habit, any one of the possible results can immediately be brought about. And presupposing an explicit habit, (1) any result can immediately be reduced to the operations by which it is brought

81   [In the margin, there appears the handwritten word 'rewrite,' with an arrow pointing to the material beginning with 'while.' The problem may have to do with the use of the words 'unconscious' (right before this material) and 'conscious,' which is different from Lonergan's strict usage (though he departs at times from this usage).]

82   [The Latin words 'integrari,' 'specializari,' 'integratur,' 'specializatur,' 'integratio,' and 'specializatio' were added by hand, with 'integrari' replacing 'evolvi,' 'integratur' replacing 'evolvitur,' and 'integratio' replacing 'evolutio.']

83   [The Latin reads 'operativo,' but it would seem Lonergan intends to say 'operatorio.' The change was made by the editors.]

operationum circulo, ad quodlibet aliud in systemate operatum certis relationibus referri potest.

Quibus perspectis, sub novo magisque fundamentali aspectu revelatur
virtus abstractionis operatoriae. Primum enim et antea consideratum huius
abstractionis gradum attendere recolimus ad structuram secundum quod
componuntur sive operationes sive operata. Sed cum iam ad habitum, circulum, systema perventum sit, ad nucleum unde omnes structurae derivantur attingimus. Nam ipsae relationes internae quibus operationes inter se
referuntur, eaedem sunt quae in variis combinationibus, permutationibus,
et repetitionibus componuntur ut concretae operationes concretaque operata habeantur.

Qui tamen abstractionis modus minime a concreto rerum processu exsu-
lat, si quidem ipsi habitus, ipsi circuli, ipsa systemata fiunt et perficiuntur,
integrantur et specializantur.[84]

[8.8] De unitate et divisione scientiarum

1 Ea quaeritur scientiarum divisio quae adeo non obscuret ut potius illumi-
net earum unitatem.

2 Scientiam dicimus habitum operatorium cognoscitivum explicitum.

Habitus: principium proximum ad operationes omnes cuiusdam circuli
eliciendas; unde et operata formant systema.

Operatorius: non ergo operativus; et ideo non necessario in una quadam
potentia subiectatur vel in uno quodam operante. Ita scientia non in solo
intellectu necessario est sed etiam in sensu et memoria sensitiva, imo et
in voluntate quae methodum eligit eamque fideliter sequitur. Praeterea,
scientia esse potest quae tanta est ut tota in unius hominis mente non contineatur.

Cognoscitivus: cuius operata sunt cognita, et operabilia cognoscibilia.

Explicitus: ipse habitus, circulus, systema in actu signato cognoscitur; et
ideo excluditur illa cognitio (intelligentia vulgaris, sensus communis) quae
in omni actu humano habetur.

3 Primam et fundamentalem credimus divisionem quae inter scientias
coordinativas et coordinatas distinguit.

about, and (2) through the circle of operations it can be related with certitude to any other resultant in the system.

From this it follows that the value of operatory abstraction is seen in a new and more fundamental light. We recall that the first degree of this abstraction that we saw earlier regards the structure of the composition either of operations or of resultants. But since we have now considered the notions of habit, circle, and system, we are touching upon the very core idea whence all structures are derived. For the internal relations themselves by which operations are interrelated are the very ones that are composed in various combinations, permutations, and repetitions to give rise to concrete operations and concrete results.

Nevertheless, this type of abstraction by no means goes beyond the limits of the concrete process of things, since it is the habits, the circles, and the systems themselves that are created and perfected, integrated and specialized.[84]

[8.8] The Unity and Division of the Sciences

1 We are seeking that division among the sciences that does not obscure but rather helps us to see their unity.

2 A science is an explicit cognitive operatory habit.

It is a habit, a proximate principle of the eliciting of all operations of a particular circle, whose results thus form a system.

It is operatory, not operative. Hence, it need not be in one particular potency as its subject, or in one particular operating subject. Thus, a science is not necessarily in the intellect alone, but can also be in the senses and the sentient memory, indeed even in the will that chooses a method and faithfully follows it. Besides, a science can be so extensive that it cannot be contained in the mind of any one person.

It is cognitive: its results are known, and its operables are knowable.

It is explicit: its habit, its circle, and its system are known explicitly. This excludes that sort of knowledge (ordinary intelligence, common sense) that is present in every human act.

3 We hold that the first and fundamental division among the sciences is between those that are coordinating and those that are coordinated.

---

84 [The Latin words 'integrantur et specializantur' are added by hand, with 'integrantur' replacing 'evolvuntur.']

Coordinativae scientiae sunt explicitae ratione sui: scilicet, ideo in eis in actu signato cognoscuntur habitus, circuli, systemata quia ipsae tamquam de obiectis tractant habitus, circulos, systemata.

Coordinatae scientiae sunt explicitae ratione alterius: ipsae enim tractant de rebus, puta, de mineralibus, plantis, animalibus, hominibus, angelis, Deo; et tamen in iis in actu signato cognoscuntur habitus, circuli, systemata, inquantum a scientiis coordinativis regulantur.

[8.9] Utrum operationes dialecticae Hegelianae circulum forment

Dubium non est circulos circulorum per hanc dialecticam intendi: vide diagramma apud H. Leisegang, *Denkformen*, Berlin, 1951², pp. 164–66.

Qui tamen circulorum circuli magis operata respiciunt quam ipsas operationes. At ipsas operationes circulum formare constat, tum ex effectu si quidem circulus operatorum[85] operationum circulationem supponit, tum etiam ex ipsis operationibus in se consideratis, si quidem contraponere ex operatione ponendi necessario oriri censetur, et ex his duabus pari necessitate habetur *Erheben,* quod novae positioni aequivalet ideoque in aliam contrapositionem conducit, etc., donec constituantur logica, natura, atque spiritus.

[8.10] Utrum alii exsistant operationum circuli praeter eos ab Hegel excogitatos

Constat multos et alios exsistere operationum circulos qui neque ab Hegel excogitati sunt neque ad circulos Hegelianos reducuntur.

Puta, mathematicam theoriam circulorum (Group Theory, Théorie des groupes, Gruppentheorie). Etiam evolutionem operationum in infantibus et pueris a Jean Piaget descriptam. Etiam circulum operationum experiendi, intelligendi, iudicandi eiusdemque evolutionem in opere *Insight* descriptam.[86]

Coordinating sciences are explicit by their very nature; that is, in them habits, circles, and systems are known explicitly because they themselves treat of habits, circles, and systems as their objects.

Coordinated sciences are explicit by reason of another science. They themselves treat of things such as minerals, plants, animals, human beings, angels, or God; yet their habits, circles, and systems are known explicitly insofar as they are governed by coordinating sciences.

[8.9] Do the Operations of Hegelian Dialectic Form a Circle?

There is no doubt that this dialectic tends towards circles of circles. See the diagram in Hans Leisegang, *Denkformen*, 2nd ed. (Berlin: W. de Gruyter, 1951) 164–66.

These circles of circles, however, regard more the results than the operations themselves. But that these operations form a circle is quite clear both from the outcome, since the circle of resultants[85] supposes the circulation of operations, and from the operations considered in themselves, since counterpositing is thought to emerge necessarily from the operation of positing, and from these two with equal necessity *Erheben* results, which is equivalent to a new position and so gives rise to another counterpositing, and so on, until logic, nature, and spirit are constituted.

[8.10] Are There Other Circles of Operations besides Those of Hegel?

Clearly, there are many other circles of operations that neither were devised by Hegel nor are reducible to Hegel's.

Take, for example, the theory of circles in mathematics (Group Theory). Then also there is the operational development in infants and children described by Jean Piaget, not to mention the circle of the operations of experiencing, understanding, and judging and its development as outlined in the book *Insight*.[86]

---

85 Lonergan's Latin has 'circuli operati,' which the editors have changed to 'circulus operatorum,' 'the circle of results,' as singular subject of the singular verb 'supponit.'
86 [See the index to Lonergan, *Insight*, s.v. 'Circuit.']

[8.11]   Utrum ipsi circuli ab Hegel propositi exsistant

Fieri potest ut aliquid quodammodo simile in hoc illove casu inveniatur. Sed generalitas, totalitas, exclusivitas quae ad dialecticam Hegelianam pertinet deneganda esse videtur; imo, nemo fere est hodie qui tertiam quandam partem operis Hegeliani, nempe, philosophiam naturae, acceptare vel defendere velit.[87]

[8.11] Do the Circles Proposed by Hegel Really Exist?

It could be that there is something like them in this or that particular case. But it seems we must deny the generality, totality, and exclusivity of Hegelian dialectic. In fact, there is practically no one today who would be willing to accept or defend the third part of Hegel's work, namely, the philosophy of nature.[87]

87 [G.W.F. Hegel, *Philosophy of Nature*, 3 vols., ed. and trans. Michael John Petry (London: G. Allen and Unwin, 1970).]

Editorial Report on the Handwritten Notes for 'De Systemate et Historia'[1]

1 Operation and Meaning (47600D0E060)

The notion of 'circle of operations' is probably the most important contribution of the notes on system and history. The first set of handwritten notes in the file 'De systemate et historia' (47600D0E060) has to do with operation and meaning.

The first two pages distinguish 'Meaning 1' and 'Meaning 2,' that is, two meanings of 'Meaning.' The basic distinction is probably identical with the more familiar distinction in some hermeneutic literature between sense and reference. 'Meaning 1' is immanent intelligibility. Thus, a sentence makes complete sense. There is also meaning in this sense of immanent

---

1 Folder 8 in batch v in the Lonergan Archives was entitled 'System and History.' It contains at least some of the notes that Lonergan wrote for his course 'De Systemate et Historia' in the fall of 1959. The clearest of these notes are the set of typed manuscripts extending from A 485 to A 488 (in the numbering followed on the archival website www.bernardlonergan.com 48500DTL050 to 48800DTL050) that were presented in the previous chapter. Some of the handwritten notes reported on in the present chapter are directly related to the course, as is clear from the notes of Rossi de Gasperis. Some do not seem to have been used directly for the course, yet because Lonergan put them together in one file that he called 'System and History,' it is likely that they formed part of his preparation for the course. The notes that precede the typed entries extend from 47600D0E060 to 48400D0L060), and those that follow the typed material extend from 48900D0L050 to 50100D0L050. What follows, then, is partly a transcription or translation of these notes (some of

315 Report on Notes for 'De Systemate et Historia'

intelligibility in non-representational art.[2] In the sense of Meaning 1, a group of operations *carries* and *reveals* a set of immanent meanings. Three terms are introduced that will carry over through much of the notes on this course, especially important to the notes on circles of operations (a term that does not appear in the present item): *operabilia, operationes,* and *operata,* that is, materials to be operated on, operations, and results of operations. The group of operations *carries* this set of immanent meanings in that the operables (*operabilia,* what are operated on), the operations, and what are operated (*operata*), that is, the results, are all interrelated. They are related, respectively, as materials, means, and ends. The group of operations *reveals* this set of immanent meanings insofar as the operables are sensed, discriminated, and selected; insofar as the operations are apposite, ordered, as through trial and error; and insofar as the things operated are anticipated, desired, sought, and found satisfactory.

'Meaning 2' is denotation. The set of meanings that a group of symbolic operations carries and reveals is not only immanent but also denotative. (1) In symbolic play children explore a universe of denotative meanings. 'Let's make believe.' (2) In mathematics there is an exploration of a universe of relational meanings. Mathematics is to quantity as psychology is to the body. (3) In system building one is exploring possible universes. (4) There is the priority of assimilation. Whatever is received, is received after the mode of the receiver. What is not assimilated is marginal, and what cannot be assimilated is beyond one's horizon. In these notes, Lonergan reveals some familiarity with Piaget, whose name will appear in 48200D0E060 below. Piaget figured in a major way in Lonergan's lectures on education in the previous summer, and that influence carries over into the notion of circles of operations. This relation of 'assimilation' to the familiar Scholastic adage 'Quidquid recipitur ...' might perhaps indicate the first way in which Piaget's work was assimilated by Lonergan himself.

So much for the first two pages of this set of notes. On the third page there is introduced the notion of the control of meaning. Discussion of it is divided into the *need* of such control, the *possibility* of it, and the *attainment* of it.

---

which are in English and others in Latin) and partly a set of comments on them. The respective numbers from the archive website are provided, so that readers may study the handwritten material directly. We take the items one by one. This editorial report was composed by Robert M. Doran.

2 See above, pp. 292–95, taken from the typed notes.

First, there is the *need* of such control. A group of operations tends to embrace the universe; that is, it tends to absorb everything. (1) There are the oral schemes of the baby, who puts everything in its mouth, creating an oral space. (2) In the neurotic the persecution complex governs everything. (3) Totemism creates a system of clan organization (exogamy), which supposes a group of real and symbolic operations, prohibition, which is also a totemic *Weltanschauung*, the formality under which everything is apprehended. It is not just a matter of materials and subsequent superimposed organization. (4) As for *Weltanshauungen* in general, we have such things as the cult of progress, Marxism, Nationalism, naturalism, historicism: in each, a basic group of real and symbolic operations that are a priori to experience create the whole of experience.[3] The analysis of horizon in these notes will later come back to these integrations, in speaking of circles of operations that attempt too much and others that narrow the scope of possibilities.[4]

Second, there is the *possibility* of the control of meaning. The control of meaning occurs through pragmatic, transcendent, and immanent sanctions.

(1) Meaning can be controlled through pragmatic sanctions. These are commented on under two headings. First, the Trobriand Islanders are an example of a pre-civilizational mode: they are quite reasonable in regard to planting and harvesting (where there are pragmatic sanctions controlling meaning), but for the rest they are lost in myth and magic. But there is also the development of civilization, and that itself is twofold. In Egypt, Babylon, and elsewhere, there is a wide expanse of human activity governed by intelligence, but the rest is ruled by myth and magic; and in empirical science, there is a great deal of pragmatic control, but for the rest there is the proscription of metaphysics. (The word 'Dread' also appears here, under empirical science and its proscription of metaphysics, and it is underlined twice.)

(2) There are transcendent sanctions (an odd use of the word 'transcendent,' meaning, it seems, the inclination of common sense and positivism *against* going beyond). One already knows the real world. One regards with skepticism any systematization, as in the sophisticated common sense of positivism. But this 'already knowing the real world' is itself just a system corresponding to a set of groups of material and symbolic operations, while

3 See below, pp. 338–39.
4 See below, pp. 338–40.

the attendant skepticism is retiring into an ivory tower, denying oneself any influence in the world that exists. One may do little harm, but one also does very little good.

(3) There are immanent sanctions. There exists an intellectual pattern of experience, which per se is uninfluenced by fears and desires. It contains its own criteria: truth and the unconditioned. It contains a basic, differentiable group of operations that yield to self-appropriated intelligent and rational self-consciousness a cognitional theory, an epistemology, a methodology, a metaphysics. This will be referred to elsewhere in these notes as the fundamental circle of operations.[5]

Finally, there is the attainment of the control of meaning. (1) The immanent sanction may be operative *in actu exercito* or *in actu signato*, insofar as it itself is or is not an *operatum* of symbolic operations, that is, insofar as the materials to be operated on have been submitted to the operations that yield an explicit result (self-appropriation).[6] (2) To discover and express an adequate account of the immanent sanction *in actu signato* has been the gradually developing, or perpetually disputed, work of philosophy. (3) The immanent sanctions *in actu exercito* as spontaneously operative may be applied to particular symbolic *operata* or to the total perspective, the *Weltanschauung*. In the former case, the *Weltanschauung* or *Weisheit* is presupposed. The latter case comes up for attention only in special circumstances, as in the contrast of different cultures; as when the Hebrew prophets ridicule idolatry, or Herodotus compares the Greeks, the Persians, and the Egyptians, or Thucydides and Plato criticize Greek culture.

2   Are Perspectives True? (47700D0EL60)

This second set of notes in the folder 'System and History' may be related to the discussion of *Weltanschauung* at the end of the previous item. This set is definitely related to the brief reference in the typed notes to perspectivism.[7]

The first point in response to the question Are perspectives true? has to do with the unconditioned. What is true is what is grasped as unconditioned, and what is grasped as unconditioned is explicitly adverted to. But

---

5 See below, pp. 342–45.
6 See Lonergan, *Method in Theology* 14: 'applying the operations as intentional to the operations as conscious.'
7 See above, pp. 256–57.

commonly the perspective within which a judgment is made is not itself under judgment. The perspective is present *in obliquo, in actu exercito,* but it is not present *in recto, in actu signato.* This is the case (1) because communication commonly takes place between people within the same perspective, (2) because the existence and the significance of perspectives have to be discovered, and (3) because the discussion of perspectives presents notable difficulties. The stranger is strange, and so we call him 'a barbarian.' Comparison by travelers contrasting cultures gives rise to reflection, as with Herodotus. Then it may be that the perspective itself comes up for judgment. But normally if a perspective is governed by myth, the myth is usually not formal error but objective error.

On a second page, Lonergan begins a three-page discussion of perspectives that is divided into nine main headings. In the first there are listed pronouns, local and temporal adverbs, and universals that abstract from the individual, from place and time, so that one can put oneself in another's place; these are not unrelated to the invariants and transformations of modern science.

The second heading treats equivalent expressions, $(x\ y\ z)$ and $(\rho\ \theta\ \varphi)$. Thus, we have the intelligibility of languages insofar as they admit adequate translation. It is far simpler to use one language or expression for some purposes, and others for other purposes.

The third heading treats the difference of viewpoint resulting from differences in legitimate interests. There is 'one's world': butcher, baker, candlestick maker. Each is incomplete, and each has different selections and emphases. All can be true as far as they go. Each contains elements of truth not otherwise attained.

The fourth heading treats the difference of viewpoint between common sense and science. For common sense the sun rises and sets; things are classified not by classical formulae but by 'practical' classification *quoad nos.* The aim of science is a deductivist structure, with reasoning, defining, and a set of definitions and axioms.

The fifth heading deals with differences of perception. (1) There are the spatial perspectives of position and distance, and the auditory perspectives of distance. (2) There is relativity of movement. (3) As for color, in the thing the higher integration dominates, whereas in the surface higher integrations are omitted. (4) There are specializations of perceptivity, the stories of people who simply could not see the tracks of animals pointed out by pygmies. Higher integration admits various specializations.

The sixth heading treats developing viewpoints, a multiplicity in time. Scientific theories are accepted not as true but as the best available probable view. Truth will be reached most expeditiously by assuming the theories and letting the consequences of the assumption reveal its inadequacy. Such theories govern conceptualization and the definition of problems

The seventh heading is on reflective multiplicity, instances of which are found in Russell's theory of types and later hierarchies of 'logical fields.'

The eighth heading treats the 'openness' of non-trivial mathematics, where reference is made to Gödel's theorem and other parallel theorems. Mathematical truth is not assured by an internal criterion.

The ninth heading deals with the development of common sense, and it does so under eight subheadings. (The last three of these are on a page in 49100D0E050, which is misplaced in the archives and really belongs rather with this item.)

(1) There is development from developing science. (a) Common sense is a specialization of intelligence for dealing with concrete situations, and the coexistence of science teaches common sense that it is not universal knowledge but only a specialization, that there are whole series of areas on which it must defer. (b) Common sense adopts (subalternate) scientific viewpoints, languages, conclusions without any deep understanding, as dictated by fashions and by practical uses.

(2) There is development from developing logic. Common sense discovers that it is not a deductivist structure, that it does not possess, and vainly would seek, mastery of accurate definitions, universal propositions. It can and does tend in this direction (logical classification, mastery in practice, language) under cultural influence, as in the French classicist mentality.

(3) There is development from developing philosophy, the transition from *mythos* to *logos*. Primitives and ancient high civilizations are embedded in myth, with a failure to distinguish: between name and science, between identity and similarity, with the existence of classes and the mode of conceiving causality, all due to the failure to distinguish judgment from understanding and experience, and to give judgment its dominant role.

(4) There is development from developing religion, as in the education of Israel by national experience, by the prophets, the Law, the writings.

(5) There is development from the practical, as in the movement from the primitive to the ancient high civilizations, from these to the Wisdom literature, and from there to the Greek *logos*.

(6) The explicitation of perspectives may be incidental or systematic. It

is incidental in clarifying statements that are disputed; it is systematic in a science, in philosophy, in history, in hermeneutics.

(7) The explicitation of perspectives implies a higher-level perspective. One is discussing not the *res* but the *rationes*.

(8) Higher-level perspectives may be more or less adequate.

There follow two very similar pages on truth and perspectives, almost two attempts to state the same thing. The next paragraph indicates what is on the first of these pages, and the succeeding paragraph what is on the second.

Truths are absolute. They rest on the grasp of an unconditioned. The unconditioned is independent, not dependent on anything else. Truths are coherent. No two truths are contradictory either explicitly or implicitly. Contradiction supposes not only real but also notional identity. '*A* is' and '*A* is not' or '*A* is *B*' and '*A* is not *B*' are contradictory if and only if both *A* means the same *re et ratione* and *B* means the same *re et ratione*. Difference of perspective involves notional diversity. The perspective is the 'ratio sub qua res consideratur' and the 'ratio quam significat nomen est rei definitio.'[8] The existence of different perspectives, of itself, does not invalidate either the absoluteness or the coherence of truth: not the coherence, because the difference *ratione* precludes contradiction; not the absoluteness, for this pertains to each truth as such.

On the second of these pages Lonergan uses numbering. (1) Truths are absolute. What is true is simply true. (2) Truths are coherent. No two truths are contradictory either implicitly or explicitly. (3) Contradiction supposes not only real but also notional identity. '*A* is' and '*A* is not' and '*A* is *B*' and '*A* is not *B*' are pairs of contradictory propositions only if there are meant the same *A re et ratione* and the same *B re et ratione*. (4) Hence, truths are perspectival. Truths may be classified not only insofar as they regard the same objects but also insofar as they regard objects *sub eadem ratione*.[9] Classification *sub eadem ratione* is perspectival. (5) Perspectives normally are implicit. Normally communication occurs between people with the same perspective, and then the perspective is present *in actu exercito* but not *in actu signato*. Only when difference arises do people begin to attend explicitly to the perspective.

8 'The formality under which the thing is considered' and 'the formality that the name signifies is the definition of the thing.'
9 'under the same formality.'

3   Religion and Metaphysics (47800DTE060)

The first two pages treat the issue of religion and metaphysics under six headings.

The first heading is philosophy of religion. For example, what are the categories involved in the interpretation of old documents and monuments? What is the relation between the absolute and the sacred? Is there any proof of the divinity of Christ from the New Testament? The relations between theology and metaphysics might show for some that Scholastic theology is too involved in metaphysical issues, that these should be short-circuited in favor of scripture, the non-metaphysical Fathers, and the imitation of Christ.

The second heading also treats philosophy of religion. While religion is prior to philosophy of religion (one can be religious without being a philosopher), yet de facto in reading or writing this article we are performing not religious acts but philosophical, theological, and scientific acts. So does philosophy of religion suppose a metaphysics, a philosophy? Is 'philosophy of ...' independent of philosophy *simpliciter*?

The third heading is 'phenomenology,' reaching the essence of concrete data. When it is reached, it is evidently the essence, i.e., there is invulnerable insight, that is, experience, insight, and truth. But phenomenology is not clear on the issue of truth. There is Husserl's epochē, but if truth is reached, then there is no epochē regarding the real, unless the real is not true but some resistance [Scheler] or some 'natürliche *Einstellung*.' Scheler is ambiguous, and this may be related to his apostasy, and van Breda does not reach reflective issues. Insofar as it is fully conscious, phenomenology involves acceptance of philosophy and negation of counter-philosophies. But insofar as it is not fully conscious, phenomenology is widely acceptable. It can be useful spadework, like measurements in science. It cannot be scientific in the full sense, but a movement towards truth.[10]

The fourth heading states that the philosopher of religion has to clarify his own polymorphism or his results will be vitiated in their origin, i.e., himself.

The fifth heading maintains that the polymorphism of philosophy and philosophy of religion are matched by the polymorphism of religion itself. There are many religions. There are many aberrant forms of religion.

10 On phenomenology, see above, pp. 280–81, and below, pp. 322–23.

Reaching the essence of religion involves at its most fundamental level the distinction between authentic and aberrant manifestations of religion; i.e., it presupposes an account of the essence of religion and verifies it, not in the sense that there are no facts to favor another view but in the sense that there are facts for this view while other views are involved in counterpositions.

The sixth heading maintains that the significance of philosophy of religion is that it claims from philosophy criteria for the interpretation of religious manifestations. Then there are three statements whose meaning is not clear:

> 'value that it supplies empirical element that indicates what categories are not only possible but also actual'
> 'value principally because latent metaphysics, undifferentiated consciousness, objective lack of explicit distinctions, forms of distinctions'
> 'relation as between empirical laws and system / in methodical science / invulnerable insights and philosophic orientation and implication.'

Possibly the last statement means something along the lines that the relation between religion and philosophy of religion is like that between empirical laws and system or between invulnerable insights and philosophic orientation and implication. But more detail would be needed to verify that interpretation.

Page 3 moves beyond these sections, but still with the heading 'Religion and Metaphysics.' True religion adds to explicit metaphysics. The latter is, in the intellectual pattern of experience, detached (not as spectator but as actor intending truth). It contemplates things in relation to one another. There is no emphasis on self. Religion takes man as he is in the concrete dramatico-practical pattern and transforms, purifies, liberates, elevates him to a concrete dramatico-practical pattern congruous with the intellectual pattern. (There is a similar comment in the summer lectures on education.)[11] Charity as love of God above all leads to detachment, and as love of neighbor as oneself it leads to objectivity. As transforming, purifying, liberating, and elevating, it is a process. Perfect charity is always a goal. As a

---

11 See Lonergan, *Topics in Education* 91.

process it has a special reference to self: humility, abasement, sorrow, detestation, purpose of amendment, hope, confidence, faith, 'I' *coram Deo* with my neighbor in the world: *Mitvollzug.*

Page 4 starts with a contrast between metaphysics as ontologically orientated, where the *priora quoad se* (i.e., God) is the focus – Lonergan mentions the names of Owens and Klubertanz – and as epistemologically orientated, with the *priora quoad nos* as the beginning point. (1) For Lonergan there is a two-way street. One can pull the sock inside out and invert it throughout. For example, the true is the correspondence of intellect to the thing, and the thing is that to which the truth corresponds. Being and the true are convertible. A certain agility is needed to adopt this position. The alternative [Owens, Klubertanz] is (2) the one-way street, where the only way is ontologically orientated.

Finally, page 5 treats polymorphism. It is not enough to affirm true propositions. There is the question of horizon, where we can cut things down to our own size. The claim 'If not empiricism, then Platonist, Augustinian, Cartesian, Kantian, Berkeleyan, Hegelian,' is a non sequitur. The page ends with 'cf. [or perhaps 'e.g.'] perception.' 'Perception' will be the topic of a distinct entry below (48000D0E060).

4   Phenomenology (479A0DTE060)

There follows a short page on phenomenology. It is related to what was said about phenomenology in the entry on religion and metaphysics.

Phenomenology deals with concrete data and moves towards invulnerable insight. Hence, it presupposes a philosophy: data-insight-judgment, and rejects a counter-philosophy that neglects concrete data, does not understand, does not require the invulnerable. Hence, it is nonsense to dispute phenomenological results because they suppose a philosophic position, and it is nonsense to attempt phenomenological study under the pretense that it is *Voraussetzungslos.*

5   Perception (480A0DTE060)

Next are two pages on perception. They probably throw light on the appearance of the word 'perception' at the very end of the entry on religion and metaphysics, since they illumine the 'non sequitur' that Lonergan mentions there.

Does perception include or exclude true judgment? James Collins, says

Lonergan, cites an article in *Revue thomiste* to support the view that it includes true judgment.[12] If it excludes true judgment, then perception is either experience and intelligence without judgment, or experience without intelligence and without judgment. If it is experience and intelligence without judgment, it is rudderless. If it is experience without intelligence and judgment, it is animal.

An objection would maintain that it does not include intelligence or judgment but that it does include Scotus's and Ockham's intellectual intuition of the existing and present qua existing and present or some less clear-headed equivalent. To this the response is that such an intuition (a) does not exist, (b) is superfluous, and (c) is merely a necessary conclusion from the fact of knowledge and a refusal to consider the facts of knowledge.

Another objection is that perception is experience and insight qua true though not reflectively known to be true. The response is that this is essentialism, since it does not regard judgment as a constitutive element in knowledge.

If perception is supposed to include true judgment, does the word 'perception' add anything to the properties of this totality of true judgments? If it adds nothing, then that is Lonergan's position. If it adds the reference to a real object, it expresses the conviction that knowing is not essentially a perfection, not radically an identity in act of knower and known, but essentially a duality of knower and known. This is Neoplatonist as opposed to Aristotelian; it fails to acknowledge what Aquinas says in *Summa theologiae*, 1, q. 14, a. 2. It leads to Scotus's formal distinction on the side of the thing and to Günther's and Rosmini's attempts to deduce the divine Word. To the objection that there is a distinction of reason between God knowing and God as known, Lonergan responds 'of true reason, No; of false reason, Yes.'

6   Being (48100D0E060)

The next item moves to the question of being.

Being is (1) what is to be known by the totality of true judgments, (2) what is to be known by understanding correctly everything about everything, (3) the objective of the pure desire to know. Equivalently (1) the

---

12 James Collins was a distinguished professor of philosophy at Saint Louis University for many years, specializing in the history of modern philosophy.

pure desire is unrestricted, (2) the pure desire moves towards its objective by raising and answering questions, and the questions are *quid sit* and *an sit.*

Why should that be being? After all, every principle presupposes a notion of being and so every argument for a notion of being is involved in a vicious circle. The objection addresses the fact that in *Summa theologiae,* 1-2, q. 66, a. 5, ad 4m, Aquinas treats wisdom. Wisdom is (1) Aristotle's first philosophy (2) a gift of the Holy Spirit. But regarding the first, an argument from authority is the weakest of all arguments. And regarding the second, we are going beyond philosophy to theology.

Lonergan asks, then, What is the genesis of wisdom? The procedure of self-appropriation in chapters 1–8 of *Insight* treats insight, in chapters 9–10 judgment, in chapter 11 self-affirmation, in chapter 12 the notion of being, in chapter 13 the notion of objectivity, in chapter 14 positions and counterpositions. Unless one says being is objective, one is in a counterposition, and so one's account of knowledge cannot be what is intelligently grasped and reasonably affirmed. It's a case of getting the skeptic to talk.

For example, one might say that being is known by the experience of resistance (Scheler): qua rationally affirmed, that is not knowledge of being; qua experience of resistance, it is not rationally affirmed; according to this position God must be not just *Geist* but *Geist und Drang.*

The force of arguments in this matter is not as though a basic notion can be derived from arguments, but that basic notions can be defended and opposed positions shown to be erroneous.

So the arguments: Either being is what is known by the totality of true judgments or being is what is known by some true judgments or being is what is known by false judgments or being is what is known without any judgment.

If being is what is known by the totality of true judgments, (1) then *veritas est adaequatio intellectus et rei,* which transposed means being is what is known by knowing truth, and truth is what is known by knowing being, and (2) since we do not reach the totality and know we do not reach it, we know that we do not know being fully.

If being is what is known by some true judgments (1) then *a pari* it is known by all; (2) otherwise which true judgments are knowledge and which are not becomes a problem, (3) [and otherwise] how can they be true if they do not correspond to being?

If being is what is known by false judgments, (1) Is this judgment false or true? If it is false, it is irrational to assert it. If it is true, then it is knowledge of nothing, for being is known not by true but by false judgments; and if

being is what is known by false judgments, (2) then being is irrational and unintelligible, e.g., '*A* can be both *B* and not-*B re et ratione*' is false, and therefore being is what is self-contradictory.

If being is what is known without judgment, then it is known by experience alone, or by experience and insight. To say it is known by experience alone is materialism; and to say that it is known by experience and insight is essentialist, Kantian, idealist, relativist, existentialist: Scheler, Heidegger, Jaspers.

Being is what is known by the totality of true judgments, if on this being there follow all the acknowledged properties of being.

7   History and System (482000D0E060)

The next item moves explicitly to the issue of history and system. (A) There is a systematic component to human living: (1) assimilation and (2) accommodation lead to a circle of operations. Piaget's name appears for the first time at this point. But reference is made also to 'mythic apprehension of world: totemistic.' (B) History is the history of systems, their development, their interpretation, their breakdown, in a basic respect. (C) The a priori of history is (B). Its a posteriori is from the data. (D) History itself is a circle of operations in the purely intellectual system: what did they experience? how did they understand?

The human good consists of (1) particular goods, (2) the good of order, civilization, a social good, where particular goods recur regularly; there are coordinated operations, habits, institutions, interpersonal relations; the good of order arises from the domination of nature through technology, from the ordering of human actions, in a domestic order, an economic order, a political order; (3) values, because of which the orders are good; values are aesthetic (the intelligible object in the sensible), ethical (the reasonable subject concerned with the true and the good), and religious (men before God in the historical world). This third level is cultural.[13]

Eras are modes of apprehension, assimilation, living, being. Eras are (1) primitive (pre-civilizational culture), (2) civilization, (3) culture, and (4)

---

13 Compare all of this with the very similar but much more elaborate position in *Topics in Education*, delivered the previous summer. See chapters 2 through 4. See also the treatment of the human good in the next item in this report.

the historical era (post-cultural civilization). The process is one of development, decline, redemption.

8   Modes of Apprehension (48300DTE060)

The notes move next to 'modes of apprehension': there is a constant passive element, and a variable active, constructive, orientative aspect. Modes of assimilation are undistinguished from modes of being. *Nomina* lead to *numina*. Just as the word mediates between meaning and what is meant, so a universe of words mediates between the mind and the world, and the mediating universe is undifferentiated from the meant.

There are stages:[14] the primitive stage, where there is hardly a division of labor or a differentiation of consciousness; the ancient high civilizations, where labor is greatly divided, where there is social evolution, the development of civilization, but where values are barely distinguished; liberal culture, where the individual stands out, where the rational and philosophy emerge, myth is expurgated, the sciences and the arts as arts are cultivated; and the modern age, where the social is transformed through historical consciousness and scientific inventions.

Again, the human good consists of (1) particular goods, (2) schemata of repetition and the order of civilization for the control of nature through technology and the domestic, economic, and political regulation of men, (3) values: aesthetic (the intelligible object), ethical (the reasonable subject), and religious (the reasonable subject before God, with others, in the historical world).

The ambiguity of the human good is seen in that it consists in particular goods, that technological and social orders are for the sake of particular goods, that values are the superstructural conditions that are based in the orders; and that the human good stands in the three levels, but in such a way that particular goods are subordinate to the social order and the social order is regulated by values; and finally that it consists in the values, since the particular goods and the social order are only the material foundation.

The basic structure of the human good, then: particular goods; schemes of recurrence for the control of nature through technology and of man through family, economy, and polity: the streams of particular goods, co-

14 Compare 'eras' at the end of the previous item.

ordinated operations, habits, institutions, capital, personal values and relations; values aesthetic, intellectual and moral, and religious.

The stages, again, are the primitive, where the circles of operations are
not specialized; the ancient high civilizations, where social circles of operations are specialized; liberal culture, where cultural circles of operations are
specialized; and the modern age, where social operations are transformed
by scientific inventions and historical consciousness, and particular goods
are multiplied.

There follows a page that begins 'Thing-colors and Surface-colors.' Perspectives are not the seen as seen but the seen as constructed. Language:
the experience of sound is the experience of meaning. What enters consciousness is what is assimilated. It may be given, but it is peripheral. (The
stress is on the influence of higher levels on the empirical level.)

The next page indicates that historical consciousness has a negative aspect and positive aspects. (1) Decisions, progress, liberalism, naturalism,
Darwin, Spencer; (2) Romanticism; (3) human philosophy; (4) history and
science; (5) history and irrationality.

The final page in this entry is incomplete. What is outside a system is
materia prima, Grenzbegriff, abstraction. (1) The first set is non-systematized,
the same for everyone; then different super-imposed systematizations. (2)
[blank – the entry ends].

9   The Circle of Operations (48400D0TL060)

Finally, there is a short page devoted to the notion of the circle of operations, which has already been mentioned more or less in passing, but which
becomes perhaps the central idea in the notes on system and history.[15] This
short page sets forth a program for much of the remainder of the notes.

The circle of operations, it states, has to be treated in itself, in the dynamics of system (sociocultural movement),[16] and in the fundamental circle,
which again is treated in itself, in the unity of the sciences, in relation to the
twofold notion of science (Greek-eternal, and modern always in motion).
Under this heading of the twofold notion of science Lonergan also writes

15 See above, pp. 298–313 and below, pp. 343–45.
16 On the dynamics of system, see below, pp. 338–41; on the fundamental
circle, see below, pp. 343–45; on the unity of the sciences, see above, pp.
308–11, and below, pp. 343–46; on the twofold notion of science, see above,
pp. 81–97, and below, pp. 416–19.

'pura objectivitas' and 'pura subjectivitas.' Then in an at least somewhat distinct thought, he write, 'ad concretam historiam' and 'ad inquisitionem historiae' ['to concrete history' and 'to historical inquiry'], possibly indicating a distinction between the history that is written about (concrete history) and the history that is written (historical inquiry).

At this point in Lonergan's folder on 'System and History,' we find the typewritten notes that have been reproduced in edited form here in the previous entry in this volume. We move now to the handwritten notes that follow the typed material.

10   The Expressive (48900D0L050)[17]

The expressive can also be representational, as in non-abstract pictures and programmatic music.[18] But essentially the expressive occurs when the artist intuits a possibility of experience and expresses it in her work, where 'experience' corresponds to composition in pure sensible forms. Thus, Wordsworth speaks of emotion recollected in tranquility, and Mozart complains of too many distractions to be able to compose.

Consciousness at the psychic dimension is somehow creative, a formation of the subject in the world towards an end. The end here is the symbolic. Sensitive life has its own proper character as life. Jung speaks of potentialities that should flourish in some complete manner, of disequilibria and their manifestations, of anticipations and their manifestations. Such symbolism is not restricted to sensitive life, which in human beings belongs by its very nature to a spiritual soul. The spiritual life of the soul is incarnated in symbols.

The importance of art: Consciousness is not a univocal function of sensible data. The censor controls what is not admitted into consciousness. We have extraordinarily different potentialities, some of them entirely rejected, such as a tendency to parricide or incest. Consciousness is selective: we walk down the street in conversation, and the continuous noise is hardly heard. The voice of our conversation partner is selected because it has a meaning. A melody is easily repeated but not a series of noises. Decoration makes a surface visible. Consciousness is formative: *Sorge*, *cura*, interest, to

17 See above, pp. 292–97, as well as the entire section on art in the previous item in this volume. See also the first item in appendix 2 below.
18 See above, p. 295 and p. 315.

be and to live: not just apprehension but projection, where the dynamism of emotions and sentiments, tendencies and values, is added.

What is art? The capacity for producing composed sensible forms. The objective meaning is what can be grasped, described, in the composition itself, leaving aside any consideration of the artist, what she suggests or intends to express. This can be said equally well of European, Asian, and African art.

The subjective meaning is known better the greater there is some empathy with the intimate experience and sentiments of the artist.

A documentary meaning, beyond the intention of the artist, reveals a vision of the world. Lonergan mentions El Greco here, with examples, and also Beethoven's 'Eroica,' symbolizing man as independent, not the domestic servant of some leader or comrade.

11   More on Art (49000D0L050)

The first page begins with the category 'technical history' aligned with: (1) mathematics, sciences, technical arts, (2) philosophies, and (3) theologies. But most of the entry has to do with art and the history of art.

The history of art is displayed in a retrospective exhibition of an individual or a school or schools, and in comparative exhibitions. If the history moves to articulate expression in language, some knowledge is supposed concerning what art is and what it manifests about man.

The second page begins with the category 'History' and the question What is man? 'Rational animal' is generic rather than specific.[19] Man becomes rational, expressive of the Greek ideal of the *zōon logikon*. Not only do science, philosophy, and the very notion of science develop, but so do those things that result from knowledge and are modified by knowledge; they develop as to their very 'quid sit': social structures, cultural forms. The very notion of himself that man forms for himself, that he actuates in his life (a) develops, (b) co-develops, (c) in such a way that what results is independent of notions, intentions, acts of will both of individuals and of all: providence, fate, 'destiny,' drama, the person before God.

Page 3 is headed 'De arte,' 'Art.' The history of art may be considered in itself, or in connection with the rest of life: with the history of human life, the primitives, the Greeks, illuminism and progress, Romanticism and irrationalism, depth psychology.

19 See below, p. 332.

There is a question whether history is rather an art; truth in speaking and truth in being; the contrast of Burckhardt and Ranke. Concrete full knowledge induces feeling, commitment, participation, the surrender of detached intellect, truth for me, my truth.

Page 4 is headed 'De momento artis,' 'the importance of art.' The sole subheading mentions 'existential habit': consciousness is not a determinate function of external data; habit involves selection, formation, vitalization; external data are conditions or opportunities by which life takes place; consciousness mediates between data and action.

Page 5 is headed 'De historia artis,' 'the history of art.' It is not for the sake of this history itself but for the sake of the fuller understanding of man and of history that can be had from the fact that there is understood what art is – analysis – and what the function of art is in human life.

Page 6 is headed 'Functio artis,' 'the function of art.' This discussion continues for two more pages, to the end of this item. It is divided into three sections.

1 The Greeks discovered the *logos* as reason, as definition, as science, and thus expelled mythos: (1) crisis and rejection, (2) new ideal of the human – *zōon logikon*, (3) new interpretation of art, that which is added to pure reason because of the sensible weakness of man; thus the rhetorical teaching about figures [of speech], tropes, metaphors; art is constrained by system.

2 The triumph of the *logos* proceeds to the point of renewing the whole of human life. Four sub-categories are supplied. (a) Illuminism – revolution: economic, political, in education. (b) Applied science – revolution: industrial, technological. (c) Romanticism senses the defect, namely, man does not live on the logical plane, but does not find the solution. (d) In our time individual and national crimes, neurosis, the mystery done by man, chaotic art. There is not sensibly, personally manifested the intelligibility of human life. Nationalism is cultivated. Man senses himself subjected to great impersonal powers. There is lacking from life the artistic element of creation.

3 Among primitives and in ancient high civilizations, dominated by myths, there was a mode of apprehending that pertains to science, philosophy, theology, religion. (The entry ends at this point.)

12   Historicism (49100D0E050)[20]

These notes are in English, except for page 3. Page 2 belongs to the treat-

20 See above, pp. 272–87.

ment of perspectivism and has been inserted into that treatment above (p. 319).

The first page has three lettered sections: (A) the discovery that man is a genus,[21] that he and his sociocultural condition are *what* they have become, 'historically determined natures,' and so, that human affairs are to be understood; (B) the priority of poetry; and (c) the repudiation of Christianity.

Page 3 is in Latin, and its heading is 'Historia tamquam categoria exsistentialis,' 'History as an existential category.' It has three numbered sections: (1) if a man suffers from amnesia, he does not know who he is, where he was born, of what nation he is a citizen, whether he has a wife and children, how he obtains his daily bread; the knowledge of one's biography is essential to ordinary life;[22] (2) but in addition we need to know something of the biographies of others; (3) and we need to know something of the common history of our group; where there is a new situation, this common mentality should be created; think of propaganda in time of war. History teaches what is to be done and how, what is to be praised and blamed.

Page 4 treats schemes of recurrence. If *A* occurs, *A* will recur. There are: the mechanical connections of the planetary system (Newton, Laplace); the circulation of water: probabilities, there are deserts; appetites and occasions, animals; with human beings there are customs, habits, institutions, habits of knowing where learning is not needed, habits of willing where persuasion is not needed, habits of doing where practice is not needed.

Page 5 is headed simply 'History.' Time is of the substance of history. What is historical is what it is because of its history, because of what it has been. What is historical has become; it is just what it has become; it could have become differently and then it would be different. Man makes himself what he is; by nature, he is a genus: rational animal, admitting as many differences as the non-rational animals. Man makes himself what he is under sociocultural conditions. His becoming is a 'becoming social.' He learns to speak not a language he invents but the language of his group. He learns not to operate but to operate with others, in a determinate material world. And the sociocultural conditions also become. These are the dimensions of choice: what I make of myself, my relations to objects, what I make of my world, my group.

---

21 An idea that will be seen several times in these notes, whether expressed in this language or not; see above, p. 330, and below, pp. 333–34.
22 See also below, p. 346.

Page 6 is headed 'Aufgabe,' 'the task.' Negatively, the problem of every generation is to discover what can be done about the mess bequeathed it by the preceding generation. People can choose (A) to do as has been done, i.e., perpetuate the mess: ideology; (B) or to act as if nothing had been done, i.e., take utopian leaps. Positively, the problem of every generation is to live. The problem of living in any given generation has a range of solutions limited by (a) the proximately potential development of the existing constellation of circles of operations, (b) the proximately potential development of existing *Weltanschauungen*, philosophies, and (c) the proximately potential development of schemes of recurrence that satisfy the equilibrium in a common run of events.

Page 7 is again headed 'History,' and has six lettered divisions. (A) The multitudinous series of multitudinous events. (B) Later ones give a new significance to earlier ones, reveal potentialities by facts. (C) The new significance is a new principle of selection. It raises some earlier events out of a 'prime matter.' (D) There is a series of later events, new significances, new solutions. (E) The chronicle is constructed out of the series of selections: the rest are not remembered. (F) Later events give a new significance, a new selection, to elements in the chronicle.

Page 8, again 'History.' What is to be done? I.e., how avoid the aimless repetition of routines that once were significant and now are not, i.e., how avoid the further expenditures of energy on projects that are just bright ideas, i.e., how discover the *Aufgabe* of present theology, philosophy, physics, Conc. Rom. ii? [Is Lonergan referring to Vatican ii, which was announced in January 1959?] The *Aufgabe* is the historian's focus on his present, at least the sociology and psychology of his knowledge, if not intended. The *Aufgabe* is the focus on the past that the historian would understand. Reference is made to romanticism: the task of constructing a new world neither Christian nor Deist.

Page 9, again 'History.' Then: 'Plus ça change, plus c'est la même chose.' But just what changes? Just what remains the same? Ideology prevents the changes, while Utopia tries to change the immutable.

13   Human Reality (49200D0L050)

'Rational animal' names only a potency, an exigence, pertaining to the soul. What a concrete human being actually *is* is determined by acquired and infused habits, which are not acquired or infused without free will.

Just as there are habits acquired by individuals, there are also habits that

are, as it were, public. There is the material evolution of a population and of capital. There is social evolution: domestic, economic, and political. There is the entire realm of culture: artistic, intellectual and moral, religious. All of these continually influence and limit choices, determine them, are constantly developing or declining through choices.

This concrete human reality is known only historically. (1) It is not known a priori by some philosophical discipline. This is not a question of what ought to be, whether from natural or positive law, but of what *is*. (2) It is not known a posteriori by empirical sciences such as psychology or sociology. These sciences throw light on aspects, but do not reach the thing itself. The form of a human act is the form understood and chosen. Such a form is always now this and now that.

This is illustrated by examples.

The state: (1) Abstraction from differences gives that which is common to every state and only to states, something that is very general, neither monarchy or tyranny, aristocracy or oligarchy, democracy or anything else.

(2) That which ought to be: utopianism.

(3) That which is: depends on past and present notions; the British, French, German, Spanish, etc., are all different. These notions determine what has been done and what is now being done.

Science: we have proposed two notions of science.

Philosophy is conceived differently as a science depending on how science itself is conceived. It is conceived differently as philosophy where attention is paid to the history of notions and to human historicity. This is especially true ever since Hegel.

The human good: the good is convertible with being; the human good is what has existed, exists now, and will exist. True and false are in the mind, good and evil are in things. The human good is dynamic, mixed with evils, limited by concrete potentialities. It is to be known historically.

Historical consciousness:[23] (1) Liberal culture was classical by its very nature. A person is free who exists for his or her own sake; a slave exists for the sake of the master. Culture is not to be measured in accord with usefulness to something else, but is rather to glory in its own uselessness. Such culture thrived from the Greeks all the way to the eighteenth century. This age is now past.

23 For much of this material and that in § 14, see above in the second item in this volume, pp. 272–87.

(2) From liberal culture itself (a) were developed the natural sciences, and from them technology and the transformation of the relations between man and nature. Also from liberal culture man arrived at the awareness of his own historicity and his own historical responsibility. Man makes man, not only by physical generation but also by educating the mind, handing on institutions, imposing his intention. What in every case happens should happen in an intelligent and reasonable manner.

(3) There is illuminism: theories, doctrines, philosophies concerning economics (Adam Smith), politics (French Revolution), education (Rousseau, Dewey), religion; concerning progress (Abbé de Saint Pierre), concerning dialectic (Hegel, Marx), concerning the mission of the white man, the Nordic race, etc. These developed minimally from books and arguments.

(4) These notions produced the actual state of the world: the cult of progress, Hegel, Marx, naturalism – every great recent movement.

This historical consciousness is above all secularist. The Hebrews and Christians did not discover history. The ancient civilizations and the higher Hellenic and Hellenistic culture had their own histories. But the Hebrews and Christians interpreted human life in a religious sense. Everything is under the hand of God – not a hair on your head will perish – who accomplishes his intentions in history, the history of Israel and the history of the church. This vision of the world Augustine expressed in a philosophical work, and it survived in the West until the *Discours sur l'histoire universelle* of Bossuet in 1681. This vision of the world was attacked indirectly by Machiavelli and Guicciardini as incomplete, and directly by Voltaire and Gibbon (*Decline and Fall of the Roman Empire*, for whom barbarism and religion conquered).

This secularist consciousness of history, because it not only prescinded from the Christian vision but positively denied it and set itself in opposition to it, assumed to itself the colors and values of a religious vision.

There was an eschatological aspect that had a missionary spirit. Rousseau: return to nature; French Revolution: the triumph of reason; the classless society of Marx; Nietzsche's *Übermensch*.

Hegel: the Christian religion within the limits of historical reason; art, religion, philosophy. Dialectic – divine wisdom; objective spirit – logos; incarnation of objective spirit – the Word made flesh; tyranny, art, law, liberty – the stages of revelation.

There appears next a page headed 'Differentiation of historical consciousness.' The treatment is very schematic, and everything in it is included in a fuller way in the next item, so it is omitted here.

14   More on Human Reality (49300D0L050)

1 Concrete human reality is known only historically. For this reality happens insofar as man understands and wills. This understanding develops and makes for new conditions of life, from which we should live and understand concrete life in a new way.

2 Man is conscious of this historicity. (a) The age of classical culture culminated at the position that human intellect is not only cultivated, but is cultivated in such a way that it can govern the conditions of life. (b) To this consciousness there is joined the negation of the Christian interpretation and a kind of imitation of the Christian interpretation. (c) This consciousness is manifested (1) by technology, industrialism, the great increase in population; (2) science and philosophy historically cultivated; (3) the practical tendency – economic, political, educational theories; (4) dynamic theories: progress, dialectic, mission – the white man, the Nordic race, this nation.

3 Differentiation of this consciousness: (1) Deism, Agnosticism; (2) Immanentism; (3) Classicism; (4) Romanticism; (5) Naturalism; (6) Historicism. (1) and (2) reject the supernatural but retain classical philosophy, with talk of being, nature, substance, God. In (2) there is a transition from substance to subject. The ultimate categories are psychological: *Phänomenologie des Geistes*; being, essence, etc., are intermediate notions; all of reality is enclosed within the limits of this world; God somehow develops; Christianity is the imagined form of philosophy; the perspective is historical. (3) and (4) Classicism retains the Graeco-Roman influence: man is the *zōon logikon*, the Greek ideal. The forms are ideal, fixed, eternal. Romanticism: concrete human beings with any and every kind of sentiment, experience, aspiration, in accord with an infinite concrete variety that evades static, general, abstract categories. This is maximally intensified by the abandonment of Christianity; God is dead. (5) and (6) Naturalism: science alone is true, with the exemplars being Newton and Darwin. All things are reduced to and explained by the mode of such science. The ideal of progress thrives. Historicism: besides the order of nature there exists another order, the intentional historical human order, where changes happen in accord with a logic that is not material but intentional.

Historical inquiry is then treated under three headings. For Romanticism there is no universal necessary or teleological structure. The historical sense resides in the very multiplicity and variety of things. Of its own accord it evades philosophical categories; it is dynamic, concrete, individual, origi-

nal. The task of historiography is to recreate the past in some way through sympathy, empathy; to put on the opinions, sentiments, etc., so that we may contemplate the past, as it was. Perhaps it is art. It certainly is not philosophy.

For others, history is a science. Ranke strikes the mean between Romantics and Hegelians. History seeks the truth: *wie es eigentlich gewesen.* Critical techniques were developed; confidence was removed from annals, chronicles, memories. Clues were sought from the writings of those who were involved in the affairs. Appeal is made to archives, diplomatic records. History was determined by what they could know about the things themselves. The entire controversial, nationalistic, etc., question was. removed. This spirit remains until today.

Finally, there are doubts about the scientific nature of history. For Burckhardt, the history of culture is the least scientific of all disciplines, but contains much that it is useful to know. There are irrationalist tendencies: Kierkegaard, Schopenhauer, Nietzsche, William James, Bergson. There are Marx, Comte, Pareto, Sorel, Freud. There are issues not only concerning that about which history was written, but also about the people who wrote, who are thought to be perhaps determined in a latent irrational manner.

Dilthey (Diaz de Cerio)[24] affirmed the relativity of every doctrine, whether metaphysical or religious. He wanted to write a Critique of Historical Reason that would be to historical science what Kant's *Critique of Pure Reason* was to mechanical science. He labored that there be a logic of the human sciences, the *Geisteswissenschaften,* that was proper not to philosophy nor to science but to human affairs. He gave no small beginning to the studies that today are known as phenomenology and existentialism.

15   Three Notions of Science (49400D0L050)

There follows one page listing the three notions of science proposed by Pierre Boutroux:[25] concerning eternal objects, concerning the genesis of objects, concerning the circle of operations. Then there appear on separate lines the words 'Math,' 'Piaget,' and '*Insight*,' corresponding respectively to each notion of science.

24 See above, p. 280.
25 Pierre Boutroux, *L'idéal scientifique des mathématiciens dans l'Antiquité et les temps modernes,* new ed. (Paris: Presses universitaires de France, 1955). Lonergan refers to these ideals in *Topics in Education* 127.

16   The Dynamics of System (49500D0L050)[26]

The dynamics of system and the movement from above in historical science: it is grounded in a twofold lack of proportion, in relation to the material and in relation to the end.

A system is something determinate and limited, for it is reduced to a determinate circle of operations.

(1) Thus, it is not equally fitting to all operables. One system will be too general, so that it does not attain the particular end. But another is too particular, and so is applied to some operables easily but not at all to others. Thus, the circles are continually being perfected, specialized, integrated, in order to achieve better adaptation and fittingness, in order more expeditiously to order more operables, etc.

(2) Human operations are not only sensitive but also intellectual. But intellect is that by which we are capable of doing and becoming all things, and the will follows the intellect both in agreeing and in rejecting. Thus, human operations extend themselves to the whole universe. They are not only material operations that consist in moving, changing, joining, and dividing things, but also symbolic operations that free things up by expressing, signifying, representing them.

A second page is again headed 'Dynamica systematis.' The dynamics of system consists in this, that habits, circles of operations, systems occur, are perfected, are integrated, are specialized. That is, the dynamics is governed through a principle of continuity. Totally new operations and circles of operations do not suddenly appear. Rather, diverse operations are slowly added to operations already exercised, until a circle emerges that is perfected to become more adept. Integration happens only to what already is in existence, and specialization happens only by the division of what already is in existence.

The third page has the same heading. There follows upon the principle of continuity a principle of inertia and of conservation. That is, whatever is received is received according to the mode of the receiver. Thus, if an operation occurs, it is not just any operation but either one of the operations already exercised, or an operation slightly different from these. And if a series of operations occurs, it occurs in accord with an already begun or attained circle of operations, or in accord with a modification or extension

26 See above, p. 328.

of a circle that has already begun or been attained. For example, an infant is both naturally drawn to sucking at the breast and naturally is able to do so and knows how to do so. Its skill in doing so soon grows; it finds the breast more easily, it returns to the breast more quickly, it recognizes the signs that nutrition is near. When it is able not only to move its arm and hand but to direct their movement, it places its hand in its mouth. When it is able to grab things with its hand, it brings them to its mouth and tries to put them in its mouth. The first human system is oral.

The fourth page is headed 'Dynamica systematis: mundus proprius' (the dynamics of system: one's own world). One's own world is set over against the universe (being = everything). One's own world arises from a tension between universal human finality and the principles of continuity, conservation, inertia. For whatever is received is received according to the mode of the receiver. But that mode will frequently be insufficient. If nonetheless something is received, there arises a premature systematization. And if there is avoidance of reception, there follows a contraction, a limited horizon, a world that is small but mine.

The fifth page is headed 'Dynamica systematis: mundus proprius: praematura systematizatio' (the dynamics of system: one's own world: premature systematization). Premature systematization shows itself in (1) the oral system of the infant, (2) neurotics, who with their persecution complex order everything by fear, (3) totemism, which, based in the horror of incest, legitimately leads to a social systematization of exogamy, but is prematurely extended to a universal mode of apprehending that governs the classification of men, animals, plants, stones, places, the formation of myths and magic, the reception of new things discovered elsewhere; people are drawn to customs that are cognate to themselves; (4) feudalism, liberalism, capitalism, socialism, nationalism, clericalism, and anticlericalism; (5) the meaning is not that the value of totemism and clericalism is the same, but that in these diverse instances there is exhibited a tendency to premature systematization on a large or small scale.

The sixth page is headed 'Dynamica systematis: mundus proprius: secundum abstinentiam a receptione' (The dynamics of system: one's own world: in terms of avoidance of reception). It is maintained that if we abstain from a premature systematization, if we do not receive, we shall not err. *Non sequitur.* For that very avoidance negates the finality of intellect to all things, and of the will with regard to all things. Thus, it creates a certain 'iron curtain,' a prematurely closed world, that is, a world worked out in infancy and childhood, traditionally communicated, born and confirmed from the

consciousness of life. Then we have a world proper to our town of birth, our own province, nation, language; one proper to priests, lawyers, doctors; or to businesspeople, workers, farmers, and so on; for whom everything else lies beyond their horizon. This is the error of the Pharisees, who had the law and the prophets, who carefully observed everything, who wanted to add nothing new, and who condemned the Lord Christ to death. It is the error of a decadent philosophic school. The school flourished at the time of the founder, or in a Renaissance, but long periods of decadence intervened, during which the words of the master were faithfully repeated by the disciples, who reduced those words to their own understanding.

The seventh page is headed 'Dynamica systematis – ut schema analysis' (The dynamics of system – as a schema of analysis). In the upper right-hand corner we have 'J. Piaget.' To have a scheme of analysis there is required (a) a method for distinguishing stages, and (b) a method for examining the process from one stage to another. (a) Stages are distinguished in accord with complete circles of operations. They are examined by observing, by discovering through experiments, whether a given circle is complete: e.g., in accord with perspective; in accord with locomotion: to return is not just another operation but an inverse operation; in accord with the use of language, notions of space, quantity, cause, chance. (b) The process has two moments: assimilation, insofar as it is an operation derived from those already exercised or similar to them; accommodation, insofar as the operation is changed in accord with the exigencies of the operable. The distinction between these may be merely conceptual: adaptation per se. Or it may be real: assimilation as in symbolic play, mathematics, systematic constructions of science, philosophy, and theology; accommodation as in imitation, practical life, positive research. (c) Education is growth of the power of assimilating languages, literatures, mathematics, philosophy.

The eighth page is headed 'Dynamica systematis – ut schema analysis – hist. humana' (The dynamics of system – as scheme of analysis – human history). It repeats what we have seen about eras or stages. Thus, the first stage is with primitives; those things that naturally occur are extended; prematurely there are developed symbolic systems that indulge in myth and magic. The second stage is found in the ancient civilizations of Egypt, Crete, Babylon, etc. There are developed technical, economic, political systems; myth and magic are adapted to these. The third stage sees myth driven out by *logos*. The capacity for assimilation grows, through symbolic operations. There flourish humane letters, philosophy, science, theology. This flourishing is praised for its lack of usefulness. The fourth stage is

the contemporary stage. Symbolic development is turned to practical ends (1) in the domain of nature, and (2) in the awareness of historical responsibility.

The ninth and final page is again headed simply 'Dynamica systematis.' 'The dynamics of system' means (1) that which happens: every event is a certain operation, supposes an operable, and terminates at something operated; (2) the mode in which it happens: not by some one operation alone, but by a conjunction, composition, of several operations. 'The dynamics of system' is applied especially to concrete, dynamic sensible realities: personal development, sociocultural development; especially to abstract realities: what is presupposed but not clearly conceived by classical logic, and what is especially fundamental in the whole of mathematics. 'The dynamics of system' explains multiplicity, diversity, mobility of cultures; permanence, conservation, inertia of cultures. 'The dynamics of system' exhibits sanctions of premature systematization and of premature closure. This poses a fundamental question: if everything is received according to the mode of the receiver, is this relativism? Is man the measure of all things?

17   Science and the Human Sciences (49600D0L050)

We begin from the notion and opposition of (1) the eternal and necessary, immobile certitude, and (2) the contingent as becoming, probability versus certitude. Now we proceed to a higher synthesis.

Generically, science is an operatory habit, a circle of operations, a system of operations.[27] Specifically, (1) it is an operatory habit that is not material but symbolic; not natural as in the digestive and vascular systems, not implicitly known *in actu exercito* but not *in actu signato*, but explicit and known *in actu signato*; (2) its end is purely intellectual. From the light of agent intellect, wonder, it asks, What? Why? Whether? and it answers exclusively from cognitive motives and means. It arises and is exercised in the intellectual pattern of experience.

The second page begins a four-page treatment of corollaries, one per page.

(1) Because science is a habit or circle or system, it is related to the knowable as to material objects, as the formal to the material, as operation to operable. Thus, a diversification first and per se from objects is merely ma-

27 On 'operatory habit' see above, pp. 304–307.

terial; it becomes formal insofar as the diversification of knowable things demands a diversification of circles of operations. Thus too, the division be-- tween objects that are eternal and necessary and objects that are contingent and in process is an opposition in the material element. Also, the diversification according to which a science is about minerals, plants, animals, men, angels, God, is a diversification that first and per se is material.

(2) Because science is not an operative but an operatory habit, it is not restricted to one potency nor is it necessarily found entirely in any one human being. De facto in science there operate not only the intellect but also sense, imagination, memory, and the will itself willing the end of science (the true) and observing faithfully the precepts of method. Besides, nothing prevents a science from being so great that it cannot be learned by any one human being (as is the case with modern mathematics).

(3) Because science is an explicit habit, science is not ordinary understanding or common sense, which is acquired from the common or special use of things, which can be entirely valid, but which lacks what is essential to a science, namely, that it exist *in actu signato* and not *in actu exercito*. Whether and to what extent common sense can be used as a mediating instrument of science is another question. See *Insight* 400, 418 [CWL ed., 425, 443].

(4) The end of science is purely intellectual: the intelligible and understood truth. Science arises and is exercised in the intellectual pattern of experience. This does not exclude an ulterior practical goal. The perfect truth and the concrete word collaborate in spirating love. We do not say 'pure reason,' which in a rationalistic or Kantian sense is a deductivism independent of concrete facts. *Insight* 402 ff [CWL ed., 427–33]. We do not say 'speculative intellect.' In the simplified Greek sense, this is abstract, eternal, necessary. In the Hegelian sense (and almost always in non-Catholic writings), it is the restoration of deductivism through another logical technique, namely, dialectic. To the objection that it would seem that it is in itself practical, for it is a habit for operations, a circle is a circle of operations, and a system is a system of things operated, Lonergan responds that if the objector means intellectual operations ordered to an intellectual end, he agrees; but if other operations are meant, he does not agree. To another objection that at least the natural sciences are merely practical, as was said by Scheler, Croce, and others, he responds that many experts in natural science think this way, but they are pragmatists; de facto, there is a clear distinction between science as pure and fundamental and science as applied; in the real experts, there shines forth an element that is purely rational, speculative, aesthetic. An underlying question is whether the human intel-

lect is intuitive or discursive, whether being is known in the exercise of true judgment or before any elicited judgment.

And so on page 6, he addresses the fundamental human cognitive circle of operations. It consists of three operations: (a) experience: that which is given by sense and by consciousness; (b) understand: what, why – direct understanding, introspective understanding: definition, hypothesis, theory; (c) reflection – is it so? reflective understanding, affirmation or negation. These make up a circle. They mutually need one another. Without experience there is nothing to inquire about, nothing in which something is understood, nothing on the basis of which something is judged. Without understanding, there is no distinction of human beings from brute animals. Without reflection, we do not distinguish true from false. They also mutually complete one another. The experienced is what is potentially intelligible. Through understanding it becomes actually understood. The understood is what is potentially affirmable or deniable. Through judgment it proceeds to known truth. And once the three are posited, the circle is closed. With the attainment of truth, the intellect rests. It may inquire further, surely, but in order to know some other truth.

Page 7 begins to treat the unity of the sciences,[28] which governs the discussion for the remainder of this item. The treatment unfolds in seven points.

(1) The differentiation of the sciences and the originating unity: the same fundamental circle is applied in different ways to different operables. Fundamental methodology addresses these diversities; it is not a matter of mere rules and conventions but of the reasons for the rules.

(a) For infrahuman realities: external experience, understanding, judgment (*Insight*);

(b) for human realities: external and internal experience (internal taking us into the very circle of operations;

(c) for superhuman realities: analogy; faith from hearing, judgments, the understanding of faith.

(2) Unity – structural unity – formal unity. This heading embraces gnoseology, epistemology, metaphysics, logic, and mathematics. Gnoseology asks about the fundamental operations themselves, about their distinction, relations, structures; a full account includes the analysis of faith. Epistemology asks about the validity, inevitability, irreformability of the fundamental operations, about the appropriation of one's own rational consciousness;

---

28 See above, pp. 308–11 and 328.

it includes an elicited act of faith. Metaphysics moves from the structure of operations to the structure of what is operated or known; there metaphysics (a) of the order of nature; (b) of man (the analogy of the subject); (c) of God: according to natural knowledge, according to the truth of faith. Logic regards the system as such; classical logic assumes its primitive terms, postulates its primitive principles, does not determine how many in individual instances, does not know the formal object; in the circle, fundamental terms are operations; fundamental properties are relations among the operations; the formal object is determined through the circle. Mathematics regards the system as such in materially many things.

Before moving to the third heading, a page is inserted on the fundamental circle and logic. It consists of a list of general points ('generalia') having to do with logic as symbolic, conceptual, and fundamental. The principle of sufficient reason is that there is no reasonable affirmation or negation without evidence. The principle of identity and noncontradiction states that it is not reasonably possible that the same thing under the same aspect be both affirmed and denied. Syllogism as proving evidence is a virtually unconditioned, a conditioned whose conditions are fulfilled. The connection is stated in the major, 'if *A* then *B*'; the fulfillment is given in the minor, 'but *A*'; the conclusion follows, 'therefore *B*.' Syllogism as explaining, as making one know, is exhibited in the example of the moon, its phases, and sphericity; in predication the same experienced data are understood, as this (subject) and as such (predicate).

(3) There is a historical unity. On this page Lonergan takes up the question whether the true is what is not hidden, what is revealed or manifested, or whether the true is the unconditioned. On the first account, the true is true for someone and indeed essentially: the experienced qua experienced, the intelligible qua intelligible, the unconditioned qua reflectively grasped. On the second account, as unconditioned, the true is independent of this or that subject, essentially communicable, public; it is never contradicted by a true assertion; it has logical connections with its presuppositions and consequences; it is an entry to the absolute order of being. The issue is one of (a) personalism versus classical ontology; (b) subject versus object; (c) history versus a system of truths already made, eternal; (d) *Dasein* versus the distinction between subject and object. Lonergan's response to the debate is very nuanced.

(1) From the analysis of habit, circle, and system, we know that operation and operated are not separated; understanding in act is the intelligible in act; rationally affirming is true, and truth formally exists in the judgment

alone. Thus, to the statement that what God reveals is true, Lonergan responds, in the divine mind, yes; in the human mind of a believer, yes; in the human mind of a nonbeliever, no. Again, the unconditioned is independent of this or that subject, yes; but that it is independent of every subject whatsoever calls for a distinction: every unknown subject, yes; every known subject, no; for the unconditioned is included among the manifested.

(2) Thus, personalism is required that there be an actual manifestation, but it is transcended to the objective order through the manifestation of the unconditioned. The ontology of the person, of the subject, supposes this transcendence if it is *truly* affirmed.

(3) The very manifestation happens under psychological, sociological, historical conditions. Thus, there is given the development of the sciences. Eternal truth (in the divine mind) is truth about the history of the human mind. God does not know through composition and division, but knows what men compose and divide.

(4) This development is in accord with alternation: going and coming; going into those things that have to do with the subject as subject, to feel compunction; returning to the objects in accordance with interdependence: one science depends on another; that is, all simultaneously form one structure, which is manifested here, and is applied there in an analogous fashion in accordance with dialectic: on account of errors, and their evil consequences. Men are compelled to consider the truth. The love of truth is not so great that men care about it for its own sake. They always believe that they have enough, and that it is useless to inquire further.

(5) This development is not systematic. On the contrary, it is the development *of systems*. The greater the manifestation grows, the more accurately and fully is the truth spoken, whether with regard to consequences or with regard to presuppositions and foundations.

(6) This development is not without a normative line. There is given a perennial philosophy and pre-philosophy, that is, before the fundamental circle is explicitly known already, it is present and operative in man. There is not given a transition from the absence to the presence of metaphysics, but a transition from latent metaphysics to metaphysics clearly known. Every development is an explicitation or differentiation of the fundamental circle.

N.B. As there is given a true perennial philosophy, also there are given false perennial philosophies, namely, constant modes to which the fundamental circle is applied: materialistic – experience; idealist – understanding; realist – judgment.

(7) Concerning the human sciences: what is the state? Abstractly, it is that which is common to primitive tribes, to ancient empires, to industrial nations; concretely, there are as many different notions of the state as there are different mentalities from the diverse political experience, intelligence, judgments, choices of life. (a) It seems it should be acknowledged that true political knowledge develops as does all true knowledge, not only in accord with what is but also in accord with what ought to be. (b) In this development there is a twofold dialectic: of error and of sin. Regarding error, we have already commented. Regarding sin, the grace of God is to be implored and the analogy of the cross is to be applied.

18   History A, B, and C (49800D0E050)

This item considers history as a form of existence (History A), history as belief (History B), and history as an empirical science (History C).

History A: History as a Form of Existence

(a) To act, I have to know who I am, what the situation is. If I suffer from amnesia, I do not know I am a Catholic, a religious, a priest, a professor, I do not know what could and could not be done, nor the consequences of my actions.

(b) For a group to act, it has to know itself and its situation. Unless it knows itself as a group, there will be no question of group action undertaken and carried through by common decision. Unless it knows its situation, its common decision will not be enlightened.

(c) Hence, (1) biography and history are the narrative form in which individuals and groups apprehend themselves and their situation. (2) This concrete narrative form of apprehension is an existential category – something that must be had if individual and group action is to occur and to be relevant, opportune, successful.[29]

History B: History as Belief

History A is a fruit of experience, memory, tradition, belief. It is communicated spontaneously as the explanation of customs, usages, modes of proce-

---

29 For material related to this, see above, p. 332.

dure. History B is a written history, the fruit of an inquiry, a more methodical and a more extensive 'narrative form.' But its methods are essentially the methods of History A. It commits to writing experiences, memory, tradition, belief; it exercises critical choices when oppositions arise if it feels competent to decide. As it essentially is a matter of believing what was said and done by whom, when, where, so it expects from its readers a similar belief.

History C: History as an Empirical Science

(1) The weakness of History B is that it is not only History A that is a form of human existence; myth-mystery is also a form of human existence.

(2) Myth-mystery is the mode of apprehension of the universe (a) prior to the reflective acknowledgment of *logos*, (b) subsequently, as the sensitive counterpart to the *logos*. It is an imaginative mode. It may be quite valid as an expression or apprehension of things as they are (mystery): but it is without resources against mere aberration in symbolic creativity.

(3) Further, History A is not less effective because its narrative has a mystery-myth dimension. On the contrary, it can be all the more effective for that reason. Effectiveness of the group in self-apprehension is not dependent on the actual occurrence of past events but on the present acceptance of itself as a group.

(4) Thus, history as an empirical science goes beyond the category of belief in tradition. It seeks a knowledge that is independent of the truthfulness of witnesses and the *bona fides* of clues.

(5) But if it is to get beyond a set of unrelated 'technical histories,' it needs an apprehension of the 'dynamics of system' as its operator from above, the mutual interaction of the dynamics of system and technical history.

19   The Problem of a Critical Sacred History (49900D0E050)

(a) The problem is solved by the conjunction of a dynamics of systems ('systems' is now used, not 'system,' as in the previous entries) and technical history. I.e., this is the form of solution for the general problem of critical history. Without the dynamics of systems there is lacking the upper operator. Without the technical history, there is lacking the lower operator.

(b) The appropriate dynamics of systems presupposes the achievement of the dynamics of systems on the natural level. That is, (1) the unification

of gnoseology, epistemology, methodology, metaphysics; (2) the formulation of their confused and latent forms; (3) the schema of their development (interaction with science); (4) the account of counterpositions and their significance in the process of development (3).

(c) The appropriate dynamics of systems presupposes the (1) development of a theology as the group theory of supernatural acts, i.e., theology as system; (2) the formulation of its confused and latent forms; (3) the schema of its development; (4) the account of counterpositions.

(d) The appropriate dynamics of systems presupposes the unification of (b) and (c) – theology as a larger group theory including (b) – as opposed to their separation by specialization and counterpositions.

20   Specialization (50100D0L050)

The last item in the folder treats specialization. Specialization happens insofar as two or even more circles of operations follow upon the task and work of one. It induces a division of labor, for not all operations do the same work, but some do one, and others do another. It induces a differentiation of consciousness. Where there is a different task and a different circle, there is also a different operatory habit and a different development, perfection, actuation of human consciousness.

Specialization supposes that human potentialities are such that they can be developed, perfected, actuated differently in different tasks. Specialization is divided by reason of a principle of developing, perfecting, actuating.

Operables, things operated ('operata') may be: aesthetic artistic – capacity of apprehending, effecting sensible forms; practical – capacity of moving and changing material things; human – the capacity according to which man influences man and undergoes influence from another; intellectual – the capacity for knowing; religious – the capacity of man to be converted to God.

Specialization is divided by reason of the work: materially, by reason of the diversity of operables, the more operations are perfected, the more they tend to form distinct circles; serially, from the multiplication of operations, the things operated in one circle become the operables of another circle; coordinatively, from the multiplication of specializations, the very coordination of circles becomes a specialized circle.

A constellation is a specialization, selection, measure, conjunction, interdependence effecting and constituting a common way of life proper to a given human society. Just as with circles of operations, so also constellations

of circles happen and are perfected, coalesce into one, and collapse when separated or divided. This process includes four principal stages: primitives, where specializations barely occur; ancient civilizations (Egypt, Mesopotamia, Crete, etc.), where specializations are multiplied by reason of the work but not much by reason of the principle; the great cultures, in which the development of the ancient high civilizations is presupposed and specializations are developed by reason of the principle: the Greeks, the Buddhists, Confucians (cf. Jaspers); modern civilizations, in which intellectual specializations are applied to transforming the conditions of human living.

Specialization happens insofar as one circle of operations is divided into two. Integration happens insofar as two circles of operations coalesce into one. Specialized circles happen in proportion to the extent to which operations extend themselves to more diverse operables. Integrated circles happen in proportion to the extent to which the operations proceed from a more perfect principle. By reason of the work, specialization induces the division of labor; integration induces a greater efficacy on the part of the operator. By reason of the operator both specialization and integration induce a differentiation of consciousness, but specialization makes for the contraction of consciousness, and integration for its extension.

A final page treats again the human good. There is the good by essence and the good by participation. The levels of the human good are: (1) the particular good, that particular thing that is desired by a particular appetite; (2) the good of order, by which there is a continuous flow of particular goods; thus civilization, the order of operations on material things, technology, the order of human beings and their operations, as social (domestic, economic, political); (3) value, by which the order itself is good; this is the cultural good: aesthetic, order as elucidating the object in sensible things; intellectual and moral, order as from perfection and for perfection of the free, ethical subject; religious, the good by participation as such and consciously such.

The stages, again, are (1) primitive: undifferentiation of consciousness, no division of labor; (2) technical and social specialization; (3) cultural specialization; (4) transformation of technology and social reality from cultural specialization.

Report on Archival Notes Relevant to the Spring 1961 Course 'De Intellectu et Methodo'[1]

1 Inquiry Concerning the Ideal of Reason (43300D0L060)[2]

It is likely that in the 1961 course entitled 'De Intellectu et Methodo' Lonergan either distributed or relied on the students notes that had been assembled for his 1959 course with the same name.[3] The first set of archival notes that are definitely related to the 1961 course is dated 20 February 1961, probably two weeks into the course. It is possible Lonergan had said something about the problems of foundation, chasm, and historicity with which he began the 1959 course, and then, either in a transition to material on the notion of science or expanding on the problem of foundation, referred to the problem of the ideal of reason, the topic of the first set of 1961 notes.

The only notes in this folder that add anything significant to what may be found in the 1959 notes are what seem to be the first four items, dated 20 February, 24 February, 27 February, and 3 March. This report is limited to those items. Translations and transcriptions of the remaining items (to 45000D0L060) may be found on the website www.bernardlonergan.com.

The notes for 20 February consist of five handwritten schematic pages. They may be found on www.bernardlonergan.com at 43300D0L060, with an

---

1 See note 147 at the very end of chapter 1, the 1959 notes on 'De Intellectu et Methodo.' This editorial report was composed by Robert M. Doran. All the footnotes are editorial.
2 Dated 20 February 1961.
3 See above, p. 227, note 147.

English translation at 43300DTE060. The heading is 'Quaeritur de ideali rationis,' 'Inquiry concerning the ideal of reason.'

The question has to do with the ideal of reason, that is, with the end or goal towards which scientific, philosophical, or theological work heads. This end is knowledge. This end is presently unknown. And yet it is also somehow known, and not just in words, feelings, and abstractions, but in such a way that precise and exact rules can be developed with regard to the process itself. Such a methodological ideal is grounded in the very nature of intellect and is conceived in different ways over the course of the ages.

At this point Lonergan makes reference to the book *La crise de la raison dans la pensée contemporaine*, Desclée 1960, by Edmond Barbotin, Jean Trouillard, Roger Verneax, Dominique Dubarle, and Stanislas Breton. Lonergan underlines Dubarle's name three times, with an arrow pointing to the name. Lonergan later reviewed this 1960 book in *Gregorianum* 1963. The review was republished in vol. 20 of Lonergan's Collected Works, *Shorter Papers*.[4] The paragraph in Lonergan's review that refers to Dubarle reads as follows.

> Dominique Dubarle envisages the issue historically in terms of the constitutions that human reason has given itself. In rapid but penetrating sketches of successive views that reason has held of reason, he tells us what *logos* was for the ancient Greeks, what *ratio* meant to Latin thought, what it became in medieval syntheses that enlightened reason by faith and, when the enlightenment of reason was sought by omitting faith, the rupture that arose not only with the medieval but also with the ancient view of reason. For modern man 'reason' is secularist self-constituting subjectivity that leaves to 'understanding' the theoretic and practical organization of the real as objectivity (pp. 80–82). Among Catholics, however, the ancient view is still alive, and even apart from religious concern one of the goals of contemporary spiritual renewal may be defined as an effective reconciliation of ancient tradition and modern discovery. For the crisis of reason in contemporary thought is simply the fact that reason has not yet given itself an adequate constitution, that its self-education remains incomplete, that as yet a fully determinate model, an explicit set of standards, an up-to-date codification does not exist (p. 113).

4 Lonergan, *Shorter Papers* 234–36.

The discussion in Lonergan's 1961 notes moves to the issue of science, and so begins to dovetail with his treatment of science in 1959. For the ancients science was certain knowledge of things through causes. Science was of the unchanging or immobile and the universal, and also of the necessary. No science considers those things that are *per accidens*. Science is speculative; it is theory; it is individualistic; and it is of absolute value. But for the moderns science is not certain. It proceeds through probable opinions to more probable opinions. It has to do with causes, but the notion of 'cause' is one thing among primitives, something else for the Greeks, something else again for the classical moderns, something else again for Einstein, and yet something else for quantum physics. Science is about laws internal to movement itself. It has to do with universals in such a way as to include particulars in their concrete development. It includes Newtonian mechanics and accounts of the genesis of the world, of the evolution of species, and of human history. Science is cooperative. It unfolds slowly over the course of time. It has to do with those intelligibles that in fact are verified. What is intelligible in this world is not necessary except 'ex suppositione.' Science indeed considers those things that are *per accidens*, as in the theory of probability. Theoretic science is a stage. It is also genetic; this is true also when it is human science. The open subject is one who makes oneself, one's society, one's scientific ideal, in free responsibility.

If the differences are so great, Lonergan goes on to ask, does there remain what traditionally is asserted of science, philosophy, theology, namely, a certain absolute value or validity? Is Western man some kind of anthropological type that differs from other types, or does he pursue an ideal that has an absolute value, that is accessible to all, and normative for all?[5] Is man a rational animal or a symbolic animal? Is the supreme science, the queen of the sciences, the sociology of knowledge? Karl Mannheim, in *Ideology and Utopia*, generalizes the Marxist notion of ideology and seeks a way of avoiding ideology. Werner Stark is also mentioned, as well as a bibliography in Merton's work. Helpful with regard to these references is the following paragraph from pp. 78–79 in *Early Works on Theological Method 1*, vol. 22 in Lonergan's Collected Works.

5 We know from elsewhere that Lonergan takes this question from Edmund Husserl, *Die Krisis der europäischen Wissenschaften und die transzendentale Phänomenologie: Eine Einleitung in die phänomenologische Philosophie*, ed. Walter Biemal (The Hague: Martinus Nijhoff, 1954). See, for example, Lonergan, *Early Works on Theological Method 1* 62–63.

There further arises the question whether theology, if it is not a science, pertains to the field of the sociology of knowledge. The sociology of knowledge was a notion developed first of all, I think, by Max Scheler in his *Die Wissensformen und Die Gesellschaft (Forms of Knowledge and Society)* and, again, *Sociologie des Wissens*. It is taken up by Karl Mannheim mainly as a generalization of the Marxian view of ideology. Marxians call everyone else's views ideology; but their own is the truth. In any case, Mannheim generalized Marx: if everything is ideology, what do you have? You have sociology of knowledge. You get the approach in *Ideology and Utopia*; there is a bibliography in it, but it regards what is before 1935. In later writings, Mannheim further developed the notion of the sociology of knowledge, and he was very keenly aware that he had to avoid a relativism because he was a Jew who had been bounced out of Germany under the Nazis, and he did not want to accept anything at all of pure relativism, but he had some difficulty getting around it. It was his problem. Similarly for Werner Stark, who teaches in England and wrote *The Sociology of Knowledge* (ca. 1957). In Robert Merton's *Social Theory and Social Structure*, which is something of a classic in contemporary sociology, there is a chapter with bibliography on the sociology of knowledge. The sociology of knowledge is what people think because of their social milieu and influences. Is Catholic doctrine that kind of thing? Or is it a matter of truth? If it is a matter of truth, you are driven into the theoretical field.[6]

Lonergan then raises the issue of science conceived as deductivist, where, once the principles are posited, the conclusions follow with necessity. With respect to this he has three subsections.

(1) There is the Euclidean scandal that

(a) in the works of Euclid, there are definitions, axioms, and postulates, and there are deduced propositions in the form of problems and theorems;

(b) the Euclidean deductions are not valid regarding the equilateral triangle and the external angle (these are examples only); for two thousand years, the deductions were faulty; what is insight and what is 'quid sit?';

(c) from other definitions, axioms, and postulates, all of Euclid's conclu-

6 The books Lonergan refers to in this paragraph are referenced in footnotes on p. 79 in *Early Works on Theological Method 1*.

sions *can* be deduced, and a system constructed; the concepts of 'between' and 'included' were omitted;[7] (d) from other definitions, axioms, and postulates there can be deduced with equal rigor non-Euclidean conclusions; there is a series of geometries;

(e) some of the known geometries can be verified empirically, whether as special or as general or as generalized;

(f) mathematics is thus not absolute knowledge but an exploration of coherent hypotheses, hypothetico-deductive.

(2) Symbolic or mathematical logic is mentioned, along with the names of the principal books on which he drew in his 1957 lectures on mathematical logic and several others.

(3) Scotus, for whom science is about possible worlds, resulting in a voluntarism, is contrasted with St Thomas, where science is a matter of drawing conclusions from principles, while understanding grasps principles and terms, and wisdom judges about the terms. Wisdom for Aquinas is acknowledged as both a gift of the Holy Spirit and the principle of philosophy. From 'the principle of philosophy' Lonergan draws an arrow in the notes to 'epistemology' and another to 'wisdom grows in the course of time.'

2   The Naturally Endowed Ideal (43600DTE060)[8]

There is a naturally endowed ideal, the speculative intellectual power, but it needs to be objectified if it is to know itself. Thus, through the mediation of objects, a lesser perfection proceeded to something more perfect: (a) myth-magic-Gnosticism; (b) Greek science: certain knowledge through causes concerning the immobile, universal, necessary, per se – theory, individualistic, of absolute value; (c) modern science: probable, cause, concerning motion itself, concerning concrete universals, empirical intelligibility, the probable, the practical, collective, of doubtful validity. The deductivist objectification ('once principles are posited, conclusions follow necessarily; but there are the principles; ergo ...') was upended by what happened

---

7 Lonergan refers to E.V. Huntington, who wrote a paper in 1913 using 'sphere' and 'inclusion' as basic terms to discuss three-dimensional Euclidean geometry; the paper was 'A Set of Postulates for Abstract Geometry, Expressed in Terms of the Simple Relation of Inclusion,' in *Mathematische Annalen* 73 (1913) 522–59. Lonergan refers as well to Henry George Forder's 1927 book *The Foundations of Euclidean Geometry* (Cambridge: Cambridge University Press).
8 These notes are dated 24 February 1961.

in geometry. There was the false appearance of deduction for two millennia, the discovery that true deduction is not unique but multiple, and finally the realization that the principles differ, and so that other geometries are equally valid. Lonergan rehearses the history of what has happened in mathematics, drawing on much of what he said at greater length in the 1957 lectures on mathematical logic. He mentions the problems of ritualism, academicism (Husserl's *Krisis*), and conventionalism. Appeal is made again to the discussion in *La crise de la raison*. The differences between Scotus and Thomas are mentioned again. The issue of whether there is a Christian philosophy is raised. For Lonergan the real question has to do with the relation of theology to philosophy to science. What appears to be his suggested response has a two-way arrow between theology and philosophy and another between philosophy and natural science; a one-way arrow from theology to existential philosophy / human science; and a two-way arrow between philosophy and existential philosophy / human science. The problem is that there is no relation between an abstract theology that treats of the supernatural and an abstract philosophy that treats of the natural. Philosophy is existential. The empirical human sciences treat of man as he actually is, at once natural, spiritual, and indigent.

The solution cannot be ahistorical; the very notion of science and of method has evolved. It cannot be left to historians; the history of mathematics can be written only by mathematicians; the history of physics only by physicists; the history of medicine only by doctors; otherwise the history of the science will omit the essentials. The blind know colors only analogically. The deaf know sounds only analogically. One who has not attended to personal experiences of understanding, etc., has no possibility except remotely and analogically of composing a science about himself or about others. Reference is made to the 'theory of true interpretation, *Insight* chapter 17.'

3   More on the Ideal of Reason (43500DTE060)[9]

These notes continue along the same lines. There is little new. On Christian philosophy, Lonergan gives his own position: If it is a matter of the concrete, the existing, then abstract deduction about natures as such and the supernatural as such is beside the point. The issue is about reformulating the notions of philosophy and science, and the conflict between ancient

9 These notes are dated 27 February 1961.

philosophy and science, on the one hand, and modern philosophy and science, on the other. As for theology, there remains the one God, but the theologies are many: dogmatic, speculative, moral, pastoral, ascetical; and there is history that is biblical, patristic, medieval, oriental, Protestant, the history of religions. Theology is poured out on many things: concrete, historical, dynamic. Unless dogmatic-speculative theology undergoes a conversion, it cannot be either the queen of the sciences or even the queen of the theologies.

4   Still More on the Ideal of Reason (43400DTE060)[10]

These notes continue to treat the ideal of reason. Some of the same problems appear.

There is an ideal of reason bestowed by nature, but it is objectified in different ways, and that is the problem. From the Greeks we have Platonic dialectic, Aristotelian logic, and such enterprises as geometry, mathematics, mechanics, medicine, history. Then there is Christian theology. And finally, there are modern methods. The Greeks and the moderns show a series of oppositions.

There is an ideal of objectification as a deductivism. Once the principles are posited, the conclusions follow. A formalization is demanded. There are posited definitions, axioms, and rules of deduction. The conclusion follows mechanically, as it were, lest acts of understanding intervene surreptitiously. I.M. Bocheński said it would take a permanent commission three or four centuries to formalize the *Summa theologiae* in this fashion.

But there are new exigencies. Mathematical postulates (so called because from them follow other things) are not proposed as necessary, absolutely universal, and evident. For what happened regarding Euclid's geometry could happen again. In physics, the intellectual ordering is ultimately grounded in an artistic or aesthetic criterion (Lindsay and Margenau). Future physics will have to satisfy all previous measurements, but it still could be different. As for philosophy, the book *La crise de la raison* manifests that some find philosophical principles on the side of objectification, and others on the side of the one who objectifies. The latter ideal is an irreformable constant, the mind itself as it demands, grounds norms, and has a nature.

The historical difference between Scotus and Aquinas is repeated in

10 Dated 3 March 1961.

these notes. As for the question of a Christian philosophy, Lonergan adds to what he said previously that the ultimate synthesis would have theology and existential philosophy, the natural and human sciences, all connected together. And as for theology, to the previous notes are added the following comments: The many theologies are all penetrated by a new historical ideal, which gives rise to serious complications. Speculative theology and positive theology have been separated, and all of this is disturbed by practical exigencies. At this point some of the issues treated in 1959 under the rubric of 'the chasm' surface: the medieval resistance against dialectic and against Aristotle; the *devotio moderna*, according to which it is better to feel compunction than to define compunction and to please the Trinity than to engage in speculation regarding the Trinity; Pietism, where biblical theology is precisely non-dogmatic; there were the questions of what is more useful for priests and missionaries (biblical and liturgical theology); there are the *priora quoad nos, quoad the apostles, quoad the ancient Hebrews*; there are historical-cultural issues, the sociology of the parish, economic concerns. The solution is impossible as long as questions regarding method are neglected. It is not enough to conceive science analogically. The question of foundations must be addressed.

De Methodo Theologiae[1]

Bibliographica

Y. Congar, art. 'Théologie,' DTC XV, 29 (1946) 341–502. Bibl. passim in articulo et post. Explicite de methodo, 462 ss.

The Method of Theology[1]

Bibliography

(Yves) M.-J. Congar, s.v. 'Théologie,' in *Dictionnaire de théologie catholique*
(DTC) XV, 29, 341–502. [In English, *A History of Theology*, trans. and ed.
Hunter Guthrie (Garden City, NY: Doubleday, 1968).] There are bibliographical references throughout the article and at the end. Method is
treated explicitly in columns 462–96 [in *A History of Theology*, pp. 226–80.]

1 [A 426 in the Lonergan Archives, 426AODTL060, 426BODTL060, and
426CODTL060 on the website www.bernardlonergan.com. These are most of
Lonergan's lecture notes for the course 'De methodo theologiae,' taught at
the Gregorian University in the spring of 1962. In the summer institute that
year at Regis College, Lonergan frequently refers to a transcription of these
notes made by students that was distributed to participants in the institute.
This edition works from Lonergan's autograph of the notes. Comparison
reveals that the student notes were copied verbatim from Lonergan's autograph, except that the last five pages (79–83) of the autograph seem not to
have been transcribed. Those of Lonergan's handwritten marginal notations
in the autograph that are not simply corrections of the text will be noted as
they occur. Translator's and editors' interpolations are placed within brackets. Lonergan's division of the text is complex, but after experimenting with
alternatives the editors decided to retain it as much as possible, since it is
clearly indicative of the organization and flow of his thought. For the sake of
clarity, the editors have placed an extra line before every paragraph beginning (a), (a'), (a"), etc. Some numbered subheadings have been added, in
brackets.]

A. Lang, art. 'Erkenntnis- und Methodenlehre,' *LThK*, III, 1003–1012.

C. Colombo, apud *Problemi ed Orientamenti*, I, 1–56; bibl., 48–56. Milano, 1957.

B. Xiberta, *Introductio in sacram theologiam*, Madrid, 1949, bibl., 34–58.

Modus Procedendi

E multis et diversis incipi posset: abstracte ut quaeratur quid sit theologia; concrete ut narrentur problemata theologica contemporanea; explicative ut causae exponantur unde problemata contemporanea sint orta.

Visum tamen est ex abrupto incipere. Primo ergo capite notiones generales de methodo traduntur. Altero exponitur prima quaedam problematica quae in antithesibus radicalibus fundatur et theologiam ut scientiam respicit. Tertio exponitur altera problematica quae in re sociali, historica, hermeneutica fundatur et theologiam respicit ut scientiam verbo Dei et corpore Christi mediatam.[2]

A. Lang, s.v. 'Erkenntnis- und Methodenlehre, Theologische E.,' in *Lexikon für Theologie und Kirche* (*LTK*), III, 1003–12.

Carlo Colombo, 'La metodologia e la sistemazione teologica,' in *Problemi e Orientamenti di Teologia Dommatica* (Milano: Carlo Marzorati, 1957), I, 1–56; bibliography, 48–56.

Bartholomaeo M. Xiberta, *Introductio in sacram theologiam* (Matriti: Consejo Superior de Investigaciones Científicas, Patronato 'Raimundo Lulio' – Instituto 'Francisco Suárez,' 1949); bibliography, 34–58.

Procedure to Be Followed

We could begin our inquiry from many different starting points. Abstractly, we could ask what theology is; concretely, we could rehearse the theological problems of the present day; or, by way of explanation, we could begin by expounding the factors that have given rise to these contemporary problems.

We think it best, however, to go directly to the question of method. The first chapter, then, will present general notions concerning method. The second will set out a first problematic, which is based upon radically antithetical positions and has to do with theology as a science. The third chapter will expound a second problematic, which is based upon society, history, and hermeneutics, and has to do with theology as a science mediated by the word of God and the Body of Christ.[2]

---

2 [It is quite likely that the materials that appear in appendix 2 below were written as Lonergan prepared his Roman course. Some of these items even include pages with the dates of the first two lectures. It is reasonable to surmise that at least these pages were early drafts of the first two lectures. In them, Lonergan experiments with the several 'different starting points' that he mentions here, which might indicate that it was only after such experimenting that he decided to 'go directly to the question of method.'

The third chapter concerned with the 'second problematic' may never have been written with the same thoroughness exhibited by chapters 1 and 2. There is in the Lonergan Archives a seventeen-page handwritten schematic outline entitled '*Problematica Altera.*' It is too difficult to decipher in some parts to be included in this volume, but it should be consulted for an indication of what Lonergan treated in the 'problematica altera.' It can be found at 45200DOL060 on the website www.bernardlonergan.com, where a transcription is also offered. An English translation appears at 45200DTE060. There are other schematic notes in the same file in the archives that may relate to this second problematic, from 45000DOL050 to 46100DOE060. These will be included in CWL vol. 25, *Archival Material*. But probably the best information on the materials intended for this third chapter can be found

Caput Primum: De Methodo in Genere[3]

1 [Theology and Method]

Theologia tractat de Deo et de aliis quae ad Deum ordinantur.[4] Consideratio methodica tractat non de obiecto sed de subiecti operationibus et de ipso subiecto seu theologo. Directe ergo non quaeritur de Deo, de scriptura, de consiliis, de patribus, de liturgia, de scholasticis, sed de TE et de TUIS operationibus.

Quod non dicit totalem obiecti neglectum. Nam sine obiecto nulla prorsus est operatio, et sine operatione redit subiectum ad statum inconscium. Quare consideratio methodica incipit quidem ab obiecto ita tamen ut in obiecto investigando non sistat sed ad operationem subiectumque redeat. Advertitur ergo ad obiecta, non propter se, sed propter mediationem quam praebent ut subiectum eiusque operationes investigentur.

2 De Operationibus in Genere

(a) Jean Piaget, *La naissance de l'intelligence chez l'enfant*, Delachaux et Niestlé, Neuchatel et Paris, 1936.

Idem, *La construction du réel chez l'enfamt*, DN, 1937.

Chapter 1: On Method in General[3]

1 [Theology and Method]

Theology treats of God and of other things in relation to God.[4] Methodical consideration does not deal with the object of a science but with the operations of a subject and with the subject, in this case the theologian. Hence, we are not directly inquiring about God or scripture or the councils or the Fathers or liturgy or the Scholastics, but about *you* and *your* operations.

This does not mean, however, that we totally neglect the object. For without an object there is no operation at all, and a subject that is not operating reverts to an unconscious state. Thus, a methodical consideration, though it begins with an investigation of the object, does not stop there but turns back to consider the operations and the subject. Hence, it attends to objects not for their own sake but as mediating the investigation of the subject and the subject's operations.

2 Operations in General

(a) Jean Piaget, *La naissance de l'intelligence chez l'enfant* (Neuchâtel and Paris: Delachaux & Niestlé, 1936 [9th ed., 1994]). [In English, *The Origins of Intelligence in Children*, trans. Margaret Cook (Madison, CT: International Universities Press, 1952, 1998).]

Jean Piaget, *La construction du réel chez l'enfant* (Neuchâtel and Paris: Delach-

---

in Lonergan's lectures in the Regis College Institute in the summer of 1962. See below, for instance, p. 387, note 36. He distributed at this institute a copy of the Latin notes that appear here, but introduced in his lectures material from the treatment of the second problematic as well. He refers there to a second set of notes on which he is drawing, in addition to the transcription of the present notes that he had distributed. See part 1 Lonergan, *Early Works on Theological Method I*, esp. p. 301, where the second set of notes is mentioned. See also p. 182, note 1, where Lonergan indicates he is moving beyond the notes that he had distributed, and probably into the material that he had intended for the third chapter in the Roman notes. Also related to this question is note 204 below, p. 577.]

3 [This part of the autograph is dated 5-2-62. The material in this chapter corresponds to that contained in the first lecture of the Regis summer institute, in *Early Works on Theological Method I* 3–29.]

4 Thomas Aquinas, *Summa theologiae* 1, q. 1, a. 7 c. and ad 2m.

Idem, *Le langage et la pensée chez l'enfant,* DN, editio secunda, 1930.

Idem, *Le jugement et le raisonnement chez l'enfant,* DN, editio secunda, 1935.

La représentation du monde chez l'enfant, Alcan Paris, 1926.

La causalité physique chez l'enfant, Alcan, 1927.

Le jugement moral chez l'enfant, Alcan, 1930, 1932.

La formation du symbole chez l'enfant, DN, 1945.

Theoria aristotelica de habitibus investigationibus empiricis completur, et quantum ad unitatem habituum perficitur.[5]

aux & Niestlé, 1937 [6th ed., 1998]. [In English, *The Child's Construction of Reality*, trans. Margaret Cook (London: Routledge & Kegan Paul, 1954, 1976. In the United States, the title is *The Construction of Reality in the Child*, trans. Margaret Cook (New York: Basic Books, 1954).]

Jean Piaget, *Le langage et la pensée chez l'enfant*, 2nd ed. (Neuchâtel and Paris: Delachaux & Niestlé, 1930 [10th ed., 1989]). [In English, *The Language and Thought of the Child*, trans. Marjorie Gabain (New York: Meridian Books, 1955; 3rd ed., rev. and enl., 1959).]

Jean Piaget, *Le jugement et le raisonnement chez l'enfant*, 2nd ed. (Neuchâtel and Paris: Delachaux & Niestlé, 1935 [8th ed., 1993].) [In English, *Judgment and Reasoning in the Child*, trans. Marjorie Warden (London: Routledge & Kegan Paul, 1928, 1959).]

Jean Piaget, *La représentation du monde chez l'enfant* (Paris: Librairie Félix Alcan, 1926 [7th ed., Paris: Presses universitaires de France, 1993]). [In English, *The Child's Conception of the World*, trans. Joan and Andrew Tomlinson (London: K. Paul, Trench, Trubner & Co.; New York: Harcourt, Brace and Co., 1929; London and New York: Routledge, 1997).]

Jean Piaget, *La causalité physique chez l'enfant, avec le concours de dix-sept collaborateurs* (Paris: Librairie Félix Alcan, 1927). [In English, *The Child's Conception of Physical Causality*, trans. Marjorie Gabain (London: K. Paul, Trench, Trubner & Co., 1930; New Brunswick, USA: Transaction Publishers, 2001).]

Jean Piaget, *Le jugement moral chez l'enfant* (Paris: Librairie Félix Alcan, 1932 [8th ed., Paris: Presses universitaires de France, 1995]). [In English, *The Moral Judgement of the Child*, trans. Marjorie Gabain (London: K. Paul, Trench, Trubner & Co., 1932; London: Routledge, 1999).]

Jean Piaget, *La formation du symbole chez l'enfant: Imitation, jeu, et rêve, image et représentation* (Neuchâtel: Delachaux & Niestlé, 1945 [8th ed., Lausanne and Paris: Delachaux & Niestlé, 1994]). [In English, *Play, Dreams, and Imitation in Childhood* (London: Routledge & Kegan Paul, 1951, 1999).]

This empirical research complements the Aristotelian theory of habits and improves upon its understanding of the unity among habits.[5]

---

5 [See also the material above, pp. 304–307, on *habitus operatorius*, a category that goes beyond the Aristotelian notion of habits, which in *Insight* Lonergan calls conjugate forms peculiar to various potencies or faculties. The notion of *habitus operatorius*, introduced in the 1959 course 'De systemate et historia,' does not seem to have been picked up on later as such, but it is connected with the notions introduced here of groups of operations and

(b) Operationes incipiunt ex naturalibus habitibus, potentiis. Quae operationes[6] tamen de se sunt approximativae, parum efficaces, parum oeconomicae. Nisu usuque fit accommodatio[7] ad obiecta particularia, unde et oritur operationum *differentiatio*: loco unius operationis inefficaciter ad multa obiecta adhibitae, habentur multae operationes paullulum inter se differentiatae quae singulae ad obiecta sua adaptantur. Sequitur *combinatio* operationum differentiatarum: quod maximum quoddam incrementum dicit (cf. mathematica de permutationibus et combinationibus). Proceditur ad *complexionem completam* combinationum operationum differentiatarum (Group Theory).[8] Ulterius proceditur ad *complexiones complexionum*.

Habitus acquisitus: quo quis sine ulteriori exercitio, addiscentia, persuasione, facile, prompte, delectabiliter ponit quamlibet combinationem operationum differentiatarum ex complexione quadam completa.

(c) Incipitur ab obiectis immediatis: quae gustantur, quae manu tanguntur, quae oculis videntur, per omnes motus corporis. Proceditur per obiecta *mediata*: non ipsa obiecta attinguntur sed eorum imago, eorum repraesentatio linguistica, eorum repraesentatio technica (mathematica, logica, scientiis). Denique ipsae operationes per se ipsas mediantur: et eiusmodi est consideratio methodica.

(b) Operations begin from natural habits and potencies. Yet these operations[6] by themselves are only approximations, and they are neither very effective nor very economical. By dint of repeated effort, an adaptation[7] to particular objects is achieved, and this in turn leads to the *differentiation* of operations: in place of one operation ineffectively directed towards many objects, there are now many operations, slightly differentiated from one another, each of which is adapted to its objects. There follows a *combination* of differentiated operations; this represents a very great step forward; consider, for example, the mathematics of permutations and combinations. The next stage in the process is a *complete group* of combinations of differentiated operations – group theory.[8] A further stage is that of the *group of groups*.

A habit is said to have been acquired when, without any further practice or learning or persuasion, one easily, promptly, and with alacrity performs any combination of differentiated operations out of some complete group.

(c) We start from immediate objects: what we taste, feel with our hands, see with our eyes, experience through our various bodily movements. Next we proceed through *mediated* objects: it is not these objects themselves that we directly attain, but their image, their linguistic representation, or their technical representation as in mathematics, logic, and the sciences. Finally, the operations themselves are mediated through themselves; a methodical consideration is of this type.

---

complete groups of combinations of differentiated operations. It is clear from 49500D0L050 on www.bernardlonergan.com that Lonergan started reading Piaget earnestly in the spring of 1959. He starts referring to Piaget extensively in the lectures on education in the summer of that year, and he refers to him again in the course 'De systemate et historia' in the fall. It is likely that his notion of 'habitus operatorius' owes much to Piaget. Lonergan's language shifted from speaking of 'circles of operations' in 'De systemate et historia' to the language that appears at this point in the present text, much of which appears later as well, including in *Method in Theology*.]

6 [The Latin word *operationes* was added by hand.]

7 ['Adaptation' is Piaget's term, and so is used to translate 'accommodatio.' See Lonergan, *Method in Theology* 27 for a brief discussion of its two steps (assimilation and adjustment) and for mention of 'group theory.']

8 Garrett Birkoff and Saunders MacLane, *A Survey of Modern Algebra*, rev. ed. (New York: Macmillan, 1953) chapters 1 and 6; Andreas Speiser, *Die Theorie der Gruppen von endlicher Ordnung, mit Anwendungen auf algebräische Zahlen und Gleichungen sowie auf die Krystallographie*, 3rd ed. (Berlin: J. Springer, 1937; New York: Dover Publications, 1945); Hans Zassenhaus, *The Theory of Groups*, trans. Saul Kravetz (New York: Chelsea Publishing Co., 1949).

(d) Brevitas considerationis methodicae: Comparate sonos alicuius linguae, omnia nomina et verba eiusdem linguae, omnes combinationes nominum et verborum; claves organi vel machinae dactylographicae, et omnia quae organo sonari, machina dactylographica exscribi, possunt; operationes fundamentales quae in opere Euclidis, in *Contra Gentes* S. Thomae adhibentur, et theoremata, argumenta, quae diversis accommodationibus, combinationibus efficiuntur.[9]

3 De Subiecto Operante in Genere

Notissimum axioma scholasticum: quidquid recipitur, ad modum recipientis recipitur.[10] Scilicet, unumquodque subiectum tales et tales habitus operandi iam acquisivit; prompte, faciliter, delectabiliter quamlibet combinationem operationum differentiatarum secundum eos habitus elicit, sive apprehendendo, sive appetendo et volendo, sive efficiendo. At novas operationes non facit nisi quatenus veteres quodammodo ad nova obiecta accommodat; indiget novo exercitio, nova addiscentia, nova persuasione (ab alio vel a seipso). Quo iunior est, eo facilius nova tentat; quo senior, eo difficilius credit se habere nova addiscenda, novam et meliorem voluntatem acquirendam, nova exercitia tentanda.

[3.1 Horizon]

Unde horizon: actualis capacitas subiecti ad operationes eliciendas definit quasi mundum quendam. Quae intra horizontem iacent, ea facillime apprehendit, appetit, facit; quae ultra horizontem iacent, ad ea vix attendit, vix attendere potest. Ei enim addiscendum, persuadendum, exercendum est, quod saltem tempus requirit, et tot tantisque negotiis iam implicatur ut tempus non habeat.

(d) The brevity of a methodical consideration: Compare the sounds of any language, all the nouns and verbs of that language, and all the combinations of nouns and verbs; the keys of an organ or a typewriter, and all the sounds that an organ can produce, or all that can be written on a typewriter; the basic operations in Euclid, or in St Thomas's *Summa contra Gentiles*, and the theorems and arguments presented in various adaptations and combinations.[9]

3   The Operating Subject in General

Recall the very familiar scholastic axiom, 'Whatever is received is received according to the manner of the receiver.'[10] In other words, any given subject has already acquired such and such habits of operating, and promptly, easily, and with alacrity performs any combination of differentiated operations in accordance with those habits, whether in apprehending or in desiring and willing or in producing something. But one does not perform new operations except insofar as one somehow adapts the old operations to new objects; one needs to practice once again, to learn new things, and to receive fresh persuasion, whether from oneself or from someone else. The younger one is, the more readily one will try something new; the older one is, the more difficulty one will have in believing that there are new things to learn, in acquiring a new willingness, and in trying something new.

[3.1 Horizon]

Thus, there arises the notion of horizon: the actual capacity a subject has to perform operations delimits the subject's 'world.' All that lie within that horizon are apprehended, desired, and done with relative ease, while one scarcely attends to or is capable of attending to whatever lies beyond it. One must continue to learn, to be persuaded, and to practice. This at least takes time, and people are so busy with so many things that there is no time left for it.

---

9 [The skill in argumentation that Thomas displayed in composing the *Summa contra Gentiles* became one of Lonergan's stock examples of how skills can be understood in terms of group theory. See, for example, Bernard Lonergan, *Method in Theology* 30.]

10 [See above, p. 315, for the use of this Scholastic expression in reference to operatory habits, and precisely in the context of discussing 'horizon,' as here.]

Qui horizon non est limes quidam absolutus: obiectum formale intellectus est ens, verum; obiectum formale voluntatis est bonum. Absolute potest
ad omne ens attendere, ad omne bonum amandum sese convertere; quod
tamen absolute potest, actu non facit sine addiscentia, persuasione, exercitio.

[3.2] De horizonte ampliando

Primo modo, augentur operationes circa obiecta immediata. Altero modo,
augentur operationes operando circa obiecta mediata; quaecumque imaginatione repraesentari possunt, lingua vulgari[11] dici possunt, modo technico
dici possunt. Tertio modo, augentur operationes operando modo reflexo
super ipsas operationes.[12] Praesupponit evolutionem circa priores duos
modos, secus neque solida est neque in ipsa operabilia[13] extendi potest.
Sed maxima generalitate atque efficacia gaudet. Nemo bene cognoscit
quamlibet scientiam donec exacte cognoscat quid praecise in ea scientia
fiat ([Eric] O'Connor, math).[14]

[3.3] De conversione subiecti

Est reorganizatio ipsius subiecti, operationum, mundi; non agitur tantummodo de horizonte ampliando (quamvis hoc quam maxime faciat), sed de

A horizon is not an absolute limit. The formal object of the intellect is being, the true, and the formal object of the will is the good. Absolutely speaking you can turn your attention to all that is, and convert yourself to loving all that is good; but what you can do absolutely speaking, you actually do not do without learning, persuasion, and practice.

[3.2] Broadening One's Horizon

A first way to broaden one's horizon is to expand one's operations regarding objects that are immediate. A second way is to expand one's operations by working on objects that are mediated. Whatever can be represented in the imagination can be expressed either in ordinary[11] speech or in technical language. A third way is to expand one's operations by reflecting upon these operations themselves.[12] This presupposes a development regarding the first two ways, for otherwise it would be neither solid nor able to be extended to the operables themselves.[13] This third way has the greatest generality and is the most effective. No one knows any science well without an accurate and thorough knowledge of what exactly is going on in that science (for example, [Eric] O'Connor, mathematics).[14]

[3.3] The Conversion of the Subject

Conversion is a reorganization of the subject, of the subject's operations, of the subject's world. It is not only a question of broadening one's horizon

---

11 [The Latin word 'vulgari' is added by hand in the autograph.]
12 [In *Method in Theology* 15, Lonergan will characterize this procedure as 'a matter of heightening one's consciousness by objectifying it,' that is, 'of applying the operations as intentional to the operations as conscious.']
13 [For the category of 'operable' see the discussion in 'System and History,' above, p. 299, note 72. This is a further indication that Lonergan is moving on here from that discussion.]
14 ['Fr. Eric O' Connor, who is quite a mathematician, remarked to me that he would never have gotten anywhere in mathematics if he had not stopped and asked himself just what he was doing. And I think that is true in any subject.' Lonergan, *Early Works on Theological Method 1* 13–14 and note 12. For some of O'Connor's occasional remarks that have made their way into print, see *Curiosity at the Center of One's Life: Statements and Questions of R. Eric O'Connor,* ed. J. Martin O'Hara (Montreal: Thomas More Institute Papers no. 84, 1987). Lonergan paid tribute to O'Connor in an obituary notice, 'Fr. R. Eric O'Connor, s.j., 1907–1980' in *Lonergan Studies Newsletter* 2:1 (1981) 2.]

mutatione perficienda in ipsa subiecti interioritate. Conversio moralis: ex obiectis desiderii, timoris, ad id quod esse debet tamquam absolutum, ad id quod valet sive placet sive non placet. Conversio intellectualis: usque ad aetatem septem annorum nondum ad usum rationis pervenimus; attamen mundum realem realiter nos cognoscere arbitramur; quae convictio fundamentalis neque revisa et correcta per reliquam vitam manere potest. *Ocularité*, Scotus et Kant de obiectivitate.[15] Conversio religiosa: ex ordine naturali humanistico ad ordinem Christianam.

[3.4] De subiecto inauthentico

Authentia, inauthentia dicitur dupliciter: relative, absolute. Relativa est secundum comparationem ad determinatam quandam doctrinam, religionem, modum vivendi, culturam. Ita sunt authentici et inauthentici Thomistae, Hegeliani, Christiani, Buddhistae, Brittanici, Americani,[16] moderni, etc.[17]

[3.5 De inauthentia relativa]

Relativa inauthentia est divergentia inter id quod subiectum re vera experitur, intelligit, verum esse iudicat, efficaciter vult et, alia ex parte, modum

(although it does this as much as can be done), but of producing a change in the very interiority of the subject. Moral conversion is a turning from objects of desire and of fear to that which ought to be as an absolute, to that which is right whether one likes it or not. As regards intellectual conversion, before the age of seven we have not attained the use of reason, and yet we think we really know the real world. This fundamental conviction can stay with us unexamined and uncorrected throughout the rest of our life. (*Ocularité*; Scotus and Kant on objectivity.)[15] Religious conversion is conversion from the natural humanistic order to the Christian order.

[3.4] The Inauthentic Subject

Authenticity and inauthenticity can be relative or absolute. They are relative in connection with some particular doctrine, religion, way of life, or culture. Thus, there are authentic and inauthentic Thomists, Hegelians, Christians, Buddhists, Englishmen, Americans,[16] moderns, etc.[17]

[3.5 Relative Inauthenticity]

Relative inauthenticity is a discrepancy between what a subject actually experiences, understands, judges to be true, and effectively wills and, on the

---

15 [The treatment is more complete at the corresponding spot in *Early Works on Theological Method 1*, but without reference to Scotus and Kant: 'Before the age of seven years we have pretty good ideas about what is really real. We can distinguish waking and dreaming, what is just a story, and what is a fib. The child, before reaching the age of reason, has arrived at certain criteria of the real. Those criteria can remain with one for all of one's life without being revised or corrected, even though one becomes a philosopher or a professor of philosophy. One can argue the thing out philosophically with a great deal of skill and subtlety, but when one gets down to the fine points, what does one appeal to? One appeals to what was the really real before one had reached the age of reason. Intellectual conversion, fundamentally, is the shift from prerational criteria of childhood to ultimate reliance upon rational criteria. It is the shift from the real as the 'already out there now' that one can put one's paw on, to the real as *id quod est*, where *id quod est* is what is rationally affirmed. The two are not exactly the same!' (14)]

16 [The autograph has 'Brittanici (Americani 100%).]

17 On these matters, see Karl Jaspers, *Psychologie der Weltanschauungen*, 3rd ed. (Berlin: Springer, 1925 [6th ed., Berlin and New York: Springer-Verlag, 1971]. [Italian translation, also mentioned by Lonergan:] *Psicologia delle visioni del mondo* (Rome: Astrolabio, 1950). [What here are called 'relative

experiendi, intelligendi, iudicandi, volendi, vivendi, agendi, qui talem doctrinam, religionem, culturam characterizat. Quae quidem divergentia non est completa: habetur series punctorum in quibus datur coincidentia, conformitas, congruentia. Propter hanc coincidentiam subiectum credit se re vera esse Thomistam, Hegelianum, Christianum, Buddhistam, etc. Unde ipse de se ipso in suo foro interiori cogitat, iudicat, quasi esset Thomista vel Hegelianus, etc.

Attamen praeter partialem coincidentiam, etiam exsistit divergentia. At ad hanc divergentiam subiectum non attendit, imo ipsa divergentia quodammodo ultra suum horizontem invenitur. Unde adhibet nomina et verba, terminos technicos, imo et principia et theoremata, non sensu obiectivo et proprio sed alio quodam qui propriae mentalitati, orientationi, modo vivendi convenit. Sequitur quasi systematica quaedam simplificatio, devalorizatio, deformatio doctrinae obiectivae. Quasi systematica: scilicet effectus est ad modum systematis, sed causa est per accidens; minime intenditur simplificatio, devalorizatio, deformatio; quinimo, ipse se credit et esse vult quam maxime authenticum, fidelissimum discipulum, ab omni originalitate et omni opinatione personali alienissimum.[18]

Quae relativa inauthentia fieri potest in solis individuis, sed ad individuos minime restringitur. Inauthenticus potest praedicare, alios dirigere, publice docere, libros componere, magna aestimatione ab aliis inauthenticis haberi, doctrinam antiquam nostris diebus modo magis accommodato sed 'omnino genuinam' uti ipse operatur exponere.[19] Sic scholae in partes scindi possunt; sic tota quaedam schola in decadentiam ruere potest; sic ordo religiosus corruptioni obnoxius est et reformatione indigere potest. Tunc securis est mittenda ad radicem, sed perpauci admodum erunt qui necessitatem securis perspiciant. Requiritur Ioannes Baptista, et sicut olim

other hand, the way of experiencing, understanding, judging, willing, living, and acting that truly characterizes that particular doctrine, religion, or culture. This discrepancy, though, is not total: there is a series of points in which there is overlapping, conformity, or congruence. Because of this overlapping, a subject believes he really is a Thomist, Hegelian, Christian, Buddhist, or whatever. Hence, in his own mind he thinks and judges about himself as if he were a Thomist, Hegelian, and so forth.

Yet besides this partial overlapping there still remains a divergence. But the subject does not advert to this divergence, and in fact the divergence itself, in a way, lies beyond his horizon. Accordingly, he uses nouns and verbs, indeed technical terms and principles and theorems, not in their objective and proper sense, but in a way that suits his own turn of mind, his own orientation or lifestyle. The result is a kind of systematic simplification, a watering down, and a distortion of the objective doctrine. We say 'a kind of systematic': that is, the result is quasi-systematic, but the cause is a cause *per accidens*, since the simplification, watering down, and distortion are not at all intentional; in fact, the inauthentic subject believes and wants himself to be a most authentic and faithful disciple, quite free of any novelty or merely personal opinion.[18]

This relative inauthenticity can be found in individuals, but it is by no means restricted to individuals. The inauthentic person can preach, direct others, teach publicly, write books, be held in highest regard by other inauthentic persons, and expound an age-old doctrine in a way that is better suited to our times but is 'entirely genuine,' as he himself believes.[19] This is how divisions can arise in schools of thought, how an entire school can become decadent, or a religious order become liable to corruption and in need of reform. Then is the time for the axe to be laid to the root, yet there are very few who see a need for the axe. That calls for a John the Baptist,

---

authenticity and inauthenticity' are related to what Lonergan later would call 'minor authenticity and inauthenticity.' See Bernard Lonergan, *Method in Theology* 80.]

18 [See Lonergan's presentation of this issue in *Early Works on Theological Method 1*, at p. 16. What here is described in Latin as 'ad modum systematis' is there more fully expressed; Lonergan uses the expression 'quasi-systematic,' which is the reason for employing it here to translate 'ad modum systematis': 'it results spontaneously and inevitably because of the divergence between his apprehension and what is to be apprehended.']

19 [The qualifying quote marks around 'omnino genuinam' and the Latin words 'uti ipse operatur' were added by hand.]

ita etiam in subsequentibus temporibus timere potest Ioannes de capite suo
ne abscindatur et in disco ponatur.[20]

[3.6] De inauthentia absoluta

Heidegger, *Sein und Zeit,* modo quodam magis absoluto inauthentiam concepit; inauthenticus est qui propriam suam responsabilitatem personalem
assumere non vult; facit quod faciunt caeteri, qui pariter faciunt; dicit quod
dicunt caeteri, qui pari modo loquuntur; vult quod volunt caeteri, qui pariter volunt; iudicat sicut iudicant caeteri, qui pariter iudicant. Nemo est qui
suo marte, propria responsabilitate, iudicat, eligit, loquitur, facit. Iterum,
inauthenticus est qui a rationalitate deficit: homo est animal rationale: animalia non-rationalia; parvuli praerationales; adulti vel rationales vel irrationales; unde dialectica.[21]

4 *De Obiectis sub Aspectu Methodologico*[22]

(a) Obiectum est vel materiale (res de qua agitur, theologia de Deo) vel

and today as in the past a John the Baptist can reasonably fear for his head, lest it be cut off and placed on a platter.[20]

[3.6] Absolute Inauthenticity

Heidegger, in *Sein und Zeit*, conceived inauthenticity in a more absolute way: the inauthentic person is one who will not assume his own personal responsibility; in what he does and says and wants and judges he follows the crowd, who do the same. There is no one who on his own and taking responsibility judges, chooses, speaks, or acts. Again, the inauthentic person is not totally rational. Man is a rational animal, non-human animals are non-rational, young children are pre-rational, and adults are either rational or irrational. This gives rise to dialectic.[21]

4 Objects Considered from a Methodological Viewpoint[22]

(a) Objects are material (the matter that is dealt with, as theology deals with

---

20 See Congar, s.v. 'Théologie,' DTC XV (29), col. 410 [in English, *A History of Theology* 141–43]; Étienne Gilson, *Le philosophe et la théologie* (Paris: Librairie Arthème Fayard, 1960) 172 [in English, *The Philosopher and Theology*, trans. Cécile Gilson (New York: Random House 1962) 156–57.] [See Lonergan, *Early Works on Theological Method 1* 16: 'When such inauthenticity arises and spreads and becomes endemic, the only thing to do is to lay the axe to the root. However, laying the axe to the root is a tricky business. One is apt to find, as St John the Baptist did, that one's head is chopped off and put on a platter.']
21 Lonergan, *Insight*, chapters 7, 18, and 20; see also chapter 14, 'The Method of Metaphysics.' [A fuller presentation of Lonergan's line of thought concerning the movement from Heidegger as he understood him to his own position appears in *Early Works on Theological Method 1* 17–18, with editorial footnote references to the two English translations of *Sein und Zeit*. It is clear there, too, that Lonergan is relying for his interpretation of Heidegger on Alphonse de Waelhens, *Le philosophie de Martin Heidegger* (Louvain: Institut supérieur de philosophie, 1942). In fact, it is questionable whether Heidegger has any criterion for authenticity matching Lonergan's nuanced notion of self-transcendence, or even if he would want that sort of criterion. At the time of these lectures, Lonergan had probably not yet articulated authenticity in terms of self-transcendence. The term does not appear here. And he does not seem to be aware of Heidegger's extreme devotion to Nazism and the possible prefiguring of that devotion in *Sein und Zeit*'s very notion of authenticity.]
22 [At this point in the autograph, the date at the top of the page switches to 12-2-62.]

formale (ratio sub qua res attingitur, ita theologia naturalis de Deo rerum omnium principio et fine, theologia dogmatica de Deo uno et trino salutis supernaturalis auctore).

(b) Obiectum formale dupliciter considerari potest, de iure, de facto: de iure, prout in definitione ponitur, prout habitu scientifico ideali, perfecto, attingeretur; de facto, prout tali complexione combinationum operationum differentiatarum de facto attingitur.

(c) Sub aspectu methodologico considerantur obiecta formalia, praecipue de facto, sed etiam de iure, secundum criteria authentiae, dialecticae. Mitigatur quod initio dictum est – methodus non de obiectis, scil., non directe de obiectis.[23]

(d) Consideratio methodologica obiectorum non solum divisionem scientiarum sed etiam earum evolutionem investigat.

Divisio: logicus est qui tali et tali operationum complexione utitur, qui sic et sic procedit; et similiter mathematicus, physicus, chemicus, biologus, psychologus, philosophus, theologus; omnes enim modo suo operantur. Necessarius modus divisionis ubi scientiae sunt non in facto esse sed in fieri.[24] Evolutio: discernuntur stadia in singulis disciplinis progredientibus vel aberrantibus: talis et talis tali tempore facta est operationum nova differentiatio, differentiatarum combinatio, combinationum aucta vel minuta complexio. Unde et scholae distingui possunt, vel scientiarum subdivisiones, partes, etc.

(e) Consideratio methodologica extenditur ultra campum scientiarum ad modos operandi non-scientificos. Homo intelligentiae vulgaris, sensus communis, tali et tali modo procedit, talibus operationum complexionibus utitur. Neque sensus communis, intelligentia vulgaris, semper et ubique una et eadem est: alia est in urbibus, alia in pagis (pagani), alia in hac natione et alia in illa; alia hoc saeculo et alia in saeculo antecedente; alia in occidente et alia in oriente; alia inter excultos et alia inter primitivos. Sicut Piaget evolutionem parvulorum, ita etiam generis humani evolutio datur: differentiatio, combinatio, combinationum complexio.

God), or formal (the special aspect under which the matter is dealt with; thus, natural theology deals with God as the principle and end of all things, while dogmatic theology treats of God as one and triune and as the author of supernatural salvation).

(b) A formal object can be considered *de iure* or *de facto: de iure*, as expressed in a definition, or as would be perfectly attained in an ideal scientific habit; *de facto*, as in actual fact it is attained in such and such a group of combinations of differentiated operations.

(c) From a methodological viewpoint, formal objects especially *de facto*, but also *de iure*, are considered according to criteria of authenticity and dialectic. This qualifies what was said at the beginning, that 'method does not deal with objects' – it does not deal *directly* with objects.[23]

(d) A methodological consideration of objects investigates not only the division of the sciences but also their development.

It investigates the division of the sciences: a logician is one who uses such and such a group of operations, who proceeds in such and such a way; likewise, a mathematician, a physicist, a chemist, a biologist, a psychologist, a philosopher, or a theologian – they all operate in their own way. This manner of division is necessary when the sciences are not in a completed state but are still in process.[24] A methodological consideration investigates the development of the sciences: various stages can be discerned in each discipline as it makes progress or goes awry; at a certain point in time there occurs a fresh differentiation of operations, or a combination of differentiated operations, or an increased or diminished group of combinations. As a result, various schools of thought can be distinguished, or various subdivisions, parts, and so forth, in the sciences themselves.

(e) A methodological consideration extends beyond the field of the sciences to nonscientific ways of operating. A person of ordinary intelligence or common sense proceeds in such and such a way, and uses certain combinations of operations. But common sense, ordinary intelligence, is not always and everywhere one and the same. It is different in cities and in the country, it differs from one nation to another; it is different in this century from what it was in the last, different in the West and in the East, different among highly civilized peoples and more primitive peoples. Just as Piaget traced development in children, so also is there development in the hu-

23 [This sentence is added by hand in the autograph.]
24 [This sentence is added by hand in the autograph.]

(f) Unde consideratio methodologica ad historiam extenditur. Historia de qua scribitur, supra;[25] quae scribitur, nunc. Historicus est qui talem operationum complexionem cum tali horizonte adhibet ut operationum complexionem atque horizontem aliorum et olim degentium investigat. E.g., exegeta Britannicus, circa annum 1910, talis religionis, talis philosophiae, talis formationis, circa talem librum VT vel NT tractans.[26] Unde scholae exegeticae, historicae, dividuntur non tantum secundum obiecta sed etiam secundum horizontem et methodum et technicas a subiectis adhibitas. Unde historia critica: quae non solum obiecta sed etiam subiecta subicit crisi.

5 *De Ipsa Consideratione Methodologica*[27]

(a) Est de operationibus immediate, mediate de subiectis et obiectis.

(b) Est comparativa, genetica, dialectica.

Comparativa: est elementum empiricum – comparantur diversa ut perspiciatur in quibus conveniant, in quibus inter se differant. Quia attenditur ad data, habetur elementum empiricum, factuale. Quia attenditur ad differentias, habetur *indicatio* circa sensum, intelligibilitatem – non sane omnis differentia est magni momenti, complures et maxime obviae non sunt nisi superficiales – sed quo magis comparatio extenditur, eo facilius

man race as a whole; there is differentiation, combination, and a group of combinations.

(f) Hence, methodological consideration extends to history. As to the history that is written about, see above.[25] Here we are dealing with the history that is written. A historian is one who employs a certain group of operations with a certain horizon to investigate the group of operations and horizon of others who lived at an earlier time. Take, for example, a British exegete, around the year 1910, belonging to a certain religious denomination, having a certain philosophy, with a certain educational background, dealing with a certain book of the Old or New Testament.[26] Hence, schools of exegesis or of history are divided not only on the basis of their objects, but also according to the horizon and method and techniques used by their subjects. Thus we have critical history, which critiques not only objects but also subjects.

5 Methodological Consideration Itself[27]

(a) Methodological consideration is immediately concerned with operations, mediately with subjects and objects.

(b) It is comparative, genetic, and dialectical.

Comparative: this is an empirical element – different things are compared in order to understand in what respects they agree and in what they differ. Because attention is given to data, there is an empirical, factual element. Because attention is given to differences, there is an *indication* as to meaning, intelligibility – not every difference, to be sure, is of great significance, and many of the more obvious ones are just superficial – but the

---

25 [It is not entirely clear to what Lonergan is referring. But the parallel discussion in *Early Works on Theological Method 1*, at p. 22, suggests that he is referring simply to what he just said about the differences of common sense in cities and other regions, in one nation and another, and so on.]

26 [See ibid.: 'For example, one can say of the value of a piece of exegesis that it was done by an Englishman in about 1910, that he was an Anglican, that he belonged to a rather idealist school of philosophy, that he studied at such a school and such a university, that he belonged to such a milieu, that he was writing on this or that book of the Old Testament which was his main object. One forms an idea of the writer and of his tendencies simply by indicating in a general way the type of operations and combinations of operations that can be expected of him.']

27 [At this point in the autograph, the date at the top of the page switches to 14-2-62.]

ordo quidam in ipsis differentiis perspicitur, hanc ab illa dependere, vel illam praesupponere.

Genetica: series chronologica in qua aliae differentiae aliis accedunt: novae differentiationes, novae combinationes, novae complexiones; ubi antiquae retinentur, modificantur, omittuntur. (Intelligentia)[28]

Dialectica: additiones et omissiones iudicantur; amittitur authentia, vel ad authentiam reditur; intrat *irrationale* obiectivum.[29]

(c) Est consideratio una, synthetica, concreta, historica.

Una: omnia considerat sub unica ratione operationis, operantis, operabilis.[30]

Synthetica: inquantum est genetico-dialectica.

Concreta: inquantum ad maxime particularia descendi potest; de differentiis linguisticis, styli, orientatione, interesse, etc., inter hanc et illam poetam, hoc vel illud poema, etc.

Historica, critico-historica: inquantum considerat operationes, (1) antiquorum, (2) historicorum secundum diversas scholas, nationes, etc.

(d) Est transcendentalis.[31] Nam considerat operationes intellectus et voluntatis, quorum obiecta sunt transcendentalia (ens, verum, bonum). Considerat operationes secundum omnes earum differentias (ens non est quid

more widespread the comparison is, the easier it is to discern the order among the differences, and to determine whether this depends upon that or presupposes it.

Genetic: a chronological series in which some differences are added to others; new differentiations, new combinations, new groups; where the old ones are retained or modified or dropped. This is a matter of understanding.[28]

Dialectical: judgments are made concerning additions and omissions; on a loss of authenticity, or a return to authenticity; an objective *irrational* enters in.[29]

(c) A methodological consideration is one, synthetic, concrete, historical.

It is one: it considers everything under the single heading of operation, the operator, operable.[30]

It is synthetic: inasmuch as it is genetic-dialectical.

It is concrete: inasmuch as it can descend to the smallest details – to differences in language, style, orientation, interest, etc., between this and that poet or this and that poem, etc.

It is historical, critical-historical: inasmuch as it considers operations (1) of people in the past, and (2) of historians with regard to their different schools, nationalities, etc.

(d) It is transcendental.[31] It considers operations of intellect and will, whose objects are the transcendentals (being, the true, the good). It considers operations according to all their differences. Being is not something

28 [The handwritten word 'Intelligentia' appears in the autograph. The comparative element is empirical, the genetic a matter of intelligence, and the dialectical a matter of judgment: 'additiones et omissiones *iudicantur.*']

29 On the objective irrational, see Lonergan, *Insight*, index, s.v. 'surd,' 'sin,' 'social.' [The words 'intrat *irrationale* obiectivum' were added by hand in the text of the autograph, along with the reference to *Insight.* In the spring course a year later, 'organic' will be added to comparative, genetic, and dialectical. See vol. 24, *Early Works on Theological Method 3.*]

30 [See the discussion above in 'System and History,' pp. 299–312, concerning 'operatio, operatum, operabile.']

31 See Emerich Coreth, *Metaphysik, eine methodisch-systematische Grundlegung* (Innsbruck: Tyrolia-Verlag, 1961 [2nd ed., 1964]). [Condensed English translation, *Metaphysics*, trans. and ed. Joseph Donceel; with a critique by Bernard J.F. Lonergan (New York: Herder and Herder, 1968).] Josef de Vries, 'Der Zugang zur Metaphysik: Objektive oder transzendentale Methode?' *Scholastik* 36 (1961) 481–96.

abstractum, nam abstractiones non exsistunt; ens est omnia circa omnia; similiter bonum et malum sunt in rebus, et in rebus non habentur abstracta).

Etiam alio sensu dici potest transcendentalis.[32] Non tam de singulis operationibus quam de earum combinationibus cogitat. Qualis autem erit combinatio operationum, talis etiam erit combinatio in operatis. E.g., similitudo inter combinationem operationum in domo aedificanda et, alia ex parte, structuram domus aedificatae; iterum similitudo inter (1) notas musicas in folio exscriptas, (2) combinationes operationum a musico peractas, (3) combinationes sonorum auditas. Praeterea, sunt combinationes operationum quae vel vi naturae oriantur vel hypothetice necessariae sint; unde necessitate quadam vel naturali vel hypothetica ponuntur tales combinationes operationum, unde similes combinationes in operatis deduci possunt. E.g., si humana cognitio obiecti proportionati per experientiam, intelligentiam, et iudicium peragitur, sequitur ipsum obiectum proportionatum esse tripliciter compositum, nempe, quidditas sive natura in materia corporali exsistens,[33] ubi quidditas sive natura per intelligentiam, materia corporalis per experientiam, exsistentia per iudicium innotescunt.

(e) Estne haec methodus transcendentalis Kantiana? Habetur aliqua similitudo inter methodum supra descriptam et methodum a Kant adhibitam. Nam secundum Kant transcendentalis est scientia seu theoria quae considerat non obiecta sed modum cognitionis, et ipsum hunc modum non qualitercumque sed secundum possibilitatem a priori.[34] Iam vero methodus supra descripta, primo, considerat non obiecta sed operationes, deinde, operationes considerat secundum combinationes quae vel naturali necessitate vel hypothetica oriuntur et ideo quodammodo a priori (ab experientia independentes) sunt. Ex tali similitudine tamen non rite concluditur ad omnimodam identitatem, cum ex elementis communibus nullatenus ad conclusiones specifice Kantianas procedi possit. Quae enim doctrinam

abstract, for abstractions do not exist; being is everything about everything. Similarly, good and evil are in things, and there are no abstractions in things.

There is also another sense in which it can be said to be transcendental.[32] It attends not so much to individual operations as to their combinations. Now, corresponding to the combination of operations there will be a similar combination of the things operated. Take, for example, the similarity between the combination of operations in building a house and, on the other hand, the structure of the completed house; or again, the similarity between (1) musical notes printed in the score, (2) the combinations of operations performed by the musician, and (3) the combinations of the sounds produced. Furthermore, there are the combinations of operations that either naturally arise or are hypothetically necessary; hence, by natural or hypothetical necessity such combinations of operations are performed that from them one can deduce similar combinations in the objects of those operations. For example, if human knowledge of a proportionate object is achieved through experience, understanding, and judgment, it follows that the proportionate object itself has a threefold composition, namely, the quiddity or nature existing in corporeal matter,[33] where quiddity or nature is known through understanding, corporeal matter through experience, and existence through judgment.

(e) Is this transcendental method Kantian? There is some similarity between the method outlined above and that of Kant. For according to Kant, that science or theory is transcendental that considers not the objects but the mode of cognition, and that mode itself not in any way at all but according to an a priori possibility.[34] Now, the method given above first of all considers not objects but operations, then considers operations according to combinations that arise either by natural or by hypothetical necessity and therefore in a way are a priori (not dependent upon experience). However, from this similarity one cannot rightly conclude to an identity in every respect, since it is quite impossible to proceed from these common elements to conclusions that are specifically Kantian. For the points that make

32 [At this point in the autograph, the date at the top of the page switches to 19-2-62.]

33 Thomas Aquinas, *Summa theologiae*, 1, q. 84, a. 7 c.

34 Immanuel Kant, *Kritik der reinen Vernunft*, B 25, A 11; Norman Kemp Smith, *A Commentary to Kant's 'Critique of Pure Reason,'* 2nd ed. rev. and enl. (London: Macmillan and Co., 1923) 74–76.

specifice Kantianam faciunt, sequentia sunt: (a) nulla est obiectivitas immediata nisi per intuitionem (*Anschauung*); (b) intuitio humana non est nisi
apparentium; (c) unde omne iudicium humanum validum necessario est
iudicium tantummodo de apparentiis; (d) et manifesta aperitudo mentis
(potens *omnia* facere et fieri) non potest esse nisi illusio transcendentalis.

Attamen aliter crisin doctrinae Kantianae faciunt realistae intuitivi et aliter realistae discursivi. Realistae intuitivi concedunt primam praemissam
Kantianam, nempe, obiectivitatem immediatam non haberi nisi per intuitionem; sed negant praemissam alteram, nam quam statuunt intuitionem
eam non apparentium sed ipsius realitatis esse asserunt. Realistae discursivi
negant tum primam tum alteram praemissam Kantianam; sane si obiectivitas esse non posset nisi quae imaginatione repraesentetur, admittenda esset
prima praemissa; sed necessitas imaginationis est necessitas mythi; et exsistentia intuitionis (quod non est confundenda cum visione oculari) prout
a Kant et a realistis intuitivis concipitur pariter mythica quaedam fabricatio
est; unde et intuitio sive apparentium Kantiana sive ipsius realitatis (intui-
tionistarum, perceptionistarum) non minus mythica est.[35] Unde et ulterior
est differentia. Qui enim obiectivitatem in intuitionibus ponunt, a priori
omnem fere methodum et non tantum transcendentalem excludunt; iis
enim alia non potest esse methodus nisi quae in eliciendis intuitionibus
consistit. Qui e contra obiectivitatem in veritate iudicii rationalis ponunt,
structuras quae de facto in cognitione humana inveniuntur agnoscere possunt, et methodum in talibus structuris fundatam adhibere.

Caput Secundum: Problematica Prima[36]

[1 The First and Second Problematics]

Omnis methodus e quaestionibus incipit ut earundem solutionem inveniat.
Quare, post indicatas notiones generalissimas de methodo, iam de quaestionibus seu problematibus determinandum est.

a doctrine specifically Kantian are the following: (a) there is no immediate objectivity except through intuition (*Anschauung*); (b) human intuition is knowledge of appearances only; (c) hence, every valid human judgment is necessarily a judgment about appearances only; (d) the obvious openness of the mind (able to make and become *all* things) can only be a transcendental illusion.

Still, intuitive realists and discursive realists have different criticisms to make regarding Kant's doctrine. Intuitive realists concede Kant's first premise, namely, that there can be no immediate objectivity except through intuition; but they deny the second premise, for they assert that the intuition they hold is not an intuition of appearances but of reality itself. Discursive realists deny both the first and the second Kantian premises. Certainly, if there can be no objectivity except that which is represented in the imagination, the first premise would have to be admitted; but the necessity of the imagination is a mythical necessity, and the existence of intuition (which is not to be confused with ocular vision) as conceived by Kant and the intuitive realists is likewise a mythical figment. Hence, intuition, whether the Kantian intuition of appearances or that of reality itself (held by intuitionists and perceptionists), is no less mythical.[35] Hence, there is a further difference. Those who attribute objectivity to intuitions exclude in principle virtually all method and not only transcendental method, since for them there can be no method except that which consists in eliciting intuitions. Those who, on the contrary, locate objectivity in the truth of a rational judgment are able to recognize those structures that in fact are found in human cognition and to make use of a method that is grounded on these structures.

Chapter 2: The First Problematic[36]

[1   The First and Second Problematics]

All method begins from questions to which an answer is to be found. Accordingly, having presented some very general notions regarding method, we must now determine what the questions or problems are.

---

35 On the nature of objectivity, see Lonergan, *Insight*, chapter 13.
36 [See above, p. 361: the first problematic 'is based upon radically antithetical positions and has to do with theology as a science.' At this point in the autograph, the date at the top of the page switches to 9-4-62. The material from

Cuius rei exemplum apud Aristotelem invenies, praecipue in *Metaphys.*, B (Latine III).[37] Eiusdem rei exemplum implicitum apud S. Thomam habes si in *Summa theologiae* miraris non ipsa sola responsa sed etiam, et forte magis, ipsam quaestionum inventionem, distinctionem, divisionem, ordinationem. Ratio autem cur de problematibus determinandum est iam ab Aristotele tradita est: qui nodum solvere vult, eum primo inspiciat qualis sit.[38]

Non quaelibet problemata a nobis sunt determinanda, sed ea quorum solutio ex ipso modo procedendi vel simpliciter vel praecipue habetur. Non enim ipsam theologiam tractamus sed theologiae methodum. Quaenam vero sint haec problemata, postea enucleandum erit. Nunc vero ad exsistentiam potius quam essentiam respicientes, dicere sufficit alia esse vetera inde a controversia mediaevali quae Augustinana-Aristotelica dicitur exorta, alia esse recentiora quae ex reorganizatione theologiae a Melchiore Cano peracta resultant, alia denique esse recentissima quae e praesenti statu rei scientificae ortum habent et maxime post constitutionem *Deus scientiarum Dominus* theologos premunt. Nostris enim temporibus florent studia positiva biblica, patristica, conciliaria, scriptorum theologicorum. Theologum premit et distrahit ingens profluvius tum monographiarum tum periodicorum. Eum de sua ignorantia illimitata convincunt encyclopaediae et bibliographiae. Tempus occupat alumnorum et mentem sollicitat series nova specializationum in re liturgica, pastorali, missionaria, catechetica, ascetica, et mystica. Novae exortae sunt philosophiae exsistentialis, personalis, phaenomenologica, unde et proveniunt difficultates, ne dicam dubia, de utilitate et valore theologiae dogmaticae. Quid ergo a dogmaticis

You will find an example of this in Aristotle, especially in *Metaphysics* B (Book III in the Latin version).[37] You will find an implicit example of the same thing in St Thomas if, in the *Summa theologiae,* you marvel not only at his responses but also, and perhaps more so, at the way he selects, distinguishes, divides, and orders the questions. The reason why we must determine what the problems are has been given by Aristotle: If you want to undo a knot, you must first know what sort of knot it is.[38]

We need not determine all the problems but only those whose solution will emerge simply, or at least mainly, from the way of proceeding itself. For it is not theology we are dealing with here but the method of theology. We shall have to explain later on what these problems are. For now, since we are looking at the existence rather than at the nature of these problems, it suffices to say that some of them are ancient problems that arose from the so-called Augustinian-Aristotelian controversy in the Middle Ages, others arose at a later date as a result of Melchior Cano's reorganization of theology, while still others have arisen quite recently as a result of the present state of scientific knowledge and, especially since the [Apostolic] Constitution *Deus scientiarum Dominus* [1931], have been demanding the urgent attention of theologians. For at the present time, studies in positive theology, of the scriptures, the Fathers, the councils, and other theological writings, have been flourishing. The theologian is weighed down and overwhelmed by a huge flood of monographs and periodicals. Encyclopedias and bibliographies make him very much aware of his wide-ranging ignorance. The students' time is taken up and their minds unsettled by a whole new series of specializations in liturgical, pastoral, missiological, catechetical, asceti-

---

here to §5 (p. 429) corresponds to that treated on pp. 42–80 in *Early Works on Theological Method 1.* The earlier material in the second lecture of the summer institute was taken from the 'problematica altera' that Lonergan has referred to. Thus, he treated the structure of the human good before he took up the radical antitheses of the sacred and the profane, the outer and the inner, the visible and the intelligible. See ibid. 34, note 5. In *Method in Theology,* of course, he once again placed the treatment of the human good immediately after the general presentation on method. While the treatment of the radical antitheses did not as such remain part of Lonergan's work on method, obviously the themes remain central.]

37 See *Aristote et les problèmes de méthode: Communications présentées au Symposium Aristotelicum tenu à Louvain du 24 août 1er septembre 1960,* ed. Suzanne Mansion (Louvain: Publications universitaires; Paris: Béatrice-Nauwelaerts, 1961).

38 Aristotle, *Metaphysics,* B, 1, 995a 27–30.

agendum sit? Sane inprimis illud exigitur ut ipsum problema quale sit investigetur. Quod duplici gressu facere conabimur. Hoc enim capite II problematicam quandam primam ponimus, sequente autem capite III alteram problematicam addemus.[39]

Prima problematica respicit theologiam ut scientiam, cuius quidem radix in antithesibus quibusdam radicalibus invenitur, quibus inter se dividuntur mundus profanus et sacer, mundus interior et exterior, mundus aspectabilis et intelligibilis. Nam omnis scientia qua scientia directe mundum intelligibilem intendit, quo tamen in mundo tum maxima hominum pars numquam versatur tum obscurus satis est regressus sive ad mundum aspectabilem, sive ad mundum interiorem, sive ad mundum sacrum. Quare, cum religio maxime mundum sacrum, interiorem, vel etiam aspectabilem dicat, theologia in mundo intelligibili exulans parum religioni conferre videtur. Unde illa dubia de valore et utilitate theologiae traditionalis, quibus in primis attendendum est ne theologia ut scientia reprobetur. Sed et stabilito theologiam esse disciplinam proprie scientificam, ulterius determinandum erit qualis scientia sit theologia, utrum nempe ad ideale scientificum Graecum, antiquum respicere debeat, an potius scientiis modernis, empiricis, probabilibus assimilanda sit.

Altera deinde problematica theologiam respicit prout est scientia subalternata. Theologia enim dogmatica de Deo tractat, non prout mediatur creatis essentiis et naturali rationis lumine, non prout mediatur ipsa divina essentia et lumine gloriae, sed prout mediatur verbo Dei revelato et ordine

cal, and mystical studies. New philosophies have arisen – existentialism, personalism, phenomenology – from which stem difficulties, not to say doubts, about the usefulness and value of dogmatic theology. What, then, is the dogmatic theologian to do? Well, surely the first thing to do is to investigate the nature of the problem. This we shall attempt to do in two steps: in this chapter 2 we state the first problematic, and in chapter 3 we shall add the second problematic.[39]

The first problematic has to do with theology as a science. The roots of the problematic are to be found in certain radical antitheses by which the world is divided into the sacred and the profane, the outer world and the inner world or world of interiority, the visible world and the intelligible world. For all science as such is directly concerned with the intelligible world, in which, however, the vast majority of humanity never set foot, or from which they shrink back into the semi-darkness of the visible or the inner or the sacred world. Now since religion has to do mainly with the sacred and the inner but also the visible world, theology, confined as it is to the intelligible world, would seem to have little to contribute to religion. Hence the doubts about the value and usefulness of traditional theology. These doubts especially must be addressed lest theology find itself utterly rejected as a science. But once it is firmly established that theology is a scientific discipline in the proper sense of the word, we shall have to further determine what sort of science theology is, that is, whether it ought to aspire to the classical Greek ideal of science or whether it ought to be more like modern sciences, which are empirical and probable.

The second problematic concerns theology as a subalternate science. For dogmatic theology treats of God not as he is mediated through created essences and by the natural light of human reason, or as he is mediated through his divine essence and by the light of glory, but as he is mediated

39 [See above note 2. Also, crossed out is the following: 'Quod duplici gressu facere conabimur; haec enim problematica prima ea considerat quae exsistentiam et naturam theologiae ut scientiae tangunt; altera autem problematica iis accedimus quae modo magis particulari theologiam respiciunt prout est scientia subalternata, quae mediatur per sensum verbi a Deo revelati et per ordinem Corporis Christi.' 'We shall try to do this in two steps. This first problematic considers those aspects that touch upon the existence and nature of theology as a science; in the second problematic we address those that more particularly regard theology as a subalternate science, mediated through the meaning of the word revealed by God and the order of the Body of Christ.']

392 De Methodo Theologiae

Corporis Christi. Iam vero *sensus* verbi divini et *ordo* Corporis Christi in eodem genere inveniuntur ac *sensus* et *ordo* rerum humanarum, qui quidem
sunt obiecta scientiarum humanarum, secundum Erich Rothacker: 'Die
Wissenschaften, welche die *Ordnungen* des Lebens in Staat, Gesellschaft,
Recht, Sitte, Erziehung, Wirtschaft, Technik, und die *Deutungen* der Welt
in Sprache, Mythus, Kunst, Religion, Philosophie, und Wissenschaft zum
Gegenstand haben, nennen wir Geisteswissenschaften.'[40] Ex quo factum est
ut omnia quae pertinent ad mediationem obiecti theologici etiam tractentur (apud acatholicos) tamquam pars quaedam obiecti scientiarum humanarum, ut scilicet ipsa religio catholica sit species quaedam subsumenda,
investiganda, diiudicanda per phaenomenologiam, psychologiam, philosophiam, sociologiam, historiam religionis. Quod quidem a catholico neque
admittitur neque admitti potest. Nec tamen ideo eliminantur problemata.
Ponitur enim quaestio apologetica, quae per totam materiam continuo recurrit. Ponitur quaestio methodologica, quo usque conveniant et ubinam
differri incipiant investigatio theologica et investigatio scientiarum humanarum. Ponuntur quaestiones theologicae quid ad suos fines assumere et
adaptare possit vel debeat theologus e conceptionibus et theorematibus et
conclusionibus scientiarum humanarum, et quemadmodum inter se habeant, mutuo influant, Corpus Christi et mundus humanus.

The Robert Mollot Collection

by the revealed word of God and the order of the Body of Christ. Now the *meaning* of the word of God and the *order* of the Body of Christ are not generically different from the *meaning* and the *order* of human realities, which in fact, according to Erich Rothacker, are the objects of the human sciences: 'Die Wissenschaften, welche die *Ordnungen* des Lebens in Staat, Gesellschaft, Recht, Sitte, Erziehung, Wirtschaft, Tecknik, und die *Deutungen* der Welt in Sprache, Mythus, Kunst, Religion, Philosophie, und Wissenschaft zum Gegenstand haben, nennen wir Geisteswissenschaften.'[40] The result of this has been that everything pertaining to the mediation of the object of theology is also (among non-Catholics) treated as a part of the object of the human sciences, so that Catholicism itself is regarded as a species to be subsumed under and investigated and judged by phenomenology, psychology, philosophy, sociology, and the history of religion. This, of course, is something that Catholics do not and cannot admit. But that does not do away with the problems. There is the question of apologetics, which continually recurs throughout the whole of this matter. There is the question of methodology, namely, to what extent theological inquiry and that of the human sciences coincide and at what point they begin to diverge. There are the theological questions as to what a theologian can and ought to adopt, and adapt to his own purposes, from the notions, theorems, and conclusions of the human sciences, and also how the Body of Christ and the human world are related to and influence each other.

40 Erich Rothacker, *Logik und Systematik der Geisteswissenschaften* (Bonn: H. Bouvier, 1947) 3. [Lonergan's emphasis. The book was first published in 1927, and reissued in 1965 (Munich: R. Oldenbourg); Lonergan's autograph refers to the 1947 edition. Lonergan typed out the table of contents, as he often did. See www.bernardlonergan.com at 19050DTG060. In *Early Works on Theological Method 1*, at p. 246, Lonergan is critical of Rothacker as 'ultimately a relativist. For him all synthesis depends upon will, is led by will ... They are unable to provide ultimate answers to say how any synthesis can arise without invoking will or something similar.' This critique is especially interesting in light of what we now know of Rothacker's involvement in Nazism. There is no indication that Lonergan was aware of this, though in hindsight it is already suggested in the title of a section ending part 1 of Rothacker's book (recall that the date was 1927): 'Methoden, Weltanschauungen, und Lebenskämpfe.']

[2 Radical Antitheses]

[2.1] Mundus sacer et profanus[41]

Pervagatur haec antithesis totam historiam religionum, totam historiam rerum humanarum et profanarum. Invenitur inde a culturis maxime primitivis.[42]

Mundus profanus est hic, praesens, vere cognitus, operationibus intelligentibus et rationabilibus dominatus, totaliter inter horizontem subiectorum. Unde insistit Malinowski primitivos qui insulam Trobriand incolunt non minus quam caeteri homines esse intelligentes et rationabiles circa terram parandam, semina spargenda, segetes metiendas, et huiusmodi.

Mundus sacer est ille non hic, incognitus, superior vel profundior, anterior vel posterior, non dominatus, nisi modo obscuro non intra horizontem subiecti. Inter primitivos nisi symbolice non apprehenditur: quod fundamentum in parte sensitiva hominis, in affectivitate, etiam hodie manet et viget.[43] At simul adest fundamentum in intellectu: naturale desiderium non quiescit donec Deus cognoscatur per essentiam;[44] in voluntate: desiderium beatitudinis; necessitas fundandi valores, ordinem rerum humanarum.

[2   Radical Antitheses]

[2.1]   The Sacred World and the Profane World[41]

The antithesis between the sacred and the profane worlds is found throughout the entire history of religions and the entire history of profane human affairs. It is found even in the most primitive cultures.[42]

The profane world is this world present and truly known, controlled by intelligent and reasonable operations, and lying entirely within the horizon of subjects. Hence, Malinowski stresses the fact that the primitive Trobrianders are no less intelligent and reasonable than the rest of mankind in tilling the soil, broadcasting seeds, harvesting the crops, and similar operations.

The sacred world is not this world of ours; it is unknown, it is at once more lofty and more profound, an earlier or later world, it is not controlled, and only dimly does it enter into the horizon of its subject. Primitive people apprehend it only by way of symbols; this foundation in the sentient part of man, in affectivity, remains strong even in our day.[43] But at the same time, it has a foundation in the intellect, whose natural desire does not rest until it knows God by his essence.[44] It also has a foundation in the will, in the desire for happiness, in the need to have a foundation for values and for order in human affairs.

41 [At this point in the autograph, the date at the top of the page switches to 21-2-62.]
42 On the primitive stages of culture: Bronislaw Malinowski, *Magic, Science and Religion, and Other Essays* (Garden City, NY: Doubleday Anchor Books, 1954), a collection of articles from 1916 on; Mircea Eliade, *Le chamanisme et les techniques archaïques de l'extase* (Paris: Payot, 1951) [in English, *Shamanism: Archaic Techniques of Ecstasy*, rev. and enl. ed., trans. Willard R.Trask (New York: Bollingen Foundation; distributed by Pantheon Books, 1964)]; Eric Voegelin, *Israel and Revelation*, vol. 1 in *Order and History* (Baton Rouge and London: Louisiana State University Press, 1956; 2nd printing, 1958; [6th printing, 1986]); see esp. Part 1, chapters 1–3 [pp. 16–115].
43 Rudolf Otto, *Das Heilige: Über das Irrationale in der Idee des Göttlichen und sein Verhältnis zum Rationalen* (Gotha: Leopold Klotz, 1926); [in English, *The Idea of the Holy: An Inquiry into the Non-Rational Factor in the Idea of the Divine and Its Relation to the Rational*, 2nd ed., trans. John W. Harvey (London: Oxford University Press, 1958). C.G. Jung, *Psychology and Religion* (New Haven: Yale University Press, 1938). Charles Baudouin, *Psychanalyse du symbole religieux* (Paris: Artheme Fayard, 1957).
44 Thomas Aquinas, *Summa theologiae*, 1-2, q. 3, a. 8; *Summa contra Gentiles* 3, cc. 25–63.

Cuius oppositionis radix est in ipso *dynamismo* conscientiae humanae: sensitiva pars est propter intellectualem; ipse intellectus tendit in ens, voluntas in bonum. Quodcumque homo attingit, semper manet ulterius attingendum; quod ipse homo optime scit. Saecularismus vult illud ulterius intra mundum profanum collocari; ita olim liberales de progressu humano, nunc communistae de societate sine classibus.

[2.1.1] INTEGRATIONES

Apud Malinowski, vita profana penetratur mythis et magia; ipsae operationes humanae rationales sunt minoris momenti; multo plus influit liturgia. Apud Eliade, shaman est quodammodo mysticus; aliqua integratio inquantum shaman est specializatio quaedam in ipsa communitate. Apud Voegelin: in Babylonia, Mesopotamia, Aegypto, maximus habebatur progressus in omni arte practica circa campos, irrigationem, architecturam, et circa dominium hominum ordine oeconomico et politico. Sed ipsa politica simul erat synthesis cosmica et religiosa mythis fundata et penetrata.[45]

[2.2] Mundus interior et exterior

Mundus exterior est obiectivus; omnia includit quae per modum obiecti apprehenduntur, appetuntur, eliguntur; etiam ipsum subiectum includit inquantum obiectivatur, in speculo, in conceptu, in affirmatione sui, in voluntate explicita suorum finium.

Mundus interior est subiecti ut subiecti. Qui mundus interior semper habetur: nam subiectum ut subiectum est subiectum ut experiens, inquirens, intelligens, cogitans, evidentiam ponderans, iudicans, appetens, volens, eligens; quod subiectum sibi praesens est, sive distincte et explicite de se cogitat sive non.[46] Attamen differentiatio inter mundum interiorem

The root of this opposition is to be found in the *dynamism* of human consciousness: the sentient component in humans exists for the sake of the intellectual; the intellect tends to being, the will tends to the good. Whatever we may grasp, there is always something further to reach for, as we know only too well. Secularism would place this 'further' within the profane world; thus, an earlier liberalism spoke of human progress, and in this century communism proclaims a classless society.

[2.1.1] INTEGRATIONS

According to Malinowski, profane activity in primitive societies is shot through with myth and magic; rational human operations are relatively unimportant, while liturgy is much more influential. According to Eliade, a shaman is a kind of mystic; there is some integration inasmuch as within the community shamanism is a specialization. According to Voegelin, great progress took place in Babylonia, Mesopotamia, and Egypt in all the practical skills regarding land, irrigation, and architecture, and in the establishment of an economic and a political order of society. But the political order itself was at the same time a cosmic and a religious synthesis founded upon and steeped in myths.[45]

[2.2] The Inner and Outer Worlds

The outer world is objective: it includes everything that is apprehended, desired, or chosen as an object. It also includes the subject himself inasmuch as he is objectified, in a mirror, in a concept, in his self-affirmation, or in the explicit willing of his ends.

The inner world is that of the subject as subject. This inner world is always present; for the subject as subject is one who is experiencing, inquiring, understanding, thinking, weighing the evidence, judging, desiring, willing, choosing. Such a subject is present to himself whether or not he is distinctly and explicitly thinking about himself.[46] Yet there was no differentiation be-

45 [The Latin words 'mythis fundata et penetrata' were added by hand in the autograph.]
46 See Bernard Lonergan, *De Verbo incarnato*, 2nd ed. (Rome: Pontificia Universitas Gregoriana, 1961) 273–90; [3rd ed. (1964) 271–88]; *The Ontological and Psychological Constitution of Christ* [trans. from the 4th ed. of *De constitutione Christi ontologica et psychologica* by Michael G. Shields, ed. Frederick E.

et exteriorem non habetur donec oriatur individualismus. Scilicet homo primitivus est collectivista: non tam ipse quam tribus, collectivitas, cognoscit, deliberat, eligit. At post disrupta magna imperia (in Sinis, in Indis, in Mesopotamia, in Aegypto) tollitur mythus cosmologicus, et homo qua individuus pro se laborare, commercia facere, etc., debuit.[47]

Thomas à Kempis, Melius est compunctionem sentire quam definire. Quando definitur compunctio, obiectivatur; ponitur in mundo exteriori; similiter quando laudatur sentimentum et reprehenditur definitio, agitur de compunctione ut obiecto. At quando sentitur compunctio, agitur de subiecto in ipso foro interno: Ego peccavi, mea culpa, Miserere mei, Deus; non agitur de his verbis, non de voluntate, iudicio, conceptione unde haec verba procedunt, sed de ipso subiecto ut subiecto compunctione commoto.

Termini sicut vita, amor, praesentia Dei non proprie apprehenduntur per definitiones vitae, amoris, praesentiae Dei. Proprie dicunt id quod antecedit omnem definitionem; ipsum subiectum qua experiens, qua vivens; ipsum subiectum qua ad aliud subiectum totaliter coniunctum (voluntas non facit ut alius sit dimidium animae meae, sed hunc statum conformare vel debilitare potest); similiter praesentia Dei de qua homines et mulieres pii, non est praesentia Dei per modum cuiusdam obiecti concepti et affirmati, sed est quodammodo ingressus in ipsam vitam, in ipsum amorem, rei divinae. Cf. gressus in contemplatione S. Ignatii ad amorem obtinendum.

Insistitur in hac interioritate: circa medium aevum: J. Leclercq, *L'amour des lettres et le désir de Dieu*, Paris, 1957. Devotio moderna contra scholasticismum decadentem. A magnis mysticis: S. Teresa, S. Ioannes a Cruce. Post negatum mundum obiectivum a Kant: apud Hegelianos, Exsistentialistas.[48]

tween the inner and the outer world until the emergence of individualism. Primitive man is a collectivist: it is not so much the individual as the tribe, the collectivity, that knows, deliberates, and chooses. But after the breakup of the great empires (China, India, Mesopotamia, Egypt), the cosmological myth was dispelled, and men as individuals had to work, to engage in trading and so forth, for themselves.[47]

Recall the dictum of Thomas à Kempis, 'I would rather feel compunction than know its definition.' When compunction is defined, it is objectified, it is placed in the outer world; likewise, when feeling compunction is extolled and defining it is deprecated, compunction is being treated as an object. But when compunction is being felt, a subject is being present to himself *in foro interno*, in the inner sanctum of his own conscience: 'I have sinned, *mea culpa*, have mercy on me, O God!' The focus here is not on these words or the will or judgment or concept from which these words proceed, but on the subject himself as a subject being moved by compunction.

Terms such as life, love, or the presence of God are not properly apprehended through definitions of life, love, or the presence of God. Properly speaking, they indicate that which precedes every definition: the subject as experiencing, as alive, the subject as entirely united to another subject (the will does not cause another person to be 'half of my soul,' *dimidium animae meae*, but it can strengthen or weaken that state). Likewise, the presence of God that devout men and women speak about is not the presence of God by way of an object that is conceived and affirmed, but is in some way an entering into the very life and love of the divine reality. See, for example, the various steps in St Ignatius's 'Contemplation for Obtaining Love.'

Great stress is laid upon this interiority by the medieval *devotio moderna* in its reaction to decadent Scholasticism, by the great mystics St Teresa and St John of the Cross, and, after Kant's denial of the objective world, by the Hegelians and existentialists.[48]

Crowe and Robert M. Doran, vol. 7 in Collected Works of Bernard Lonergan (Toronto: University of Toronto Press, 2002)], part 5 [pp. 156–89]; *Insight*, chapter 11 [pp. 343–71].

47 Karl Jaspers, *Vom Ursprung und Ziel der Geschichte* (München: R. Piper, 1949, 1950); [in English, *The Origin and Goal of History*, trans. Michael Bullock (New Haven: Yale University Press, 1953).]

48 Jean Leclercq, *L'amour des lettres et le désir de Dieu: Initiation aux auteurs monastiques du Moyen Age* (Paris: Les Éditions du Cerf, 1957) [in English, *The Love of Learning and the Desire for God: A Study of Monastic Culture* (New York: Fordham University Library, 1961)]. Gaston Fessard, *De l'actualité historique.*

[2.3] Mundus aspectabilis et intelligibilis[49]

Differentiatio oritur inquantum cognitio scientifica attingitur, quae quidem a cognitione vulgari differt.

Fine: quaeritur verum intelligibile; cognitio vulgaris quaerit verum quatenus utile est ad fines practicos vitae humanae; et quaerit intelligibile quatenus in sensibilibus inspicitur et statim ad praxin deduci potest.

Obiecto: quoad se, res secundum earum habitudines inter se; cognitio vulgaris considerat tantum quoad nos, res secundum habitudinem ad nostros sensus et appetitus.

Lingua: invenit terminos technicos, procedit technice secundum logicam, methodologiam; cognitio vulgaris linguam ordinariam adhibet, rhetorice procedit.

Structura conscientiae: intellectus fit finis; caeterae potentiae non operantur nisi secundum exigentias ipsius intellectus; cognitio vulgaris habet et usurpat intellectum ut partem hominis functionalem, finis est dramatico-practicus, quid cui faciam, dicam. Thales, puella; Newton; Socrates, Athenienses.[50]

[2.3] The Visible World and the Intelligible World[49]

This differentiation arises as scientific knowledge is acquired, which differs from ordinary everyday knowledge.

It differs in its *end*: science aims at intelligible truth; ordinary knowledge seeks truth inasmuch as it is useful for the practical purposes of everyday living, and it seeks intelligibility inasmuch as this is discernible in sensible data and can be of immediate practical application.

It differs in its *object*: scientific knowledge regards things as they are in themselves, according to their relations to one another; ordinary knowledge considers them only as they are with respect to us, according to their relation to our senses and desires.

It differs in its *language*: science coins technical terms, and proceeds in a technical way according to logic and methodology; ordinary knowledge uses ordinary language, and proceeds rhetorically.

It differs in the *structure of consciousness*: in science, intellect becomes the end; other faculties operate only in accordance with the requirements of the intellect itself. Ordinary knowledge possesses and uses the intellect as a functional part of a person; its end is dramatic-practical: 'What should I do or say and to whom?' Examples: Thales and the milkmaid; Newton; Socrates and the Athenians.[50]

---

vol. 1, *À la recherche d'une méthode*; vol. 2, *Progressisme chrétien et apostolat ouvrier* (Paris: Desclée de Brouwer, 1960). Gaston Fessard, *La dialectique des 'Exercices spirituels' de Saint Ignace de Loyola* (Paris: Aubier, 1956). Georges Morel, *Le sens de l'existence selon Saint Jean de la Croix*: vol. 1, *Problématique*; vol. 2, *Logique*; vol. 3, *Symbolique* (Paris: Aubier-Montaigne, 1960–61).

On Hegel: Wilhelm Dilthey, *Die Jugendgeschichte Hegels und andere Abhandlungen zur Geschichte des deutschen Idealismus*, vol. 4 in his *Gesammelte Schriften*, ed. Herman Nohl (Leipzig: B.G. Teubner, 1921). Paul Asveld, *La pensée religieuse du jeune Hegel: Liberté et aliénation* (Louvain-Paris: Publications universitaires de Louvain, 1953); includes a bibliography.

49 [At this point in the autograph, the date at the top of the page switches to 25-2-62.]

50 [The Latin words 'contra quem scripsisti' were added by hand after 'quid cui faciam, dicam.' It is not clear what they refer to, and they have been dropped here. As for 'Thales and the milkmaid,' 'puella' does not translate directly as 'milkmaid' but as 'girl.' However, Lonergan frequently refers in English to the story of Thales and the milkmaid; in fact, the lecture in the summer of 1962 on this very material uses that expression; see Bernard Lonergan, *Early Works on Theological Method 1* 51.]

Obscuratur haec differentiatio per *culturam*, scilicet, per vulgarizationem quae fit ephemeridibus, articulis, libris, scholis elementaribus, mediis, disciplinis auxiliariis, professoribus secundi et tertii ordinis; per culturam clericalem, ubi aliae scientiae non coluntur nisi philosophica et theologica, utraque facillime modo non scientifico.

Non loquimur de mundo intelligibili, vel eo ipso quod agnoscimus exsistentiam Dei, angelorum, animae nostrae immaterialis vel eo ipso quod loquimur de materia et forma, essentia et exsistentia, substantia et accidentibus: possumus haec omnia modo quodam confuso concipere, quia ex mundo aspectabili ad intelligibilem exire nolumus vel ignoramus.

[3] Reflexio super Praecedentia (mundum sacrum, profanum, interiorem, exteriorem, aspectabilem, intelligibilem)

[3.1] Quid mundus?

Mundus non est obiectum quoddam sed potius obiectorum complexio, neque tantum obiectorum actu cognitorum, sed potius obiectorum quae cognosci possint. Comparatur ergo mundus ad obiecta sicut complexio combinationum operationum differentiatarum ad combinationes quasdam determinatas. Sicut singula obiecta combinatione determinata operationum attinguntur, ita mundus correspondet complexioni combinationum possibilium.

[3.2] Differentiatio mundorum

Facta est secundum dynamismum conscientiae, structuram conscientiae, technicam evolutionem conscientiae.[51]

This differentiation is obscured by *culture*, that is, in the popularization that takes place through magazines, articles, books, elementary schools, the media, auxiliary subjects, second- and third-rate professors; and by clerical culture, where the only branches of knowledge cultivated are philosophy and theology, and these very often in an easy-going and nonscientific way.

We do not speak of the intelligible world just because we acknowledge the existence of God and angels and an immaterial human soul, or because we talk about matter and form, essence and existence, substance and accidents; for we can have woolly notions about all of these realities, because we either will not move, or do not know how to move, from the visible into the intelligible world.

[3] Further Reflection on These Various 'Worlds'

[3.1] What Do We Mean by a 'World'?

A world is not some particular object but rather a group of objects, and not only of objects that are actually known, but even more of objects that can be known. A world, therefore, is to its objects as a group of combinations of differentiated operations is to certain determinate combinations. Just as individual objects are attained by a determinate combination of operations, so a world corresponds to a group of possible combinations.

[3.2] The Differentiation of Worlds

Differentiation takes place in accordance with the dynamism of consciousness, the structure of consciousness, and the technical development of consciousness.[51]

---

51 [This is explained more clearly in *Early Works on Theological Method 1* 60: '... the differentiation of the worlds rests upon differentiations in the subject. The *dynamism* of consciousness leads to the opposition between the ultimate and the proximate; the *structure* of consciousness leads to the opposition between subject and object; the subject is never conscious unless he is dealing with some object, but the subject as subject never is an object; and finally, the *specialization* of consciousness leads to the movement from the milkmaid to Thales, from the Athenians to Socrates.' Thus (a), (b), and (c) here refer respectively to dynamism, structure, and development or specialization.]

(a) Alia est complexio combinationum operationum differentiarum quam adhibemus mane in oratione, in missa, in recitatione breviarii, in secessu annuali, et alia est complexio in studio, inter scholas, scribendo, in conversatione, inter edendum et bibendum. Laudatur sane praesentia Dei perpetua, sed communior est oscillatio inter sacrum et profanum; imo in ipsis sacris peragendis, facillime ad profana redimus (distractiones mentis); rarius in profanis peragendis distrahimur ad sacra; quod si fit, nos iam in via perfectionis credimus. S. Teresa tandem denique eo pervenit ut simul ad profana attenderet et a statu mystico non discederet; ubi tamen ipsa se divisam experta est.

(b) Alia est complexio operationum, eaque maxima, quibus circa mundum exteriorem occupamur: omnia quae imaginatione repraesentamus, intellectu concipimus, iudicio affirmamus vel negamus, voluntate volumus vel nolumus, deliberatione eligimus, verbis dicimus, manibus vel pedibus corpore peragimus. Sed alius est reditus in se ipsum suasque operationes neque facilis est, neque perdurans; perdurat subiectum ut subiectum, ad se non attendens.[52] Facilior quidem est reditus in se sensitive operantem, e.g., aperiendo et claudendo oculos attentionem dirigo in me videntem et non videntem, ab obiecto viso attentionem amoveo, sed fere statim ipsum me et meam visonem per modum obiecti imaginati, vel concepti, vel affirmati considero. Difficilior est reditus ad operationes intellectuales – quid commune inter opera *Verbum*[53] et *Insight*; in utroque agitur de interioritate; emanatio intelligibilis et actus intelligendi unde emanatio intelligibilis non prout obiective concipitur, affirmatur, nisi per prius ut factum immediatum experitur; 'quilibet in se ipso experiri potest.'[54] Minus difficilis est reditus ad operationes voluntatis, qui tamen suam difficultatem habet: an consensisti, an deliberate fecisti? Nisi oscillatione non attenditur ad interiorem et exteriorem mundum.

(a) We use one group of combinations of differentiated operations in our morning prayer, at Mass, in saying the breviary, in our annual retreat, and another group in studying, in class, in writing, in conversing, and in eating and drinking. The continuous presence of God is praiseworthy, to be sure, but much more common is our going back and forth between the sacred and the profane. Indeed, in performing these sacred duties we slip very easily back into the profane (mental distractions). More rarely are we distracted by holy thoughts in the midst of our profane activities; and if this happens, we may consider ourselves to be already on the way of perfection. St Teresa finally reached the point where she was able to attend to profane concerns without leaving the mystical state; and yet even at those times she experienced herself as divided.

(b) The group of operations (the largest one) that we use when engaged in dealing with the outer world is one thing: all that we represent in our imagination, all that we conceive by our intellect, all that we affirm or deny in our judgments, all that we want or do not want by our will, and all that we choose in our deliberations, utter by our words, and perform by our hands or feet or other physical movements. The reflective activity in which we direct our attention back to ourselves and our operations is something quite different. It is neither easy nor long-lasting. (The subject as subject continues, of course, even when not attending to himself.)[52] This reflecting upon oneself is relatively easy in the matter of sentient operations; for example, in opening and closing my eyes I direct my attention to myself as seeing or not seeing, removing my attention away from the object seen; yet almost immediately I am considering myself and my vision as an object imagined or conceived or affirmed. More difficult is reflection upon our intellectual operations. This is a theme common to *Verbum*[53] and *Insight*, as both deal with interiority. Intelligible emanation and the act of understanding that grounds intelligible emanation are not conceived and affirmed objectively until first experienced as an immediate fact: 'Anyone can experience within himself ...'[54] Less difficult is the reflection upon the operations of the will, although it does have a difficulty of its own: did you consent, did you act deliberately or not? One can attend to both the inner and the outer world only by oscillating between them.

---

52 [The Latin words 'perdurat subiectum ut subiectum, ad se non attendens' were added by hand in the autograph.]
53 See above, p. 63, note 47.
54 [Thomas Aquinas, *Summa theologiae*, 1, q. 84, a. 7 c.]

(c) Manifestissima est oppositio inter mundum aspectabilem et intelligibilem; maxima pars hominum, imo excultorum, ad mundum intelligibilem haud pervenit.

[3.3] Analogia mundorum

Non consistit in similitudine inter mundum sacrum huius et illius, primitivi et mystici, et sic de aliis: ex parte obiecti maxima dissimilitudo inveniri potest. Sed consistit in similitudine ex parte subiecti, scilicet tali operationum complexione utitur quae ab aliis distinguitur secundum dynamismum conscientiae, structuram conscientiae, technicam evolutionem conscientiae.[55]

[3.4] Concreta mundorum consideratio[56]

A nullo aspectu mundi abstrahitur, sed semper considerandus est mundus hic profanus, etc., secundum omnes suas determinationes; scilicet, terminus habetur universalis, non abstrahendo a quadam determinatione mundi, sed referendo mundum ad complexionem operationum; ipsaque complexio concipitur universaliter, non abstrahendo a qualibet determinatione sed opponendo eam relative ad complexionem oppositam.

[3.5] Historica mundorum consideratio

Quia concreta est consideratio, etiam includit aspectum historicum, determinationes particulares ex loco, tempore, stirpe, etc., provenientes. Historia

(c) The most obvious opposition is that between the visible and the intelligible worlds; the vast majority of people, even of the educated, never get to the intelligible world.

[3.3] The Analogy of Worlds

This analogy does not consist in the similarity between this and that sacred world, between the sacred world of primitive people and that of the mystics, and likewise for the others; for on the part of the object one can find a very great dissimilarity. The analogy consists rather in the similarity on the part of the subject; that is, the subject uses a certain group of operations that differs from others with respect to the dynamism of consciousness, the structure of consciousness, and the technical development of consciousness.[55]

[3.4] The Concrete Study of Worlds[56]

No abstraction is made from any aspect of a world; rather, this profane world and the rest are to be considered in all their determinations. In other words, we have a universal term, not by abstracting from some particular determination of a world, but by relating that world to a certain group of operations; and this group itself is conceived in a universal way, not by abstracting from any determination but by considering it in relation to its opposite group.

[3.5] The Historical Study of Worlds

Since this study is concrete, it also includes a historical aspect, the particular determinations resulting from place, time, race, and so forth. 'History'

55 [Perhaps the statement in *Early Works on Theological Method 1* 60–61, is clearer: 'The religious world of one person is not the same as that of another. The religious world of the shaman is not the religious world of St Teresa of Avila. They are analogous, and the analogy does not lie in comparing the properties of the two worlds. It is an analogy not of attribution but of proportion: what is ultimate for the shaman is his religious world, and what is ultimate for St Teresa of Avila is her religious world.']
56 [Entered by hand: 'Quomodo concreta? Paucissima cognoscimus! Definitio heuristica, quae est fallax nostra cognitio concreti (=ens).' 'How concrete? We know so few things! Heuristic definition, which is our fallible knowledge of the concrete (= being).']

(secundum quam historica est consideratio) non est historia quae scribitur sed est historia de qua scribitur; iterum non est historia quae cognoscitur sed est historia de qua quaeritur, [seu] totalitas actionum humanarum.[57]

Quia est concreta et historica, includit considerationem motus, mutationis, evolutionis: motus enim non fit in conceptibus sed in rebus concretis, et tantummodo in iis. Unde evitamus difficultatem eorum qui evolutionem dogmatum, evolutionem theologiae, in abstracto, secundum principia generalia considerant, et difficultates sat graves inde patiuntur: in abstracto enim nihil movetur.

[3.6] Mundorum mobilitas

Additis novis differentiationibus, integrationibus (i.e., evolutione ulteriori): ex aperitudine ·mentis, ex voluntate rationem sequente, ex aperitudine societatis. Quamvis excludatur evolutio in hoc homine, in hac societate, alibi fieri potest; unde et postea fere constringitur homo, societas, ad evolutionem acceptandam; ita scientiae modernae in civilizatione occidentali evolutae sunt, sed sese omnibus culturis hodie imponunt.

Non solum evolvendo sed etiam regrediendo mutantur mundi *inauthentia*;[58] *formalismo*: observantur conventiones, technicae, sed praetermittitur interioritas unde sensum, vitam, habent (logica symbolica, scientiae humanae ad modum scientiae naturalis excultae, philosophia, theologia, sine interioritate); *pathos*: abundat interioritas, sed deest peritia ad accuratas definitiones, scientificam rei ordinationem (Scheeben);[59] *intellectualismus, anti-intellectualismus*: praetermittitur, despicitur, reprehenditur, mundus aspectabilis, *beziehungsweise*, intelligibilis; *archaismus, anachronismus*: omnia

in this historical study is not the history that is written but history that is written about; and again, it is not history that is known but history that is the object of inquiry: the totality of human actions.[57]

Since it is concrete and historical, it also includes a consideration of movement, of change, of development. Movement is not to be found in concepts, but in concrete realities, and only in them. In this way we avoid the problem had by those who consider the development of dogmas and of theology in the abstract according to general principles, and so get into serious difficulty; for in the realm of the abstract, nothing moves.

[3.6] Movement in Worlds

Movement in worlds arises from the addition of new determinations and integrations (in other words, ongoing development): from openness of mind, from a will that follows reason, from openness in a society. Although there may be no development in this particular person or that particular society, there can be development elsewhere, and so eventually this person or society is virtually constrained to accept the development. Thus, for example, modern sciences developed in the West, but now are spreading to all cultures.

Worlds change not only by developing but also by regression, by *inauthenticity*;[58] for example, by *formalism*: conventions are observed, techniques followed, but the interiority that gives them meaning and vitality is disregarded (as in symbolic logic, human sciences patterned after the natural sciences, philosophy and theology without interiority); by *sentiment*: interiority abounds, but the ability to formulate accurate definitions and to order material scientifically is lacking (Scheeben);[59] by *intellectualism or anti-intellectualism*: ignoring, despising, condemning the visible and the intelligible

---

57 [The Latin words '= totalitas actionum humanarum' are added by hand in the autograph.]

58 [In the autograph at this point Lonergan inserts 'fides scientifica' ('scientific faith') in the left margin Latin. The student notes insert 'fides scientifica' at the end of the treatment of formalism. For an instance of 'scientific faith,' see below, p. 469.]

59 [See *Early Works on Theological Method 1* 63: 'Just as there can be complete competence of the formalist, so there can be the man who really gets hold of the problems and really has felt his way towards their solution, but cannot give any theoretically or technically competent account or expression of his findings. For example, Scheeben ...']

semper eodem modo se habent, eodem modo apprehenduntur; quare si facta est evolutio, aut ad sola priora ut authentica attendendum est, aut ipsa priora exacte uti hodierna fuisse affirmantur; *regressivitate:* sicut in pathologia psychica difficultates evitantur redeundo ad stadium prius puerile, infantile, ita in genere problemata evitari possunt redeundo ad statum naturae primitivum vel saltem ad aliquid minus complicatum quam mundus modernus est.

[3.7] Mundorum integratio

Apparens per suppressionem, negligentiam, euphemizationem vel alterius membri vel ipsius oppositionis. Ita si omittuntur mundus intelligibilis, mundus interior, et mundus sacer, sat facile in unum coincidunt mundus profanus, exterior, aspectabilis – mundus journalisticus – educatio pro vita, practica.[60] Si tollitur illud 'aut-aut' quod ad mundorum oppositionem constituendam pertinet. Hegel, Kierkegaard.[61]

Simplificata: in Brahmanismo adsunt oppositiones quae tamen ad unam reducuntur: mundus sacer, interior, intelligibilis est subiectum absolutum, Atman, in quo absorptio, nirvana, optatur; mundus profanus, exterior, aspectabilis est Maya, campus apparentiarum, karmae, metempsychosis.

Dynamica integratio habetur inquantum inter extrema oscillatur, ita tempus orationis et tempus studii; Toynbee, Withdrawal & Return; Tao, Via quae oscillatur inter extrema symbolice repraesentata per Caelum et terram, Diem et noctem, Marem et feminam, Siccum et aridum.[62]

Transpositione, sublimatione, reconciliatione. Exemplo sit (1) S. Georgius et draco, (2) Ionas et magnus piscis, (3) oscillatio, (4) Christianismus, unicum malum est peccatum; sicut caritas excludit peccatum, ita foras expellit timorem; unde qui timet non est perfectus in caritate. Ita tollitur radix prioris oscillationis, sed oritur nova in alio campo: num re vera ego habeo caritatem, nonne sum peccator, hoc feci et faciam, quod tamen forte pec-

worlds respectively; by *archaism or anachronism*: everything is always the same and apprehended in the same way; therefore, if there has been development, either things are to be regarded as authentic only as they were in the earlier stage, or else they are judged to have been in that earlier stage exactly as they are understood to be today; by *regression*: just as the mentally ill avoid problems by regressing to the puerile or infantile stage, so problems in general can be avoided by returning to a primitive state of nature or at least to something that is less complicated than the modern world.

[3.7] The Integration of Worlds

There is an *apparent* integration by way of suppressing, neglecting, or euphemizing either one or other of the opposing worlds or their mutual opposition itself. Thus, if the intelligible, inner, and sacred worlds are ignored, the visible, outer, and profane worlds are quite easily lumped together: the journalistic world, education for life, for the practical;[60] again, the 'either-or' that constitutes the opposition between worlds can be denied. Hegel, Kierkegaard.[61]

There can be a *simplified* integration. Thus, in Brahmanism there are opposites that, however, can be brought into unity: the sacred, inner, and intelligible world is an absolute subject, Atman, absorption into which, or nirvana, is to be desired; the profane, outer, visible world is Maya, the realm of appearances, of karma, and of the transmigration of souls.

Dynamic integration takes place when there is oscillation between the extremes; for example, between prayer and study; Toynbee's 'Withdrawal and Return'; Tao, the Way that oscillates between extremes symbolically represented by heaven and earth, day and night, male and female, dry and wet.[62]

There can be integration by *transposition, sublimation, reconciliation*: for example, (1) St George and the dragon, (2) Jonah and the whale, (3) oscillation, (4) Christianity: the sole evil is sin; just as love excludes sin, so does it cast out fear; hence, one who fears has not perfect love. In this way the root of the previous oscillation is removed, but a new one springs up in another area: do I really have love, am I not a sinner? I have done such and

---

60 [The words 'educatio pro vita, practica' were added by hand in the autograph.]
61 [The words 'Hegel, Kierkegaard' were added by hand in the autograph.]
62 [For 'wet' Lonergan typed *aridum*, another word for 'dry.' He surely meant to write *humidum*, 'wet.' See Lonergan, *Early Works on Theological Method* 64.]

catum est – scrupulositas, vel conscientia indurata. Confugiendum est ad
Dominum in oratione, ad interioritatem. Aliud exemplum: problema transportationis; invenitur currus automobilis; tot fiunt ut viae publicae fere im-
passibiles reddantur; multiplicantur viae sed augetur currorum numerus;
problema transportationis non est tantum quaestio de vehiculis et viis, sed
etiam de urbibus, et forte ulterius de mundo profano, aspectabili, exteriori,
in quo localis motus fere principalis quaedam est operationum conditio.

[3.8] Integrationum mobilitas

Nisi modo generalissimo integrationes non consideravimus. Sed non minus sunt concretae quaedam oscillationes dynamicae, concretae quaedam
problematum transpositiones, sublimationes, quae fiunt in adiunctis concretis, secundum intelligibiltatem non necessariam sed de facto (empiricam), secundum iudicium prudens, secundum electionem liberam.

Integrationes concrete consideratae tam sunt mobiles quam sunt mundi integrandi. Sicut ipsi mundi, ita etiam integrationes non sunt obiecta
scientiae cuiusdam universalis, necessariae, per se, essentiarum aeternarum
et immobilium, sed inveniuntur in contingenti, particulari, per accidens,
evolventis et decadentis.

[3.9] Integrationis locus

Integratio de qua agitur non est synthesis quaedam obiectiva in mundo
intelligibili, pulcherrima quaedam theoria quae omnia considerat, ordinat,
inter se componit. Nam mundus intelligiblis ipse non est nisi elementum
quoddam materiale quod cum aliis elementis (sacro, profano, interiori, aspectabili) integrandum est.

Ulterius, non tam ipsi mundi quam complexiones operationum subiecti
sunt integrandae. Ipsi mundi non dicunt nisi totalitatem quandam obiectorum quae per talem operationum complexionem attingi potest. Integratio
quae quaeritur maxime ipsas complexiones respicit, et ipsum subiectum
quod ex alia complexione in aliam potius salit quam transit.

Tum propter integritatem subiecti, ne personalitatem divisam, multiplicem, habeat; tum propter authenticitatem erga ipsos mundos: sine sacro,

such and will do so in the future, and perhaps it is a sin: either scrupulosity or a hardened conscience. One must flee to the Lord in prayer, take refuge in interiority. Another example: the problem of transportation. Since automobiles were invented, they have become so numerous that the streets have become virtually impassable. More and more roads are being built, but there are more and more cars. But the problem of transportation is not just a matter of vehicles and roads, but of cities, and perhaps ultimately a matter of the profane, visible, and outer world in which mobility is a prime condition of operations.

[3.8] The Changeability of Integrations

We have been considering integrations only in a most general way. But no less concrete are certain dynamic oscillations, certain concrete transpositions and sublimations of problems that are carried out in concrete circumstances, not according to necessary intelligibility but according to *de facto* (empirical) intelligibility, and according to prudent judgment and free choice.

Considered concretely, integrations are as changeable as there are worlds to be integrated. Like the worlds themselves, integrations also are not objects of some science that is universal, necessary, *per se*, a science of eternal and immutable essences; they are found in that which is contingent, particular, *per accidens*, progressing and declining.

[3.9] The Place of Integration

The integration we are talking about here is not some objective synthesis in the intelligible world, some beautiful theory that considers, arranges, and connects everything together. For the intelligible world itself is but one material element that must be integrated with the other elements (the sacred, profane, inner, and visible worlds).

Furthermore, it is not so much the worlds themselves as the groups of operations of the subject that have to be integrated. The worlds themselves refer only to a totality of objects that can be attained through a particular group of operations. The integration we seek regards mainly those groups themselves and the subject who jumps rather than simply moves from one group to another.

[Such integration is sought] both for the sake of the integrity of the subject, to avoid having a split or a multiple personality, and for the sake of the

ita profanum omnia occupat ut homo dignitate sua privetur; sine interiori, mundus exterior in vanitatem et vacuitatem decidit; sine intelligibili, mundus aspectabilis mentalitate mythica apprehenditur et completur.[63]

4 Problematica Theologica in Antithesibus (Mundis) Fundata[64]

[4.1 Problem Not Religious]

1 Problema non est in ipsa religione christiana, quae de se quam maxime diversos mundos inter se unit.

(a) Est sacralizatio mundi profani: Verbum caro factum est; ecclesia est corpus Christi; vivit ecclesia per dirigentem inhabitantem Spiritum sanctum.

(b) Quae sacralizatio mundum interiorem penetrat: paenitentia de peccatis, perpetua quaedam conversio (oratio et ieiunium), fides, spes, caritas uniunt subiectum ad Deum, ad ecclesiam, ad homines singulos.

(c) Quae mundum exteriorem aspectabilem occupat: hierarchia, successio apostolica; kerygma, praedicatio, missiones; sacrificium, sacramenta, liturgia; familia, moralitas, societas, educatio,[65] status, ius, ordo socialis catholicus omnes habent sensum determinatum.

(d) Quae in mundum intelligibilem transit: evolutio dogmatica: *homoousion*, una persona in duabus naturis, supernaturale, sacramenta; evolutio theologica: quaestiones, distinctiones, systemata.

[4.2 Problem Theological]

2 Problema est theologicum, scilicet, illud religionis christianae quod ad mundum intelligibilem pertinent.

(a) Problema fundamentale methodologicum: controversia mediaevalis

authenticity of the subject with regard to the worlds themselves; for without the sacred, the profane world takes over everything so completely that man is deprived of his dignity; without the inner world, the outer world degenerates into vanity and emptiness; and without the intelligible world, the visible world is apprehended and completed[63] by a pervasive mythic mentality.

4 The Theological Problematic Based upon the Antitheses (Worlds)[64]

[4.1] Problem Not Religious

1 The problem is not with the Christian religion itself, which unites within itself worlds that are most diverse.

(a) It is the sacralization of the profane world: the Word was made flesh; the church is the body of Christ; the church lives through the guidance of the indwelling Holy Spirit.

(b) This sacralization penetrates the inner world: repentance for sin, ongoing conversion (prayer and fasting), faith, hope, and charity unite the subject to God, to the church, to individual persons.

(c) It enters into the visible world: hierarchy, apostolic succession; *kerygma*, preaching, missions; sacrifice, sacraments, liturgy; the Catholic family, morality, society, education,[65] state, law, and social order all have a well-defined meaning.

(d) It influences the intelligible world by dogmatic development: *homoousion*, one person in two natures, supernatural, sacraments; and by theological development: questions, distinctions, systems.

[4.2] Problem Theological

2 The problem is theological; that is, it concerns that aspect of the Christian religion that pertains to the intelligible world.

(a) A fundamental methodological problem is found in the medieval

---

63 [The Latin words 'et completur' were added by hand in the autograph.]
64 [At this point in the autograph the date at the top of the page switches back to 21-3-62.]
65 [The Latin word 'educatio' was added by hand in the autograph, replacing 'moralitas,' which was crossed out.]

aristotelica-augustiniana: Ut distinctiones inter se cohaereant, ne tantum verbales sint et problemata potius augeant quam minuant, requiritur systema, scilicet, omnium conceptuum ordinata atque unita quaedam formatio; quam systematizationem effecit Aquinas assumendo et transformando Aristotelismum; contra quem processerunt Augustiniani: noluerunt scientiam paganam, acceperunt logicam Aristotelis, ideale scientificum, sed non philosophiam, non scientiam.[66]

(b) Ipse aristotelismus est doctrina integrata sed incompleta.

(a′) Integrantur mundus aspectabilis-intellibigibilis: hylemorphismus est quaedam horum compenetratio (contra separationem platonicam inter *ta ontōs onta* et *ta mē onta*); substantiae separatae sunt motores immobiles mundi aspectabilis, plus minus quinquaginta, unde uti dictum est habetur polytheismus quidam demythologizatus; e contra disputatur utrum ideae platonicae sint realitates an normae quaedam.

(b′) Integrantur quodammodo mundus interior et exterior, per obiectificationem mundi interioris: principia per se nota, logica, psychologia, metaphysica, ethica, politica, rhetorica, poetica; ubi tamen habetur periculum inauthentiae: omisso, oblito mundo interiori, eius obiectificatio fit aes sonans et cymbalum tinniens; quod factum est saepius.

(c′) Sed ideale scientificum est incompletum: scientia aristotelica est certa, de immobilibus, per se, necessariis, universalibus; e contra, scientiae modernae sunt non certae sed probabiles; sunt de ipso motu: calculus infinitesimalis, genetica, dialectica; sunt de per accidens: statistica, tendentiae; sunt circa intelligibilitatem non necessariam sed de facto, empiricam; sunt circa particularia, nam de motu, qui nisi in particularibus non fit: e.g., systema planetarium, genesis mundi, evolutio specierum.

(c) Cum hac moderna[67] scientiae notione coniunguntur scientiae humanae empiricae, in quibus non agitur de homine abstracto, in statu naturae

controversy between the Augustinians and the Aristotelians. In order that distinctions be mutually coherent and not merely verbal, in which case they would simply aggravate rather than mitigate the problems, system is required, that is, a well-ordered and unified formation of all concepts. This systematization was worked out by Aquinas by adopting and transforming Aristotelianism. The Augustinians reacted against this systematization: they would have nothing to do with 'pagan' science; they accepted Aristotle's logic as a scientific ideal, but not his philosophy or his science.[66]

(b) Aristotelianism itself is integrated but incomplete.

(a′) In it are integrated the visible and intelligible worlds: hylomorphism is the compenetration of both of these aspects (against the Platonic separation between *ta ontōs onta* and *ta mē onta*, the 'really real' and the 'non-real'); separate substances are the unmoved movers of the visible world, about 50 in number, what has been called a demythologized polytheism. On the other hand, it was a matter of debate whether the Platonic Ideas were realities or norms of some sort.

(b′) It integrates in a way the inner and outer worlds through the objectification of the inner world: self-evident principles, logic, psychology, metaphysics, ethics, politics, rhetoric, poetics. Yet here there is a danger of inauthenticity: when the inner world is left out or forgotten, its objectification becomes as sounding brass or tinkling cymbal – which has happened quite often.

(c′) But its scientific ideal is incomplete: Aristotelian science is certain, and has to do with the immobile, the *per se*, the necessary, the universal. Modern sciences, by contrarst, are not certain but probable; they are concerned with motion itself: infinitesimal calculus, genetic and dialectical methods; with the *per accidens*: statistics, trends; not with necessary but with *de facto* or empirical intelligibility; with particulars, for they deal with motion, which belongs only to particular things: e.g., the planetary system, the origin of the world, the evolution of species.

(c) The empirical human sciences are closely connected with this modern[67] notion of science. In these sciences it is not man in the abstract that

---

66 See Roger Marston, *Quaestiones disputatae: De emanatione aeterna, De statu naturae lapsae, et De anima* (Ad Clares Aquas, Florentiae: Ex typographia Collegii S. Bonaventurae, 1932). [The reference to Marston was added by hand in the autograph.]

67 [The Latin word 'moderna' was added by hand in the autograph.]

purae, sine peccato originali, sine indigentia divinae gratiae, eiusque acceptatione vel reiectione; agitur tantummodo de hominibus qui fuerunt, sunt, erunt; non agitur de familia ideali, de societate ideali, de moralitate ideali, de educatione ideali, de statu vel iure ideali, de oeconomia vel technica ideali; agitur de iis quae sunt, prout de facto inveniuntur, prout empirice intelliguntur. Augustinus: non homo prout est sed prout sempiternis rationibus esse debeat; moderni sempiternas rationes ignorant, facta et factorum intelligibilitatem empiricam quaerunt, et secundum eam vivere volunt. Aquinas: synthesis, theologia, philosophia, scientiae aristotelicae; apud modernos, scientiae humanae empiricae non subsunt philosophiae de homine abstracto; imo ipsa philosophia fit exsistentialis et eo ipso[68] campum theologicum invadit.

(d) Accedit quae dicitur conscientia historica.

(a′) Homo suo intellectu, suo libero arbitrio, sua responsabilitate facit mundum suum; et homo modernus conscie suum mundum fecit: itinera et novarum terrarum inventio, novae linguae vernaculares, novae litteraturae (non iam disputatur de meritis antiquorum et recentium auctorum); novae artes: architectura, plastica, repraesentativa, musica; novae scientiae, novae philosophiae, novae religiones, novae formae politicae, novae oecomonia, industria, commercium, technica; nova educatio, moralitas, saepe familia. Nulla dirimitur quaestio vel theoretica vel practica eo quod sic et sic olim fiebat, olim dicebatur.

(b′) Invaduntur fontes theologiae. Examinantur scripturae, scripta patristica, mediaevalia, recentiora,[69] orthodoxa et haeretica, methodo historico-critica, scilicet criteriis litterariis et historicis, et ideo sicut et aliud quodlibet scriptum, documentum, monumentum; an inserendum sit a priori theologicum, quodnam, quomodo.[70]

is their subject-matter, man in a state of 'pure nature,' without original sin, without need of divine grace and its acceptance or rejection; they deal only with human beings who have lived, are living, and will be living. They do not concern themselves with the ideal family, the ideal society, ideal morality, ideal education, the ideal polity or legal system, the ideal economy or technology; they deal with things that exist, things as they are actually found to be and are understood empirically. Augustine appealed not to people as they are but as they ought to be according to 'eternal ideals'; moderns ignore eternal ideals, look for facts and the empirical understanding of them, and want to live in accordance with that understanding. Aquinas provides a synthesis of theology, philosophy, and Aristotelian science; for moderns, the empirical human sciences are not subsumed in a philosophy of man in the abstract; in fact, philosophy is becoming existential, and by that fact[68] is invading the field of theology.

(d) To this is added 'historical consciousness.'

(a′) By our own intellect, our own free will, our own responsible choices, we make our world; and modern man has consciously made his own world through voyages and discovery of new lands, new vernacular languages, new literatures (no longer is there the dispute about the merits of ancient and modern authors); new arts: architecture, the plastic arts, representational art, music; new sciences, new philosophies, new religions, new political systems, new economics, industry, commerce, technology; new forms of education, morality, family. No longer are questions, whether of theory or practice, cut short by an appeal to what was done or said in the past.

(b′) The sources of theology are invaded by historical consciousness. Scripture, the writings of the Fathers, medieval and modern writings,[69] both orthodox and heretical, are scrutinized by the method of historical criticism, that is, according to literary and historical criteria, and so are subject to examination like all other historical writings, documents, or other evidences of the past. The question is, should some theological *a priori* be introduced here, and if so, what, and how?[70]

---

68 [The Latin words 'et eo ipso' were added by hand in the autograph.]

69 [The Latin word 'recentiora' was added by hand in the autograph.]

70 See Albert Descamps, 'Réflections sur la méthode en théologie biblique,' in *Sacra pagina: Miscellanae biblica congressus internationalis catholici de re biblica*, vol. 1, ed. J.Coppens, A. Descamps, É. Massaux (Paris: Gabalda, and Gembloux: J. Duculot, 1959) 132–57; and Máximo Peinador, 'La integración

(c′) Invaditur ipsa doctrina theologica. Olim ponebatur rei definitio, de qua non disputabatur. Hodie ponitur notionis historia: e.g., persona (critici litterarii; notio heuristica Augustini; definitiones Boethii, Richardi a S. Victore, S. Thomae; theoriae metaphysicae Scoti, Capreoli, Caietani, Tiphani, Suarezii; notio psychologica subiecti; notio phaenomenologica Ego-Tu). Quod de omnibus notionibus, omnibus theorematibus, fit vel fieri debet, unde tollitur doctrina fere et traditur doctrinae historia. Secundum CIC, theologia doceri debet ad principia rationem doctrinam S. Thomae; quomodo procedendum est ne doctrina S. Thomae sit tantummodo pars historiae doctrinalis, imo ne loco doctrinae S. Thomae ponatur inquisitio historico-critica circa mentem S. Thomae.[71]

(e)[72] Coluntur phaenomenologia, existentialismus, personalismus. Quibus commune eat quod ex immediatis, concretis, in mundo aspectabili sine difficultate apprehensis, statim ad mundum interiorem proceditur, omissa omni consideratione abstracta, pure theoretica, speculativa, systematica. Excluditur fere mundus intelligibilis.

Apud E. Husserl methodus phaenomenologica reductione triplici constat: reductione phaenomenologica qua praescinditur a sensu realitatis (*natürliche Einstellung*); reductione eidetica qua ad essentiam, sensum, significationem immediatam attenditur; reductione transcendentali qua ex obiecto ad subiectum, obiecti principium, receditur; quibus omnibus illud unum intenditur, ut omissis contingentibus ad necessitatem stricte dictam, scientiarum fundamentum, perveniatur.

(c′) Theological doctrine itself is invaded by historical consciousness. One used to state the definition of something, about which there was no dispute. But today the history of the notion is set forth: for example, the history of 'person' (literary critics; Augustine's heuristic notion; definitions by Boethius, Richard of St Victor, St Thomas; the metaphysical theories of Scotus, Capreolus, Cajetan, Tiphanus, Suárez; the psychological notion of subject; the phenomenological notion of 'I-Thou'). And the same is being done or needs to be done for all other notions and theorems. Hence, doctrines are being replaced by the history of doctrines. The [1917] *Code of Canon Law* [canon 1366, §2] states that theology is to be taught according to the principles, method, and doctrine of St Thomas. But how is one to go about doing this without his teaching becoming but a part of the history of doctrine, and indeed without replacing it with a historical-critical investigation into the thought of Thomas himself?[71]

(e)[72] The philosophies of phenomenology, existentialism, and personalism are cultivated. Common to these three is the fact that from what is immediate, concrete, and readily apprehended in the visible world they proceed straightaway into the inner world of interiority, bypassing all abstract, purely theoretical, speculative, and systematic study. The intelligible world is virtually shut out.

In Husserl, phenomenological method consists of a threefold reduction: phenomenological reduction, by which one prescinds from the sense of what is real (*natürliche Einstellung*); eidetic reduction, by which one attends to the immediate essence, meaning, and signification of a thing; transcendental reduction, by which one goes back from the object to the subject, the principle of the object. All of these reductions have one objective, namely, that having set aside all that is contingent, one arrive at necessity in the strict sense, the foundation of the sciences.

----

de la exégesis en la teología, Hacia una auténtica "Teología bíblica",' ibid. 158–79. [This is one of the earliest references (perhaps the earliest) to Descamps's work by Lonergan; it was to prove an important paper for him as he formulated the approach to hermeneutics that would appear in *Method in Theology*.] For the importance of this work of historical criticism, see Berthold Altaner, *Patrologie*, 5th ed. (Freiburg im Breisgau, 1958), Introduction [§3], pp. 9–37. [In English, *Patrology*, trans. Hilda C. Graef (New York: Herder and Herder, 1960), Introduction, §3, pp. 12–44.]

71 [The Latin words 'imo ne loco doctrinae S. Thomae ponatur inquisitio historico-critica circa mentem S. Thomae' were added by hand in the autograph.]

72 [In the autograph, '(e)' to the end of '(g)' consist of two undated pages.]

Latius sumitur phaenomenologia tamquam immediatorum descriptio, quae ipsam operationem, eventum, rem, sese manifestare permittit, quae per hanc immediatam evidentiam ad indubiam quandam essentiae, sensus, significationis, momenti humani apprehensionem procedit. Max Scheler eam adhibuit ad manifestanda intersubiectiva, sentimenta, valores, rem religiosam.[73] M. Heidegger intelligentiam entis et esse quaerit, inprimis esse humani; principium ponit illam esse humani intelligentiam quae eo ipso datur quod quis homo est; quam immediatam experientiam et intelligentiam (inauthenticam, authenticam) accurate distinguit ab eiusdem elucidatione conceptuali (*existenziell, existenzial*). Cui inhaeret R. Bultmann exegesin S. Pauli efficiens secundum praeintelligentiam existentialem.[74]

Unde permulti auctores[75] circa intersubiectiva, sentimenta, symbolica, aesthetica, moralia, personalia, ritualia, liturgica, religiosa, circa situationem humanam, dialecticam concretam evolutionis personalis (Hegel servus-dominus; Fessard Judaeus-Paganus coram Christo).[76]

Quibus omnibus ita lucupletior, magis concreta, magis personalis, magis ad captum omnium res theologica reddi potest, ut tamen simul superfluere videatur vetus illa theologia, dubie scientifica, per ontologiam graecam, hellenisticam, deviata, scientiis humanis nihil conferens, quaestionibus historicis vel dissipata vel obruta. Quinimo, ipsa dogmata, quamvis minime negentur, tamen minus in vita interiori et religiosa efficere videntur quam a theologis dogmaticis opinari solet. Unde inculcatur vita interior. 'Plus il s'agit de ce que *je suis* et non de ce que *j'ai*, plus questions et réponses perdent toute signification. Quand on me demande, ou quand je me demande, en quoi je crois, je ne puis me contenter d'énumérer un certain

Phenomenology in a broader sense is taken to mean the description of immediate data that allows the operation or event or thing to reveal itself, and that proceeds from this immediate evidence to an undoubted apprehension of its essence, meaning, significance, and importance. Max Scheler has used phenomenology for manifesting the intersubjective, feelings, values, religion.[73] Martin Heidegger seeks an understanding of being and existence, especially human existence; he lays down as a principle that understanding of human existence which is given by the very fact that one is human; and this immediate experience and understanding (inauthentic, authentic) he accurately distinguishes from its conceptual elucidation (*existenziell, existenzial*). He is followed by Rudolf Bultmann, who carries out his exegesis of St Paul according to an existential preunderstanding.[74]

Accordingly, a host of authors[75] have written about intersubjectivity, feelings, the symbolic, aesthetics, morality, person, ritual, liturgy, religion, the human condition, the concrete dialectic of personal development (Hegel: master-slave; Fessard: Jew-Pagan confronting Christ).[76]

By means of all of these, theology can be rendered more rich, more concrete, more personal, and more within the grasp of everyone, so that traditional theology seems superfluous, doubtfully scientific, derailed by Greek and Hellenistic ontology, having nothing to contribute to the human sciences, and being now in disarray or quite overwhelmed by historical questions. As a matter of fact, the dogmas themselves, though not at all denied, nevertheless seem to have less effect upon the interior and religious life than dogmatic theologians generally imagine. Hence, the interior life is strongly recommended. 'Plus il s'agit de ce que *je suis* et non de ce que *j'ai*, plus questions et réponses perdent toute signification. Quand on

73 Heinrich Fries, *Die katholische Religionsphilosophie der Gegenwart, der Einfluss Max Schelers auf ihre Formen und Gestalten: Eine problemgeschichtliche Studie* (Heidelberg: F.H. Kerle, 1949); Maurice Dupuy, *La philosophie de Max Scheler: Son évolution et son unité*, 2 vols. (Paris: Presses universitaires de France, 1959); idem, *La philosophie de la religion chez Max Scheler* (Paris: Presses universitaires de France, 1959).

74 For a comparative study of Heidegger and Bultmann, see John Macquarrie, *An Existentialist Theology* (London: SCM, 1955, 1960).

75 [The Latin word 'auctores' is added by hand in the autograph.]

76 [See G.W.F Hegel, *Phänomenologie des Geistes* (Frankfurt am Main: Suhrkamp, 1970) 145–55; in English, *Phenomenology of Spirit*, trans. A.V. Miller (Oxford: Clarendon Press, 1977) 111–19. Gaston Fessard, *De l'actualité historique*, 2 vols. (Paris: Desclée de Brouwer, 1960).]

nombre de propositions auxquelles je souscris; ces formules, de toute évidence, traduisent une réalité beaucoup plus profonde, plus intime: le fait d'être en circuit ouvert par rapport à la Réalité transcendante reconnue comme un *Tu*.'[77]

Unde et laudatur magis theologia genuflectens et orans quam speculans et disputans (H. Urs von Balthasar). Pariter laudatur theologia kerygmatica (*Verkundigungstheologie*) quae ad captum omnium loquitur, verbum Dei annuntiat, magis praedicat quam docet.[78]

(f) E contra, si theologia renuntiat aspirationes suas speculativas, concedit se non esse scientiam stricte dictam, attitudinem subiecto theoretico propriam omittit, a mundo intelligibili recedit, tunc tria sat inconvenientia sequuntur.

(a′) Cum theologis protestantibus et liberalissimis concordat, e.g., Ernst Troeltsch: So ist die Dogmatik ein Stück der praktischen Theologie und keine eigentliche Wissenschaft.[79] Scilicet dogmatica subordinatur scientiae humanae cui nomen, religionis scientia, psychologia, philosophia, historia, phaenomenologia.

me demande, ou quand je me demande, en quoi je crois, je ne puis me contenter d'énumérer un certain nombre de propositions auxquelles je souscris; ces formules, de toute évidence, traduisent une réalité beaucoup plus profonde, plus intime: le fait d'être en circuit ouvert par rapport à la Réalité transcendante reconnue comme un *Tu*.'[77]

Hence also, 'theology that kneels and prays' (Hans Urs von Balthasar) is more highly praised than theology that speculates and disputes. Kerygmatic theology (*Verkundigungstheologie*) is likewise extolled for communicating at the level of Everyman, proclaiming the word of God, and preaching rather than teaching.[78]

(f) On the other hand, if theology renounces its speculative aspirations, concedes that it is not strictly speaking a science, lacks the proper attitude towards a theoretical subject, and withdraws from the intelligible world, there follow three rather awkward consequences:

(a') Its position coincides with that of Protestant liberal theology; for example, Ernst Troeltsch: 'So ist die Dogmatik ein Stück der praktischen Theologie und keine eigentliche Wissenschaft.'[79] In other words, dogmatics is subordinated to a human science called the science, psychology, philosophy, history, phenomenology of religion.

77 Gabriel Marcel, in Roger Troisfontaines, *De l'existence à l'être: La philosophie de Gabriel Marcel*, tome II (Louvain: E. Nauwelaerts; Paris: J. Vrin, 1953) 352. [Lonergan translates this in the existentialism lectures: 'The more the question is one of what I am and not of what I have, the more the whole business of questions and answers loses all meaning. When someone asks me or when I ask myself what I believe in, I cannot be content to enumerate a certain number of propositions to which I subscribe. Quite clearly, such formulae are the translation of a reality that is much more profound, more intimate: the fact of being in open communication with a transcendent reality that I recognize as a Thou.' See Bernard Lonergan, *Phenomenology and Logic* 228. There is another translation given in *Early Works on Theological Method 1* 77.]

78 See Xiberta, *Introductio in sacram theologiam*, bibliography, s.v. 'Theologia kerygmatica,' pp. 54–55; Colombo, 'La metodologia e la sistemazione teologica,' in *Problemi e Orientamenti di Teologia Dommatica* I, bibliography, s.v. 'La "teologia kerigmatica,"' pp. 54–55.

79 Ernst Troeltsch, 'Die Dogmatik der "religionsgeschichtlichen Schule,"'in *Zur religiösen Lage, Religionsphilosophie und Ethik*, Neudruck der 2. Auflage 1922, vol. 2 in *Gesammelte Schriften* (Aalen: Scientia Verlag, 1962) 500–24, at 515. See 'Was heisst "Wesen des Christentums?"' ibid. 386–451; and 'Wesen der Religion und der Religionswissenschaft, ibid. 452–99. [Lonergan translates the quoted sentence in *Early Works on Theological Method 1* 77: 'Dogmatics is a piece of practical theology and no real science.']

(b′) Cum Henry Duméry concordat qui, cum dogmaticam nisi practicam esse censuerit, crisin quandam stricte philosophicam religionis, imprimis catholicae, instaurare voluit; cuius opera principalia statim in indicem librorum prohibitorum relata sunt.[80]

(c′) Religio catholica intellectualiter inermis relinquitur. E.g., quid intercedat inter nuperrime citata ex G. Marcel et modernismum? Utraque doctrina insistit in realitate quadam profundiori experientae internae quae exprimitur per symbola fidei. Modernismus hanc experientiam internam tamquam solam originem et causam religionis tum alterius tum catholicae agnoscit. Marcel minime ad talem conclusionem pervenit: praeter ea quae ipse est, etiam sunt quae ipse habet; secundum id quod est, habetur illa realitas profundior secundum quam Deum ut personam apprehendit et cum eo colloquitur; secundum ea quae habet, formulas fidei recitat.

Breviter, praetermisso ente, praetermisso assensu intellectuali vero quo dicitur 'est,' non apprehenditur divinitas Christi, scilicet, veritas huius asserti quod Iesus Nazarenus est Deus. Qua de re, Anglicanorum experientiam sat tristem exposuit acatholicus J.S. Lawton.[81]

(g) Tendentiis supra descriptis (notio scientiae nova, scientia humana empirica, historia doctrinae loco doctrinae, cultus immediatorum, renuntiatio theologiae stricte scientificae, speculativae) accedit problema fundamentale et philosophicum. Sensu priori et latiori criticismus Kantianus quaerit qua ratione philosophia (metaphysica) veram scientiae rationem attingere possit. Quae quidem quaestio omnino distinguenda est ab alia, utrum sit philosophia, metaphysica, quae et vera et certa sit; nam fieri potest ut sit philosophia et vera et certa quae tamen sensu communi vel alia via neque methodica neque stricte scientifica attingatur. Momentum

(b′) It agrees with Henry Duméry who, by declaring dogmatics to be a practical science, wanted to inaugurate a strictly philosophical critique of religion, especially Catholicism; his most important works were promptly placed on the *Index Librorum Prohibitorum*.[80]

(c′) The Catholic religion is left intellectually defenseless. What is the difference, for example, between the above quotation from Gabriel Marcel and Modernism? Both positions insist on some deeper reality of inner experience that is expressed in the articles of faith. Modernism recognizes this inner experience to be the sole origin and cause of religion, Catholic and others. Marcel certainly does not arrive at this conclusion. Besides those things that he himself is, there are those things that he has; as to what he is, there is present that deeper reality by way of which he apprehends God as a person and converses with him; as to what he has, he recites the formulas of faith.

Briefly, if one ignores being, if one ignores that true assent of the intellect in which one says, 'It is,' then there is no apprehending the divinity of Christ – that is, the truth of the assertion 'Jesus of Nazareth is God.' On this point, a non-Catholic author has described the sad experience within Anglicanism.[81]

(g) In addition to the above-mentioned tendencies – a new notion of science, empirical human sciences, the history of doctrines instead of doctrines, the cult of the immediate, the dismissal of a theology that is strictly scientific and speculative – there is a fundamental philosophical problem. In an earlier and broader sense, the Kantian critique asks in what way philosophy (metaphysics) can arrive at being a true science. Now this question is quite different from another question, namely, whether there is such a thing as a philosophy or metaphysics that is true and certain; for it is possible for a philosophy to be true and certain without succeeding in being

80 [Lonergan had in mind works by Duméry such as *Critique et religion: Problèmes de méthode en philosophie* (Paris: Société d'édition d'enseignement supérieur, 1957) and *Philosophie de la religion: Essai sur la signification du christianisme* (Paris: Presses universitaries de France, 1957). Lonergan refers to these two books and to Duméry's 'practical' view of dogma in *The Triune God: Doctrines* 634–35 and note 76. At the end of the note, Lonergan remarks that these books 'were placed on the index.' See also Lonergan, *Early Works on Theological Method 1* 78 and note 20.]

81 John Stewart Lawton, *Conflict in Christology: A Study of British and American Christology from 1889–1914* (London: Society for Promoting Christian Knowledge, 1947).

huius quaestionis theologicum est duplex: primo, si non datur philosophia vere methodica et stricte scientifica, haud datur theologia vere methodica et stricte scientifica, nam in multis similes sunt theologia et philosophia; deinde, cum philosophia sit ancilla theologiae, per ancillam non scientificam ad theologiam scientificam haud perveniri potest.

5 Ad Problematicam Theologicam in Antitithesibus Fundatam Responsa Quaedam Generaliora[82]

[5.1 Theology as a Strict Science]

Retinenda est theologia quae est scientia stricte dicta, a subiecto theoretico peracta, circa mundum intelligibilem tractans.

(a) Nam aliud est solvere et aliud supprimere problema integrationis; omissa scientia stricte dicta, non solvitur sed supprimitur problema. Omnis enim evolutio est processus quidam differentiationis et integrationis: ubi prius habebatur unum et confusum, nunc inveniuntur plura et distincta, quae inter se componenda sunt.

Recentissima evolutio ad vitam interiorem et ad mundum immediatum, aspectabilem, modo magis explicito, pleniori, exacto, fructuoso attendit. Quae tamen integrari debet cum iis quae iam pridem habentur; secus specie progressus, re vera nisi regressio quaedam ad stadium minus evolutum efficitur. Adeo non solvitur ut potius supprimatur integrationis problema.

Quod si quis dicit primaevam ecclesiam theologia dogmatica caruisse, nihil suadetur nisi archaismus (uti ante aliquot saecula a Protestantibus factum est).

(b) Quod non nullos forte decipit in eo est quod actuale integrationis problema non intra mundum intelligibilem per theoremata vel distinctiones solvendum est, sed e contra in ultimis quibusdam antithesibus consistit

methodical and strictly scientific in the ordinary sense or some other way. The importance of this question for theology is twofold: first, if there is no such thing as a truly methodical and strictly scientific philosophy, there will be no theology that is truly methodical and strictly scientific, since the two are similar in so many ways; second, since philosophy is the handmaid of theology, one will hardly arrive at a scientific theology by way of a non-scientific handmaid.

5 *Some General Answers to the Theological Problematic Rooted in the Antitheses*[82]

[5.1 Theology as a Strict Science]

Theology as a science in the strict sense, performed by a theoretic subject, and dealing with the intelligible world, must be retained.

(a) It is one thing to solve and quite another to suppress the problem of integration. If science in the strict sense is disregarded, the problem will be suppressed, not solved. For every development is a process of differentiation and integration: where formerly there was a single undifferentiated reality, now there are several distinct realities that have to be brought into synthesis.

The most recent development is one that pays attention to the interior life and to the immediate visible world in a fuller, more explicit, more exact and fruitful way. But it must be integrated with long-standing elements; otherwise there is but the appearance of progress, while in reality there results only a regression to a less developed stage. Not only is the problem not solved, but rather the problem of integration is suppressed.

And anyone who says that the early church had no dogmatic theology is advocating archaism (like the earlier Protestants).

(b) What has led many astray is this, that the present problem of integration is not to be solved within the intelligible world by means of theorems or distinctions; on the contrary, it lies in certain ultimate antitheses that

82 [At this point in the autograph the date at the top of the page switches to 27-3-62. Corresponding material through § 5.3 may be found in *Early Works on Theological Method 1* 81–102.]

quae inter se modo radicali mundum interiorem, aspectabilem, intelligibilem separant. Non solvitur intra ipsum mundum intelligibilem: nam omnis
talis solutio esset theoretica; sed problema respicit habitudinem inter theoriam obiectivam, subiectum interius, et mundum aspectabilem.

Sed communius solvitur oscillatione quadam, secundum divisionem temporis, ut nunc magis ad interiora, nunc magis ad practica, nunc at theoretica convertimur. Cf. Eccl. 3.1–8: 'Omnia tempus habent, et suis spatiis
transeunt universa sub caelo. Tempus nascendi et tempus moriendi, tempus planandi et tempus evellendi quod plantatum est, tempus occidendi et
tempus sanandi, tempus destruendi et tempus aedificandi ...'

(c) Propter hanc radicalem differentiam, re vera mirum non est quod inter se tam diversa videantur vera religio catholica et opera theologica stricte
scientifica. Sane descriptio phaenomenologica hominis sancti et theologi
eximii duos typos prorsus fere diversos exhibet. Sanctus ita cum Deo occupatur interius ut in omni actione, in omni loquela, spiret bonum odorem
Christi. Theologus e contra ita est subiectum theoreticum, ita mundo intelligibili inhaeret, ita normas scientificas in omnibus observat, ut mundanam
quandam sapientiam quaerere videatur. Quam oppositionem inculcant qui
cum Pascal repetunt Deum Abraham, Isaac, Iacob, patrum nostrorum et,
alia ex parte, Deum philosophorum; vel qui quaerunt, quis orat motorem
immobilem, quis laudat ipsum esse subsistens, quis relationes subsistentes
adorat. At eiusmodi antitheses nisi modo particulari non dicunt quam iam
pridem et agnoscimus et docemus exsistere antitheses. Qui tamen inde
concluderet seligendum esse inter hoc et illud, ut ecclesia vel sanctos habeat et nullos theologos, vel theologos habeat et nullos sanctos, ipsas limitationes naturae humanae agnoscere non vult. Talis enim est natura humana
ut omnia simul peragere non potest, ut ita perficiatur per differentiationes
et integrationes, ut tamen ipsae integrationes non sint simultanea quaedam
totius perfectionis humanae usurpatio atque fruitio sed successiva et debitis
temporibus divisa.

(d) Quinimo, ad ipsam perfectionem religionis catholicae pertinet ut
theologiam habeat stricte scientificam. Religio enim catholica ita totam vitam humanam penetrat et ordinat ut non solum sit mundi profani sacralizatio, non solum sit vitae interioris transformatio, non solum profundum
quendam atque continuum influxum in mundum aspectabilem exerceat,
sed etiam suam partem, eamque supremam, in ipso mundo intelligibili sibi

together radically separate the inner, the visible, and the intelligible worlds. It is not solved within the intelligible world itself; such a solution would be theoretical. The problem is with the relation between objective theory, the interior subject, and the visible world.

More commonly it is solved by a certain temporal oscillation, so that we turn more at a certain time to interior realities and at another time to practical matters, and at still another to theoretical considerations. 'For everything there is a season, an allotted span for every creature under heaven: a time to be born and a time to die, a time for planting and a time for uprooting what has been planted, a time for killing and a time for healing, a time for tearing down and a time for building ...' (Ecclesiastes 3.1–8).

(c) Because of this radical difference, it is really no wonder that genuine Catholic religion and the work of strictly scientific theology seem to be so very different. It is true that phenomenological descriptions of a holy man and of a great theologian exhibit two very different types of persons. One who is holy is so absorbed with God in his interior life that in his every action and word he breathes forth the good odor of Christ. The theologian, by contrast, as a theoretic subject is so deeply immersed in the intelligible world and so observant of scientific norms in everything that he seems to be seeking a worldly wisdom. This opposition is emphasized by those who quote Pascal's dictum about the God of Abraham, Isaac, and Jacob and the God of our fathers and, by contrast, the God of the philosophers; or by those who ask who ever prays to the unmoved mover, praises self-subsistent being, or adores subsistent relations. But these antitheses simply state in a particular way what we have been acknowledging and teaching all along, namely, that antitheses exist. Yet whoever would conclude from this that a choice must be made of one or the other, that the church must have either holy persons and no theologians or theologians and no holy persons, fails to recognize the limitations of human nature. For human nature is such that it cannot accomplish everything at once; hence, it works by way of differentiations and integrations, yet in such a way that those integrations are not a simultaneous but rather a successive and periodic use and enjoyment of all that humanity has accomplished.

(d) In fact, it is a feature of the excellence of the Catholic religion that it has a strictly scientific theology. The Catholic religion so thoroughly enters into and regulates the whole of human life that it not only sacralizes the profane world, not only transforms the interior life, and not only exerts a profound and constant influence upon the visible world, but also claims a role, and indeed the leading role, in the intelligible world. The church

vindicet. Quem influxum in theoriam, in mundum intelligibilem, nisi pedetentim exercere non incepit ecclesia. Quod tamen ita sub ductu Spiritus sancti, ita solide et irrevocabiliter factum est, ut de eo omittendo seria esse non potest quaestio. Non enim concilia graeca contaminationem quandam religionis et fidei perfecerunt, uti saepius inde ab A. Harnack repetitur, sed potius eiusmodi contaminationem excluserunt. Quod in Nicaena synodo definitum est 'homoousion' nihil aliud dicit quam quod in praefatione SS. Trinitatis canitur: Quod enim de tua *gloria* (kabôd Iahwe) *revelante* te *credimus*, hoc de Filio tuo, hoc de Spiritu Sancto ... Quod quidem excludit rationalismum Arii, Platonismum Origenis, stoicismum Tertulliani, quod pariter instauravit metaphysicam philosophiae christianae, nempe, realitatem, entia, non experientia externa vel interna, non nescio quo intuitu intellectuali, sed per veritatem veri assensus nobis innotescere.

Religio catholica, fides, dogmata, philosophia christiana, ita inter se connectuntur ut iam pridem de iis separandis, de mundo intelligibili praetermittendo, ab ipsa ecclesia non admittitur.

(e) Quibus positis et retentis, ad verum problema discernendum et determinandum procedi oportet. Quod si retinenda est theologia stricte scientifica, non ideo despicienda vel reicienda sunt quae novis methodis et technicis modo magis explicito, systematico, fructuoso coluntur. Sicut integratio non excludit mundum intelligibilem, ita non excludit vel mundum interiorem vel mundum aspectabilem. Quod si integratio non in ipso mundo intelligibili efficienda est, sed potius in oscillatione quadam, ita novus quidam modus omnia inter se conciliandi, ordinandi, inveniri debet. Olim habebatur theologia scientiarum regina, et intelligebatur regimen deductivum, quasi omnia in ipso mundo intelligibili continerentur. Quod verum est, non simpliciter sed secundum quid. Omnia in mundo intelligibili continentur, sed tantummodo per modum obiecti scientifice apprehensi. Praeter quam apprehensionem exsistunt et aliae, suo valore praeditae neque vel ignorandae vel praetermittendae, nempe, immediata illa mundi aspectabilis apprehensio, immediata et interior sui ipsius conscientia, et utriusque ad Deum quasi experta atque viva (*erlebt*) habitudo.

(f) Quinam autem sit valor harum aliarum apprehensionum, vel breviter perstringi oportet. Per phaenomenologiam ergo attingitur ille actus intelligendi, inde ab Aristotele notus, qui in ipsis sensibilibus intelligibile attin-

began to exert this influence upon theory, upon the intelligible world, only gradually. Yet what has been done is so solid and irreversible and so clearly directed by the Holy Spirit that there can be no serious question of dropping it. The Greek councils were not a contamination of Christian faith and religion, as has been so often said, beginning with Harnack; on the contrary, they prevented that sort of contamination. What Nicea defined as *homoousion* is simply another way of stating what is expressed in the Preface of the Holy Trinity: 'Quod enim de tua *gloria* (Heb., kabôd Yahweh) *revelante* te *credimus*, hoc de Filio tuo, hoc de Spiritu Sancto ...': 'For what we *believe* through your *revelation* about your *glory*, we hold the same about your Son and the same about the Holy Spirit ...' This in fact excludes Arius's rationalism, Origen's Platonism, and Tertullian's Stoicism; it likewise laid the foundations for metaphysics in Christian philosophy, namely, that reality, beings, are known not by experience, external or internal, nor by some sort of intellectual intuition, but through the truth of a true assent.

The Catholic religion, faith, dogmas, and Christian philosophy are so intertwined that the church itself has long refused to allow them to be separated, and the intelligible world to be ignored.

(e) Keeping all this in mind, we must go on now to discern and determine the real problem. If we must hold to a strictly scientific theology, it does not follow that studies that rely upon new methods and techniques more explicitly, more systematically, and with better results are to be despised or rejected. Just as integration does not exclude the intelligible world, neither does it exclude either the inner world or the visible world. But if integration is to be realized not in the intelligible world by itself but rather in an oscillation between worlds, some new way of reconciling all these elements and putting them in their proper order will have to be found. In the past, theology was regarded as the queen of the sciences and was understood as a deductive process, as if everything were contained in the intelligible world itself. This is true, indeed, but not without qualification. All things are contained in the intelligible world, but only as an object apprehended scientifically. Besides this apprehension, however, there exist other kinds, each with its own proper value, that are not to be ignored or overlooked, namely, the immediate apprehension of the visible world, the immediate interior consciousness of self, and, so to speak, the experienced and living (*erlebt*) relationship of both of these to God.

(f) We must now briefly touch upon the value of these other kinds of apprehension. Phenomenology, then, does attain that act of understanding, known since Aristotle, that apprehends the intelligible in sense data. Thus

git. Unde S. Thomas, *Sum. theol.*, I, q. 85, a. 1, ad 5m: 'intellectus noster et abstrahit species intelligibiles a phantasmatibus ... et tamen intelligit eas in phantasmatibus ...'[83] Quo tamen actu non perficitur cognitio humana, quae quasi tribus contignationibus constat, nempe, experientia, intelligentia, iudicio. Ex actu intelligendi procedit verbum incomplexum, quod vel scientifica rei definitio esse potest, plena universalitate gaudens, vel sufficiens quaedam ad praesentem considerationem et usum expressio, uti fit in cognitione vulgari; unde Athenienses et Socrates, quorum utrique virtutem quandam, e.g., temperantiam, fortitudinem, intelligebant, illi modo vulgari rem exprimebant, hic autem definitionem universaliter validam exigebat. Exemplum ex circulo; definitio incompleta; definitio completa; quaestio de exsistentia.[84] At praeterea requiritur iudicium, utrum res prout intelligitur atque definitur exsistat.

Phaenomenologia facile ita adhibetur ut omittatur definitio re vera universalis atque lenior illa scrutatio quae ad iudicium universale requiruntur. Unde H. Fries crisin doctrinae M. Scheler ex hoc puncto incipit. 'Derselbe Scheler ist aber auch ein Beispiel dafür, wie leicht und häufig die Gefahr der Willkür auftaucht und wie man mit derselben Methode zu ganz verschiedenen "evidenten" Resultaten kommen kann. Mit Recht hat die Kritik darauf den Finger gelegt. So genial und fructbar die "Wesensschau" sein kann, sie bedarf der erkenntniskritischen Sicherung der Kritik der Vernunft.'[85] 'Die Grenze der Phänomenologie liegt noch auf einem anderen Gebiet. Sie kann das Gesamtphänomen des Seins, die Einheit des Seienden aus Sosein und Dasein nicht erfassen, weil ihr die Erkenntnis des Daseins verwehrt ist. Die phänomenologische Methode kann nur diese Frage mit Husserl einklammern.'[86] Unde satis elucet per phaenomenologiam minime ad exclusionem mundi intelligibilis concludi potest, nisi quis vult portas ad omnes errores admittendos latissime patere.

St Thomas: 'Our intellect both abstracts intelligible species from phantasms … and yet understands them in the phantasms …'[83] This act, however, is not the whole of human cognition, which is a three-storey edifice of experience, understanding, and judgment. From the act of understanding there proceeds a simple word, which can be either a scientific definition of something, having full universality, or an expression that suffices for immediate consideration and use, which is the case in ordinary everyday knowledge. Hence, though Socrates and the Athenians both understood what a particular virtue was – temperance, for example, or fortitude – the Athenians expressed its meaning in a commonsense way, while Socrates demanded a definition of it that would be universally valid. See, for example, the definition of a circle: an incomplete definition; a complete definition; the question of its existence.[84] But beyond that there is need of a judgment, that is, whether a certain thing exists in the way it is understood and defined.

Phenomenology easily lends itself to being used in such a way as to omit both a truly universal definition and that fuller scrutiny, which are both required for a universal judgment. Hence, Heinrich Fries takes this as the starting point for his critique of the doctrine of Max Scheler: 'Derselbe Scheler ist aber auch ein Beispiel dafür, wie leicht und häufig die Gefahr der Willkür auftaucht und wie man mit derselben Methode zu ganz verschiedenen "evidenten" Resultaten kommen kann. Mit Recht hat die Kritik darauf den Finger gelegt. So genial und fruchtbar die "Wesensschau" sein kann, sie bedarf der erkenntniskritischen Sicherung der Kritik der Vernunft.'[85] 'Die Grenze der Phänomenologie liegt noch auf einem anderen Gebiet. Sie kann das Gesamtphänomen des Seins, die Einheit des Seienden aus Sosein und Dasein nicht erfassen, weil ihr die Erkenntnis das Daseins verwehrt ist. Die phänomenologische Methode kann nun diese Frage mit Husserl einklammern.'[86] From this it is quite clear that one can by no means conclude through phenomenology to the exclusion of the intelligible world, unless one wishes to open wide the door to all sorts of errors.

83 Thomas Aquinas, *Summa theologiae*, 1, q. 85, a. 1, ad 5m.
84 [In *Insight* 31–37, Lonergan discusses what he means by a scientific 'definition,' beginning with the definition of a circle as an example. In *Understanding and Being* 40–43, using the same example as an illustration, he presents what amounts to a brief discussion of incomplete definitions.]
85 Fries, *Die katholische religionsphilosophie der Gegenwart* 141.
86 Ibid. [*Early Works on Theological Method 1* 87 presents Lonergan's own summary statement and near translation of these two quotations from Scheler: 'Scheler himself is an example of how easily and frequently the danger of

[5.2 A New Differentiation of Science in Theology]

Nova[87] scientiae differentiatio ita admittenda atque acceptanda est, ut tamen cum doctrina traditionali integretur.

(a) Admittenda atque acceptanda est, quia in multis magis cum doctrina catholica consonat quam ideale scientificum aristotelicum, praesertim ubi hoc magis ad litteram quam ad sensum intelligitur.

(a′) Circa certitudinem, quae in theologia sunt theoretica et systematica, communius etiam sunt non certa sed probabilia. Requiritur ergo methodus quae non supponit omne vere scientificum etiam esse certum.

(b′) Circa universalitatem: ipse Dominus Noster Iesus Christus, facta in scripturis narrata, traditio catholica, facta dogmatica, non sunt universalia sed singularia. Neque dici potest haec singularia ad theologiam pertinere per modum exemplorum.[88] Requiritur ergo methodus quae non supponit omne vere scientificum esse non singulare sed universale.

[5.2 A New Differentiation of Science in Theology]

A[87] new differentiation of science is to be admitted and welcomed, so long as it is integrated with traditional doctrine.

(a) It is to be admitted and welcomed, because in many respects this new differentiation is better suited to Catholic doctrine than the Aristotelian ideal of science, especially when the latter is understood more according to the letter than according to its true meaning.

(a′) With regard to certitude, those elements in theology that are theoretical and systematic are also more commonly not certain but probable. What is needed, then, is a method that does not suppose every scientific truth to be also certain.

(b′) As for universality, our Lord himself, facts related in the bible, Catholic tradition, dogmatic facts, are not universals but singulars. Nor can it be said that these singulars belong to theology only as examples.[88] A method, then, is needed that does not suppose every scientific truth to be universal rather than singular.

---

arbitrariness breaks out and how one can use exactly the same phenomenological method to reach contradictory "evident" results. In other words, when you are dealing with concrete human affairs and getting insight into them and seeing what is obvious, one man can apply the phenomenological method to bring out something and make it very evident, and someone else can apply the same method to get contrary results. Phenomenology gives insights. It is illuminating. It is helpful. It opens up windows. But it has to be submitted to the further test of rational judgment, and that is the element that gets eclipsed. As Fries says, however genial and fruitful the grasp of essence may be, it needs the control of rational criticism. Then he goes on to the other limitation of phenomenology: because phenomenology operates on the level of sense and understanding without paying attention to the critical control of rational judgment, all it can do about the question of existence is, as Husserl did, to put it in brackets. Husserl prescinds systematically from questions of existence. And, as Fries remarks, that is the only way that the phenomenologist can proceed. It means that he cannot deal with the existential in an adequate fashion. And if he cannot do that, whether he is dealing merely with bright ideas or with something that is true is something that he cannot determine.']

87 [At this point in the autograph, the date at the top of the pages switches to 28-3-62.]
88 Thomas Aquinas, *Summa theologiae*, 1, q. 1, a. 2, ad 2m.

(c') Circa immobilitatem: non immobilia sed historica, mobilia, contingentia sunt quae ad ordinem salutis, ad *Heilsgeschichte*, pertinent; habetur enim evolutio revelationis in vt, ex vt ad nt, etiam inter libros ipsius nt; habetur evolutio dogmatum, evolutio theologiae, evolutio praxeos ecclesiae; et ideo requiritur methodus quae scientificum non in immobili ponit sed etiam in mobilibus agnoscit, quaerit, invenit.[89]

NB: Ubi excluditur intelligibilitas in ipso motu, ibi facile recurritur ad falsum quendam abstractionismum qui separat verum aeternum a temporali contingenti, et hoc respuit, illud vero solum acceptare vult. Ita indifferentismus religiosus qui religionem quandam naturalem, ratione fundatam, admittit, sed religiones positivas rebus mutabilibus immixtas, adiunctis adaptatas, nisi valoris cuiusdam relativi non agnoscit.[90]

(d') Circa necessitatem: quae ad ordinem salutis pertinent, non absolute necessaria sunt sed contingentia quibus competit intelligibilitas quaedam de facto seu empirica. Non absoluta necessitate facta est Incarnatio, Redemptio, ecclesiae institutio, librorum sacrorum inspiratio et inerrantia, septenarius sacramentorum numerus. Imo, iis omnibus suppositis, absolute fieri potuissent aliter quam de facto facta sunt. Requiritur ergo methodus quae aliud scientificum agnoscit praeter necessitatem absolutam.

(e') Dixerit quispiam haec omnia iam pridem a theologis optime cognosci, methodi aristotelicae adaptationes iam pridem esse factas, etc. Respondetur nos minime dixisse theologos haec ignorare, nullam adaptationem fecisse. Ultro fatemur eos quam plurimas fecisse adaptationes, eos singulas quaestiones secundum propriam earum naturam tractare posse. Sed quaestionem de methodo ponimus, et ipsam cumulatam adaptationum multitudinem parum ducimus methodicam ubi una quaedam sufficeret adaptatio eaque systematica.

(c′) Regarding immobility, it is not immobile realities but mobile ones, historical and contingent, that pertain to the order of salvation, to *Heilsgeschichte*. Revelation undergoes development within the Old Testament, from the Old Testament to the New, and even within the books of the New Testament itself; in the church there is development in dogma, in theology, and in practice, and so there is need of a method that does not place the scientific in the category of the immobile or unchangeable, but that also acknowledges, seeks, and finds it in changeable things.[89]

Note here that when intelligibility is denied to motion itself, one easily falls into a false abstractionism that separates eternal truth and temporal contingency and, rejecting the latter, will accept only the former. This opens the way to religious indifferentism, which admits a natural sort of religion based upon reason but attributes only a relative value to positive religions that include many mutable elements and are adapted to changing circumstances.[90]

(d′) As for necessity, what pertain to the order of salvation are not absolutely necessary but rather contingent realities having a *de facto*, empirical necessity. The incarnation, the redemption, the institution of the church, the inspiration and inerrancy of sacred scripture, the fact that there are seven sacraments, do not exist with absolute necessity; absolutely speaking, they all could have been different from what they are *de facto*. What is required, then, is a method that recognizes that the scientific is something other than the realm of absolute necessity.

(e′) At this point someone may say that theologians have known all this for a long time now, that certain adaptations in the Aristotelian method have been made, etc. Our reply to this is that we do not at all deny that theologians are aware of this and that many adaptations have been made. We will go so far as to admit that they have made as many adaptations as possible, and are able to treat each question as the nature of that question requires. But the issue here is method, and we maintain that the accumulation of a multitude of adaptations is not very methodical when one systematic adaptation would suffice.

89 [The Latin words 'quaerit' and 'invenit' were added by hand in the autograph.]
90 See Immanuel Kant, *Die Religion innerhalb der Grenzen der blossen Vernunft* (Hamburg: F. Meiner, 1956). [In English, *Religion within the Limits of Reason Alone*, trans. Theodore M. Greene and Hoyt H. Hudson (New York: Harper & Row, 1960).]

(b) Ipsa nova scientiae differentiatio ita admittenda est ut cum doctrina traditionali integretur.

(a′) Eiusmodi enim est natura omnis evolutionis quae non solum in differentiatione sed etiam in differentiatorum integratione consistit.

(b′) Caeterum patet tum vetera non esse derelinquenda tum nova non eo modo esse acceptanda quomodo in scientiis naturalibus communius intelliguntur atque adhibentur. Vetera non esse derelinquenda, cum reapse sint vera necessaria, vera in immutabilibus, vera universalia, vera certissima. Neque nova sine correctione esse admittenda; quemadmodum enim methodus scientifica moderna communius in scientiis intelligitur et adhibetur, variis erroribus admiscetur, uti mechanismo, positivismo, phaenomenismo, pragmatismo.

(c′) Perficitur haec integratio quatenus nova differentiatio ex radicibus derivatur quae iam in doctrina aristotelica et thomistica prostant. Cuius asserti sensus minime est vel Aristotelem vel S. Thomam omnia anticipasse et explicite dixisse quae de intellectu eiusque natura e scientiis modernis collegi possunt. Eiusdem asserti sensus est eos ea posuisse fundamenta unde derivari, iudicari, corrigi possunt quae postea magis explicita sunt facta. Eiusdem asserti probatio est obvia: si enim nova differentiatio ex doctrina aristotelica et thomistica derivatur, iudicatur, corrigitur, necessario cum illa doctrina cohaeret.

(c) Integrata novae differentiationis acceptatio duobus maxime constat, quorum primum quaestionem, quid sit, alterum autem quaestionem, an sit, respiciunt. Quae sane divisio in doctrina aristotelica et thomistica habetur, et quidem explicite.

(d) Circa quaestionem, quid sit: Nova differentiatio essentialiter dicit duo: aliud circa rem, aliud circa rei cognitionem.

Circa rem dicit exsistere intelligibilitatem, non necessariam sed empiricam, quae in ipso motu discernitur, quae temporum decursu evolvitur. E.g., exsistere processum quendam intelligibilem ex NT ad concilium Nicaenum; hanc intelligibilitatem non esse absolutam quandam necessitatem ita ut res aliter fieri non potuisset; hanc intelligibilitatem perspici non in abstracta quadam speculatione de dogmatum evolutione sed in ipsis factis concretis historice investigatis; qua intelligibilitate hoc in casu perspecta, non habetur praemissa universalis unde de omni alia dogmatis evolutio-

(b) This new differentiation of science ought to be admitted in such a way as to integrate it with traditional teaching.

(a′) It is the nature of every development to consist not only in a differentiation but also in an integration of differentiations.

(b′) Besides, it is clear both that the old must not be abandoned and that the new elements are not to be admitted in the way the modern natural sciences generally understand and use them. The old elements must not be abandoned, since in fact there are necessary truths, truths in immutable things, universal truths, absolutely certain truths. And the new elements are not to be admitted without some correction; for according to the way modern scientific method is commonly understood and employed in the sciences, various errors are present, such as mechanism, positivism, phenomenalism, pragmatism.

(c′) This integration takes place inasmuch as the new differentiation is derived from roots that are already set forth in the doctrine of Aristotle and St Thomas. The meaning of this statement is certainly not that Aristotle or Thomas anticipated and explicitly taught everything about the intellect and its nature that can be gathered from the modern sciences. It means that they laid the foundations from which one can derive, judge, and correct what have subsequently been made more explicit. The proof of this statement is obvious: if a new differentiation is derived from and judged and corrected by means of Aristotelian and Thomistic doctrine, it must necessarily be coherent with that doctrine.

(c) An integrated acceptance of a new differentiation consists mainly of two elements, the first of which regards the question What is it? and the second, the question Is it? This division is certainly present, and explicitly so, in the doctrine of Aristotle and St Thomas.

(d) Concerning the question What is it? a new differentiation essentially means two things: one that concerns the matter and the other that concerns knowledge of the matter.

Concerning the matter itself, it means that there is an intelligibility that is not necessary but empirical, that is discernible in movement itself, and that develops in the course of time. For example, it means that there is an intelligible process from the New Testament to the Council of Nicea; that this intelligibility is not one of absolute necessity, as if things could not have been otherwise; that this intelligibility is grasped not in some abstract speculation about the development of dogmas, but in the concrete facts themselves as determined by historical research; and that after grasping the intelligibility

ne deducitur, sed reliqua dogmata simili modo investigata suam et aliam pariter concretam intelligibilitatem habere, ut ipse modus quo evolvuntur dogmata evolvatur.

Circa rei cognitionem dicit eiusmodi intelligibilitatem non uno quodam intuitu a maximo quodam ingenio inveniri, sed eiusdem inventionem paulatim crescere. Primo enim dissita elementa seorsim perspiciuntur, deinde ab alio perspecta ab aliis reexaminantur atque corriguntur, idque non semel sed saepius; unde augente intelligentia elementa colligi et inter se comparari incipiunt, ut comparata magis in unum conflentur, et conflata nunc alio nunc alio modo denique tandem ad talem coniunctionem conducant quae omnibus fere quaestionibus satisfacere videatur.

Cuius rei exemplum sit progressus in intelligendo motu ex NT usque ad c. Nicaenum, qui quidem progressus inde a Petavio incipit et usque ad nostra tempora extenditur. Quod exemplum satis complexum est, sed pariter esset omne fere aliud. Quemadmodum proceditur? Incipitur a contemporanea quadam *solutione*, eius elementa formalia et materialia enumerantur; quemadmodum inter se cohaereant et solutionem faciant perspicitur; quaeritur deinde unde desumpta sint elementa formalia, unde desumpta sint elementa materialia; quod quidem repetitur usque ad Petavium.

Diximus qualis sit illa intelligibilitas quae ad quaestionem quid sit respondet, secundum novam scientiae differentiationem. Est nempe non necessaria sed empirica, est non in immobilibus sed in mobilibus, est non universalis sed sese historice evolvens, neque uno quodam intuitu invenitur sed pedetentim decursu temporum ex multis et dissitis factis in unum conflatis et ordinatis attingitur.[91]

Iam vero an doctrina eiusmodi radicem suam in Aristotele vel Aquinate habet? Sane docent intellectum nostrum in ipsis sensibilibus intelligibilitatem perspicere. Sane sciunt ex collectis et comparatis priorum docto-

in this particular case, one does not have universal premises from which to deduce all other cases of dogmatic development, but all the other dogmas when similarly investigated have their own proper intelligibilities that are different and concrete as well, so that the way in which dogmas develop itself undergoes development.

Concerning knowledge of the matter, it means that this sort of intelligibility is not something to be discovered by some great genius in some single intuition, but rather that its discovery dawns gradually. First, disparate elements are grasped one by one; then, having been understood by one person they are re-examined and corrected by others, not once but several times; whereupon, as understanding grows, the various elements begin to be grouped together and compared to one another, so that being thus compared they become more and more harmonized, and thus harmonized in various ways they finally come together in a unity that seems to answer virtually all questions.

A good example of this would be the progress made in understanding the movement from the New Testament to Nicea. This progressive understanding began with Petavius and has continued down to our own day. This example is fairly complicated, but so would be almost any of the others. How does this process go? It begins with a contemporary *solution*; its formal and material elements are listed; the way in which they fit together and arrive at a solution is grasped; the question is then asked where the formal elements and where the material elements came from. This process goes all the way back to Petavius.

We have explained the nature of the intelligibility that answers the question What is it? in terms of a new differentiation of science. It is an intelligibility that is not necessary but empirical, not found in unchangeable realities but in the changeable, not universal but developing historically, not hit upon in one single intuition but arrived at gradually over time from many disparate facts that are brought together into one ordered unity.[91]

But does this doctrine have its roots in Aristotle and Aquinas? Well, they certainly teach that our intellect grasps intelligibility in sense data. They certainly know that collecting and comparing the opinions of previous thinkers

91 [Lonergan's own detailed account of dogmatic development with regard to the Trinity is, of course, to be found in *The Triune God: Doctrines*, with honorable mention given to Petavius in the opening sentence of Part 1 (pp. 28–29).]

rum sententiis non parvum colligi fructum ad quaestiones solvendas. Sane sciunt intellectum humanum esse potentialem, neque quemquam ita perfecte omnes solvere quaestiones ut nihil a posteris inveniendum relinquatur. Sane sciunt quemadmodum fit actus intelligendi: quilibet in se ipso experiri potest quod quando aliquid intelligere studet, format sibi aliqua phantasmata per modum exemplorum in quibus quasi inspicit quod intelligere studet.[92] Sane sciunt ipsum actum intelligendi non statim attingi sed pedetentim: cf. descriptionem Aristotelis in qua comparat addiscentiam cum processu quo milites e proelio fugientes et ab hostibus secuti interdum stant atque resistunt, ubi unus primo stat, deinde accedit alius, brevi simul multi uniuntur, et hostes persequentes sed dispersos vincunt.[93] Quod apud eos deest, minime consistit in eo quod nesciunt intelligibile in sensibilibus particularibus perspici vel paulatim augeri. Eis deest anticipatio collaborationis scientificae, eis deest anticipatae collaborationis methodica regulatio, eis deest fructuum praevisio qui ex methodica collaboratione oriuntur.

(e) Circa quaestionem, an sit: Cum haec quaestio longe sit complexior, sub alio et distincto asserto consideratur.

[5.3 Wisdom, Wise Judgment, and the Integration of the New Differentiation]

Haec[94] novae differentiationis cum doctrina traditionali integratio accuratam quandam atque plenam exigit iudicii sapientis analysin.

(a) Ipsum factum evidens est. Ubi enim scientia in empiricis, particularibus, mobilibus versatur, ibi non agitur de conclusionibus universalibus, necessariis, immobilibus, quae ex principiis per se notis infallibiliter deducantur. Quare, nova scientiae differentiatio aut certitudinem simpliciter praetermittit (quod in re theologica haud toleratur) aut eam ex iudicio sapienti repetit.

is quite helpful in settling questions. They certainly know that the human intellect is potential and that no one ever settles questions so completely that there is nothing left for those who come after them to discover. They certainly know how the act of understanding takes place: 'Anyone can experience in himself the fact that when he is trying to understand something he forms images to serve as examples in which he sees, as it were, what he wants to understand.'[92] They certainly know that the act of understanding is not attained immediately but step by step. Recall Aristotle's comparison of growth in knowledge to the process in which soldiers being routed and pursued by the enemy sometimes stop and offer resistance, when first one soldier makes a stand and then another one joins him, and soon many join together, scatter their pursuers, and win the day.[93] Aristotle and St Thomas by no means lacked knowledge of the fact that the intelligible is grasped in sensible particulars or that understanding grows gradually. What they did lack, however, were an anticipation of collaboration among scientists, an anticipation of the methodical regulation of such collaboration, and a foreknowledge of the benefits to be derived from methodical collaboration.

(e) Concerning the question 'Is it?' This is a far more complicated matter, and so will be dealt with in a separate assertion, in [sub]section 5.3, which immediately follows.

[5.3   Wisdom, Wise Judgment, and the Integration of the New
        Differentiation]

This[94] integration of a new differentiation with traditional doctrine calls for a full and careful analysis of wise judgment.

(a) The fact itself is evident. When a science is dealing with empirical, particular, and changeable realities, there is no question of universal, necessary, and immutable conclusions infallibly deduced from self-evident principles. Hence, a new differentiation of science either simply disregards certitude (something that theology finds intolerable), or else gets it through a wise judgment.

92 Thomas Aquinas, *Summa theologiae*, 1, q. 84, a. 7 c.
93 [See Aristotle, *Posterior Analytics*, II, 19, 100a, 12 – 100b, 5.]
94 [At this point in the autograph, the date at the top of the page switches to
     3-4-62.]

(b) Quid sit iudicium? Iudicium est actus (1) quo quaestioni, An sit, Utrum ita res se habeat, affirmando vel negando respondetur, (2) quo iudicans ad verbum exterius prolatum comparatur ut assentiens vel dissentiens, (3) quo interius dicitur, Est, Non est.[95]

Iudicium non est actus voluntatis (electio, decisio, *Entscheidung*) quae bonum appetit, ei complacet, agendum vel faciendum decernit, sed est actus intellectus qui verum respicit.

Iudicium non pertinet ad primam intellectus operationem quae quaerit, perspicit, concipit synthesin (sive datorum sive conceptuum sive totius cuiusdam systematis) sed pertinet ad alteram intellectus operationem quae synthesin iam perspectam atque conceptam absolute ponit vel absolute reicit. An ego loquor? Sane. An manus habeo? Utique. Sed sola synthesis nisi hypothesis non est.[96]

Quae quidem positio est absoluta, scilicet, sine qualificatione vel reservatione. Quando enim iudicamus, dicimus rem, non imaginatione repraesentari, non affectu desiderari vel timeri, non conceptu cogitari, non huic vel illi videri, sed (sine addito) esse. Cui absolutae positioni mens absolute adhaeret. Non enim secundum plus et minus, secundum gradus quosdam, affirmamus vel negamus, sed simpliciter. Quod quidem docet Newman etiam de iudiciis modalibus: scilicet affirmare rem esse probabilem non est debilior quaedam affirmatio exsistentiae rei sed absoluta positio probabilitatis.[97]

(b) What is judgment? Judgment is an act (1) in which the question Is it? Is it so? is answered either affirmatively or negatively, (2) in which the one who judges assents to or dissents from the exteriorly uttered word, and (3) in which 'It is' or 'It is not' is said interiorly.[95]

Judgment is not an act of the will (a choice, a decision, *Entscheidung*), which desires good, enjoys it, decides what ought to be done or made; rather, it is an act of the intellect, which is concerned with truth.

Judgment does not belong to the first intellectual operation, which inquires, grasps the point, conceives a synthesis (of data or of concepts or of an entire system); it belongs to the second intellectual operation, which posits absolutely or rejects absolutely the synthesis understood and conceived. 'Am I talking?' – 'Certainly.' 'Do I have a hand?' – 'Yes.' But a synthesis by itself is only a hypothesis.[96]

This positing is absolute, that is, made without qualification or reservation. When we make a judgment we say, not that something is being imagined or desired or feared or being thought about or that it seems so to this person or that, but simply that it is. The mind adheres absolutely to this absolute positing. To affirm or to deny is not a matter of more or less, a matter of degree; when we affirm or deny we do so simply, without any additional qualification. Newman, in fact, in *Grammar of Assent*, makes this point even about modal judgments: to assert that a thing is probable is not a weaker affirmation of its existence but is an absolute positing of its probability.[97]

95 Modal judgments, such as 'perhaps it is,' 'it probably is,' 'maybe,' need not be dealt with here. They are generally reducible either to a reluctance to judge ('perhaps it is' = 'I don't know') or to an assertion that is not about existence itself but about what is related to existence ('it could be' = 'there exists the potentiality whereby this can come into existence'). [Lonergan's Latin for this note, contained in parentheses in the text: 'Circa iudicia modalia (forte est, probabiliter est, esse potest) hic non est agendum: in genere reducuntur vel in evitationem iudicii (forte est = nescio), vel in assertum non ipsius esse sed eius quod ad esse refertur (esse potest = exsistit potentia unde hoc aliquid fieri potest).']

96 [The Latin words 'Sed sola synthesis nisi hypothesis non est' were added by hand in the autograph.]

97 ['... assents to the plausibility, probability, doubtfulness, or untrustworthiness, of a proposition ... [are] not variations of assent to an inference, but assents to a variation in inferences. When I assent to a doubtfulness, or to a probability, my assent, as such, is as complete as if I assented to a truth; it is not a certain degree of assent.' John Henry Newman, *An Essay in Aid of a Grammar of Assent*, chapter 6, §1, no. 2.]

Quae absoluta mentis adhaesio (vel non-adhaesio) sicut intellectualem cuiusque probitatem exercet ita personalem eius responsabilitatem implicat. Cuius signum est verbum de la Rochefoucauld: 'Tout le monde se plaint de sa mémoire mais personne de son jugement.'[98]

Denique ipse iudicandi actus est intrinsece rationalis; procedit ex perspecta rei evidentia propter perspectam rei evidentiam, non mechanice, non vitaliter, sed rationaliter.[99]

(c) Quid sit evidentia sufficiens?[100] Mensura sufficientiae est syllogismus explicitus vel implicitus ut, scilicet, sufficit evidentia affirmandi B ubi habentur 'si A tunc B; atque A; ergo B.' In syllogismo explicito praemissae sunt propositiones verbis expressae atque iudicio interiori affirmatae (negatae). In syllogismo implicito vel altera vel utraque praemissa aut non exprimitur aut in stadio cognitionis invenitur quod iudicio praeit.

Duplex est syllogismi (expliciti vel impliciti) interpretatio: alia est kantiana ut syllogismus non sit nisi initium regressus infiniti prosyllogismorum;

Just as this absolute adherence (or non-adherence) of the mind exercises a person's intellectual honesty, so also does it involve one's personal responsibility. As de La Rochefoucauld observed, 'Everyone complains about his memory but no one ever complains about his judgment.'[98]

Finally, the act of judging is intrinsically rational; it proceeds from the grasp of the evidence of the thing precisely on account of this grasp of the evidence, not mechanically, not vitally, but rationally.[99]

(c) What is sufficient evidence?[100] The measure of sufficiency is an explicit or implicit syllogism, so that there is sufficient evidence for affirming *B* when there is realized the following: 'If *A*, then *B*; but *A*; therefore *B*.' In an explicit syllogism the premises are expressed verbally and are affirmed or denied in an interior judgment. In an implicit syllogism at least one of the premises is either not so expressed or is still in that stage of the cognitional process that precedes judgment.

There are two interpretations for syllogisms, whether explicit or implicit. One is the Kantian interpretation that a syllogism is only the beginning of

98 [Quoted in Lonergan, *Insight* 297, with source information given in a footnote, and mentioned again in Lonergan, *Understanding and Being* 113.]

99 On this intelligible emanation, see Bernard Lonergan, 'The Concept of *Verbum* in the Writings of St Thomas Aquinas,' *Theological Studies* 7:3 (1946) 380–91 [see Lonergan, *Verbum* 46–59]; *Divinarum personarum* 57–61 [*The Triune God: Systematics* 134–43]. On the notion of judgment in St Thomas: Lonergan, 'The Concept of *Verbum* in the Writings of St Thomas Aquinas: II,' *Theological Studies* 8:1 (1947) 35–79 [*Verbum* 60–105]; Peter Hoenen, *La théorie du jugement d'après St Thomas d'Aquin* (Rome: Gregorian University Press, 1946) [in English, *Reality and Judgment according to St Thomas*, trans. Henry F. Tiblier (Chicago: Henry Regnery Co., 1952).] On judgment in general, see Lonergan, *Insight*, chapters 9–10. [The contrast Lonergan has in mind in his remark that the act of judgment proceeds 'not vitally but rationally' is at least partly indicated when he writes: '... within consciousness act originates from act: a real, natural, conscious act from a real, natural, conscious act. Thus if one see a large fierce-looking dog without a leash, one spontaneously feels fear ... [W]hen act consciously originates from act, sensitive consciousness mediates in one way and intellectual consciousness in another. A sensitive act originates from another sensitive act according to a particular law of nature. But an intellectual act originates from another intellectual act in accordance with the conscious, transcendental exigencies of the intellect itself, which are not bound to any particular nature but are ordered to all that is intelligible, all that is true, all that is being, all that is good ... [W]e judge *because* we grasp evidence as sufficient and *in accordance with* the evidence we have grasped.' *The Triune God: Systematics* 143.]

100 [At this point in the autograph, the date at the top of the page switches to 4-4-62.]

alia autem dicit syllogismum exhibere conclusionem ut virtualiter incondi-
tionatam. Inconditionatum est duplex, formaliter et virtualiter: formaliter
inconditionatum nullas prorsus habet conditiones, et eiusmodi est Deus,
isque solus; virtualiter inconditionatum conditiones quidem habet quae
tamen de facto sunt impletae. Ita in syllogismo maior praemissa exhibet B
ut conditionatum (si A, tunc B); minor praemissa exhibet conditiones ut
impletas (atqui A); conclusio exhibet B ut virtualiter inconditionatum.

Virtualiter inconditionatum intellectu perspectum constituit evidentiam
sufficientem. Nam ubi B perspicitur uti virtualiter inconditionatum, habetur motivum et sufficiens et cogens ut assensu absoluto absolute ponatur
B. Sine virtualiter inconditionato non habetur evidentia sufficiens. Ubi
enim B non perspicitur ut inconditionatum, non perspicitur utrum sint
conditiones quae non implentur. Quo non perspecto, iudicium ponere esset temerarium.

Quemadmodum haec analysis variis iudicii typis applicetur, alibi diximus.[101] Exemplo tamen sit typus fundamentalis[102] in quo: impletio conditionum, A, habetur ex ipsis datis qua datis (sive sensibilitatis sive conscientiae);
nexus, si A tunc B, habetur ex ipso processu intellectuali debite peracto ex
datis, A, ad synthesin conceptualem, B; qui quidem processus consistit in inquisitione circa data, in aliquali intelligentia datorum, in conceptione eius
quod in datis intelligitur; qui processus debite peragitur quatenus normis
atque exigentiis luminis intellectualis satisfacit.

an infinite regress of prosyllogisms; the other states that the syllogism expresses a conclusion as virtually unconditioned. There are two ways of being unconditioned, formally and virtually. The formally unconditioned has no conditions whatsoever, and that is God alone; the virtually unconditioned has conditions that, however, are in fact fulfilled. Thus, in a syllogism the major premise expresses *B* as conditioned (if *A*, then *B*); the minor premise expresses the conditions as fulfilled (but *A*); so the conclusion expresses *B* as virtually unconditioned.

The virtually unconditioned grasped by the intellect constitutes sufficient evidence. For when *B* is grasped as being virtually unconditioned, there is a sufficient and compelling motive for positing *B* absolutely in an absolute assent. Without a virtually unconditioned, sufficient evidence is lacking. For when *B* is not grasped as unconditioned, it is not grasped whether there are conditions that have not been fulfilled. If that is not grasped, it would be rash to make a judgment.

We have indicated elsewhere[101] how this analysis can be applied to various types of judgment. But here is an example of the basic type,[102] in which the fulfillment of the conditions, *A*, is found in the data themselves precisely as data, as the given (either the data of sense or data of consciousness); the nexus, 'if *A*, then *B*,' is found in the intellectual procedure duly followed in going from the data, *A*, to the conceptual synthesis, *B*; which procedure consists in an inquiry into the data, some understanding of the data, and conceiving what has been understood in the data; and this procedure is duly followed insofar as it satisfies the norms and requirements of intellectual light.

---

101 Lonergan, *Insight,* chapter 10.
102 [The example itself is not given in the text. At the point in *Early Works on Theological Method 1* where he is treating this material, after giving the concrete example of the correct judgment, 'The microphone is here,' Lonergan says, 'That analysis in chapter 10 of *Insight* I apply to a series of instances. That is the fundamental case of the emergence of a judgment as a virtually unconditioned. There are different kinds of judgments, and I line them up in the tenth chapter and apply the same analysis to each case.' It is likely that 'Exemplo sit' in the Latin text refers to some similar concrete instance that he employed to manifest 'the fundamental case,' 'the basic type.' See Lonergan, *Early Works on Theological Method 1* 99–100. It is not impossible that 'Exemplo sit' here refers to the example in chapter 10 of *Insight* of the man coming home from work to find his house in disarray and making the judgment of fact, 'Something happened.']

Qua ex analysi fundamentali distinguuntur tria quae obiectivitatem cognitionis humanae faciunt.[103] *Obiectivitas experientialis,* quae eo ipso habetur quod data dantur (ubi nulla est admittenda distinctio valoris inter data, cum omnia pariter dentur, quamvis alia fundent iudicia de rebus materialibus et alia fundent iudicia de psychologia abnormali). *Obiectivitas normative,* quae ipso lumine intellectuali constituitur, iis scilicet normis atque exigentiis quibus naturaliter regitur processus intellectualis, et quidem non mechanice, caece, vitaliter, sed conscie, intellectualiter, rationaliter regitur, dirigitur, gubernatur, cogitur. *Obiectivitas absoluta,* quae perspecto virtualiter incondicionato attingitur, quae ex obiectivitate experientiali (*A*) et normativa (si *A* tunc *B*) resultat.

(d) Quid logica, methodologia, 'esprit de finesse,' 'illative sense.' Non propter auctoritatem Aristotelis logicam accipimus, sed ideo Aristoteles auctoritate gaudet quia logica exprimit ea quae ipso lumine intellectuali iam cognoscimus. Differunt tamen inter se ipsum lumen intellectuale et logica sicut et differunt subiectum et obiectum. Lumen enim intellectuale nihil aliud dicit nisi subiectum humanum conscium quatenus ab animali bruto differt, quatenus non absolute stupidum est, quatenus non insipiens prorsus est. Logica autem dicit obiectificatio quaedam (per conceptus et iudicia) ipsius luminis intellectualis. Propter quam differentiam debemus logicam addiscere, non quidem ut lumen intellectuale consequamur, sed ut lumen intellectuale naturaliter habitum obiective per conceptus et iudicia apprehendamus.

Sicut logica, ita etiam methodologia est obiectiva quaedam luminis intellectualis expressio atque manifestatio. Quae tamen inter se differunt, quatenus logica de cognitione in facto esse tractat, methodologia autem de cognitione in fieri. Logica enim supponit conceptus iam formatos, iudicia iam elicita; quibus suppositis, alios conceptus quemadmodum definiantur, et alia iudicia quemadmodum deducantur, explicat, ordinat, regit. Methodologia autem ipsam conceptionum formationem aggreditur, ipsam iudiciorum praeparationem debitumque exercitium. Cumque aliter in aliis scientiis formentur conceptus et eliciantur iudicia, distinguuntur methodologia generalis quae omnes pariter scientias (uti in fieri) respicit, et methodologiae speciales quae differentias particularium scientiarum (uti in fieri) considerat.

From this fundamental analysis we can distinguish three elements that make up the objectivity of human knowledge.[103] *Experiential objectivity* is had from the very fact that data are given. (There is no difference in value among the data since all are equally given, even though some may form the basis of judgments about material things and others may form the basis of judgments about abnormal psychology.) *Normative objectivity* is constituted by intellectual light itself, that is to say, by those norms and requirements that naturally govern the intellectual process; they do so not mechanically, blindly, or vitally; rather they consciously, intellectually, and rationally govern, direct, control, and drive that process. *Absolute objectivity* is attained in grasping the virtually unconditioned, and results from experiential objectivity (*A*) plus normative objectivity (if *A*, then *B*).

(d) What are logic, methodology, the '*esprit de finesse*,' 'illative sense'? We do not accept logic merely on account of the authority of Aristotle; but Aristotle has authority because in his logic he expresses what we already know by our intellectual light itself. But the difference between intellectual light and logic is the difference between subject and object. For by 'intellectual light' we mean simply the conscious human subject insofar as that subject differs from a brute animal, is not utterly stupid or quite silly. Logic is an objectification, by way of concepts and judgments, of this intellectual light. Because of this difference we have to learn logic, not in order to acquire intellectual light, but to apprehend objectively through concepts and judgments the intellectual light with which we are endowed by nature.

As logic, so also methodology is an objective expression and manifestation of intellectual light. The difference between them is that logic treats of knowledge as an accomplished fact while methodology treats of knowledge in process. Logic presupposes concepts already formed and judgments already made; and with these being presupposed, it explains, orders, and regulates the way in which other concepts are defined and other judgments deduced. Methodology, however, addresses the very formation of concepts and the preparation for and the proper way to make judgments. And since the concepts are formed and judgments elicited in different ways in different sciences, we distinguish between general methodology, which applies in the same way to all sciences as being in process, and special methodologies, which take into account the differences peculiar to the various sciences in process.

103 Lonergan, *Insight* chapter 13.

Luminis intellectualis tota vis atque virtus per logicam et methodologiam non exhauritur. Tam enim methodologia quam logica nisi generaliora, communiora, utiliora exponere non possunt; quinimo quo magis omnium consensum atque approbationem quaerunt, eo magis tardioribus mentibus necessario cedunt, eaque omittunt quae quamvis generalitate non careant tamen difficilius perspiciantur.

Quam ob causam, etiam sunt agnoscenda quae dicuntur 'esprit de finesse' (Pascal) vel 'illative sense' (Newman). Quae quidem dicunt ipsum lumen intellectuale prout in empiricis, contingentibus, mobilibus excercetur, et quidem prout subtilius, celerius, accuratius procedit quam ut legibus universalibus concipi et dici possit. Quo enim magis quaestio ad formam geometricam accedit, eo facilius omnis rei aspectus accurate concipitur, omnis nexus perfecte exprimitur, omnis usus luminis intellectualis ad legem quandam generalem et obiectificatam reducitur. E contra, quo magis quaestio a forma geometrica recedit, quo magis empiricis, contingentibus, mobilibus, iisque non paucis sed permultis simul, involvitur, eo subtilius totam inquisitionem pervadit, dirigit, gubernat lumen intellectuale. Quae quidem omnium penetratio, directio, gubernatio adeo huic materiae, huic elementorum coniunctioni particulari, adaptatur, ut non obiective exponatur nisi per expositionem ipsius totius processus secundum omnes et singulas suas ambages.

(e) Quid sapientia.[104]

(a′) Sicut scientia est de conclusionibus, intellectus de principiis, ita sapientia seligit terminos quibus positis elucent principia. Exemplo sit notio entis, quae aliter concipitur apud Parmenidem, Platonem, Aristotelem, Plotinum, Avicennam, Averroem, Aquinatem, Scotum, Hegel, Heidegger. Inter quas diversas notiones non caece seligendam est. Neque per prima principia seligi potest. Nam ipsa prima principia diversum induunt sensum prout diverso modo exponitur entis notio. Neque solo et quasi nudo lumine intellectuali seligi potest. Hoc enim lumen ex parte subiecti invenitur et donec obiectificetur nondum clare et distincte constat quid praecise exigat, quid vetet. Caeterum, solum et nudum lumen intellectuale, sicut infantibus

The power and effectiveness of our intellectual light is not wholly accounted for by logic and methodology. Both methodology and logic can only express generalities and the more common and useful elements; in fact, the more they seek universal agreement and approval, the more they will have to make concessions to duller minds and leave out elements that, while not lacking in generality, are nevertheless more difficult to grasp.

For this reason we must also note what Pascal calls '*esprit de finesse*,' and Newman 'illative sense.' These expressions refer to intellectual light as brought to bear upon empirical, contingent, and changeable realities, and indeed as it proceeds more subtly, more expeditiously, and more accurately than can be conceived and expressed in universal laws. The more a question is geometrical in its form, the easier it is for all the aspects of the matter to be accurately conceived, every nexus perfectly expressed, and every exercise of intellectual light reduced to some general objectified law. Conversely, the less its exposition resembles that of geometry, and the more it is involved with empirical, contingent, and changeable data, and with a large number of these at the same time, the more subtly does intellectual light enter into, direct, and control the entire process of inquiry. Indeed, this all-pervasive direction and control adapts itself so well to this sort of material and this particular combination of elements that no objective account of it can be given except by describing the whole process in all of its many twists and turns.

(e) What is wisdom?[104]

(a′) As science is about conclusions and understanding is about principles, so wisdom selects the terms by means of which principles become clear. An example would be the notion of being, which is understood differently by Parmenides, Plato, Aristotle, Plotinus, Avicenna, Averroes, Aquinas, Scotus, Hegel, and Heidegger. Selection among these various notions must not be done blindly. They cannot be selected by recourse to first principles. For first principles themselves take on a meaning in accordance with the different ways in which the notion of being is explained. Nor can this selection be made by mere intellectual light alone. For this light is found on the side of the subject, and until it is objectified one cannot know clearly and distinctly what precisely it requires and what it rejects. Moreover, bare

104 [See also Lonergan's discussion of wisdom in *Verbum* 78–87 and *Insight* 432 and the treatment of 'Foundation' in the first item in this volume.]

et parvulis non deest, ita nec magnis illis nominibus nuperrime recitatis.[105] Quibus perspectis, cum Aquinate dicendum est sapientiam iudicare de ente, non-ente, iisque quae per se sunt entis.[106]

(b′) At qualis sit illa sapientia? Sapientis esse dicitur 'ordinare omnia.' Quae omnium ordinatio non ex superiori quodam principio (nobis immanente) procedit, uti ex superius dictis constat, sed ipsum supremum principium dicit, lumen nempe intellectuale nostrum, idque non solum et nudum, sed prout ad omnia extenditur iisque applicatur.

(c′) Qualis sit necessitas illius ordinationis? Quamvis superius analysin iudicii fecerimus quasi eventus quidam isolatus esset, omne tamen iudicium intra contextum aliorum iudiciorum fit, quibus sensus iudicii facti elucidatur et explicatur, veritas eiusdam probatur et defenditur, antecedentia et consequentia adducuntur ut ipsum iudicium reddatur manifestius. Cui contextui iudiciorum correspondet ipsa rerum interconnexio, interdependentia, similitudinis et dissimilitudinis multiplex relatio. Quare, tum propter connexionem iudiciorum inter se, tum propter connexionem rerum inter se, tum propter correspondentiam inter vera iudicia et ipsas res, omne iudicium supponit omnium quandam ordinationem.

(d′) Qualis sit genesis eiusdem ordinationis? Paradoxon enim statuisse videmur. Ut bene iudicemus, praerequiritur sapientia. Sed ipsa sapientia in quadam omnium ordinatione consistit, quae sane cognosci non potest nisi per vera iudicia eaque permulta. Iam vero paradoxon non excludit factum. Parvulis non negamus lumen intellectuale, et tamen eos ad usum rationis pervenisse non censemus ante annum septimum. Adulescentibus non negamus vel lumen intellectuale vel usum rationis, et tamen eos coram lege plene responsabiles non reputamus ante annum primum et vigesimum. Iuvenibus non negamus vel lumen intellectuale, vel usum rationis, vel responsabilitatem plenam coram lege, et eos tamen minus aptos ad scientiam ethicam examinandam duxit Aristoteles propter defectum experientiae rerum humanarum. Cur? Quia sunt gradus sapientiae, quia sunt 'omnium ordinationes' vel valde imperfectae in pueris, vel imperfectiores

457   The Method of Theology

intellectual light by itself is present in infants and children as well as in the famous philosophers just mentioned.[105] Accordingly we must say with Aquinas that wisdom makes judgments about being and non-being and those things that *per se* pertain to being.[106]

(b') But what is the nature of this wisdom? It is characteristic of the wise 'to order all things.' This ordering of all things does not proceed from some higher principle immanent within us, as is clear from what we have said above, but expresses the supreme principle itself, namely, our intellectual light, and not that bare light by itself but rather as it extends to and is applied to all things.

(c') What is the necessity for this ordering? Although we have analyzed judgment above as if it were an isolated event, yet every judgment is made within the context of other judgments by which the sense of the judgment in question is clarified and explained, its truth proven and defended, and its antecedents and consequents adduced in order to clarify it further. Corresponding to this network of judgments is the interconnection, the interdependence, and the multiple relations of similarity and dissimilarity in things themselves. Therefore, because of the mutual connections among judgments, the mutual connections among things, and the correspondence between true judgments and the things themselves, all judgment presupposes an ordering of all things.

(d') What is the genesis of this ordering? It looks as if we have set up a paradox. Wisdom is a prerequisite for judging well, yet wisdom itself consists in ordering all things, which ordering surely cannot be known except through good judgments, and several of them at that. But a paradox does not eliminate an actual fact. We do not deny that children possess intellectual light, even though we do not consider them as having reached the age of reason before their seventh year. We do not deny adolescents either intellectual light or the use of reason, even though we do not account them fully responsible before the law until they reach the age of majority. We do not deny young men and women intellectual light, the use of reason, and full responsibility before the law, and yet Aristotle considered them unfit to study ethics on account of their lack of experience in human affairs. Why is this? Because there are degrees of wisdom, because these 'orderings of all

---

105 [The Latin words 'clare et distincte' and 'nec' were added by hand in the autograph.]
106 Thomas Aquinas, *Summa theologiae*, 1-2, q. 66, a. 5, ad 4m.

etsi aliquatenus sufficientes in adolescentibus, vel ad plenam perfectionem nondum adductae in iuvenibus. Quae quidem ordinationes pedetentim acquiruntur, ut per iudicia minus bene facta denique tandem ad iudicia bene facienda perveniamus.

(e′) Quare, apte recolitur pyramis illa aristotelica[107] secundum quam ex multis sensationibus una fit memoria, ex multis memoriis unum fit experimentum, ex multis experimentis una fit causae cognitio, et quo altius in causas cognoscendas proceditur eo perfectius ad sapientiam simpliciter dictam pervenitur.

(f) De divisione sapientiae

(a′) Alia est sapientia simplicitur, quae omnia simpliciter ordinat, et alia est sapientia secundum quid (vel sapientia particularis) quae omnia in determinato quodam genere vel campo ordinat.

(b′) Ita sapientia sutoris est sapientia secundum quid; omnia enim ordinat quae calceamenta respiciunt, et ideo de calceamentis bene iudicat; at 'sutor ne supra crepidam.' Similiter, omnes qui specialistae dicuntur, sapientes secundum quid sunt; ita historicus circa historica, exegeta circa exegetica, physicus circa physica, etc. Qui omnes, quatenus propriam materiam exploratam atque perspectam habent, omnia ad eam pertinentia ordinant et de omnibus illis bene iudicare possunt.

(c′) At praeter particulares has sapientiae partes etiam exsistit sapientia simpliciter quae omnia simpliciter considerat et ordinat. Qualis in primis est ipsa divina sapientia quae totum posse divinae potentiae comprehendit.[108] Qualis deinde est visio beata Domini Nostri Iesu Christi, quae non solum ipsam divinam essentiam immediate apprehendit sed etiam omnia actualia in eadem essentia videt.[109] Cui proxime accedit visio Dei caeterorum beatorum, quae pro perfectione visionis plura ad Deum ordinata tamquam obiectum visionis secundarium perspiciunt.

(d′) Cui divinae et beatorum sapientiae proxime accedunt participationes quaedam vel positivae vel negativae quae hominibus hac in vita divini-

things' are found to be very imperfect in young children, rather imperfect though somewhat sufficient in adolescents, and not yet fully developed in young adults. These orderings are acquired gradually, so that by way of judgments made less well we eventually arrive at making good judgments.

(e′) Hence it will be pertinent to recall here Aristotle's 'pyramid'[107] in which many sensations go to form one memory, many memories go to form one experience, many experiences go to form one knowledge of a cause, and the higher one goes in one's knowledge of causes the more perfectly does one arrive at wisdom simply so called.

(f) There are different kinds of wisdom.

(a′) There is wisdom simply so called, which orders absolutely all things, and there is wisdom in some respect, particular wisdom, which orders all things within a determinate category or field.

(b′) Thus, the wisdom of a shoemaker is an example of particular wisdom; it orders everything that has to do with shoes and so makes sound judgments about shoes; but, 'Cobbler, stick to your last!' In the same way, all specialists are wise in some particular field: a historian in history, an exegete in exegesis, a physicist in physics, and so forth. Inasmuch as they all have a thorough knowledge of their material, they order everything that pertains to it and are thus able to make good judgments about all those matters.

(c′) But besides these instances of particular wisdom there is, as we have noted, wisdom without qualification, which considers and orders absolutely all things. Such above all is divine wisdom, which comprehends absolutely all that the divine power is capable of doing.[108] Such again is Christ's beatific vision, which not only directly apprehends the divine essence but also beholds in that essence all actually existing realities.[109] Not far inferior to Christ's vision is the vision of God that the blessed enjoy, who in proportion to the perfection of their vision behold many things related to God as the secondary object of their vision.

(d′) Closely approximating this wisdom of God and the blessed are certain positive or negative participations in it granted by God to mortals. The

107 Aristotle, *Metaphysics*, I, 1, 980a – 982a; Thomas Aquinas, *In 1 Metaphys.*, lect. 1. [See also Aristotle, *Posterior Analytics*, II, 19, 99b, 35 – 100a, 12.]
108 Thomas Aquinas, *Summa theologiae*, 1, q. 25, a. 5.
109 Ibid. 3, q. 10, a. 2.

tus conceduntur. Positivae quidem sunt quae a Deo revelantur, et praecipue eae quae ad revelationem publicam vt et nt pertinent, uti prophetiae, librorum sacrorum inspiratio et inerrantia, apostolorum charismata. Negativae autem sunt in primis illa divinae providentiae assistentia quae impedit quominus in rebus fidei et morum magisterium ecclesiae erret.

(e′) Iam vero ad sapientiam divinam et beatorum comparatur sapientia theologica, sicut ad scientiam subalternantem (puta geometriam) comparatur scientia subalternata (puta perspectivam non modernam sed antiquam).[110] Quae quidem similitudo non perfecta est sed analogica, cum theologia christiana categorias aristotelicas excedat. Similitudo quidem invenitur secundum quod theologus a Deo revelante accipit quae suum captum atque iudicium excedunt, sicut etiam scientia subalternata a scientia subalternante accipit. Dissimilitudo autem in eo est quod, qui perspectivam addiscit, etiam geometriam addiscere potest; sed qui theologiam addiscit, visionem beatam addiscere non potest sed tantummodo eandem sperare in vita futura a se acceptum iri.

(f′) Unde et concludes theologum numquam suae sapientiae nimis confidere, semperque suum iudicium iudicio ecclesiae submittere. Quae enim considerat mysteria in Deo abscondita, secundum sapientiam proportionatam non ordinantur et iudicantur nisi sit sapientia vel divina vel beatorum. Quod autem magisterium exercet ecclesia Dei, illud divinitus adiuvatur ne in rebus fidei et morum erret, et quidem infallibiliter.

(g′)[111] Etiam philosophia est sapientia quae omnia respicit. Et quidem si homo esset in statu naturae purae, philosophia esset suprema sapientia humana, uti docuit Aristoteles. In ordine autem actuali sapientia philosophica ita omnia respicit (ens enim transcendentale est) ut tamen aperta esse debeat ad intimiorem coniunctionem cum ipsa divina sapientia quae supernaturaliter se revelat, per fidem creditur, per theologiam in totum campum intelligibilem redundat.

(g) Quemadmodum haec de iudicio, de evidentia sufficienti, de sapientia, comparentur ad antiqua? Manifestum est Aristotelem fuisse auctorem doctrinae tum de syllogismo tum de sapientia. Praecipua differentia in eo est quod, post admissam novam scientiae differentiationem, ea quae olim

positive participations are God's revelations, especially those of the Old and New Testaments, such as prophecies, the inspiration and inerrancy of scripture, and the charisms of the apostles. Negative participations are especially those helps afforded by divine providence that prevent the teaching office of the church from erring in matters of faith and morals.

(e′) Theological wisdom is to the wisdom of God and of the blessed as a subalternate, or derivative, science is to its subalternating, or principal, science. For example, the ancient (not the modern) science of perspective is to geometry as subalternate to its subalternating science.[110] This comparison, however, is not perfect but analogical, since Christian theology goes beyond Aristotelian categories. The similarity lies in the fact that the theologian accepts from God's revelation matters that exceed his own capacity and judgment, just as a subalternate science is a derivative of its subalternating science. The dissimilarity lies in the fact that one who learns perspective can also learn geometry; but one who learns theology cannot learn the beatific vision but can only hope to obtain it in the next life.

(f′) Hence, one may conclude that theologians should never trust too much in their own wisdom, but always submit their judgment to that of the church. For the mysteries hidden in God are to be ordered and judged by a proportionate wisdom, which can only be that of God and the blessed. The teaching office of the church, however, is divinely assisted, and indeed infallibly so, to prevent it from erring in matters of faith and morals.

(g′)[111] Philosophy also is a wisdom that regards all things. Indeed, if humanity were in a state of pure nature, philosophy would be the supreme human wisdom, as Aristotle teaches. In the present order of reality, however, though philosophical wisdom regards all things, for being is transcendental, yet at the same time it ought to be open to a closer relationship with that divine wisdom which reveals itself supernaturally, is believed through faith, and through theology enters into the whole field of the intelligible.

(g) How do these notions about judgment, about sufficient evidence, and about wisdom compare with the ancient notions? Obviously Aristotle has been the source of our teaching both about the syllogism and about wisdom. The main difference is that after admitting a new differentiation

110 Ibid. 1, q. 1. a. 2. See also C. Dumont, 'La réflexion sur la méthode théologique,' *Nouvelle Revue Théologique* 84 (1962) 17–35.
111 [At this point in the autograph, the date at the top of the page switches to 9-4-62.]

de prudentia dicebantur,[112] iam ad complementum sapientiae esse adaptanda. Prudentia (recta ratio agibilium) respicit mobilia, contingentia, particularia, per accidens, sed eam tantummodo veritatem quaerit quae 'practica' dicitur, nempe, quae de hic et nunc dicendis, agendis, faciendis determinat. Ubi autem admittitur scientia veri nominis quae empirice de homine tractat, ibi etiam excolenda est sapientia quae ita *omnia* ordinat ut etiam mobilia, contingentia, particularia, per accidens includat.

Quae sapientiae perfectio ea lege haberi potest ut:

(a′) agnoscatur 'esprit de finesse,' 'illative sense,'
(b′) excolantur sapientiae particulares, scilicet, specialistarum,
(c′) inter se ordinentur, coniungantur, quodammodo in unum conflentur tum sapientia theologica tum hae sapientiae particulares.

Quemadmodum vero ad hunc finem procedatur, postea convenientius dicetur, ubi de divisione scientiarum agendum erit.[113]

[5.4 The Exclusion of Extrinsicism and of Immanentism][114]

Quibus[115] excluduntur tum extrinsecismus tum immanentismus, omnesque quaestiones ad duo fundamentalia reducuntur, nempe, quid sit, et an sit.

(a) 'Quibus,' i.e., assertis praecedentibus de admittenda nova scientiae differentiatione et de necessitate iudicii sapientis.

of science, what used to be said about prudence[112] now has to be adapted to being complemented by wisdom. Prudence ('right reason concerning what is to be done') has to do with the changeable, the contingent, the particular, and the *per accidens*, but seeks only that truth which is called 'practical,' namely, that which determines what ought to be said or done here and now. But wherever you have a true science that deals with humans empirically, you will also have to cultivate the wisdom that regards *all things*, so that it also includes the changeable, the contingent, the particular, and the *per accidens*.

This perfection of wisdom can be had on the following terms:

(a′) that the *esprit de finesse*, or illative sense, is recognized;

(b′) that particular forms of wisdom, those of specialists, are cultivated;

(c′) that both theological wisdom and these particular wisdoms are related to each other, linked together, and in some way brought into unity.

How to proceed to this end will more appropriately be dealt with later, when we come to treat of the various kinds of sciences.[113]

[5.4 The Exclusion of Extrinsicism and of Immanentism][114]

The foregoing[115] rule out both extrinsicism and immanentism and reduce all questions to two basic ones, namely, What is it? and, Is it?

(a) 'The foregoing' refers to the previous assertions about admitting a new differentiation of science and about the need for wise judgment.

---

112 Thomas Aquinas, *Summa theologiae*, 2-2, qq. 47–56.

113 [Lonergan is probably referring to the material below in section 8, 'Distinctions within the Unity of Knowledge.' Notice, though, that discussion of the human sciences is there left to the 'second problematic.']

114 [The material in *Early Works on Theological Method 1* corresponding to section 5.4 may be found in chapter 1962-5, 'Beyond Extrinsicism and Immanentism.']

115 [At this point in the autograph the date at the top of a single page switches back to 4-4-62. It would appear that '(f) (g′)' and '(g),' above, which cover a single page in the autograph, were composed on or for 9 April 1962 (a Monday) and inserted into the text that was composed on or for 4 April 1962 (the prior Wednesday). Further, the fact that a crossed-out version of '(f) (g′)' and '(g)' appears immediately prior to the present '(f) (g′)' and '(g),' under the date of 4 April, provides further evidence that Lonergan rewrote these two items on or for 9 April 1962 and inserted them into the text composed on or for 4 April, which is resumed here.]

(b) Excluditur extrinsecismus, et quidem quadruplex, nempe, deductivisticus, operativus, metaphysicus, et intuitivus.

(a′) Extrinsecismus in genere est oblivio suae et propriae mentis;[116] quae
quidem oblivio suas habet rationes quae tamen taceri solent, scilicet, timor
intelligendi et fuga a responsabilitate iudicandi.

(b′) Extrinsecismus deductivisticus non consistit in eo quod deductiones
adhibentur, eaeque vel longiores, systematicae, subtiliores, sed consistit in
eo quod scientia reponitur, non in habitu intellectus, sed in processu quodam externo qui in libro exscribitur neque operationem intellectus nisi per
accidens exigit.[117]

Exemplo sit auditor vel lector criticus qui semper et de omnibus idem
fert iudicium, Res non demonstratur. Iterum, exemplo sint theologi saec.
XIV qui singulas probationes in theologia naturali examinaverunt et, decursu temporum, semper plura divina attributa iudicaverunt indemonstrabi-
lia.[118] 'Tout se passe comme si un théologien ... ne disposait ... que d'un
instrument, la raison, que la logique où il s'est formé à penser, lui a appris
à manier et à définir.'[119]

Quod aliunde non oritur nisi ex natura syllogismi non perspecta. Duo
enim sunt syllogismi munera: aliud circa quaestionem, quid sit, propter
quid res ita se habeat; aliud circa quaestionem, an sit.[120]

Circa quaestionem, quid, propter quid, syllogismus (qui dicitur *epistēmonikos*, 'faciens scire') per medium terminum exhibet causam cur praedicatum insit subiecto; causam autem numquam cognoscimus nisi quatenus
intelligimus. Propter quid scimus lunam esse sphericam? Propter phases.
Unde syllogismus: Si luna per phases transit, necessario spherica est; atqui

(b) Four different forms of extrinsicism are ruled out: deductivist, operational, metaphysical, and intuitionist.

(a') Extrinsicism in general is being oblivious of one's own mind.[116] The reasons for such oblivion, namely, fear of understanding and flight from the responsibility of judging, usually remain secret.

(b') Deductivist extrinsicism does not consist in the simple fact of using quite lengthy, systematic, and overly subtle deductions, but in placing knowledge not in a habit of the intellect but in some external process written down in a book and only *per accidens* requiring an operating intellect.[117]

An example of this would be a critical listener or reader who always renders the same judgment about everything, namely, 'The point is not proven.' Another example would be the fourteenth-century theologians who scrutinized all the proofs in natural theology and as time went on declared more and more divine attributes to be unprovable.[118] 'Tout se passe comme si un théologien ... ne disposait ... que d'un instrument, la raison, que la logique, où il s'est formé à penser, lui a appris à manier et à définir.'[119]

The source of this error is nothing other than the failure to understand the nature of a syllogism. Syllogisms have two functions: one concerns the question What is it? or Why is a thing as it is? and the other the question, Is it?[120]

As to the question What? or Why?, the syllogism (which is called *epistēmonikos*, 'knowledge-producing,' or explanatory) shows by its middle term the cause, the reason, for a predicate being part of the subject. But we know a cause only insofar as we understand. Why do we know that the moon is a sphere? Because of its phases. Hence the syllogism: If the moon passes

---

116 [The Latin words 'suae et propriae' were added by hand in the autograph.]
117 [A useful supplementary discussion here is Lonergan's assessment in *Insight* 427–33 of the adequacy of deduction as the one proper method for metaphysics.]
118 See P. Vignaux, s.v. 'Nominalisme,' DTC XI (21) cols. 717–84, at col. 782.
119 ['Everything goes on as if a theologian ... had only one instrument at his disposal, namely, reason, which logic, by which he has trained himself to think, has shown him how to wield and delimit.'] Ibid. col. 779.
120 [For the same point, see Bernard Lonergan, 'Theology and Understanding,' in *Collection* 117–18.]

per phases transit; ergo necessario spherica est. Qui[121] syllogismus sensum alicui non habet nisi ipse intelligit nexum inter phases et sphericitatem; quod quidem non intelligit nisi experimenta vel fingit vel facit; scilicet, superficies plana aut tota illuminatur aut nulla eius pars; superficies cylindrica illuminatur vel tota vel pars prout ex alia vel alia directione advenit lux, sed phases non sunt sicut in luna; etc. Unde addisces: syllogismus *epistēmonikos*, seu faciens scire, eatenus scire facit quatenus *aliquis* causam, rationem, *addiscit*; si modo extrinseco consideratur, si a subiecto addiscente praescinditur quasi ab eo quod est per accidens, syllogismus evanescit; fit aes sonans et cymbalum tinniens. Unde etiam addisces: quod intendit syllogismus faciens scire est, primo et per se, intelligentiae communicationem; vult ut alius addiscat et intelligat, ut quaestioni propter quid respondere possit. Etiam quidem certitudinem intendit, sed secundario, vel ut finem ulteriorem, qui non attingitur nisi mediante intelligentia causae.

Circa quaestionem, An sit, Utrum sic se habeat, syllogismus non est obiectivus quidam processus qui sine mente procedit, sicuti fit in processu mechanico, physico, chimico, biologico. Quinimo, syllogismus non est nisi medium quo intellectui reflexo exhibetur inconditionatum virtuale. Quae quidem exhibitio utilis est, sed tantum obiectivam non vero formalem evidentiam constituit. Formalis enim evidentia eatenus attingitur, quatenus a subiecto inconditionatum ut inconditionatum perspicitur. Quam perspicientiam iam diximus supponere (in ultima analysi) tum dari data omnia quae ad rem pertinent tum non dari quae rei obstant tum illam ordinantem sapientiam quae debite ex datis ad conceptiones, syntheses, theorias, systemata procedit.

Quod si quis neque ad data attendit neque genesin sapientiae in se ipso curat sed omnia, quasi gratiae gratis dandae essent, ex demonstrante exspectat, nullam umquam conclusionem demonstratam habebit.

Unde et addisces: sicut in eo qui extrinsecismum prorsus fugit invenitur syllogismus instrumentum scientiae augendae, ita in eo qui extrinsecismo indulget invenitur syllogismus instrumentum scepticismi. Quale instrumentum in saec. XIV factum est.

through phases, it must be spherical; but it does pass through phases; therefore it must be spherical. This[121] syllogism will not make sense to anyone who does not understand the connection between phases and sphericity; and one will not understand this connection without imagining or performing some experiments. A plane surface is either totally illuminated or not at all; a cylindrical surface is illuminated either totally or partially depending upon the direction from which the light strikes it, but its phases are not like those of the moon; and so forth. From this we learn the following: an *epistēmonikos* or explanatory syllogism produces knowledge only insofar as there is *someone* who *learns* the cause, the reason. If it is considered in an extrinsicist manner, if one prescinds from the learning subject as if from something *per accidens*, the syllogism is empty; it becomes as 'sounding brass or tinkling cymbal.' And from this we further learn that what an explanatory syllogism primarily and *per se* aims at is to communicate understanding. It wants another person to learn and understand and so be able to answer the question 'Why?' True, it also aims at certitude, but secondarily, or as a further objective that is not attained except by means of an understanding of the cause.

As to the question Is it? or Is it so?, a syllogism is not some objective process carried on outside a mind, like some mechanical, physical, chemical, or biological process. The syllogism, in fact, is but a means by which a virtually unconditioned is manifested to a reflective intellect. This manifestation is useful, of course, but it constitutes only objective, not formal, evidence. Formal evidence is attained insofar as a subject grasps the unconditioned as unconditioned. As we have said, this grasp supposes, in the final analysis, that all the pertinent data are present, that there is nothing there to the contrary, and that there is also present that ordering wisdom which proceeds in due course from data to concepts, syntheses, theories, and systems.

But if you neither attend to the data nor care about the genesis of wisdom within yourself, but expect everything to come from the person demonstrating like graces from on high, you will never have any conclusion proven.

From this you can see that, just as for one who totally rejects extrinsicism a syllogism is an instrument for increasing knowledge, so for one who is given to extrinsicism the syllogism becomes an instrument of skepticism. Just such an instrument was fashioned in the fourteenth century.

121 [At this point in the autograph, the date at the top of the page switches to 5-4-62.]

Fallacias extrinsecismi iam notavimus. In eo scilicet consistunt quod de 'vero,' 'certo,' 'evidente' disputatur quasi haec 'obiectiva' essent quin tamen in ullo intellectu fuissent. E.g., quod Deus revelat est verum; atqui hoc Deus revelavit; ergo hoc est verum. Maior constat ex theologia naturali; minor constat ex apologetica quae naturali rationis lumine peragitur; conclusio demonstrat praeter fidem auctoritatis etiam exsistere fidem scientificam, obiective demonstratam, in mysteria revelata.

Distinguenda est maior et pariter conclusio: est verum, in mente divina, C, in mente humana, sub-dist., credente, C, infideli, N.[122]

At fallaciae eiusmodi vix manifestant quam perniciosus sit extrinsecismus deductivisticus. Praetermissa enim mente, etiam praetermittitur omne augmentum intelligentiae, scientiae, sapientiae, quod tamen exsistit tum in ordine naturali tum etiam fatente ipso c. Vaticano (DB 1800) in ordine supernaturali. Quo augmento praetermisso, pariter praetermittitur evolutio conceptuum, accuratior principiorum enuntiatio, plenior et exactior conclusionum deductio. Quibus praetermissis, iam excluditur omnis historia doctrinalis. Sicut ideae platonicae sunt aeternae et immobiles, ita etiam sunt conceptus qui dicuntur 'obiectivi' (scilicet, in nulla mente) et ideo sub omni respectu similes prorsus sive ante duo millia annorum intendebantur sive ante mille sive hodie. Quod si conceptus sunt immobiles, idem pariter de principiis est dicendum. Quod de conceptibus et principiis fingitur, etiam de 'probationibus' pariter retinendum est; exsistit ergo de singulis rebus vera quaedam atque obiectiva probatio, quae vel umbram mutabilitatis pati non potest; totis viribus nitendum est ut illa probatio inveniatur; totis deinceps viribus nitendum est ne inventa per quamlibet vel levissimam mutationem corrumpatur.

Neque sufficit haec historiae doctrinalis exclusio, haec factorum manifestorum negatio. Illi conceptus, illa principia, illae probationes, quae ideo

We have noted the fallacies in extrinsicism. They consist in arguing about what is 'true' or 'certain' or 'evident' as if these were 'objective' realities never found in any intellect. An example of this would be: 'What God reveals is true; but God has revealed this; therefore this is true.' The major premise is clear from natural theology; the minor is clear from apologetics, which uses the natural light of reason; the conclusion shows that besides faith in authority there exists also scientific faith, objectively demonstrated, in the revealed mysteries.

The major premise has to be distinguished and the conclusion distinguished accordingly: it is true in the mind of God, granted; in a human mind, we sub-distinguish: of a believer, granted; of a non-believer, we deny.[122]

Fallacies of this sort scarcely begin to show how pernicious deductivist extrinsicism is. Ignore the mind, and you ignore all growth in understanding, in science, and in wisdom, a growth that exists not only in the natural order but also, according to the [First] Vatican Council (DB 1800, DS 3020, ND 136), in the supernatural order. Ignore this growth, and you will similarly ignore all development in concepts, the increasingly accurate enunciation of principles, and the fuller and more exact drawing of conclusions. If all these are ignored, there can be no history of doctrines. Like Plato's eternal and unchangeable Ideas, so-called objective concepts ('objective' meaning 'not existing in any mind') are absolutely the same in every respect whether they were conceived two thousand years ago or a thousand years ago or only yesterday. But if concepts are unchangeable, so must principles be. And what is imagined to be true of concepts and principles must likewise be maintained concerning 'proofs.' Hence, every single thing has a true and objective proof, which cannot be allowed to suffer the least shadow of change. One must bend every effort to discover that proof; and once it is found, one must bend every effort to see that it not be corrupted by any change, no matter how slight.

As if this rejection of the history of doctrines, this denial of obvious facts, were not enough, those concepts and principles and proofs that are so ob-

---

122 [On scientific faith, see also www.bernardlonergan.com at 15500DTL050, 'Notes on faith,' where the first page (numbered 6) begins with a discussion of this issue. Also, Lonergan's position is succinctly stated in 'The Subject,' in *A Second Collection: Papers by Bernard J.F. Lonergan, S.J.*, ed. William F.J. Ryan and Bernard J. Tyrrell, s.j. (Philadelphia: The Westminster Press, 1974; reprint ed., Toronto: University of Toronto Press, 1996) 71–72.]

sunt obiectivae quia in nulla mente sunt, etiam ideo sunt ab omnibus agnoscendae ne triumphet relativismus. Quod quidem neque relativismum refutat neque relativismi refutationem tolerat et ideo quam maxime in relativismum stabiliendum atque disseminandum tendit.

Relativismum non refutat: relativistae enim docent relativitatem non conceptuum, principiorum, probationum, quae in nulla mente exsistant, sed eorum quae in mentibus humanis inveniuntur.

Relativismi refutationem non tolerat. Non enim eum tolerat qui ab extrinsecismo recedit, sed statim eum relativismi reum habet. Sed nemo potest relativismum refutare nisi qui conceptus in mentibus humanis considerat; et ipsa haec consideratio eo ipso est extrinsecismi derelictio et, secundum extrinsecistas, relativismi crimen.

(c′)[123] Accedit extrinsecismus *operativus*. Qui a praecedenti et deductivistico differt, non ratione, sed instrumento. Ubi enim alii loco mentis volunt syllogismum exterius dictum vel scriptum, alii loco mentis volunt methodum fideliter observatam. Fiant operationes secundum regulas methodicas, et eo ipso progredietur scientia. Neque tantummodo superfluit quidquam de intelligente et rationali subiecto cogitare, sed omnis talis cogitatio ipsam scientiae obiectivitatem obscurat, impedit, destruit. Eiusmodi enim concipitur esse 'obiectivitas' ut in ipso processu externo attingatur, consistat, salvetur.[124]

Ita quae dicitur logica vel symbolica vel mathematica suam sane et validitatem et utilitatem eamque magnam habet. At ea mente intelligi, suscipi, adhiberi potest, ut fiat non instrumentum mentis sed rationalitatis criterion atque mensura. Ita, etsi modo inarticulato, Alfred Tarski contra F. Gonseth.[125]

jective that they exist in no mind whatever must be acknowledged by everyone lest relativism triumph. But in fact this neither refutes relativism nor does it tolerate a refutation of relativism, and so it tends very greatly towards the establishment and dissemination of relativism.

It does not refute relativism; for relativists teach the relativity not of concepts, principles, and proofs that exist in no one's mind, but of those that are found in human minds.

It does not tolerate a refutation of relativism either; for it does not tolerate anyone who strays from extrinsicism, but immediately accuses such a one of relativism. But no one can refute relativism unless one considers concepts that are in human minds; yet this very consideration in itself is an abandonment of extrinsicism and this, according to extrinsicists, is the crime of relativism.

(c′) [123] Operational extrinsicism differs from the foregoing deductivist extrinsicism not in its essential meaning but in the instrument it uses. Where deductive extrinsicists would replace mind by an externally spoken or written syllogism, operational extrinsicists would substitute a method faithfully followed. Let operations be done according to methodical rules, and by that very fact knowledge will advance. To give any thought to an intelligent and rational subject is not only quite superfluous, but all such thinking obscures, obstructs, and nullifies the very objectivity of knowledge. Conceived in this way, 'objectivity' is attained, consists of, and is preserved in the external process itself. [124]

Symbolic or mathematical logic certainly does have its own validity and utility, and very much so. But it can be understood, adopted, and used with the intent of making it not an instrument of the mind but the criterion and measure of rationality. This we see in Alfred Tarski's rather inarticulate reply to Ferdinand Gonseth. [125]

---

123 [At this point in the autograph, the date at the top of the page switches to 10-4-62.]

124 [In *Method in Theology* 5–6, Lonergan compares the understanding of method in terms of a set of rules to 'The New Method Laundry,' and it is said to be inadequate 'if progressive and cumulative results are expected,' for 'neither discovery nor synthesis is at the beck and call of any set of rules.']

125 See 'Discussion' (Colloque International de Logique), *Revue Internationale de Philosophie* 8 (1954) 46–64. [See also Lonergan's discussion of this exchange between Tarski and Gonseth in a lecture he gave on 11 July 1957, published now in *Phenomenology and Logic* 98–100. Editorial note 20 on p. 99 provides some further information.]

Simili quodam modo in scientiis naturalibus bona reputatur investigatio quae viam aperit ad multas et alias investigationes peragendas, quae sua vice bonae sunt quatenus iterum vias aperiunt ad multas et alias investigationes ulteriores. Sane non fit scientia sine usu mentis; sed ipsa interioritas praetermittitur; tota attentio concentratur in iis quae vel sensibiliter dantur vel enuntiationibus proponuntur, ut progressus scientiae in eo consistat ut semper augeantur quae sibi mutuo correspondent data et enuntiata.

At ulterius inter 'naturalistas' scientiae humanae eatenus vere scientificae reputantur quatenus ad methodum scientiarum naturalium accedunt. Unde et quaeruntur 'leges' ad modum legum physicarum, chimicarum, biologicarum, ut omittatur quod specifice humanum est. Neque ipsa haec omissio apprehenditur quia scientia modo extrinseco intellecta et exercita etiam praetermittit quod specifice humanum est.

Qui sane errores ab iis evitantur qui maxime ex motu romantico vel idealistico oriundi, scientiis spiritualibus (*Geisteswissenschaften*) operam dant. Quod tamen alios errores non excludit; ita recentius H.G. Gadamer, *Wahrheit und Methode,*[126] hermeneuticam romanticam (interpres ita mentem auctoris penetrat ut quasi cum auctore totum opus reproducat) ideo impugnavit quod talis interpres sui oblitus in difficultates historismi ruit: 'Die Naivität des sogenannten Historismus besteht darin, dass er sich einer solchen Reflexion entzieht und im Vertrauen auf die Methodik seines Verfahrens seine eigene Geschichtlichkeit vergisst.'[127] Quod sane nihil aliud est quam extrinsecismus, nempe, ita methodo confidere ut propria mens praetermittatur.

Momentum huius extrinsecismi in eo est quod non parum influit in illam sententiam confirmandam atque disseminandam, nempe, scientias empiricas nisi probabiles non esse. Re vera, extrinsecismus sicut mentem ita etiam iudicium investigantis praetermittit; quo iudicio praetermisso, non solum certitudo sed etiam cognita probabilitas tollitur. Reiecto autem extrinseci-

In a similar way, research in the natural sciences is considered good if it opens the way to many different avenues of research, which in turn are good if they lead to many further ones. Science, of course, is not carried on without using one's mind; but this very interiority is quite overlooked. All attention is concentrated on what is presented to the senses or set forth in propositions, so that progress in science consists in the constant accumulation of interrelated data and propositions.

In addition, 'naturalists' consider the human sciences to be truly scientific only inasmuch as their method approaches that of the natural sciences. Hence, they look for 'laws' like those of physics, chemistry, and biology, so that they leave out what is specifically human. And this omission itself is not even noticed, because a science understood and practiced in an extrinsicist way also overlooks what is specifically human.

These errors are, it is true, avoided by those who, especially from a background of romanticism or idealism, devote themselves to the 'spiritual sciences' (*Geisteswissenschaften*). But this does not prevent other errors from being made. Recently H.-G. Gadamer, in *Wahrheit und Methode*[126] criticized Romantic hermeneutics (i.e., that the interpreter penetrates the mind of an author so completely that along with the author he could almost reproduce the entire work) on the grounds that such an interpreter in his self-forgetfulness falls into the difficulties of historicism: 'Die Naivität des sogennanten Historismus besteht darin, dass er sich einer solchen Reflexion entzieht und im Vertrauen auf die Methodik seines Verfahrens seine eigene Geschichtlichkeit vergisst.'[127] This is surely a case of extrinsicism, relying so much on one's method as to quite overlook one's own mind.

The importance of this extrinsicism lies in the fact that it bolsters and propagates the opinion that the empirical sciences are only probable. But actually, extrinsicism, in overlooking the mind of the investigator, also overlooks the investigator's judgment; and when judgment is overlooked, not only is certitude eliminated but also probable knowledge. When, however,

---

126 Hans-Georg Gadamer, *Wahrheit und Methode: Grundzüge einer philosophischen Hermeneutik* (Tübingen: J.C.B. Mohr, 1960; [2nd ed., 1965]). [In English, *Truth and Method*, trans. Joel Weinsheimer and Donald G. Marshall (New York: Crossroad, 1989.]

127 Gadamer, *Wahrheit und Methode* 283. [*Truth and Method* 299: 'The naivete of so-called historicism consists in the fact that it does not undertake this reflection, and in trusting to the fact that its procedure is methodical, it forgets its own historicity.']

smo, et in honorem revocato illo actu personali quo iudicatur, satis perspici potest non solum probabilia sed etiam in multis certa iudicia in scientiis empiricis ferri posse.

Et in primis antiquatae seu superatae hypotheses et theoriae non probabiliter tantum sed etiam certo reiciuntur. Deinde in ipsis theoriis, quae hodie uti 'optimae opiniones quae cognoscuntur' valent, etsi totum nisi probabile non sit, partes tamen omnes non ideo certitudine carent. Quod data occasione etiam a scientificis agnoscitur: ita cum theoria newtoniana theoriae Einsteinianae locum cessit,[128] illud ab omnibus agnitum est, mensurationes iam factas non esse reficiendas, cum nova theoria novum processum mensurandi non determinarit. Sed et aliud exemplum sit valor tabulae periodicae, quae per centum circiter elementa plus ter centena millia compositorum (non mixtorum) explicat: iam vero nemo diceret theorias subatomicas non posse theoriam elementorum mutare; quod tamen si fieret, ita fieri deberet ut salvae manerent quae iam sunt verificatae habitudines inter centum elementa et ter centena millia compositorum. Unde et illud generalius dici potest: ita superata theoria novae theoriae locum cedit, ut tamen ipsa nova theoria salvare debet tum phaenomena iam pridem accurate descripta, tum mensurationes et experimenta iam rite peracta, tum correlationes quae proxime ipsis mensurationibus inhaerent. Quid praecise per illud 'salvare debet' in singulis casibus significet nisi iudicio sapiente non dicitur. Sed iudicium sapiens haberi potest, non sane per deductionem necessariam et universalem, non per regulas cuiuslibet methodi, sed per agnitam prioritatem ipsius interioris mentis et per sapientiam particularem quae nisi lente, nisi per longum exercitium, singulis materiis adaptata non acquiritur.

(d') Accedit extrinsecismus *metaphysicus*. Intelligentia vulgari cognoscuntur *res quoad nos*, scilicet res cum habitudinibus suis ad nostros sensus, appetitus, emotiones, sentimenta, usus, fines. Per scientias cognoscuntur *res quoad se*, scilicet res cum habitudinibus ad alias res eiusdem ordinis; ita per tabulam periodicam cognoscuntur elementa secundum relationes uniuscuiusque ad caetera. Per abstractionem quandam considerari potest res praecisis omnibus relationibus sive ad nos sive ad alias res eiusdem or-

extrinsicism is rejected and that personal act by which we judge is restored to its place of honor, it becomes clear enough that in the sciences not only probable judgments can be made, but in many instances certain judgments as well.

First, antiquated or superseded hypotheses and theories are not only probably but indeed certainly discarded. Again, in the case of theories that are valid today as being 'the best opinion available,' even though the theory as a whole may be only probable, it does not follow that all of its parts lack certitude. On occasion this is acknowledged even by scientists: so, for example, when Newton's theory gave way to Einstein's,[128] all agreed that previous measurements need not be repeated, since the new theory had not determined a new procedure for measuring. Another example would be that of the validity of the periodic table, which explains more than 300,000 chemical compounds (not mixtures) by approximately 100 elements. Now, no one would say that subatomic theories could not modify the theory of the elements; but if that were to happen, it would have to be done in such a way as to retain the already verified relations between the 100 elements and the 300,000 compounds. This point, therefore, can be stated more generally as follows: an older theory is superseded by a new theory in such a way that the new theory must retain the phenomena already accurately described, the measurements and experiments that were properly done, and the correlations that are most closely involved with those measurements. What precisely the phrase 'must retain' may mean in each case is a matter for a wise judgment to determine. But wise judgments are possible, not, of course, through necessary and universal deductions, nor according to the rules of any method, but by acknowledging the priority of one's interior mental processes and by a particular wisdom that is acquired only gradually over time by years of practice in dealing with its specific subject matter.

(d') Metaphysical extrinsicism: Through ordinary everyday understanding we come to know things as they are *with respect to us*, that is to say, things in their various relationships to our senses, appetites, emotions, feelings, needs, and purposes. Through the sciences we come to know things as they are *with respect to themselves*, that is, things in their relationships to other realities of the same order; so through the periodic table we know elements according to the relations each one has to the others. Through abstraction

128 [At this point in the autograph, the date at the top of the page switches to 11-4-62.]

dinis, et sic concipitur *res-in-se*. E.g., anima prout praescinditur a duplici definitione aristotelica, (1) anima est actus primus corporis potentia vitam habentis, (2) anima est primum quo vivimus, sentimus, intelligimus.[129]

Iam vero eadem res est et quoad nos et quoad se; praeterea, altera cognita in cognitionem alterius ducit; ita ex cognitione rerum-quoad-nos proceditur in cognitionem scientificam; et ex cognitione scientifica reditur ad applicationes practicas. E contra, res-in-se non est nisi abstractio; abstractiones non exsistunt nisi in mente; neque cognoscuntur nisi ut entia rationis. Imo[130] res-in-se illicitam abstractionem importat ut potius merum nomen quam verus conceptus dicenda sit. Quod enim alicui essentiale est, ab eo illicite praescinditur; ipsa enim praecisio est implicita quaedam ipsius essentiae negatio. Ita anima humana est per se et essentialiter forma corporis (DB 481); et ideo ubi praescinditur ab habitudine animae ad corpus, ibi tollitur ipsa ratio animae. Pariter, manus est essentialiter organum, et organum est essentialiter pars corporis organici; unde conceptus manus-in-se importat negationem eius quod est manui essentiale. Pariter, omnis essentia finita est natura, seu principium intrinsecum remotum operationum; quae quidem operationes sunt vel transeuntes vel immanentes; et transeuntes eiusmodi sunt ut alias res afficiant aptae natae sunt, immanentes vero eiusmodi ut alias res cognoscant et appetant. Essentia-finita-in-se ergo vel negat rationem naturae, ut nullam habitudinem ad operationes habeat, vel negat rationem operationis ut nullam habitudinem ad alias res habeat.

Quibus secundum veritatem positis, nihilominus fatendum est iam per saecula de re-in-se et fusius scribi et acrius disputari. Quaenam praecise fuerint confusiones apud quosnam auctores, nisi per longiorem investigationem historicam non dicitur. Sed sequentia animadvertenda esse videntur.

we can consider things apart from all their relations both to us and to other realities of the same order, and so conceive the *thing-in-itself*. An example would be 'soul,' when one prescinds from both Aristotelian definitions: (1) the soul as the first act of a body capable of having life, and (2) the soul as the principle by which we live, sense, and understand.[129]

Now it is the very same things that are known both with respect to us and with respect to themselves. Besides, the knowledge of one leads to knowledge of the other; thus, knowledge of things as they are with respect to us leads to scientific knowledge, and scientific knowledge in turn leads to practical applications. On the other hand, a thing-in-itself is just an abstraction; abstractions exist only in the mind and are not known except as conceptual beings. In fact,[130] to speak of a thing-in-itself implies an illegitimate abstraction, which must accordingly be said to be a mere name rather than a true concept. It is illegitimate to prescind from an essential element of a thing, for such an abstraction is an implicit denial of the essence itself. Thus, the human soul is of itself and essentially the form of the body (DB 481, DS 902, ND 405); hence, in prescinding from its relation to the body, the essential notion of soul is denied. Similarly, the hand is essentially an organ and an organ is essentially a part of an organic body, and so the concept of 'hand-in-itself' implies a negation of what is essential to a hand. Similarly, every finite essence is a nature, that is, the remote intrinsic principle of operations. These operations are either transient or immanent; transient operations are those whose nature it is to affect other things, while immanent operations are those by which we know and desire other things. 'Finite-essence-in-itself,' therefore, either denies the notion of nature so as to deny its relation to operations, or it denies the notion of operation so as to deny its relation to other things.

Having stated these points in accordance with the dictates of truth, we must admit, however, that over the centuries there has been much ink spilled and much acrimonious debate over the 'thing-in-itself.' It would take a very lengthy historical investigation to tell just what were the confused notions entertained and by which writers. But the following observations would seem to be in order.

129 [For slightly more on the two definitions of 'soul' in Aristotle, see Lonergan, *Verbum* 32–33, with sources in Aristotle and for commentaries by Thomas on these sources given in footnotes.]

130 [At this point in the autograph, the date at the top of the page switches to 13-4-62.]

Ne confundentur res quoad se et res in se: neutra dicit habitudinem immediatam ad nostros sensus, sentimenta, usus; sed illa est obiectum scientiarum; haec autem ens rationis dubii valoris. Quod nullam habet habitudinem ad nostros sensus, sensibus non apparet; unde res in se opponitur meris apparentiis. E contra, res quoad nos dicit habitudinem ad nostros sensus; sed non ideo sequitur cognitionem rei quoad nos esse cognitionem apparentiarum. Falso laudantur scientiae quasi per ipsas cognoscantur res in se dum cognitio vulgaris nisi apparentias non cognoscit. Immerito concluderetur idealismus ex eo quod res in se neque cognosci potest neque exsistit. Inepte ad defensionem realismi laboraret qui rem in se et valide cognosci et realiter exsistere et strenuo assereret et diligenter probaret. Quinimo, argumenta idealistis praeberet. Inepte concipitur metaphysica uti scientia rerum in se; et falso inde concluderetur, sicut res-in-se nullam ad aliud quidquam habitudinem habeat, ita metaphysicam scientiam nullatenus habitudines habere sive ad cognitionem nostram sive ad obiecta aliarum scientiarum sed securissimam in nescio qua turri eburnea reponi.

(e′) Accedit extrinsecismus *intuitivus.* Huius tendentiae radix est epistemologica. Ad quaestionem criticam (quemadmodum fieri possit ut·obiectum cognoscatur) respondet: tum nos ideo obiecta cognoscere quia ea videmus, percipimus, inspicimus, intuemur, tum nos non posse immediate obiectum cognoscere nisi ea videmus, percipimus, inspicimus, intuemur.

Verba haec (videre, percipere, inspicere, intueri, et similia) sumuntur non sensu proprio sed analogico. Sensu proprio visionem ocularem dicunt. Sensu analogico de aliis actibus cognoscitivis adhibentur quatenus visioni oculari partim sunt similes et partim dissimiles. Ipsa similitudo non ex factis psychologicis investigatis manifestatur sed ex necessitate epistemologica concluditur. Scilicet, per se evidens reputatur subiectum non posse obiectum realiter distinctum immediate cognoscere nisi per actum qui aliquo modo similis sit visioni oculari. Nam sine tali similitudine non esset transcendens, et sine transcendentia non esset cognoscitivus. Sicut videre ergo, etiam audire, tangere, olfacere, gustare, conscium esse, intelligere, iudicare dicuntur vel dici possunt videre, percipere, conspicere, intueri. Quibus nominibus significatur (1) hos actus esse transcendentes, obiectorum cognoscitivos, et (2) nullam dari posse transcendentiam nisi per aliquam similitudinem ad visionem ocularem.

One must not confuse things as they are with respect to themselves and things-in-themselves. Neither of these indicates an immediate relation to our senses, feelings, and needs. But the former is the object of the sciences; the latter is a conceptual being of doubtful value. That which has no relation to our senses is not perceptible to the senses; hence, a thing-in-itself is opposed to mere appearances. A thing as it is with respect to us, by contrast, indicates a relation to our senses; but it does not follow from this that knowledge of a thing as it is with respect to us is knowledge of appearances. It is erroneous to extol the sciences as if they know things-in-themselves while ordinary knowledge knows only appearances. It would be wrong to conclude to idealism from the fact that a thing-in-itself is not knowable and does not exist. It would be a wrong-headed defense of realism to assert vehemently and take great pains to prove that things-in-themselves are validly known and really exist. In fact, such an attempt would furnish idealists with arguments. It would likewise be quite wrong to conceive metaphysics as the science of things-in-themselves, and to draw from this the false conclusion that as a thing-in-itself has no relation to anything else, so the science of metaphysics has no relation either to our knowledge or to the objects of other sciences, but dwells safely locked away in some ivory tower.

(e′) Intuitionist extrinsicism: The root of this tendency is epistemological. To the critical question How is it possible to know an object? it responds: We know objects because we see them, perceive them, look at them, intuit them, and we cannot have immediate knowledge of objects without seeing, perceiving, looking at, intuiting them.

These verbs (to see, perceive, look at, intuit, and similar ones) are used not in their literal sense but analogously. Properly speaking they refer to ocular vision. In an analogous sense they are used to refer to other cognitive acts as being partly like and partly unlike ocular vision. This similarity is not arrived at by investigating psychological facts, but is concluded to from epistemological necessity. That is, it is thought to be self-evident that a subject cannot immediately know an object really distinct from itself except by an act that is in some way similar to ocular vision. For without such a similarity the act would not be transcendent, and without transcendence it would not be cognitive. In like manner, therefore, hearing, touching, smelling, tasting, being conscious, understanding, and judging are also said to be, or can be said to be, a seeing, a perceiving, a looking, an intuiting. These words signify (1) that these acts are transcendent, knowing objects, and (2) that no transcendence is possible except through something similar to ocular vision.

Quod epistemologicum intuitionismi principium non reputamus nisi mythum. Verum est nos non posse *imaginatione repraesentare* transcendentiam cognitionis nisi per imaginem visionis ocularis vel alterius similis. Falsum est transcendentiam in eo consistere quod sic imaginatione repraesentatur; nam re vera ideo cognitio humana (non dico animalem cognitionem) est transcendens quia inconditionatum attingit; quod enim inconditionatum est, conditiones iam non habet; quod conditiones non iam habet, sicut ab aliis ita etiam a subiecto cognoscente independens est; quod ita est independens, subiectum transcendit.

Qui tamen mythus non parum influit in theorias cognitionis tum realisticas tum idealisticas. Realistae asserunt nos videre, intueri, non meras apparentias sed ipsam realitatem, et quidem nos videre, percipere, non solum sensibus sed etiam intellectu. Exemplo sit E. Gilson, *Réalisme thomiste et critique de la connaissance*, Paris, Vrin, 1939.[131] P. 203: 'Ainsi, de quelque manière et à quelque profondeur de plan que nous lui posions la question: comment savoir qu'une chose existe? le réalisme répond: en la percevant.' P. 215: 'On peut donc tenir pour certain, dès le début de cette nouvelle enquête, que l'apprehension de l'être par l'intellect consiste à *voir* directement le concept d'être dans n'importe quelle donnée sensible.'[132] P. 225: 'Mais l'intellect peut *voir* l'être dans le sensible que nous percevons.'[133] P. 225 s.: '... le jugement qui prédique l'être de cet existant le lui attribue tel que le conçoit l'intellect, c'est à dire comme "vu" dans le sensible donné dont il l'abstrait.'

Our position is that the epistemological foundation of intuitionism is simply a myth. It is true that we cannot *imagine* the transcendent nature of knowledge except by way of a likeness to ocular vision or something similar. But it is false to think that transcendence consists in what we imagine it to be. The fact is that human knowledge (we are not talking about animal knowledge) is transcendent because it attains the unconditioned. For what is unconditioned no longer has conditions; what no longer has conditions is independent of a knowing subject just as it is of other things; and what is thus independent transcends the subject.

This myth has exerted enormous influence upon both realist and idealist theories of knowledge. Realists assert that we see, intuit, not mere appearances but reality itself, and indeed that we see and perceive not only by our senses but also by our intellect. See, for example, Étienne Gilson, *Réalisme thomiste et critique de la connaissance.*[131] P. 203: 'Ainsi, de quelque manière et à quelque profondeur de plan que nous lui posions la question: comment savoir qu'une chose existe? le réalisme répond: en la percevant.' [P. 186: 'Thus, no matter in what manner nor with what profundity we may pose the question as to how we know that something exists, realism will always respond: by perceiving it.'] P. 215: 'On peut donc tenir pour certain, dès le début de cette nouvelle enquête, que l'appréhension de l'être par l'intellect consiste à *voir* directement le concept d'être dans n'importe quelle donnée sensible.' [P. 197: 'This much is certain, then, from the beginning of this new inquiry: the apprehension of being by the intellect consists of directly seeing the concept of being in some sensible datum.'][132] P. 225: 'Mais l'intellect peut *voir* l'être dans le sensible que nous percevons.' [P. 205: 'But the intellect is able to see being in the sensible objects we perceive.'][133] Pp. 225–26: '... le jugement qui prédique l'être de cet existant le lui attribue tel que le conçoit l'intellect, c'est-à-dire comme "vu" dans le sensible donné dont il l'abstrait.' [P. 205: '... the judgment which predicates being of this

---

131 Étienne Gilson, *Réalisme thomiste et critique de la connaissance* (Paris: Librairie philosophique J. Vrin, 1939). [In English, *Thomist Realism and the Critique of Knowledge*, trans. Mark A. Wauck (San Francisco: Ignatius Press, 1986). The English translations of the French texts cited by Lonergan are included in brackets after the French texts, along with the page numbers of the translation from *Thomist Realism*.]

132 [In *Réalisme thomiste* Gilson italicized 'voir,' but in Wauck's translation 'seeing' is not italicized.]

133 [Again, in *Réalisme thomiste* Gilson italicized 'voir,' but Wauck's translation does not italicize 'see.']

E contra Kant in sua *Kritik der reinen Vernunft* quamvis formas sensibilitatis, categorias intellectus, ideas rationis habeat a priori, quamvis asserat omnem nostram intuitionem non esse nisi apparentium, tamen principio generali de necessitate intuitionis omnino cum Gilson concordat. Incipit transcendentalis aesthetica: 'Auf welche Art und durch welche Mittel sich auch immer eine Erkenntnis auf Gegenstände beziehen mag, so ist doch diejenige, wodurch sie sich auf dieselbe unmittelbar bezieht, und worauf alles Denken als Mittel absweckt, die Anshauung.' A 19; B 33; Akd. IV, 29; III, 49.[134] Initio logicae transcendentalis: 'Anschauung und Begriffe machen also die Elemente aller unserer Erkenntnis aus ...' 'Gedanken ohne Inhalt sind leer, Anschauungen ohne Begriffe sind blind.' A 50 s.; B 74 s.; Akd. IV, 47 s.; III, 74 s.[135]

Quia sola immediata obiecti cognitio est intuitio, iudicium nisi mediatam cognitionem non praestat: 'Das Urteil ist also die mittelbare Erkenntnis eines Gegenstands, mithin die Vorstellung einer Vorstellung desselben.' A 68; B 93; Akd. IV, 58; III, 85.[136] Unde et ideae rationis longius ab obiecto cognoscendo inveniuntur cum immediate nisi intellectum eiusque usum non attingunt: 'Die Vernunft bezieht sich niemals geradezu auf einen Gegenstand, sondern lediglich auf den Verstand und vermittelst desselben auf ihren eigenen empirischen Gebrauch.' B 671; Akd. III, 427; A 643.[137]

existent attributes being to it according to the way it is conceived by the intellect, namely as "seen" in the sensible datum from which it is abstracted.']

On the other hand, although Kant, in his *Kritik der reinen Vernunft*, posits *a priori* forms of sensibility, intellectual categories, and ideas of reason, and although he asserts that all our intuiting is of appearances only, nevertheless in his general principle about the necessity of intuition he and Gilson are in complete agreement. His transcendental aesthetic begins thus: 'Auf welche Art und durch welche Mittel sich auch immer eine Erkenntnis auf Gegenstände beziehen mag, so ist doch diejenige, wodurch sie sich auf dieselbe unmittelbar bezieht, und worauf alles Denken als Mittel absweckt, die Anschauung' (A 19; B 33). ['In whatever manner and by whatever means a mode of knowledge may relate to objects, *intuition* is that through which it is in immediate relation to them, and to which all thought as a means is directed.']¹³⁴ And at the beginning of his transcendental logic: 'Anschauung und Begriffe machen also die Elemente aller unserer Erkenntnis aus …' 'Gedanken ohne Inhalt sind leer, Anschauungen ohne Begriffe sind blind' (A 50, 51; B 74, 75). ['Intuition and concept constitute, therefore, the elements of all our knowledge … Thoughts without content are empty, intuitions without concepts are blind.']¹³⁵

Because intuition is the sole immediate knowledge of an object, Kant holds judgment to be but a mediated knowledge: 'Das Urteil ist also die mittelbare Erkenntnis eines Gegenstands, mithin die Vorstellung einer Vorstellung desselben' (A 68; B 93). ['Judgment is therefore the mediate knowledge of an object, that is, the representation of a representation of it.']¹³⁶ Hence, the ideas of reason are found at a further remove from the object to be known since they immediately touch only the intellect and its function: 'Die Vernunft bezieht sich niemals geradezu auf einen Gegenstand, sondern lediglich auf den Verstand und vermittelst desselben auf ihren eigenen empirischen Gebrauch …' (A 643, B 671). ['Reason is never in immediate relation to an object, but only to the understanding, and it is only through the understanding that it has its own (specific) empirical employment.']¹³⁷

---

134 [Translation here and following are by Norman Kemp Smith. See Immanuel Kant, *Critique of Pure Reason*, unabr. ed., trans. Norman Kemp Smith (New York: St Martin's Press, 1965) 65.]
135 [Ibid. 92, 93.]
136 [Ibid. 105.]
137 [Ibid. 532–33.]

Breviter: nulla est immediata relatio cognitionis ad obiectum nisi per intuitionem; iudicia nisi mediate obiecta non attingunt; ideae rationis duplici mediatione indigent tum intellectus tum ipsius intuitionis. Quam ob causam, cum omnis nostra intuitio (*Anschauung*) non sit nisi apparentium, ipse validus et legitimus usus intellectus et rationis non potest conducere nisi ad validitatem quandam phaenomenalem; et ulterius, cum sine intuitione nullum prorsus attingatur obiectum, usus rationis ultra campum phaenomenalem reputatur illusio transcendentalis.

Unde concludes: idem principium epistemologicum (nempe, *voir, percevoir, anschauen* esse conditionem necessariam possibilitatis obiectum cognoscendi) dupliciter adhiberi posse: uno modo, a realista uti E. Gilson, qui quandam entis visionem intellectui humano astruat; alio modo, a Kant, qui intuitiones nostras ad apparentias restringat.

Ulterius concludes: sententiam a Gilson propugnatam – realismum criticum esse contradictionem; doctrinam aut esse realisticam et non criticam, aut criticam et tunc non realisticam[138] – fundari secundum quid sed non simpliciter. Fundatur secundum quid, quatenus per nomen realismi intelligitur realismus intuitivus; supposita enim necessitate transcendentali intuitionis, id quod per intuitionem videtur, conspicitur, percipitur, necessario est aut reale aut apparentia. Non fundatur simpliciter, nam uti iam diximus, asserta necessitas intuitionis (ut cognitio obiecti sit possibilis) non est nisi mythus.

Ulterius concludes: realismum criticum non dicere contradictionem. Realismus quidem est quia ens per verum iudicium cognoscit. Criticus est quia mythum reicit sive a realistis intuitivis sive ab idealistis criticis propugnatur.

Ulterius concludes: realismum criticum magis quam realismum intuitivum a doctrina Kantiana recedere. Realismus enim intuitivus concedit praemissam maiorem Kantianam, necessariam esse intuitionem, et tantummodo negat praemissam minorem, intuitionem nostram esse apparentium. Realismus autem criticus negat tum maiorem Kantianam tum minorem: cognitio humana est transcendens, non propter imaginem intuitionis, sed propter inconditionatum virtuale actu intelligendi reflexo perspectum; experientia humana sensitiva non est apparentium sed datorum; quinimo

In short: there is no immediate relation of knowledge to an object except through intuition; judgments reach their objects only mediately; ideas of reason need the twofold mediation of the intellect and the intuition itself. For this reason, since all our intuition (*Anschauung*) is of appearances only, the valid and legitimate use of the intellect and of reason can lead to only phenomenal validity; and furthermore, since without intuition no object whatsoever is arrived at, the use of reason beyond the field of phenomena is to be regarded as a transcendental illusion.

From this we conclude that the same epistemological principle, namely, that seeing, *voir, percevoir, anschauen,* is the necessary condition of the possibility of knowing an object, can be used in two different ways: by realists like Gilson, who give to the human intellect a vision of being, and by Kant, who restricts our intuitions to appearances.

We conclude further that Gilson's opinion that critical realism is a contradiction, that a position is either realistic and non-critical, or is critical and non-realistic,[138] has a foundation in a qualified sense only and not absolutely. It has a foundation in a qualified sense if by realism one means intuitive realism: supposing the transcendental necessity of intuition, what is seen, looked at, and perceived by an intuition is necessarily either real or apparent. But it is without foundation absolutely speaking, for, as we have said, the assertion that intuition is necessary for an object to be knowable is but a myth.

We further conclude that critical realism is not a contradiction. It is realism because it knows being through true judgment; it is critical because it rejects the myth defended by both the intuitive realists and the critical idealists.

We further conclude that critical realism is farther from the Kantian position than intuitive realism is. For intuitive realism concedes Kant's major premise, that intuition is necessary, and denies only his minor premise, that our intuition is of appearances. Critical realism, however, denies both Kantian premises: human knowledge is transcendent not because of a similarity to intuition but because of its grasp of a virtually unconditioned in a reflective act of understanding; human sense experience is not an experience of appearances but of data; as a matter of fact, it cannot be an experience of

138 Gilson, *Réalisme thomiste et critique de la connaissance* 38 note, 39, 44–45, 77–78, 128, 154, 160 note, 161–62, 179 note, 182. [*Thomist Realism* 51–52, note 32, 53, 57–58, 83–85, 126–27, 147–48, 152 note 2, 153–54, 166–67 (probably) note 7, 169–70.]

apparentium esse non potest, nam distinctio inter id quod est et id quod tantum apparet non fit a sensu sed a iudicio rationali (e.g., baculus est rectus sed aquae immersus apparet [= non est] curvus).

Momentum huius disputationis, quantum rem methodologicam attinet, maximum est. Eatenus enim methodologia accurate determinari potest, quatenus facta circa intelligentiam et rationalitatem humanam accurate concipiuntur et vere dicuntur. Iam vero mythica illa necessitas, omnem actum cognoscitivum visioni oculari quodammodo esse similem, continuo veritatem psychologicam impedit et fictiones fabricationesque suadet. Neque tantum in campo psychologico sed etiam in campo hermeneutico: exemplo sit C.R. Fay,[139] qui in sensu contradictorio interpretatus est *De ver.* q. 1, a. 9; ubi S. Thomas dicit veritatem actus cognosci non posse nisi cognita natura actus, et naturam actus cognosci non posse nisi cognoscatur natura principii activi, ille dicit naturam principii activi cognosci non posse nisi perspecta ipsa re et perspecta conformitate intellectus ad rem; quod quidem asserit, per modum interpretationis manifestae.

(c) Excluditur immanentismus.

(a′) Sicut extrinsecismus ita mundis aspectabili et intelligibili inhaeret ut mundum interiorem praetermittat, ita immanentismus ita mundo interiori includitur ut mundum exteriorem aspectabilem vel intelligibilem attingere non valeat.

Transitus ex extrinsecismo in immanentismum fit per problema criticum. Exigentia enim critica est ne quis de iis loquatur quae neque scit neque scire potest. Cui exigentiae satis fieri non potest nisi extrinsecismus deponitur, ad interioritatem reditur, et actus cognoscitivi indicantur quibus unumquodque, de quo quis loquitur, vel cognoscitur vel saltem cognosci potest.

At ipsa haec exigentia critica sat facile errorem et malum oppositum inducit. Arduum enim et longum est ad claram distinctamque notitiam cognitionis humanae pervenire. Neque enim ipsi actus cognoscitivi ut actus facile observantur et inter se ordinantur. Neque idem actus qua cognoscitivi facile explicantur quemadmodum obiecta attingunt. Accedit quod inter se dependent solutio prioris et psychologicae quaestionis et solutio posterioris

appearances, for the distinction between what is and what only appears to be is not made by the senses but by rational judgment (for example, that a straight stick thrust into water only looks, i.e., is not, bent).

The importance of this dispute as it touches upon methodology is immense. A methodology can be accurately established only insofar as the facts about human intelligence and rationality are accurately conceived and correctly enunciated. But that mythical necessity of thinking that all cognitional acts are in some way similar to ocular vision gets continually in the way of psychological truth and fosters figments and fabrications. And this is true not only in the area of psychology, but also in that of hermeneutics: for example, C.R. Fay, who has interpreted *De veritate*, q. 1, a. 9, in a contradictory sense.[139] Where St Thomas says that the truth of an act cannot be known unless the nature of that act is known, and the nature of an act cannot be known unless the nature of the active principle is known, Fay states that the nature of the active principle cannot be known unless both the thing itself is grasped and also the conformity of the intellect to the thing. In fact, he asserts this as an obvious interpretation.

(c) Immanentism is ruled out.

(a′) As extrinsicism is so closely bound up with the visible and intelligible worlds that it overlooks the world of interiority, so immanentism is so confined to the world of interiority that it cannot reach the visible or intelligible external worlds.

The transition from extrinsicism to immanentism is made by way of the critical problem. The critical exigence requires that one should not speak about what one neither knows nor is able to know. This exigence cannot be satisfied unless one abandons extrinsicism, returns to interiority, and indicates the cognitive acts by which one knows, or at least can know, everything about which one speaks.

This critical exigence, however, quite easily leads to the opposite error and evil. For it is an arduous and lengthy task to arrive at a clear and distinct knowledge of human cognition. Cognitive acts as acts are not easily observed and related to one another. Nor, again, is it easy to explain how these same acts as cognitive reach their objects. In addition, there is the fact that the solution to the prior psychological question and the solution to the

---

139 Cornelius Ryan Fay, 'Fr. Lonergan and the Participation School,' *The New Scholasticism* 34 (1960) 461–87, at 483–84.

et epistemologicae quaestionis; ut qui solutionem epistemologicam ignorat, facta psychologica vix observare possit; et qui facta psychologica ignorat, solutionem epistemologicam vix concipere possit. Neque haec sufficiunt. Ut de ipsis factis psychologicis disseras, ut de obiectis eorumque ad actus psychologicos habitudine loquaris, theoriam quandam metaphysicam saltem implicite adhibeas necesse est. Quare, quamvis breviter et rationabiliter exigentia critica proponatur, ei tamen non satis fit nisi simul fere solvuntur quaestiones maxime fundamentales et psychologicae et epistemologicae et metaphysicae. Quibus vel nullatenus vel imperfecte solutis exigentia critica ita extrinsecismum tollit ut immanentismum imponat.

(b′)[140] Ad immanentismum excludendum gressus fundamentalis est iam peracta iudicii analysis, quae simul psychologica, epistemologica, et metaphysica quasi in radice tangit.

Haec enim analysis psychologica est quatenus narrat facta: nos quaerere an sit (utrum, e.g., haec iudicii analysis vera sit); nos evidentiam eamque sufficientem exigere; syllogismo sive explicito sive implicito proponi inconditionatum quoddam virtuale; conditionatum quidem sufficere non posse, inconditionatum vero non posse non sufficere ad iudicium absolute ponendum; nos per iudicium absolute ponere quod iam perspeximus esse inconditionatum, et quidem necessitate rationali.

Eadem analysis epistemologica est. Nam eatenus cognitio nostra subiectum transcendit, quatenus inconditionatum attingitur. Quod enim inconditionatum virtuale est, illud conditiones non iam habet; quod conditiones non iam habet, neque in aliis rebus neque in ipso subiecto conditiones iam habet; quod in ipso subiecto conditiones iam non habet, subiectum transcendit, ab eo independens est, ex-sistit.

(Obici potest sic haberi transcendentiam non absolutam sed relativam, ut scilicet affectiones, modificationes, desideria, timores, subiectivitas cognoscentis transcendantur, sed relativitas ad modum cognoscendi humanum maneat. Respondetur modum cognoscendi humanum esse ut ita dicam transparentem; eiusmodi scilicet esse ut conditiones cognoscendi sint ipsae conditiones transcendendi. Radicitus enim conditiones cognitionis humanae sunt duae: proxima, ut iudicium ex perspecto inconditionato procedat;

subsequent epistemological question depend upon each other. Thus, one who does not know the epistemological solution will hardly be able to observe the psychological facts, and one who is ignorant of the psychological facts will hardly be able to conceive the epistemological solution. And that is not all. In order to discuss these psychological facts, to speak about their objects and their relation to psychological acts, one necessarily uses, at least implicitly, some metaphysical theory. Accordingly, even though the critical exigence is briefly and reasonably proposed, it will not be satisfied unless the most basic questions of psychology, epistemology, and metaphysics are fairly well solved at the same time. If these questions are not solved, or if they are solved only imperfectly, the critical exigence will banish extrinsicism only to bring in immanentism in its place.

(b')[140] The fundamental step in ruling out immanentism is our previous analysis of judgment, which simultaneously goes to the root of psychology, epistemology, and metaphysics.

This analysis is psychological inasmuch as it narrates facts: the fact that we ask, 'Is it so?' (whether, for example, this analysis of judgment is true); that we demand evidence, evidence that is sufficient; that in a syllogism, either explicit or implicit, we propose a virtually unconditioned; that a conditioned cannot suffice, but that an unconditioned cannot not suffice for making a judgment absolutely; that we posit absolutely through judgment, and this by rational necessity, what we have grasped as unconditioned.

This same analysis is epistemological. For insofar as our knowledge attains the unconditioned, it transcends the subject. What is virtually unconditioned no longer has conditions; that which no longer has conditions has no conditions either in other things or in the subject; and that which no longer has conditions in the subject is independent of that subject, it transcends the subject, it 'ex-sists.'

(One might object that here there is only relative, not absolute, transcendence, that is, that the feelings, moods, desires, fears, and subjectivity of the knower are transcended, but that relativity to the human manner of knowing remains. To this we would reply that the human manner of knowing is, so to speak, transparent; that is, it is such that the conditions of knowledge are the very conditions of transcendence. Radically there are two conditions of human knowledge: a proximate condition, that judgment

140 [At this point in the autograph, the date at the top of the page switches to 15-4-62.]

remota, ut totus cognoscendi processus per non restrictam capacitatem et exigentiam regatur, scilicet, per intellectum qui est potens omnia facere et fieri, per animam quae est quodammodo omnia, per naturale cognoscendi desiderium quod de omnibus, etiam de Deo infinito, quaerit quid sit, et de omni quidditate dubitet an sit. Iam vero hae cognoscendi conditiones etiam transcendendi conditiones sunt: absolutae enim transcendentiae proportionantur tum non restricta capacitas et exigentia tum huius capacitatis ad unum determinatio per inconditionatum.)

Eadem denique analysis metaphysica est. Quod enim iudicio ponitur, per 'esse' ponitur; iudicamus enim quatenus affirmamus, Est, vel Non est. Quod autem per 'esse' ponitur, est ens: nam ens ab esse dicitur; vel ens est cui suo modo competit esse. Quod denique metaphysica tractat, nihil est aliud quam ens.

(c′) Quod si excluditur immanentismus per analysin iudicii rite peractam, sequitur omnis immanentismi radicem in eadem analysi non rite peracta reponi.

Unde concludes non ipsum morbum sed morbi tantummodo symptoma eo inveniri ubi sensibilia reputantur mere apparentia vel ubi impugnatur intuitionismus. Ubi enim rite peragitur iudicii analysis, statim perspicitur sensibilia non qua sensa sed qua iudicata dici apparentia, vel reiecto intuitionismo minime ideo esse reiciendum realismum.

E contra, ubi deponuntur illusiones circa rem-in-se, circa sensibilia uti mere apparentia, circa intuitionismum, ibi non ideo ab immanentismo receditur. Cogita Hegelianos, apud quos tamen iudicium non est nisi conceptuum compositio, et alia quidem alia perfectior donec ad perfectissimam perveniatur quae in identitate intelligibilitatis consistat, e.g., hominem esse rationalem.[141]

(d′) Sed et subtilior quaedam est recens immanentismi forma sui parum conscia, quae fortiter sese idealismo opponit, non quia inconditionatum, transcendens, verum, ens attigerit, sed quia vel (1) realitatem in experto, vel (2) esse in viso reponit.

Qui realitatem in experto reponit, Deum se cognoscere opinatur, non

proceed from a grasp of the unconditioned; and a remote condition, that the whole cognitional process be governed by an unrestricted capacity and exigence, that is, by an intellect that is in potency to make and become all things, by a soul that is in a way all things through its natural desire to know that asks about everything, even about an infinite God, What is it?, and wonders about every quiddity, Is it really so? Now these conditions of knowledge are also conditions of transcendence, for both this unrestricted capacity and exigence and the determination of this capacity to one thing through an unconditioned are proportioned to absolute transcendence.)

Finally, this analysis is metaphysical. What is stated in a judgment is stated in terms of 'to be,' for we judge inasmuch as we affirm, 'It is,' or, 'It is not.' Now, what is affirmed in terms of 'to be' is being, for being is expressed in terms of 'to be': being is that to which it belongs to be in its own proper way. And metaphysics treats of nothing other than being.

(c′) If immanentism is rejected through a correct analysis of judgment, it follows that the root of all immanentism lies in a faulty analysis of judgment.

Hence, we may conclude that it is not the morbid condition itself but only a symptom of it that is found where sensible realities are looked upon as mere appearances or where intuitionism is attacked. For when an analysis of judgment is done correctly, it is immediately clear that sensible realities are said to be appearances not as sensed but as judged, or that the rejection of intuitionism by no means entails the rejection of realism.

On the other hand, dispelling illusions about things-in-themselves, about sensible realities as being mere appearances, and about intuitionism, does not by that fact mean a retreat from immanentism. Think of the Hegelians, for whom judgment is only a composition of concepts, one more perfect than the other until the most perfect one is reached, which consists in the identity of intelligibility, for example, that man is rational.[141]

(d′) But more recently there has emerged a subtler form of immanentism, scarcely aware of itself, that strenuously opposes idealism, not because it has reached the unconditioned, the transcendent, truth, and being, but because it either (1) identifies the real with that which is experienced or (2) identifies existence with that which is seen.

Those for whom reality is what is experienced are of the opinion that

---

141   W.T. Stace, *The Philosophy of Hegel: A Systematic Exposition* (London: Macmillan and Co., 1924, and New York: Dover, 1955) 231-47.

quia per verum iudicium apprehendat ens, non quia per assensum intellectualem fidei in dogmata Auctorem salutis cognoscat, sed quia ei tam realis
est vita sua religiosa quam reliqua quam agit vita. Recole quae superius e
Gabriel Marcel citavimus; vel eos cogita quos allicit titulus, *Our Experience of
God*, auctore H.D. Lewis;[142] vel etiam seminaristas, ne dicam theologiae professores, qui antiquam theologiam ab ontologia hellenistica et mediaevali
quodammodo purgandam esse censeant. Sed contra Aquinas qui reputavit
nos esse divinum cognoscere quatenus veram cognoscimus esse propositionem, Deus est.[143]

Qua in re omnino distinguendum est inter (1) errorem theologicum et
(2) defectum evolutionis seu conversionis intellectualis. Error in eo consistit quod negantur quae in Vaticano docentur, DB 1789, 1792, 1820. Defectus
evolutionis seu conversionis intellectualis in eo consistit quod mirum, imo
incredibile, homini videtur se 'realiter realia' realiter cognoscere per mera
iudicia vera. Qui defectus rarius et difficilius corrigitur. Quem enim parvuli
realitatis sensum ante usum rationis formavimus, eundem per reliquam vitam invincibili quodam instinctu aestimamus tutissimum et securissimum.
Tam enim per animalitatem quam per rationalitatem definitur homo.

Qui vero esse in viso, perspecto, reponunt, non solum sensum videntem
sed etiam intellectum in sensibilibus intelligentem significant. Ultra phaenomenologiam procedunt ut ontologicam quandam statuant. Quae tamen
a Thomistica differt, cum verum et ens in illo intelligibili sese manifestante
inveniatur quod in ipsis sensibilibus elucet. Ita opus artis homini attenden-
ti, intelligenti, contemplanti manifestat pulchrum, verum in sensibilibus,
possibilitatem secundum quam quis homo *esse* possit. Quod tamen verum
intuitioni per artem exhibetur, idem a philosopho reflectente et indagante
quaeritur, idemque a philosopho attingitur quatenus tum ad esse (humanum) tum ad se ipsum intelligendum pervenit.[144] Quae tamen esse et sui
ipsius intelligentia non hypothesis habetur inconditionato mensuranda et

they know God, not because they apprehend being by a true judgment, nor because they know the Author of salvation through an intellectual assent of faith to dogmas, but because for them their religious life is as real as all the other aspects of their life. Recall the quotation from Gabriel Marcel, above; or think of those intrigued by the title of a book, *Our Experience of God* by H.D. Lewis;[142] or even seminarians, not to mention professors of theology, who think that an age-old theology needs somehow to be purged of Hellenistic and medieval ontology. But on the other side, think of Aquinas who considered that we know the existence of the divine inasmuch as we know that the proposition 'God is' is true.[143]

In this matter it is of utmost importance to distinguish between (1) theological error, and (2) a lack of development or intellectual conversion. Error consists in denying what the [First] Vatican Council teaches (DB 1789, 1792, 1820; DS 3008, 3011, 3045; ND 118, 121, 140). The lack of development or intellectual conversion consists in the fact that people think it extraordinary, indeed incredible, that they really know the 'really real' simply by true judgments. This defect is quite rarely and only with considerable difficulty corrected. By some ineradicable instinct, we adults consider to be absolutely safe and sound through the rest of our lives that sense of reality that we formed as little children before attaining the use of reason. After all, animality enters as much into the definition of man as rationality.

But those who place existence in what is seen or perceived are referring not only to the sense seeing but also to the intellect understanding in sense data. They go beyond phenomenology to set up an ontology. The ontology, however, differs from Thomist ontology, since [for it] truth and being are found in the manifesting of the same intelligibility that shines out in the sensible data. Thus, to one who attends to, understands, and contemplates it, a work of art manifests the beautiful, the true in sensible data, and the potentiality by which any person can *be*. The same truth that is apprehended by intuition through art is sought by a philosopher who reflects and inquires, and is attained by him inasmuch as he arrives both at (human) existence and at his own self-understanding.[144] Yet this existence

---

142 [Hywel David Lewis, *Our Experience of God* (London: Allen & Unwin; New York: Macmillan and Co., 1959).]
143 Thomas Aquinas, *Summa theologiae*, 1, q. 3, a. 4, ad 2m.
144 Rudolf Bultmann, 'Das Problem der Hermeneutik,' *Zeitschrift für Theologie und Kirche* 47 (1950) 47–69, at 56–57; reprinted in *Glauben und Verstehen*, vol. 2 (Tübingen: J.C.B. Mohr [Paul Siebeck], 1961) 211–35, at 221–23. [In

iudicio affirmanda vel neganda sed, his gressibus oblitis, ad ordinem voluntarium statim proceditur ut quis eligat utrum talem possibilitatem humanam in se ipso efficere decernat, vel, ut rem religiosam tangam, utrum
occasione praedicationis evangelicae per fidem quandem fiducialem ad
Deum voluntarius accedat.

Iam vero, ubi verum, esse, onticum, ontologicum ita concipiuntur, nominibus et verbis potius quam re et veritate ab immanentismo receditur.
Quam enim identificationem realitatis et rationalitatis tum obiective tum
subiective tum absolute posuit Hegel (illa nempe quae conceptum antecedit et ad conceptum tendit), eadem fere hic repetitur, non tamen generaliter, sed quatenus genesin (eamque in ordine practico) respicit nunc huius
nunc illius libere electae ideae *tou* hominem esse.

(d) Omnesque quaestiones ad duas reducantur, Quid sit, et An sit.[145]
Ea scilicet lege integrari potest nova scientiae differentiatio cum doctrina
traditionali, ut ad radicem priorem et communem reducantur quae inter
se contradictorie opponuntur, uti necessarium et contingens, universale et
singulare, immobile et motus, per se et per accidens.

Quae quidem radix praeconceptualis sit, necesse est, nam conceptus
contradictorie opponuntur. Praeconceptualia autem sunt tum ipsae quaestiones tum intelligendi actus: ideo enim formantur conceptus ut quaestionibus respondeatur et quod intellectum est exprimatur.

Et quaestiones quidem ita ad responsa conducunt ut eadem non determinant. Qui enim quaerit quid sit, intelligibilitatem quaerit, neque a priori
determinat utrum quaesita intelligibilitas sit necessaria an empirica, universalis in multis an singularis in exemplo unico, immobilis per omnia tempora vel temporum decursu sese evolvens, per se uti in lege classica vel ex ipsis
quae per accidens sunt hausta uti in lege statistica.

Qui autem intelligibilitatem quandam attingit perfectam vel imperfectam, essentialem vel analogicam, ordinis vel naturalis vel supernaturalis,
non ideo ad ens et verum pertingit sed ad synthesin quandam quae, utrum

and self-understanding are not had as a hypothesis to be measured by the unconditioned and affirmed or denied by a judgment; instead, oblivious to these steps, people proceed immediately to the volitional order to decide whether they should choose to actualize this human potentiality in themselves, or, in reference to religion, whether on the occasion of hearing the gospel they should willingly approach God by a trusting faith.

Now when truth, existence, the ontic, and the ontological are thus conceived, the retreat from immanentism is more a matter of vocabulary than of truth and reality. For the identity between reality and rationality that Hegel asserted objectively, subjectively, and absolutely (namely, the identity that precedes a concept and tends towards a concept), is virtually repeated here, not, however, in a general sense, but insofar as it regards the genesis, in the practical order, of now this person's and now that person's freely chosen idea of 'to be human.'

(d) All questions are reducible to two: What is it? and Is it so?[145]

The law that makes it possible for a new differentiation of science to be integrated with traditional teaching is that what are contradictorily opposed to each other, such as the necessary and the contingent, the universal and the singular, the unchangeable and change, the *per se* and the *per accidens*, can be reduced to a prior common root.

This root must be preconceptual, for the concepts are mutually contradictory. The preconceptual elements are the questions themselves and the acts of understanding; for concepts are formed to answer questions and express what has been understood.

Questions lead to but do not determine answers. For when one asks, What is it?, one is seeking intelligibility, and does not predetermine whether the intelligibility one is seeking is necessary or empirical, a universal found in many instances or a singular present in a unique instance, absolutely unchangeable or evolving in the course of time, obtained from what is *per se*, as in classical laws, or from what is *per accidens*, as in statistical laws.

However, even if one attains some intelligibility, perfect or imperfect, essential or analogical, in the natural or supernatural order, it does not follow that one has thereby reached being and truth; one has reached a

---

English, 'The Problem of Hermeneutics (1950),' in *New Testament and Mythology and Other Basic Writings*, selected, ed., and trans. by Schubert M. Ogden (Philadelphia: Fortress Press, 1984) 69–93, at 77–79.

145 [Chapter 1962-6 in *Early Works on Theological Method 1* corresponds to some material from this point to the end of the present text. See below, note 152.]

realiter exsistat, per ulteriorem quaestionem, An sit, investigandum est. Numquam enim illi extrinsecismo indulgendum est qui evidens sine evidentiam perspiciente, verum sine sapienter reflectente, certum sine responsabiliter iudicante astruat.

(e) Qua reductione peracta, fundatur unitas non solum theologiae sed et omnis cognitionis proprie humanae.

(a') Omnis enim quaestio (quid sit, an sit) intendit 'ens.' Omne iudicium affirmat vel negat 'esse.' Omnis conceptus, sicut ad praeparandum iudicium ordinatur, ita etiam ad 'esse' ordinatur; quod autem ad 'esse' ordinatur, est 'ens'; et ideo omnis conceptus saltem implicite est conceptus entis.

(b') Proinde, cognitio proprie humana non atomistica est sed composita. Non enim rationaliter iudicatur nisi intelligitur aliquo saltem modo quid sit de quo fertur iudicium; neque intelligitur nisi praemittitur eius experientia quod intelligendum est.

Pariter, quamvis sola experientia, externa vel interna, cognitionem in animali constituit, non ideo sola experientia sine intelligentia vel iudicio dici potest cognitio proprie humana. Neque sufficit ut intelligentia experientiae accedat quin fiat iudicium; sic enim inter realitatem et apparentias, inter astrologiam et astronomiam, inter alchimiam et chimiam, inter mythum et historiam, non distinguitur.

(c') Unde et excluditur exaggerata illa distinctio et separatio obiectorum quae ex influxu Max Scheler valde diffunditur. Re vera, modus cognoscendi humanus subtiliter differentiatur secundum diversitatem obiectorum. Quam differentiationem in clara luce ita posuit Scheler ut tamen, synthesi non adepta, radicalem quandam separationem suadere videatur.

> Scheler hat ... die verschiedenen Sphären des Seins gesehen und ihnen eine sehr differentzierte 'sphärenkongeniale Erkenntnis' zugeordnet: Der Sphäre der Werte das intentionale Fühlen, der Sphäre des Göttlichen den religiösen Akt, der Sphäre des Personalen den Mitvollzug der Akte, der Sphäre der Realität den Widerstand, der Sphäre der Wissenschaft die Akte des Anschauens und Denkens.

synthesis, and a further question, Is it so? is needed to determine whether or not it really does exist. One must never indulge in that extrinsicism that would entertain evidence without one who grasps evidence, truth without one who wisely reflects, or certitude without one who responsibly judges.

(e) When the reduction of all questions to two has been achieved, the unity not only of theology but of all properly human knowledge is grounded.

(a′) Every question (What is it? Is it so?) intends 'being.' Every judgment affirms or denies 'to be.' Every concept, since it is ordered towards the preparation of a judgment, is thereby also ordered to 'to be.' But what is ordered to 'to be' is 'being,' and therefore every concept is at least implicitly a concept of being.

(b′) Accordingly, properly human knowledge does not consist of indivisible units, but is a composite whole. No one rationally judges without at least some understanding of that about which the judgment is being made, and one does not understand without having had an experience of that which was to be understood.

Similarly, although experience alone, external or internal, constitutes knowledge in an animal, this does not mean that experience alone without understanding or judgment can be said to be proper knowledge for a human being. Nor does it suffice if understanding without judgment is added to experience; for without judging there can be no distinguishing between reality and appearances, between astrology and astronomy, between alchemy and chemistry, between myth and history.

(c′) For this reason we must also reject that exaggerated distinction and separation of objects that has become so widespread through the influence of Max Scheler. It is true that the ways of human knowing are subtly differentiated according to the diversity of their objects. This differentiation has been so emphasized by Scheler that, not having achieved a synthesis, he seems to be arguing for a radical separation.

> Scheler hat ... die verschiedenen Sphären des Seins gesehen und ihnen eine sehr differentzierte 'sphärenkongeniale Erkenntnis' zugeordnet: der Sphäre der Werte das intentionale Fühlen, der Sphäre des Göttlichen den religiösen Akt, der Sphäre des Personalen den Mitvollzug der Akte, der Sphäre der Realität den Widerstand, der Sphäre der Wessenheit die Akte des Anschauens und Denkens.

Aber Scheler, der die Besonderheit der Sphären nach Akt und Gegenstand erkannte, betonte ihre Unableitbarkeit so sehr, dass er nicht nur die zwischen den Sphären bestehende Gemeinsamkeit aus den Augen verlor, sondern auch ihren letzten Zusammenhang mit dem Sein. Schelers grosse Konzeption der Sphären barg auch die Gefahr und Grenze seiner Philosophie: den Umschlag des Pluralismus in einen abgründigen Dualismus. Und Scheler ist diesen Weg gegangen.[146]

(d')[147] Quam apud Scheler irreductibilem differentiationem notavit H. Fries, multis et aliis modis apud alios invenitur, modo momentum iudicii vel praetermittant vel falso concipiant.

Nam experientia externa et interna pro diversitate obiectorum diversificatur; intelligentia pariter pro diversa obiectorum intelligibilitate variatur. Quare, quamdiu ad experientiam et intelligentiam restringitur attentio, tamdiu non inveniuntur nisi aliae et aliae experientiae, quibuscum concordant, ut formae materiis, aliae et aliae intelligibilitates.

Quod cognitionem humanam unit, in intentione finis et in ipso fine invenitur. Finis autem in singulis processibus cognoscitivis est iudicium, quo semper idem ponitur aut Est aut Non est. Intentio autem finis in quaestionibus invenitur; quae quidem intentio per quaestionem, quid sit, data externa et interna promovet ut intelligibilitas in iis quaeratur et inventa concipiatur; unde et eadem finis intentio per quaestionem, an sit, conceptam intelligibilitatem promovet ad ordinem veri et entis.

(f) Quae fundata unitas cognitionis proprie humanae et analogica est et analogiae entis correspondet.

Analogica est et quidem analogia proportionis. Non enim idem semper est obiectum experientiae, idem obiectum intelligentiae, idem quod iudicio affirmatur, sed eaedem semper sunt operationes, nempe, experiendi, intelligendi, iudicandi.

Analogiae entis correspondet: nam illud ens, quod nostrae cognitionis hac in vita est obiectum proprium, est quidditas sive natura in materia

> Aber Scheler, der die Besonderheit der Sphären nach Akt und
> Gegenstand erkannte, betonte ihre Unableitbarkeit so sehr, dass er
> nicht nur die zwischen den Sphären bestehende Gemeinsamkeit aus
> den Augen verlor, sondern auch ihren letzten Zusammenhang mit
> dem Sein. Schelers grosse Konzeption der Sphären barg auch die
> Gefahr und Grenze seiner Philosophie: den Umschlag des Pluralis-
> mus in einen abgründigen Dualismus. Und Scheler ist diesen Weg
> gegangen.[146]

(d')[147] This irreducible differentiation of Scheler's noted by Fries is found in other thinkers in many different forms, since they either ignore or wrongly conceive the importance of judgment.

Experience, external and internal, varies according to the diversity of its objects; understanding likewise varies according to the intelligibility of its objects. Hence, as long as attention is directed to experience and understanding alone, one will find only a variety of experiences along with a variety of intelligibilities corresponding to them as forms to their respective matters.

What unifies human knowledge is to be found in the intention of the end and in that end itself. In every cognitional process the end is judgment, by which the same thing is always posited, either 'It is' or 'It is not.' The intention of the end, however, is to be found in questions: the intention expressed in the question What is it? brings forward external and internal data for the intelligibility in them to be searched for and, once found, to be conceived; then the same intention of the end expressed in the question Is it so? brings this conceived intelligibility up to the level of truth and being.

(f) This solidly grounded unity of properly human knowledge is analogical and corresponds to the analogy of being.

It is analogical by the analogy of proportion. For the objects of experience or of understanding or of judgment are not always the same, but the operations themselves – experiencing, understanding, and judging – are always the same.

It corresponds to the analogy of being: for that being that is the proper object of our knowledge in this life is a quiddity, or nature, existing in cor-

---

146 Fries, *Die katholische Religionsphilosophie der Gegenwart* 139, 140. [In *Early Works on Theological Method I* 134, Lonergan summarizes and again all but translates this citation.]
147 [In the autograph, two undated typed pages begin at this point.]

corporali exsistens.[148] Ubi materia corporalis correspondet experientiae, quidditas sive natura correspondet intelligentiae, exsistentia denique correspondet iudicio.

Ens autem ultra proportionem obiecti proprii humani est duplex, angelus nempe et Deus. Neque enim de angelo hac in vita intelligere possumus quid sit[149] neque de Deo.[150] Sed eos cognoscimus quod sunt et quod quidditatem sive naturam habent. Inter quos tamen illa demonstratur differentia quod in angelo aliud est essentia et allud esse sed in Deo eadem est essentia ac esse; et iterum quod in angelo aliud est esse et aliud intelligere, sed in Deo idem est esse ac intelligere.[151]

Qua perspecta correspondentia concludes: sicut analogia entis omnia includit, ita etiam consideratio methodologica quae in operationibus fundatur quibus ens cognoscitur; quinimo, ipsae operationes fundamentales experiendi, intelligendi, iudicandi, fundamentalibus categoriis metaphysicis correspondent, nempe, potentiae, formae, et actui; sed et ulterius, sicut unum ens materiale e tribus componitur, materia nempe et forma et esse, ita una cognitio humana e tribus componitur, nempe, experientia, intelligentia, iudicio.

[5.5 Distinctions within the Unity of Human Knowledge][152]

Posita unitate tum metaphysica ex parte obiecti tum methodologica ex parte operationum cognoscitivarum, ad distinctiones intra hanc unitatem proceditur, ut inter se distinguantur sensus communis (= intelligentia vulgaris), scientiae naturales, philosophia, fides, theologia, theologia positiva, theologia systematica.

(a) Posita unitate: cf. numerum praecedentem ad finem.

Inter se distinguuntur: notate omissionem scientiarum humanarum, quae propter specialem difficultatem in altera problematica consideran-

poreal matter.[148] Corporeal matter corresponds to experience, quiddity or nature corresponds to understanding, and existence corresponds to judgment.

Being that lies beyond the scope of properly human knowledge is two-fold, namely, the angels and God. In this life we cannot understand either what an angel is[149] or what God is.[150] But we do know that they exist and that they have a quiddity or nature. There is, however, this difference between them, that in an angel essence and existence are different, whereas in God they are the same; and, again, that in an angel existence and understanding are different, whereas in God they are the same.[151]

Having grasped this correspondence, we may draw the following conclusions. As the analogy of being includes all things, so also does a methodological consideration based upon the operations by which being is known. Indeed, these fundamental operations of experiencing, understanding, and judging correspond to the fundamental categories of metaphysics, namely, potency, form, and act. Furthermore, as one material being is a composite of three elements, namely, matter, form, and existence, so one human knowledge is a composite of the three elements of experience, understanding, and judgment.

[5.5 Distinctions within the Unity of Human Knowledge][152]

Given the unity both metaphysical on the part of the object and methodological on the part of cognitional operations, we proceed now to distinctions within this unity, distinguishing between common sense (= ordinary understanding), natural sciences, philosophy, faith, theology, positive theology, and systematic theology.

(a) 'Given the unity': see the last part of the previous section.

'Distinguishing between …': note the omission of the human sciences, which on account of the difficulty peculiar to them are considered in the

148 Thomas Aquinas, *Summa theologiae*, 1, q. 84, a. 7.
149 Ibid. q. 88, a. 2.
150 Ibid. a. 3; see q. 2, a. 1.
151 Ibid. q. 3, a. 4; q. 14, aa. 2 and 4; q. 54, aa. 1 and 2.
152 [Chapters 1962-6 and 1962-7 in *Early Works on Theological Method 1* have some correspondence to the material presented from this point to the end of these notes on the 1962 course 'De methodo theologiae.']

tur.[153] Etiam notate distinctionem esse methodologicam, i.e., secundum operationes modumque operandi.

(b) Distinguuntur sensus communis et scientia natualis.

Narrat Aristoteles (*Metaphys.*, M, 4, 1078b 17 ss.), etsi Democritus et Pythagoraei quasdam posuerint definitiones, Socrati tamen recte duo attribui, nempe, ratiocinia inductiva (*epaktikoi logoi*) et definitiones universales.

Iam vero qui definitiones universales ponere vult, sensim sine sensu ad systema excogitandum cogitur. Non enim minus priores termini quam posteriores determinationem exactam flagitant, neque ipsi primi aliter quam per mutuas habitudines exactam determinationem habere possunt. Qui autem primos terminos per mutuas suas habitudines determinatos ponit, systema ponit unde systematice omnes alios terminos per primorum compositionem definire potest.

E.g., in metaphysica Aristotelica-Thomistica omnes primi termini etiam bini sunt et per mutuas habitudines, scilicet per mutuam proportionem seu analogiam, determinantur; ita potentia et actus, materia et forma, essentia et esse, substantia et accidens. Cui systemati metaphysico supra addidimus systema methodologicum atque correspondens.

Illud ergo inter sensum communem et scientiam naturalem intercedit, quod sensus communis ad systema conceptuale efformandum non tendit, sed scientia ad systema efformandum cogitur.

Quae quidem differentia ipsum modum concipiendi afficit. Tam sensus communis quam scientia naturalis data sensibilia intelligit. Ubi autem sensus communis exprimit quod intelligit tum lingua ordinaria tum eo modo quo alii quam facillime sensum verborum[154] perspiciant, scientia ideale quoddam logicum et systematicum respiciens ad linguam technicam confugit, facilitatem addiscendi praetermittit, univocitatem, rigorem, exactitudinem, possibilitatem deductionis longioris super omnia aestimat.

Quae differentia in obiecto intelligendo et concipiendo aliam in ipsa structura conscientiae subiecti inducit.

Qui enim modo vulgari cognoscit, intellectum et cognitionem non ponit finem humanum cui caetera subordinantur; sed finis est finis hominis

second problematic.[153] Note also that the distinction is methodological, that is, according to operations and the way of operating.

(b) Common sense and natural science are distinguished.

Aristotle (*Metaphysics*, XIII, 4, 1078 b 17–25) notes that, although Democritus and the Pythagoreans posited some definitions, two things are rightly attributed to Socrates, namely, inductive reasoning (*epaktikoi logoi*) and universal definitions.

Now, whoever wants to posit universal definitions will gradually and imperceptibly be led to devise a system. For prior terms no less than subsequent terms demand exact determination, and even primitive terms themselves cannot have an exact determination otherwise than through their mutual relations. But whoever posits primitive terms determined through their mutual relations posits a system whence all other terms can be systematically defined through the composition of primitive terms.

For example, in Aristotelian-Thomist metaphysics all primitive terms are paired and are determined through their mutual relations, that is, through their mutual proportion or analogy: potency and act, matter and form, essence and existence, substance and accident. To this metaphysical system we have added above a corresponding methodological system.

The difference between common sense and natural science is this, that common sense does not tend to form a conceptual system, whereas science is forced to do so.

This difference affects their way of conceiving. Both common sense and natural science understand sensible data. But where common sense expresses its understanding in ordinary language and in such a way that others can as easily as possible understand the meaning of the words,[154] science, intent upon following a logical and systematic ideal, uses technical terminology, is unconcerned about making things easy to learn, and places a premium on univocity, rigor, exactitude, and the possibility of lengthy deduction.

This difference in understanding and conceiving their objects leads to another difference in the very structure of the consciousness of their subjects.

One whose knowledge is of the ordinary kind does not make intellect and knowledge a human end to which all other ends are subordinate; such

---

153 [See above, p. 361, note 2. There is far more about the human sciences in the entries that appear in vol. 24, *Early Works on Theological Method 3*.]

154 [The Latin word 'verborum' was added by hand in the autograph.]

in quem tendit totus simul homo, cuius tantummodo pars est intellectus. Quare qui sensu communi cognoscit, vere quidem cognoscit et permulta quae aliter cognosci non possunt; attamen quae practica non sunt, quae ad finem hominis non directe respiciunt, ea inutiliter cognosci dicit.

E contra,[155] qui modo scientifico cognoscit, quatenus sic cognoscit, ei cognitio est finis cui caeterae potentiae subordinantur. Cogita mathematicum qui totus occupatur in symbolis exscribendis, intelligendis, et aliter rescribendis. Quam technicam conscientiae transformationem supra notavimus, ubi de mundo intelligibili diximus. Mundus enim intelligibilis est systematicus, in quo e primis quibusdam caetera derivantur et ipsa prima per mutuas habitudines determinantur; ad quem mundum apprehendendum exigitur subiectum, non curis cotidianis immersum, sed his resectis et dimissis totum fini intellectuali intentum.

Unde notantur:

Non alius est mundus aspectabilis sensu communi apprehensus et alius intelligibilis intelligentia scientifica conceptus, sed idem prorsus mundus aliter et aliter apprehenditur. Per conscientiam in schemate dramatico-practico apprehenditur mundus quoad nos; per conscientiam in schemate intellectuali apprehenditur mundus quoad se.[156]

Mundus intelligibilis sensui communi ultra horizontem iacet. Quod enim dicit sensus communis, inutiliter cognosci non-practica, manifeste falsum est, uti demonstrant scientiae applicatae. Attamen non simpliciter errat sensus communis; quamvis enim inutilitatem dicendo erret, tamen suam incapacitatem dicendo non erraret; per sensum communem enim cognosci non potest mundus quoad se, seu mundus intelligibilis. Quinimo, ad sanitatem ipsius sensus communis pertinet ut a re theoretica prorsus

a person's aim is the end of an individual towards which the whole person at once is directed, of whom intellect is only a part. Hence, one who knows in a commonsense way really does know, and indeed knows a great many things that could not be known otherwise; nevertheless, whatever is not practical and has no direct bearing upon the end of an individual is declared to be useless knowledge.

On the contrary,[155] for one who knows in a scientific way, and precisely as knowing scientifically, knowledge is an end to which all other faculties are subordinate. Think of a mathematician who is wholly occupied in writing and understanding and rewriting symbols. This technical transformation of consciousness we noted above when we spoke about the intelligible world. For the intelligible world is a world of system, one in which everything else is derived from certain primitive notions and the primitive notions themselves are determined by their mutual relations. To apprehend this world requires a subject who is not immersed in the cares of daily life, but having put them aside is wholly intent upon an intellectual aim.

Note, therefore, the following:

> The visible world apprehended by commonsense knowledge and the intelligible world conceived by scientific understanding are not two different worlds but the very same world known in different ways. Through consciousness in a dramatic-practical pattern we apprehend the world with respect to us, *quoad nos*; through consciousness in an intellectual pattern we apprehend the world with respect to itself, *quoad se*.[156]

The intelligible world lies outside the commonsense horizon. What common sense says about the uselessness of knowing non-practical things is patently false, as the applied sciences demonstrate. And yet common sense is not simply wrong; for although it errs in declaring the uselessness of such knowledge, it would not be mistaken in declaring its own limitation, for common sense cannot know the world *quoad se*, that is, the intelligible world. In fact, it would be conducive to its sanity for common sense to ab-

---

155 [At this point in the autograph the second of the aforementioned two undated pages ends and the date at the top of the next page appears as 17-4-62.]

156 On the patterns of consciousness, see *Insight*, chapter 6, § 2. [In *Insight* these are called 'patterns of experience.']

abstineat; ubi enim theoreticis sese immiscet, in insaniam ruit, uti multis et diversis exemplis nostri temporis sat manifestum est.

(c) A sensu communi et scientia naturali distinguitur philosophia.

Qui scientias perspectas et exploratas habet, non ideo sensu communi caret. Sed, sicut idem est mundus aspectabilis et intelligibilis, ita idem est subiectum, nunc scientificum mundo intelligibili intentum, nunc in mundo aspectabili vivens et schemate conscientiae dramatico-practico utens.

At quamvis idem sit mundus intelligibilis et aspectabilis, attamen non eadem eiusdem regio in scientiis et in sensu communi principaliter consideratur. Et quamvis idem sit subiectum quod nunc schemate conscientiae intellectuali, nunc schemate dramatico-practico utitur, nemo tamen utroque schemate simul uti potest.

Unde agnoscenda est duplex scissio: scissio obiecti, cum systema quod primum est in consideratione scientifica longissime distet ab iis quae sensui communi sunt immediata; et praeterea scissio subiecti, qui inter diversa conscientiae schemata oscillatur.

Cui duplici scissioni advenit philosophia. Et scissioni quidem subiecti advenit quatenus e mundis intelligibili et aspectabili recedit in mundum interiorem. Scissioni autem obiecti advenit quatenus totum obiectum cognitionis humanae, nempe ens, facit suum et proprium.

Recedit in mundum interiorem. Sicut enim exigentia systematica cogit scientificum in mundum intelligibilem, ita exigentia critica cogit philosophum in mundum interiorem.

Exigentia enim critica est: *negative*, ne quis de iis loquatur quae non cognoscit et multo minus de iis quae cognoscere potest (puta extrinsecistam qui de entibus loquitur prout a Deo sunt facta, prout a Deo sunt cognita; qui modus loquendi Deo quidem convenit sed non philosopho qui omnia quae cognoscit modo humano cognoscit); *positive*, exigentia critica est ut pro singulis obiectis de quibus fit sermo etiam indicantur actus quibus obiecta vel cognoscuntur vel saltem cognosci possunt. Quae actuum indicatio supponit mundum interiorem perspectum et exploratum.

Qui tamen in mundum interiorem reditus ab omni immanentismo libe-

stain completely from the theoretical; for when it involves itself in matters theoretical, it goes crazy, a fact amply illustrated by sundry examples in our own day.

(c) Philosophy is distinguished from both common sense and natural science.

One who has a thorough grasp of science is not on that account devoid of common sense. But just as the visible and the intelligible worlds are the same world, so is their subject the same, now a scientist studying the intelligible world and now someone living in the visible world and using the dramatic-practical pattern of consciousness.

But although the intelligible and visible worlds are the same, nevertheless it is not the same region of this one world that is principally addressed by science and by commonsense knowledge. And although it is the same subject who uses now the intellectual pattern of consciousness and now the dramatic-practical pattern, one cannot function in both patterns at the same time.

Hence, we must recognize a twofold split: a split in the object, since system, which is of paramount importance to science, is far removed from what is of immediate concern to common sense; and also a split in the subject, who moves back and forth between these diverse patterns of consciousness.

This twofold split is where philosophy comes in. It addresses the split in the subject inasmuch as it withdraws from the intelligible and visible worlds into the world of interiority; and it addresses the split in the object inasmuch as it makes its own proper object the entire object of human knowledge, being.

It withdraws into the world of interiority. Just as the systematic exigence forces the scientist into the intelligible world, so the critical exigence forces the philosopher into the world of interiority.

This exigence is critical (1) *negatively*, in the sense that no one should speak about what one does not know, much less about what one cannot know (such as extrinsicists, who talk about beings as they are made by God or known by God – a way of speaking that is all right for God but not for a philosopher who knows all that he knows in a human manner); and (2) *positively*, in that the critical exigence requires that for each object being treated there should also be indicated the acts by which the objects are known or at least can be known. Indicating these acts presupposes a thorough grasp of the world of interiority.

This return to the world of interiority, however, must be free of all imma-

rari debet. Quamvis enim actus cognoscitivi per conscientiam subiecto dentur, tamen cognitio proprie humana neque per sola data, neque per data
intellecta, sed per data ita intellecta ut fiat iudicium verum constituitur.
Quod si cognitio proprie humana non ante constituitur quam ad iudicium
verum perveniatur, frangitur omnis immanentismus; nam iudicium verum
affirmat esse de ente (non esse de non-ente), et adeo ens in subiecto non
continetur ut subiectum, tamquam pars prorsus minor, in ente contineatur.

Imo, cum ens (collective) dicat omnia, in ente continentur tum mundus
interior, tum mundus aspectabilis, tum mundus intelligibilis. De singulis
enim et de omnibus eorum partibus et aspectibus eatenus cognoscimus
quatenus vere dicimus ea esse.

Philosophus ergo scissionem obiecti et subiecti superat quatenus (1)
intra mundum interiorem conscius est tum actuum cognoscitivorum tum
diversorum conscientiae schematum (scilicet, dramatico-practici in mundo
aspectabili, theoretici in mundo intelligibili, introspectivi in mundo interiori) unius subiecti secundum diversa tempora diversosque fines intentos, et
(2) cum mundum interiorem per verum transcenderit, intra ens cognoscit
tam mundum intelligibilem quam mundum aspectabilem et mundum interiorem.

Sed et ulterius structuras notat earumque isomorphismum. Sicut enim
subiectum cognoscit quatenus et experitur et intelligit et iudicat, ita ens subiecto proportionatum componitur potentia, forma, et actu, tum in ordine
substantiali tum in ordine accidentali (puta, materiam primam, formam
substantialem, esse; intellectus, habitus, actus intelligendi; oculus, visus, actus vivendi; etc.)

Praeter isomorphismum structuralem, notat materialem correspondentiam. Quamvis enim alia facilius secundum priora quoad nos, alia facilius
secundum priora quoad se concipiantur et cognoscantur, nihil tamen ita
est quoad se quin transponi possit ad ea quae sunt quoad nos, et nihil adeo
quoad nos quin transponi possit ad quae sunt quoad se. Quod enim in alio
est prius, in alio posterius est.

Similiter, quodcumque ab homine cognoscitur sive in mundo intelligibili sive in mundo aspectabili, idem tamquam obiectum per determinatos
subiecti actus cognoscitur; et ita ex mundo vel intelligibili vel aspectabili in
mundum interiorem semper redire possumus.

Praeter isomorphismum structuralem et materialem correspondentiam,

nentism. For although the cognitive acts of a subject are data that are presented to that subject through consciousness, knowledge that is properly human is not constituted by data alone nor by data that are understood, but by data understood in such a way that a true judgment is made. Now if properly human knowledge is not fully constituted until a true judgment is arrived at, there is no room for immanentism; for a true judgment affirms the existence of what is and the non-existence of what is not, and being is so far from being contained in the subject that the subject is contained in being as a very minor part of it.

Indeed, since being, collectively considered, denotes all things, the world of interiority, the visible world, and the intelligible world are all contained in being. We know each of them and all of their parts and aspects to the extent that we can truly say that they exist.

A philosopher overcomes the split in the object and the subject insofar as (1) within the world of interiority he is conscious both of his cognitive acts and of the various patterns of consciousness (namely, the dramatic-practical in the visible world, the theoretic in the intelligible world, and the introspective in the world of interiority) in one and the same subject at different times and according to his different aims; and (2) when he has transcended the world of interiority through truth, he knows within being the intelligible world, the visible world, and the world of interiority.

But he also notes structures and their isomorphism. For just as a subject knows inasmuch as he experiences, understands, and judges, so being that is proportionate to a subject is composed of potency, form, and act, both in the substantial and in the accidental order (such as prime matter, substantial form, and the act of existence; intellect, habit of understanding, and the act of understanding; eye, sight, and seeing; and so forth).

Besides structural isomorphism, he notes a material correspondence. For although some things are more easily conceived and known with respect to us (*quoad nos*), while others are more easily conceived and known with respect to themselves (*quoad se*), nevertheless nothing is so *quoad se* that it cannot be transposed to the *quoad nos* and nothing is so *quoad nos* that it cannot be transposed to the *quoad se*. For what is prior in one case is posterior in the other.

Similarly, whatever is known either in the intelligible or in the visible world is known as an object through the determinate acts of a subject; and thus we can always go from the intelligible or the visible world into the world of interiority.

Besides this structural isomorphism and material correspondence, he

notat processum geneticum. Exigentia enim systematica cogit inquirentem
ex mundo aspectabili in mundun intelligibilem; exigentia critica cogit inquirentem e mundo vel aspectabili vel intelligibili vel utroque in mundum
interiorem; exigentia methodica facit ut reflexe cognoscatur processus cognoscendi adhibitus circa mundum aspectabilam, intelligibilem, interiorem,
et ulterius ut haec reflexa cognitio gubernet atque ordinet operationes ulteriores quae in his mundis cognoscendis exercentur.

Quae quidem omnia aspectum inversum habent. Mundus enim aspectabilis est quasi medium quo in mundum intelligibilem proceditur; mundus
intelligibilis est quasi medium quo in subiectum accurate cognoscendum
reditur; mundus interior denique est medium quo reflexe cognoscitur sensus communis et methodice exploratur sive mundus a sensu communi cognitus sive mundus intelligibilis sive mundus interior.

Qui duplex circulus geneticus non semel pro semper circuitur sed saepius. Singulis enim vicibus plenius satisfit exigentiis systematicis, criticis,
methodicis. Singulis pariter vicibus et plenius et accuratius cognoscuntur
obiecta, clarificantur actus et structurae subiecti, extenduntur structurae
isomorphicae, augentur correspondentiae materiales, et ipse processus historicus quo haec omnia perficiuntur in clariori ponitur luce.

Praeter isomorphismum structuralem, correspondentiam materialem,
processum geneticum, notat elementum dialecticum. Quem enim diximus
processum geneticum, linea quaedam idealis seu prima quaedam approxi-
matio est. Quatenus autem actualis rerum cursus per extrinsecismum vel
immanentismum ab hac linea aberratur, oriuntur scholae per diametrum
oppositae, quae verum falsis admiscent, surdum quendam irrationalitatis in
se continent et hoc tamen surdum qua irrationale agnoscere vel non possunt vel nolunt, quamvis continuo fere doctrinam suam nunc hic, nunc ibi,
modificare cogantur quin umquam securim ad radicem mittere valeant.

Unde et concluditur ad profundiorem quandam criticam, eamque dialecticam, quae omnia dicta, vel omnes theses, inter positiones et contra-positiones dividit, et illas quidem definit per actus cognoscitivos rite adhibitos
et exercitos, has autem per eorundem actuum quemlibet defectum. Qua
distinctione perspecta et explorata, scholarum oppositarum sententias ita
examinat ut quid positionis, quid contra-positionis, contineant determinet.

notes a genetic process. The systematic exigence forces an inquirer to go from the visible world into the intelligible world; the critical exigence forces an inquirer to go from the visible or the intelligible world or from both into the world of interiority; the methodical exigence makes the cognitional process used in knowing the visible or intelligible or interior world to be known reflectively and, further, makes this reflective knowledge govern and order any further operations to be performed in knowing these worlds.

There is an inverse aspect to all this. The visible world is a quasi-medium by which one proceeds into the intelligible world; the intelligible world is a quasi-medium by which one returns to obtain accurate knowledge of the subject; and the world of interiority is a medium by which common sense is known reflectively, and by which the world known by common sense, the intelligible world, and the world of interiority are explored in a methodical way.

This double genetic circle is something for one to go around not once for all, but repeatedly. For every time it is traversed, the systematic, critical, and methodical exigences are more fully satisfied. Likewise, for every time it is traversed, objects are more fully and more accurately known, the acts and structures of the subject are clarified, the isomorphic structures are extended, material correspondences are increased, and the historical process itself by which all these things are brought about is more clearly brought to light.

Besides this structural isomorphism, material correspondence, and genetic process, the philosopher notes a dialectical element. The above-mentioned genetic process is an ideal line, a first approximation. Insofar as the actual course of events deviates from that line because of extrinsicism or immanentism, diametrically opposed schools of thought emerge with their mixture of the true and the false, containing within themselves the surd of irrationality, and yet unable or unwilling to acknowledge that surd as irrational, even though they are almost continually forced to modify their doctrine now on one point and now on another without ever being able to lay the axe to the root.

All this results in a more profound critique, a dialectical one, that separates all statements or all theses into positions and counterpositions, defining the former by reason of cognitive acts correctly used and performed, and the latter by way of any defect in those same acts. With this distinction thoroughly understood, one may go on to examine the opinions of opposing schools in order to determine to what extent they contain positions or

Qua peracta determinatione, nihil remanet ut positiones quidem ad ulteriorem perfectionem producantur, contra-positiones autem per eliminationem elementi irrationalis in positiones convertantur.[157]

(d) Distinguuntur fides et cognitio.[158]

(a′) Excluso extrinsecismo, nullum est verum nisi in aliqua mente. Unde si nullus intellectus esset aeternus, nulla veritas esset aeterna. Sed quia solus intellectus divinus est aeternus, in ipso solo veritas aeternitatem habet.[159]

(b′) Aliter verum alteri intellectui inest.

Alteri enim inest ut *cognoscenti*; ipse scilicet expertus est, ipse inquisivit et intellexit, ipse concepit, ponderavit, iudicavit; unde per proprium suum cognoscendi processum ipse eo pervenit ut hoc aliquid esse verum cognoscat.

Alteri autem inest ut *credenti*; credens nempe per proprium cognoscendi processum non eo pervenit ut hoc aliquid esse verum cognoscat ipse; ei deest *vel* experientia, quia numquam in Asia fuit, *vel* intelligentia, quia quamquam augumenta perlegit, vim argumenti cur $E = mc^2$ perspicere non valuit, *vel* evidentiae sufficientia, quia quamvis experientiam habuerit et consecutionem argumentorum intellexerit, eo tamem non pervenit ut certum iudicium efformare potuerit. Attamen, credens, quamvis ipse non cognoscat, alteri tamen cognoscenti credit; habet in suo intellectu ut verum quod in intellectu non suo sed alterius est cognitum; e.g., tabulas mathematicas mathematici omnes habent ut veras, quas tamen admodum perpauci veras esse cognoscunt.

(c′) Fides extensionem veri valde auget. Per extensionem veri significamus numerum mentium in quibus hoc aliquid verum inest. Iam vero sine fide sola ea vera in singulis essent mentibus ad quae certo cognoscenda singulae per proprium cognoscendi processum pervenerunt. Per fidem autem fit ut quod verum est in hoc aliquo intellectu etiam in omnibus credentibus sit verum.

(d′) Fides sensum 'veri' facit duplicem. Excluso enim extrinsecismo, nul-

counterpositions. Once this determination has been made, it remains simply to improve the positions and to convert counterpositions to positions by purging them of their irrational element.[157]

(d) Faith and knowledge are distinguished.[158]

(a′) Having rejected extrinsicism, we affirm that there is no truth except in some mind. Hence if no intellect were eternal, no truth would be eternal. But since only the divine intellect is eternal, in it alone does truth possess eternity.[159]

(b′) Truth is in the intellect in different ways.

In one way it is in the intellect as *knowing*. A knower has experienced, has inquired and understood, has conceived, has weighed the evidence and judged; hence, through his own cognitional process he has come to know that this particular thing is true.

In a different way truth is in the intellect as *believing*. A believer has not come to know that this particular thing is true through his own cognitional processes. For *either* he lacks experience, because he has never been, say, in Asia, *or* he lacks understanding, because even after studying the theory he has not been able to understand why $E = mc^2$, *or* he lacks sufficient evidence, because even though he has experienced and has understood the course of the argument, he has not yet reached the point of being able with certitude to pronounce a judgment. Nevertheless one who believes, even though he himself does not know, believes one who does know; he has in his intellect a truth that is known in an intellect that is not his but another's. A good example would be mathematical tables, which all mathematicians accept as true, though very few of them *know* that they are true.

(c′) Faith greatly extends the extension of truth. By the 'extension of truth' we mean the number of minds in which a truth is present. Without faith, only those truths would be present in individual minds that those individual minds have arrived at through their own cognitional processes. But faith makes it possible for a truth in this particular intellect also to be present as true in the minds of all who believe it.

(d′) The fact of faith means that 'truth' has two meanings. Contrary to

---

157 On this whole topic, see *Insight.* [For relevant pages, see the Index, s.v. 'Positions.']
158 [At this point in the autograph, the date at the top of the page switches to 18-4-62.]
159 See Thomas Aquinas, *Summa theologiae,* 1, q. 16, a. 7 c.

lum est verum nisi in aliqua mente. Per fidem autem fit ut vera dupliciter huic intellectui inesse possint, nempe, ut cognita, vel ut credita. Attamen, primo et per se 'verum' significat verum cognitum; secundario autem 'verum' significat verum creditum. Nisi enim esset qui cognosceret, non haberetur cui credi posset. Numquam denique verum significat quod neque cognoscitur neque creditur; secus in extrinsecismun relaberemur.

(e′) Processus ergo fidei est (1) ex vero cognito ab illo (2) ad verum creditam ab hoc. Principium ergo processus est verum cognoscens et dicens. Terminus processus est verum audiens et credens. Ipse processus est mediatio inter principium et terminum.

Abstracte, mediatio invenitur in ratione boni intellectualis. Scilicet, ideo fieri potest transitus ex vero cognito ad verum creditum quia intervenit ratio boni intellectualis. Quamvis primo et per se verum sit tantummodo verum cognitum, tamen secundario verum cognitum est bonum non tantum intellectus cognoscentis sed etiam alterius intellectus.

Concrete, mediatio consistit in operationibus credentis qui (1) verum ab alio cognitum apprehendit ut bonum sibi intellectuale; (2) hoc bonum apprehensum suo intellectui conferre vult; (3) suus intellectus, a voluntate sua motus, vero ab alio cognito assentit.

Notate, interventum voluntatis necessario sequi ex eo quod verum ab alio cognitum mediante ratione boni in verum creditum transit. Quare nihil refert utrum omnino evidens sit scientia et attestatio cognoscentis; semper enim interventus voluntatis requiritur.

(f′) Centralem locum in processu psychologico ad fidem tenet actus intelligendi reflexus. Obiectum fidei est id quod creditur; e.g., tabulas mathematicas esse veras. Motivum fidei est cur credatur; quod motivum est scientia cognoscentis et veracitas dicentis; e.g., qui fecit tabulas neque fallitur neque fallit. Actus fidei est assensus intellectus ad obiectum propter motivum; credo tabulas esse veras quia a sciente et verace sunt confectae. Electio fidei est actus voluntatis: volo credere obiectum propter motivum.

extrinsicism, there is no truth except in a mind. Faith, however, means that there is not one way but two ways in which truths exist in a particular mind, namely, as known or as believed. Still, primarily and *per se*, 'true' signifies truth that is known; secondarily 'true' signifies truth that is believed. For unless there were someone who knows, there would be no one to be believed. But 'true' never signifies what is neither known nor believed; otherwise we should relapse into extrinsicism.

(e') The faith process, therefore, is from a truth known by one person to this same truth believed by another person. Thus, the origin of this process is the one who knows and speaks a truth. The term of the process is the one who hears and believes the truth. The process itself is a mediation between the origin and the term.

Abstractly, the mediation involves the formality of intellectual good. That is, the passage from a truth that is known to a truth that is believed is made possible by the intervention of the formality of intellectual good. Although primarily and *per se* truth is only truth that is known, yet secondarily a truth that is known is a good not only of the intellect of the one who knows it but also of the intellect of someone else.

Concretely, this mediation consists in the operations of a believer who (1) apprehends a truth known by another as an intellectual good for himself and (2) wishes to confer upon his own intellect this good he has apprehended; (3) his intellect, moved by his will, assents to the truth known by the other.

Note that the intervention of the will necessarily follows from the fact that a truth known by another becomes a believed truth by the mediation of the formality of the good. That is why it does not matter whether the knowledge and testimony of the knower is completely evident or not; an intervention on the part of the will is always required.

(f') A reflective act of understanding holds the central place in the psychological process towards faith. The object of faith is that which is believed; for example, that the mathematical tables are true. The motive of faith is why one believes. This motive is the knowledge of the knower together with the truthfulness of the speaker – for example, that the person who drew up the mathematical tables was neither ignorant nor mistaken nor untruthful. An act of faith is an assent of the intellect on account of the motive: I believe these tables to be true because they have been drawn up by one who knows and is truthful. The decision to believe is an act of the will: I will to believe the object because of the motive. The judgment of credibility

Iudicium credibilitatis et credenditatis[160] est iudicium verum de bono, de valore: possum et debeo velle credere obiectum propter motivum.

Actus intelligendi reflexus est quo perspicitur evidentiam sufficere ut ponatur iudicium credibilitatis et credenditatis: perspicio evidentiam sufficere ut iudicem me posse et debere velle credere tabulas esse veras propter scientiam et veracitatem eius qui tabulas confecit.

Praeambula fidei dicunt evidentiam cuius sufficientia in actu intelligendi reflexo perspicitur. Sunt nempe praemissae alicuius syllogismi expliciti vel impliciti qui manifestat inconditionatum virtuale esse quod in actu reflexo perspicitur, in iudicio credibilitatis affirmatur.

Iam vero actus fidei ex electione sequitur et in electione praecontinetur. Credo quia volo credere. Electio fidei ex iudicio credibilitatis et credenditatis sequitur et in eo praecontinetur. Volo credere quia possum et debeo velle credere. Iudicium credibilitatis et credenditatis ex actu intelligendi reflexo sequitur et in eo praecontinetur. Iudico me posse et debere velle credere, quia perspicio evidentiam sufficere ut ita iudicem.

Sed[161] actus intelligendi reflexus non ita praecontinetur in praeambulis neque ita ex iis sequitur. Praeambula enim dicunt evidentiam, cuius tamen sufficientia ab actu reflexo perspicienda est. Et secundum hoc praeambula comparantur ad actum reflexum sicut materia comparatur ad formam, vel melius sicut forma comparatur ad actum. Praeambula iterum dicunt praemissas syllogismi cuius conclusio est iudicium credibilitatis et credenditatis. Sed inter praemissas syllogismi et eiusdem conclusionem intercedit actus reflexus quo perspicitur syllogismum valere; et sine illa perspicientia nihil in mente fit sed tantummodo habetur processus quidam verbalis et exterior.

Quia ergo actus intelligendi reflexus ita actus subsequentes praecontinet atque fundat, ut tamen ipse in praeambulis non ita praecontineatur vel fundetur, habetur intentum: actum intelligendi reflexum in processu psychologico ad fidem locum quendam centralem obtinere.

(e) Distinguuntur fides humana et fides divina.

and credendity[160] is a true judgment about good, a judgment of value: I can and I ought to will to believe the object because of the motive.

The reflective act of understanding is that in which one grasps that the evidence is sufficient for making a judgment of credibility and credendity: I grasp that the evidence is sufficient for me to judge that I can and ought to will to believe that those tables are true on account of the knowledge and the truthfulness of the one who drew them up.

The preambles of faith refer to the evidence whose sufficiency is grasped in the reflective act of understanding. They are the premises of an explicit or implicit syllogism which manifests the fact that there is a virtually unconditioned to be grasped in a reflective act and affirmed in a judgment of credibility.

The act of faith follows from a decision and is precontained in the decision. I believe because I will to believe. The decision to believe follows from the judgment of credibility and credendity and is precontained in it. I will to believe because I can and ought to will to believe. The judgment of credibility and credendity follows from the reflective act of understanding and is precontained in it. I judge that I can and ought to will to believe because I grasp that there is sufficient evidence for me so to judge.

But[161] the reflective act of understanding is not so precontained in the preambles nor does it follow from them. For the preambles state the evidence whose sufficiency is to be grasped by a reflective act. Accordingly, the preambles are to the reflective act as matter is to form, or better, as form is to act. Again, the preambles state the premises of a syllogism whose conclusion is a judgment of credibility and credendity. But between the premises of this syllogism and its conclusion there is a reflective act that grasps the validity of the syllogism; and without that grasp nothing takes place in the mind; there is only an external verbal process.

Therefore, because a reflective act of understanding precontains and grounds subsequent acts without itself being precontained or grounded in the preambles, we have attained what we set out to establish: that the reflective act of understanding occupies the central place in the psychological process towards faith.

(e) Human and divine faith are distinguished.

---

160 [Formed from the Latin *credendum*, 'that which ought to be believed.']
161 [At this point in the autograph, the date at the top of the page switches to 19-4-62.]

(a′) Fidei divinae definitio (DB 1789), rationabilitas (DB 1790), gratuitas (DB 1791), obiectum (DB 1792), necessitas (DB 1793), auxilia interna et externa (DB 1794), comparatio cum ratione humana (DB 1795).

(b′) Fides dicitur divina vel propter motivum vel propter obiectum.

Est divina propter motivum, ubi Deus est fidei principium, ille scilicet qui verum cognoscit et dicit. Et secundum hoc fide divina creduntur omnia a Deo revelata, sive sunt ordinis supernaturalis, sive sunt ordinis naturalis sed non ab omnibus expedite, firma certitudine, et nullo admixto errore cognoscuntur (DB 1786).

Est divina propter obiectum, quatenus obiectum est mysteria ita in Deo abscondita ut nisi divinitus revelarentur nobis innotescere non possent (DB 1795).

Ad simplicitatem argumenti confert ut de fide divina tum propter motivum tum propter obiectum fiat sermo.

Fides humana etiam est humana vel propter motivum vel propter obiectum. Simplicitatis causa sermo erit de fide humana tum propter obiectum tum propter motivum.

Per fidem humanam creditur homini quod ab homine cognosci potest; e.g., tabulas mathematicas esse veras, vel '$E = mc^2$,' quamvis ipsi neque hoc neque illud per proprium experiendi, intelligendi, iudicandi processum cognoscamus.

Per fidem divinam creditur Deo quod a solo Deo cognosci potest; e.g., Deum esse trinum, hominem ad visionem Dei aeternam gratuito ordinari.

(c′) Sicut in fide humana, ita etiam in fide divina, verificantur quae superius sunt posita, nempe, per fidem valde augeri extensionem veri, duplicem fieri sensum 'veri,' processum esse ex cognoscente et dicente ad audientem et credentem, mediationem esse per rationem boni, locum centralem obtineri ab actu intelligendi reflexo.

Quae tamen omnia aliter in fide divina, aliter in fide humana, verificantur.

Per fidem enim divinam fit ut extensio veri dicat inclusionem ordinis supernaturalis; fide enim divina creduntur quae naturaliter ab homine cognosci non possunt. Iterum, per fidem divinam fit alia duplicatio sensus

(a′) The definition of divine faith (DB 1789, DS 3008, ND 118), its reasonableness (DB 1790, DS 3009, ND 119), its gratuitousness (DB 1791, DS 3010, ND 120), its object (DB 1792, DS 3011, ND 121), its necessity (DB 1793, DS 3012, ND 122), its internal and external helps (DB 1794, DS 3013, 3014, ND 123, 124), its comparison with human reason (DB 1795, DS 3015, ND 131).

(b′) Faith is said to be divine either by reason of its motive or by reason of its object.

It is divine by reason of its motive when God is the origin of faith, that is, the one who knows and speaks what is true. In this case there are believed by divine faith all that have been revealed by God, either belonging to the supernatural order, or else belonging to the natural order but not readily known by all with firm certitude and entirely free from error (DB 1786, DS 3005, ND 114).

It is divine by reason of its object, inasmuch as its object is the mysteries so hidden in God that without divine revelation they could never become known to us (DB 1795, DS 3015, ND 131).

It would simplify things here to speak of faith that is divine by reason of both its motive and its object.

Human faith also is human either by reason of its motive or by reason of its object. Again, for the sake of simplicity let us speak of faith that is human by reason of both its motive and its object.

By human faith we believe a person with respect to what a human being can know: for example, that the mathematical tables are true, or that $E = mc^2$, even though we ourselves do not know these things through our own process of experiencing, understanding, and judging.

By divine faith we believe God with respect to what God alone can know: for example, that God is triune, and that man is by God's free gift ordered to the vision of God.

(c′) In the case of both divine and human faith those statements we made above are verified, namely, that through faith the domain of truth is greatly extended, that the word 'true' has two meanings, that the faith process goes from the knower and speaker to the hearer and believer, that there is a mediation through the formality of the good, and that the reflective act of understanding holds the central place in this process.

All of the above, however, are verified in different ways in divine faith and in human faith.

Divine faith extends truth to include the supernatural order; for by divine faith are believed those truths that we cannot know naturally. Again, in divine faith the twofold meaning of 'true' is different; for what is believed

'veri': quod enim fide humana creditur, idem ipsum a credente cognosci potest; e.g., quamvis credo tabulas mathematicas esse veras, tamen addiscere possum calculationis principia et ipsam calculationem perficere. Quod autem fide divina creditur, idem a credente secundum suam naturam cognosci non potest; mysteria enim divina suapte natura intellectum creatum excedunt (DB 1796). Iterum, per fidem divinam mediatio ita in ratione boni consistit, ut tamen illud bonum non homini naturale sed ultra eius proportionem inveniatur. Iterum, in fide divina actus intelligendi reflexus ita locum centralem obtinet ut tamen sine lumine fidei supernaturali et gratuito ipse actus non perficiatur.

Quod hoc lumen supernaturale est, ex noto principio concluditur, actus per obiecta specificari. Iam vero credere mysteria propter auctoritatem divinam est actus supernaturalis, uti ex obiecto, 'mysteria,' patet. Pariter ergo supernaturales sunt actus quibus *volo* credere mysteria, *iudico* me posse et debere velle credere mysteria, et *perspicio* evidentiam sufficere ut iudicem me posse et debere velle credere mysteria. Idem enim est in singulis obiectum, mysteria.

Idem concluditur ex eo quod actus fidei, electio fidei, iudicium credibilitatis et credenditatis ex actu reflexo sequuntur et in actu reflexo praecontinentur. Nisi enim ex actu supernaturali non sequuntur actus supernaturales, et nisi in actu supernaturali non praecontinentur actus supernaturales. Secus destrueretur ille duplex ordo, principio et obiecto distinctus, de quo DB 1795.

E contra, sicut actus intelligendi reflexus non praecontinetur in praeambulis neque ex iis sequitur, per se non requiritur lumen supernaturale ad praeambula fidei peragenda. Exemplo sit revelatio divina quae nihil contineret nisi quod naturaliter ab homine cognosci potest etsi non ab omnibus, expedite, firma certitudine, et nullo admixto errore. Quae revelatio per signa externa actualibus signis simillima confirmari posset. Neque tamen lumen supernaturale exigeretur sive circa signa sive circa ipsa revelata.

(d') Quid faciat lumen fidei

(a″) Intelligimus lumen fidei radicale, scilicet, quod in actu intelligendi reflexo invenitur. Momentum quaestionis in eo est quod ipsum transitum

by human faith is something that the believer is capable of knowing. For example, even though I believe that the mathematical tables are true, nevertheless I can learn the principles of calculation and do the calculation itself. But what is believed by divine faith cannot be known by the believer in accordance with his nature, since the divine mysteries by their very nature are beyond any created intellect (DB 1796, DS 3016, ND 132). Again, in divine faith the mediation, while it consists in the formality of the good, is nevertheless a good that is not a natural human good but lies beyond what is proportionate to man. Further, in divine faith the reflective act of understanding holds the central place, but it is not completed without the free gift of the supernatural light of faith.

That this light is supernatural is deduced from the well-known principle that acts are specified by their objects. Now, to believe the mysteries on account of the authority of God is a supernatural act, as is clear from its object, the 'mysteries.' Equally supernatural are the acts by which I *will* to believe the mysteries, *judge* that I can and ought to will to believe the mysteries, and *grasp* that there is sufficient evidence for me to judge that I can and ought to will to believe the mysteries. For to each of these acts there is the same object, the mysteries of faith.

The same conclusion can be drawn from the fact that the act of faith, the decision to believe, and the judgment of credibility and credendity follow from the reflective act and are precontained in it. For supernatural acts are consequent only upon a supernatural act, and supernatural acts are precontained only in a supernatural act. Otherwise the distinction between the natural and the supernatural orders as to both their origin and their object would cease to exist; see DB 1795, DS 3015, ND 131.

On the other hand, as the reflective act of understanding is not precontained in the preambles and does not follow from them, supernatural light is not required *per se* for the preambles of faith. Take, for example, a divinely revealed truth containing only what could be naturally known by us yet is not readily known by everyone with firm certitude and without any admixture of error. Such a revealed truth could be confirmed by external signs that are very similar to the actual signs. Still, supernatural light would not be required either with regard to those signs or with regard to the revealed truths themselves.

(d') What the light of faith does.

(a″) We understand here a light of faith that is radical, that is, found in the reflective act of understanding. The importance of this question lies in

ex ordine naturali ad supernaturalem (quantum cognitionem attinet) in clara luce ponit.

(b″) Lumen fidei respicit quaestionem, an sit, non quaestionem, quid sit. Respicit quaestionem, an sit. Nam fundat iudicium credibilitatis et credenditatis. Et iudicium respondet quaestioni, an sit. Non respicit quaestionem, quid sit. Differt ergo a lumine gloriae quo Deum per essentiam seu quidditatem cognoscimus. Differt pariter a scientia per se infusa, per quem naturas seu quidditates intelligimus quae proportionem nostri intellectus excedunt. Quam ob causam, theologus nisi imperfectam quandam mysteriorum intelligentiam attingere non potest, eamque ex analogia eorum quae naturaliter cognoscit (DB 1796).

Quia non respicit quaestionem, quid sit, differt ab illo lumine quod docuit P. Rousselot, 'Les yeux de la foi.'[162] Hoc enim lumen non solum ad sufficientiam evidentiae perspiciendam sed etiam ad ipsam evidentiam perspiciendam ponitur; et ideo non solum quaestionem, an sit, respicit, sed etiam quaestionem, quid sit, quae in praeambulis peragendis ponitur.

(c″)[163] Lumen fidei efficit transitum ex vero humano ad verum divinum.

Verum humanum est quod homo per propriam experientiam, intelligentiam, iudicium cognoscere potest ut verum. Quod verum humanum quodammodo verum divinum includit et quodammodo non includit: includit quatenus naturali rationis lumine concludere possumus exsistere aliquod

the fact that it explains clearly the transition (as far as knowledge is concerned) from the natural to the supernatural order.

(b″) The light of faith regards the question Is it? and not the question What is it? It regards the question Is it? since it grounds the judgment of credibility and credendity, and a judgment answers the question Is it? It does not regard the question What is it? It is different, therefore, from the light of glory by which we know God in his essence or quiddity. It differs likewise from knowledge that is *per se* infused, by means of which we may understand natures or quiddities that lie beyond the scope of our intellect. Hence, a theologian can attain only an imperfect understanding of the mysteries, and does so by way of analogy with truths that he knows naturally (DB 1796, DS 3016, ND 132).

Because it does not regard the question What is it? it differs also from that light which Rousselot speaks of in *Les yeux de la foi*.[162] This light is posited not only for grasping the sufficiency of the evidence but also for understanding the evidence itself; hence, it regards not only the question Is it? but also the question What is it?, which is posed in going through the preambles of faith.

(c″)[163] The light of faith effects the transition from human truth to divine truth.

Human truth is what one can know as true from one's own experiencing, understanding, and judging. In one way human truth includes divine truth, and in another way it does not. It includes it inasmuch as by the natural light of reason we can conclude to the existence of some divine truth

---

162 Pierre Rousselot, 'Les yeux de la foi,' *Recherches de Science Religieuse* 1 (1910) 241–59, 444–75; 'Remarques sur l'histoire de la notion de foi naturelle,' ibid. 4 (1913) 1–36; 'Réponse à deux attaques,' ibid. 5 (1914) 57–69; 'La vraie pensée de Bautain,' ibid. 5 (1914) 453–58; [in book form, *Les yeux de la foi, suivé d'une note historique sur le concept de la foi scientifique* (Paris: Bureaux des Recherches de Science Religieuse, 1913); in English, *The Eyes of Faith*, trans. Joseph Donceel, with an introduction by John M. McDermott, together with *Answer to Two Attacks*, trans., with an introduction by Avery Dulles (New York: Fordham University Press, 1990).] *L'intellectualisme de Saint Thomas, precédée d'une notice sur l'auteur et d'une bibliographie*, 3rd ed. (Paris: G. Beauchesen, 1936). [In English, translation of an earlier edition, *The Intellectualism of Saint Thomas*, trans. with a foreword by James E. O'Mahoney (London and New York: Sheed & Ward, 1935, 1965).]

163 [At this point in the autograph, the date at the top of the page switches to 4-5-62. Easter Sunday occurred on 22 April in 1962, so the celebration of Easter probably accounts for the gap in dates.]

verum divinum quod analogice concipimus; non includit quatenus illa cognitio est analogica, et omnis cognitio analogica duplicem importat ignorantiam (nempe, in quo non simile sed dissimile sit obiectum analogice cognitum, et quanti momenti sit haec dissimilitudo).

Per lumen fidei promovemur ad verum divinum quatenus non includitur in vero humano; scilicet ea ut vera habemus quae ultra campum veri humani iacent, quae nisi divinitus revelata essent nobis innotescere non possent (DB 1795).

Unde concludes: motivum fidei non potest esse nisi ipsa veritas divina. Aliter, fides reduci non potest ad motivum quod intra campum veri humani iacet. Aliter, non solum obiectum sed etiam motivum fidei creditur.

Iterum concludes: sicut fides humana, ita fides divina auget *extensionem* veri, scilicet, numerum mentium in quibus propositiones habentur ut verae; sed ulterius fides divina auget *campum* veri, scilicet, numerum propositionum quae in mente humana ut verae haberi possunt.

Ulterius concludes: ideo fides divina est supernaturalis quia campum veri auget; dicit enim accessum ad eam regionem veri quae ultra vires humanas invenitur.

(d″) Lumini fidei opponitur rationalismus. Nam per lumen fidei iudicamus nos posse et debere velle ea credere quae ab homine naturaliter cognosci non possunt. Sed rationalismus contradictorium docet: nos nec posse nec debere pro veris habere ea quae ab homine cognosci non possunt.

(e″) Lumen fidei et criticismus: Per criticismum non intelligimus speciem particularem, kantianam, immanentisticam, sed exigentiam illam generalem, nempe, hominem loqui non debere de iis quae non cognoscit et ideo determinandas esse naturam, extensionem, limitationes intellectus humani, ultra quas non est procedendum.

Notatur primo exigentiam criticam non eo sensu esse admittendam ut excludatur sermo de iis quae homo credit. Secus in rationalismum relaberemur. Notate deinde non directe opponi exigentiam criticam et fidem; fides enim non dicit se cognoscere mysteria sed ea credere. Notate tertio hominem naturaliter desiderare visionem Dei immediatam sed naturaliter eam non posse consequi.[164] Quo naturali desiderio critice stabiliri potest

conceived analogically; it does not include it inasmuch as that knowledge is analogical, and all analogical knowledge implies a twofold ignorance, namely, of the way in which the analogically known object is not similar but dissimilar, and of the importance of this dissimilarity.

Through the light of faith we are raised up to divine truth insofar as it is not included in human truth; that is to say, we hold as true truths that lie beyond the field of human truth, truths that we could never come to know unless they were divinely revealed to us (DB 1795, DS 3015, ND 131).

From this we conclude that the motive of faith can only be divine truth itself. In other words, faith cannot be reduced to a motive that lies within the field of human truth; or, to put it in still another way, not only the object but also the motive of faith is believed.

Again, we conclude that, as human faith increases the *extension* of truth, so also does divine faith increase it; that is to say, it increases the number of minds in which propositions are held as true; but divine faith also enlarges the *domain* of truth, for it increases the number of propositions that the human mind can hold as true.

Further, we conclude that divine faith is supernatural because it enlarges the domain of truth; for it gives access to that realm of truth that is beyond the capability of man to discover.

(d″) Rationalism is opposed to the light of faith. By the light of faith we judge that we can and ought to will to believe things that cannot naturally be known by us. But rationalism asserts the exact opposite of this, namely, that we cannot and ought not hold as true what cannot be known by us.

(e″) Criticism and the light of faith: By 'criticism' we do not mean any particular criticism, Kantian, or immanentist, but that general exigence, namely, that one ought not to speak about things that one does not know, and hence the necessity of determining the nature, scope, and limitations of the human intellect beyond which one must not go.

Note the following: First, a critical exigence that would exclude all mention of those things that are believed is inadmissible. Otherwise we should lapse into rationalism. Second, faith and the critical exigence are not directly opposed. For faith does not mean knowing the mysteries but believing them. Third, man has a natural desire for the immediate vision of God, but cannot by his natural power attain that vision.[164] By reason of this natu-

---

164 Thomas Aquinas, *Summa theologiae*, 1-2, q. 3, a. 8; q. 5, a. 5.

possibilitas ordinis supernaturalis (uti patet, possibilitas hic intelligitur non sensu logico, non sensu metaphysico, sed sensu critico), non tamen a philosopho, sed a theologo.

(f) Comparantur theologia, fides divina, cognitio humana

(a′) In genere, theologia est scientia de Deo. In specie, distinguuntur theologia naturalis, theologia viae, theologia patriae, quarum unaquaeque est scientia de Deo, sed diverso utitur medio tum subiectivo tum obiectivo.

Theologia naturalis Deum attingit mediantibus rebus creatis per naturale lumen rationis. Theologia viae Deum attingit mediantibus verbo Dei et ordine Corporis Christi per rationem fide illustratam. Theologia patriae Deum attingit mediante ipsa divina essentia per lumen rationis lumine gloriae confortatum.[165]

Deinceps nomen, theologia, dicet theologiam viae.

Haec viae theologia duplicem habet aspectum: prout est particularis quaedam scientia, est scientia de Deo et de aliis quae ad Deum referuntur;[166] prout locum quendam tenet inter caeteras scientias humanas, '… haec doctrina maxime sapientia est inter omnes sapientias humanas, non quidem in aliquo genere tantum sed simpliciter. Cum enim sapientis sit ordinare et iudicare, iudicium autem per altiorem causam de inferioribus habetur; ille sapiens dicitur in unoquoque genere, qui considerat causam altissimam illius generis … Ille igitur qui considerat simpliciter altissimam causam totius universi, quae Deus est, maxime sapiens dicitur …'[167]

(b′) Comparationem quam volumus inter theologiam, fidem divinam, et cognitionem humanam invenimus in Vaticano, DB 1795, 1796, 1800, 1820.

ral desire the possibility of a supernatural order – obviously, we understand 'possibility' here not in a logical sense nor in a metaphysical sense, but in a critical sense – can be critically established, not, however, by a philosopher but by a theologian.

(f) Comparison between theology, divine faith, and human knowledge

(a′) In general terms, theology is knowledge of God. Specifically, we may distinguish natural theology, the theology of wayfarers, and the theology of the blessed, each of which is knowledge of God but makes use of different means, both objective and subjective.

Natural theology attains knowledge of God by the mediation of created things through the natural light of reason. The theology of wayfarers attains knowledge of God by the mediation of the word of God and the order of the Body of Christ through human reason enlightened by faith. The theology of the blessed attains knowledge of God by the mediation of the divine essence itself through the light of reason strengthened by the light of glory.[165]

Henceforth 'theology' will refer to the theology of wayfarers.

There is a twofold aspect to this theology: (1) as a particular branch of knowledge, it is the science of God and of all other things as related to God;[166] (2) as having a place among the other human sciences, '... this doctrine is in the highest degree a wisdom above all other forms of human wisdom, not in any particular category, but absolutely speaking. For since it is the mark of a wise man to set in order and to make judgments, and judgments about inferior matters are made on the basis of some higher principle, a wise man in any particular field is said to be one who considers the highest principle in that field ... One, therefore, who considers absolutely the highest principle of the entire universe, which is God, is said to be the wisest of all ...'[167]

(b′) The comparison we are seeking between theology, divine faith, and human knowledge is found in Vatican I, DB 1795, 1796, 1800, 1820; DS 3015, 3016, 3020, 3045; ND 131, 132, 136, 140.

165 Ibid. 1, q. 12, a. 5 c. and ad 2m.
166 Ibid. q. 1, aa. 3 and 7.
167 Ibid. a. 6 c.

	Principium	**Obiectum**
Cognitio naturalis	Naturale lumen rationis	Naturaliter cognoscibilia
Fides divina	Lumen fidei	Mysteria[168]
Theologia	Ratio per fidem illustrata	Mysteria imperfecte intellecta

(c′) Notate aliter ad fidem et theologiam comparari cognitionem humanam, et aliter ad easdem comparari intellectum humanum. Tam fides quam theologia sunt habitus et operationes intellectus humani, sed non ideo sunt operationes cognitionis humanae.

Cuius differentiae fundamentum est quod intellectus humanus plura naturaliter desiderat quam naturaliter consequi potest. Intellectus enim humanus *ut intellectus* habet obiectum formale (omnibus intellectibus commune) quod est ens; idem intellectus humanus *ut humanus* habet obiectum proprium quod est quidditas sive natura in materia corporali exsistens. Propter obiectum formale, intellectus humanus in omnia tendit, omnia est potens facere et fieri, anima est quodammodo omnia, de omnibus quaerere potest, omnia (= ens) cognoscere desiderat. Propter obiectum proprium, non omnia consequi potest intellectus humanus suis propriis viribus; sed tamen lumine fidei adiutus ea credere potest quae Deus revelat; et lumine gloriae confortatus ipsam divinam essentiam per ipsam divinam essentiam intelligere potest.

Fides ergo excedit cognitionem humanam tum principio tum obiecto, principio quatenus lumen fidei est supernaturale, obiecto quatenus mysteria nisi divinitus revelantur nobis innotescere non possunt (DB 1795). Pariter theologia excedit cognitionem humanam, et quidem iisdem rationibus; nam utitur lumine fidei et tractat obiectum fidei.

Sed fides non simpliciter excedit intellectum humanum: nam potentia intellectus seu eius naturale desiderium extenditur ad omne ens, quod includit obiectum fidei; neque per fidem intellectui infunditur species proportionata obiecto fidei, quae species esset sola divina essentia,[169] et ideo nisi analogice non intelligimus mysteria (DB 1796). Fides ergo intellectum humanum excedit secundum hoc quod per lumen fidei credere possumus verum divinun quod extra et ultra campum veri humani iacet.

	Principle	Object
Natural knowledge	Natural light of reason	Naturally knowable
Divine faith	Light of faith	Mysteries[168]
Theology	Reason enlightened by faith	Mysteries imperfectly understood

(c′) Note that human knowledge is related to faith and theology differently from the way in which the human intellect is related to them. Both faith and theology are habits and operations of the human intellect, but it does not follow that they are operations of human knowledge.

The basis for this difference is the fact that the human intellect naturally desires more than it can naturally attain. For the human intellect *as intellect* has a formal object, common to all intellects, which is being. But this same human intellect *as human* has a proper object, which is the quiddity or nature existing in corporeal matter. Because of its formal object, the human intellect tends towards all things, is able to make and become all things, can inquire about all things, desires to know all things (= being): the human soul is in a way all things. Because of its proper object, however, the human intellect cannot attain all things by its own powers. Nevertheless, aided by the light of faith it can believe what God has revealed; and strengthened by the light of glory it is able to understand the divine essence through the divine essence itself.

Faith, therefore, exceeds human knowledge in both its principle and its object: in its principle inasmuch as the light of faith is supernatural, and in its object inasmuch as the mysteries cannot become known to us without divine revelation (DB 1795, DS 3015, ND 131). Similarly, theology exceeds human knowledge, and for the same reasons; for it uses the light of faith and treats the object of faith.

But faith does not absolutely exceed the human intellect; for the power of the intellect, its natural desire, extends to all being, which includes the object of faith. Yet faith does not infuse the intellect with that *species* that is proportionate to the object of faith, which *species* would be the divine essence alone,[169] and for this reason we have only an analogical understanding of the mysteries (DB 1796). Hence, faith exceeds the human intellect in that through the light of faith we are enabled to believe a divine truth that lies above and beyond the field of human truth.

168 See DB 1792, 1820; DS 3011, 3045; ND 219, 140.
169 Thomas Aquinas, *Summa theologiae*, q. 12, a. 5 c.

Similiter theologia non simpliciter excedit intellectum humanum, et ii-sdem quidem rationibus uti antea circa fidem.

(d′) Comparantur deinde fides et theologia, quarum differentia in eo est quod fides tantum credit sed theologia ad intelligentiam quandam imper-fectam eorum pertingit quae fides credit (DB 1796).[170]

Quae quidem intelligentia decursu temporum augetur; aucta autem in-telligentia, augetur consequenter scientia; et auctis tam intelligentia quam scientia, augetur illa capacitas omnia ordinandi et iudicandi quae est sa-pientia (DB 1800).

N.B. S. Thomas: 'Quaedam enim disputatio ordinatur ad removendum dubitationem an ita sit; et in tali disputatione theologica maxime utendum est auctoritatibus ... Quaedam vero disputatio est magistralis in scholis non ad removendum errorem sed ad instruendum auditores ut inducantur ad intellectum veritatis quam intendit: et tunc oportet rationibus inniti inve-stigantibus veritatis radicem, et facientibus scire quomodo sit verum quod dicitur: alioquin si nudis auctoritatibus magister quaestionem determinet, certificabitur quidem auditor quod ita est, sed nihil scientiae vel intellectus acquiret et vacuus abscedet.'[171]

(e′)[172] Quare reicienda esse videtur illa methodus theologica quae *unice* consistit in auctoritatibus citandis et auditoribus certificandis (positivismus Christianus, *Denzingertheologie*).

Primo arguitur ex Vaticano quod docet theologiam posse et debere ali-quam mysteriorum intelligentiam assequi: theologia enim potest, quia ratio per fidem illustrata potest (DB 1796); theologia etiam debet, nam illa in-telligentia est fructuosissima, et theologia non debet esse minus fructuosa quam esse potest.

Deinde arguitur ex contradictionibus internis istius methodi positivisti-cae.

Prima contradictio in eo est quod ipsae auctoritates quam maxime

Theology likewise does not absolutely exceed the human intellect, for the same reasons as given above in regard to faith.

(d') Let us now compare faith and theology, whose difference lies in this, that faith simply believes while theology attains an imperfect understanding of the truths believed by faith (DB 1796, DS 3016, ND 132).[170]

This understanding of the truths of faith grows in the course of time. With growth in understanding there is a consequent growth in knowledge; and with growth in both understanding and knowledge there is growth in that ability to order and judge all things, which is wisdom (DB 1800, DS 3020, ND 136).

Note here the words of St Thomas: 'One kind of argument is directed to removing doubts as to whether something is so. In such arguments in theology, one relies especially on the authorities ... But another kind of argument is that of the teacher in the schools. It seeks not to remove error but to instruct the students so that they understand the truth that the teacher hopes to convey. In such cases it is important to base one's argument on reasons that go to the root of the truth in question, that make hearers understand how what is said is true. Otherwise, if the teacher settles a question simply by an appeal to authorities, the students will have their certitude that the facts are indeed as stated; but they will acquire no knowledge or understanding, and they will go away empty.'[171]

(e')[172] We must therefore reject that theological method that consists *solely* in quoting authorities and filling students with certitudes (Christian positivism, *Denzingertheologie*).

Our first reason for saying this is that Vatican I teaches that theology can and ought to acquire some understanding of the mysteries. Theology can, because reason enlightened by faith can do so (DB 1796, DS 3016, ND 132). It also ought to, for such an understanding is very fruitful, and theology ought not to be less fruitful than it can possibly be.

Our second reason is that that sort of positivistic method contains internal contradictions.

One contradiction lies in the fact that [ecclesiastical] authorities them-

---

170 On this, see Lonergan, *Divinarum personarum* 7–51; [*The Triune God: Systematics* 6–123. 'DB 1796' was added by hand in the autograph.]

171 Thomas Aquinas, *Quaestiones quodlibetales* 4, q. 9, a. 3. [See above, p. 17, note 22.]

172 [At this point in the autograph, the date at the top of the page switches to 5-5-62.]

laudant theologiam S. Thomae, quinimo praecipiunt ut theologia doceatur secundum principia, rationem, doctrinam S. Thomae.[173] Si ergo audiuntur auctoritates, etiam auditur S. Thomas, qui tamen explicite docuit nudis auctoritatibus procedere 'nihil scientiae vel intellectus' continere sed auditores 'vacuos' relinquere.

Altera contradictio in eo est quod, praetermissa intelligentia mysteriorum, etiam intelligentia auctoritatum praetermittatur necesse est. Non enim alia est intelligentia mysteriorum laudata post initium, et alia crescens intelligentia laudata ad finem cap. 4, sess. III, c. Vaticani (DB 1796, 1800), sed una eademque est et mysteriorum et decursu temporum crescens. Neque crevit haec intelligentia contra auctoritates vel praeter auctoritates, sed in ipsis auctoritatibus hoc augmentum quam maxime est perspicuum; nihil enim aliud est quam dogmatum evolutio. Qui ergo intelligentiam mysteriorum non vult, intelligentiam dogmatis evolventis non vult; qui intelligentiam dogmatis evolventis non vult, intelligentiam auctoritatum non vult. Quomodo ergo in auctoritatibus fundari potest theologia quae ipsas auctoritates intelligere non vult? Per contradictionem. Undenam contradictio? Quia contra auctoritates praetermittitur doctrina S. Thomae et placita positivistica intellectu obnubilato acceptantur.

(g) Transitus ex fide divina in theologiam[174]

(a') Post comparationem quasi staticam inter fidem et theologiam, ad comparationem dynamicam transeundum est. Quae dynamica comparatio duplici perficitur gressu, alio generico qui similes transitus in aliis materiis etiam considerat, alio specifico, qui ad differentias motui ex fide in theologiam proprias attendit.

(b') Generice ergo distingui possunt (1) terminus a quo, (2) terminus ad quem, (3) principium transitus, (4) finis transitus, et (5) reditus.

selves have the highest praise for the theology of St Thomas, and in fact ordain that theology be taught according to the principles, method, and doctrine of St Thomas.[173] If, then, we heed these authorities, we shall also be listening to Thomas as he explicitly teaches that theology by authorities alone contains 'no knowledge or understanding' and so leaves its students similarly 'empty.'

A second contradiction is this, that if you disregard an understanding of the mysteries you will necessarily disregard an understanding of the authorities. For the understanding of the mysteries mentioned near the beginning of Vatican I, sess. III, chapter 4 (DB 1796, DS 3016, ND 132) and that growing understanding mentioned at the end of the chapter (DB 1800, DS 3020, ND 136) are not two different things, but it is one and the same that is an understanding of the mysteries and that grows in the course of time. Now this understanding has not grown in a way contrary to or apart from authorities; rather, this growth is most evident in these authorities themselves, for it is nothing other than the development of dogmas. Hence, whoever rejects an understanding of the mysteries rejects an understanding of developing dogmas; and whoever rejects an understanding of developing dogmas rejects an understanding of the authorities. How, then, can theology be based upon authorities if it will not understand the authorities themselves? Only by being self-contradictory. And whence does this contradiction arise? From the fact that contrary to the [ecclesiastical] authorities, the teaching of St Thomas is ignored, and with this intellectual obfuscation the erroneous notions of positivism gain acceptance.

(g) Transition from divine faith to theology[174]

(a′) After a static comparison, as it were, between faith and theology, we turn now to a dynamic comparison. This dynamic comparison will be made in two steps, first generically, by considering similar transitions in other fields, and then specifically, by noting the differences proper to the movement from faith to theology.

(b′) Generically speaking, then, we can distinguish (1) the terminus-from-which, (2) the terminus-to-which, (3) the principle of the transition, (4) the term of the transition, and (5) the return.

173 [See the reference to canon 1366, §2 of the 1917 Code of Canon Law on p. 421 above.]
174 [For corresponding material in *Early Works on Theological Method 1*, see chapter 1962-7.]

Comparantur terminus-a-quo et terminus-ad-quem uti (1) implicitum et explicitum, (2) actus exercitus et actus signatus, (3) *le vécu et le thématique*, (4) *verstehen und erklären*, (5) *existenziell und existenzial*, (6) vita et theoria, (7) experientia et experimentum, (8) subiectum dramatico-practicum et subiectum theoreticum, (9) mundus vel aspectabilis vel interior et mundus intelligibilis.

Principium motus ex termino-a-quo ad terminum-ad-quem est admiratio (initium omnis philosophiae et scientiae,[175] quaestio, problema, *Fragestellung.*

Finis motus seu transitus attingitur, quatenus pervenitur ad explicitum, signatum, thematizatum, explicatum, existentialia, theoriam, experimentum, subiectum theoreticum, mundum intelligibilem. Pervenitur autem duplici gressu, nempe, concipiendo ut dicatur quid sit, et iudicando ut dicatur utrum res se habeat sicut concepta est.

Reditus denique est applicatio expliciti, theoriae, etc., ad casus concretos.

(c′) Circa terminum a quo et ad quem, principium et finem motus, et reditum seu applicationem, notantur in genere:

Pro diversis rerum aspectibus diversae fieri possunt explicitationes seu explicationes quarum singulae sunt validae et verae. E.g., incipiendo a NT fieri potest grammatica NT, lexicon NT, studium linguisticum, studium stylisticum, studium compositionis quoad modum, quoad tempus, quoad fontes, quoad auctores, quoad notiones geographicas, historicas, morales, doctrinales, etc., etc.

Eiusmodi diversa studia eiusdem rei poni possunt (1) in contextu ampliori (ex grammatica NT ad grammaticam comparativam, ex linguistica NT ad linguisticam comparativam, etc., etc.), vel (2) possunt mutuo se opitulari secundum organicam quandam interdependentiam diversorum aspectuum eiusdem rei. Studia possunt esse vel minora, quae ab uno quodam homine perficiuntur, vel maiora quae nisi saeculorum decursu non absolvuntur.

Ipse transitus seu motus potest fieri per modum actus exerciti, per modum vitae, per modum experientiae, per modum intelligentiae. E contra,

The terminus-from-which and the terminus-to-which are comparable to each other as (1) the implicit and the explicit, (2) *actus exercitus* and *actus signatus*, (3) *le vécu* and *le thématique*, (4) *verstehen* and *erklären*, (5) *existenziell* and *existenzial*, (6) life and theory, (7) experience and experiment, (8) the dramatic-practical subject and the theoretic subject, (9) the visible world or the world of interiority and the intelligible world.

The principle of the movement from the terminus-from-which to the terminus-to-which is wonder, the beginning of all philosophy and science,[175] a question, a problem, *Fragestellung*.

The term of the movement or transition is attained when one arrives at the explicit, the conceptualized, the thematized, the explained, the *existenzial*, theory, experiment, the theoretic subject, the intelligible world. One arrives at this point in two steps, namely, by forming a concept to say what something is, and by making a judgment to say whether the thing really is as it has been conceived to be.

The return movement is the application of the explicit, the theory, and so forth, to concrete cases.

(c′) Regarding the terminus-from-which and the terminus-to-which, the principle and term of the movement, and the return or application, we have the following general observations to make.

According to the various aspects of things, different explicitations or explications can be made, all of which are valid and true. For example, from the text of the New Testament one can derive a New Testament grammar, a New Testament lexicon, a linguistic study, a stylistic study, a study of the composition of the New Testament as to the type of composition, the various times of composition, the sources, the authors, and with regard to geographical, historical, moral, and doctrinal notions, and so on.

Such varied studies of the same object can be placed (1) in a broader context – moving from New Testament grammar to comparative grammar, from New Testament linguistics to comparative linguistics, and so on – or (2) they can enrich one another through the organic interdependence of various aspects of the same reality. These studies can be minor ones, carried out by one person, or major ones that are carried on over the course of centuries.

This transition or movement can be made in actual practice, in daily living, through actual experience and understanding. On the other hand,

---

175 Aristotle, *Metaphysics*, I, 2, 982 b 11–13

ipse transitus potest fieri explicite, signate, thematice, methodice, sub ductu theoriae. Quo in casu, ipsa transitus explicitatio, signatio, thematizatio, explicatio, theoria, methodus, potest esse erronea vel vera, inadaequata vel adaequata; et ubi vel erronea vel inadaequata est, sequi potest minor vel maior corruptio ipsius transitus. Unde oriuntur disputationes de methodo, invocantur theoriae philosophicae, et ipsae diversae philosophiae ad problema criticum coguntur.

Ubi studium est maius, priora stadia explicationis fieri possunt implicite, exercite, per modum vitae, intelligentiae, experientiae, et solummodo stadia posteriora, ex interventu reflexionis methodologicae, explicite, signate, thematice, sub ductu methodi et theoriae fiunt.

Progrediente studio, tum ex thematizatione et explicatione rei iam peractis, tum ex thematizatione et explicatione ipsius processus thematizandi et explicandi, etiam fit progressus ex simplici et quasi nativa admiratione ad quaestiones exacte positas, debite ordinatas, in finem heuristice definitum methodice conducentes.

(d′) Quae superius (a′ et b′) diximus, nunc exemplis illustramus.

Petrus morbo laborans Paulum medicum consulit. Morbus ei est in actu exercito; intelligit quidem se morbo laborare quem clare et distincte experitur; sed signare nequit qualis sit morbus, explicare non potest qualis sit eius causa qualeve remedium sit adhibendum. Petrum de suis malis narrantem attente audit Paulus; Petro credit Paulus non tamen simpliciter sed secundum quid; quae enim Petrus magni momenti aestimat, ea nullius vel minoris momenti forte iudicat Paulus; quae parvi vel nullius momenti aestimat Petrus, ea magni forte facit Paulus. Sed ulterius Paulus Petrum interrogat, et quidem de iis de quibus non cogitavit Petrus, de iis quae nullatenus cum morbo connexa esse duxit Petrus. Quae signa a Petro narrantur, a Paulo intelliguntur ut symptomata accurate concepta, interrogationibus identificanda, morborum discretiva. Quem morbum non experitur Paulus, non per modum experientiae, sympathiae, empathiae, intuitionis, sed per modum experimenti (exactis positis quaestionibus quibus respondetur Ita vel Non) cognoscit Paulus.

Paulum finximus medicum qui tantummodo scientiam iam acquisitam casui particulari applicat. At ipsa scientia medica evolvi debuit. Technica interrogandi patientes elaborari debuit. In ipso casu Petri adesse potuit ele-

it can be made explicitly, reflectively, thematically, methodically, guided by theory. In this case the explicitation, reflection, thematization, explanation, theory, and method of the transition can be erroneous or correct, inadequate or adequate; and when it is erroneous or inadequate, a greater or lesser corruption of that transition can result. This gives rise to disputes about method; appeals are made to philosophical theories, and the different philosophies have to face the critical problem.

In the case of a major study, the earlier stages of its explication can be carried out implicitly, in actual practice, in daily living, in concrete experience and understanding, and only the later stages emerge as a result of methodological reflection, explicitly, reflectively, thematically, guided by method and theory.

As the study progresses, as a result both of the thematization and explication of the subject already completed and of the thematization and explication of the thematizing and explicating process itself, there is also a progression from a simple and rather naïve wonder to questions that are exactly posed and properly ordered, and that lead methodically to a heuristically defined end.

(d') Let us now give examples to illustrate what we have said above in sections (a') and (b').

Peter is ill, and consults Paul, a physician. His illness is a lived reality; he understands that he is ill with an illness that he clearly and distinctly experiences; but he cannot indicate what kind of illness it is, nor can he explain its cause or know what remedy to use. Paul listens carefully as Peter tells him about his illness. Paul believes Peter, not absolutely however, but with some qualification; for what Peter considers to be quite important, Paul may perhaps consider of little or no importance; and what Peter considers to be of little or no importance Paul may regard as very significant. But Paul questions Peter further, and indeed about things that Peter never even thought about, things that Peter thought had no connection at all with his illness. The signs of his illness that Peter relates Paul understands as symptoms accurately conceived, to be identified through a process of questioning, and essential for diagnosing illnesses. Paul does not experience the illness by way of either personal experience, sympathy, empathy, or intuition, but knows it by way of experiment, that is, by asking exact questions to be answered by a 'yes' or a 'no.'

Paul, our fictitious doctor, simply applies the knowledge that he has acquired to a particular case. But medical science itself had to develop. The technique of questioning patients had to be worked out. And in Peter's case

mentum scientiae medicae ignotum quod Paulus invenit, examinat, explorat, unde et articulum ad periodicam medicam mittit.

Aliud exemplum sit Petrus testis coram Paulo iudice. Iterum Paulus narrationem Petri per interrogationes complet. Et interrogat quidem non ut ius legesque addiscat sed ut facta determinentur. Quamvis Petrus facta melius quam Paulo ignorante cognoscat, interrogat tamen Paulus ut facta cognoscat, non uti a Petro apprehenduntur sed uti sunt iuridica, uti sub legibus cadunt. Ex factis exercitis ad facta iuridice signata proceditur; ex tragedia vitae humanae ad thematizationem legalem transitur; ex intellecta iniustitia ad crimen codice explicatum et definitum movetur; ex experientia ordinaria et confusa ad cognitionem per modum experimenti (singulis elementis seorsum determinatis ex claris et distinctis indiciis) proceditur.

Quo ex exemplo transiri potest ad historiam iuris, ad fundamenta seu philosophiam iuris, ad intelligentiam historiae per fundamenta; unde et colligi potest quae dicitur die *Wendung zur Idee,* scilicet, tendentia ex vita in theoriam, influxus theoriae in vitam, tensio inter vitam et theoriam, processus denique quo pedetentim ipsa vita magis magisque per theoriam informatur et vicissim ipsa theoria, etsi in altissimis principiis fundata, magis magisque particulariter determinatur et exigentiis vitae adaptatur.

Tertium sit exemplum unusquisque sibi ubi dicit 'ego': e.g., ego adsum, ego sum fatigatus, interesse admodum parvum in hac materia habeo ego. Omnes dicimus 'ego'; et dicentes, optime intelligimus quid significemus; iam pridem intelligimus; neminem umquam invenimus qui nesciat quid significet quando 'ego' dicat. Adeo obvium atque manifestum est 'ego' ut insanire videatur qui de eo dubitaret, quaeret, investiget. Ad illud rerum genus sane pertinet quae sunt 'taken for granted,' 'tout naturel,' '*selbstverständlich.*'

Quae quidem omnia verissima sunt quoad actum exercitum, *le vécu, verstehen, existenziell,* vitam, experientiam, subiectum dramatico-practicum. At hoc minime impedit quominus fiat transitus ad actus signatos, ad *le thématique,* ad *erklären,* ad *existenzial,* ad theoriam, ad ea quae per modum experimenti quodammodo verificantur, ad subiectum theoreticum mundumque intelligibilem.

At ipse hic transitus diversimode effici potest: metaphysice, gnoseologice, psychologice, phaenomenologice, linguistice. Singuli transitus terminan-

there could well have been some element hitherto unknown to medical science that Paul discovers, examines, and researches, the results of which research he submits as an article to a medical journal.

In our second example, let us imagine that Peter is a witness at a trial before Paul as the judge. Again Paul fills out Peter's story by means of questions. He questions him, not to learn what the law is but to determine the facts of the case. Although Peter knows the facts better than Paul, Paul interrogates him in order to know the facts, not as Peter apprehends them, but as they are in relation to the law and jurisprudence. There is a process here from deeds as done to deeds as juridically significant. There is a transition from a tragic episode in life to juridical thematization, a movement from a deed recognized as an offence to a crime defined in a code of law, a process from an ordinary and somewhat unclear experience to knowledge acquired by way of experiment through the separate determination of each element of the case from clear and distinct pieces of evidence.

From this example we can go on to the history of law, to the fundamentals or philosophy of law, and to an understanding of its history through its fundamentals. From all this one can gather what is meant by *die Wendung zur Idee*, that is, the movement from daily living to theory, the influence of theory on living, the tension between living and theory, and the process in which living gradually becomes more and more informed by theory, and theory in turn, even if founded upon the highest principles, is elaborated in ever greater detail and adapted to the demands of everyday life.

The third example is something that we can all do for ourselves when we say the word 'I': 'I am present,' 'I am tired,' 'I have very little interest in this stuff.' We all say 'I,' and as we say it, we all know perfectly well what we mean. We have understood its meaning for a long time; I have never found anyone who does not know what they mean when they say 'I.' So obvious is the meaning of 'I' that anyone who would have doubts about it or question it or investigate it would seem to be crazy. It surely belongs to that class of things that are 'taken for granted,' '*tout naturel*,' '*selbstverständlich.*'

This is all perfectly true with regard to the act performed, the *vécu, verstehen*, the *existenziell*, daily living, experience, the dramatic-practical subject. But this by no means prevents the transition to reflection upon the action as meaningful, to the *thématique*, the *erklären*, the *existenzial*, to theory, to what are verified in some way through experiment, to the theoretic subject in the intelligible world.

Now this transition itself can occur in various ways: metaphysically, gnoseologically, psychologically, phenomenologically, linguistically. Each

tur ad contextum longe maiorem pure metaphysicum, pure gnoseologicum, pure psychologicum, pure phaenomenologicum, pure linguisticum. At iterum omnes transitus, quatenus ad concretum reducuntur, mutuo se opitulantur quatenus diversos eiusdem rei aspectus illuminant, et etiam mutuo sibi pugnant quatenus synthesin quandam concretam diversorum aspectuum exigunt.

Sed et ulterius in historiam thematizationis *tou* 'ego' regredi potest. Diu dicebatur 'ego' quin thematizaretur. Primo, forte, grammatice facta est thematizatio: 'ego' est pronomen personale primam personam denotans. At implicita forte iam aderat thematizatio sub alio nomine, puta, in mythis de umbris, de psyche, de immortalitate,[176] sicut postea in philosophicis speculationibus de iisdem, in psychologia S. Augustini quae de 'mente' quam plurima disseruit. Etc., Etc.

(e') Mens symbolica, cultura classica, conscientia historica: Hos adhibemus terminos (1) ut diversas habitudines inter vitam et theoriam significemus et (2) ut consequentes tendentias designemus quae diversa stadia in historia generis humani modo quodam schematico distinguamus.

Mens ergo symbolica est ubi vivitur sine theoria, ubi signatio, thematizatio, explicatio vel nullae sunt vel minimae. Quod tamen non facit ut nulla sit admiratio, nullae quaestiones, nulla problemata. Tantummodo facit ut quaestiones et responsa, problemata et solutiones, symbolice evolvuntur.

Cultura classica non tantum vivit sed etiam theoriam colit. Quod tamen ita facit ut antitheses inter vitam et theoriam vel mitigentur vel supprimantur. Theoria re vera in magnis philosophis et in veris scientiarum cultoribus habetur; sed eadem ab 'excultis' participatur, non qua theoria est, non quae subiectum theoreticum in mundo intelligibili versans exigit, sed prout a scholarum magistris ad captum discipulorum docetur, prout intra limites sensus communis quodammodo recipitur, prout facta est '*la haute vulgarisation.*' E contra, vita in sua diversitate, multiplicitate, mobilitate, particularitate, spontaneitate, irrationalitate ita vivitur et agnoscitur ut tamen

of these transitions terminates in a much larger context that is purely meta-physical, purely gnoseological, purely psychological, purely phenomeno-logical, purely linguistic. But again, all these transitions, in being brought back to the concrete, enrich one another insofar as they throw light on different aspects of the same reality, yet also conflict with one another insofar as they demand a concrete synthesis of those various aspects.

But we can go farther back into the history of the thematization of the word 'I.' 'I' was uttered for a long time without being thematized. The first thematization was perhaps done by grammar: 'I' is the personal pronoun denoting the first person singular. But there may well have already been an implicit thematization under another name, such as in myths about the 'shades,' the soul, or immortality,[176] just as later on these same notions became the subject of philosophical speculation, of Augustine's psychology with its frequent mention of 'mind,' and so on.

(e') The symbolic mind, classical culture, and historical consciousness: We are using these terms (1) to express the various relationships between life and theory, and (2) to designate the resulting tendencies by which in a rather schematic fashion different stages in human history can be distinguished.

The mind is symbolic when life is lived without theory, where reflective conceptualization, thematization, and explanation are minimal or non-existent. This does not mean, however, that there is no wondering, that there are no questions, no problems. It simply means that questions and answers, problems and solutions, are developed by way of symbols.

Classical culture not only lives, it also cultivates theory. But it does so in such a way that the antitheses between life and theory are minimized or simply suppressed. There really is theory present in the major philosophers and in the genuine practitioners of the sciences. But 'educated' people also share in this same theory, not as theory, however, not as something requiring a theoretic subject in the intelligible world, but as something taught by schoolmasters according to the capacity of their students and received somehow or other within the limits of common sense and propagated by '*haute vulgarisation*.' On the other hand, human life in all its diversity, mul-

---

176 [In *Method in Theology* 88, Lonergan will give the example of how, in the course of the development of language, referring to oneself is sometimes achieved by pointing 'to one's head or neck or chest or stomach or arms or legs or feet or hands or whole body.']

haec omnia, quippe temporalia et contingentia, quodammodo praetermittantur et ipsa vita per principia generalia, per idealia, per exemplaria, per praecepta, per 'hominen prout sempiternis rationibus esse debeat' apprehendatur. *'Plus ça change, plus c'est la même chose.'*

Conscientia historica non solum theoriam vitae addit sed etiam antitheses inter vitam et theoriam in clara luce ponit. Thematizatur processus thematizandi, signatur processus actum exercitum signandi, explicantur tum intelligentia quae technice non explicat tum intelligentia quae technice explicat (*verstehen und erklären*), methodi procedendi e vita in theoriam methodice excoluntur, subiectum fit conscium sui tum ut dramatico-practicum, tum ut theoreticum, tum ut interius principium obiectivandi mundum aspectabilem, mundum theoreticum, mundum interiorem, etc.

Theoria excolitur secundum proprias exigentias, secundum antithesin ad vitam: cogita quam abstrusa sit logica moderna, philosophia moderna systematica, critica, transcendentalis, methodica, scientiae modernae in parte sua theoretica, uti physica, chimia, etc. Vita agnoscitur in ipsa sua tensione cum theoria, simul cum tendentia ad theoriam et exigentia theoriae. Agnoscitur in ipsa sua multiplicitate, diversitate, mobilitate, particularitate, spontaneitate, irrationalitate. Scientia vitae quaeritur, non per abstractionem a temporalibus et contingentibus sed per intelligentiam et explicationem ipsorum temporalium et contingentium, secundum eorum evolutionem historicam. Ipse philosophus vel scientificus ipse se cogitat (1) ut inconscie productum ab ambiente historico-sociali, quamdiu ad conscientiam historicam non pervenerat, et (2) quam primum ad conscientiam historicam pervenit, ut investigatorem criticum, iudicem, actorem eiusdem processus historico-socialis.

(f') His in genere positis de transitu, iam specifice considerandus est transitus ex fide divina in theologiam. Primo, ponitur exemplum quoddam contemporaneum. Deinde, idem exemplum analysi subicitur secundum topica generica iam indicata. Tertio, ad considerationem generalem transitus ad theologiam proceditur.

(g') Exemplo sit argumentum circa conscientiam Christi humanam ab E. Gutwenger positum, *Bewusstsein und Wissen Christi*, Innsbruck, 1960, pp. 47–78, ubi tria sunt capita, nempe, I, 3: Die Ichaussagen Christi in den Evan-

tiplicity, changeability, particularity, spontaneity, and irrationality is lived and acknowledged, but in such a way that all of these qualities, being temporal and contingent, are somehow ignored, and life itself is apprehended in terms of general principles, ideals, models, precepts, 'man as he ought to be according to eternal reasons.' *Plus ça change, plus c'est la même chose.*

Historical consciousness not only adds theory to life, but also clearly brings to light the antitheses between life and theory. Thematization is itself thematized, the process of reflection upon life is itself reflected upon, both the understanding that does not explain things in technical terms and that which does – *verstehen* and *erklären* – are themselves explained, methods are developed for proceeding methodically from life to theory, the subject is made conscious of self as a dramatic-practical subject, as a theoretic subject, as the interior principle of the objectification of the visible world, the world of theory, the world of interiority, and so on.

Theory is pursued according to its proper exigencies, according to its antithesis to life. Think of how abstruse are modern logic, modern systematic, critical, transcendental, and methodical philosophy, and the theoretical part of modern sciences such as physics, chemistry, and so on. Life is recognized in its tension with theory, along with its tendency to theory and its exigency for theory. It is seen in its multiplicity, diversity, changeability, particularity, spontaneity, and irrationality. A science of life is sought, not by abstracting from the temporal and the contingent, but through an understanding and explanation of those very temporal and contingent elements according to their historical development. As long as they have not yet arrived at historical consciousness themselves, philosophers or scientists think of themselves as brought up unawares in a historical-social milieu, but as soon as they do arrive at historical consciousness, they think of themselves as investigators, critics, judges, and active participants in this same historical-social process.

(f') Having made these general observations about this transition, we must now consider specifically the transition from divine faith to theology. First, we shall give a contemporary example; next, we shall analyze this example according to the general topics already mentioned; third, we shall go on to consider in a general way the transition to theology.

(g') Our example will be Engelbert Gutwenger's argument concerning the human consciousness of Christ, in *Bewusstsein und Wissen Christi: Eine dogmatische Studie* (Innsbruck: Verlag Felizian Rauch, 1960), pp. 47–78, set out in three chapters: ɪ, 3; pp. 47–55: 'I' spoken by Christ in the Gospels; ɪ,

gelien, pp. 47–55; I, 4: Das Ich in der psychologischen Erfahrung, pp. 55–68; I, 5: Die menschliche Icherfahrung Christi, pp. 68–78.[177]

Quae tria capita ad hoc fere schema logicum reducuntur, ut capite tertio proponitur praemissa minor, nempe, haec et haec tali sensu a Christo homine esse dicta, capite quarto proponitur praemissa maior, nempe, quemadmodum e dictis ad ipsam experientiam psychologicam concludendam procedendum sit, et capite quinto concluditur de conscientia Christi humana.

Re vera tamen ipsum schema logicum naturam argumenti parum manifestat. Id quod fit est signatio et thematizatio et explicatio datorum evangelicorum in quibus Christus 'ego' dixit. Quae quidem explicatio non per se sola et isolata stat, quasi nemo umquam dicta vel facta Christi thematizavit, sed maximum quendam praesupponit contextum dogmaticum atque theologicum, unde et habetur elaboratissima *Fragestellung*, et urgetur valde complicata cohaerentiae exigentia.

Unde quattuor distinguenda veniunt: ipsa generalis quaestio (a″); quaestio quae P. Gutwenger occurrit (b″); responsum ab evangelistis quaesitum (c″); responsum a P. Gutwenger datum (d″).

(a″) Omnes semper Christiani et legebant et intelligebant loca evangelica in quibus 'ego' a Christo homine dicitur: Ego dico vobis; Sitio; Antequam Abraham fieret ego sum; Ego in Patre et Pater in me est; etc. Eadem loca a Patribus thematizata sunt in controversiis et conciliis christologicis et, ulterius, a theologis qui de ontologia unionis hypostaticae disputaverunt. At nisi his ultimis decenniis inter theologos catholicos eadem loca sub aspectu psychologico non sunt thematizata.

Quam ob causam, ipsa generalis quaestio est nova et ideo nobis exemplum praebet in quo thematizatio examinari potest quin longiora atque difficiliora studia historica fiant.

Quaestionis generalis elementa fere sunt: dogmata Christologica inter catholicos recepta; diversae sententiae theologorum circa unionem hypostaticam; problema determinandi quid praecise sit subiectum psychologi-

4; pp. 55–68: 'I' in psychological experience; I, 5; pp. 68–78: Christ's human experience of 'I.'[177]

These three chapters can be summarized schematically in the following logical form: I, 3 states the minor premise, namely, Christ as man said this and that with this meaning; I, 4 states the major premise, that is, how one should proceed from what Christ said to drawing conclusions about what he experienced psychologically; and I, 5 states the author's conclusions about Christ's human consciousness.

In fact, however, this logical scheme tells us little about the nature of his argument. What we have here is a reflection upon the data, the gospel passages in which Christ said 'I,' and a thematization and explication of them. This explication does not stand alone and isolated, as if no one else ever thematized Christ's words or deeds. But it presupposes an enormous dogmatic and theological context; hence, there is an extremely elaborate *Fragestellung* and the need for a very complicated exigency for coherence.

Thus, we find that there are four things to be distinguished: (a″) the general question; (b″) the question that occurred to Gutwenger; (c″) the answer sought from the evangelists; (d″) the answer given by Gutwenger.

(a″) All Christians at all times have read and understood the gospel passages in which the word 'I' is uttered by Christ the man: 'I say to you'; 'I thirst'; 'Before Abraham was, I am'; 'I am in the Father and the Father is in me'; and so on. These same passages were thematized by the Fathers in the Christological controversies and councils and further thematized by theologians in their disputations about the ontology of the hypostatic union. But it is only in these last few decades that these passages have been thematized by Catholic theologians under their psychological aspect.

Hence, the general question itself is a new one and thus provides us with a good test case for examining thematization without going into fairly lengthy and difficult historical studies.

These are the elements of the general question: the Christological dogmas accepted by Catholics; the various opinions of theologians concerning the hypostatic union; the problem of determining precisely what is a psy-

177 [See also Lonergan's 1962 notes for a lecture at a seminar of professors from the Gregorian University and Biblical Institute, Rome, published now as 'De Argumento Theologico ex Sacra Scriptura,' 'The Theological Argument from Sacred Scripture,' in Bernard Lonergan, *Shorter Papers* 247–55.]

cum; problema integrandi theoriam psychologicam de subiecto cum theoria metaphysica de subsistente; problema procedendi analogice ex theoria de subiecto et subsistente ad illud subiectum subsistens quod est Christus Deus et homo.

(b″) P. Gutwenger, vestigiis P. Galtier premens, pariter tenet Tiphanum caeteris theologis melius exposuisse unionem hypostaticam. Ubi autem P. Galtier concludit personam Christi non inter data conscientiae Christi hominis dari, quia persona uti a Tiphano concipitur ordinis non psychologici sed tantummodo ontologici est, dubitat P. Gutwenger. Nam qui experientiam suam psychologicam vel leviter examinat, alio modo 'tu' et alio modo 'ego' conscientiae humanae advenire iudicat; quod enim ut 'tu' experimur, illud ex parte obiecti nobis sistitur; quod autem ut 'ego' experimur, illud ex adversa parte subiecti sistitur. Ulterius, si in conscientia Christi humana non adest divina persona nisi per visionem beatam (uti voluit P. Galtier), sequitur divinam personam non adesse nisi per modum obiecti, nisi per modum alicuius 'tu.'[178] Unde oritur quaestio prout a P. Gutwenger evangelistis ponitur: An dixerit Christus homo 'ego' eo sensu quo persona ut persona significetur?

(c″) Cui quaestioni exacte propositae respondent evangelistae abundanter. Longior series textuum citatur in quibus 'ego' a Christo dicitur et persona ut persona (e.g., relationibus interpersonalibus implicata) significatur, pp. 50–55.

Qui quidem usus sacrae scipturae *ad modum experimenti* est. Sicut medicus patientem interrogat, non ut mentem eius exploret, non ut sentimenta eius participet, sed ut signa a patiente nota interpretetur et morbi symptomata pedetentim colligat; vel iterum, sicut iudex testem interrogat ut ea facta eaque sola cognoscat quae ad legalem rei conceptionem faciant; ita P. Gutwenger quaestionem exacte conceptam evangelistis proponit. 'Hier

chological subject; the problem of integrating the psychological theory of the subject with the metaphysical theory of the subsistent; and the problem of proceeding analogically from a theory of the subject and of the subsistent to that subsistent subject who is Christ, God and man.

(b″) Gutwenger, following Paul Galtier, holds that Tiphanus had the best explanation of the hypostatic union of any theologian. But when Galtier concludes that Christ's person was not part of the data of his human consciousness, on the grounds that his person, as conceived by Tiphanus, belongs only to the ontological order and not to the psychological, Gutwenger hesitates. Anyone who even cursorily examines his or her own psychological experience will judge that the way 'you' come into human consciousness is different from the way 'I' do; for what we experience as 'you' stands before us on the side of the object, while what we experience as 'I' lies on the opposite side, the side of the subject. Furthermore, if, as Galtier would have it, the divine person is present in Christ's human consciousness only through the beatific vision, it follows that the divine person is present there only as an object, only as a 'you.'[178] From this there arises the question that Gutwenger puts to the evangelists: Did the man Christ say 'I' in the sense that a person as person was being signified?

(c″) This very precisely stated question has been answered abundantly by the evangelists. A lengthy series of texts are quoted (pp. 50–55) in which Christ says 'I' and a person as person (implied, for example, in interpersonal relationships) is signified.

Now this is using sacred Scripture *in the manner of an experiment.* It is just like the doctor who questions the patient, not to explore his mind or share his feelings, but to interpret the signs of illness noted by the patient and so gradually come to recognize the disease by its symptoms; or again, it is like the judge interrogating the witness in order to determine those facts and those alone that make for an understanding of the case from a legal standpoint. This is how Gutwenger has precisely formulated his question and posed it to the evangelists. 'Hier kommt es lediglich darauf an, festzus-

---

178 [See Lonergan's treatment of Gutwenger's relation to Galtier in *Early Works on Theological Method 1* 167. See also his presentation and criticism of Galtier's position in *The Ontological and Psychological Constitution of Christ* 269–77. Tiphanus's position on the ontological constitution of Christ is mentioned briefly in the latter work at 117.]

kommt es lediglich darauf an, festzustellen, was Christus meinte, wenn er in seinen Aussagen das Wörtlein 'Ich' verwendete.'[179]

Quia interrogatio evangelistarum est ad modum experimenti, ea seliguntur loca scripturistica quae fini experimenti satisfaciunt; sufficeret quidem unus locus in quo indubie 'ego' a Christo dictum personam ut personam significaret; sed multitudinem invenit P. Gutwenger eaque sub variis capitibus ordinata seriatim cum brevissimo commentario citat.

Quare ipse suum procedendi modum sic descripsit: 'Im folgenden soll nun ein schematischer, durchaus nicht alles umfassender Überblick über die Personalprädikationen Christi geboten werden. Das Material, das sich anführen lässt, ist derart überwältigend, dass sich kein berichtigter Zweifel gegen die Tatsache vorbringen lässt, dass mit dem Gebrauch des Wörtleins 'Ich' in den Selbstaussagen Christi nur eines bezweckt ist, nämlich die Person Christi zu bezeichnen.'[180]

Pariter missas facit omnes quaestiones, quas ob alios fines movere possunt exegetae, circa Formgeschichte, modum compositionis, chronologiam, etc. Unum tantum vult, nempe, Christum ea substantialiter dixisse quae in evangeliis ei attribuuntur.[181] Cuius omissionis ratio est, eadem verba multis et diversis modis ad thematizationem produci posse, neque tamen ideo omnes modos semper esse adhibendos, sed eos tantum qui ad finem inquisitionis faciunt.

(d″) Ex responso evangelistarum ad responsum suum denique procedit P. Gutwenger. Sicut enim alio in contextu signa morbi a patiente narrantur, et alio in contextu eoque scientifico a medico collocantur, sicut pariter alio in contextu testimonium a teste concipitur, et in alium contextum eumque iuridicum a iudice transfertur, ita pariter procedit P. Gutwenger. Quod intra contextum vitae et actu exercito a Christo dictum est, quod intra contextum vitae et actu exercito ab evangelistis narratum est, hoc a P. Gutwenger in contextum dogmaticum, theologicum, metaphysicum, psy-

tellen, was Christus meinte, wenn er in seinen Aussagen das Wörtlein "Ich" verwendete.'[179]

Because his interrogation of the evangelists is done as an experiment, he selects those scriptural passages that suit the purpose of the experiment. One text would indeed be enough to show beyond doubt that Christ said 'I' to signify his person as a person; but Gutwenger has found a large number of them, has arranged them under various headings and quoted them in order along with a brief commentary.

Gutwenger himself has thus described his way of proceeding: 'Im folgenden soll nun ein schematischer, durchaus nicht alles umfassender Überblick über die Personalprädikationen Christi geboten werden. Das Material, das sich anführen lässt, ist derart überwältigend, dass kein berechtigter Zweifel gegen die Tatsache vorbringen lässt, dass mit dem Gebrauch des Wörtleins "Ich" in den Selbstaussagen Christi nur eines bezweckt ist, nämlich die Person Christi zu bezeichnen.'[180]

Similarly, he sets aside other questions that for different purposes exegetes ask concerning *Formgeschichte*, manner of composition, chronology, etc. He wants only one thing, namely, that Christ said substantially what the gospels attribute to him.[181] The reason for this omission is that the same words can be thematized in different ways, and therefore not all ways are to be followed, but only those that are conducive to the aim of the particular inquiry.

(d″) Gutwenger then proceeds from the answer of the evangelists to his own answer. Just as the signs of the illness are related by the patient in one context and are placed by the physician in another context, a scientific one, and again, just as the witness conceived his testimony in one context and the judge transfers it to a juridical context, so has Gutwenger proceeded. What Christ said in actual conversation within the context of everyday life and what the evangelists actually narrated in the context of their lives Gut-

---

179 ['Here we are concerned only with ascertaining what Christ intended when in his utterances he used the pronoun "I."' Gutwenger, *Bewusstsein und Wissen Christi* 48.]

180 Ibid. 50. ['What follows will now be a schematic overview of Christ's personal statements, an overview that cannot be all-inclusive. The material at our disposal is so overwhelming as to leave no reasonable doubt about the fact that in the use of the word "I" in Christ's statements about himself only one thing was intended, namely, to indicate the person of Christ.']

181 Ibid. 47.

chologicum transfertur. Sicut concipit Tiphanus unionem hypostaticam
tamquam totum ex natura humana et persona aeterna Verbi constitutum,
ita P. Gutwenger totum quoddam compositum sed psychologicum concludit in quo in Christo homine habentur tum centrum actuum humanorum
tum etiam huius centri adunatio ad Verbum praesens ex parte subiecti.

(h′) De transitu in theologiam modo generali:[182] Quae iam in casu particulari vidimus, iam modo generaliori sunt dicenda. Primo, ergo, de con-
stantibus seu invariantibus elementis dicemus, nempe, (a″) de contextu
praesupposito, (b″) de modo thematizandi, et (c″) de usu fontium. Deinde,
ulteriora addentur circa ipsam methodum temporum decursu sese evolventem.

(a″) De contextu praesupposito: NT praesupponit VT. Fides ecclesiae praesupponit et scripturas et traditionem apostolicam. Incipiens theologia
supponit fidem ecclesiae. Theologia incepta supponit et fidem et praeviam
theologiam et philosophiam illam christianam quae implicite in theologia
continetur.

Contextum quendam praesupponi constans et invariabile est. Sed ipse
qui praesupponitur contextus temporum decursu per evolutionem dogmatum et profectum theologiae continuo augetur. Quinam sit ille contextus,
quemadmodum auctus sit, quali certitudine vel probabilitate singula eius
elementa recipiantur, quaerunt, disputant, docent theologi.

Quo ex contextu procedit omnis quaestio nova tum quoad definitionem
quaestionis tum quoad criteria quae solutionem perpendunt, ponderant,
iudicant. Quem in contextum recipitur novae cuiusque quaestionis solutio,
et quidem uti possibilis, vel probabilis, vel certa, vel theologice certa, vel de
fide definita, etc. At omnis quae consideratur quaestio aut nunc aut olim
nova erat quaestio. Quam ob causam, totus contextus theologicus quasi
summatio quaedam et integratio est omnium solutionum quae aliquando
intra contextum sunt receptae.

Iam vero clarius quodammodo et distinctius perspicitur transitus e fide
in theologiam, ubi nova ponitur quaestio et nova recipitur solutio, ubi augetur contextus theologicus, quam iis in exemplis ubi acute, sane, et soller-

wenger transfers to a doctrinal, theological, metaphysical, and psychological context. As Tiphanus conceived the hypostatic union as a whole constituted by the human nature and the eternal person of the Word, so does Gutwenger conclude to a composite psychological whole in which there is in Christ as man both a center of human acts and also the union of this center to the Word present on the side of the subject.

(h') The transition to theology in general:[182] What we have seen in a particular case must now be expressed in general terms. First, then, we shall speak about the constant or invariant elements, namely, (a″) the presupposed context, (b″) the mode of thematization, and (c″) the use of sources. Then we shall add some further points concerning developments in the method itself over the course of time.

(a″) The presupposed context: The New Testament presupposes the Old. The faith of the church presupposes the scriptures and apostolic tradition. Theology when beginning presupposes the faith of the church. Once begun, theology supposes faith plus previous theology, as well as that Christian philosophy which is contained implicitly in theology.

The fact that some context is presupposed is a constant, an invariable. But the presupposed context itself continually grows over time through the development of dogmas and the progress of theology. What this context is, how it grows, and with what degree of probability or certitude its various elements are accepted is a matter that theologians inquire into, discuss, and teach.

Out of this context every new question arises, both as to the definition of the question and as to the criteria for considering, weighing, and judging its solution. Into this context the solution to each new question enters, whether it is possible, or probable, or certain, or theologically certain, or defined as a matter of faith, and so forth. But every question under consideration either is now or once was a new question. Therefore, the whole context of theology is, as it were, the summation and integration of all the solutions accepted at any time within that context.

Now, this transition from faith to theology is, in a way, more clearly and distinctly discernible when a new question is posed, a new solution accepted, and the theological context thus enlarged, than in those instances when

---

182 [At this point in the autograph, the date at the top of the page switches to 10-5-62.]

ter arguitur sed nihil fere efficitur nisi illa theologicae traditionis repetitio quam nova quaeque exigit generatio. Quam ob causam exemplum posuimus ex recentissima quaestione de conscientia Christi; et pariter in aliis exemplis historice ad illud tempus recurremus quo primo mota et soluta est nova quaedam quaestio.

Haec contextus praesuppositio non solum facit ut inquisitio theologica numquam sine suppositis fiat sed etiam post inceptam theologiam semper augeat, ut ita dicam, distantiam inter contextum originalem et biblicum et contextum postea auctum et theologicum. Quo autem magis augetur haec distantia eo clarius et distinctius apparet theologum scripturas adire easque scrutari atque interpretari, non ad modum discipuli cuius intellectus fere tabula rasa est in qua nihil est scriptum sed ad modum medici vel iudicis qui verba patientis vel testis in suas categorias transponit.

Quem enim in P. Gutwenger procedendi modum deprehendimus, ut ex recenti quadam occasione problema habuerit, ut luce contextus dogmatici, theologici, philosophici, psychologici determinatam quandam quaestionem formularit, ut ex scripturis non repetierit nisi isolati cuiusdam facti claram certamque determinationem, ut hanc determinationem e contextu biblico in suum et praeformatum contextum transtulerit, eundem fere procedendi modum, pro diversitate temporum vel minus vel plus explicitum, sive in Patribus, sive in Scholasticis, sive in subsequentibus theologorum aetatibus, observatum invenies.

Quod positive probabis legendo Tertullianum adversus Praxean, Athanasium adversus Arianos, Basilium de Spiritu sancto, Cyrillum adversus Nestorium, Augustinum contra Pelagianos, Leontium de Monophysitis, Maximum Confessorem de Monotheletis. Quod in ipsa technica quaestionis mediaevalis conspicitur, quae ex oppositis testimoniis problema ducebat et in iisdem speculative reconciliandis solutionem quaerebat. Quod denique in tractatibus, commentariis, manualibus theologicis communiter inveniebatur et recentius a rei biblicae peritis impugnatum est, sane phantasma non fuit sed realitas quae mutanda ducebatur.

Idem etiam negative concluditur. Quae enim dicitur conscientia historica, quae sedulo diversos et sibi succedentes contextus distinguit, non omnium temporum est sed recentioris. Quare, qui conscientiam historicam habet, similem Patribus et Scholasticis non attribuit; qui vero non habet, Patres et Scholasticos sibi similes dubitare non potest.

the matter is, no doubt, argued with acumen and astuteness, yet with virtually no result except a repetition of the theological tradition that each new generation demands. It was for this reason that we took as our example the very recent question about the consciousness of Christ; and we shall similarly have recourse to other examples from a time in the past when some new question was first mooted and solved.

This presupposition of a context means that theological inquiry is not only never without presuppositions but also that, once theology has begun, it always increases, so to speak, the distance between the initial biblical context and the subsequently enlarged theological context. The greater this distance becomes, the more clearly and distinctly evident it is that a theologian should go to the scriptures to study and interpret them, not like a schoolboy, however, whose intellect is a clean slate upon which nothing has been written, but like a physician or a judge who transposes into his own categories what a patient or a witness has told him.

Gutwenger's mode of proceeding, which we have dwelt upon, namely, that he addressed a problem that had recently emerged, that in the light of a dogmatic, theological, philosophical, and psychological context he formulated a very precise question, that he repeated nothing from scripture except the clear and certain determination of an isolated fact and transposed that determination from the biblical context to his own predetermined context, is the very same mode of proceeding you will find to have been followed, more or less explicitly according to the various historical periods, by the Fathers, by the Scholastics, and by theologians in later centuries.

You will find positive proof of this if you read Tertullian against Praxeas, Athanasius against the Arians, Basil on the Holy Spirit, Cyril against Nestorius, Augustine against the Pelagians, Leontius on the Monophysites, and Maximus the Confessor on the Monothelites. It is especially clear in the medieval technique of the question, which proposed a problem arising out of contradictory quotations and then sought the solution by speculatively reconciling them. And what was very commonly found in treatises and commentaries and theological manuals, and more recently has been under attack by biblical scholars, was surely no figment of the imagination but a reality that it has been deemed necessary to change.

The same conclusion can be reached in a negative way. For what is called 'historical consciousness,' which carefully distinguishes a succession of different contexts, is something that is of more recent origin. Accordingly, one who has a historical consciousness will not make the mistake of attributing a similar consciousness to the Fathers or the Scholastics; on the other

(b″) De modo thematizandi theologico:[183] Idem textus in multos et diversos fines adhiberi potest, e.g., NT ut grammaticam scribas, ut lexicon componas, ut mentem Palaestinensem vel Hellenisticam investiges, etc.

Theologo dogmatico textus NT est verbum Dei qua verum.

Verbum (signum articulatum cum sensu, elemento intentionali) sumi potest (1) ut eventus, (2) ut expressio, vel (3) ut occursus.

Ut eventus, consideratur historice. An Paulus re vera scripsit? An tali tempore, tali intentione, ad tales? An ipsa haec verba scripsit?

Ut expressio, consideratur psychologice. Ex qua mente, quo affectu, qua sensibilitate, qua voluntate processerunt haec verba? Ita maxime in hermeneutica romantica (Winckelmann, Schleiermacher, Dilthey) qui interpretem voluerunt per empathiam quandam (*Einfühlen*) ita mentem, affectum, sensum, voluntatem auctoris penetrare, ut dicere possit cur singulae fere phrases sic et non aliter sint formatae.

Ut occursus (*Begegnung*, meeting), consideratur secundum relationes interpersonales, de quibus abundanter personalistae, phaenomenologici, et psychiatrae. Quo in casu thematizatio considerat mutuum influxum personae in personam qui mediantibus verbis producitur. Est consideratio psychologica quasi duplicata, cum duae personae secundum psychologiam considerantur et secundum mutuum influxum psychologicum.[184]

Praeter quos aspectus (qui omnes valide per modum thematis sumi possunt) manet aspectus verbi ad rem quae intenditur, dicitur; secundum quem aspectum verbum aut verum est aut falsum.

hand, those who do not have it will have no doubt that the Fathers and Scholastics were just like themselves.

(b″) The theological way of thematization:[183] The same New Testament text can be used for many different purposes, for example, to compose a New Testament grammar, to compile a New Testament lexicon, to investigate the Palestinian or Hellenistic mentality, and the like.

To a dogmatic theologian the New Testament text is the word of God as true.

The word, an articulated sign with a meaning, an intentional element, can be taken in three ways: (1) as an event, (2) as an expression, or (3) as an encounter.

As an event, it is considered from an historical viewpoint. Did Paul really write this, at this time, with this intention, to these people? Did he write these very words himself?

As an expression, it is considered from a psychological viewpoint. Out of what sort of mentality, what feelings, what sensibility, what intent did these words proceed? Thus, especially a Romantic hermeneutics (as in Winckelmann, Schleiermacher, Dilthey) would have the interpreter so thoroughly enter into the mind, feelings, sensibility, and intent of the writer by way of a certain empathy (*Einfühlen*) as to be able to say why virtually every single phrase was expressed in that particular way and not some other way.

As an encounter (*Begegnung*) it is considered according to interpersonal relations, about which the personalists, phenomenologists, and psychiatrists have had a great deal to say. In this case, thematization considers the influence persons have on one another that occurs through the mediation of words. It is, so to speak, a double psychological consideration, since it considers two persons according to their psychology and according to their psychological influence upon each other.[184]

In addition to these aspects, all of which can be validly taken as a theme, there remains that aspect of a word that regards the thing that is intended or expressed; according to this aspect a word is either true or false.

---

183 [At this point in the autograph, the date at the top of the page switches back to 9-5-62. It is clear, though, that these pages were originally written to follow immediately upon the material preceding the previous section (a″), 'The Presupposed Context,' which was written later and inserted into the notes.]

184 [It would not be long before these particular ideas took shape in the category of mutual self-mediation. See Bernard Lonergan, 'The Mediation of Christ in Prayer,' in *Philosophical and Theological Papers 1958–1964* 174–76.]

Iam vero dogmaticus ideo scripturas adit ut addiscat id quod a Deo dicitur, id quod a Deo docetur. Quod sibi per modum thematis assumit est verum a Deo revelatum.

Ita P. Gutwenger eventum aliunde stabilitum supponit, nempe, Christum dixisse 'ego,' quaestionem psychologicam ponit, nempe, ex qua experientia interna processerit illud dicere 'ego,' sed hanc quaestionem psychologicam non per hermeneuticam romanticam resolvit sed per sensum eius quod in scripturis dicitur et per veritatem istius sensus.

Quod autem a P. Gutwenger factum est, idem universaliter apud Patres et theologos invenies. Assumunt scripturas in thema prout sunt verbum Dei, cui nefas est contradicere, cui ab omnibus fidelibus consentiendum est. Unde et formula illa quam maxime dogmatica, 'Si quis dixerit ... anathema sit.'

Ubi tria praecipue sunt notanda.

Primo, aliud est explicite assignare modum thematizandi theologicum; aliud est talem modum adhibere, quin tamen explicite signetur; tertium denique est verbum Dei invocare, quin de fine theologico cogitetur, imo quin explicite de veritate verbi Dei quidquam dicatur. Quibus distinctis, procedere poteris ab iis quae sunt quam maxime implicita ad ea quae sunt quam maxime explicita. E.g., ubi Paulus, Gal 1.8: 'Sed licet nos aut angelus de caelo evangelizet vobis praeterquam quod evangelizavimus vobis, anathema sit.' Non explicite dicitur quidquam de veritate, de immutabilitate veritatis, de veritate evangelii iam evangelizati, sed eo modo concrete procedit qui theoretice iustificatur per immutabilem evangelii veritatem.[185]

Deinde, ubi in thema assumitur verbum qua verum, eo ipso assumitur quod de contextu in contextum transferri potest. Quod verum de contextu in contextum transferri potest, ex ipsa veri transcendentia habetur. Quod enim verum est, independens a subiecto est, rationem quandam inconditionati et absoluti habet. Quod autem ita independens, inconditionatum, absolutum est, illud non ita huic tali contextui religatur ut idem in alio contextu dici non possit. Quam sane translationem non admittit verbum

Thus, the dogmatic theologian approaches the scriptures to learn what is said by God, what is taught by God. What he takes as his theme is truth revealed by God.

Accordingly, Gutwenger presupposes an event already established elsewhere, namely, that Christ did say 'I.' Then he asks a psychological question, namely, from what interior experience that saying 'I' proceeded; but he answers this psychological question not through a Romantic hermeneutic but through the meaning of what is said in scripture and through the truth of that meaning.

Now, what Gutwenger has done you will find to have been done universally throughout the writings of the Fathers and theologians. They take the scriptures for a theme as being the word of God that it is impious to contradict and to which all the faithful must assent. Whence that most dogmatic of all formulas, 'If anyone says ..., let that one be anathema.'

There are three points especially that are to be noted here.

First, it is one thing to explicitly designate the theological way of thematizing and another to make use of this way without explicitly designating it; and it is still another to appeal to the word of God without having a theological purpose in mind, indeed without anything explicitly being said about the truth of the word of God. Having made these distinctions, you will be able to proceed from the most implicit to the most explicit. Take, for example, Paul's statement in Galatians 1.8: 'Even if we ourselves or an angel from heaven preach a gospel to you different from the one we have preached, let that person be anathema.' Nothing here is said explicitly about truth, about the immutability of truth, about the truth of the gospel already preached, but Paul proceeds concretely in a manner theoretically justified by the immutable truth of the gospel.[185]

Second, when a word as true is taken as a theme, it is taken by that very fact that it can be transferred from one context to another. The fact that what is true can be transferred from one context to another is a result of the very transcendence of truth. For what is true is independent of the subject; it has the note of being unconditioned and absolute. What is thus independent, unconditioned, and absolute is not so tied to one particular context that it cannot be spoken in another. Word as event, as expression, or as

185 You will find further stages of this indicated in Bernard Lonergan, *De Deo Trino: Pars Analytica* (Rome: Gregorian University Press, 1961) 132–37; 88–95. [The 1964 edition of this work, re-titled *De Deo Trino: Pars dogmatica*, is available now as *The Triune God: Doctrines*. See also below, note 207.]

ut eventus, ut expressio, ut occursus; quod enim circa haec transfertur est verum de eventu, verum de expressione, verum de occursu. Neque translatio fundatur nisi in veritate iudicii, in vero quod dicit independentiam a subiecto, inconditionatum, absolutum; ita ubi verum intelligitur ut res sese manifestans, ut obiectum experientiae et intelligentiae, ut rectitudo inquirentis, ibi non habetur transcendentia quae in veritate iudicii invenitur et translationem in alium contextum admittit. Quare sedulo notandum est quantum differt hic processus dogmaticus in transcendentia veri fundatus a processu hermeneuticae romanticae qui in reproductione quadam consistit. Scilicet, interpres secundum principia romantica ad interpretationem adaequatam pervenit ubi in se reproducere potest quod in auctore factum est. In processu dogmatico per transcendentiam veri legitimatur transitus e contextu in contextum. In processu romantico, quantum fieri potest, eliminatur diversitas contextus. Denique, quamvis possibilitatem transitus e contextu in contextum in transcendentia veri fundemus, minime inde concludere licet sensum eius quod est verum aliunde repeti quam e contextu originali in quo verum primo enuntiatur. Interpres primo debet intelligere sensum auctoris ad mentem auctoris et deinde debet secundum exigentias alterius contextus illum iam determinatum sensum verum exprimere. Nihil plus per transcendentiam veri legitimatur.

Tertio, aliud est datum in thema assumere et aliud est verum in thema assumere. Qui datum in thema assumit ut illud intelligat atque explicet, in via est ad verum quoddam inveniendum. Quod quidem primo inveniet quando reflectitur super datum intellectum et explicatum, evidentiam ponderat, iudicat. Qui autem verum in thema assumit ut illud intelligat et explicet, verum inde ab initio habet, neque in aliud tendit nisi in idem verum plenius per intelligentiam et explicationem possidendum. Ita qui methodo philologico-historica utitur et evangelia considerat, problema synopticum invenit. Evangelia ei sunt ut data, quae per theoriam vel fontium vel formarum secundum modum compositionis intelliguntur et explicantur; at haec intelligentia, haec explicatio, non est veri quod ab evangelistis dicitur, quamvis esse possit verum quod in evangeliis ut datis fundetur. E contra, dogmaticus intelligentiam quaerit, non evangeliorum ut datorum, sed illius veri quod in evangeliis a Deo dici et doceri creditur.

encounter, of course, does not allow this transference; for concerning these aspects what is transferred is the truth of the event, the truth of the expression, the truth of the encounter. This transference is founded solely upon the truth of a judgment, upon a truth that asserts independence from a subject, an unconditioned, an absolute. Thus, when the true is understood as a thing manifesting itself, or as an object of experience and understanding, or as the integrity of the inquirer, there is then not that transcendence that is found in the truth of a judgment and allows transference to another context. Accordingly, one must note carefully how great the difference is between this dogmatic process founded upon the transcendence of truth and the process of Romantic hermeneutics, which consists in a sort of reproduction. That is to say, interpreters belonging to the school of Romantic hermeneutics attain a satisfactory interpretation when able to reproduce in themselves what took place in the author. In the dogmatic process the transition from one context to another is legitimated by the transcendence of truth. In the Romantic process the diversity of contexts is eliminated as much as possible. Finally, although we ground the possibility of this transition from context to context upon the transcendence of truth, one may by no means conclude from this that the meaning of the true statement is to be got from some source other than the context in which the truth was originally stated. The interpreter must first understand the meaning of the author according to the mind of the author and then having determined the true meaning, express it according to the exigencies of the other context. Only this is legitimated by the transcendence of truth.

Third, it is one thing to take a datum as a theme and quite another to take a truth as a theme. One who takes a datum as a theme in order to understand and explain it is on the way towards discovering some truth. This truth will be discovered first when one reflects upon the datum that one has understood and explained, weighs the evidence, and makes a judgment. One who takes a truth as a theme in order to understand and explain it possesses the truth from the outset and is moving only to a fuller possession of it through understanding and explanation. Thus, whoever uses a philological-historical method and is studying the gospels comes upon the synoptic problem. For such a one the gospels are the data that are understood and explained by means of a theory of sources or of literary forms according to the manner of composition. But this understanding, this explanation, is not an understanding and explanation of a truth expressed by the evangelists, although it could be a truth that is based upon the gospels as data. The dogmatic theologian, by contrast, seeks an understanding, not of the gospels as

(c″) De usu fontium et in primis scripturae:[186] Quo magis contextus biblicus et contextus theologicus distinguuntur atque separantur, eo magis etiam distinguuntur et separantur scientia biblica et theologia dogmatica. Qua distinctione et separatione peracta, interpretatio scripturae ad exegetam pertinet, neque plus facit dogmaticus quam *usum* scripturae interpretatae.

Sane omnis differentiatio integrationem praeparat atque exigit; de praesenti tamen agitur de ipsis integrandis clare et distincte apprehendendis, ut postea de earum integratione tractetur ubi de theologia positiva et de theologia ut sapientia.[187]

Qui quidem usus est ad modum experimenti. Quod quid significet per comparationem experientiae et experimenti declarari oportet. Vivendo experimur. Ortis quaestionibus, sponte ad experientiam attendimus et secundum eam iudicamus. Quae tamen attentio, qui experientiae usus, minime thematizatur nisi forte per transennam. Quo tamen modo omnia fere addiscimus, omnem peritiam acquirimus, omnem inventionem facimus. Qui autem experimentum facit, ipsam experientiam in thema assumit. Ex elaborata conceptualizatione procedit, quaestiones distinguit, easque exacte definit et secundum progressum quendam inter se ordinat. Quibus rite peractis, ad experientiam redit ut ea seligat quae ad suam rem faciunt, ut e selectis et accurate examinatis quasi responsum seu decisionem exhauriat ad suas quaestiones resolvendas.

At ipse hic usus ad modum experimenti supponit textum iam opere exegetico interpretatum. Quod tamen suppositum saepe eo modo verificatur ut complures sint interpretationes eiusdem loci. Quinimo, etiam ubi non habeatur nisi unica loci interpretatio, verendum est ne ea non sit nisi probabilis; sicut enim caeterae scientiae empiricae, ita etiam exegetica ea lege efformatur et progreditur ut theorias probabiles per probabiliores perpetuo corrigat quin unquam ad plenam certitudinem perveniat.

data, but of that truth which is believed to have been spoken and taught by God in the gospels.

(c″) The use of the sources, especially scripture:[186] The more the biblical and theological contexts are distinguished and separated, the greater is the distinction and separation between biblical studies and dogmatic theology. With this distinction and separation, the task of interpreting scripture belongs to the exegete, and the dogmatic theologian simply uses the scriptures thus interpreted.

Certainly every differentiation prepares for and calls for integration; for the present, however, we are concerned with clearly and distinctly understanding what are to be integrated, so that later we may deal with their integration, when we speak about positive theology and about theology as wisdom.[187]

This use of scripture is by way of experiment. What this means needs to be clarified by comparing experience and experiment. Experience is part of everyday life. When questions arise, we automatically attend to our experience and judge accordingly. This attending, this use of experience, is scarcely thematized except incidentally. Nevertheless, this is the way we gain virtually all new knowledge, acquire all expertise, and make all our discoveries. One who experiments, however, takes this same experience as a theme. He proceeds from a detailed conceptualization, he distinguishes questions, and he defines them accurately and puts them in order according to a certain progression. When this has all been duly carried out, he returns to his experience in order to select those things that are relevant, so that finally from what he has selected and carefully examined he might draw forth, as it were, the answer or decision to solve his questions.

But this use of experiment supposes a text already interpreted through the work of exegesis. This supposition, however, is often verified in this way, that there are several interpretations of the same passage. In fact, even where there is only one interpretation of a particular passage, the fear is that it may be only a probable interpretation; for just like the other empirical sciences, exegesis develops and proceeds according to the law that probable theories are continually being corrected by more probable ones without full and complete certitude ever being attained.

---

186 [At this point in the autograph, the date at the top of the page switches back to 10-5-62.]
187 [See the discussion below on positive and systematic theology, beginning on p. 581.]

Scientia enim exegetica notissimo circulo hermeneutico fertur. In obiecto enim intentionali non solum sensus totius e partibus dependet sed etiam sensus partium e sensu totius. Neque ipsum totum nisi modo quodam relativo 'totum' est: omnis enim contextus ut pars maioris cuiusdam contextus considerari potest, ut iterum et aliter oriatur mutua dependentia partium et totius.

Quibus perspectis, dogmaticus non otiosus exspectat donec scientia exegetica omnibus numeris absoluta perficiatur; sic enim ad diem iudicii ultimi forte exspectaret. Sed ea quaerit et adhibet artificia quibus aliquid certum, etsi breve et tenue, iam nunc determinari possit.

(α)[188] Ita definitiones adhibet heuristicas quae non solum futurum scientiae exegeticae progressum effugiunt sed etiam obscuriora ad clariora reducunt. E.g., quid in prologo Ioannis significetur per *Logon*? Respondetur: in prologo Ioannis *Logos* est *X*. Et ex ipso prologo Ioannis non pauca de hoc *X* cognoscimus. *X* enim erat in principio, erat apud Deum, erat Deus; per *X* omnia facta sunt; et caetera quae in ipso prologo leguntur. Quae quidem notionis Logou determinatio futurum scientiae exegeticae progressum effugit. Omnis enim exegeta futurus ex ipso textu incipere debebit et ea ipsa, quae in textu dicuntur, non eliminare sed explicare. Scilicet eandem definitionem *Logou* heuristicam accipiet, qua iam utitur dogmaticus.

Sed praeterea haec definitio heuristica reducit obscuriora in clariora. Etsi enim de sensu nominis *Logos* dubitemus, minus tamen de 'principio,' de 'apud,' de 'Deo,' de eo per quem omnia facta sunt, dubitare possumus.

(β) Ita enumerationes eiusdem facit.

E.g., si vel unico in loco Christus 'ego' dixisse et personam significasse exhiberetur, intentum suum habuisset P. Gutwenger. At permulta eiusmodi loca invenit, et permulta recitavit. Quae enumeratio logicam argumenti vim non auget, sed fundamentum valde confirmat. Si enim unicus esset locus, exceptionem suspicaremur. Si perpauci essent loci, brevior et facilior esset labor refutantis. Ubi continuo idem recurrit, ibi habetur argumenti

Exegetical knowledge goes around in the famous hermeneutic circle. For in an intentional object not only does the meaning of the whole depend upon that of the parts, but also the meaning of the parts depends upon that of the whole. And this 'whole' is only relatively speaking a whole; for every context can be considered as part of a larger context, so that repeatedly and in different ways the mutual dependence of parts and the whole comes to light.

In view of all this, dogmatic theologians do not sit back and wait for exegetical knowledge to reach absolute perfection in every way; otherwise they would be waiting till doomsday. But they do look for and use techniques that will enable them eventually to determine something that is certain, however brief and small.

(α) [188] Thus, dogmatic theologians use heuristic definitions that not only are immune from any future development in exegesis but that also clarify obscurities. For example, what does John mean by *Logos* in the prologue of his gospel? Answer: in the prologue of John, *Logos* is X. And from this prologue we know quite a few things about this X. X was in the beginning, was with God, was God; through X all things were made; and so on for the rest of the prologue. This determination of the notion of *Logos* is free from any future advance in exegesis. For all future exegetes will have to start from this very text and not eliminate anything but explain just what the text says. That is to say, they will accept the same heuristic definition of *Logos* as dogmatic theologians already use.

But further, this heuristic definition clarifies obscurities. For although we may not be sure about the meaning of the title *Logos*, we can scarcely doubt about the meaning of 'beginning' and 'with' and 'God' and of 'the one through whom all things were made.'

(β) Dogmatic theologians enumerate identical expressions.

If, for example, there were only one passage in which Christ indicated his person by saying 'I,' Gutwenger would still have attained his objective. But he found many passages and listed them. Such an enumeration does not enhance the logic of the argument, but it greatly strengthens its foundation. For if there were but one such passage, we might suspect it to be an exception. If there were very few, refutation would be quicker and easier.

---

188 [At this point in the autograph, the date at the top of the page switches to 11-5-62. The Greek lettering for these four subsections is editorial. Lonergan had 'a)', etc., but it is difficult to distinguish such subsections clearly from those with the letters (a), (a′), and (a″), etc.

fundamentum tam alte in ipsis datis repositum ut in subsequente scientiae exegeticae progressu potius datum explicandum quam explicatio corrigenda consideretur.

(γ) Ita similia cumulat.

Ipsum enim NT non perpetuo alia et nova proponit, sed potius eadem ex diversis perspectivis pro diversis adiunctis in diversos fines recitat. Quod factum in suam utilitatem vertit dogmaticus. Quae enim ita repetuntur, longe difficilius in diversas partes easque semper mobiles ab exegetis trahi possunt, quam quae semel dicuntur, per transennam tanguntur, vel aliter minus arcte cum reliquo NT contexuntur.

(δ) Ita notiones sese evolventes exhibet.

E.g., quisnam sit Iesus? Cui quaestioni in NT multipliciter respondetur. Per modum actus exerciti, implicite, per modum vitae: ubi exhibetur potestas miraculorum, potestas remittendi peccata, auctoritas corrigendi VT, auctoritas exigendi amorem et servitutem omnium hominum, potestas redemptoris, potestas iudicis universalis. Deinde thematice sed ad modum sensus communis per titulos et honores, et quidem secundum diversas perspectivas exspectationis (Messias), originis, vitae praesentis, anticipati futuri (Filius hominis), inthronizationis messianicae (Dominus, Filius Dei), etc. Denique per modum inceptae theologiae: per quem omnia, in forma Dei, Logos, Filius sine addito, Patri aequalis, unum cum Patre.

Quod argumenti genus ab opere exegetico distingui oportet, quamvis ei propius accedere videatur. Ubi enim dogmaticus e proprio suo et theologico contextu quaestiones haurit et criteria definit ut responsa e scripturis accepta in contextum theologicum transferantur, exegeta quaestiones suas et proprias ex ipsis scripturis habet. Ubi dogmaticus suis artificiis nisi minimum quendam sensum eumque certum non quaerit, exegeta omnia colligit quae ex diversis thematizationibus concluduntur, et plenum et accuratissime distinctum sensum uniuscuiusque loci vult. Ubi dogmaticus ad nudum fere factum evolventis apprehensionis attendit, ut illud determinet quod tam alte in fontibus reponatur ut potius datum explicandum quam explicatio vel amplianda vel corrigenda considerari debeat, exegeta genesin notionis vel apprehensionis quasi ultimum quendam et supremum fructum attingit qui in toto suo praevio labore circa singula loca fundatur et quasi sponte sua ex iis locis exsurgit.

When the same thing occurs over and over again, the foundation of the argument is so deeply embedded in the data themselves that with any subsequent advance in exegesis the data would be considered as needing explanation rather than the explanation considered as needing correction.

(γ) Dogmatic theologians group together similar passages.

The New Testament itself is not continually expressing something new and different, but rather repeats the same things from different perspectives according to different circumstances and for different ends. This fact dogmatic theologians turn to their own advantage. For it is much more difficult for an exegete to give divergent and ever-changing interpretations to such repetitions than to ideas expressed only once, or only indirectly alluded to, or otherwise less closely tied in with the rest of the New Testament.

(δ) Dogmatic theologians set forth the development of ideas.

For example, who is Jesus? There are many answers to this question in the New Testament. First, in actual performance, implicitly, and in everyday life: passages that express his miraculous powers, his power to forgive sins, his authority to correct the Old Testament, his authority to command love and service from all mankind, his power as redeemer, and his authority to be the universal judge. Second, in a thematic way but in a commonsense mode: through his titles and honors, and indeed according to the different perspectives of expectation ('Messiah'), of origin, of this present life, of an anticipated future ('Son of man'), of his messianic enthronement ('Lord,' 'Son of God'), and so forth. Finally, by way of an inchoate theology: 'through whom all things,' 'in the form of God,' '*Logos*,' 'Son' without further qualification, 'equal to the Father,' 'one with the Father.'

This kind of argument must be distinguished from that of the exegete, even though it may seem to resemble it closely. For while dogmatic theologians derive their questions from their proper theological context and set up the criteria for transferring the scriptural answers to a theological context, exegetes get their proper questions from the scriptures themselves. While dogmatic theologians in using their own techniques seek only a minimal meaning that is also certain, exegetes collect all the conclusions from various thematizations and aim at the full and most carefully distinguished meaning of each passage. While dogmatic theologians attend only to the bare fact of a developing understanding of a passage in order to determine something that is so deeply embedded in the sources of revelation that it ought to be considered a datum to be explained rather than an explanation to be expanded or corrected, exegetes get to the genesis of a notion or of an understanding as the ultimate and supreme fruit of their labors that

Dogmaticus utens scriptura : exegeta :: iudicans quid certi in chimia: investigans, perficiens chimiam. *Momentum*: debita libertas scientiae exegeticae; processus per imperfecta ad adaequata.[189]

(d″) Differentiae decursu temporum ortae: Consideravimus processum e fide in theologiam, tum in casu particulari et recentissimo, tum modo generaliori secundum tria elementa, nempe, contextus, thematizationis, et usus scripturae. At haec tria non semper eodem modo fiebant, et ideo nunc eadem considerare debemus prout decursu temporum factus est processus differentiationis et integrationis.

(α) Circa contextum quattuor distinguimus tempora, patristicum, mediaevale, theologiam modernam, et theologiam recentem.

In aetate patristica per concilia trinitaria et christologica et per condemnationes Pelagianorum evolutus est contextus dogmaticus, qui tamen ut contextus distinctus a biblico vel apostolico latebat. E.g., Athanasius minime suspicatus est c. Nicaenum fundamentum posuisse unde totus contextus dogmaticus esset surrecturus; concessit formulas fidei verbis scripturisticis exponi debere; nisi unam exceptionem, *homoousion*, propter necessitatem ex Arianis ortam non defendebat. C. Chalcedonense minime suspicatum est se vocem *physis* eo sensu adhibere qui radicaliter differret a sensu eiusdem vocis prout apud Patres (Athan., Basil., Nyss., Cyr. Alex.) adhibebatur; nisi saeculo subsequenti non est perspecta necessitas distinguendi inter naturam *enupostaton* et *anupostaton*, et quidem propter decretum Chalcedonense. Medio aevo technica quaestionis universaliter applicata sponte sua ad libros sententiarum et ad summas conducebat. Ipsae summae, cum nihil efficerent nisi systema quoddam notionum adinvenirent, ad systemata excogitanda et quidem ad praeformatum et Aristotelicum adaptandum cogebantur.

Ita est ortus contextus non solum dogmaticus sed etiam theologicus, qui tamen in propria sua ratione parum perspiciebatur. Acerrime disputatum est sub fine saec. XIII inter Aristotelicos et Augustinianos. Sed vera quaestio

stems from all their previous labors over each particular passage and that spontaneously, as it were, emerges from those passages themselves.

The dogmatic theologian using scripture : exegete :: judge of what is certain in chemistry : the researcher, perfecting chemistry. *Importance* of this: due freedom for the science of exegesis; process through what is imperfect to what is satisfactory.[189]

(d″) Differences that have arisen in the course of time: We have been considering the process from faith to theology, both in a recent particular case and in a more general way according to three elements, namely, context, thematization, and the use of scripture. But these three were not always done in the same way, and so we must now consider them according to the way the process of differentiation and integration took place over the course of time.

(α) As to context, we distinguish four periods, the patristic, the medieval, modern theology, and recent theology.

In the patristic period, the dogmatic context developed through the trinitarian and Christological councils and the condemnations of the Pelagians; this context, however, was previously latent as a context distinct from the biblical or apostolic. Athanasius, for example, had not the least suspicion that the Council of Nicea had laid the foundation upon which the entire dogmatic context would be built. He conceded that the creedal formulas should be expressed in scriptural terminology; but he defended one exception to this rule, the word *homoousion*, on the grounds that Arianism made it necessary. The Council of Chalcedon had not the least suspicion that it was using the word *physis* in a radically different sense from that of the Fathers (Athanasius, Basil, Gregory of Nyssa, Cyril of Alexandria); and only in the next century did the need for distinguishing between *enhypostaton* and *anhypostaton* become evident, precisely because of the decree of Chalcedon. In the Middle Ages the universal application of the technique of the question led naturally to the books of the Sentences and the *Summas*. The *Summas* themselves, since their only function was to systematize ideas, were compelled to devise systems and to adapt to an already established system, the Aristotelian.

In this way there emerged not only a dogmatic but also a theological context, although its true and proper character was little understood. Towards the end of the thirteenth century a bitter dispute arose between the Aristo-

---

189 [The material in this paragraph was added by hand in the autograph.]

erat de legitimitate contextus theologici et systematici. Minor et subordinata omnino erat quaestio utrum systema e Patre ecclesiae, Augustino, an e pagano Aristotele hauriri oporteret.

Ortis et distinctis scholis theologicis (Thomistica, Scotistica, Nominalium) manifesta erat differentia inter contextum theologicum disputationibus plenum et simplicem planumque sensum scripturae. Impugnabatur scholasticismus tum variis in tendentiis renascentiae tum ab aliis haereticis et maxime a Protestantibus. Conciliationem quandam inter scholasticismum et nova studia quaerebat Melchior Cano, *De locis theologicis.*[190]

Quae tamen tempora haud propitia erant ut inter catholicos inveniretur distinctio inter contextum biblicum et contextum dogmatico-theologicum, tum propter suspicionem haereseos protestanticae quae inter verbum Dei et adinventiones humanas et scholasticas polemice distinguebat, tum propter classicismum qui ad idealia, exemplaria, normativa, praecepta, leges, universalia magis attendit quam ad differentias contingentes et temporales, tum propter conceptualismum quendam qui conceptus dogmaticos et theologicos implicite in conceptibus scripturisticis inveniendos arbitrabatur.

Recentius autem classicismo derelicto et renovatis studiis philosophicis conscientia historica repanditur et ab Ecclesia per *Deus scientiarum Dominus* et *Divino afflante Spiritu* in theologiam et in studia biblica debitis cum cautelis introducta est. Exegesis desinit scripturas per notiones dogmaticas et theologicas exponere. Theologia biblica florere incepit. Dogmatici naturam propriae methodi clarius perspiciunt. Differentiatio iam pridem facta nunc agnita est, et ponitur potius quaestio circa integrationem.

569   The Method of Theology

telians and the Augustinians. But the real issue was about the legitimacy of a systematic theological context. The minor and quite secondary issue was whether the system was to be derived from a Father of the church, namely Augustine, or from the pagan Aristotle.

With the emergence of different schools of theology (Thomists, Scotists, Nominalists), the difference between the theological context with all its disputes and the plain and simple meaning of the bible became obvious. Scholasticism was under attack from various Renaissance currents of thought and from heretics and especially from the Protestants. Melchior Cano, in his *De locis theologiae*, sought to reconcile Scholasticism and the new learning.[190]

Because of the suspicion of the Protestants, who in a polemical manner distinguished between the word of God and the human inventions of the schools, because of classicism, which paid much more attention to ideals, models, the normative, precepts, laws, and universals than to contingent temporal differences, and because of a conceptualism that thought that dogmatic and theological concepts were to be found implicitly contained in biblical concepts, those times were hardly favorable for Catholics to develop the distinction between the biblical context and the dogmatic-theological context.

More recently, however, with the abandonment of classicism and a renewal of philosophical studies, an expansion of historical consciousness has occurred and, with due safeguards, has been introduced into theology and into biblical studies by the church in *Deus scientiarum Dominus* [1931] and *Divino afflante Spiritu* [1943]. Exegesis has stopped expounding scripture by way of dogmatic and theological notions. Biblical theology has begun to flourish. Dogmatic theologians have a clearer understanding of the nature of the method proper to them. The differentiation that had been going on for a long time has now been acknowledged, and the question now is rather that of integration.

---

190 See Albert Lang, *Die Loci theologici des Melchior Cano und die Methode des dogmatischen Beweises: ein Beitrag zur theologischen Methodologie und ihrer Geschichte* (München, J. Kösel & F. Pustet, 1925); Congar, DTC XV (29) s.v. 'Théologie,' cols. 421–22 [*A History of Theology* 163–65]; A. Gardeil, DTC IX (17) s.v. 'Lieux théologiques,' cols. 712–47; Eugène Marcotte, *De la nature de la théologie d'après Melchior Cano* (Ottawa: Scolasticat Saint-Joseph; Éditions de l'Université, 1949; includes bibliography on pp. 11–16); Jean-Marie Levasseur, *Le lieu théologique, "histoire": Contribution à une ontologie et introduction à une méthodologie* (Trois-Rivières: Éditions du Bien public, 1960).

Collected Works of Bernard Lonergan

(β) Thematizatio dogmatico-theologica verbum Dei assumit ut verum.

Verbum Dei, evangelii, gratiae, etc., *ut praedicandum et audiendum*, saepe recurrit in NT. Cf. Concordantiam s.v. *logos*; TWNT *legō, akouō*. Ipsum factum praedicationis et auditus est centrum nascentis et crescentis ecclesiae, quae per oecumenen diffusa unitatem doctrinae ex unitate originis apostolicae retinuit. Quod multis et diversis factis illustratur: *kerygma, didakhē*, catechumeni, baptismus, liturgia, episcopatus, traditio, martyres, formatio canonis, symbolum dictum apostolicum, concilia localia, apologetae. Sicut inter Hebraeos ad ipsum sensum Legis pertinebat ut observaretur, ita inter fideles ad ipsum sensum verbi Dei pertinebat ut ei crederetur, non contradiceretur. Fides ex auditu. Qui sensus concretus modo practico in thema assumitur per formulam dogmaticam, 'Si quis dixerit ..., anathema sit.'

Cui sensui concreto accedit extensio ex ipsis scripturis, tum practica et moralis circa modum fructuose suscipiendi verbum Dei, tum etiam in theoriam tendens circa veritatem, imo Veritatem, quae per evangelium communicatur.

Thematizatio dogmatico-theologica novam specializationem accepit inde a *Sic et non* Abaelardi qui auctoritates citavit in utrasque contradictionis partes circa plus centum quinquaginta propositiones. Unde quaestiones: Videtur quod non ... Sed contra est ... Respondeo ... Ad primum ... Ad ea quae in contrarium ...[191]

Unde[192] duplex motus: alius ad auctoritates colligendas et ordinandas, Libri sententiarum; alius ad distinctiones systematice evolvendas, Summae. Quorum hic longe maiorem attentionem et laborem accepit, ut fere quingenti sunt commentarii in Sententias Lombardi. Ultimus commentarios in Lombardum composuit Estius (publici iuris factos anno 1616, tres annos post eius mortem). Scripserat Lombardus c. 1150.

Quo motu scholastico in thema assumitur verbum Dei praecise *ut verum*, et eo quidem modo ut ad cohaerentiam, contradictionis exclusionem,

(β) Dogmatic-theological thematization takes the word of God as true.

The word of God, of the gospel, of grace, and so on, *as something to be preached and heard*, is a recurrent notion in the New Testament. See the concordance, s.v. *logos*; TWNT [in English, TDNT], s.v. *legō, akouō*. This fact of preaching and hearing was a central feature of the nascent and growing church, which, while spreading throughout the *oikumenē*, kept its unity of doctrine through the unity of its apostolic origins. This is illustrated by a number of different features: *kerygma, didachē*, catechumens, baptism, liturgy, episcopacy, tradition, martyrs, the formation of the biblical canon, the Apostles' Creed, local councils, apologists. As among the Jews observance of the Law was an essential element of its meaning, so among Christians the meaning of the word of God was something to be believed and not challenged. 'Faith from hearing.' This concrete meaning is taken as a theme in a practical way through the dogmatic formula 'If anyone says …, let that one be anathema.'

To this concrete meaning there is a further addition taken from the scriptures themselves, a practical moral addition regarding the manner of fruitfully receiving the word of God, and also a tendency towards theory regarding the truth, indeed the Truth, communicated through the gospel.

Dogmatic-theological thematization acquired a new specialization when Abelard in his *Sic et non* quoted authorities on both sides of a contradiction involving more than 150 propositions. Hence the questions: *Videtur quod non … Sed contra est … Respondeo … Ad primum … Ad ea quae in contrarium* …[191]

Hence,[192] there are two movements here, one towards the collection and arrangement of authorities, the 'Books of Sentences,' and the other towards systematically developing distinctions, the *Summas*. Of the first group, the one that received by far the most attention and study was Peter Lombard's *Sentences*, with about 500 commentaries on it. The last one to write a commentary on Lombard was Estius; it was published in 1616, three years after his death. Lombard wrote ca. 1150.

This Scholastic movement takes as a theme the word of God precisely *as true*, and indeed in such a way as to attend most of all to coherence, the

---

191 Congar, DTC XV (29) s.v. 'Théologie,' cols. 370–73 [*A History of Theology* 80–84. The reference to Congar was added by hand in the autograph.]

192 [At this point in the autograph, the date at the top of the page switches to 12-5-62.]

maxime attenderetur. Ubi huic thematizationi accedit extrinsecismus, ut ad verum attenderetur quod in nulla mente est, iam ad inauthentiam, decadentiam, perventum est. E contra, ubi extrinsecismus per immanentismum corrigitur, ibi tollitur ipsa thematizatio dogmatico-theologica. Haec inter extrema procedit qui verum in mente, et quidem in iudicio, invenit et quidem sub duplici aspectu (1) conversionis intellectualis per quam homo non sensui, sentimento, fictis intuitionibus, sed vero se submittit et (2) medii in quo, sicut apprehenditur ens, ita etiam fit occursus cum Deo sese manifestante.

Incompletam esse hanc thematizationem verbi ut veri suadent multiplicatae divisiones theologiae. 'Très tôt, le travail théologique perd son unité et se morcelle en spécialités.'[193]

Theologiae scholasticae accessit theologia quae dicebatur mystica, spiritualis, ascetica, affectiva. Influxerunt opera SS. Ignatii de Loyola, Ioannis a Cruce, Francisci de Sales. Nominantur L. Bail, Contenson, Massoulié, Chardon. Secundum P. Congar: 'C'est une théologie dont le "lieu théologique" finalement décisif est l'experience des "âmes saintes," et non la pure vérité révélée, objectivement contenue dans les lieux théologiques classiques.'[194]

Theologiae dogmaticae accessit theologia moralis, quae elementum morale e theologia scholastica sibi assumpsit et periculum induxit subalternandi hanc doctrinam moralem philosophiae morali et principiis iuris.[195]

Theologiae scholasticae accessit theologia positiva, quae primo intelligebatur theologia PP., uti Augustini, Hieronymi, Gregorii, et potius modum

exclusion of contradiction. But when extrinsicism is added to this thematization, so that attention is directed to truth that is found in no one's mind, the result is inauthenticity and decadence. On the other hand, when this extrinsicism is corrected by immanentism, dogmatic-theological thematization itself vanishes. Between these extremes is the position that locates truth in the mind, indeed in the judgment, and that under a twofold aspect: (1) intellectual conversion, by which one submits not to the senses, feelings, fictitious intuitions, but to truth, and (2) the medium in which, just as being is apprehended, so also God is encountered in his self-revelation.

The multiplication of branches of theology suggests that this thematization of the word as true is not finished. '*Tres tôt, le travail théologique perd son unité et se morcelle en spécialités.*'[193]

In addition to Scholastic theology there were mystical theology, spiritual theology, ascetical theology, affective theology. Influential here are the works of St Ignatius Loyola, St John of the Cross, and St Francis de Sales. Among the names one could mention are Louis Bail [1610–69], Vincent Contenson [1641–74], Antoine Massoulié [1632–1706], Louis Chardon [1595–1651]. In the words of Congar, 'C'est une théologie dont le "lieu théologique" finalement décisif est l'expérience des "âmes saintes" et non la pure vérité révélée, objectivement contenue dans les lieux théologiques classiques.'[194]

Besides dogmatic theology there was moral theology, which takes the moral element from Scholastic theology and runs the risk of subordinating this moral doctrine to moral philosophy and jurisprudence.[195]

Still another addition to Scholastic theology was positive theology, which was first understood as the theology of the Fathers, such as Augustine, Jer-

---

193 ['Very soon, the theological work loses its unity and breaks down into specialties.'] Congar, DTC XV (29) s.v. 'Théologie,' col. 423. [See *A History of Theology* 165.]

194 ['It is then a theology whose finally decisive "theological *locus*" is the experience of "holy souls" and not the pure, revealed truth, objectively contained in the classical, theological loci.'] Ibid. col. 424. [See *A History of Theology* 167.]

195 Ibid. col. 426. ['Already Vásquez sees in the analysis of morality and the kinds of virtues and sins nothing but pure philosophy and, for this reason, considers the moral part of theology as subalternate to moral philosophy, or quite simply as belonging to philosophy.' Congar, *A History of Theology* 170. Congar's discussion of dogmatic theology and moral theology here begins on p. 168 and ends on p. 170.]

reflectionis theologicae litterarium respiciebat, quae brevi etiam ad defendendam continuitatem historicam doctrinae catholicae contra haereticos dirigebatur.[196]

A theologia positiva differt apologetica, quae non fidem sed rationem supponit, neque dogma in fontes revelatos reducit, sed de valore ipsius revelationis et dogmatis quaerit. Quatenus haec apologetica aestimatur fundamentum totius theologiae, nominatur fundamentalis; quae tamen est opinio varie concepta et disputata.[197] Re vera, apologetica fundat non veritatem mysteriorum sed rationabilitatem credendi.[198]

Recentius accesserunt theologia biblica, patristica, liturgica, pastoralis, missionaria, kerygmatica.

Quae omnes eo tendunt ut verbum Dei non tantum sistatur in mundo intelligibili ante subiectum theoreticum sed etiam pro subiectis dramatico-practicis vel vitae interiori deditis locum in mundo aspectabili vel interiori inveniat.

(γ)[199] De usu fontium, praecipue scripturarum, differentiae. Non agitur de historia exegeseos[200] sed de momentis novis praecipuis circa usum scripturarum in fines theologicos.

Magisterium: 2 Pet 1.20: hoc primum intelligentes quod omnis prophetia Scripturae propria interpretatione non fit.

Symbolismus: tendentia Iudaeo-Christiana (Daniélou)[201] et Gnostica contra quam invocat Irenaeus traditionem apostolicam in omnibus ecclesiis servatam, Clemens Alex. docet (a) symbola ad litteram non esse sumenda

ome, and Gregory, and was concerned more with the literary mode of theological reflection, but which soon was directed also towards defending the
historical continuity of Catholic doctrine against heretics.[196]

The difference between positive theology and apologetics is that the latter supposes not faith but reason, does not trace dogmas to the sources
of revelation, but inquires into the validity of revelation and dogma. Inasmuch as apologetics is considered the foundation of all theology it is called
fundamental theology; this point, however, is variously understood and is
disputed.[197] In fact, apologetics provides a foundation not for the truth of
the mysteries of faith but for the reasonableness of believing.[198]

More recent additions are biblical, patristic, liturgical, pastoral, missiological, and kerygmatic theology.

The tendency of all of the above is to situate the word of God not only in
the intelligible world in front of a theoretic subject, but also, for the sake
of dramatic-practical subjects and those given to the interior life, to find a
place for it in the visible world and in the world of interiority.

(γ)[199] Differences in the use of the sources, especially scripture: We are
not dealing here with the history of exegesis,[200] but with the more important new movements as to their use of scripture for theological purposes.

The magisterium: 2 Peter 1.20: '... understanding above all that no
prophecy in scripture is a matter of one's personal interpretation.'

Symbolism, a Judeo-Christian and gnostic tendency; see Daniélou.[201]
Against this Irenaeus appeals to the apostolic tradition observed in all the
churches, and Clement of Alexandria teaches (a) that symbols are not to be

---

196 Ibid. cols. 426–30. [*A History of Theology* 170–75.]
197 Ibid. col. 431. [See Congar, *A History of Theology* 175–76. Note, however, that
     Guthrie's translation is somewhat truncated at this point.]
198 [This Latin sentence is added by hand in the autograph.]
199 [At this point in the autograph, the date at the top of the page switches to
     16-5-62.]
200 See R. Schnackenburg, J. Schmid, K.H. Schelkle, H.-G. Beck, J. Assfalg, A.
     Kleinhans, H. Greeven, s.v. 'Exegese,' *Lexikon für Theologie und Kirch* III, cols.
     1273–93.
201 [Presumably, Lonergan has in mind such works by Jean Daniélou as *Théolo-
     gie du judéo-christianisme* (Tournai-Paris: Desclée & Cie, 1958; in English, *The
     Theology of Jewish Christianity*, trans. and ed. John A. Baker (London: Darton,
     Longman & Todd, and Chicago: The Henry Regnery Company, 1964). See
     also Lonergan's discussion of the Judeo-Christians, which draws heavily on
     Daniélou's writings, in *The Triune God: Doctrines* 54–71.]

(Strom. v) et (b) methodum definiendi, definiti exsistentiam determinandi, etc. (Strom. viii).²⁰²

Dogmatismus: *homoousion*, eadem de Filio quae de Patre dicuntur; una Christi persona, voces apostolicas et evangelicas non dividendas inter duas personas, subsistentias (DB 116).

Oppositio ad realismum nativum Tertulliani, Platonismum Origenis.

Cohaerentiae exigentia: Gratianus, *Concordia discordantium canonum*; Abaelardus, *Sic et non*; technica quaestionis; libri sententiarum; summae.²⁰³

Theoriae de theologia ut scientia, in obliquo determinaverunt usum scripturae, conceptum probationis theologicae.

Conscientiae historicae opponebantur: simultaneitas logica disputationis; indifferentia classica erga temporalia et contingentia; theoria conceptualistica scientiae quae conceptus dogmaticos et theologicos in ipsis verbis scripturisticis implicite contentos voluit.

(i) Theologia positiva et systematica²⁰⁴

taken literally (*Stromata* v) and (b) the method of defining, of determining the existence of what was defined, etc. (*Stromata* VIII).[202]

Dogmatism: *homoousion*, that the same things are predicated of the Son as of the Father; one person in Christ: the words of the apostles and evangelists are not to be divided between two persons, two subsistences (DB 116, DS 255, ND 606/4).

Opposition to the naive realism of Tertullian and Origen's Platonism.

The need for coherence: Gratian, *Concordia discordantium canonum*, and Abelard, *Sic et non*; the technique of the question; books of Sentences; Summas.[203]

Theories about theology as a science have determined indirectly the way in which scripture is used and the concept of theological proof.

The following militated against historical consciousness: the atemporal logic of a disputation; classical indifference towards the temporal and contingent; the conceptualistic theory of science that would have the concepts of dogma and theology implicitly contained in the very words of scripture.

   (i) Positive and systematic theology[204]

202 [For more on Clement of Alexandria's approach, see Lonergan, *The Triune God: Doctrines* 210–25.]

203 See M.-D. Chenu, *Introduction à l'étude de Saint Thomas d'Aquin* (Paris: Librairie Philosophique J. Vrin; Montréal: Institut d'Études Médiévales, 1950) 106–31 [in English, *Toward Understanding Saint Thomas*, trans. with authorized corrections and bibliographic additions by A.M. Landry and D. Hughes (Chicago: Henry Regnery Company, 1964) 126–55]; Ceslas Spicq, *Esquisse d'une histoire de l'exégèse latine au moyen âge* (Paris: Librarie Philosophique J. Vrin, 1944).

204 [At this point in the autograph, the date at the top of the page switches to 28-5-62, that is, from a Wednesday to a Monday, with a break of a full week between. Note, too, that there is no subsection (h). These notes on positive and systematic theology were not part of what Lonergan's students transcribed from his autograph. *Early Works on Theological Method 1* 183, note 1, at the beginning of a lecture on 'positive and systematic theology, and meaning,' notes that 'Lonergan began by indicating that he was now moving beyond the notes that he had distributed.' It is entirely possible that in the Gregorian course he had moved to the 'second problematic,' and inserted these notes into that context. Note what he says below: 'A fuller treatment of this matter belongs to the second problematic.' See also www.bernard-lonergan.com at 45200DOL060 (translated at 45200DTE060), where it is clear that the first item taken up in the 'problematica altera' was positive theology and the development of dogmas and theology. At any rate, it is likely that something is missing from the record of his notes for the Roman course: the break of a full week in the dating of the notes and the movement from (g) to (i) in Lonergan's lettering would indicate as much.]

(a′) Cumulative per repetitos transitus ex fide in theologiam ortus est contextus dogmatico-theologicus: qui in scholis theologicis docetur et addiscitur; unde inter catholicos supponitur et assumitur; inter eos est *selbstverständlich*; qui constituit semper 'reliquum' quod sensum determinat eius quod hic et nunc a catholico dicitur; unde 'secundum analogiam fidei' Rom 12.6; DB 2146; sensus ecclesiae, sensus fidelium; eo sensu quo definitum est, DB 2314; quo sensu? eo qui ab omnibus catholicis intelligitur; consulat probatos auctores; qui ab haereticis praetermittitur; qui enim haeretico falluntur spiritu, non falsum prorsus dicunt sed verum quoddam, ita tamen ut alia et non omittenda omittant; cuius praehistoria, cuius materia in thema assumpta, cuius suppositum est verbum Dei scriptum et traditum; quod verbum reicere est nefas, unde dogmata, 'si quis dixerit … anathema sit'; cuius formatio a PP effecta est occasionaliter, cuius explicatio a Scholasticis exquisita est systematice, cuius derivatio historica a modernis investigatur, cuius veritas a fidelibus creditur; cuius fontes numquam exhauriuntur, DB 2314, et ideo semper orandum et optandum est in ecclesia augmentum intelligentiae, scientiae, sapientiae, DB 1800.

(b′) Videri potest investigatio eiusmodi contextus pertinere ad sociologiam cognitionis.[205]

Plenior huius rei consideratio pertinet ad alteram problematicam.[206] Brevissime: eo magis valet sociologia cognitionis quo minus homines pro se ipsis, suo marte, inquirunt, intelligunt, iudicant. Fundamentum cognitionis

(a′) From the accumulation of repeated transitions from faith to theology there has emerged the dogmatic-theological context. It is taught and learned in schools of theology; hence, it is presupposed and taken for granted by Catholics, for whom it is *selbstverständlich*. It always constitutes the 'remainder' that determines the meaning of what is said here and now by a Catholic; hence, 'according to the analogy of faith,' Romans 12.6, DB 2146, DS 3546, ND 143/9; the mind of the church, the sense of the faithful; 'in the sense in which it was defined,' DB 2314, DS 3886, ND 859; in what sense? in the sense in which it is understood by all Catholics – consult the approved authors. It is disregarded by heretics; for those who are led astray by a heretical spirit, although their statements are not totally false but contain some truth, nevertheless omit other points that ought not to be omitted. Its prehistory, its matter taken as a theme, its presupposition, is the word of God in scripture and tradition, a word that it is impious to reject, hence the dogmatic formula, 'If anyone says ..., let that one be anathema.' Its formation was shaped on particular occasions by the Fathers, its explanation was worked out systematically by the Scholastics, its historical derivation is being investigated by modern theologians, and its truth is believed by the faithful. Its sources will never run dry (DB 2314, DS 3886, ND 859), so that growth in understanding, knowledge, and wisdom in the church (DB 1800, DS 3020, ND 136) is ever to be earnestly prayed for and devoutly to be wished.

(b′) Investigation into this context can be seen as belonging to the sociology of knowledge.[205]

A fuller treatment of this matter belongs to the second problematic.[206] But very briefly: the sociology of knowledge is all the more valid as people are less and less able to investigate, understand, and judge for themselves,

---

205 See Max Scheler, *Die Wissensformen und die Gesellschaft*, 2nd ed., vol. 8 in *Gesammelte Werke* (Bern: Francke Verlag, 1960) [in English, *Problems of a Sociology of Knowledge*, trans. Manfred S. Frings, ed. with an intro. by Kenneth W. Stikkers (London: Routledge & Kegan Paul, 1980)]; idem, *Schriften zur Soziologie und Weltanschauungslehre* (Leipzig: Der Neue Geist-Verlag, 1923–24) [2nd ed., vol. 6 in *Gesammelte Werke* (Bern: Francke Verlag, 1963)]; Karl Mannheim, *Ideology and Utopia: An Introduction to the Sociology of Knowledge* (New York: Harcourt, Brace & Co., 1936, 7th impression, 1954; includes bibliography); Werner Stark, *The Sociology of Knowledge: An Essay in Aid of a Deeper Understanding of the History of Ideas* (London: Routledge and Kegan Paul, 1958; Glencoe, IL: The Free Press, 1957; Robert King Merton, *Social Theory and Social Structure*, rev. and enl. ed. (Glencoe, IL: The Free Press, 1957).

206 [See above, p. 361, note 2.]

socialis est in transcendentia veri; nam quia verum dicit inconditionatum, a subiecto independens, (a) idem verum a pluribus cognosci potest; (b) idem verum ab aliis cognosci et ab aliis credi potest; (c) idem verum ex alio in alium contextum transferri potest.

(c′) Contextus ergo dogmatico-theologicus considerari potest dupliciter; uno modo secundum originem, unde 'theologia positiva'; alio modo secundum finem, scilicet, ut augentur intelligentia, scientia, sapientia circa doctrinam fidei, unde 'theologia systematica.'

(d′) Theologia positiva duas praecipue ponit quaestiones: primo, circa criterion continuitatis; deinde, circa ordinem considerationis.

(a″) Circa criterion continuitatis: In documentis ecclesiae saepe legitur illud, 'semper tenuit et tenet sancta Mater Ecclesia …' Secundum Pium XII eiusque praedecessores, legitur nobilissimum munus theologi esse ut ostendatur quemadmodum doctrina definita in fontibus contineatur, et quidem eo sensu quo definitum est (DB 2314). Quaestio de criterio continuitatis est quemadmodum sciatur, quemadmodum procedatur, ut eluceat doctrinam definitam esse eo sensu quo revelata est.

Cuius quaestionis alia est solutio dogmatica et alia solutio theologica, et quidem theologiae positivae.

Solutio dogmatica notissima est: Spiritum sanctum ita assistere docenti ecclesiae ut in rebus fidei et morum doctrina definita sit infallibilis.

Solutio tamen theologica etiam requiritur, secundum illud supra citatum ex Pio XII.

(b″) Criterion continuitatis in theologia positiva: In eo est quod historia doctrinae ad doctrinam terminatur. Quod assertum quid dicere velit perpendendum est.

Iam vidimus transitum ex fide in theologiam esse per modum thematizationis. Iam vero *per se* thematizatio neque mutat rem cognitam neque mutat rei cognitionem sed cognitione rei utitur ut per aliam technicam eadem res plenius cognoscatur. Recole exempla iam data, medici, iudicis, cognitionis subiecti psychologici. Attamen *per accidens* thematizatio in errorem conducere potest, nam quidquid recipitur ad modum recipientis recipitur.

on their own. The foundation of social knowledge is the transcendence of truth; since 'true' means unconditioned, independent of a subject, then (a) the same truth can be known by many; (b) the same truth can be known by some and believed by others; (c) the same truth can be transferred from one context to another.

(c′) Hence, the dogmatic-theological context can be considered in two ways: according to its origin, hence as 'positive theology,' and according to its goal, that is, the growth in understanding, knowledge, and wisdom about the teachings of the faith, hence as 'systematic theology.'

(d′) Positive theology mainly asks two questions: first, about the criterion of continuity; second, about the order to be followed in investigating a question.

(a″) The criterion of continuity: In the documents of the church we often read the following: 'Holy Mother Church has always held and does now hold …' According to Pius XII and his predecessors, we read that the noblest task of a theologian is to show how a defined doctrine is contained in the sources and indeed in the sense in which it has been defined (DB 2314, DS 3886, ND 859). The question about the criterion of continuity is how to know, how to proceed, so as to show clearly that a doctrine has been defined in the same sense as that in which it was revealed.

To this question there is a dogmatic solution and a theological solution, indeed that of positive theology.

The dogmatic solution is very well known: the Holy Spirit assists the teaching church so that any defined doctrine in matters of belief and morals is infallible.

Nevertheless, a theological solution is also called for, in accordance with the above quotation from Pius XII.

(b″) The criterion of continuity in positive theology is in this, that the history of a doctrine terminates at that doctrine. Let us now see what this statement means.

We have already seen that the transition from faith to theology occurs by way of thematization. Now, *per se* thematization changes neither the object known nor the knowledge of the object, but uses the knowledge of the object in order to come to a fuller knowledge of the same object by means of another technique. Recall the examples we gave of a physician, a judge, and the knowledge of the psychological subject. *Per accidens*, however, thematization could lead one into error, for whatever is received is received according to the dispositions of the receiver.

Qui tamen modi investigari possunt: in genere sunt horizontes; in specie, horizon recipientis receptionem veram impedit quatenus adest inauthentia, quatenus deest conversio vel intellectualis, vel moralis, vel religiosa.

Quibus positis, habetur criterion continuitatis. Datur enim continuitas ubi constat thematizationem fuisse per se, fuisse receptionem quae per modum subiecti non corrumpebatur. Non datur continuitas ubi constat thematizationem fuisse per accidens, fuisse receptionem quae per modum subiecti corrumpebatur.

Quod criterion secundum utrumque suum aspectum ipsi historiae doctrinali applicari potest.

Unde ex ipsis factis exsurget alios auctores evidenter per accidens processisse, alios autem per se.

Unde historia doctrinae ad ipsam doctrinam terminatur, scilicet quatenus doctrinarum oppositiones et successiones manifestant processum geneticum et dialecticum, in ipsis factis invenitur norma quaedam seu criterion.

(c″) Applicatio huius criterii illustratur, sane imperfecte, in iis quae de structura motus antenicaeni collegi:[207]

Quis Christus? Respondetur symbolice a Iudaeo-Christianis et a Gnosticis. Respondetur secundum realismum nativum a Tertulliano. Respondetur secundum placita Platonismi medii ab Origene. Respondetur rationalistice ab Arianis. Respondetur dogmatice ab Athanasio et subsequenti ecclesia, quo in responso continetur realismus dogmaticus qui tum puro symbolismo tum realismo nativo tum platonismo tum rationalismo opponitur.

An unus sit Christus? Apollinaristae, Diodorus et Theodorus, Nestorius, Cyrillus, Orientales, Leo Magnus, etc.

DB 2318: deploratur perversio notionis satisfactionis. Quaenam sit notio non perversa: cf. investigatio, *De Verbo Incarnato*, pp. 447–86; ex historia doctrinae ad doctrinam proceditur.

These dispositions can be investigated. In general terms, they are horizons; specifically, the horizon of the receiver can interfere with true reception to the extent that there is an absence of authenticity, an absence of intellectual or moral or religious conversion.

When these conditions are present, you have the criterion of continuity. For there is continuity when the thematization was clearly a *per se* thematization, when the reception was not distorted by the disposition of the subject. There is no continuity when the thematization was clearly a *per accidens* thematization, when the reception was distorted by the disposition of the subject.

This criterion in both of its aspects can be applied to the history of doctrine.

Hence, it becomes clear from the facts themselves that some authors in their thematizing proceeded *per accidens* and others *per se*.

Hence, the history of doctrine terminates at the doctrine itself; that is, inasmuch as the opposite positions and the successive stages in doctrines exhibit a genetic and dialectical process, it is in these very facts that the norm or criterion is to be found.

(c″) The application of this criterion is illustrated – imperfectly, it is true – in the elements of the structure of the ante-Nicene movement that I have collected:[207]

Who is Christ? This question the Jewish Christians and the Gnostics answer by way of symbolism. Tertullian's answer is that of naive realism. Origen answers according to the notions of middle Platonism, and the Arians give a rationalistic answer. The answer of Athanasius and subsequently of the church is a dogmatic answer, the answer of dogmatic realism which is opposed to pure symbolism, to naive realism, to Platonism, and to rationalism.

Is Christ one? Here you have the Apollinarists, Diodore and Theodore, Nestorius, Cyril, the Orientals, Leo the Great, and others.

The encyclical *Humani generis* (DB 2318, DS 3891) deplores a distorted notion of satisfaction. But what is the notion that is not distorted? See the investigation of this question in *De Verbo Incarnato*, [2nd ed., 1961], pp. 447–86; from the history of a doctrine one proceeds to the doctrine itself.

207 [A reference, it seems, to *De Deo Trino: Pars analytica* (1961). Note that the *Praemittenda* in both the 1961 and 1964 edition culminates in a § 10, which has the heading '*Motus Antenicaeni Structura.*' See *The Triune God: Doctrines* 288–303, 206–25.]

(d″) Unde quodammodo elucet distinctio inter theologiam dogmaticam positivam et theologias magis specializatas, uti biblicam, patristicam, mediaevalem, recentiorem.

Exemplo sit transformatio axium, coordinatorum: Glenn, Carpenter, primo secundum axes fixos in superficie terrae; deinde secundum axes fixos in centro telluris; tertio, si ad lunam pergeretur,[208] secundum axes fixos aliter in centro telluris, vel etiam in centro solis.[209]

Theologia positiva dogmatica praecipue occupatur circa ipsas transformationes ex alio in alium contextum; theologiae positivae et specializatae praecipue occupantur circa ipsos contextus particulares.

(e″) Theoria generalis, cf. *Insight*, cap. XVII, de veritate interpretationis.

(f″) Deinde quaerendum erat de ordine quo quaestiones investigantur; scilicet, de quo primo quaerendum sit utrum criteriis continuitatis satisfaciat; de quo deinde, de quo tertio, etc.

In cuius intelligentiam duo ordines distingui debent: alius enim est ordo magis chronologicus, et alius magis logicus.

Ordo *chronologicus* considerat elementa contextus dogmatico-theologici ea consecutione seu serie in qua chronologice facta sunt explicata, signata.

Ordo *logicus* in actuali contextu dogmatico-theologico distinguit inter ea quae sunt magis fundamentalia et ea quae ex fundamentalibus vel derivantur vel alio modo dependent.

Qui duo ordines quodammodo conflantur ubi quaestio ponitur de genesi categoriarum theologicarum. Sunt enim in contextu theologico-dogmatico notiones quaedam et fundamentales et propriae, quae pedetentim in ecclesia factae sunt explicitae, quae deinceps influxum quendam omnino fundamentalem in reliquas notiones exercuerunt. Quae notiones nominari possunt categoriae theologicae.

(g″) De genesi categoriarum

Distinguendum est inter categorias iam explicitas et alia ex parte catego-

(d″) This helps to clarify the distinction between positive dogmatic theology and the more specialized theologies such as biblical, patristic, medieval, and modern theology.

Take, for example, the transformation of axes, of coordinates: [the astronauts] [John] Glenn and [M. Scott] Carpenter, first, according to axes fixed on the surface of the earth, next, according to axes fixed in the center of the earth, and third, if they were going to the moon,[208] according to axes fixed differently in the center of the earth, or even in the center of the sun.[209]

Positive dogmatic theology is chiefly concerned with the transformations from one context to another; specialized positive theologies are chiefly concerned with those particular contexts themselves.

(e″) For the general theory, see *Insight*, chapter 17, [§3] on the truth of interpretation.

(f″) Our second question was about the order in which to investigate questions; that is, about what to ask first in order to satisfy the criterion of continuity; what to ask about next, then third, and so forth.

To understand this, two orders must be kept distinct, one a more chronological order, the other a more logical order.

The *chronological* order considers the elements of the dogmatic-theological context by way of a sequence or series according to the time in which facts were explained, or became thematic.

The *logical* order makes a distinction in the actual dogmatic-theological context between what are more fundamental and what derive from or depend upon those fundamentals.

These two orders are in a sense combined when the question is asked concerning the genesis of theological categories. For in the dogmatic-theological context there are certain notions that are fundamental and proper to it that have gradually become explicit in the church and that subsequently have had an absolutely fundamental influence upon all the other notions. Those fundamental notions can be called 'theological categories.'

(g″) The genesis of the categories

A distinction must be drawn between categories that are already explicit

---

208 [Note that this was written in May 1962, seven years before the first landing on the moon.]

209 [In the margin opposite this paragraph there are some handwritten words: 'axes, group of transf., series of …']

rias quae quamvis usurpentur tamen ad accuratam quandam explicitationem nondum pervenerunt.

Categoriae iam pridem explicitae: *homoousion*: quod enim de tua gloria
revelante te credimus hoc de Filio ...; unde tres *hypostaseis*, una *ousia*; tres
personae, una substantia; unde relationes, processiones, etc. Una persona:
apostolicae et evangelicae voces non duobus assignantur; unde duae naturae post unionem, duae naturales proprietates, etc., DB 116. Supernaturale:
secundum applicationes ad gratiam, ad oeconomiam salutis, ad methodum
theologiae.

Categoriae plus minus implicitae: habetur aliqua thematizatio, sed vix ad
totam rei plenitudinem concipiendam sufficit. Subiectum, interioritas, religio, symbolum, sociale, historicum, verbum Dei, evolutio, differentiatio, integratio, continuitas; brevi, omnia quae respiciunt particularia, contingentia, mobilia, concreta, etc., quae ad alteram problematicam remisimus.[210]

Circa has categorias notate eas esse quam maxime in usu: nihil magis
est historicum quam ecclesia catholica, quae quasi monolithica per duo
millennia lux elevata in gentibus iam exsistit;[211] nullatenus habent catholici problema historicum quale habent Protestantes vel liberales, qui vel
totam vel maiorem partem historiae Christianae per modum aberrationis
interpretari debent; et tamen ante hoc nostrum saeculum categoriae historicae vix in scholis theologicis et catholicis serio sunt consideratae; e.g.,
Journet[212] locutus est de necessitate categoriis addendi dimensionem temporis S. Thomae; neque imaginari debetis hanc necessitatem vel ab omni-

and, on the other hand, those that, although they are used, nevertheless have not yet become carefully explicitated.

Categories already explicit for some time: *Homoousion*: 'what we believe ... concerning your glory, we believe about your Son and about the Holy Spirit ...;' hence three *hypostaseis*, one *ousia*; three persons, one substance; hence the relations, the processions, etc. One person: DB 116, DS 255, ND 606/4: words in the writings of the apostles and the gospels are not to be attributed to two; hence two natures, two natural properties, etc. in Christ. Supernatural: according to application to grace, to the economy of salvation, to the method of theology.

Categories that are more or less implicit: there is some thematization here, but hardly enough for a full and complete conception of the matter: personal, subject, interiority, religion, symbol, social, historical, word of God, development, differentiation, integration, continuity; in short, all that have to do with the particular, the contingent, the changeable, the concrete, and so forth, which we shall deal with in the second problematic.[210]

Note that these categories are very much in use. Nothing is more historical than the Catholic Church, which for two millennia has stood like a monumental stele, raised up as a beacon to all the world.[211] Catholics do not have the problem with history that Protestants or liberals have, who must interpret all or most of the history of Christianity as an aberration; and yet prior to this century historical categories were scarcely given serious consideration in Catholic schools of theology. For example, see Journet,[212] who speaks of the need to add the dimension of time to the categories of St Thomas. You must not imagine that this need has either been universally

---

210 [See above, p. 361 note 2.]

211 [See DB 1794, DS 3014, ND 123. The allusion is probably to Isaiah 11.12.]

212 Charles Journet, *Introduction à la théologie* (Paris: Desclée de Brouwer, 1947). [In English, *The Wisdom of the Faith: An Introduction to Theology*, trans. R.F. Smith (Westminster, MD: The Newman Press, 1952.) Lonergan cites no page in support of his claim. Perhaps the following from p. 90 of the English translation (translating from p. 160 of the original) by implication provides some support: 'Historical theology ... if it is to be thought that its purpose is to put into operation an intention that was roughly sketched in *The City of God, has not yet been founded*; nor is it so easy to conceive its nature with great preciseness. Nevertheless, it is worth our while to attempt of see what it is.' *The Wisdom of Faith* 90 (italics added). Note finally that a little further on in the discussion (*Introduction à la théologie* 180–85; *The Wisdom of Faith* 104–107), Journet tends to emphasize Thomas's contribution to the development of a historical theology.]

---

bus esse agnitam vel ab omnibus agnoscentibus authentice intelligi; non pauci sunt qui differentiam inter conscientiam historicam et relativismum perspicere non valeant, qui hanc suam incapacitatem seu horizontem vel ipsam regulam fidei esse arbitrentur.

Problema ergo in eo est quod (1) praeter genesin categoriarum iam pridem generatarum habetur etiam genesis categoriarum quae nostris temporibus incipitur et (2) hae categoriae nunc in fieri quodamodo sunt magis fundamentales quam categoriae iam generatae.

V.g. *homoousion*, una persona in Christo, fundantur in verbo Dei; verbum Dei est locutio Dei intra contextum humanum historico-socialem atque religiosum.

(h″) Theologia systematica

Est quae quaerit finem contextus dogmatico-theologici, qui quidem finis est illa intelligentia imperfecta et fructuosissima mysteriorum in Vaticano laudata (DB 1796, 1800).

Ubi in primis desideratur methodus critica, unde systematice, methodice, eliminantur opiniones et disputationes quae ex inauthentia et horizonte et defectu conversionis opinantium et disputantium oriuntur. Quod primum desideratum modo quam maxime intimo cohaeret cum iis quae diximus circa criterion continuitatis: quod enim in positiva ad alios et antiquos applicatur, in systematica ad ipsum theologum applicandus est.

At deinde desideratur analogias repeti secundum Vaticanum (DB 1796) ex iis quae naturaliter cognoscuntur. Non pauci videntur theologi erubescere si ex ipsa cognitione naturali procedunt ut fundamentum analogiarum ponant solidum et verum. Ita nuperrime de conscientia Christi disputatum est, et humillimo meo iudicio ideo praecipue quod theologi ad munus mere philosophicum, mere psychologicum, attentionem dare noluerint. Ipsi sunt theologi; quid sit conscientia, nihil refert.

acknowledged or correctly understood by those who have acknowledged it; there are quite a few who are unable to grasp the difference between historical consciousness and relativism, and who imagine this inability, this horizon of theirs, to be the very rule of faith.

The problem, therefore, lies in the fact that (1) besides the genesis of categories that have already arisen there is also the genesis of categories that are beginning to emerge in our day, and (2) these categories now in the process of emerging are in a way more fundamental than those that have already emerged.

For example, *homoousion* and the one person in Christ: these are founded upon the word of God; and the word of God is the utterance of God within the human historical-social and religious context.

(h″) Systematic theology

This is that theology that seeks to fulfill the purpose of the dogmatic-theological context, which is that imperfect and most fruitful understanding of the mysteries mentioned in Vatican I (DB 1796, DS 3016, ND 132; DB 1800, DS 3020, ND 136).

What is desired here first of all is a critical method whereby systematically, methodically, those opinions and arguments are eliminated that stem from the inauthenticity and horizon and lack of conversion on the part of those who hold those opinions and make those arguments. This first desideratum is most closely connected with what we have said about the criterion of continuity; for that criterion that in positive theology is applied to other theologians and to those of the past, in systematic theology is to be applied to theologians themselves.

The next desideratum is, in accordance with Vatican I (DS 1796, DS 3016, ND 132) to obtain analogies from what we know naturally. Quite a few theologians seem to be ashamed to proceed from natural knowledge in order to lay a true and solid foundation of analogies. Such has been the case recently with regard to the dispute about the consciousness of Christ, which in my humble opinion exists mainly because theologians have refused to give themselves to a task that is purely philosophical or purely psychological. After all, they are theologians; the nature of consciousness is of no interest to them.

Appendix 1:
Introductio in notionem et problema methodi[1]

[1] Quaestio
[2] Seriatio quaestionum
[3] Responsorum ordinatio
[4] Seriatio ordinationum
[5] Criterion ordinationis novae
[6] Problema fundamenti
[7] Problema historicitatis
[8] Problema khasmatis[2]

[1]   Quaestio

1 Exsistit quaestio ubi adesse videntur rationes cogentes tam ad affirmandam quam ad negandam unam eandemque propositionem. Unde con-

Appendix 1:
Introduction to the Notion and Problem of Method[1]

[1]   The Question

1 A question exists when there seem to be cogent reasons for both affirming and denying one and the same proposition. Hence, there is no question,

---

1 [These undated notes correspond roughly to the first chapter of the *reportatio* 'De Intellectu et methodo' ('Understanding and Method'), titled 'De notione quaestionis,' which appears above, pp. 4–79. In view of what Lonergan says at the very end of this present text, it may be an earlier attempt to put together that first chapter. But it may also contain the notes he used in lecturing on the material. The notes that constitute 'Understanding and Method' were assembled by students and then approved by Lonergan and used by him in the 1961 course of the same name. So they have a more 'official' status than the present portion, even if the present document is from Lonergan's own hand. Unless otherwise indicated, translator's and editors' interpolations are in square brackets. Lonergan's handwritten marginal notes will be indicated.]

cludes: non esse quaestionem ubi non de eadem propositione agitur, ubi rationes in unam tantummmodo partem mentem inclinant vel in neutram, ubi rationes non sunt seriae, cogentes.

2 Ita definitur quaestio apud Gilbertum Porreta et alios.³

3 Colligebantur quaestiones cum rationibus oppositis: Gratianus, *Decretum*; Abaelardus, *Sic et non*.⁴

4 Technica quaestionis perspicitur in articulis S. Thomae: Videtur quod non, Sed contra, Respondeo. Dicendum quod ... Ad primum dicendum ... In *Summa* [*Theologiae*] generatim schematica tantum adhibetur technica quaestionis. Serie usurpatur alibi:⁵ cf. *Super II Sent.*, d. 28, q.1, a. 2; *De Ver.*, q. 24, a. 12. 'Gratia Operans,' *Theological Studies*, 1941–42.⁶

5 Quaestiones sine technica inde ab initiis ecclesiae; e.g., an sint duo dei? Iust., *Dial.* 58; Tert., *Adv. Praxean*; Hipp., *Contra haeresin Noeti*; Orig, *In Ioan.*, II, 2; Novatianus, *De trin.*, cap. ult.; Dion. Rom., DB 48–51; Arius, Opitz,

[a] when the discussion is not about the same proposition; [b] when the reasons incline the mind to only one side of the issue, or to neither side; [c] when the reasons are not serious and compelling.

2 This is how the question was defined by Gilbert de la Porrée and others.[3]

3 Collections of questions with reasons on opposite sides can be found in Gratian, *Decretum,* and Abelard, *Sic et non.*[4]

4 The technique of the question is very clear in St Thomas: *Videtur quod non* (It seems that ... not ...); *Sed contra* (But on the contrary ...); *Respondeo. Dicendum* (I reply. It must be said that ...); *Ad primum* (In response to the first objection) ... In the *Summa* [*theologiae*] generally the technique of the question is used only schematically. It is employed seriously elsewhere:[5] See Thomas Aquinas, *Super II Sententiarum,* d. 28, q. 1, a. 2; *De veritate,* q. 24, a. 12. [See Bernard Lonergan, 'St Thomas' Thought on] *Gratia Operans,' Theological Studies* 2 (1941) 289–324; 3 (1942) 69–88, 375–402, 533–78.[6]

5 Questions without this technique have emerged from the very beginnings of the church; for example, 'Are there two gods?' Justin, *Dialogus cum Tryphone Iudaeo,* 58; Tertullian, *Adversus Praxean;* Hippolytus, *Contra haeresin Noeti;* Origen, *Commentariorum in Evangelium Johannis,* ii, 2; Novatian, *De Trinitate,* last chapter; Dionysius of Rome, DB 48–51, DS 112–15, ND 301–303;

2 [The numbers of the sections are added by the editors. What here are sections 9–12 were not listed by Lonergan at the beginning, but have the same status in the document as the first eight sections. There are some minor discrepancies between the list above and the list that appears in 'Understanding and Method.' In particular, the last three items listed above appear in 'Understanding and Method' as one item with three aspects. In addition, what is called in the list above 'The Problem of the Chasm [*Khasmatis*]' in 'Understanding and Method' is called the problem of separation (*separationis*), though Lonergan switches to *chasma* for the remainder of the document. The numbering is editorial, and numbers from 9 to 12 have been added in the text.]

3 See (Yves) M.-J. Congar, 'Le développement de la QUAESTIO,' in *Dictionnaire de théologie catholique* [DTC] XV (29), s.v. 'Théologie,' 370–74, especially 371.

4 See Gratian, *Decretum,* ML 187; Peter Abelard, *Sic et non;* ML 178, cols. 1329–1610.

5 [The Latin from 'In Summa ...' was added by hand in the text.]

6 [Available now as part 1 in *Grace and Freedom* (see above, p. 47, note 40). See 'Understanding and Method,' pp. 6–7 above, where Lonergan states his point more fully and more clearly.]

Athanasius Werke, Urkunde,[7] Euseb. Caes., *De eccl. theol.*; Conciliabula ariana vel minus orthodoxa, Hahn.[8]

6 Quinam sit nexus inter quaestiones mediaevales et fontes revelationis? Non clare apparet: reformatores, Baianistae, Iansenistae, murmurantes contra scholasticismum. Re vera exsistit: si quis ex qq mediaevalibus ad fontes SScr et PP investigatione historica ascendit.[9]

[2]   De Seriatione Quaestionum

1 Primo modo. Soluta una quaestione, oritur alia. Ita postquam divinitas Christi fuit definita, quaerebatur utrum etiam Spiritus Sanctus fuerit Deus, utrum Christus re vera fuerit homo, utrum habuerit duas naturas, duas voluntates, duas operationes, utrum unica persona fuerit divina; utrum Spiritus Sanctus a Filio procedat.

2 Altero modo. Reiecta et damnata quadam haeresi, sub alia forma resurgit. Pelagiani: sicut Stoici, a diis petitur non virtus sed fortuna; si exsistit gratia, saltem non est necessaria, vel necessaria ad facilius posse;[10] si gratia absolute[11] necessaria est, consistit in lege, in cognitione legis, in natura, in libero arbitrio, in remissione peccatorum; si ad bonum opus necessaria, homini datur secundum merita; si gratia praevenit opera bona, datur secundum merita bonae voluntatis; si interdum ipsam bonam voluntatem praevenit, interdum a bona voluntate praevenitur.

3 Tertio modo. Reiecta haeresi, in oppositam confugitur. Si necessaria est gratia, non exsistit libertas. Si necessaria est gratia, saltem superiores subditos corrigere et castigare non debent. Augustinus, *De gratia et libero arbitrio, De correptione et gratia.* Protestantes negant organizationem eccle-

Arius, Opitz, *Athanasius Werke, Urkunde* [Documents];[7] Eusebius of Caesarea, *De ecclesiastica theologia.* Arian or less orthodox councils, Hahn.[8]

6 What is the connection between the medieval questions and the sources of revelation? The matter is not clear: the Reformers, Baianists, Jansenists, those who inveigh against Scholasticism. But a connection really does exist, if one through historical investigation traces the medieval questions back to the biblical sources and the Fathers.[9]

[2] The Serial Arrangement of Questions

1 *First way*: when one question is solved, another emerges. Thus, after the divinity of Christ was defined, the question arose whether the Holy Spirit also was God; whether Christ was truly man; whether he had two natures, two wills, two operations; whether the one person in Christ was divine; whether the Holy Spirit proceeds from the Son.

2 *Second way*: when a heresy is rejected and condemned, it emerges again in another form. The Pelagians, like the Stoics, prayed for good fortune, not virtue. If grace exists, at least it is not necessary or only necessary to be able more easily [to act];[10] but if it is absolutely[11] necessary, it consists in law, in a knowledge of the law, in nature, in free will, in the forgiveness of sins; but if it is necessary for doing good, it is given in accordance with one's merits; but if grace is antecedent to good works, it is granted according to the merits of a good will; and if sometimes it is antecedent to good will, sometimes good will precedes it.

3 *Third way*: with the rejection of a heresy, there is a rush to the opposite extreme. If grace is necessary, there is no freedom. If grace is necessary, at least superiors should not correct and punish their subjects. Augustine, *De gratia et libero arbitrio* and *De correptione et gratia.* Protestants deny the external

7 [Hans-Georg Opitz, ed., *Athanasius Werke, hrsg. im auftrage der Kirchenväterkommission der Preussischen akademie der wissenschaften,* 3 vols (Berlin and Leipzig: W. De Gruyter and Co., 1934–41).]
8 [August Hahn, *Bibliothek der Symbole und Glaubensregeln der Apostolisch-katholischen Kirche* (Breslau: Grass & Barth, 1842); 2nd ed., *Bibliothek der Symbole und Glaubensregeln der alten Kirche* (Breslau: E. Morgenstern, 1877); 3rd ed., 1897; repr. ed., Hildesheim: Georg Olms Verlagsbuchhandlung, 1962].
9 See Lonergan, 'St Thomas' Thought on *Gratia operans,*' 1941 [*Grace and Freedom* 3–43.]
10 [The Latin words 'vel necessaria ad facilius posse' were added by hand in the autograph.]
11 [The Latin word 'absolute' was added by hand in the autograph.]

siae externam et iuridicam, sacerdotium, missae sacrificium, sacramenta. Catholici ita in his insistunt ut vitam interiorem minus colant. Liberales-Modernistae studiis biblicis, historiae incumbunt.

4 Quarto modo. Clarissime excluduntur omnes haereses cum omnibus suis variationibus. Pariter excluduntur errores e diametro oppositi. Sed exclusio fit secundum Mt 5.37: 'Sit sermo vester est, est; non, non; quod enim abundantius est, a malo est.' Et secundum 1 Cor 8.1: scientia inflat (*hē gnōsis physioi*). S. Anselmus, *Tract. de Concord. Praescientiae*, 11, ML 158, 522. Aquinas, Quodl. IV, 18. Vaticanum, DB 1796, 1800.

Auctoritas quaestionem facti dirimit: sunt rationes in utramque partem; sed creditur quaenam sit pars vera, quaenam falsa. Fide certissima creditur; sed manent difficultates. Fides quaerit intellectum, solutionem rationum. Unde maximus labor clarificationum, definitionum, investigationis eorum quae supponuntur, consequuntur.

[3]   De Responsis Ordinandis

1 Quo magis sese extendit quaestionum seriatio, eo magis exigitur responsorum ordinatio.

2 Ordinatio in primis est 'logica,' ubi invenitur technica derivationis terminorum (definitio) et propositionum (deductio); unde distingui possunt tam termini quam propositiones primitivae et derivatae,[12] et concipi potest *systema* seu virtualis quaedam propositionum totalitas quae mediante technica derivationis eaque sola per primitiva determinatur.

NB: Euclides ad systema formandum non pervenit; eumque non pervenisse usque ad tempora recentiora ignoratum est.

and juridical organization of the church, the priesthood, the sacrifice of the Mass, sacraments. Catholics lay so much emphasis on these things that they pay less attention to the cultivation of the interior life. Liberals/Modernists devote themselves to scriptural and historical studies.

4 *Fourth way:* clearly exclude all heresies with all their variations, as well as the errors diametrically opposed to them. But this exclusion is done in accordance with Matthew 5.37: 'Let your word be "Yes, Yes," and "No, No"; anything more than this is from the evil one.' And, according to 1 Corinthians 8.1: 'knowledge puffs up' *(hē gnōsis physioi)*. St Anselm, *De concordia praescientiae et praedestinationis nec non gratiae Dei cum libero arbitrio,* q. 3, c. 1; ML 158, 522. Thomas Aquinas, *Quaestiones quodlibetum,* IV, q. 9, a. 3 (18). [First] Vatican [Council], DB 1796, 1800; DS 3016, 3020, ND 132, 136.

Questions of fact are settled by appealing to authorities: there are reasons on both sides, but which side is right and which wrong is a matter of faith. It is believed with faith that is most certain; but difficulties remain. Faith seeks understanding, a solution based on reasons. Hence the laborious task of clarifying, defining, and investigating the presuppositions of a position and its consequences.

[3]   Ordering the Answers

1 The more extensive the serial arrangement of questions is, the more urgent is the need for an ordering of the answers.

2 The ordering is first of all 'logical,' where the technique of the derivation of terms (definition) and of propositions (deduction) is used. Hence the possibility of distinguishing both terms and propositions as primitive and derived,[12] and of conceiving a *system,* a virtual totality of propositions determined by the primitive terms and propositions through the mediation of the technique and that alone.

Note that Euclid did not arrive at the formation of a system; and the fact that he did not do so was unknown until recently.

12 In the stricter and merely formal sense, not about concepts, judgments, intelligibles, truths, but about terms, propositions. Otherwise never any clear notion of *method.* [This was added by hand in the autograph: 'sensu strictiori mere formali non de conceptibus, iudiciis, intelligibilibus veris, sed de terminis, propositionibus. Secus nulla umquam clara notio *methodi.*' It is possible that 'secus ...' belongs with 3, on coherence.]

3 *Cohaerens* est systema quod non continet KpNp.[13] Cum 'systema' in genere non sit nisi ideale, datur motus ad ideale attingendum; qui motus in primis regitur per principium contradictionis; unde habetur *dialectica* quaedam *interior*.

4 *Sensus realis* habetur in systemate ubi determinari potest quid realiter intercedat inter p et Np. Unde semantica, metaphysica: distinctio inter entia realia et rationis, inter distinctiones reales et rationis; et harum ad omnia applicatio systematica.

NB: M.-J. Congar tria stadia evolutionis mediaevalis distinguit: sub regimine grammaticae, ab Alcuino;[14] sub regimine dialecticae, ab Abaelardo;[15] sub regimine metaphysicae (init Gul. Altiss., Phil. Can., Alb., Aq.)[16]

5 *Aequivalentia* sunt systemata quae eandem propositionum totalitatem diversimode ordinant. Quod maxime respicit valorem scientificum, explicativum, systematis. Incipitur enim ex prioribus quoad nos (via inventionis, resolutionis) ut perveniatur ad priora quoad se. Unde incipitur iterum ex prioribus quoad se (via doctrinae, compositionis) ut redeatur ad priora quoad nos.

NB: S. Thomas in *C. Gent.* concludit ad revelata (Hinc est quod dicitur …; visio beata, III, 25–63, necessitas gratiae, III, 147 s). *Summa* tota est in ordine doctrinae (I, qq. 27–43).[17] Unde concludes: dari punctum inflexionis; dari principia proprie theologica (non 'ex revelatis vel ex philosophia'); erroneam esse methodum Ioan a STh.[18]

3 A system that does not contain 'KpNp' is *coherent*.[13] Although 'system' in general is only an ideal, there is a movement towards attaining the ideal. This movement is first of all guided by the principle of contradiction: hence, there is had an *internal dialectic*.

4 A *real meaning* is present in a system when one can determine the real difference between p and Np. From this, semantics and metaphysics: the distinction between real beings and conceptual beings, between real distinctions and notional distinctions, and their systematic application to everything.

Note: Congar has distinguished three stages of medieval development: under the dominance of grammar, from Alcuin;[14] under the dominance of dialectic, from Abelard;[15] under the dominance of metaphysics (beginning with William of Auxerre, Philip the Chancellor; Albert, Aquinas).[16]

5 Systems that order the same totality of proposition in different ways are *equivalent*. This regards most of all the scientific or explanatory value of a system. One begins from what are first with respect to us (the way of discovery, of analysis, of resolution into causes) to arrive at what are first with respect to themselves. From here one begins again from what are first with respect to themselves (the way of teaching, of composition) to return to what are first with respect to us.

Note that St Thomas in the *Summa contra Gentiles* ends with the truths of revelation ('Hence there is what is said ...'; the beatific vision, 3, cc. 25–63; the necessity of grace, ibid. cc.147–48). The entire *Summa [theologiae]* is ordered according to the way of teaching (1, qq. 27–43).[17] Hence we conclude: there is a turning point; there are principles that are properly theological (not 'from revelation or philosophy'); John of St Thomas's method is wrong.[18]

---

13 [Lonergan is using Jan Łukasiewicz's Polish notation.]

14 Congar, 'Théologie,' DTC XV (29) 360–64 [*A History of Theology* 61–67].

15 Ibid. 364–74 [*A History of Theology* 69–84].

16 Ibid. 374–92 [*A History of Theology* 85–114. On the left of this paragraph, Lonergan wrote: 'Eunomius, *Apologeticus*, PG [MG] 30: 837 ff.' To clarify his point, see the reference to Eunomius in *Understanding and Method*, pp. 22–23 above.]

17 [The corresponding sentence in 'Understanding and Method' has 'according to the synthetic way.' See above, p. 25.]

18 Congar, 'Théologie,' DTC XV (29) 418–21 [*A History of Theology* 157–62. On p. 162, Congar writes: 'When John of Saint-Thomas ... expresses the function of the theology in these terms: "supernatural things treated in the fashion of metaphysical science and discussed in natural terms ..." he denounced any potential deviation from this important and legitimate function. The

[4]   De Seriatione Ordinationum

1 Sicut soluta una quaestione, oritur alia, ita soluta quaestionum serie, oriuntur quaestiones ulteriores. *C. Gent.* III, 48, ¶12, §2257; DB 1800. Verbum Dei scriptum et traditum 'tot tantosque continet thesauros veritatis, ut numquam reapse exhauriatur'; 'sacrorum fontium studio sacrae disciplinae semper iuvenescunt.'[19]

2 Sicut prioribus quaestionibus responsum est, ita etiam posterioribus respondendum erit; et sicut priora responsa sunt ordinata per quoddam systema, pari ratione etiam posteriora erunt ordinanda.

3 Nova tamen responsa triplici modo se habere possunt ad ordinationem prius factam. Primo modo, non sunt nisi conclusiones ex priori ordinatione: scil. oritur nova quaestio cuius tamen solutio habetur per solam derivationis technicam ex terminis et propositionibus primitivis iam positis. Altero modo, novae quaestioni non respondetur sufficienter ex ordinatione iam facta et per solam technicam derivationis; sed tamen ei responderi potest si paulum evolvitur ordinatio iam facta; scilicet, adduntur novi termini primitivi, novae propositiones primitivae, sive explicite, sive modo latente et tecte per additas distinctiones prius non factas. Tertio modo, novae quaestioni non respondetur sufficienter sive ex ordinatione iam facta et per solam technicam derivationis sive per evolutionem quandam ordinationis iam factae, sed requiritur novus procedendi modus qui essentialiter differt a modo superius exposito.

[4]   The Serial Arrangement of the Orderings

1 Just as when one question is settled another emerges, so when one series of questions is settled further questions arise. See Thomas Aquinas, *Summa contra Gentiles*, 3, c. 48, ¶12, §2257; DB 1800, DS 3020, ND 136. The word of God in scripture and tradition 'contains so many and such great treasures of truth that it will never be really exhausted.' Hence, 'the sacred disciplines are always being rejuvenated by the study of the sacred sources.'[19]

2 As the prior questions were answered, so should the subsequent questions also be answered. And just as the prior answers were arranged through some system, so with equal reason are the subsequent answers to be arranged.

3 Newer answers, however, can be related to a previous ordering in three ways. In the first way, they are simply conclusions from the previous ordering: that is, a new question arises whose answer is obtained solely through the technique of derivation from the primitive terms and propositions already laid down. In the second way, a new question is not adequately answered from the previous ordering and through the technique of derivation alone. But it can be answered if there is some slight development in the ordering already made; that is, new primitive terms and new primitive propositions are added, either explicitly or in a hidden manner through the addition of distinctions not previously made. In the third way, a new question is not adequately answered either from the previous ordering and the technique of derivation alone, or through a development in that ordering. What is required here is a new way of proceeding that differs essentially from the way expounded above.

---

real danger exists of considering the role of faith in theology merely as preliminary, necessary to furnish the starting point, but truly borderline and extrinsic, while the real theological work is then done by the simple application of metaphysics to this datum held as true. How then, while constructing a rational interpretation, can theology preserve for that Christian datum its specificity, its character of a whole, and its original reality?'].

19 *Acta Apostolicae Sedis* XLII (1950) 568 [DB 2314, DS 3886, ND 859]. [At this point in the text, Lonergan inserts by hand: 'Ratio intrinsica: cf. folium additum – 'Intrinsic reason: cf. added sheet.' This page may be missing; but the 'added sheet' may be the following one, titled '*De quaestionibus quae ex doctrina NT oriuntur,*' 'Questions Arising out of the Teaching of the New Testament,' on which are listed 13 questions regarding the meaning of biblical doctrines; see below, §4.1.]

4 Quamdiu sufficit primus modus, non oritur quaestio methodologica; sufficit logica systematis. Quam primun in secundum et praesertim in tertium modum transgreditur, oritur quaestio methodologica. Quare, aliquid clarius et distinctius ponendum est circa distinctionem secundi modi a primo et tertii modi a secundo. Agitur enim de exsistentia quaestionis methodologicae.

[4.1] De quaestionibus quae ex doctrinae NT oriuntur

1 Quod de facto ortae sunt quaestiones, dubitari non potest. (a) Conflictus cum Iudaeis orthodoxis: S. Paulus et Iudaizantes; primum quod dicitur concilium Hierosolymitanum. (b) Conflictus cun Iudaeis heterodoxis: Daniélou, *Théologie du Judéo-christianisme* (Tournai-Paris: Desclée & Cie 1958).[20] Ebionitae, Elkesaïtae, Cerinthus, gnosticismus Samaritanus. (c) Gnosticismus, Montantismus, patripassianismus, adoptionismus, Sabellianismus. (d) Ariani, Semi-Ariani, conservatores exaggerati; Pelagiani; Nestoriani; Monophysitae; Monothelitae; schisma ecclesiae orientalis. (e) Reformatio, rationalismus, liberalismus, modernismus, etc.

2 Quod ortae sunt quaestiones ex ipsa natura doctrinae NT. (a) Secus superfluisset ecclesia docens, magisterium infallibile; erronea fuisset dogmatum evolutio; aberratio fuisset omnis theologia. (b) Qui aliter opinantur, intrinsecam idearum historicitatem non capiunt. Ex intelligentia procedit verbum; quo perfectior est intelligentia, eo accuratiora sunt verba; et intelligentia augetur decursu saeculorum, secundum Vaticanum, DB 1800. Formae Platonicae non sunt reales; species non sunt fixae. (c) Doctrina NT exprimitur terminis qui intra ipsum NT evolvuntur atque perficiuntur. Acts 2; 1 et 2 Cor; Phil et Col; Hebr 1; John 1. (d) Ipsa haec evolutio fiebat intra culturam non solum antiquam sed etiam particularem; fiebat secundum separationem a notionibus illi culturae alte fixis: novum vinum veteres utres explodebat. (e) E contra, ipsa doctrina est universalistica: docete omnes gentes … ego vobiscum sum omnibus diebus usque ad consummationem saeculi. (f) Ipsa doctrina est summi momenti: margarita magni pretii; qui non crediderit condemnabitur. (g) Ipsa doctrina est radicalis et compre-

4 As long as the first way is sufficient, the methodological question does not arise; the logic of the system suffices. As soon as there is a transition to the second and especially to the third way, the methodological question does arise. Therefore, something more clear and more distinct must be determined concerning the difference between the first and second way and between the second and third way. For the issue is about the existence of the methodological question.

[4.1]   Questions Arising Out of the Teaching of the New Testament

1 That in fact questions have arisen is beyond doubt. (a) Conflicts with orthodox Jews: St Paul and the Judaizers; the so-called first Council of Jerusalem. (b) Conflicts with heterodox Jews: Jean Daniélou, *Théologie du Judéo-christianisme* (Tournai-Paris: Desclée & Cie 1958).[20] Ebionites, Elkaisites, Cerinthus, Samaritan gnosticism. (c) Gnosticism, Montanism, patripassianism, adoptionism, Sabellianism. (d) Arians, semi-Arians, ultraconservatives; Pelagians; Nestorians; Monophysites; Monothelites; schism of the Eastern church. (e) Reformation, rationalism, liberalism, modernism, etc.

2 Questions have arisen from the very nature of the teaching of the New Testament. (a) Otherwise a teaching church and infallible magisterium would have been superfluous; dogmatic development would have been erroneous; all theology would have been an aberration. (b) Those who think otherwise do not grasp the intrinsic historicity of ideas. From understanding there proceeds an inner word; the more perfect is the understanding, the more accurate are the words; and understanding increases through the course of centuries, according to the [First] Vatican Council, DB 1800, DS 3020, ND 136. Platonic Forms are not real; species are not fixed. (c) The teaching of the New Testament is expressed in terms that within the New Testament itself evolve and are perfected. Acts 2; 1 and 2 Corinthians; Philippians and Colossians; Hebrews 1; John 1. (d) This development took place in a culture that is not only ancient but also quite particular; it took place by getting away from the ideas that were deeply embedded in that culture: new wine burst the old wineskins. (e) On the other hand, the

---

20 [In English, *The Theology of Jewish Christianity*, trans. and ed. John A. Baker (London: Darton, Longman & Todd, and Chicago: The Henry Regnery Company, 1964).]

hensiva: non iam sibi vivant sed ei qui pro ipsis mortuus est et resurrexit (2 Cor 5.15). (h) Doctrina universalistica, summi momenti, radicalis et comprehensiva, si intra limites culturae particularis atque antiquissimae exponitur atque evolvitur, ex ipsa sua ratione est fons quidam perpetuus quaestionum.

[5]   Criterion Ordinationis Novae

1 In particulari, nullum est problema. Habetur nova ordinatio ubi habetur nova quaedam totalitas virtualis propositionum. Et habetur nova totalitas virtualis ubi novi accedunt termini primitivi, novae propositiones primitivae, vel forte nova technica derivationis.

2 At generalis etiam est huius rei consideratio, si quidem (a) in omni actuali totalitate propositionum (b) adhibita technica derivationis (definitio, deductio) (c) distingui possunt termini derivati et non derivati (d) et pariter propositiones derivatae et non derivatae, unde fieri possunt collectiones sequentes: (e) ex terminis non derivatis seu primitivis, mediante technica derivationis, formari possunt omnes termini possibiles intra ordinatiomm, Σt;[21] (f) ex collectione terminorum possibilium, Σt, formari potest collectio propositionum possibilium, seu quaestionum, Σq;[22] (g) et comparari potest totalitas virtualis quaestionum, Σq, cum virtuali totalitate systematis, Σr,[23] scilicet, propositionum primitivarum una cum propositionibus derivatis mediante technica derivationis eaque sola; unde distingui

teaching itself is universalist: 'teach all nations ... I am with you always until the end of the world' [Matthew 28.19–20]. (f) This teaching is of supreme importance: the 'pearl of great value' [Matthew 13.45–46]; 'one who does not believe shall be condemned' [Mark 16.16]. (g) This teaching is radical and comprehensive: 'that they might live no longer for themselves but for him who for them died and rose' (2 Corinthians 5.15). (h) A doctrine that is universalist, of supreme importance, radical, and comprehensive, if it is expounded and developed within the limitations of a particular and very ancient culture, by its very nature will be a perpetual source of questions.

[5]   The Criterion of a New Ordering

1 In an individual case, there is no problem. There is a new ordering when there is a new virtual totality of propositions. And there is a new virtual totality when there are new primitive terms, new primitive propositions, or perhaps a new technique of derivation.

2 But there is also a general consideration of this matter, since (a) in every actual totality of propositions (b) when the technique of derivation (definition, deduction) is used, (c) derived and non-derived terms can be distinguished, (d) and similarly also derived and non-derived propositions, whence the following collections can be made: (e) from non-derived, or primitive, terms, through the mediation of the technique of derivation, all possible terms within the ordering can be drawn up, Σt;[21] (f) from this collection of possible terms, Σt, a collection of possible propositions, or questions, can be drawn up, Σq;[22] (g) and the virtual totality of questions, Σq, can be compared with the virtual totality of the system, Σr,[23] that is, of the primitive propositions together with the derived propositions through the

---

21 [Lonergan actually typed 'St'; 'Σt' was written in the left margin. It seems likely that he used 'S' simply because the typewriter he was using did not permit him to type 'Σ.' Accordingly, in these symbolic expressions, 'Σ' has been substituted here wherever 'S' appears in the original document. See 'Understanding and Method' above, pp. 32–33.]

22 [Lonergan actually typed 'SQp.' In the left margin, however, he wrote 'Σq,' which corresponds better with what is found in 'Understanding and Method.' In addition, it avoids having 'ΣQp' do double duty, standing in (f) for 'a collection of possible propositions, or questions,' and in (g) for just 'the virtual totality of questions.']

23 [Again, Lonergan actually typed 'SRp,' but inserted 'Σr' by hand in the left margin.]

possunt (h) systemata clausa in quibus $\Sigma q = \Sigma r$,[24] (i) systemata aperta in quibus $\Sigma q > \Sigma r$.[25]

3 Unde inter logicos recentiores investigantur systemata secundum quod sunt clausa vel aperta (secundum quod solvere possunt problema decisionis necne).[26] Inter quos constat:[27] (a) calculum propositionum esse clausum; (b) calculum functionalem secundi vel altioris ordinis esse apertum;[28] (c) arithmeticam (si includitur theorema de factoribus et similia quaedam) aut esse contradictoriam aut apertam, modo non adhibeantur operationes logicae infinite repetitae; (d) exsistere seriem theorematum typi Gödel.[29]

Unde concedendum videtur systema aut esse triviale aut apertum; unde Wang concipit mathesin tamquam seriem apertam systematum apertorum. Vide apud Ladrière.[30]

mediation of the technique of derivation, and that alone. Whence a distinction can be made between (h) closed systems, in which $\Sigma r = \Sigma q$[24] [and] (i) open systems, in which $\Sigma q > \Sigma r$.[25]

3 Hence it is that recent logicians are inquiring into systems as to whether they are closed or open (according as to whether they can solve the problem of decision).[26] They agree that:[27] (a) the calculus of propositions is closed; (b) the functional calculus of the second or higher order is open;[28] (c) arithmetic (if one includes the theorem of factors and similar things) is either contradictory or open, so long as logical operations repeated an infinite number of times are not used; (d) there exists a series of theorems of the type of Gödel's theorem.[29]

Hence, it seems it must be granted that a system is either trivial or it is open. Thus, Hao Wang conceived mathematics as an open system of open systems;[30] see Ladrière on this point.

24 [Lonergan actually typed 'SRp = SQp,' but next to this expression he inserted '$\Sigma q = \Sigma r$,' which is what is found in 'Understanding and Method.']
25 [Lonergan actually typed, 'SRp < SQp,' but next to this expression he inserted '$\Sigma q > \Sigma r$,' by hand, as in 'Understanding and Method.']
26 ['These are the fundamental questions asked about deductive systems. First, can you prove all the propositions in the system (completeness)? Second, if you can prove all of them, are you sure that you will not prove too many, namely, two contradictories (coherence)? And third, can you solve mechanically all the problems that arise in the system? This is called the decision problem: is there some standard procedure that will solve any problem that arises on this level of logic.' Lonergan, *Phenomenology and Logic* 5; see also 55, 320. In the left margin at this point wrote: 'definitiones per connotationem[,] per denotationem' 'definition by connotation[,] by denotation.' The term 'decision problem' (*Entscheidungsproblem*) would seem to derive from David Hilbert.]
27 [At this point, Lonergan adds on the right side of the page a general references to Joseph Bocheński, ed., *Bibliographische Einführungen in das Studium der Philosophie* (Bern: A. Francke (1948–53) and to A.N. Prior, *Formal Logic* (Oxford: Clarendon Press, 1955 [2nd ed., 1962]). Lonergan does not assign pages with either reference, but at least as regards the work edited by Bocheński, if footnote 25 on p. 50 in *Phenomenology and Logic* (CWL 18) is any indication, he had in mind E.W. Beth's bibliography in *Symbolische Logik und Grundlegung der exakten Wissenschaften*, fasc. 3 in *Bibliographische Einführungen*, 1–27 (independent pagination). Note, finally, that at this point in 'Understanding and Method' Lonergan cites not this work edited by Bocheński, but Bocheński's own book *Formale Logik*.]
28 Church, *Introduction to Mathematical Logic*.
29 See Jean Ladrière, *Les limitations internes des formalismes*.
30 [The reference may be to Hao Wang, 'The Formalization of Mathematics,' *Journal of Symbolic Logic* 19 (1954) 241–66. There is a written insertion at this

[5.1]   Momentum praecedentis considerationis generalis pro scholasticis

Generatim scholastici non explicite ponunt ordinationem logicam, sicut quodammodo fecerunt Euclides, Spinoza, et accurate tantummodo logici et mathematici recentiores. Apud eos systema logicum est aliquid implicitum, potentiale, quod fieri posset sed non fit. Unde I. Bocheński opinatus est *Summam theologiae* S. Thomae formalizari posse intra duo vel tria saecula si formaretur commissio quaedam permanens specialistarum in hunc finem.[31]

Ubi deest completa enumeratio terminorum primitivorum et exacta determinatio technicae derivationis terminorum, ubi deest completa enumeratio propositionum primitivarum et exacta determinatio technicae derivationis propositionum, vix determinatur exacte quandonam ex alia ordinatione logica in aliam transeatur.

Admittunt scholastici omnes principium medii exclusi (EpNp), non tamen rigide sicut inter logicos recentiores, sed per modum cuiusdam idealis, unde et valet principium sed semper fieri potest conveniens distinctio si occurrit, neque requiritur ut conveniens distinctio praecontineatur in terminis primitivis complete enumeratis, cum desit talis enumeratio. Unde facillime sed modo latente et tecte fieri potest transitus ex alia in aliam ordinationem.

Factum quaestionum disputatarum, quae quidem per saecula iam sunt disputatae, neque finis et fructus praevidetur, indicat inter scholasticos non sine utilitate fieri posse seriam considerationem quaestionis, utrum habeant systemata aperta, quid per talia systemata determinari possit, quid per talia systemata determinari non possit.

Magis fundamentaliter quaeri potest utrum re vera methodus scholastica sit ad normas ordinationis logicae (quod equidem negarem); si re vera est

[5.1]   The Importance of the Foregoing Topic for Scholasticism

Scholastics generally do not explicitly order their material logically, as Euclid and Spinoza did in some manner, and as only logicians and more recent mathematicians do in an accurate manner. For the Scholastics a logical system is something implicit and potential, something that could be done but is not done. Hence, J. Bocheński was of the opinion that the *Summa theologiae* of St Thomas could be formalized in two or three centuries if a permanent commission of specialists were set up for this purpose.[31]

When a complete enumeration of primitive terms and an exact determination of the technique of derivation of terms is lacking, and when a complete enumeration of primitive propositions and an exact determination of the technique of derivation of propositions is lacking, one can hardly determine exactly when the transition is made from one logical ordering to another.

Scholastics all admit the principle of the excluded middle (EpNp), yet not rigidly like the more recent logicians, but by way of a certain ideal; therefore, the principle is valid, but if it does occur, an appropriate distinction can always be made. Nor is it requisite that this appropriate distinction be precontained in the complete enumeration of primitive terms, since such an enumeration is lacking. Hence, the transition from one ordering to another can be made very easily but go unnoticed.

The fact of disputed questions, disputed indeed for centuries, and without the prospect of any end to the disputes or any benefit from them, is an indication that Scholastics might find it rather useful to seriously consider whether they have open systems, and what can be determined through such systems and what cannot.

A more fundamental question can be asked, namely, whether the Scholastic method really accords with the norms of logical ordering (which I

---

point, several words of which are barely decipherable: 'Leicester – such a series ??? of systems whose meaning is found in a further system whose meaning is found in a further [system] (Dialectica, 195?).' The first word would seem to be 'Leicester,' and the journal referred to is *Dialectica*, though the precise year from the 1950s is not completely clear. Circumstantial evidence, namely, the mention of Leicester after the author's name and the title and topic of the paper, suggests that Lonergan may have had in mind the article by R.L. Goodstein, 'On the Nature of Mathematical Systems,' *Dialectica* 12:3–4 (1958) 296–315.]

31 [See 'Understanding and Method' above, pp. 32–35 and note 33.]

ad normas talis ordinationis, debent scholastici suas doctrinas formalizare et problemata talis formalizationis acceptare; si re vera non est ad normas talis ordinationis, debent scholastici clarius determinare ad quasnam normas procedant, et quid ex tali modo procedendi haberi possit, quid autem ex tali modo procedendi haberi non possit.

Aliis verbis, vestrae considerationis hanc quaestionem propono, an exsistat in scholasticismo conflictus methodologicus an modus procedendi per quaestiones et modus procedendi per ordinationem logicam inter se clare distinguuntur an forte confundantur.[32]

[6]   Problema Fundamenti

1 Problema fundamenti potest esse particulare vel generale. Particulare est ubi quaeritur fundamentum huius particularis ordinationis factae a tali viro, tali tempore, in tali ambiente, sub influxu talium quaestionum, talium auctorum, etc. Problema generale ponitur quando quaeritur de transitu ex qualibet particulari ordinatione in aliam.

2 Exsistit problema generale: quia semper oriuntur novae quaestiones; nec quisquam potest anticipare virtualiter solutionem omnium quaestionum usque ad diem iudicii; si posset, nullum iam erit verum augmentum sapientiae et intelligentiae in ecclesia; et superflueret oratio concilii Vaticani.[33]

3 Idem problema generale proponi potest diversimode.

Primo modo, sit ordinatio accepta, O, et sit novum problema, P, quod non solvitur per solam technicam derivationis ex suppositis ordinationis O. Sint multae solutiones, evolutiones alternativae, ut O fiat vel O^1, vel O^2, vel O^3, ... Quaeritur in genere quibusnam criteriis eligitur una evolutio possibilis prae aliis. Quaecumque sunt criteria, non potest criterion esse applicatio technicae derivationis ex O; quia O non solvit problema. Et ideo

would deny). If it really does accord with these norms, Scholastics need to formalize their doctrine and accept the problems involved in this formalization; but if it really does not accord with these norms, Scholastics need to determine more clearly the norms according to which they proceed, and what can be had from such a way of proceeding and what cannot.

In other words, I propose this question for your consideration, whether there exists in Scholasticism a methodological conflict, or whether the way of proceeding by questions and the way of proceeding through a logical ordering are clearly distinguished from each other, or are perhaps confused.[32]

[6]   The Problem of Foundation

1 The problem of foundation can be particular or general. It is particular when one is seeking the foundation of this particular ordering made by such and such a person, at such a time, in such a milieu, under the influence of such questions, such authors, and so on. To inquire about the transition from any particular ordering to another one is to state the general problem.

2 The general problem exists. New questions are constantly coming up, nor can anyone anticipate the solution to virtually all the questions from now to judgment day. If that were possible, there would no longer be any real increase of wisdom and understanding in the church, and the prayer of the Vatican Council would be superfluous.[33]

3 This same general problem can be expressed in different ways.

A first way: take a certain ordering, O, and a new problem, P, which is not solved solely by the technique of derivation from the suppositions of the ordering O. Let there be a number of solutions, alternative developments, so that O becomes O^1 or O^2 or O^3, ... Ask in general by what criteria one possible development is chosen in preference to others. Whatever the criteria are, no criterion can be the application of the technique of derivation from O, because O does not solve the problem. Therefore, from O one cannot conclude to the premises of a system in which [the question] Q is solved

32 This sentence is a handwritten insertion by Lonergan.
33 [The reference is to DB 1800. See above, p. 37, note 34.]

ex *O* non concludi possunt praemissae systematis in quo deductive solvitur *Q*.[34] Quare oritur problema novi ordinis, methodologicum.

Altero modo, tota historia praeterita atque futura concipi potest tamquam successio ordinationum. Sit successio quaedam cui nomen philosophia perennis. Sint aliae successiones quae etiam sibi idem nomen vindicant. Sit successio quaedam cui nomen solida doctrina catholica. Sint aliae successiones quae sibi idem nomen vindicant. Iam vero eiusmodi successiones non sunt nisi problema transitus multipliciter repetitum. Quaeritur ergo de criteriis praeferendi unam scholam prae alia. Quaeritur ulterius cur sint praeter perennem philosophiam, praeter solidam theologiam, tot aliae orthodoxae et etiam heterodoxae. Quae quidem quaestio non solvitur per deductionem ex propositionibus primitivis: nam propositiones primitivae aut coincidunt cum primitivis alicuius scholae aut non; si coincidunt, praesupponitur solutio quaestionis; si non coincidunt, introducitur nova schola ut problema adeo non solvatur sed potius augeatur.

[7]   Problema Historicitatis

1 Superius dixi vim explicativam, scientificam, haberi inquantum ordinatio logica eiusdem systematis est multiplex; magis particulariter, inquantum distinguuntur via analytica et via synthetica; sed iam notandum est hanc viam explicativam non per se solum esse sufficientem.

2 *C. Gent.* passim: Hinc est quod dicitur … Sed distingui oportet inter textum prout eius sensus determinatur ex constructione explicativa totius *C Gent.* et eundem textum secundum mentem auctoris inspirati. En problema historicitatis: quinam sit nexus inter primum et alterum? Si est simpliciter saltus, tunc quando proceditur ex Sacra Scriptura vel ex Patribus ad fundamentum theologiae systematicae, iterum fieri debet saltus in directione tamen opposita; quod est inconveniens, quia tollit fundamentum scripturisticum.

Iterum, *S.T.*, I, qq. 27–43, incipiunt ex conclusione Augustini de analogia psychologica et terminantur ad missiones, sed ad missiones systematice conceptas, neque sic concipiebantur a primaevis Christianis, quamvis forte

deductively.[34] For this reason there arises the problem of a new order, a methodological problem.

A second way: the whole of past history and of the future can be conceived as a succession of orderings. Let there be a succession called *philosophia perennis*. Let there be other successions claiming the same name. Let there be a succession called 'solid Catholic doctrine.' Let there be other successions claiming this title. Now, successions of this kind are simply the frequently recurring problem of transition. The question arises, then, about the criteria by which one school of thought is preferred to another. Then there is the further question why in addition to *philosophia perennis* and solid theology there are so many other orthodox and even heterodox positions. This question is not solved through deduction from primitive propositions; for primitive propositions either coincide with the primitive propositions of some school or they do not; if they do, the solution to the question is presupposed; if they do not, a new school comes into being, so that the problem is not only not solved but rather enlarged.

[7]   The Problem of Historicity

1 I said above that an explanatory or scientific way is had inasmuch as the logical ordering of the same system is manifold; more particularly, inasmuch as the analytic way and the synthetic way are distinguished. But now we must note that this explanatory way by itself alone is not sufficient.

2 In the *Contra Gentiles,* passim: 'Hence, there is what is said [in scripture] ...' But one must distinguish between the text insofar as its meaning is determined from the explanatory construction of the whole of the *Contra Gentiles*, and the same text according to the mind of the inspired author. This, then, is the problem of historicity: what is the connection between the first and the second? If there is simply a leap, then when one goes from scripture or the Fathers to the foundation of systematic theology, a second leap will have to be made in the opposite direction. But this cannot be admitted, because it would destroy the scriptural foundation.

Again, [Thomas Aquinas, *Summa theologiae*] 1, qq. 27–43, begins from Augustine's conclusion about the psychological analogy and ends at the [divine] missions – but at the missions conceived systematically. However, the

---

34 [The Latin words from 'Et ideo' were written by hand in the autograph.]

ipse S. Paulus per scientiam infusam eas ita concipere potuit, quin tamen ullum signum talis conceptionis manifestavit. Habetur vel saltus vel processus – saltus tollit fundamentum, processus non est stricte deductivus.[35]

3 Quod problema est notissimum: renascentia, studia textualia, historica, biblica, historiae litterarum, historiae religionum, historiae dogmatum, historiae theologiae. Totum ponitur sub rubrica theologiae positivae, quae fit non modo scholastico sed scientifice (uti theologi positivi dicunt). Scatet subdivisionibus et subsubdivisionibus, pro singulis auctoribus utriusque Testamenti, pro singulis fere patribus, conciliis et sessionibus conciliorum, pro aetatibus theologorum minorum, pro singulis fere operibus theologorum maiorum. In dies multiplicatur litteratura, ut specialista partem suam legere et serio iudicare vix possit.

Attamen agitur de ipsis fundamentis theologiae systematicae, dogmaticae; sine fundamento methodologico valido, facillime abit in placita positivistarum, relativistarum: Videant dogmatici.

4 En problema methodologicum: non solvitur per solam technicam derivationis ex propositionibus primitivis; (hanc ob causam theologia positiva est disciplina fere separata et independens quod dogmatici, philosophi, non satis attendunt ad problema non logicum sed methodologicum). Secus deduci posset historia contingens. Nisi integrantur theologia systematica et positiva, systematica caret fundamento, positiva caret directione, forma, fine. Fiunt specialistae: omnis conclusio probabilis, plus minus, reformabilis, [?] reformata.[36]

[8]   **Problema Khasmatis**

Lc 16.26: 'inter nos et vos magnum chaos firmatum est, ut hi qui hinc transire ad vos non possint, neque inde huc transmeare.'

early Christians had no such conceptions about them, unless perhaps Paul could have conceived them in this way through some infused knowledge, though he never gave any indication of such an understanding. There is either a leap or a process – the leap destroys the foundation, and the process is not strictly deductive.[35]

3 This problem is very familiar: the Renaissance, textual, historical, biblical studies, histories of literature, of religions, of dogmas, of theology. The whole falls under the heading of positive theology, which is carried on not in the Scholastic manner but (according to positive theologians) scientifically. It abounds with subdivisions and subsections, for each author of both Testaments, for just about every one of the Fathers, for the councils and the conciliar sessions, for the life and times of minor theologians, and for virtually every work of the major theologians. The literature increases daily, so that a specialist can hardly read all that is written about his own area and make serious judgments upon it.

Yet what is at issue here is the very foundation of systematic and dogmatic theology. Without a valid methodological foundation, the opinions of positivists and relativists very easily begin to appear. Dogmatic theologians, take note!

4 This is the methodological problem: it is not solved solely through the technique of derivation from primitive propositions; (this is why positive theology is a virtually separate and independent discipline, because dogmatic theologians and philosophers do not pay enough attention to the problem, which is not logical but methodological). Otherwise [i.e., if it could be solved through derivation], contingent history could be deduced. Unless systematic and positive theology are integrated, systematic theology will lack a foundation, and positive theology will lack direction, form, and purpose. Specialists emerge: every conclusion is more or less probable, reformable, [?] reformed.[36]

[8]   The Problem of the Chasm

> Luke 16.26: 'Between us and you a great chasm has been fixed, so that those who would pass over from here to you cannot do so, nor go from there to here.'

35 [The last sentence in this paragraph was a handwritten addition in the autograph.]
36 [The Latin words from 'Secus ...' are entered by hand in the autograph.]

1 Hoc problema notissimun est. Athanasius, *De decr Nic. Syn.*, per modum exceptionis omnino lamentatae defendit usum vocis non-scripturisticae in formula fidei, quia secus Arianismus non efficaciter excluderetur.[37] Severus Antiochenus impugnavit concilium Chalcedonense quia usurpavit vocem *physis* alio sensu quam in Patribus receptus erat.[38] Theologia mediaevalis, quae systematicam omnium quaestionum solutionem quaerebat, multas et alias novas categorias introduxit.[39] Controversia Augustiniana-Aristotelica radicitus erat de usu categoriarum (non logicarum sed scientificarum et philosophicarum) Aristotelis.[40] Devotio moderna parum laudabat definitiones et disputationes. *Imitatio Christi*: melius sentire quam definire compunctionem; melius adorare quam disputare de Trinitate. Reformatio praedicabat reditum ad puram fidem evangelicam. Baianistae et Iansenistae praedicabant reditum ad Augustinum. Theologia ascetica, mystica, moralis, pastoralis, liturgica, missiologica,[41] kerygmatica, personalistica, paullum existentialistica separantur a dogmatica ut indigentiis fidelium occurrant imo et quaeri potest quinam sit nexus in ipso theologo speculativo inter opera sua erudita et subtilia et orationem suam personalem ad Deum personalem.

2 Iam vero respondendo quaestionibus oriuntur seriationes quaestio-

1 This problem is a very familiar one. In his 'Letter on the Decrees of the Council of Nicea,' Athanasius defended as an exception, however regrettable, the use of a nonscriptural word in formulating the faith, on the grounds that otherwise Arianism would not be effectively ruled out.[37] Severus of Antioch attacked the Council of Chalcedon for having used the word *physis* with a meaning different from that accepted by the church Fathers.[38] Medieval theology, in seeking a systematic solution to all questions, introduced many other new categories.[39] The Augustinian-Aristotelian controversy was at bottom a dispute about the use of the categories (not the logical, but the scientific and philosophical) of Aristotle.[40] *Devotio moderna* had little good to say for definitions and disputations. *The Imitation of Christ*: 'It is better to feel compunction than to define it, better to adore than to argue about the Trinity.' The Reformation preached a return to the pure gospel faith. The Baianists and Jansenists preached a return to Augustine. Moral, pastoral, ascetical, mystical, liturgical, missiological,[41] kerygmatic, personalistic theology, all somewhat existentialist, are separated from dogmatic theology, in order to cater to the needs of the faithful. In fact, one may even ask what connection there is between the learned work of a speculative theologian and his personal prayer to a personal God.

2 Now, in answering questions there arise seriations of questions, whence

37 [See Athanasius, *Epistola de decretis Nicaenae synodi* 32; MG 25, 474 D – 475 A.]
38 ['Lebon' is added by hand in the autograph at this point. See above, p. 45, note 38.]
39 [In the margin: 'Exemplum ?? Lottin de Ghellinck.' 'Exemplum' may refer to what Lonergan regarded as Aquinas's problematic answer to the objection that theology cannot be a science because it is concerned with individual cases: 'Sacred doctrine sets out individual cases, not as being preoccupied with them, but in order both to introduce them as examples for our own lives … and to proclaim the authority of those through whom divine revelation has come down to us.' *Summa theologiae*, 1, q. 1, a. 2, ad 2m. As for Lottin and de Ghellinck, see above, p. 45, note 40.]
40 ['Roger Marston' was added by hand in the autograph at this point. In his *Quaestiones disputatae*, this Franciscan author from the last third of the thirteenth century (d. ca. 1303) expresses his opposition to some of Aquinas's positions. See J. Cairola, 'L'opposizione a S. Tommaso nelle "*Questiones disputatae*" di Ruggero Marston,' in *Scholastica ratione historico-critica instauranda: Acta Congressus Scholastici International Romae anno sancto* MCML *celebrati* (Rome: Pontificium Athenaeum Antonianum, 1951) 447–60. It seems Marston's only other surviving work are four *Quodlibeta*, though it is known that he wrote a commentary on Peter Lombard's *Sentences*.]
41 [The word 'missiologica' was added by hand in the autograph.]

num, unde exigitur ordinatio quaestionum saltem logica (ne fiant repe-
titiones sine fine), cohaerens, cum sensu reali, et cum valore explicativo
(iam habetur tota *Summa* S. Thomae); quibus introducuntur novi termini
technici logici, metaphysici, scientifici; eorumque extensio ad ordinem supernaturalem mysteriorum; sed ordinationes multiplicantur; additur novum problema fundamenti generalis et immensum problema historicitatis;
maxima quaedam superstructura intellectualistica habetur, sed re vera cui
bono?

3 Problema ergo khasmatis iacet inter simplex evangelium et semper
eruditiorem theologiam; quemadmodum inter se uniri possint, ut perspici possit nexus realis, concretus, inter haec tria: evangelium, theologiam,
et hominem particularem parum intellectualisticum; quod problema non
solvitur applicando technicam derivationis ex propositionibus primitivis;
ideoque methodologicum est.

[9]   Versus Solutionem Problematum: Gressus Initialis

1 Primo considerandum esse videtur in quonam rerum genere ponatur
fundamentum. Utrum sit in nominibus et verbis et propositionibus. Utrum
forte altius ascendendum sit in conceptus ipsi menti internos et in iudicia
in mente elicita.[42] Utrum denique remotius est inquirendum in ipsum intellectum, in habitus intellectuales speculativos eorumque actus, nempe,
scientiae, intelligentiae, sapientiae.

2 Quid sibi velit hoc tertium. Scientia consideratur dupliciter: in fieri est
processus ex principiis in conclusiones; in facto esse est intelligentia conclusionum in principiis, ut per modum unius apprehendantur tam conclusiones quam principia. Intelligentia consideratur dupliciter: consequenter,
in terminis perspicit principia; antecedenter, in ipsis sensibilibus perspicit intelligibilem unitatem vel relationem (obiectum proprium intellectus
nostri hac in vita) unde concipit tam nexus quam terminos et, augente

the need of an ordering, at least logical, of the questions (to avoid endless repetition), an ordering that is coherent, with real meaning, and with an explanatory value (present now in the whole of St Thomas's *Summa*); thus there are introduced new technical terms, logical, metaphysical, and scientific, and their extension to the supernatural order of the mysteries; but orderings multiply; the new problem of a general foundation arises, as well as the immense problem of historicity; there is, indeed, a vast intellectualistic superstructure – but to whose benefit, really?

3 The problem of the chasm, therefore, is that of the gap between the simple gospel and an increasingly sophisticated theology: how to bring them together, so that the real concrete connection between these three may be grasped – the gospel, theology, and an individual human being who is not very intellectualistic. This problem is not solved by applying the technique of derivation from primitive propositions; it is, therefore, a problem of methodology.

[9]   Towards a Solution to These Problems: A First Step

1 It seems that the first point to consider is in what category of reality foundation is to be placed. We must determine whether it is to be placed in terms and propositions; or whether we should go higher, perhaps, and place it in concepts within the mind itself and in judgments elicited in the mind;[42] or, finally, whether we must investigate more remotely the intellect itself, the speculative intellectual habits, namely, science, understanding, and wisdom, and their acts.

2 What this third alternative means: Science can be considered in two ways: *in fieri*, as a process from principles to conclusions; and *in facto esse*, as an accomplished fact, an understanding of conclusions in their principles, so that both conclusions and their principles are apprehended as a unity. Understanding can be considered in two ways: in its consequences, when it grasps principles in their terms; in its antecedents, when it grasps an intelligible unity or relation in the sensible data themselves (the proper object of our intellect in this life), whence it conceives both connections and terms,

---

42 [Handwritten in the text: '(privatum cui ? publicum)', that is, perhaps, the private mental acts to which public language corresponds. In this sense the first possible locus for foundations is public, the second private. See Lonergan's later response to Edward MacKinnon on this issue, in *Method in Theology* 254–62.]

intelligentia, concipit nexus latiores subtiliores et terminos accuratiores, distinctiores.

Sapientia est principium ordinis et iudicii, nobis immanens. Unde (a) est principium iudicii de ipsis primis terminis in unaquaque disciplina, quinam sint et quonam sensu sint adhibendi; e.g., multipliciter concipitur ens (Parmenides, Plato, Aristotle, Plotinus, Avicenna, Aquinas, Scotus, Hegel); (b) est principiun iudicii de intelligentia utrum apprehensa intelligibilitas sit necessaria an contingens (empirica) et, si contingens est, utrum de facto sit vera an falsa; (c) est principium iudicii de ratiociniis, utrum unum sufficiat an requirantur multa, utrum multa sint expetenda ex unico quodam fonte an forte ex multis et diversis simul fontibus, utrum multa argumenta in unum quoddam formandum coalescant, utrum generent probabilitatem an ad certitudinem pertingant; (d) est principium iudicii de ordinatione, quotupliciter eadem propositionum totalitas ordinari possit, quosnam in fines diversae ordinationes sint aptiores, quinam finis hic et nunc maiori attentione indigeat, quandonam vetus ordinatio plus vel minus corrigenda, amplificanda videatur.

3 Comparantur diversa fundamentorum genera.

(a) Sufficit primum genus, modo (1) quaestio non ponatur nisi iis qui de primitivis terminis et propositionibus consentiant, et (2) ipsi cur consentiant non inquirant, et (3) nulla ponatur quaestio nisi ea quae intra systema suppositum solvi possit. Sed nulla est collectio terminorum et propositionum de quibus nemo prorsus dubitat. Et etiam ii qui non dubitant non rationaliter sine ratione assentant. Et semper novae oriuntur quaestiones.

(b) Sufficit alterum genus, donec inveniatur ipsos primos terminos multipliciter concipi posse: triangulus: absolute apud Euclidem = hodie Euclidianus;[43] ens: Parmenides, Plato, Aristotle, Avicenna, Aquinas, Scotus, Caietanus, Hegel.[44]

Sufficit, donec ponuntur quaestiones, non de nexibus necessariis, sed tamen intelligibilibus et de facto veris; leges scientificae empiricae; postulata

and, with growth in understanding, it conceives broader and more subtle connections and more accurate and distinct terms.

Wisdom is the principle of order and judgment, immanent in us. Hence: (a) It is the principle of judging about the primitive terms in every discipline, what they are and in what sense they are to be used. Being, for example, has been conceived in many different ways (Parmenides, Plato, Aristotle, Plotinus, Avicenna, Aquinas, Scotus, Hegel). (b) It is the principle of judging about understanding, whether an apprehended intelligibility is necessary or contingent (empirical) and, if contingent, whether it is in fact true or false. (c) It is the principle of judging about reasonings, whether one process of reasoning or many are needed, whether many are to be sought from a single source or from many different sources together, whether many arguments come together to form a single argument, and whether they generate probability or arrive at certitude. (d) It is the principle of judging about ordering, about how many ways the same totality of propositions can be ordered, for what purposes various orderings are more suitable, what purpose here and now needs greater attention, and when a long-standing ordering seems to need more or less correction or enlargement.

3 Comparison between the different kinds of foundations:

(a) The first kind suffices, provided (1) that a question is posed only to those who are in agreement about primitive terms and propositions, (2) that they do not ask why they agree, and (3) that no question is asked except those that can be answered within the given system. But there is no such thing as a collection of terms and propositions about which no one has any doubts whatever. And even those who have no doubts do not rationally assent without a reason. And, finally, new questions are always emerging.

(b) The second kind suffices, until it is discovered that primitive terms can be conceived in different ways. 'Triangle': absolutely for Euclid = today Euclidean.[43] 'Being': Parmenides, Plato, Aristotle, Avicenna, Aquinas, Scotus, Cajetan, Hegel.[44]

The second kind suffices until questions are asked, not about necessary connections, but about ones that are intelligible and true *de facto*. Empiri-

---

43 [A shorthand way of saying that today the triangle as conceived in Euclidean geometry is but one conception in one of many geometries in which some or all Euclidean presuppositions no longer hold. See his corresponding remarks in 'Understanding and Method,' p. 53 above.]

44 See Thomas Aquinas, *Summa theologiae*, 1-2, q. 66, a. 5, ad 4m. [See also Lonergan, *Insight* 388–98.]

mathematica (parallelarum); convenientia apud Aquinas = voluntarismus apud Scotum; omnis intelligibilitas historica; omnis intelligibilitas hominis concreti exsistentis: natura, gratia.[45]

Sufficit donec fiant argumenta multa ex diversis fontibus quae tamen in unum quoddam coalescent.

Sufficit donec quaeratur de iis quae intra systema determinari non possunt.

Sufficit donec quaeratur de problemate transitus ex uno systemate in aliud, de problemate multarum scholarum, etc.

(c) Sufficit tertium genus, ubi sufficit primum vel alterum. Intellectus enim est principium scientiae, intelligentiae, sapientiae; quae sunt principia conceptuum et iudiciorum; quae sunt principia terminorum et propositionum.

Sufficit tertium genus ubi deficit primum vel alterum: progrediente intelligentia: perficiuntur conceptus, principia; progrediente sapientia: perficiuntur ordinationes. Praeterea, ipsa intelligentia tam est de concretis quam de abstractis, tam de empiricis quam de necessariis intelligibilibus. Praeterea, ipse intellectus est in nobis ultimum in quod caetera reducuntur, cur ita concipiamus, iudicemus, ordinemus.

Sed forte dicendum est, non 'sufficit' sed 'sufficeret.' Si enim dicitur 'sufficit,' supponitur homines habere sapientiam: quod valde dubium est. Uti enim perpetuo repetebat Aquinas, 'Stultorum numerus est infinitus.'[46]

4 De possibilitate tertii fundamenti, nempe, sapientialis[47]

(a) Non enim nascimur sapientes: initio enim intellectus humanus est sicut tabula rasa in qua nihil est scriptum. Neque naturali quadam necessitate fimus sapientes: quod enim naturali necessitate fit, semper fit vel saltem fit in pluribus. Sed sapientia reputatur non in maiori hominum parte inveniri sed potius in minori, imo in minima. Neque consilio et voluntate possumus nos reddere sapientes. Si enim iam sumus sapientes, superfluunt

cal scientific laws; mathematical postulates (of parallels). [Arguments of] fittingness [*convenientiae*] in Aquinas = voluntarism in Scotus. All historical intelligibility. All intelligibility about concretely existing human beings: nature, grace.[45]

It suffices until arguments are brought up from a variety of sources that nevertheless coalesce in a unity.

It suffices until there is a question about things that cannot be determined within the system.

It suffices until a question arises about the transition from one system to another, about the problem of many different schools, and so forth.

(c) The third kind suffices when the first and second suffice. For intellect is the principle of science, understanding, and wisdom; and these are the principles of concepts and judgments, which are the principles of terms and propositions.

The third kind suffices when the first and second fail: with a growth in understanding: concepts and principles are perfected; with growth in wisdom, orderings are perfected. Besides, understanding is as much about the concrete as about the abstract, about empirical intelligibles as about necessary intelligibles. Furthermore, our understanding is the ultimate to which all else is reducible, why we conceive, judge, and order in such a way.

But perhaps we ought to say 'would suffice' rather than 'suffices.' For if we say, 'It suffices,' we are supposing that people have wisdom; this, however, is quite doubtful. As Aquinas used often to say, 'The number of fools is infinite.'[46]

4 The possibility of the third foundation, the sapiential.[47]

(a) We are not born wise: in the beginning, the human intellect is a *tabula rasa*, a clean slate upon which nothing has been written. Nor do we become wise through some necessity of nature: for what happens by natural necessity happens always, or at least for the most part. But it is generally acknowledged that wisdom is to be found not in the majority of human beings but in a minority, indeed, a very small number. Nor can we make ourselves

---

45 [The words 'natura gratia' are added by hand in the autograph.]
46 [The expression *stultorum infinitus est numerus* would seem to occur about twenty-five times in Aquinas's writings, usually with reference to Ecclesiastes 1.15. In 'Understanding and Method' Lonergan drops any reference to Aquinas and has simply, 'But alas, *numerus stultorum infinitus.*' See p. 57 above.]
47 [There follow five objections against wisdom as a foundation.]

illud consilium illaque voluntas. Sin autem nondum sapientes invenimur, sumus insipientes ut longe probabilius illud consilium etiam sit insipiens et consequens voluntas vana.

(b) Praeterea, fundamentum praeiacere debet ut caeterum opus supra fundamentum construatur. Sed sapientia non praeiacet. Ergo non est fundamentum.

Maior videtur evidens. Minor facile probabur, tum ex antecessis (4, a), tum ex analysi. Nam illa sapientia quae omnia ordinat et de omnibus iudicat non praehabetur inquisitioni sed potius est ultimus fructus perfectissimus ex absoluta omni inquisitione gignendus. Qui enim omnia ordinare potest non omnia ignorat, neque maiorem rerum partem ignorat, neque vel minimam partem ignorat, sed omnia prorsus scire debet tum in se ipsis tum in singulorum habitudine ad alias quascumque res. Qui ita omnium ordinem scit, etiam de omnibus iudicare potest.

(c) Praeterea, inutilis videtur recursus ad magna auctoritatis nomina: ut agnoscantur Aristoteles, Augustinus, Aquinas fuisse sapientissimi: ut ipsi dicamur eorum discipuli atque sequaces fidelissimi. Nam si ipsi sumus sapientes, superfluunt auctoritates. Sin autem insipientes sumus, certo certius male intelligemus et male interpretemur et Aristotelem et Augustinum et Aquinatem. Quod factis constat, cum tot tamque diversae sunt scholae Aristotelicae, Augustinianae, Thomisticae.

(d) Praeterea, insufficiens videtur effugium quod in nomine philosophiae praebetur, nempe, nos quamvis nondum simus sapientes, tamen sapientiam diligimus et ad eam habendam totis viribus incumbimus. Nam aut habetur sapientia aut non habetur. Si habetur, recte diligitur. Si non habetur, falsa quaedam sapientiae species probabilius diligitur et in eam acquirendam totis viribus incumbitur.

(e) Praeterea, uti argumentis constat, vanum est fundamentum in sapientia positum; ideoque ad sapientiam confugere nihil aliud est quam specioso quodam nomine relativismum tecte et latenter introducere. Sed relativismus certo est condemnatus. Ergo redeundum est ad alterum vel primum fundamentum, et quantum ad problemata (quae sic solvi non possunt) simpliciter dicendum est nos in multis ignorantia contentos esse debere. Altiora te ne quaesieris, uti docent tam SScr quam Horatius.

5 De possibilitate tertii fundamenti, responsum partiale.

wise simply by deliberating and willing to do so. If we are already wise, such deliberation and willing are unnecessary. But if we are not yet wise, then our lack of wisdom makes it far more probable that our deliberation will be unwise and our consequent willing foolish.

(b) Besides, a foundation has to be laid first so that the rest of the enterprise may be built upon it. But wisdom is not something that is laid down first; therefore, it is not foundational.

The major premise is evident. The minor is easily proved, both from what has been said above in (a) and by an analysis. The wisdom that orders all things and judges about all things is not had before inquiry is begun, but rather is the final and most perfect fruit to be garnered through the completion of all inquiry. One who is capable of ordering all things is one who knows all things, is not ignorant of most or even of the smallest part of reality, but must know absolutely everything about everything both in themselves and in the relations of each and every one. One who has such knowledge of the order of all reality is also able to judge about all things.

(c) Moreover, it seems useless to have recourse to weighty authorities – that Aristotle, Augustine, and Aquinas be acknowledged as having been most wise, and that we ourselves claim to be their faithful disciples and followers. For if we ourselves are wise, we have no need of these authorities. But if we are unwise, as sure as anything we are misunderstanding and misinterpreting Aristotle, Augustine, and Aquinas. This is proven by the facts, since there are so many different Aristotelian, Augustinian, and Thomistic schools of thought.

(d) Furthermore, for us to give ourselves the name 'philosophers,' that is, 'lovers of wisdom,' seems a rather poor disclaimer: although we are not yet wise, we love wisdom and do all we can to acquire it. For we either have wisdom or do not have it. If we have it, we love it correctly. If we do not have it, we are more likely to love some false kind of wisdom and do all we can to acquire that.

(e) Again, as the arguments prove, to make wisdom a foundation is fruitless. To take refuge in wisdom, therefore, is but to sneak relativism in under a fine-sounding name. But relativism has certainly been condemned. Therefore, one must return to the second or first foundation; and as to the problems (which cannot be solved that way), one must simply say that we have to be content to be ignorant of many things. As both the bible [Psalm 131] and Horace [*Odes* I, 11] tell us, do not seek things above and beyond yourself.

5 The possibility of the third foundation: a partial answer.

Responsum. In primis notandum est quod de vero problemate et non de ficto agitur, ideoque responsum adaequatum brevi expositione dari non potest.[48]

Primum responsi elementum respicit modum quo augetur scientia humana. Illud enim augmentum non mera additione fit, ut antequam fiat quid sit prorsus ignoretur. Sed principaliter fit dividendo aliquod totum quodammodo praeiacens.

Quod enim primum in intellectus apprehensione cadit est ens, quod omnia dicit, omniaque in se concludit. Quae deinceps cognitione adduntur, non extra ens iacent ut ei addi possint, sed intra ens inveniuntur et per entis divisionem cognoscuntur. Praeterea, haec entis divisio semper completa esse potest, nam per contradictorias differentias arbor quaedam Porphyriana erigi potest, ut ens dividatur in immateriale et materiale, materiale dividatur in non-vivens et vivens, vivens dividatur in sentiens et non sentiens, sentiens dividatur in rationale et non-rationale, et ita porro.

Quibus perspectis, elucet homini semper adesse posse quandam totius entis apprehensionem eamque ordinatam atque suo modo permanentem atque immutabilem. Quo concesso, etiam concedendum est homini semper adesse posse minimam quandam sapientiam quae modo quodam universaliori omnia ordinat et de omnibus ita generaliter conceptis iudicare potest. Quo posito, ulterius concedendum est sapientiam eo modo augeri posse per divisionem entis eiusque ordinationem, ut quod recentius addatur non prius habitum destruat sed potius salvet atque ampliet.

Unde unusquisque pro modulo et mensura propriae sapientiae posse et quaedam satis ordinare atque iudicare et maiori indigere sapientia antequam alia ordinare et iudicare audeat: unde simul salvantur et certitudines vitae humanae necessariae et modestia illa intellectualis non minus necessaria quae inflationi vanae et perniciosae opponitur (1 Cor 8.1).

First of all, it must be noted that we are dealing here with a real problem, not a fictitious one, and therefore we cannot answer it adequately in a brief exposition.[48]

The first element of our answer has to do with the way in which human knowledge grows. This growth does not take place through simple accretion, so that our new knowledge is of something about which we were totally ignorant before. Rather, it takes place principally by dividing some pre-existing whole.

What is first apprehended by the intellect is being, which means all things and includes all things within itself. Subsequent additions to our knowledge do not lie outside the ambit of being as something that can be added to it, but are found within being and come to be known through a division of being. Besides, this division of being can always be complete, for a Porphyrian Tree can be erected through contradictory differences, so that being is divided into material and immaterial, material is divided into non-living and living, living is divided into sentient and non-sentient, sentient is divided into rational and non-rational, and so on.

Once this is understood, it is clear that man can always have some apprehension of all being, one that is ordered and in its own way permanent and immutable. And once this is granted, one must also grant that some minimal wisdom is always available to a person, a wisdom that in a more general way orders all things and can make judgments about them as understood in this general way. This being the case, then, one must further grant that wisdom can thus grow through the division of being and its ordering, so that a recent addition to knowledge does not dismantle what was previously known, but rather secures and enlarges it.

Therefore, each person according to the manner and measure of his or her own personal wisdom can both order and judge some things well enough and at the same time need more wisdom before venturing to order and judge other matters; thus are safeguarded both those certainties necessary for human living and that equally necessary intellectual modesty that is the opposite of foolish and pernicious knowledge that puffs one up with pride (1 Corinthians 8.1).

48 See *Insight.* [Presumably, Lonergan is suggesting that some indication of the problem and a more lengthy response to the problem can be found in *Insight.* Wisdom is explicitly mentioned in *Insight* on a number of occasions, but it is likely that he means the whole book. Numerous references to Aquinas's discussions of the role of wisdom in its various forms can be found in Lonergan, *Verbum.* See the index, s.v. 'Wisdom.']

Quod tamen responsum, de praesenti sufficiens, non simpliciter sufficiens est. Valor enim divisionis per dichotomiam non solum in valore principii contradictionis fundatur sed etiam in valore differentiae quae seligitur et cui principium contradictionis applicatur. Aeque bene divideretur ens per dichotomiam in entia quae (1) habent tam alas quam pedes, vel (2) neutras habent, vel (3) habent pedes sed non alas, vel (4) habent alas sed non pedes. Unde distinguendum est inter differentias classificatorias (uti in botania) et explicativas (uti in physica, chimia, &c); et ulterius determinandum est quid permanens et quid fluens in explicatione scientifica inveniatur.[49]

6 De possibilitate tertii fundamenti, solvuntur obiectiones.

(a) Conceditur nos non nasci sapientes sed fieri, neque naturali necessitate fieri sapientes. E contra, asseritur nos naturali inclinatione et tendentia in sapientiam acquirendam moveri; quae inclinatio atque tendentia per consilium et voluntatem confirmari atque adiuvari potest. Et ad rationem additam, negatur suppositum; nempe, dicimus sapientiam in indivisibili non stare, ideoque non valere distinctionem nos aut sapientes esse aut insipientes. Possumus enim parvam quandam sapientiam habere quae ad maiorem habendam (modo adest humilitas et modestia – 'sedulo, pie, sobrie quaerat') nos praeparat atque iuvat.

(b) Fundamentum praeiacere debet secundum modum fundamenti. Si fundamentum ponitur in primitivis terminis et propositionibus, praeiacere debent haec primitiva. Si fundamentum ponitur in conceptibus et iudiciis unde caetera certo concluduntur, praeiacere debent hi conceptus haecque iudicia. Si fundamentum ponitur in intellectu in quo pedetentim augentur intelligentia, scientia, sapientia, praeiacere debet talis intellectus. Proinde

Yet, this answer, while sufficient for our present purposes, is not sufficient in every respect. For the validity of dichotomy by division depends not only on the validity of the principle of contradiction but also on the validity of the difference that is selected and to which the principle of contradiction is applied. Being could equally well be divided into beings which (1) have both wings and feet, or (2) have neither, or (3) have feet but no wings, or (4) have wings but no feet. Hence, we need to distinguish between classifying difference, as in botany, and explanatory difference, as in physics, chemistry, etc.; and we must further determine what is permanent and what transitory in a scientific explanation.[49]

6 Solution to the objections concerning the possibility of the third foundation.

(a) We grant that we are not born wise but become so, and that we do not become wise through natural necessity. On the other hand, we maintain that we have a natural inclination and tendency towards the acquisition of wisdom; this inclination and tendency can be strengthened and assisted by deliberation and will. And as for the added reason, we deny the supposition; that is, we affirm that wisdom is not a matter of all or nothing, and therefore the disjunction that we are either wise or unwise is invalid. We can have a certain modicum of wisdom that disposes and helps us to acquire greater wisdom (provided we have humility and modesty – let one seek it 'reverently, diligently, and judiciously' [DB 1796, DS 3016, ND 132]).

(b) A foundation must have been laid already in accordance with the kind of foundation. If the foundation is placed in primitive terms and propositions, these primitive elements must already be present. If the foundation is placed in concepts and judgments from which all the rest follow with certitude, these concepts and judgments must already be present. If the foundation is placed in the intellect, in which understanding, science, and

---

49 On these points, see *Insight*.
   [The following, hard-to-decipher handwritten and oddly ordered insertion occurs at this point:
   '(3) Question: What is mutable in the positive sciences? What is permanent?
   '(1) Question: concerning being: many concepts: many reflex analyses, yet one natural notion (see *Insight*, chapter 12) [which is] implicit in everyone speaking [or] writing;
   '(2) Question: what is science? notion quasi per accidens ??? scientifically ordered ??? (E. Husserl, *Die Krisis der europäischen Wissenschaften und die transzendentale Phänomenologie. Eine Einleitung in dei phänomenologische Philosophie* (Den Hag: Nijhoff, 1954.)']

ad rationem additam dicendum est unumquemque pro modulo et mensura suae sapientiae omnia ordinare atque iudicare posse, et pro defectu suae sapientiae modeste et humiliter ab ordinando et iudicando abstinere debere.

Quod in vita humana clarissime perspicitur. Pueri septennes ad aetatem rationis pervenisse dicuntur quia ante omnia satis ordinata non habuerunt ut de bono et malo, de voluntario et involuntario, de libero et spontaneo iudicare potuerint. Adulescentes ab Aristotele inepti ad rem ethicam examinandam iudicabantur, quia iis defuit illa experientiae extensio atque varietas quae ad actus humanos virtutesque et vitia ordinandos et iudicandos requiritur. In singulis rebus maximi aestimatur iudicium illius qui in illo rerum genere et scientia eminet et experientia ipsa eruditus invenitur. Denique tandem experimur omnes in nova materia addiscenda, neque statim ab initio nos eam satis ordinare et iudicare posse, et tamen in eadem materia ordinanda et iudicanda gradatim proficere, ut denique tandem et ipsi professores et doctores esse possimus.

(c) Quantum ad maxima auctoritatis nomina invocanda, dicendum est non ibi haberi remedium efficax contra omnimodam stultitiam: non ideo enim quis aestimandus est sapientiae Aristotelicae, Augustinianae, Thomisticae particeps qui litteras Graecas vel Latinas legere potest; neque ideo quia magna quadam diligentia multa loca ex istis auctoribus in unum collexit et suas conclusiones inde deduxit; neque ideo quia ab iis auctoribus quaerit quod ipsi minime tractaverunt ('Le scoutisme d'après S. Thomas d'Aquin').[50] Sed nullum est remedium efficax contra insipientiam. Abusus tamen non tollit usum: maximi pretii esse iudico verum et constantem et diuturnum nisum quo quis pedetentim progreditur ad Aristotelis sapientiam, Augustini, Aquinatis, quodammodo participandam.

(d) Obiectio contra nomen philosophiae ideo non valet quia disiunctionem facit inter insipientiam perfectam et sapientiam perfectissimam: dantur positiones intermediae, in quibus homines omnes invenimur; quae intermediae positiones, cum aliquantulam sapientiam includant, a scepticismo nos salvant; et cum a perfecta sapientia deficiant, ab inflata et absurda mentis superbia nos retinent.

wisdom gradually increase, this intellect must already be present. Then, with respect to the added reason it must be said that each one in accordance with the manner and measure of one's wisdom is capable of ordering and judging all things, and in accordance with what is lacking in their wisdom must modestly and humbly refrain from ordering and judging.

This fact is clearly seen in human life. Seven-year-olds are said to have reached the age of reason because previously they did not have everything ordered well enough to be able to make judgments about what is good or evil, voluntary or involuntary, free or spontaneous. Aristotle considered adolescents unfit to study ethics because they lack breadth and variety of experience, which is required for ordering and judging human actions and virtues and vices. In each particular field the judgment most highly prized is that of the person who in that field is outstanding for his knowledge and is found to be well versed in it through experience. Finally, we all have the experience of learning new material, and of the fact that we cannot right from the outset order and judge it adequately; yet by degrees we make progress in doing so, so that finally we may ourselves become teachers and professors of it.

(c) As far as invoking the weightiest authorities goes, we must say that in this we do not have an efficacious remedy against all forms of stupidity. No one should be considered to have appropriated some of the wisdom of Aristotle, Augustine, and Aquinas simply because he can read Greek or Latin; or because he has with great diligence made a collection of numerous passages from these authors and drawn his own conclusions from them; or because he looks in those writers for topics they never dealt with ([for example,] *Le scoutisme d'après S. Thomas d'Aquin*).[50] But there is no sure antidote to lack of wisdom. However, the abuse of something should not cause it to be rejected: I place the highest value on a genuine and constant and persevering effort to advance step by step towards appropriating in some measure the wisdom of Aristotle, Augustine, and Aquinas.

(d) The objection to the word 'philosophy' is invalid because it makes a disjunction between perfect foolishness and consummate wisdom. There are intermediate positions, in which all of us can be found. These intermediate positions, since they include a small amount of wisdom, save us from skepticism; and since they fall short of perfect wisdom, they save us from the absurdity of puffed-up intellectual pride.

---

50 [There is in fact a book by Réginald Héret, *La loi scoute: Commentaire d'après saint Thomas d'Aquin* (Paris: Éditions Spec, 1924; later, enl. ed., 1945.)]

(e) Relativismus non consistit in eo quod negatur omnes homines omnis temporis esse sapientes sapientia quadam divina. E contra, confugere ad deductivismum sive propositionalem sive conceptualisticum nihil est aliud quam res prout de facto sunt derelinquere, problemata quae urgent negligere, in turrim quandam eburneam illusionibus fundatam confugere; scilicet in universalia et necessaria, ubi quaeritur undique de concretis, de historicis, de socialibus, de individualibus, de empirice intelligibilibus et veris.

(f) Posuimus quaestionem de possibilitate per modum expositionis responsi. Attamen quando vere dubitatur, sic non est procedendum. Nam ex esse ad posse valet illatio. Ex esse cognitionis concludere possumus quemadmodum exacte cognitio fieri possit. Sed ubi deest cognitio, deest fundamentum unde perspici possit quemadmodum talis cognitio sit possibilis.

Aliis verbis, circa cognitionem, longe difficilius est scire ipsam scientiae possibilitatem quam scire ipsam scientiam. Et qui prius de possibilitate scientiae quaerit quam ipsam scientiam, viam parat latam et planam ad scepticismum. Intrate ergo semper per portam angustam.

[10] Problema khasmatis: gressus initialis

1 Simplici fideli, qua fideli et simplici, competit simplex fides. Sed etiam simplex fidelis est homo, naturaliter intellectu praeditus, ad quaestiones suas ponendas naturaliter motus. Cui qua tali competit intelligentia fidei, secundum illud SS. Augustini et Anselmi, 'Crede ut intelligas.'[51]

2 Quod problema acuitatem quandam specialem nostris temporibus habet, ubi educatio quaedam est universalis et obligatoria, ubi educatio productior est valde communis, ubi multiplicantur libri stylo populari conscripti ad notitiam mathematicam et scientificam, socialem, historicam, culturalem divulgandam.[52]

3 Cuius problematis solutio duo requirit: ut ipsi theologi scientificam

(e) Relativism does not consist in denying that all men of every age are wise with a certain godlike wisdom. On the contrary, to have recourse to deductivism, whether propositional or conceptualist, is simply to ignore things as they really are, to neglect pressing problems, to take refuge in an ivory tower founded upon illusions, namely, in universals and necessaries, when on all sides people are asking about concrete reality, historical questions, social questions, about individuals, about what is empirically intelligible and true.

(f) We have put the question about the possibility [of the third kind of foundation] by way of an explanation of its answer. Nevertheless, this is not the way to proceed when one is truly in doubt. For one may validly reason from existence to possibility. From the existence of knowledge we can deduce exactly how knowledge can come into existence. But when knowledge is lacking, there is also lacking a foundation for being able to understand how such knowledge is possible.

In other words, concerning knowing as a process, it is far more difficult to know the possibility of a science than to know that science itself; and one who would inquire into the possibility of a science before knowing that science itself is starting out on the broad and level road to skepticism. Always enter, therefore, by the narrow gate!

[10] The Problem of the Chasm: A First Step

1 For the simple faithful, as such, a simple faith is quite appropriate. But the simple faithful too are human, and are thus naturally endowed with an intellect and naturally moved to ask questions. An understanding of the faith is thus appropriate for them to have, according to the mind of Augustine and Anselm, *Crede ut intelligas*, 'Believe, that you may understand.'[51]

2 This problem is particularly acute in our day, when there is universal compulsory education, when prolonged education is very common, and when there is a flood of books and magazines that popularize and disseminate knowledge of mathematics, science, society, history, and culture.[52]

3 Two things are required for a solution to this problem: that theolo-

---

51 [Handwritten here: pie sedulo sobrie (reverently, diligently, and judiciously), referring to Vatican I: DB 1796, DS 3016, ND 132.]
52 [The words 'socialem,' 'historicam,' and 'culturalem' are added by hand in the margin of the autograph.]

suam fidei intelligentiam intendant atque acquirant; ut hanc scientificam fidei intelligentiam ad usum hominum secundum diversos gradus culturae adaptare possint.

4 Ad primum requiritur ut agnoscatur in tractatu theologico punctum inflexionis, scilicet, reici oportet illam aberrationem quae theologiam semper remotiorem a fontibus revelatis facit neque ullum tentare vult reditum ex conclusionibus in ipsos fontes intelligendos.

5 Ad alterum requiritur ut eliminetur khasma inter intellectum et sensum, scilicet, intellectus occupatur unice de universalibus et necessariis; praetermittitur simpliciter intelligentia quae habetur in ipsis sensibilibus; praetermittitur multiplex ille influxus mutuus quo sensus et intellectus sponte et natura cooperantur et unam conscientiam humanam tam sensibilem quam intellectualem formant. Quare, evolvi debet psychologia 'spiritus incarnati'; theoria artis pictoriae, plasticae, musicae, litterariae; theoria mentis primitivae, mythicae, popularis, semi-educatae;[53] quae quidem omnia cum theologia integrari debent: Christologia, gratia, ascetica et mystica, moralis et pastoralis, liturgica, personalistica, existentialistica, ecclesiologia, quod multum simul confert ad problema historicitatis solvendum.

[11] Problema Historicitatis: Gressus Initialis

1 Ideae Platonicae tempore non evolvuntur neque perficiuntur. Conceptus humani, sub aspectu logico, sunt aeterni et immutabiles: id quod intenditur qua tale semper est idem; e.g., triangulus in spatio Euclidiano est univocus.

Sed ipsa humana intentio non semper fit, neque semper fit eodem modo. Non semper fit, quia non semper intendimus in unumquodque. Non semper fit eodem modo, nam conceptus procedit de actu intelligendi, et ideo, quotiescumque perficitur vel augetur intelligentia, diversificatur conceptus.

gians themselves strive for and acquire their own scientific understanding of the faith; and that they be able to adapt their scientific understanding of the faith to the needs of the people in keeping with their various levels of culture.

4 The first of these requires that there be acknowledged in a theological treatise the turning point or pivotal point; that is to say, the abandonment of the aberration that makes theology ever more and more remote from the revealed sources and never tries to make the return trip from its conclusions to a deeper understanding of those very sources.

5 The second of these requires the elimination of the chasm or gap between intellect and the senses. This means [to abandon the false notion that] the intellect has to do solely with universals and necessaries, utterly ignoring the fact that understanding is had in sensible data, as well as the fact of the manifold mutual influence by which the intellect and the senses spontaneously and naturally work together to form a single human consciousness that is both sentient and intellectual. There must be developed, therefore, a psychology of the 'incarnate spirit'; a theory of the pictorial and plastic arts, of music and literature; a theory of the primitive, the mythic, the popular, and the semi-educated mentality.[53] All of these must be integrated with theology, with Christology, [the theology of] grace, ascetical and mystical theology, moral theology, pastoral, liturgical, personalistic, existentialistic theology, ecclesiology. All this together would contribute greatly to solving the problem of historicity.

[11] The Problem of Historicity: A First Step

1 Platonic Ideas do not develop nor are they perfected in the course of time. Human concepts, from the point of view of logic, are eternal and immutable: what they intend as such is always the same. For example, a triangle in Euclidean space is univocal.

But this human intending is not always happening, or always happening in the same way. It is not always happening, because we are not always intending something. It is not always happening in the same way, for a concept proceeds from an act of understanding, and therefore as often as understanding improves and grows, so is the concept modified.

---

53 [The names 'Marcel, Merleau-Ponty, De Waelhens' are inserted by hand in the left margin at this point.]

Quare quod olim ponebatur de triangulo universaliter nunc etiam dicitur, non tamen universaliter, sed tantummodo de triangulo in spatio Euclidiano. Quod si movetur geometria, multo magis caetera.

2 Radicitus evitatur omne problema historicitatis si supponitur conceptus non procedere ex actibus intelligendi sed, mediante quodam mechanismo metaphysico, fixo et immutabili, immediate ex ipsis rebus quae non mutantur. Radicitus evitato omni possibili problemate historicitatis, facilius solvuntur problemata epistemologica, et tutius evitatur omnis vel species relativismi.[54]

Sed falsitas neque vere prodest neque simpliciter prodest: negligi debet omne serium studium fontium revelatorum et traditionis catholicae; negligi debet omne serium fundamentum theologicae systematicae in fontibus secundum sensum historicum fontium; semper augebitur theologia positiva, et semper minuetur influxus et aestimatio theologiae systematicae seu scholasticae; semper audactius professores in materia positiva aperte in scholis dicent auditoribus quod id quod in schola dogmatica assumitur tamquam fundamentum aliud fundamentum non habet nisi crassam quandam ignorantiam.

3 Si factum historicitatis agnoscitur,

(a) debet agnosci vera criteriologia (valde complexa); in re exegetica, historica, non fiunt demonstrationes ex principiis necessariis; agitur de intelligibilitate empirica (contingente sed vera) quae innotescit ex convenientia multorum indiciorum, quae non probatur in decem momentis examinis sed breviter et schematice indicatur;

(b) extendi debet methodologia viae inventionis; processus ex fontibus in thesin dogmaticam plus minus coincidit cum processu historico.

This is why what used to be said universally about a triangle is also said today, yet not universally, but only about a triangle 'in Euclidean space.' If geometry changes, all the more so do other things.

2 The whole problem of historicity is radically avoided if one supposes that concepts do not proceed from acts of understanding, but rather, through some sort of metaphysical mechanism that is fixed and immutable, proceed immediately from things themselves that do not change. Every possible problem of historicity having been radically avoided, epistemological problems are more easily solved, and all relativism and even the semblance of it is more surely avoided.[54]

But a false position is neither truly helpful nor simply helpful: all serious study of the sources of revelation and Catholic tradition must be neglected; the whole of systematic theology's solid foundation in the sources according to the historical meaning of the sources must be neglected; positive theology will ever increase, and the influence of and esteem for systematic or Scholastic theology will go on diminishing; professors in the fields of positive theology will ever more boldly and openly tell their students that what in their course in dogmatic theology is assumed as a foundation has really no foundation other than crass ignorance.

3 If the fact of historicity is recognized:

(a) true criteriology (very complex) must be acknowledged; in exegesis and in matters of history one does not deduce proofs from necessary principles; these are matters of empirical intelligibility (contingent but true), which comes to be known from the convergence of many pieces of evidence, and which is not proven in a ten-minute examination but is indicated briefly and schematically;

(b) the methodology of the analytic way, the 'way of discovery,' must be extended; the process from the sources of revelation to the dogmatic thesis more or less coincides with the historical process.

54 [Handwritten in the margin: 'non paucis verbis exponitur solutio eius quod et datur evolutio vera et relativismus est falsus Insight 342 ff. Tota secunda pars' – 'A fairly lengthy solution is given of the fact that there is a development that is true and that relativism is false: see Lonergan, *Insight* 366–71 – the whole second part.' Collected Works pagination has been substituted for the pagination Lonergan gave, '342 ff.']

II.I Problema historicitatis[55]

1 Radicale: (a) augentur sapientia, intelligentia, scientia; (b) nexus subtiliores perspiciuntur, conceptus accuratiores formantur.

2 Tempori comparatur: (a) progressus exsistit atque regressus; e.g. xiv:
coluit logicam; scepticismus; neglexit intelligentiam; (b) progressus in uno
campo, regressus in alio; determinismus mechanisticus a xvi ad xx; (c) stadia fundamentalia distinguuntur, saltem principia distinctionis; non phae-
nomenalis: conceptus 'Hebraicus' 'Graecus'; sed principalis; (d) deducuntur singulis stadiis modi cogitandi, percipiendi, vivendi; E.Cassirer : myth ::
Kant : Newton.[56]

Quod problema excluditur (a) si conceptus habentur non ex intelligentia rerum sed ex ipsis rebus, (b) si nihil scientificum nisi quod necessario
concluditur ex principiis necessariis, per se notis, certis, a nullo disputatis.
Nemo cogitur ad sapientiam: qui vult cogi, manebit cum parva sua sapientia –
maximum damnum ecclesiae infert.

Problema historicitatis: (a) progrediente intelligentia plenius, accuratius
percipiuntur nexus, formantur conceptus; (b) ipse intellectus et se et partem sensitivam cognoscit ex 'per se' ad 'concretum,' historicum.

Exclusio historicitatis: omittitur plenior intelligentia; plenissime iam est
habita apud Ar. Aug. Aq.; omittitur concretum, quaestionum classificatio;
conjungitur ad per se.

[12] De Unitate Solutionis[57]

1 Quoddam solutionis initium indicavimus circa triplex problema fundamenti, khasmatis, historicitatis. At illud in primis notari oportet

11.1 The Problem of Historicity[55]

1 Radical: (a) wisdom, understanding, science increase; (b) more subtle connections are understood, more accurate concepts are formulated.

2 Is related to a period of time: (a) there is progress, and also regression; e.g., fourteenth century, cultivation of logic; skepticism; neglect of understanding; (b) progress in one field, regression in another: mechanist determinism from fourteenth to twentieth century; (c) fundamental stages are distinguished, at least the principles of the distinction: not phenomenal, such as the concepts 'Hebrew' and 'Greek,' but principal; (d) in each stage are deduced the modes of thinking, perceiving, living. E. Cassirer : myth :: Kant : Newton.[56]

This problem is excluded (a) if concepts are had not from an understanding of things but from things themselves; (b) if there is nothing scientific except what is concluded necessarily from principles that are necessary, known *per se*, certain, disputed by no one. *No one is forced towards wisdom*: whoever wants to be forced will end up with his little bit of wisdom and do great harm to the church.

The problem of historicity: (a) as understanding progresses, connections are understood, and concepts formulated, more fully and accurately; (b) the intellect knows both itself and the sensitive dimension; from the *per se* to the *concrete, historical.*

The exclusion of historicity: fuller understanding is omitted; understanding is already most fully had in Aristotle, Augustine, Aquinas; the concrete, the classification of questions, is omitted; there is a link to the *per se*.

[12] The Unity of the Solution[57]

1 We have indicated the beginning of a solution to the threefold problem of the foundation, the chasm, and historicity. But this above all should be

---

55 [The material in this subsection appears on two handwritten pages inserted in Lonergan's manuscript at this point. These pages correspond roughly to the material worked out more fully in 'Understanding and Method.' See above, pp. 74–79.]

56 [In 'Understanding and Method' above, p. 71, Lonergan expressed his meaning this way: 'What Kant did with regard to Newtonian mechanics, Cassirer has tried to do with regard to the mythic mentality.']

57 [Lonergan's typed text resumes at this point.]

idem in tribus esse solutionis initium, nempe, intellectum humanum potentiale.

2 Quia enim potentialis est intellectus humanus, progreditur intelligentia, scientia, et sapientia. Ex quo progressu repetita est solutio problematis
fundamenti.

3 Quia humanus est hic noster intellectus potentialis, cum vita sensitiva
modo maxime intimo coniungitur. Ex qua unione repetita est solutio problematis khasmatis.

4 Quia in intima unione cum vita sensitiva progreditur noster intellectus,
modo historico progreditur, scilicet, sub conditionibus socialibus, cultura-
libus, secundum limitationes earundem conditionum, maxime secundum
exigentias harum conditionum; exteriores enim conditiones sociales et
culturales sunt effectus quidam ipsius intellectus; manifestant tum verum
quod ab intellectu perspicitur tum falsum in quod intellectus aberrat; unde
dialectica quaedam est interactio inter intellectum progredientem et conditiones culturales et sociales, et ideo ad intellectum sensu unitum et historico modo progredientem confugimus ut quaeramus solutionem problematis historicitatis.

5 Proinde notandum est hoc solutionis initium non esse nisi prolonga-
tionem quandam et continuationem eius quod iam pridem ab Aristotelicis
et Thomistis agnoscitur, nempe, intellectum humanum esse potentialem,
quam intime cum vita sensitiva uniri, totam suam perfectionem hac in vita
habere non posse, progredi ex magis universalibus in magis particularia, ...

6 Unde quodammodo potest titulus: 'De intellectu et methodo.' Methodus enim ordinat media in finem; ubi finis est scientia non inventa sed
invenienda, finis ignoratur; attamen in lumine intellectus agentis omnis
scientia est nobis originaliter indita; et ideo ex ipso intellectu quaerenda est
methodus, ordinatio mediorum in finem scientiae acquirendae.

noted, that the beginning of the solution to all three is the same, namely, the potential human intellect.

2 It is because the human intellect is potential that there is progress in understanding, science, and wisdom. The solution to the problem of the foundation has been sought from the fact of this progress.

3 Because this potential intellect of ours is human, it is most intimately connected with our sense life. The solution to the problem of the chasm has been sought from this intimate union.

4 Because our intellect progresses in this intimate union with our sense life, it progresses historically; that is, conditioned by cultural and social factors, according to the limitations of those conditions, most of all according to the demands of these conditions, for these external social and cultural conditions are the effects of our intellect itself, and manifest both whatever truth our intellect has grasped and whatever error it has deviated into, whence there is a certain dialectical interaction between the intellect as it progresses and cultural and social conditions; therefore, we go to the intellect united with sense and progressing historically for the solution to the problem of historicity.

5 Now it is to be noted that this beginning of a solution is but a further development and continuation of what Aristotelians and Thomists recognized long ago: that the human intellect is potential, that it is intimately united with the life of the senses, that it cannot attain its full perfection in this life, that it progresses from the more universal to the more particular, and so on.

6 From this you can see in a way why we have titled our treatise 'Understanding and Method.' For method orders means to an end. When the end is knowledge that is not yet found but is to be discovered, that end is not known; nevertheless, all knowledge is imparted to us in the light of the agent intellect as its origin. That is why it is from the intellect itself that we are to seek method, the ordering of means to that end which is the acquisition of knowledge.

Appendix 2 – Items Related to 'De Methodo Theologiae'[1]

---

1   De Expressione[2]

1 Expressio aut discursiva est aut practica aut artistica aut his mixta.
  2 Expressio discursiva est cognitionis intellectualis. Obiectum intellectus

Appendix 2 – Items Related to 'De Methodo Theologiae'[1]

1   Expression[2]

1 Expression can be discursive or practical or artistic or a mixture of these.
  2 Discursive expression is the expression of intellectual knowledge. The

1 [The items in this second appendix have some relation to 'De methodo theologiae,' the fifth item in this collection, and in some instances to other items in this volume. The first seven items were found in the same folder as the autograph of Lonergan's notes 'De methodo theologiae,' immediately preceding that lengthy document. The last four of these seven have dates that indicate they were composed in connection with that course. The first three may not be directly related to the course, but they are included here not only because of their location in Lonergan's file but also since they represent views that are reflected in the notes for the course and elsewhere in the volume. They may be part of a project to try to understand the way of discovery in terms of a movement from the implicit to the explicit. This project is reflected in the archival document A 467, now available on www. bernardlonergan.com at 46700D0LE60 and in transcription at 46700DTLE60. This item was too schematic and in places too indecipherable to be put in the Collected Works, but may be fruitfully studied for the light that it throws on Lonergan's talk of 'implicit' and 'explicit.' It would seem that differentiations of consciousness came to be viewed as a better way of explaining the way of discovery than the more logical consideration of implicit and explicit. See Lonergan, *Method in Theology* 353: '... the shift from a predominately logical to a basically methodical viewpoint may involve a revision of the view that doctrinal developments were "implicitly" revealed.' The final four items in this appendix were found elsewhere in the archives, but dates on the pages place them with the same course.]
  2 ['De expressione' is the first item in folder 1 of batch V in the Lonergan

est ens, intelligibile, verum. Expressio discursiva supponit ergo obiectum quoddam attingi et quidem sub ratione entis, intelligibilis, veri.

Ipsa expressio consistit in nominibus verbisque propriis apte ordinatis sive ore prolatis sive scriptis quae idem obiectum directe respiciunt.

Qua in expressione distingui possunt: ordinabilia (nomina, verba), ordinatio, et positio (prolatio, scriptio). Quod analogice quodammodo se habet ad triplex elementum constitutivum cognitionis humanae: experientia, intelligentia, iudicium.

3 Expressio practica finem quendam ulteriorem intendit praeter cognitionis intellectualis declarationem. Puta loquentem vel scribentem docere, persuadere, orare, optare, imperare, etc.

4 Expressio artistica sicut discursiva triplici constat elemento: ordinabile (soni, colores et figurae, sculptibile, aedificabile, nomina verbaque), ordo intelligibilis, et positio (ipsum artis opus). Quibus tamen alio quodam modo utitur.

(a) In expressione discursiva elementa ordinabilia associantur cum rebus, tamquam signa cum significatis. Quam ob causam expressio discursiva potest esse reflexiva, scilicet de ipsa expressione (grammatica) et de principio expressionis (psychologia).

In expressione artistica elementa ordinabilia aut nullo modo sunt signa (colores, soni, volumina spatialia) aut significant non res sed imaginabilia (poesis).

Quare opus artisticum dissociatur a mundo reali, a vita practica: a tali mundo talique vita est aliud, extraneum, separatum. Unde sequitur ulterius opus artis, praecise quia non cum mundo reali, vita practica integratur, propter se ipsum attentionem solicitat et magis videtur, magis auditur, etc., quam caetera quae non videntur neque audiuntur nisi per transennam ut statim alibi dirigatur attentio.

(b) In expressione discursiva ordo quidam imponitur nominibus ver-

object of the intellect is being, the intelligible, the true. Discursive expression supposes, therefore, that the intellect has attained some object and attained it precisely as being, as intelligible, as true.

The expression itself consists in appropriate nouns and verbs, suitably arranged and either spoken or written, that directly refer to that same object.

Three elements, then, can be distinguished in such expression: the things to be arranged (nouns, verbs), their arrangement, and their statement (orally uttered or in writing). There is a certain analogy to the three elements constitutive of human knowledge: experience, understanding, judgment.

3 Practical expression has some further purpose beyond the manifestation of intellectual knowledge – such as the aim of the speaker or writer to instruct, persuade, pray, express a wish or command, etc.

4 Artistic expression, like the discursive, consists of three elements: the matter to be given a certain form or order (sounds, colors and shapes, material for sculpting or building, verbs and nouns), an intelligible order, and the artistic statement (the work of art itself). However, it uses these in a different way.

(a) In a discursive expression, the elements to be ordered are associated with things as are signs with what they signify. Discursive expression, therefore, can be reflexive, that is, about the expression itself (grammar) or about the principle of the expression (psychology).

In artistic expression the materials to be ordered either are not signs in any sense (colors, sounds, spaces), or else signify not things themselves but what can be imagined (poetry).

Thus, a work of art is dissociated from the real world, from practical life: it is something different, foreign, separated from this world and this life. Hence, precisely because art is not involved in the real world or practical living, it attracts attention to itself and is more closely looked at or more intently listened to, and so on, than other things, which are seen or heard only *en passant*, so that one's attention is immediately diverted elsewhere.

(b) In discursive expression a certain order is imposed upon nouns and

Archives. Its connection with the course 'De methodo theologiae' may be nothing more than that it was found as the first item in the folder that contains the notes for that course. It was assigned the archival number A 422, and can be found at 42200DTL060 on the website www.bernardlonergan.com. And see also above, p. 293, for a possible connection with other material.]

bisque, qui tamen maxime attendit ad ordinem significatorum, et variatur pro diverso fine loquentis et pro diversa capacitate audientium.

In expressione artistica ordo est quam maxime immanens ipsis ordinatis. Nullatenus invenitur in ordine abstracto: e.g., idem est abstractus ordo tum in annotatione musica tum in sonis secundum annotationem emissis; sed ordo artisticus solummodo in sonis actu emissis invenitur. Scilicet, constat ordo expressionis artisticae in relationibus quae ipsis ordinabilibus sunt internae, quae pertinent ad colores, ad spatia, ad sonos.

(c) Ordo discursivus ad revelandam ordinem intelligibilem ipsis rebus inhaerentem dirigitur.

Sed ordo artisticus ipse est finis expressionis. Scil., hic ordo determinat selectionem et mensuram ordinabilium. Iterum, ipse hic ordo (non pigmenta, non soni separati, non lapis marmoreus) est id quod in opere artis qua tali perspicitur. Iterum, ipse hic ordo intelligibilis est id quod artista producit et quasi creat. Est *symbolum*.

(d) Positio discursiva (Est, est; Non, non) mensuratur secundum verum. Verum autem sumitur secundum criterion et secundum definitionem. Secundum criterion mensura habetur ex debito modo procedendi intellectus: ita inquisivit ut perspici possit evidentiam sufficere, quod quidem perspicitur. Secundum definitionem mensura habetur ex ipsis rebus quibus intellectus se adaequat.

Positio artistica (ipsum opus secundum fieri et factum esse) habet suum criterion. Scil., artista iudicat quemadmodum ordo poni debeat, quemadmodum positus sit; et similiter critici. Quod tamen criterion non est aliquid ulterius significatum, rebus conformem (sicut in positione discursiva), sed est ipsum quod exprimendum erat (quasi in discursu adfuit criterion veritatis sine definitione veritatis).

(e) Quid exprimendum?

Intelligibile se habet ad sensibile dupliciter. Primo modo, secundum originem, intelligibile perspicitur in sensibilibus, scil. in eo quod per sensus, phantasma, repraesentatur, quare dicitur intellectus sine organo, quia materiale eius est non ipse sensus sed intentionale sensu vel phantasia repraesentatum.

Alio modo, secundum effectum, nam homo intelligit, iudicat, vult, consiliatur, eligit, ut agat; per quam actionem imponitur intelligibile appre-

verbs, which order, however, pays the closest attention to the order of the things signified and varies according to the different purposes of the speaker and the nature of the audience.

The order in artistic expression is as much as possible immanent in the ordered elements themselves. It is not found at all in the abstract order: for example, there is the same abstract order in both a musical score and in the sounds emitted according to that score, but the artistic order is found only in the sounds as actually emitted. In other words, the order of an artistic expression consists in the relations that are intrinsic to the ordered elements themselves, which belong to colors, spaces, sounds.

(c) The discursive order is aimed at manifesting the intelligible order inherent in the things themselves.

But the artistic order itself is the goal of [artistic] expression; that is, this order determines the selection and measure of the elements to be ordered. Also, this order itself (not the paint, the individual sounds, or the marble block) is that which is grasped in the work of art as such. And it is this intelligible order that the artist produces, and in a sense, creates. It is a *symbol*.

(d) The measure of a discursive statement ('It is'; 'No, it is not') is truth. But truth can be taken according to its criterion or according to its definition. According to the criterion, its measure is obtained from the intellect's proper way of proceeding: it inquires in order to be able to grasp that the evidence is sufficient, and this in fact is grasped. According to its definition, the measure of truth is taken from the things themselves to which the intellect corresponds.

An artistic statement (the work of art in its coming-to-be and as completed) has its own criterion. That is to say, the artist judges how an order ought to be stated, how it has been stated – and so also do the critics. But this criterion is not something further signified corresponding to things (as in a discursive statement); rather, it is the very thing that was to be expressed (as if in a discursive statement the criterion of truth had been present without the definition of truth).

(e) What is to be expressed?

The intelligible is related to the sensible in two ways. First, according to its origin, the intelligible is grasped in sensible data, namely, in that which is represented through the senses or phantasm; hence, the intellect is said to be lacking an organ, since its material is not the sense itself but the intentional represented by the sense or phantasm.

Second, according to its effect, for a person understands, judges, wills, deliberates, and chooses in order to act; and through this action the intelli-

hensum ipsi suae vitae sensitivae; imponitur ergo non in intentionalibus tantum sed in naturalibus, in animi motibus, passionibus, affectibus, sentimentis, motibus corporis.

Quod quidem intelligibile se habet ad motus internos, sicut se habet ordo symboli ad ordinabilia artistica. Intelligibile artisticum oritur ex vita subiecti interna, et exprimitur in ordinabilibus: neque prius perfecte habetur et deinde exprimitur (cf. histrio qui partes suas didicit), sed ipsum fit prout exprimitur (cf. drama vitae).

Quare, imprimis, le style, c'est l'homme. Primum (primitivum) opus artis est ipsa concreta vita humana, et primum (primitivum) ordinabile est corpus humanum quod saltare, movere, cantare, etc., potest. Proprie autem opus artis non est vivere: sicut expressio discursiva communicat non res sed ideas de rebus, ita etiam ars dicit intelligentiam vitae, feeling, Gefühl.

2   De Explicito et Implicito[3]

1 Explicitum simpliciter et explicite cognoscitur et explicite dicitur.

Explicite cognoscitur quod in se clare distincteque concipitur et aut affirmatur aut negatur. Quare non explicite cognoscitur quod (1) non in se sed in alio cognoscitur vel (2) non ex parte obiecti vel non per intellectum cognoscitur.

Explicite dicitur quod propriis nominibus verbisque in recto enuntiatur.

2 Implicitum est quod vere quodammodo sed non explicite vel cognoscitur vel dicitur. Modos fundamentales quibus invenitur implicitum distinguimus quattuor: litterarium nempe, logicum, psychologicum, et gnoseologicum. Quibus postea accedent modi compositi, nempe, historicus, religiosus, theologicus.

3 Litterarie implicitum dicimus quod ratione enuntiationis ab explicito deficit. Est ergo quod non propriis sed translatis dicitur nominibus verbisve, quod in obliquo potius quam in recto ponitur, ad quod fit allusio, quod paucis tamquam notum recolitur, quod suggeritur, quod intenditur et intelligitur quin tamen dicatur.

gible that is apprehended is imposed upon one's sentient life. It is imposed, therefore, not in the intentional order only but in the natural order, in emotions, passions, feelings, sentiments, bodily movements.

This intelligibility is to interior movements as the order of a symbol is to things that can be ordered artistically. Artistic intelligibility arises from the interior life of a subject and is expressed in things capable of being ordered. It is not first possessed perfectly and then expressed, like an actor who has learned his part, but comes into being as it is actually being expressed: the drama of life.

Hence, first of all, *le style, c'est l'homme.* The first and primal work of art is concrete human living, and the first and primal thing to be ordered is the human body in its ability to dance, gesture, sing, and so forth. However, a work of art in the proper sense is not actual living: just as discursive expression communicates not things themselves but ideas about them, so does art express an understanding of life, feeling, *Gefühl.*

2   The Explicit and the Implicit[3]

1 The simply explicit is both explicitly known and explicitly expressed.

That is explicitly known which in itself is clearly and distinctly conceived and either affirmed or denied. Therefore, whatever (1) is known not in itself but in another, or (2) is not known on the side of the object or through the intellect, is not known explicitly.

That is explicitly expressed which is enunciated directly in appropriate nouns and verbs.

2 The implicit is what is truly known or expressed in some way, but not explicitly. We distinguish four basic ways in which something can be implicit: literary, logical, psychological, and gnoseological. To these will be added later compound ways, namely, historical, religious, theological.

3 We term literarily implicit what lacks explicitness in enunciation: what is expressed not in literal but in metaphorical nouns and verbs, what is expressed indirectly rather than directly, what is alluded to, what is recognized by few, what is suggested, what is intended and understood without being stated.

---

3 ['De explicito et implicito' is the second item in folder 1 of batch v in the Lonergan Archives. This item was assigned the archival number A 423, and can be found at 42300DTL060 on the website www.bernardlonergan.com.]

4 Logice implicitum dicimus quod in alio explicite cognito logice continetur. Illud continetur logice in alio quod ex alio concluditur necessario
sive per modum consequentis sive per modum praesuppositi.

5 Psychologice implicitum dicimus quod in se cognoscitur sed potius per
intersubiectivitatem quandam seu empathiam quam per intellectum et sub
ratione entis, intelligibilis, et veri.

Alios scilicet intelligimus et cognoscimus dupliciter: *primo modo*, per signa
articulata, quibus communicatur quod sub ratione entis, intelligibilis, veri
ab intellectu attingitur; qua in cognitione requiruntur ut alius non decipia-
tur neque mentiatur et ut ipsi intelligamus et sapiamus; *alio modo*, inquantum ipsam aliorum experientiam quodammodo participamus, sive quia ipsi
similia experti sumus, sive quia naturali quodam animi motu quasi sentire possumus quid sentiremus si similia experiremur; inter empathiam et
sympathiam (compassionem) illud intercedit quod sympathia veros animi
motus realiter in nobis inducit, dum empathia magis notitiam status alterius generat quam similem quodammodo statum in nobis reproducit. Psychiatrus utitur non sympathia sed empathia. Empathia : sympathia :: imaginatio : sensus – non imaginationis, sensationis, actionis meae sed alterius.[4]

Scilicet homo est spiritus incarnatus: unde cognitio humana duplici componitur elemento, alio magis spirituali et intellectuali, alio autem magis
corporali et sensitivo. Utrumque elementum et complet et exigit alterum.
Sed alia et alia mensura fit duorum compositio: cf. opus dramaticum scriptum et lectum et idem opus repraesentatum, visum, auditum; similiter, tractatum et lectionem coram; amicorum epistulas et eorundem praesentiam.

Iam vero scientia psychologica progrediente, explicite cognitum fit per
conceptus et iudicia quod iam per ipsam vitam implicite vivendo, experiendo cognoscitur.

Iterum, qui verba alterius audit vel scripta eius legit, in iis explicite dictis
vel scriptis aliud invenit psychologice implicitum, nempe, loquentis vel scri-
bentis motus animi, sentimenta, humanitatem.

4 We term logically implicit what is logically contained in something else that is known explicitly. That is said to be logically contained in another which is necessarily deduced from another either as a consequence or as a presupposition.

5 We term psychologically implicit what is indeed known in itself but known through intersubjectivity or empathy rather than intellectually and under the formality of being, the intelligible, and the true.

We understand and know other persons in two ways: (1) through articulated signs that communicate what is attained by the intellect as being, intelligible, and true; this knowledge requires that the other person not be deceived or lying, and that we on our part understand and know; (2) inasmuch as we in some way participate in what another is experiencing, whether because we have experienced something similar ourselves, or because through some natural interior movement we are in some way capable of feeling what we would be feeling were we experiencing something similar. The difference between empathy and sympathy (compassion) is that sympathy really evokes true interior movements within us, while empathy is more a matter of generating in us an awareness of the state of the other person than of somehow reproducing in us a similar state. A psychiatrist uses empathy, not sympathy. Empathy is to sympathy as imagination is to the senses: not the imagination of my sensations and actions but of another's.[4]

Now, human beings are incarnate spirits. Hence, human knowledge is composed of two elements, one that is more spiritual and intellectual, the other more bodily and sentient. These elements complement and need each other. But these two ingredients can be combined in different measures: for example, a play as written and read and the same play as presented on the stage and seen and heard; likewise, a treatise on some subject and a lecture on the same subject; or a letter from a friend and the presence of that friend.

With the advances in the science of psychology, what is already known implicitly in the experience of human living becomes explicitly known through concepts and judgments.

Also, one who hears the words of another or reads what he has written finds in those explicit statements something else that is psychologically implicit, that is, the emotions, the feelings, the humanity of the speaker or writer.

---

4 [The Latin words from 'Psychiatrus' to the end of the paragraph were added by hand in the autograph.]

Quod psychologice implicitum ipse forte vel implicite tantum cognoscit vel, si psychologus est, etiam explicite concipit et affirmat.

Quibus perspectis, dicendum est illud esse psychologice implicitum quod (1) per scientiam psychologicam fit explicitum; (2) implicitum est inquantum cognoscitur sed non sub ratione entis, intelligibilis, veri; (3) potest implicite a loquente et scribente cognosci, implicite communicari, et implicite ab audiente vel legente cognosci (unde arcte connectitur cum implicito litterario sincere); (4) brevi dicitur elementum resonantiae, humanitatis, intersubiectivitatis, sensibilitatis, empathiae, sympathiae, artis; (5) quando explicite cognoscitur et dicitur, quodammodo potius tollitur quam confirmatur.

6 Gnoseologice implicitum dicimus quod in se cognoscitur et per intellectum, non tamen sub ratione entis, intelligibilis, veri, sed sub ratione experti.

Est illa admiratio quae initium dicitur omnis scientiae et philosophiae. Est inquisitio intelligens, experientia intelligendi, emanatio intelligibilis verbi, reflexio critica, intelligibilis emanatio iudicii, experientia principii liberi, responsabilis, moralis, experientia conflictus, tensionis, vincentis vel victi.

Est notitia subiecti qua subiecti.

Est id quod fit explicitum cum ex parte obiecti ponuntur logica, epistemologia, metaphysica, ethica, psychologia rationalis, naturale desiderium videndi Deum per essentiam.

3   De Explicito et Implicito Historico[5]

1 Nobis non solum notissimae sunt sed et tritae distinctiones [1] inter animam et corpus; [2] inter cognitionem, appetitionem, actionem; [3] inter

This psychologically implicit reality one will perhaps know only implicitly, but, if one is a psychologist, one will perhaps also have an explicit conception and judgment about it.

From the above, we say that the psychologically implicit is what (1) becomes explicit through the science of psychology, (2) is implicit inasmuch as it is known but not known under the formality of being, the intelligible, and the true, (3) can be known implicitly by the speaker or writer, implicitly communicated, and implicitly known by the hearer or reader (hence, it is closely connected with the sincere literary implicit), (4) is, in a word, the element of resonance, of humanity, of intersubjectivity, of sensibility, of empathy, of sympathy, of art, and (5) when it comes to be known and expressed explicitly, it, in a way, vanishes rather than being strengthened.

6 We term the gnoseologically implicit what is known in itself and through the intellect, but not under the formality of being, the intelligible, and the true, but under the formality of the experienced.

It is that wonder that is said to be the starting point of all science and philosophy. It is intelligent inquiry, the experience of understanding, the intellectual emanation of a word, critical reflection, the intellectual emanation of a judgment, the experience of a free and responsible moral principle, the experience of conflict, of tension, of triumph and defeat.

It is the awareness of the subject as subject.

It is what becomes explicit when there are put forth on the side of the object logic, epistemology, metaphysics, ethics, rational psychology, and the natural desire to see God through his essence.

3   The Historical Explicit and Implicit[5]

1 The following distinctions are not only extremely well known, but even trite: (1) between soul and body; (2) between knowledge, appetition, and

---

5 ['De explicito et implicito historico' is the third item in folder 1 of batch V in the Lonergan Archives. It was assigned the archival number A 424, and can be found at 42400DTL060 on the website www.bernardlonergan.com. Recall Lonergan saying in 'De explicito et implicito' above that to the four basic ways in which something can be implicit there will be added later compound ways, namely, *historical*, religious, theological. This item at least begins to treat the first of these compound ways. At the end of the first paragraph the autograph has the word 'psychicam,' which the editors have changed to 'physicam,' in light of the fact that it is followed by the words 'chimicam' and 'biologicam.']

sensitivum, intellectivum, rationale, liberum, morale; [4] inter subiectum et obiectum; [5] inter individuum et consociationem; [6] inter consociationem domesticam, tribalem, technologicam, oeconomicam, politicam, culturalem, scientificam, religiosam; [7] inter artes practicas et liberales, inter pictoriam, plasticam, constructivam, litterariam, inter genera litteraria; [8] inter theologiam, philosophiam, physicam, chimicam, biologicam, etc.

2 Quibus in distinctionibus fundantur et quodammodo consistunt multae et diversae structurae specializatae et articulatae: tota explicita cognitio quam de nobis ipsis et de aliis habemus; tota organizatio scientiarum, bibliothecarum, scholarum; innumerae structurae technologicae, oeconomicae, politicae, medicorum et clinicorum, recreationis, laboris, religionis, etc.

3 Quae omnes distinctiones et consequentes specializationes et specialistarum organizationes et articulationes quandoque erant novae, inauditae, neque ullo usu comprobatae. E.g., industria et commercium modernum non essent sine scientiis modernis; et sine industria et commercio moderno non esset vita nostra urbana, maxima telluris populatio humana, problemata socialia et politica et internationalia.

Nobis notissimum est aliam esse scientiam et aliam philosophiam: inter eas distinxit clarissime Newton qui tamen opus suum celeberrimum nominavit 'philosophiae naturalis principia mathematica.' Cartesius, quamvis theologiam et philosophiam prorsus separavit, inter philosophiam et scientiam non satis distinxit: probat conservationem momenti ex immutabilitate Dei. Aquinas inter philosophiam et theologiam distinxit sed eas minime separavit; S. Anselmus ipsam distinctionem parum novit.

Hebraei inter cognitionem, appetitionem, operationem parum distinxerunt.[6]

4 Sicut distinctiones erant quandoque inveniendae, ita etiam generalizationes. Quid magis obvium quam numerous 'duo': sed anglice manent nomina 'team,' 'pair,' 'couple,' 'brace,' quae denotant non 'duo' quodlibet sed 'duo' determinati cuiusdam generis. E. Cassirer, *Philosophie der Symbolischen Formen, 1. Grammatica*.[7] complicatur secundum personam qui loquitur, quibuscum loquitur, de quibus loquitur (dual, trial, plural; etc.).

action; (3) between sentient, intellectual, rational, free, moral; (4) between subject and object; (5) between individual and group; (6) between domestic, tribal, technological, economic, political, cultural, scientific, and religious groups; (7) between the practical and liberal arts, between the pictorial, plastic, constructive and literary arts, between literary genres; (8) between theology, philosophy, physics, chemistry, biology, etc.

2 In these distinctions many diverse specialized and articulated structures are grounded and, in a way, hold together: all the explicit knowledge we have of ourselves and of others; the entire organization of the sciences, of libraries, of schools; the multitude of technological, economic, political, medical, clinical, recreational, industrial, religious structures.

3 All these distinctions and their consequent specializations with their various organizations and articulations of specialists were once quite new, unheard of, and unproven by use. For example, modern industry and commerce would not exist without the modern sciences; and without modern industry and commerce, our urban way of life, the majority of human beings on earth, along with all the social, political, and international problems, would not exist.

We are quite familiar with the distinction between science and philosophy; Newton very clearly distinguished the two, yet titled his famous work *Philosophiae Naturalis Principia Mathematica*. Descartes, although he completely separated theology and philosophy, did not sufficiently distinguish between philosophy and science: his proof for the conservation of momentum was based upon God's immutability. Aquinas distinguished between philosophy and theology, but did not separate them; and St Anselm had little knowledge of this distinction.

The Hebrews made little distinction between knowledge, appetition, and operation.[6]

4 Just as new distinctions had to be made at times, so also did generalizations. What is more obvious than the number 'two'? But in English we have the words 'team,' 'pair,' 'couple,' 'brace,' all denoting not any two whatever, but two of a determinate kind. Ernst Cassirer, *Philosophie der Symbolischen Formen, 1. Grammatica*:[7] it is complicated according to the one speaking,

---

6 See TWNT, I, 688–719 [TDNT, I, 689–719] s.v. γινώσκω (R. Bultmann); see also Susanne K. Langer, *Feeling and Form*.
7 [In English, *The Philosophy of Symbolic Forms*, vol. 1: *Language*. Lonergan gives no page numbers, but in the English translation chapter 3, § 3, pp. 226–49, is concerned with 'The Linguistic Development of the Concept of Number.']

4   De Problemate Theologico[8]

1 Accurata huius problematis intelligentia tradi non potest inde ab initio. Nihil hic intendimus nisi generales quasdam indicationes praebere, quae nostrum procedendi modum aliquatenus fundent atque explicent.

2 Praeter theologiam quae in libris sacris VT et NT iam contineri dicitur, distingui possunt theologia patristica, theologia mediaevalis, theologia classica (inde a saec. XVI), et theologia contemporanea.

(a) Theologia patristica maxime in determinationibus conciliariis continetur: de divinitate Filii, de divinitate Spiritus sancti, de unione hypostatica seu personali, de duabus Christi naturis, proprietatibus, operationibus naturalibus et voluntatibus, de peccato originali et de gratia praeveniente. Praesertim theologia Graeca novos terminos non-biblicos introduxit: *homoousion, hypostasis, physis, energein, thelein.*

(b) Theologia mediaevalis quaestionibus satisfacere voluit. Modo pure speculativo: ita Anselmus qui omnes quaestiones difficiliores et speculativas movit, de Trinitate, de fine Incarnationis, de lapsu angelorum, de peccato originali, de praescientia divina, de praedestinatione, de gratia et libero arbitrio. Modo magis concreto, qui documentis inhaeret: Abaelardus, *Sic et non*, 158 propositiones earumque contradictoria, stabiliuntur ex scr., PP., rationibus. Gilbertus Porretanus: exsistit quaestio si et solummodo si auctoritates vel rationes solidae adduci possunt pro utraque parte contradictionis. Unde quaestio: Videtur quod non ... Sed contra est ... Respondeo ... Ad primum ... Ad primum alterius partis ...[9]

Unde summae: ut multis quaestionibus cohaerenter respondeatur, requiritur terminorum fundamentalium complexio sibi cohaerens.

Unde usus Aristotelis: apud S. Thomam termini fundamentales sumuntur ex Aristotele vel analogice construuntur ex terminis Aristotelicis.

those with whom one speaks, and the subject spoken about (dual, triple, plural; etc.).

4   The Theological Problem[8]

1 We cannot present an accurate understanding of this problem right at the outset. All we intend here is to suggest some general points that will to some extent ground and explain our way of proceeding.

2 Besides the theology that is said to be contained in scripture, both Old and New Testaments, we can distinguish patristic theology, medieval theology, classical theology (the sixteenth and following centuries), and contemporary theology.

(a) Patristic theology is to be found especially in the decisions of the councils: concerning the divinity of the Son, the divinity of the Holy Spirit, the hypostatic or personal union, the two natures, properties, natural operations, and wills in Christ, original sin, and prevenient grace. New non-biblical terminology was introduced into theology mainly by the Greeks: such terms as *homoousion, hypostasis, physis, energein, thelein.*

(b) Medieval theologians wanted to give satisfactory answers to questions. In a purely speculative vein we have Anselm, who brought up all the more difficult speculative questions: about the Trinity, the purpose of the Incarnation, the fall of the angels, original sin, divine foreknowledge, predestination, grace and free will. More concretely, in a manner that holds to documents, we have Abelard, *Sic et non,* and 158 propositions with their contradictories, all based upon scripture, the Fathers, or reason; Gilbert de la Porrée, for whom a question exists if and only if sound authorities or reasons can be adduced in favor of both sides of a contradiction; hence the *quaestio:* '*Videtur quod non … Sed contra est … Respondeo … Ad primum … Ad primum alterius partis …*'[9]

Hence the *Summas:* in order to give coherent answers to a multitude of questions, a coherent system of basic terms is needed.

Hence the use of Aristotle: in St Thomas the basic terms are taken from Aristotle or are derived analogically from his terms.

---

8 ['De problemate theologico' is the fourth item in folder 1 of batch V in the Lonergan Archives. It was assigned the archival number A 425a, and can be found at 425AODTL060 on the website http://www.bernardlonergan.com.]

9 See Thomas Aquinas, *De veritate,* q. 24, a. 12.

Unde conflictus Augustino-Aristotelicus: Thomistae utuntur tamquam ancillis non solum logica sed etiam philosophia et scientiis Aristotelicis; Scotistae logicam accipiunt, philosophiam et scientiam respuunt.

Unde habentur: theologia ut intelligentia fidei (participatio scientiae divinae et beatorum) analogiis naturaliter notis et cohaerentia mysteriorum inter se utens; theologia ut logica fidei: notae theologicae summa cura determinatae; quaestiones de absoluta possibilitate huius, de demonstrabilitate illius; omissa cura intelligendi, principia evanescunt, et oritur scepticismus saec. XIV.

(c) Theologia classica. Tridentinum reaffirmat positiones scholasticas de traditione, justificatione, sacramentis.[10] Tit 1.9: ut potens sit exhortari in doctrina sana et eos qui contradicunt arguere. Paulus de episcopo (v. 7); Cano de theologo.[11] Decem loca: Scriptura, Traditiones Christi et Apostolorum, Doctrina ecclesiae, conciliorum, RR. PP., Patrum, Scholasticorum, disciplinae humanae, philosophi, historici.

(d) Theologia contemporanea. Vaticanum, *De fide et ratione. Aeterni Patris. Pascendi. Deus scientiarum Dominus. Divino afflante Spiritu. Humani generis.*

Transitum est ex ideali scientifico Aristotelica ad realitatem scientiae modernae: certa rerum per causas cognitio: scientia est non certa sed semper probabilior; non tam est per causas quam per fixas quasdam relationes inter magnitudines ($s = gt^2/2$); motus ex termino intelligitur: motus in se ipso per calculum infinitesimalem intelligitur; nulla scientia tractat illud quod est per accidens: dantur scientiae statisticae, leges statisticae; scientia est de necessariis: scientia est de intelligibilitate empirica, de conveniente, de eo quod aliter esse posset sed de facto sic est; scientia est de universalibus: scientia procedit ex universalibus abstractis per intellectum motus, per accidens, ad genesin rerum et eventuum concretam.

Hence the conflict between the Augustinians and the Aristotelians: the Thomists take as a help not only Aristotle's logic but also his philosophy and science; the Scotists accept his logic while rejecting his philosophy and science.

Hence we have theology as the understanding of the faith (a participation in God's knowledge and that of the blessed) by making use of analogies naturally known and the coherence of the mysteries among themselves; and theology as the logic of faith, where theological notes are determined with the utmost care, questions are asked about the absolute possibility of this and the demonstrability of that; with the neglect of understanding, principles vanish and skepticism emerges in the fourteenth century.

(c) Classical theology. (Trent reaffirms the Scholastic positions on tradition, justification, and the sacraments.)[10] St Paul, with reference to a bishop: 'to be able to preach sound doctrine and refute those who contradict it' (Titus 1.7–9); compare [Melchior] Cano with reference to a theologian.[11] Ten theological topics [*loca theologica*]: scripture, the traditions of Christ and the Apostles, the teaching of the church, of the councils, of the Popes, of the Fathers, of the Scholastic theologians, the human sciences, the philosophers, the historians.

(d) Contemporary theology. The [First] Vatican Council, chapter on faith and reason; the papal documents *Aeterni Patris* [1879], *Pascendi* [1907], *Deus scientiarum Dominus* [1931], *Divino afflante Spiritu* [1943], *Humani generis* [1950].

There is a transition from the Aristotelian ideal of science to the reality of modern science: [from] 'the certain knowledge of things through their causes' [to] science is not certitude but always a matter of greater probability; nor is it so much knowledge through causes as through certain constant relations between magnitudes ($s = gt^2/2$); [from] 'motion is understood from its term' [to] motion is understood in itself through the infinitesimal calculus; [from] 'science does not deal with what is *per accidens*' [to] there are statistical sciences, statistical laws; [from] 'science is about the necessary' [to] science is about empirical intelligibility, about what is fitting, about what could be otherwise but in fact is so; [from] 'science is

10 [The sentence within parentheses was added by hand in Latin in the autograph.]
11 Eugène Marcotte, *De la nature de la théologie d'après Melchior Cano* 87; see also pp. 90–91; theologian a soldier of Christ, pp. 94–95.

Transitum est ex conceptualismo classico circa res humanas ad cognitionem historicam civilizationum, culturarum, religionum, idearum, philosophiarum, scientiarum, artium. Conceptualismus classicus concipit hominem ut semper essentialiter eundem, animal rationale; concipit iura hominis universalia secundum constructionem quandam idealem de eo quod esse debet; caetera habet ut per accidens, positiva, minoris nomenti. In forma catholica: conservare ecclesiam traditionalem, monarchiam traditionalem, consuetudines traditionales; nihil novi admittere nisi omnibus manifestum sit eius praestantia. In forma deistica: religio naturalis (ex sola ratione); status secundum naturam humanam (aequalitas, libertas, fraternitas).

E contra romanticismus: ad particularia, singularia, positiva, subiectiva, etc., quam maxime recurrebat iisque delectabatur.

Philologia (F. Wolf): ex lingua exacte cognita totam culturam alicuius populi secundum omnes aspectus reconstituere; unde ideale studii historici circa legem, statum, religionem, moralitatem, artem, litteraturam, oeconomiam, etc.

Unde intelligitur homo secundum particularitatem epochae, culturae, nationis, occupationis; homo concretus non est abstractum quoddam ideale (animal rationale) sed evolvitur in ambiente contingenti secundum suam libertatem.

In rebus humanis, positiva, per accidens, pertinent ad concretam essentiam; quae tamen sine libertate non determinantur. Scientia non solum est tantummodo probabilis sed etiam obiectum scientiae non est aeterna quaedam essentia sed temporaliter, contingenter, libere evolvens individuorum successio atque evolutio.[12]

Transitum est ex philosophia Graeca, ex realismo dogmatico (verbi Dei, dogmatum, methodi scholasticae) ad philosophias quae cum scientiis modernis earumque methodis arcte connectuntur. Descartes (Galileo, *Methode*), Spinoza (*De emendatione intellectus*), Leibnitz (mathematicus notabilis), Kant (methodus transcendentalis, arcte cum mechanica Newto-

about universals' [to] science proceeds from abstract universals abstracted through the understanding of motion, *per accidens*, to the concrete genesis of things and events.

There is a transition from classical conceptualism regarding human affairs to a historical knowledge of civilizations, cultures, religions, ideas, philosophies, sciences, and the arts. Classical conceptualism conceives man as always essentially the same, a 'rational animal.' It conceives human laws as universal, in accordance with some ideal construct about what ought to be; it considers the rest as *per accidens*, positive, less important. As found in Catholicism it is concerned to preserve the traditional church, the traditional monarchy, and traditional customs; to admit nothing new unless it is clear to all that it is better. In deism it manifests itself in natural religion, that is, religion based on reason alone, and in a state that is in accord with human nature (liberty, equality, fraternity).

Opposed to this is Romanticism, which turns as much as possible to the particular, the singular, the positive, the subjective, etc., and delights in these.

Philology (Friedrich Wolf) is concerned to reconstruct from an accurate knowledge of their language the whole culture of any people in all its aspects; hence the ideal of historical studies regarding law, state, religion, morality, art, literature, economy, etc.

In this way man is understood according to the particularity of time, culture, nation, and occupation. Man is concrete, not some abstract ideal (rational animal) but evolving in a contingent context in freedom.

In human matters the positive and *per accidens* factors belong to a concrete essence; nevertheless, they are not determined without freedom. Not only is science just probable, but also the object of [human] science is not some eternal essence, but a temporally, contingently, freely evolving succession of individuals.[12]

There is a transition from Greek philosophy and from dogmatic realism (of the word of God, of dogmas, of the Scholastic method) to philosophies that are closely connected to the modern sciences and their methods. Galileo, Descartes (*Méthode*), Spinoza (*De emendatione intellectus*), Leibniz (an outstanding mathematician), Kant (transcendental method, closely con-

---

12 [The Latin words 'contingenter' and 'libere' are added by hand in the autograph.]

niana), Hegel (cum interioritate, cum historia, cum scientia humana sui temporis).[13]

5   De Theologia[14]

Brevissime recoluntur notiones quaedam: quaestio de methodo non est introductoria in theologiam sed reflexiva super theologiam iam cognitam; intendit non iam scita repetere sed futuras investigationes dirigere; ideoque recoluntur notiones quaedam.

Theologia tractat de Deo et de aliis prout ad Deum referuntur, ordinantur.[15]

Dividi solet in theologiam naturalem et dogmaticam quibus commune est quod Deum immediate non cognoscunt; nam hac in vita quid sit Deus nescimus, Deum per essentiam non cognoscimus.[16] Quare utraque est scientia mediata.

Differunt principio, obiecto, mediatione, concretione. Principio: naturale rationis lumen, revelatio et fides – ratio per fidem illustratra; obiecto: quae naturaliter cognosci possunt, quae nisi divinitus revelata nobis innotescere non possunt (DB 1795s.); mediatione: per ea quae facta sunt, per verbum Dei revelatum; concretione: ex parte *subiecti* – homo sine gratia solo rationis lumine utens est quodammodo homo abstractus; hac enim in vita omnes habent peccatum originale, gratia Dei indigent, gratiam Dei recipiunt, ea vel bene vel male utantur; ex parte *obiecti* – nam Deus unus praecisione facta a Trinitate, Incarnatione, Redemptione, Fine ultimo, est

nected with Newtonian mechanics), Hegel (with interiority, with history, and with the human sciences of his day).[13]

5   Theology[14]

Let us briefly recall certain notions: the question of method is not part of the introduction to theology but rather a reflection upon theological knowledge already possessed. It is intended not for rehearsing what is already known, but for directing the course of further investigation. Therefore we *recall* certain notions.

Theology treats God and other things as referred or ordered to God.[15]

It is customarily divided into natural and dogmatic theology. What is common to both is the fact that God is not immediately known; for in this life we do not know what God is, we do not know God through his essence.[16] Hence, both of these kinds of theology are mediated sciences.

They differ as to their principle, their object, their mediation, their concreteness. They differ as to their principle: the natural light of reason, revelation and faith – reason illumined by faith; as to their object: what can be known naturally, what can be known by us only through divine revelation (DB 1795–96, DS 3015–16, ND 131–32); as to their mediation: through created things, through the revealed word of God; as to their concreteness: on the part of the *subject* – man apart from grace and using only the light of reason is in a sense an abstraction; for in this life all have original sin, need God's grace, and receive God's grace and use it either well or badly; on the part of the *object* – God as one, prescinding from the Trinity, the Incarna-

---

13 [There follows a handwritten schematic page, 'Theologia,' which can be found on www.bernardlonergan.com at 425B0D0L060.]

14 [This item is dated 5-2-62, indicating that it belongs to the main set of notes for the course 'De methodo theologiae.' This is the date that also appears at the beginning of the main set of notes, so this item may well be an earlier set of notes for the very introduction to the course. It is likely that the same is true for the next two items, 'Theological Operations' and 'The Order of Exposition.' At the top of the page, there are some handwritten words, distinguishing theology as science and as wisdom. As science, theology is concerned with God and with all else as ordered to God. As wisdom, theology is said to be queen of the sciences. For further details, see 42500DTE060 on www.bernardlonergan.com.]

15 Thomas Aquinas, *Summa theologiae*, 1, q. 1, a. 7 c. and ad 2m.

16 Ibid. q. 2, a. 1; q. 12.

Deus abstracte consideratus; *ex parte mediationis* – nam cognoscere Deum per creaturas, praecisione facta a religionibus humanis, ab earum natura, historia, etc., est consideratio abstracta.

Distinguuntur theologia naturalis et dogmatica, ne quidem confundantur, sed non ut prorsus separentur. Ne confundantur: utraque enim habet proprium principium, obiectum, mediationem, gradum concretionis. Non ut separentur: exsistunt enim in eadem mente et de eodem Deo; alia super aliam non addit nisi novam mediationem et maiorem concretionem. Sicut mathematicus cognoscit et systematice adhibet logicam, sicut physicus mathesin, sicut chimicus physicam, sicut biologus chimiam, sicut psychologus sensitivae partis biologiam, ita multo magis theologus dogmaticus cognoscere et adhibere debet theologiam naturalem. Similiter, quia scientiae omnes distinguuntur ut inter se ordinentur et ordinata simul ad concretum cognoscendum adhibeantur. Magis, quia math addit super logicam, etc., sed theologia naturalis per transcendentalia (ens, unum, verum, bonum) Deum cognoscit, sed supernaturale non est super ens sed intra ens.

Sicut theologia dogmatica cum naturali connectitur ratione obiecti (Deus), ita ratione mediationis connectitur cum scientiis humanis (*Geisteswissenschaften*). Scientiae enim humanae tractant de *ordine* vitae humanae in familia, moralitate, societate, educatione, statu, iure, oeconomia, technologia, et de *sensu* vitae humanae prout in intersubiectivitate, in symbolis, in artibus, in litteratura, in historia, in religione, in philosophia, in scientiis deprehenditur.[17] Theologia dogmatica attingit obiectum suum mediantibus *ordine* corporis Christi mystici (theologus est membrum huius corporis, sub magisterio laborat, de ipso corpore mystico inquirit) et *sensu* verbi Dei revelati.[18]

Quare theologia dogmatica analogice se habet ad scientias humanas. Adest similitudo: utraque enim de *sensu* et de *ordine* vitae humanae; adest differentia: scientiae humanae de sensu et ordine tractant tamquam de *obie-*

tion, redemption, and man's ultimate end, is God considered abstractly; on the part of the *mediation* – for to know God through creatures, prescinding from human religions and from their nature and history and so on, is an abstract consideration.

We distinguish between natural theology and dogmatic theology to avoid confusing them, not to separate them completely. To avoid confusing them: each one has its own principle, object, mediation, and degree of concreteness. Not to separate them: for these two theologies exist in the same mind and are about the same God; the second adds to the first only a new mediation and a greater concreteness. Just as a mathematician knows and systematically uses logic, and just as a physicist knows and uses mathematics, a chemist physics, a biologist chemistry, and a psychologist biology, so likewise but much more so must a dogmatic theologian know and use natural theology; similarly, because all sciences are distinct from one another but in such a way that they are ordered to one another, and being so interrelated are used together to attain knowledge of concrete reality; but more so, because while mathematics adds to logic, and so on, natural theology knows God through the transcendentals (being, one, true, good), and the supernatural order is not above being but within being.

Just as dogmatic theology is connected with natural theology by reason of their object, God, so by reason of mediation it is connected with the human sciences, the *Geisteswissenschaften*. For the human sciences treat the *order* of human life in terms of the family, morality, society, education, state, law, economy, and technology, and the *meaning* of human life as found in intersubjectivity, in symbols, in the arts, in literature, in history, in religion, in philosophy, and in the sciences.[17] Dogmatic theology attains its object through the mediation of the *order* of the mystical body of Christ – a theologian is a member of this body, but his work is subordinate to the teaching office of the church and he inquires into the mystical body itself – and the *meaning* of the revealed word of God.[18]

Therefore, dogmatic theology is related analogically to the human sciences. There is a similarity: each deals with the *meaning* and the *order* of human life; but there is also a difference, in that the human sciences treat

17 Erich Rothacker, *Einleitung in die Geisteswissenschaften* (Tübingen: Mohr, 1930).
18 [The material in this paragraph became the core element in the 'problematica altera' of the course 'De methodo theologiae.' See above, p. 361, note 2.]

cto; theologia adhibet sensum quendam divinitus revelatum, ordinem divinitus effectum, tamquam *media* ad obiectum attingendum. Unde DB 2314: 'theologia … positiva … scientiae dumtaxat historicae aequari nequit.' Nam historia tractat de sensu et ordine ut de obiecto; theologia positiva tractat de sensu quodam particulari et de ordine quodam particulari tamquam de mediis ad obiectum cognoscendum.

Praeter hanc analogiam, multipliciter inter se connectuntur theologia dogmatica et scientiae humanae.

Sit *A* sensus verbi Dei et ordo corporis mystici; sit *B* sensus et ordines per scientias humanas investigati. Tunc: Exsistimus secundum *A* inquantum ex *B* convertimur; difficultates et obstacula ex *B* superamus – theologia moralis, ascetico-mystica. Floret *A* inquantum transformat *B*: inquantum facit familiam, moralitatem, societatem, educationem, statum, ius, oeconomiam, intersubiectivitatem, artes, symbola, litteraturas, etc., vere Christianas – theologia pastoralis latissimo sensu.

Universalitas *A* habetur inquantum in qualibet societate, cultura, cuiuslibet gradus perfectionis, introduci, stabiliri, evolvi possit – theologia missionaria.

Methodus determinandi de *A* non est simpliciter alia ac methodus determinandi de *B*; nam datur analogia.

Apologetice: incipimus ex mundo *B* ut ad existentiam *A* probandam procedamus.

Speculative: theologia dogmatica nullas novas species accipit; quoad modum est supernaturalis nam fidem supponit; sed quoad substantiam est naturalis; quare nisi per analogias ex *B* possumus intelligere et concipere notiones *A* proprias, e.g., familia Christiana, educatio Christiana, litteratura Christiana, virtutes Christianas.

Historice investigatur *A* intra contextum concretum quem supplet *B*.

Exsistentia *tou A* ex *B*, in contextu *B*, per transformationem *B*, est de ipsa ratione *A*; est redemptio hominis lapsi; est lex crucis; est bonus odor Christi in mundo.

Haec multiplex interconnexio inter *A* et *B* est radix actualis problematis de methodo theologiae. Non enim evolvi inceperunt istae scientiae humanae empiricae nisi saeculo XIX, et quidem de duplici radice, alia naturalistica (Comte, *Sociologie*), alia idealistica (ex Hegel, eius sequacibus et adversariis). Unde duplex difficultas: alia theoretica (nova scientiae notio) et alia materialis (obruitur theologia inquisitionibus positivis).

meaning and order as their *object*, whereas theology uses a divinely revealed meaning and a divinely established order as the *means* of attaining its object. Hence DB 2314, DS 3886, ND 859: '… positive theology … cannot … be put on a level with the merely historical sciences.' For history deals with meaning and order as its object; positive theology treats of a particular meaning and a particular order as means for attaining a knowledge of its object.

Besides this analogy, dogmatic theology and the human sciences are connected in many ways.

Let *A* be the meaning of the word of God and the order of the mystical body; let *B* be the meanings and orders investigated by the human sciences. Then: We exist according to *A* inasmuch as we are converted from *B*; we overcome the difficulties and obstacles arising from *B* – moral and ascetical-mystical theology. *A* flourishes inasmuch as it transforms *B*: inasmuch as it makes a family, morality, society, education, the state, law, economics, intersubjectivity, the arts, symbols, literature, etc., truly Christian – pastoral theology in the widest sense.

A possesses universality inasmuch as it can be introduced, take root in, and thrive in any society and culture at whatever level of development – missiology.

The method of determining *A* is not simply different from the method of determining *B*, for there is an analogy here.

In apologetics: we begin from the world of *B* to go on to prove the existence of *A*.

Speculatively: dogmatic theology does not admit of any new species. As to its manner it is supernatural, for it presupposes faith; but as to its substance it is natural. Therefore, it is only through analogies taken from *B* that we can understand and form concepts proper to *A*: for example, the Christian family, Christian education, Christian literature, Christian virtues.

A is studied historically within the concrete context supplied by *B*.

The existence of *A* from *B*, in the context of *B*, through the transformation of *B*, is of the very essence of *A*. It is the redemption of fallen man; it is the Law of the Cross; it is the good odor of Christ in the world.

This manifold interconnection between *A* and *B* is the root of the present problem of the method of theology. For those empirical human sciences developed only in the nineteenth century, and indeed from two different roots, one naturalistic (Comte, *Sociologie*) and the other idealistic (from Hegel and his followers and adversaries). Two difficulties, therefore, one theoretical (a new notion of science), the other material (theology overwhelmed by positive research).

Unde ad quaestiones quaedam recentiores.

De novo obiecto theologiae. Christus totus. Ita E. Mersch, NRT 61 (1934) 449–75; *RechScRel* 26 (1936) 129–57; *La théologie du corps mystique,* Bruxelles, 1944, I, 5–156. Ita qui de theologia kerygmatica: cf. C. Colombo, *Problemi e Orientamenti* I, 54 s. (Lakner, Dander, H. Rahner, J. R. Geiselmann).

Contra Y. Congar, DTC, XV, 456–59.

Deus est obiectum theologiae: ratio ultima semper est Deus, et quidem qui hac in vita quid sit nescimus. Quod obiectum in theologia naturali per creaturas, in theologia dogmatica per sensum verbi Dei et per ordinem corporis Christi mediatur. Agitur de mediatione obiecti, qua in mediatione utique Christus locum prorsus centralem tenet.

De nova theologia (C. Colombo, *Problemi,* I, 53;[19] Xiberta, 56 s.[20]). Plane adsunt nova: studia scripturistica, patristica, mediaevalia, conciliaria, ascetica, pastoralia, cathechetica, missiologica, liturgica, etc., sine fine multiplicantur. Non eodem modo proceditur in DTC ac in manualibus saec XIX. *Deus scientiarum Dominus, Divino afflante Spiritu,* nova continent. Pius XII, AAS 35 1943 319 (*Divino afflante*): 'omnes Ecclesiae filii ... ab illo haud satis prudenti studio abhorrere debent, quo quidquid novum est, ob hoc ipsum censetur esse impugnandum, aut in suspicionem adducendum.'

Hence, regarding certain recent questions:

Concerning the new object of theology: the whole Christ. Thus, Émile Mersch, 'Le Christ mystique centre de la théologie comme science,' *Nouvelle revue théologique* 61:5 (1934) 449–75; 'L'Objet de la théologie et le "Christus Totus,"' *Recherches de science religieuse* 26 (1936) 129–57; *La théologie du corps mystique* (Paris: Desclée de Brouwer; Bruxelles: L'Édition universelle, 1944; [4th ed., 1954]) I, 5–156. [In English, *The Theology of the Mystical Body*, trans. Cyril Vollert (London and St Louis: B. Herder Book Co., 1962) 3–128.] Thus also those who speak of kerygmatic theology: see Carlo Colombo, 'La metodologia e la sistemazione teologica,' in *Problemi e Orientamenti di Teologia Dommatica* (Milano: Carlo Marzorati, 1957) I, 54–55; the bibliography on these pages includes references to works by Lakner, Dander, H. Rahner, J.R. Geiselmann.

For the contrary position, Yves M.-J. Congar, s.v. 'Théologie,' in *Dictionnaire de théologie catholique* (DTC) xv, 29, cols. 456–59. [*A History of Theology* 217–21.]

God is the object of theology: its ultimate meaning is always God, and in this life we do not know what God is. In natural theology this object is mediated to us through creatures, and in dogmatic theology through the meaning of the word of God and the order of the mystical body of Christ. It is a question of the mediation of the object, and in this mediation Christ is absolutely central.

Concerning the new theology: Colombo, 'La metodologia e la sistemazione teologica,' in *Problemi ...* I, 53;[19] Bartholomaeo M. Xiberta, *Introductio in sacram theologiam* (Matriti: Consejo Superior de Investigaciones Científicas, Patronato Raimundo Lulio – Instituto Francisco Suárez, 1949); bibliographic references on pp. 56–57.[20] Obviously there are new elements: studies in scripture, patristics, the Middle Ages, the councils, ascetical theology, pastoral theology, catechetics, missiology, liturgy, etc., are multiplying endlessly. The procedure in the *Dictionnaire de théologie catholique* is not the same as

19 [Lonergan would seem to be referring to that part of the bibliography at the end of Colombo's article which is headed 'V. Teologia Positiva e Teologia Scolastica; Natura della Teologia Positiva.' It appears on pp. 52–53.]

20 [All Lonergan has here is 'Xiberta, 56 f.' However, in the bibliography placed at the beginning of *De methodo theologiae*, after listing Colombo's article, Lonergan lists the book by Xiberta inserted above. It seems a safe surmise, then, that he is referring to some or all of the items listed in that part of the bibliography that appears on pp. 56–57 of *Introductio in sacram theologiam*.]

Sed quae nova sunt non nova dogmata, nova theolgia, sed nova problemata, novae divitiae, nova vitalitas.

6   De Operationibus Theologicis[21]

Nisi in fine huius inquisitionis non dicetur quaenam exacte sint operationes
theologicae. Attamen brevissima quaedam huius rei determinatio etiam
praerequiritur ne finem nostrum theologicum praetermittere videamur.

In genere ergo operationes theologicae ex obiecto specificantur; theologiae autem obiectum est in primis Deus, deinde alia quae ad Deum ordinantur.[22] Quare, illae certe sunt operationes theologicae quae tractant de
Deo uno et trino, de creatione, de incarnatione et redemptione, de missione Spiritus sancti et de ecclesia Dei, de gratia, de virtutibus infusis, de
sacramentis, et novissimis.

At ulterius theologia attingit Deum, obiectum suum, non immediate sed
mediate. Hac enim in vita nescimus quid sit Deus, seu per essentiam Deum
non cognoscimus, seu visionem beatam nondum habemus.[23] Huius autem
obiecti mediatio est duplex: alia enim fit mediantibus creaturis, et sic in theologia naturali proceditur; alia autem fit mediante verbo Dei revelato per
ecclesiam nobis proposito (DB 1792), et sic in theologia dogmatica. Quare
etiam theologicae sunt operationes quae respiciunt verbum Dei, nempe,
revelationem, inspirationem sacrae scripturae, eiusdem interpretationem,
traditionem catholicam, ecclesiae magisterium.

Praeterea, theologia non solum particularis quaedam scientia est sed
etiam sapientia. Prout scientia est, de proprio obiecto inquirit; sed prout sa-

that of the nineteenth-century manuals. The papal documents *Deus scientiarum Dominus* and *Divino afflante Spiritu* contain new elements. Pius XII, *Divine afflante Spiritu, Acta Apostolicae Sedis* 35 (1943) 319: 'all sons of the Church ... should abhor that less than prudent zeal by which anything new would for that very reason be considered as deserving of condemnation, or at least suspect.'

But the new things are not new dogmas or new theology; they are new problems, new riches, new vitality.

6   Theological Operations[21]

Only at the end of this study will we be able to say what exactly theological operations are. Nevertheless, some brief preliminary remarks are in order first, lest we seem to lose sight of our theological purpose.

In general, then, theological operations are specified by their object. The object of theology is primarily God, and then all other things ordered to God.[22] Hence, operations that deal with God, both as one and as a Trinity, with creation, the Incarnation and the redemption, the sending of the Holy Spirit and the church of God, grace, the infused virtues, the sacraments, and the last things are certainly theological operations.

But further, theology attains its object, God, not immediately but mediately. For in this life we do not know what God is; that is, we do not know him through his essence, for we do not yet enjoy the beatific vision.[23] But this object is mediated to us in two ways: one mediation is through creatures, and so we have natural theology; the other is through the revealed word of God as communicated to us through the Church (DB 1792, DS 3011, ND 121), and so we have dogmatic theology. Those operations, therefore, that deal with the word of God, that is, with revelation, the inspiration and interpretation of the bible, and Catholic tradition and the teaching office of the church, are also theological operations.

Again, theology is not only a particular science but also wisdom. As a science, it investigates its proper object; but as wisdom it orders all things and

---

21 [This item is dated 7-2-62 at the top of each page. Thus, it probably represents a set of earlier notes for the second class in the course 'De methodo theologiae.' See above p. 361, note 2.]

22 Thomas Aquinas, *Summa theologiae,* 1, q. 1, a. 7 c and ad 2m.

23 Ibid q. 2, a. 1; q. 12.

pientia est, omnia ordinat et omnia iudicat.[24] Unde et dicitur theologia esse regina quaedam scientiarum. Quare et theologicae etiam sunt operationes quibus de loco theologiae inter totum scientiarum circulum determinatur, quibus de valore et limitibus aliarum scientiarum iudicatur, quibus theologia in suos fines sibi assumit non caece sed critice quae in aliis scientiis determinantur.

Iam vero, ubi de aliis scientiis theologice tractatur, maxime ad duo genera attendendum est.

Inprimis ad disciplinas philosophicas: in statu enim naturae purae, non theologia sed philosophia fuisset regina scientiarum; quinimo, etiam in actuali rerum ordine, non desunt qui philosophiae primum locum attribuunt uti Hegeliani, vel philosophiam parvi pendentes scientiis positivis summum honorem tribuunt.

Deinde etiam ad scientias humanas: eiusmodi enim scientiae tractant de *sensu* et *ordine* humanae vitae: de sensu prout intersubiectivitate, symbolis, artibus, linguis, litteraturis, historiis, philosophiis, scientiis, religionibus manifestatur; de ordine prout in familia, in moralitate, in societate, in educatione, in statu, in iure, in oeconomia, in technicis artibus exhibetur.[25]

Quibus scientiis quam proxime ad theologiam accedunt, quippe quae de *sensu* verbi Dei et de *ordine* corporis Christi mystici tractat.

7   De Ordine Expositionis[26]

Duplici ordine procedi potest in exponendis operationibus theologicis: primo, enim, ex maxime particularibus incipi potest, ut deinde ad generaliora, denique ad generalissima procedatur; et ita primo quis exponeret operationes circa ipsum Deum, deinde operationes circa ea quae supernaturalia sunt et immediatius ad Deum referuntur, tertio denique ad remotissima accederetur quae theologiam uti sapientiam respiciunt; deinde, autem, incipi posset ex maxime generalibus ut postea pedetentim ad particulariora procederetur; et sic inciperetur de operationibus humanis ut deinceps de operationibus humanis atque theologicis diceretur.

judges all things.[24] Accordingly, theology is said to be queen of the sciences. Therefore, those operations also are theological that determine the place of theology within the whole circle of sciences, that judge the value and limits of the other sciences, and by which theology adopts for its own purposes, not blindly but critically, the findings of other sciences.

Now when other disciplines are being treated theologically, one must note very carefully two different kinds.

First, the philosophical disciplines: in a state of pure nature, philosophy, not theology, would be queen of the sciences. In fact, even in this present order of things there are those who give pride of place to philosophy, such as the Hegelians, and those who disparage philosophy while giving top honors to the positive sciences.

Second, the human sciences: these are those disciplines that have to do with the *meaning* and the *order* of human life: meaning, as manifested in intersubjectivity, in symbols, the arts, languages, literatures, histories, philosophies, sciences, and religions; order, as found in family life, morality, society, education, the state, law, economy, and technology.[25]

Theology comes as close as possible to these sciences, treating as it does the *meaning* of the word of God and the *order* of the mystical body of Christ.

7   The Order of Exposition[26]

In explaining theological operations we can follow two different orders. First, we can proceed from the most particular to the more general and then to the most general. Following this order, one would first expound the operations concerning God himself, then the operations concerning supernatural realities that refer more directly to God, and third go on to those things that are most remote, which regard theology as wisdom. Second, however, one could begin from the most general and proceed to the more particular; in this way one would begin with human operations and go on from there to speak about human theological operations.

---

24 Ibid. q. 1, a. 6.
25 Rothacker, *Einleitung in die Geisteswissenschaften*; *Logik und Systematik der Geisteswissenschaften*.
26 [This item is dated 7-2-62 at the top of the page. Again, the surmise is that we have here an earlier set of notes for at least part of the second lecture in the course 'De methodo theologiae.']

Prior quidem ordo ideo praestare videtur quia auditor haud dubitare posset de iis tractari quae re vera ad theologiam pertineant; sin autem ex generalissimis inciperetur, maxima ei et continua essent dubia cursum esse de methodo non in genere sed theologica.

Alius autem ordo etiam sua habet emolumenta.

Nam primo non intelligitur quid sit operatio humana et theologica nisi per prius intelligatur quid sit operatio humana.

Deinde, quamvis maxime theologicae sunt operationes quae ipsum Deum respiciunt, hae tamen in theologia non immediate sed mediate Deum attingunt, nempe, mediantibus verbo Dei revelato et magisterio ecclesiae.

Tertio, ipsum verbum Dei revelatum, ipsaque ecclesia, non in vacuo quodam inveniuntur sed multis et diversis modis iisque minime extrinsecis connectuntur cum iis quae ad scientias humanas pertineant: sit enim *A* sensus verbi Dei et ordo corporis Christi; sit *B* sensus vitae humanae eiusque ordo, de quibus in scientiis humanis; tunc secundum *B* sumus omnes peccatores (Rom 1.18 ss., 7), sed secundum *A* ex *B* convertimur individualiter dum socialiter transformationem quandam efficimus *tou B* ut familia, moralitas, societas, educatio, status, ius, oeconomia, technica fiant Christiana, ut similiter artes, symbola, litteraturae, historiae, culturae fiant Christianae. Quae quidem habitudo non extrinseca et per accidens est; gratia enim qua elevans perficit naturam, qua sanans indigentiis naturae advenit; redemptio non solum est fundatio ecclesiae sed etiam est redemptio generis humani, cum missione prorsus universali. Praeterea, tota theologia apologetica ex *B* incipi debet ut exsistentiam *tou A* probaret; et tota theologia speculativa nihil de *A* intelligit (non enim novas accipimus species supernaturales) nisi secundum analogiam *tou B*.

Quarto, totum problema methodologicum nostri temporis non tam ex interna quadam evolutione theologica ortum suum duxit quam ex influxu externo ex novis scientiis philologicis, historicis, psychologicis: quaerimus de methodo theologiae *quia* invaditur theologia per nova studia scripturistica, patristica, conciliaria, mediaevalia, liturgica, symbolica, *quia* ipsa haec invasio facilius attendit ad normas philosophicas et methodologicas sui originis, i.e., idealisticas, Kantianas, naturalisticas, positivisticas, quam ad normas theologice determinatas.

Quibus perspectis, videtur dicendum quod, si ad finem investigationis

The first of these procedures seems to be preferable, because then the student could hardly doubt that what truly pertains to theology is being dealt with; whereas if we were to begin from what are most general, he might have a serious nagging doubt about the course as apparently being about method in general instead of theological method.

However, the second order or procedure also has its advantages.

First, you will not understand human theological operations unless you first understand what human operation is.

Second, although those operations that have to do with God himself are the most theological, nevertheless they attain God not immediately but mediately, that is, through the mediation of the revealed word of God and the teaching office of the church.

Third, both the revealed word of God and the church herself do not exist in a vacuum, but are connected in many different and by no means extrinsic ways with what pertain to the human sciences. For let A stand for the word of God and the order of the body of Christ, and let B stand for the meaning and the order in human living that the human sciences are about. Then according to B we are all sinners (Romans 1.18–32; 7), but according to A we are individually converted from B while socially we bring about a transformation of B in making the family, morality, society, education, the state, law, economics, and technology Christian, so that the arts, symbols, literatures, histories, and cultures may likewise become Christian. This relation is not extrinsic or *per accidens*. Grace as elevating perfects nature and as healing brings to nature what it needs. Redemption is not just the foundation of the church but also the redemption of the whole human race with a mission that is absolutely universal. Besides, the whole of apologetics has to begin from B in order to prove the existence of A; and the whole of speculative theology understands nothing about A (for we do not receive new supernatural *species*) except by analogy with B.

Fourth, the whole methodological problem of our time arises not so much from the internal development in theology itself as from the external influences upon it from recent advances in philological, historical, and psychological sciences. We ask about the method of theology *because* theology is inundated with new studies in scripture, patristics, the councils, the Middle Ages, liturgy, and symbolism, and *because* this inundation itself more readily follows the philosophical and methodological norms of its origin, namely, idealism, Kantianism, naturalism, and positivism, than norms that are theologically determined.

From all the foregoing it seems clear that if we put off to the end of our

tamquam de re minoris momenti remitteretur consideratio scientiarum affinium, totum problema methodologicum potius negligeretur quam serio consideraretur. Quod facile illustratur quaestionibus fundamentalibus nostri temporis: Vaticanum *De fide et ratione, Aeterni Patris, Pascendi, Deus scientiarum Dominus, Divino afflante Spiritu, Humani generis,* sunt documenta methodologica principalia, omniaque respiciunt quaestiones philosophicas et quaestiones ex novis scientiis humanis ortas.[27]

8   Hermeneutica Est Ars Intelligendi Textum, Documentum[28]

1 *Erklären, Verstehen*
(a) Primo modo accipitur haec distinctio quatenus obiectum scientiae naturalis non constituitur per actus humanos intentionales (intelligendi, concipiendi, significandi); obiectum scientiae humanae (*Geisteswissenschaften*) vel partim vel totaliter constituitur per actus humanos intentionales.

E.g., tribunal, processus, condemnatio, exsecutio, si sola phaenomena considerantur et a sensu, elemento intentionali humano praescinditur, non sunt nisi sonus et furia; sicut in scientiis naturalibus ita in humanis fieri possunt investigationes secundum methodum empiricam; sed in his praesupponi debet ut intellecta ipsa constitutio intentionalis.

(b) Altero modo accipitur eadem distinctio quatenus actus humani intentionales et obiectorum constitutivi sunt actus intelligentiae non scientificae sed vulgaris (sensus communis).
Intelligentia scientifica et vulgaris duobus differunt: primo, ex parte

inquiry the consideration of related disciplines as being of lesser importance, then we are neglecting the whole problem of method rather than
giving it serious attention. This is well illustrated by the fundamental questions of our time: Vatican I on faith and reason [DB 1789–1800, DS 3008–20,
ND 118–36], *Aeterni Patris, Pascendi, Deus scientiarum Dominus, Divino afflante
Spiritu,* and *Humani generis* are the principal methodological documents,
and they all deal with philosophical questions and questions arising from
the human sciences in recent times.[27]

8   Hermeneutics Is the Art of Understanding a Text or a Document[28]

1 *Erklären, Verstehen*
(a) Taken in the first way, the distinction is accepted insofar as the object
of natural science is not constituted by the intentional human acts of understanding, conceiving, and signifying, [and] the object of human science
(*Geisteswissenschaften*) is either partly or totally constituted by intentional
human acts.

For example, take the case of a tribunal with a trial, condemnation, and
execution. If only phenomena are considered and no account is taken of
meaning, the intentional human element, it is nothing but sound and fury.
As in the natural sciences so also in the human sciences, investigations can
be carried out according to an empirical method; but in the case of the latter, it must be presupposed that this intentional constitution is understood.

(b) Taken in the second way, the same distinction is accepted insofar as
intentional human acts constitutive of objects are acts not of scientific understanding but of commonsense understanding.

Scientific understanding and commonsense understanding are different

27 [It would seem that after giving the reasons pro and con for treating the
   relation of theology to other disciplines first, Lonergan resolved the question by putting off these issues so that they became part of his 'problematica
   altera.']
28 [This incomplete item appears in the Lonergan Archives at A 462
   (46200DTL060 on www.bernardlonergan.com), surrounded by other, handwritten notes on hermeneutics. It was dated 23-4-62, and has the Latin title
   'Hermeneutica est ars intelligendi textum, documentum.' It is connected
   with the 'problematica altera' of the 1962 course 'De methodo theologiae.'
   This item and the surrounding notes may be regarded as stepping stones
   towards the document on hermeneutics distributed at the summer institute
   at Regis College (now the appendix in *Early Works on Theological Method 1.*]

obiecti, uti Socrates et Athenienses: intelligentia scientifica ad systema cogitur, ad terminos universaliter definitos, ad divisionem terminorum in
primos et derivatos, ad divisionem propositionum in primas et derivatas,
in acceptionem omnium quae systemate praesupponuntur vel implicantur;
e contra, intelligentia vulgaris non cogitur versus systema; ea intelligere
studet unde prompte, faciliter, delectabiliter videat quid dicendum, quid
faciendum, in qualibet e situationibus ordinariis; et plura intelligere super-
fluum, inutile, periculosum iudicat.

Deinde, ex parte subiecti, Thales et puella: intellectus scientificus non
est tantummodo pars alicuius totius operantis, sed ipse est finis, dominans,
ut caeterae hominis partes vel intra parentheses contineantur vel prorsus
fini intellectuali subordinentur; intellectus autem vulgaris non est nisi pars
totius, non quaerit nisi fines totius, non caetera sibi subordinat, sed ipse toti
viventi subordinatur.

(c) Prout primo modo accipitur, distinctio omnino valet. Sed prout altero modo sumitur, reservationes addendae sunt.

(a′) Nisi aliter constat (e.g., in tractatu scientifico), intelligentia vulgaris
est fons tou esse intentionalis et constitutivi communiter, substantialiter,
primo, per se.

(b′) Attamen adesse potest qui dicitur 'motus in ideam' (*die Wendung zur
Idee*), ubi motus intelligitur proprie dictus ut 'actus exsistentis in potentia
prout huiusmodi,' oculus in foetu.

E.g., circa proelium distingue (1) theoria pura bellica, (2) huius theoriae
intelligentia imperfecta et applicatio imperfecta ab utroque duce ante proelium, (3) ipsum proelium prout fit secundum imperfectam (valde imperfectam in vincto) realizationem ideae imperfectae. Notate theoriam puram
bellicam esse ortam non ante omnia proelia sed post permulta, eamque
etiam ex subsequentibus perfici.

E.g., de Christo domino in NT (1) loquuntur facta quasi theophania quaedam, (2) loquuntur tituli, (3) adduntur conceptiones. Cf. *De Verbo Incarnato*.

(c′) Qui motus, quae tendentia in ideam, ex parte obiecti intelligendi observatur, multo magis ex parte subiecti interpretantis invenitur. Quam ob
causam, philosophia hermeneutica restringi non debet ad *Lebensphilosophie*.

Interpres enim magis assimilatur Thali quam puellae: quaerit veritatem

in two ways. The first is on the side of the object, as in the case of Socrates versus the Athenians: scientific understanding is driven towards system, to universally defined terms, to the division of terms into primitive and derived, to the acceptance of all that is presupposed or implied by the system. Commonsense understanding, on the other hand, is not driven towards system: it strives to understand whatever would enable it to see readily, easily, and with satisfaction what should be said or done in any ordinary situation. Anything more than that it considers superfluous, useless, or dangerous.

The second difference is on the side of the subject, as illustrated by Thales and the milkmaid: scientific understanding is not just part of some operating whole but is the end, overriding all else, so that all other aspects of the person are either bracketed or wholly subordinated to its intellectual purpose. Commonsense understanding, however, is but a part of the whole; it seeks only the ends of the whole, and does not subordinate all else to itself but is itself subordinated to the whole living person.

(c) Taken according to the first way, the distinction is entirely valid. Taken in the second way, however, there are some reservations to be made.

(a′) Except in certain cases (in scientific treatises, for example), commonsense understanding is the source of intentional, constitutive existence, universally, substantially, primarily, and per se.

(b′) Nevertheless there can be present what is called the movement towards the idea, *die Wendung zum Idee*, where the movement is understood to be a movement in the proper sense of the word as 'the act of a being in potency as such' – for example, the eye in a fetus.

In the case of a battle, for instance, distinguish between (1) a pure theory of war, (2) an imperfect understanding of this theory and an imperfect application of it by both commanders before the battle, (3) the battle itself as fought in accordance with the imperfect realization (very imperfect in the case of the loser) of the imperfect idea. Note that a pure theory of warfare developed not before all battles but only after a large number of them had been fought and was perfected as a result of subsequent battles.

Concerning Christ in the New Testament, for example: (1) some events are spoken of as seeming theophanies, (2) certain titles are mentioned, and (3) conceptions are added. See *De Verbo incarnato*.

(c′) This movement, this tendency towards the idea, is observed on the side of the object to be understood, and much more clearly found on the side of the interpreting subject. For this reason, hermeneutic philosophy must not be restricted to *Lebensphilosophie*.

For an interpreter is more like Thales than the milkmaid: he seeks objec-

obiectivam; non continetur finibus propriae vitae; quod a Bultmann minus perspici videtur. Quamvis singuli textus secundum intelligibilitatem intelligentiae vulgaris sint intelligendi, tamen sat conspicuus est motus in ideam quatenus series vel totalitas textuum considerantur. Technice enim distinguuntur sensus litteralis et figurativus, genera litteraria, evolutio linguarum, litteraturarum, idearum, etc.

(d′) Hic motus in ideam ex parte interpretum non unicus quidam solusque invenitur …

9   De Genesi Categoriarum Theologicarum[29]

Categoriae adhuc fere implicitae. *Religio*: Eliade, Jung Morel.[30]

1 *Sum. theol.*, I, 44, 4, 3m: '… omnia appetunt Deum ut finem, appetendo quodcumque bonum, sive appetitu intelligibili, sive sensibili, sive naturali qui est sine cognitione: quia nihil habet rationem boni et appetibilis nisi secundum quod participat Dei similitudinem.'

Unde concludes sensum ultimum, intelligibilitatem completam, omnis motus vel processus, omnis gaudii et tristitiae, omnis desiderii vel timoris, omnis inquisitionis et consilii, esse religiosum.

2 Diximus 'ultimum' sensum, 'completam' intelligibilitatem; quae tamen adiecta supponunt iam peractam esse differentiationem mundi profani et mundi sacri; tacite enim assumitur mundum profanum sensum quendam proprium habere, qui tamen ultimatim cum sensu religioso complendus est, e.g., quia omne bonum rationem boni habet quia bonitatem divinam participat. At ipsa haec differentiatio S. Thomam a S. Bonaventura distinguit, cf. Y. Congar, DTC XV (29), 388; etiam 386–88; 396.[31]

tive truth, and is not content with the ends of his own everyday life – something that Bultmann seems to have poorly grasped. Although each text is to be understood according to the intelligibility of commonsense understanding, still there is a quite evident movement towards the idea insofar as a series or totality of texts are considered. For there is a technical distinction between the literal and the figurative senses, the literary genres, the development of languages, of literatures, of ideas, and so forth.

(d') This movement towards idea is not found uniquely and solely on the part of the interpreters [sentence ends]

9   The Genesis of Theological Categories[29]

Categories still largely implicit. Religion: Eliade, Jung, Morel.[30]

1 *Summa theologiae*, 1, q. 44, a. 4, ad 3m: '... in desiring anything that is good, all things are desiring God as their end, whether they do so by intellectual desire or sentient desire or noncognitional natural desire; because nothing possesses the note of goodness and desirability except according to its likeness to God.'

From this it follows that the ultimate meaning, the complete intelligibility, of all movement or process, all joy and sorrow, all desire and fear, all inquiry and deliberation, is religious.

2 We say 'ultimate' meaning, 'complete' intelligibility. These adjectives, however, suppose that the differentiation between the profane world and the sacred world has already been accomplished; for we assume that, while the profane world does have its own proper meaning, it must nevertheless ultimately be completed by a religious meaning, since every good has its goodness because it participates in divine goodness. But that very differentiation distinguishes St Thomas from St Bonaventure; see Yves Congar, DTC xv (29) col. 388; also cols. 386–88 and 396.[31]

---

29 [Lonergan Archive document A 857. This and the next two items were relocated by Lonergan in a folder labeled 'Various Papers,' which contains material that seems to have been used both in his lectures on 'Knowledge and Learning' at Gonzaga University in 1963 and in the 1964 institute on method at Georgetown University. The three papers are related to the 'problematica altera' in the spring course 'De methodo theologiae.' This item is dated at the top of the page 22.5.62, and so was used late in the course.]

30 [The three names are handwritten in the autograph.]

31 [*A History of Theology* 107; also 103–107, 120–21.]

388: 'Comme celles-ci [sciences, philosophie] ne valent que dans leur rapport à Dieu, les sciences n'apporteront pas à la sagesse chrétienne une connaissance de la nature des choses en elle-même, mais des exemples et des illustrations; elles ont une valeur symbolique pour aider à l'intelligence de la vraie révélation, laquelle vient d'en haut et est spirituelle. Ceci nous fait comprendre encore en quel sens les augustiniens parleront de la philosophie *ancilla theologiae*: les sciences n'existent que pour servir et on ne leur demande que de servir, non d'apporter quelque vérité en leur nom propre. Tel est bien le sens de l'expression, par exemple, dans les lettres de Grégoire ix et d'Alexandre iv à l'université de Paris.'[32] Ex alia parte apud Albertum et Thomam, uti voluit Gilson 'pour meiux s'assurer les services de son esclave, la théologie vient de commencer par l'affranchir.'[33]

3 At ipsa positio Augustiniana non simpliciter praetermittit vel ignorat sive differentiationem mundi sacri et profani, sive distinctionem cognitionis profanae et sacrae (rationis superioris et inferioris); tantummodo exprimit iudicium 'veritatis' et valoris circa rationem inferiorem. Longe aliter res se habet apud hominem 'archaicum' ubi nondum facta est differentiatio mundi sacri et profani.[34]

10   De Bono Humano[35]

1 Verum et falsum sunt in mente; bonum et malum sunt in rebus. Quare, qui de bono quaerit, de concreto, actuali quaerit.

Col. 388: 'As these [sciences, philosophy] have validity or meaning only in their relation to God, so the sciences will not convey to Christian wisdom a knowledge of the nature of things in itself but only examples and illustrations. They have a symbolic value to assist the understanding of true Revelation, which comes from on high and is spiritual. We also see in what sense the Augustinians will talk of philosophy as the "handmaid of theology." The sciences exist only to serve, and they may be asked only for that. Certainly they are not expected to impart any truth of their own. Such is very likely the meaning of the expression in the letters of Gregory IX and Alexander IV to the University of Paris.'[32] For Albert and Thomas, on the other hand, as Gilson put it, 'In order to better secure the services of her handmaid, theology is now just beginning to give her her freedom.'[33]

3 The Augustinian position, however, neither simply disregards nor is ignorant of either the differentiation of the sacred and profane worlds or the distinction between profane and sacred learning (the lower and the higher reason); it merely pronounces a judgment of 'truth' and of value upon the lower reason. This is far removed from the situation of so-called primitive man, where the differentiation of sacred and profane worlds has not yet been made.[34]

10   The Human Good[35]

1 The true and the false are in the mind; good and evil are in things. Hence, one who asks about good is asking about what is concrete, actually existing.

---

32 [Ibid. 107.]

33 [Congar gives the source in Gilson's writings in the original article at the bottom of col. 388.]

34 [The remainder of this document consist of a series of quotations from Mircea Eliade, *Forgerons et alchimistes* (Paris: Ernest Flammarion, 1956) and Georges Morel, *Le sens de l'existence selon S. Jean de la Croix*, vol. III: *Symbolique* (Paris: Aubier, 1961). The quoted texts may be found at item 85700DTL060 on the website www.bernardlonergan.com.]

35 [Lonergan Archives document A 858. This document is dated at the top of the page 27.2.62. This places it early in the 1962 course 'De methodo theologiae,' at least in one of Lonergan's outlines of the course. It is likely that he did not use this material, at least early in the course, but rather that, if it was used at all, it figured in the 'Problematica altera' material that he introduced towards the end. The uncertainty as to where precisely to locate this material is reflected in the summer course at Regis College that year, where material on the human good appears early, but with some hesitation as to

2 Bonum humanum: non totum bonum respicit, uti in ontologia boni, sed illud tantum quod ex analysi rerum humanarum manifestatur.

3 Schema:

Subiecti potentia	Actus	Mediatio socialis	Obiectum
indigentia-capacitas	operatio	cooperatio	bonum particulare
perfectibilitas	habitus acquisitus	instituta	bonum ordinis
libertas	orientatio	relationes interpersonales	valores terminales

4 *Annotationes*

(a) Indigentia-capacitas, e.g., fames est indigentia, cui correspondet capacitas cibos quaerendi, manducandi.

Operatio, cooperatio, e.g., Robinson Crusoe, vel membrum societatis.

Bona particularia: quae in se sunt particularia, et indigentiis particularibus respondent; ita hoc pomum, hoc prandium, haec visio beata.

(b) Transitur ex prima ad secundam lineam quia in genere bona particularia non sunt aeterna sicut visio beata sed transeuntia; homo vult non tantummodo hoc prandium sed prandium cotidianum.

Bonum ordinis: *materialiter* dicit non tantum appetibilia (bona particularia) sed etiam appetentes, appetitus, appetitiones, media quibus appetibilia attinguntur; *formaliter* dicit talem ordinem de facto effectivum ut recurrentibus indigentiis recurrunt etiam bona particularia.

Quare minime agitur de ideali quodam, de eo quod esse debeat sed de facto non est, quod efficax esse debeat sed efficax non est; sed unice agitur de illo ordine, illa ordinationum complexione, unde de facto in hac societate hic et nunc bona particularia recurrunt.

2 Human good: does not extend to all good, as in the ontology of good, but only to that which becomes known from an analysis of all that is human.

3 Schematic outline:

Potency of subject	Act	Social mediation	Object
need-ability	operation	cooperation	particular good
perfectibility	acquired habit	institutions	good of order
freedom	orientation	interpersonal relations	terminal values

4 Notes:

(a) *Need-ability*: for example, hunger is a need, to which there corresponds the ability for seeking and eating food.

Operation, cooperation: e.g., Robinson Crusoe; member of society.

Particular goods: those which in themselves are particular and respond to particular needs: thus, this apple, this dinner, this beatific vision.

(b) We move from the first to the second line above, because particular goods are generally not eternal, as the beatific vision is, but are transitory; a man wants not only this particular dinner but dinner every day.

The *good of order*: *materially* it refers not only to what are desirable (particular goods) but also to desirers, appetites, desires, and the means by which the desirable are attained; *formally* it refers to an order that is in fact effective in satisfying recurring needs with recurring particular goods.

Thus, it is not at all a question of some ideal, of what ought to be and in fact is not, of what ought to be effective but is not. At issue here is only that order of things, that complex of orderings, whereby in this society here and now particular goods recur.

---

whether that is the best place to put it. Lonergan mentions there that he has two sets of notes (where the first is presumably chapters 1 and 2 constituting the first problematic, and the second are notes towards chapter 3, the second problematic, from the Gregorian course). See Bernard Lonergan, *Early Works on Theological Method 1* 34–40 and especially 301: 'I have two packs of notes! One corresponds to the typewritten stuff [i.e., the notes distributed from the Roman course] and the other, equally big, which I hope to work in some time in the course of these two weeks. The stuff on the human good was pulled out of the second stack.' While there is a notion of the invariant structure of the human good earlier in Lonergan's work, where the structure is determined by the threefold division of particular goods, the good of order, and values, this may just be the first appearance of a schematic presentation. The presentation eventually assumed eighteen terms. See Lonergan, *Method in Theology* 48.]

Non agitur de illo ordine prout theoretice concipitur; eiusmodi conceptiones possunt esse verae vel falsae, et semper sunt magis abstractae quam
actualis ordo, magis fixae et immutabiles quam actualis ordo.

Instituta sunt: familia, societas, educatio, moralitas, status, ius, oeconomia, technica. Sunt bases difficile mobiles et communiter agnitae unde
fiunt cooperationes et unde habetur bonum ordinis. Non sunt vel ipsae
cooperationes vel ipsum bonum ordinis, sed ad haec comparantur sicut
potentia ad actum, sicut conditio ad conditionatum.

E.g., institutum familiale non facit ut singuli homines uxores ducant, sed
facit ut talis sit familia si matrimonium ineatur; pariter, stante eodem instituto familiali, aliud et aliud est bonum ordinis in diversis familiis. Instituta
oeconomica non faciunt ut homines laborent sed determinant quid emolu-
menti percipiant si laborant; et eodem manente instituto tempora bona et
depressiones oeconomicae sibi succedunt (h.e., bonum ordinis nunc floret
et mox decidit).

Perfectibilitas, habitus acquisiti, iam superius explicati sunt.[36] Homo est per-
fectibilis inquantum per exercitium, addiscentiam, persuasionem eo pervenit ut prompte, faciliter, delectabiliter ponat quamlibet ex complexione
combinationum operationum differentiatarum.

Specializatio est ordinatio particularis ad munus quoddam determinatum
in institutis exercendum. Ita a puero quaeritur quid futurus sis. Qui respondet se fore astronautam, vehiculi publici conductorem, Romanum Ponti-
ficem, etc. Specializatio est vel a natura (mas, femina; dona particularia;
aptitudo naturalis) vel ex habitibus acquisitis.

(c) *Transitur* ex secunda linea ad tertiam quando observatur nulla instituta, nullum ordinis bonum, esse unicum possibile. Familia potest esse
patriarchalis vel matriarchalis, monogamica et polygamica, monogamia
permanens et monogamia serialis. Educatio potest esse classica, philologi-
ca, moderna, scientifica, technica. Ius potest vel quam maxime consuetudi-
narium, unde iudices magnam discretionem personalem adhibere possunt,
vel potest esse quam maxime codificatum unde iudices nisi determinationes legales sequi neque debent neque possunt. Multi sunt gradus interme-
dii; neque codices omnes eadem de omnibus determinant. Capitalismus,
socialismus; democratia, totalitarianismus; ...

The question is not about that order as conceived theoretically. Such conceptions can be true or false and are always more abstract than the actual order, and more fixed and immutable than the actual order.

Institutions: the family, society, education, morality, the state, law, the economy, technology. These are the foundations not easily changed and commonly recognized as fostering cooperative efforts and hence the good of order. They are not the cooperative efforts themselves or the good of order itself, but are related to these as potency to act, as condition to conditioned.

The institution of the family, for example, does not cause people to marry; rather, marriage results in a family; also, while the institution of the family remains the same, different families have different goods of order. Economic institutions do not cause people to work, but determine what benefit they will receive if they do work; and while the economic institution remains the same, good times and depressions follow each other – that is, the good of order now flourishes but soon declines.

Perfectibility and *acquired habits* have been explained above.[36] One is perfectible inasmuch as through practice, additional learning, and persuasion one becomes able to perform any of the complex of combinations of differentiated operations promptly, easily and with enjoyment.

Specialization is a particular ordination to a determinate function to be performed in a given institution. A boy is asked what he is going to be when he grows up. He answers: an astronaut, a streetcar driver, the pope, etc. Specialization results either from nature (male, female; particular goods; natural aptitude) or from acquired habits.

(c) We move from the second line to the third when we observe that no institution, no good of order, is the only one possible. A family can be patriarchal or matriarchal, monogamous or polygamous, permanently monogamous or serially monogamous. Education can be classical, philological, modern, scientific, technical. Law can be either mostly a matter of custom, giving judges considerable personal discretion, or it can be very strictly codified so that judges must follow only what the laws have determined. There are many intermediate types of law, and not all law codes make the same determinations about everything. [Economic and political institutions] Capitalism, socialism; democracy, totalitarianism; ...

36 [This is likely a reference to the material on Piaget in the main set of notes; see above, pp. 362–69. This would confirm the view that these notes on the human good were originally written to be introduced early in the course.]

Iam vero pueri de bonis particularibus disputant, pugnant; homines de bono ordinis; ...

Valor, valores, dicunt cur hic ordo potius quam ille eligendus sit; valor ergo est ratio proxima rationalem appetitum movens.

Diversimode a diversis concipitur. Reductionistae valorem ponunt in quadam maximizatione bonorum particularium; Bentham, 'greatest happiness of the greatest number'; calculus hedonisticus. Quibus opponnutur qui ideale quoddam agnoscunt aestheticum, intellectuale, morale, religiosum, unde 'id quod esse debet' sensum habet qui ad maximizationem bonorum particularium reduci non potest.

Orientatio, scilicet, directio in quam tendit usus libertatis. Nulla directio, homo inauthenticus, non vult nisi illa quae caeteri volunt; et caeteri similiter. Orientatio deliberata, vel in maximizationem bonorum meorum, vel in maximizationem bonorum pro omnibus, vel in ideale quoddam aestheticum, intellectuale, morale, religiosum.

Ipsa orientatio est valor originalis, originans, secundum illud Kant, nihil est simpliciter bona nisi bona voluntas. Unde distinguitur a valoribus terminalibus, socialismus, monogamia, ... Hic recurrunt omnia quae de subiecto diximus, de eius horizonte, de eius conversione, de eius authentia vel inauthentia.[37]

Relationes interpersonales (concreta apprehensio ordinis vitae humanae).[38] Oriuntur ex statu, (role), in institutis: ita vir, uxor, pater, mater, filius, filia, frater, soror; professor, auditor; confessor, paenitens; ...

Oriuntur ex orientatione libertatis, et mutantur mutata hac orientatione.

Priores secundum potentialitatem reiectam, suppressam, examinantur theoria Freudiana, secundum varia crimina familiae Laii.[39]

Posteriores examinantur dialectica interpersonali: Dominus-servus, Hegel, *Phänomenologie;* Fessard: Iudaeus – Paganus.[40]

Boys argue and fight over particular goods, men over the good of order.

Value, and values, are the reasons why this order is preferable to another. Value, therefore, is the proximate reason that moves the rational appetite.

Value is conceived differently by different people. Reductionists place value in the maximization of particular goods; Bentham, 'the greatest happiness of the greatest number'; hedonistic calculus. The opposite view is held by those who acknowledge an aesthetic, intellectual, moral, or religious ideal, in which 'ought' has a meaning that cannot be reduced to the maximization of particular goods.

Orientation: the direction in which the exercise of freedom tends. Lack of direction: the inauthentic person, one who wants only what the others want; and similarly for the rest. Deliberate orientation: either towards the maximization of my goods, or towards the maximization of goods for all, or towards some aesthetic, intellectual, moral, or religious ideal.

An orientation itself is an original and originating value; as Kant remarked, nothing is simply good except a good will. Hence, it is to be distinguished from terminal values, such as socialism, monogamy ... All that we have said about the subject, about the subject's horizon, conversion, authenticity or lack thereof, comes up again here.[37]

Interpersonal relations (concrete apprehension of the order of human life).[38] Some relationships result from one's role in institutions: husband, wife, father, mother, son, daughter, brother, sister; professor, student; confessor, penitent; ...

Others result from the orientation of freedom, and change along with a change in that orientation.

The former relationships with respect to the rejection or suppression of their potentiality are examined in Freudian theory, dealing with the various crimes in Laius's family.[39]

The latter are examined by interpersonal dialectic: master-slave (Hegel, *Phenomenology*); [Gaston] Fessard: Jew-pagan.[40]

---

37 [Another reference to material in the main set of notes.]
38 [The Latin words 'concreta apprehensio ordinis vitae humanae' are handwritten in the autograph.]
39 [A reference to Sophocles' play *Oedipus Rex* and to the use Freud made of it in developing his theories.]
40 [See Gaston Fessard, *De l'actualité historique* 40–52.]

11   Sensus[41]

1 Gradus: intersubiectivus, symbolicus, artisticus, linguisticus.[42]

(a) *Sensus intersubiectivus.*

Intersubiectivitas: quo unum sumus – quasi daretur gradus conscientiae quae distinctionem inter 'ego' et 'tu' antecedit; sicut manus mea sponte ad caput meum protegendum movetur, ita etiam ad alios adiuvandos, protegendos, movetur.[43]

Sensus intersubiectivus perspicitur in vultu, motibus oculorum, labiorum, musculorum facialium, capitis, digitorum, manuum, brachiorum, corporis, pedum. Evolvitur in saltationibus, ritibus, caeremoniis, salutationibus.

Exemplo sit surrisus (smile).

(a') Habet sensum; non est tantummodo motus labiorum, oculorum; quia habet sensum, non plateas circuimus omnibus arridentes; male intelligeremur; qui sensus ad motus faciales comparatur sicut forma ad materiam.

(b') Unde surrisus facillime apprehenditur. Apprehensio non est functio undularum luminis, soni, quae nos afficiunt; est activa quaedam selectio ut, ex omnibus sonis platearum, vocem socii seligimus ut ea fere sola audiatur – quod fieri potest praecise quia sensum habet illa vox; si sine sensu loqueretur, non magis eum audiremus quam caetera. Apprehensio surrisus

11   Meaning[41]

1 Degrees: intersubjective, symbolic, artistic, linguistic.[42]

(a) Intersubjective meaning.

Intersubjectivity: by which we are one – as if there were a level of consciousness prior to the distinction between 'I' and 'you.' Just as my hand moves spontaneously to protect my head, so also does it move to help or protect others.[43]

Intersubjective meaning is present in one's facial expression, the movements of one's eyes, lips, facial muscles, head, fingers, hands, arms, body, feet. It is further developed in dances, rituals, ceremonies, formal salutations.

Let us take the smile as an example.

(a′) A smile has a meaning. It is not just a movement of the lips and eyes. And because it has a meaning, we do not go around the streets smiling at everyone; if we did, we should be misunderstood. Its meaning is to the facial movements as form to matter.

(b′) Hence, a smile is easily apprehended. Apprehending is not a function of light waves or sound waves acting upon us; rather, it is an active selection, so that of all the street noises we hear we can single out the voice of a companion in such a way as to hear him alone. This is possible precisely because that voice has a meaning; if he were speaking without a meaning, we should not hear him any more than the other sounds. The apprehen-

---

41 [Archive document A 870 (87000DTL060), dated at the top of the page 19-5-62. This date places this material towards the end of the Gregorian course, but it is interesting that these notes are found in the archives in the same file as the previous section on the human good, whose date places it early in the course, at least as Lonergan conceived it. Material on meaning follows Lonergan's treatment of the human good in the 1962 summer institute at Regis College; see Lonergan, *Early Works on Theological Method 1* 40–42, where it forms part of the second 'stack' of notes that he was trying to integrate with the main set of notes he had distributed. These are very early notes towards the lengthy chapter on meaning that would appear ten years later in *Method in Theology*, after the chapter on the human good.]

42 [These 'degrees' or 'levels' become 'carriers' in the chapter on meaning in *Method in Theology*.]

43 See Max Scheler, *Wesen und Formen der Sympathie: Der 'Phänomenologie und Theorie der Sympathiegefühle,'* 5th ed. (Frankfurt/Main: Verlag G. Schulte-Bulmke, 1948). [In English, *The Nature of Sympathy* (Hamden, CT: Archon Books, 1954).]

non est conclusio ex motibus facialibus deducta; si tales et tales sunt motus, habetur surrisus; atqui … ergo … Habetur intelligentia in ipsis sensibilibus; intelligentia incarnata alteri incarnatae intelligentiae sese manifestat.

(c′) Sensus in surrisu contentus est naturalis, spontaneus. Addiscimus ambulare, loqui, natare; sed arridere non addiscimus; imo, surrisus authenticus fit sine advertentia, sine intentione praevia. Sensus subridendi non addiscitur, sicut sensus vocabulorum; unusquisque quasi ipse primus sensum subridendi invenit. Sensus subridendi in alium non reducitur, per alium non elucidatur; iacet intra campum intentionalitatis, constituitur tamen per intentionalitatem non conceptualem sed incarnatae intelligentiae.

(d′) Comparantur sensus intersubiectivus et sensus conceptualis.

Conceptualis univocitatem vult; surrisus multa et diversa exprimit, agnitionem, welcome, amicitiam, amorem, gaudium, delectationem, satisfactionem, pacem, irrisionem, ironiam, resignationem, defatigationem, tristitiam; risus sardonius, aenigmaticus.

Conceptualis potest esse non solum verax vel mendax sed etiam verus vel falsus; surrisus potest esse verax vel mendax, non autem verus aut falsus; sensus in surrisu contentus est sensus potius rei, facti, personae, quam sensus verbi.

Conceptualis sese distinguit: concipimus distincte quae sentimus, desideramus, timemus, cogitamus, cognoscimus, volumus, iubemus, intendimus. Sensus intersubiectivus est indifferentiatus, est sensus personae in habitudine ad aliam personam.

Conceptualis est de rebus, obiectivus; intersubiectivus situationem supponit (occurrere, adesse, habitudines praevias), situationem interpersonalem agnoscit, confitetur, situationem determinat, est elementum quasi constitutivum situationis interpersonalis actualis, subiectum potius trahit quam describit, subiectum revelat: non fit deductio ex surrisu in statum animae, sed ipsa persona fit transparens, sese manifestat; pertinet ad gradum communicationis quae antecedit distinctionem inter signum et significatum, corpus et animam.

(b) Sensus aestheticus.[44]

sion of a smile is not a conclusion deduced from facial expressions: If there is this or that movement, it is a smile; but there is such a movement; therefore ... Understanding is had in the very data of sense; one incarnate understanding manifests itself to another incarnate understanding.

(c′) The meaning of a smile is natural and spontaneous. We learn to walk, to speak, to swim; but we do not learn to smile. A genuine smile occurs inadvertently, without any previous intention. Nor is the meaning of a smile something we learn, like the meaning of words. Each person discovers by himself the meaning of a smile as if he or she were the first to do so. Its meaning is not reducible to any other meaning, is not clarified or explained by any other meaning. It lies within the field of intentionality, yet it is constituted not by conceptual intentionality but by the intentionality of incarnate understanding.

(d′) Comparison between intersubjective and conceptual meaning.

Conceptual meaning desires univocity, whereas a smile can express many things: recognition, welcome, friendship, love, joy, delight, satisfaction, peace, derision, irony, resignation, weariness, sadness; and there are sardonic smiles and enigmatic smiles.

Conceptual meaning can be not only sincere or deceptive but also true or false; a smile can be sincere or deceptive but not true or false, for the meaning contained in a smile is the meaning of a thing, a deed, a person, rather than the meaning of a word.

There are several kinds of conceptual meaning. We conceive in different ways what we feel, desire, fear, think, know, will, order, and intend. Intersubjective meaning is undifferentiated; it is the meaning of one person in relation to another.

Conceptual meaning is about things, is objective. Intersubjective meaning supposes a situation (encounter, presence, previous relationships); it recognizes and acknowledges the interpersonal situation and determines it; it is as it were a constitutive element of an actual interpersonal situation; it attracts rather than describes a subject. It reveals a subject: there is no deduction made from a smile to the state of one's soul, but one becomes transparent, reveals oneself; it belongs to the degree of communication that is prior to the distinction between a sign and the signified, between body and soul.

(b) Aesthetic meaning.[44]

---

44 See Susanne K. Langer, *Feeling and Form.* [The reference to Langer is added by hand in the autograph.]

Art: obiectification of a purely experiential pattern. Ars obiectificat schema experiendi purum. Schema abstractum: uti in foliis musicis; indenta-
tiones in disco gramophonico. Schema concretum: uti in ipsis percipiendi
actibus, in motibus corporis, in sonis audiendis, in coloribus videndis, etc.

Schema experiendi: experientia non est chaos quod per omnia et quaelibet obiecta externa in nobis producitur, sed est selectio atque organizatio
quae facit differentiam inter ea quibus attendimus et alia, pariter praesentia, quae praetermittimus.

Unde facile melodiam, minime strepitum urbis, repetimus; facile versus
addiscimus; facile superficiem decoratam videmus. Sicut arbor e trunco
per ramos ad folia modo organico extenditur atque unitur, ita decoratio
e minoribus variationibus per complexitatem crescentem ad unum totum
organizatum maximeque perceptibile pervenit.

Schema experiendi purum: aliud est experiri, et aliud est experientia uti
in ordine ad fines ulteriores. Sensus fieri possunt quasi apparatus quo subiecta ad uniformitatem reducta in mundo mechanizato agunt: automatic
behaviour of a ready-made subiect in a ready-made world. Sensus fieri possunt instrumenta intelligentiae scientificae, quae statim pergit ad momentum expertorum relate ad theoriam. Sensus e nativa sua operatione detrudi
possunt per theorias physicas, physiologicas, epistemologicas, utilitarianas.

Schema experiendi purum est operatio sensitiva secundum proprias suas
leges in proprias suos fines; accedunt associationes naturales ipsa vita se-
lectae, emotiones et affectus ipsi rei visae qua visibili, ipsis sonis qua audi-
bilibus, convenientes; est vita sensitiva in propria sua aperitudine, caeteris
omissis quae hanc vitam ad meram instrumentalitatem reducunt.

Quod schema purum, ab aliis curis liberatum, sua spontaneitate, vitalita-
te, sese extendit, evolvit, organizat, finalitatem suam attingit. Ita rhythmus
habetur ubi prior quique motus subsequentem necessitat (exspirare, inspirare); construuntur tensiones ut resolvantur.

Sensus huius schematis est elementaris, non denotativus, sed immanens;
est sensus vitae. Sicut tamen est liberatio sensus ab instrumentalizatione,
ita etiam est quasi transformatio mundi: unde aestheticum habetur vel ut
illusorium vel ut magis reale quam quae vulgo realitas habetur; revelatur
mundus alius, diversus, inusitatus, mirus, novus, remotus et tamen intimus.

Sicut transformatur mundus, ita transformatur subiectum; desinit autom-

Art: objectification of a purely experiential pattern. Abstract pattern: as in musical scores, or the grooves in phonograph records. Concrete pattern: as in the acts of perceiving themselves, in movements of the body, in sounds to be heard, in colors to be seen, etc.

Experiential pattern: experience is not a chaos produced in us by any and every external object, but is a selection and organization that differentiates between what we pay attention to and all other objects, equally present, which we ignore.

Hence, we can easily repeat a melody but not street noises; we easily learn poetry and notice a decorated wall. Just as a tree organically extends from its trunk through its branches to the leaves, so does a decoration grow from minor variations through complexity to arrive at one organized and most easily perceptible whole.

A purely experiential pattern: experiencing is one thing, but it is quite another to use experience towards ulterior ends. The senses can become like mechanisms whereby subjects are reduced to uniformity to act in a mechanized world: automatic behavior of a ready-made subject in a ready-made world. The senses can become instruments of scientific intelligence, which immediately head towards those experiences that are important for theory. The senses can be forced out of their native operation by physical, physiological, epistemological, or utilitarian theories.

A purely experiential pattern is an operation of the senses that follows its own laws for its proper ends. In addition, there are natural associations chosen by life itself, emotions and feelings that are in accord with a visible object itself as visible and with sounds as audible. That is the life of the senses in its proper openness, without anything else that would reduce this life to mere instrumentality.

This pure pattern, freed from other concerns, by reason of its spontaneity and vitality, grows, develops, organizes, and attains its finality. In this way there is produced a rhythm in which each prior movement necessitates a subsequent (breathing out, breathing in); tensions are set up to be resolved.

The meaning of this pattern is elemental, not denotative but immanent; it is the meaning of life. Just as it is a freeing of the senses from instrumentalization, so also it is a sort of transformation of the world. Hence, the aesthetic is held to be either illusory or more real than what is commonly regarded as reality. Another, a different, world is revealed, one that is unusual, wonderful, new, remote, and yet intimate.

As the world is transformed, so is the subject; one ceases to be an au-

aton bene adaptatum ad omnes usus vitae quotidianae; oritur subiectum emergens, ex-sistens, mirans, originale, originans.[45]

Quod schema experiendi purum obiectificatur. De se experitur, sed tantummodo experitur; est intra subiectum conscium, sed sine obiectificatione manet quodammodo implicitum, velatum, absconditum; ut revelatur, inspiciatur, repetatur, fruitione detur, transponitur ex parte subiecti ad partem obiecti. Quae obiectificatio abstrahit ab experientia actuali, ea seligit quae maioris momenti videntur, quae clarius sensum vitae manifestant; abstrahitur forma, non tamen concipiendo, sed faciendo.

(c) Sensus symbolicus; Newman: Cor ad cor lquitur; Pascal: le coeur a ses raisons que la raison ne connaît pas.[46]

Sensus symbolicus ipsis affectibus inest; sed affectibus *et* ipsi disponimur, orientamur, dirigimur *et* erga mundum, vitam, personas, res nos habemus.

Symbolum ergo est imago (1) quae affectum vel inducit vel exprimit et (2) quale sit subiectum in quali mundo revelat.

Affectum inducit: sicut obiectum reale, ita etiam imago eius affectum quendam excitat, et quidem vel modo opinato (times sed habes quod timendum est) vel modo inopinato (parvuli tenebras timent quia mundus visibilis disparet sed mundus audibilis manet quin obiecta videri et identificari possint). Affectum exprimit: imago sponte formata manifestat statum subiecti affectivum (dispositiones, habitus, capacitates, indigentias, nisus, finalitatem). Subiectum suumque mundum revelat: unde in symbolis sensus profundior esse potest (omnia Deum appetunt), sicut etiam eorum sensus graviores perturbationes et aberrationes indicare potest.

In unoquoque est vita affectiva, in tali stadio suae evolutionis seu maturationis, nunc cum minoribus nunc cum maioribus defectibus. Manifestationes vitae affectivae examinantur clinice (Freud, etc.), vel anthropologice,[47] vel studiis litterariis, mysticis, etc. Revelatur influxus affectivus in

tomaton well adapted to all the uses of daily living. There arises the subject: emergent, 'ex-sisting,' filled with wonder, original, originating.[45]

This purely experiential pattern is objectified. Of itself it is experienced, but it is only experienced; it is within the conscious subject, but without objectification it remains somehow implicit, veiled, hidden. In order that it be revealed, looked at, repeated, and enjoyed, it is transposed from the side of the subject to that of the object. This objectification abstracts from the actual experience; it selects the elements that seem more important, those that manifest the meaning of life more clearly. Form is abstracted, not by conceiving, but by making.

(c) Symbolic meaning. Newman: 'Cor ad cor loquitur.' Pascal: 'Le coeur a ses raisons que la raison ne connaît pas.'[46]

Symbolic meaning is inherent in feelings themselves; but by those feelings *both* we ourselves are disposed, orientated, directed, *and* we are related towards the world, towards life, towards persons, towards things.

A symbol, therefore, is an image that (1) evokes or expresses a feeling, and (2) reveals what the subject and the subject's world is like.

It evokes a feeling: just as the real object, so also the image of it elicits a certain feeling, and does so either as expected (you are afraid, but you have good reason to be) or as unexpected (children fear the dark because the visible world has disappeared while the audible world remains without any object being seen or able to be identified). It expresses the feeling: a spontaneously formed image manifests the affective state of the subject (dispositions, habits, capacities, needs, drives, finality). It reveals the subject and the subject's world; hence, in symbols there can be a deeper meaning (all things desire God), just as their meaning can indicate more serious disturbances and aberrations.

Each one has an affective life at a certain stage of development or maturity, at times with greater and at other times with lesser defects. The manifestations of the affective life are examined clinically (Freud, etc.), or anthropologically,[47] or in literary studies, or mystical studies, and so on. The

45 [On *Existenz*, see Lonergan's discussion in *The Ontological and Psychological Constitution of Christ* 18–31.]
46 [The references to Newman and Pascal are entered by hand in the autograph.]
47 Gilbert Durand, *Les structures anthropologiques de l'imaginaire: Introduction à l'archétypologie générale* (Paris: Presses universitaires de France, 1960). [In English: *The Anthropological Structures of the Imaginary* (Brisbane: Boombana Publications, 1999).]

usu linguistico ubi universale, classis, locum cedit figurae repraesentativae, ubi univocitas locum cedit pluribus simul sensibus, ubi probatio locum cedit repetitionibus, variationibus, etc., eiusdem, ubi principium tertii exclusi locum cedit superdeterminationi quae opposita coniungit, ubi negatio locum cedit nisui superandi, obruendi, supprimendi, ubi unicum thema locum cedit condensationi quae multa simul themata evolvit.[48]

Negatio[49] per positionem oppositorum eorumque ablationem: ita Swinburne, 'The Garden of Proserpine':

> Then star nor sun shall waken,
> Nor any change of light:
> Nor sound of waters shaken,
> Nor any sound or sight:
> Nor wintry leaves nor vernal;
> Nor days nor things diurnal;
> Only the sleep eternal
> In an eternal night.[50]

Condensatio diversorum thematum:

> And Pity, like a naked newborn babe,
> Striding the blast, or Heaven's Cherubin, hors'd
> Upon the sightless couriers of the air,
> Shall blow the horrid deed in every eye
> That tears shall drown the wind.[51]

(d) Sensus linguisticus (Helen Keller).

Sensus liberatur a limitationibus partis materialis: sensus intersubiectivus non habetur nisi in situatione interpersonali; sensus aestheticus non habetur nisi in vivente; sensus symbolicus non habetur nisi in affectibus; sed sensus linguisticus sibi assumit substratum conventionale quod indefinite

influence of feelings appears in the use of language, when universals or
class names give way to representative figures, when univocity gives way to
several meanings at the same time, when proof gives way to repetitions,
variations, etc., of the same theme, when the principle of the excluded
middle gives way to an overdetermination that combines opposites, when
a negation gives way to an effort to overcome, overwhelm, suppress, when
a single theme gives way to a condensation that develops many themes simultaneously.[48]

For a negation[49] through the positing of opposites and their ablation, see
Swinburne, 'The Garden of Proserpine':

> Then star nor sun shall waken,
> Nor any change of light:
> Nor sound of waters shaken,
> Nor any sound or sight:
> Nor wintry leaves nor vernal;
> Nor days nor things diurnal;
> Only the sleep eternal
> In an eternal night.[50]

For the condensation of diverse themes:

> And Pity, like a naked newborn babe,
> Striding the blast, or Heaven's Cherubin, hors'd
> Upon the sightless couriers of the air,
> Shall blow the horrid deed in every eye
> That tears shall drown the wind.[51]

(d) Linguistic meaning (Helen Keller).

Meaning is freed from the limitations of its material element: intersubjective meaning is had only in an interpersonal situation; aesthetic meaning
is had only in what is living; symbolic meaning is had only in affectivity; but
linguistic meaning takes to itself a conventional substratum capable of in-

---

48 [At the bottom of the page Lonergan writes: 'any object of fear as symbol of
   fear: mythological monster as art ...']
49 [At this point, the date at the top of the page switches to 20-5-62.]
50 Quoted in Langer, *Feeling and Form* 243.
51 Quoted ibid. 244. [These lines are from *Macbeth*, act 1, scene 7.]

evolvi, adaptari, perfici potest. Linguae pedetentim fiunt instrumenta intellectus.

De evolutione linguarum, E. Cassirer, *Philosophie der symbolischen Formen*, vol. 1.[52] Non parvi momenti est intelligere quam lente linguae evolutae sint a primitiva particularitate, concretione, incapacitate generalitatis, ad formas recentiores.

(e) Opus hermeneuticum et theologicum, quod in transcendentia veri fundatur, quam accuratissime distinguere debet inter diversos gradus seu fontes unde sensus loci invenitur. E.g., quid apud S. Paulum sit 'corpus Christi'; quanti momenti sit sensus intersubiectivus, symbolicus, aestheticus; quo usque hi sensus in modum loquendi, in id ipsum quod dicitur, influant.[53]

(f) Reditus e systemate theologico ad praedicandum reassumere debet modos significandi concretos, intersubiectivum, aestheticum, symbolicum.

2 Momentum sensus

(a) Sensus, esse intentionale, est quasi substantia evolutionis individualis. Si omnis aufertur sensus, vel ad statum parvulorum vel amentium reducimur. Docuit Nietzsche Deum esse mortuum, scilicet, in saec. xix disparebat omnis sensus vitae humanae qui in fide Christiana vel in philosophia deistica fundatus erat. Nihilistae sunt qui nullum sensum in metaphysica, in ethica, in vita humana practica, aesthetica, speculativa inveniunt. Tristes confitentur 'omnia permitti.'

(b) Obiectificatio sensus est conditio possibilitatis evolutionis. Inquantum sensus ex parte obiecti sistitur, inspici potest, inter elementa meliora et peiora distingui potest, quid auferendum et quid addendum perspici potest. Non omnis obiectificatio quasi in eodem plano est sed ex alio in aliud et superius pedetentim ascenditur. Scilicet, in unoquoque gradu sunt quae monstrari sed non dici possunt (Wittgenstein); e.g., exemplum contradictionis risum excitat; sed ut sermo fiat de contradictione ipsa, ad planum logicum ascendendum est. Eo maxime perfici possumus quod ipsi nos cognoscimus. Sed nos cognoscimus per obiectificationem eorum quae in nobis procedunt; et prout obiectificationes ascendunt ex alio in aliud pla-

definite development, adaptation, and improvement. Languages gradually become instruments of the intellect.

On the development of languages, see E[rnst] Cassirer, *Philosophie der symbolischen Formen*, vol. 1.[52] It is of no small importance to understand how slowly languages have evolved to their recent forms from their primitive particularism, concreteness, and inability to generalize.

(e) The task of hermeneutics in theology, which is based upon the transcendence of truth, must distinguish as accurately as possible between the various degrees or sources in which the meaning of a passage is to be found. For example, what St Paul means by 'the body of Christ,' how important is the intersubjective, the symbolic, the aesthetic meaning; to what extent these meanings have an influence upon the manner of speaking, upon what is actually said.[53]

(f) In the return from systematics to preaching one must go back to using concrete, intersubjective, aesthetic, and symbolic modes of expression.

2 The Importance of Meaning

(a) Meaning, intentional *esse*, is as it were the very substance of individual development. If there is no meaning, we are reduced to the state of children or the insane. Nietzsche taught that God was dead: that is, in the nineteenth century the whole meaning of human life as grounded on Christian faith or deistic philosophy was vanishing. Nihilists are those who find no meaning in metaphysics, in ethics, in the practical, the aesthetic, the intellectual aspects of human living. Sadly, they acknowledge that 'everything is permitted.'

(b) The objectification of meaning is the condition for the possibility of development. As meaning is situated on the side of the object, it can be investigated, its better or worse elements can be distinguished, and it is possible to see what must be added and what removed. Not all objectification is on the same level, but there is a gradual movement from one level to a higher one. That is to say, at each level there are things that can be pointed out but not expressed (Wittgenstein). For example, a contradiction evokes laughter; but when one discusses that contradiction itself, one rises to the level of logic. It is through self-knowledge most of all that we are capable of developing. But we know ourselves by objectifying what is going on within

52 [Cassirer, *Philosophie der symbolischen Formen*, vol. 1: *De Sprache, The Philosophy of Symbolic Forms*, vol. 1: *Language*.]
53 On literary genres, see Lonergan, *Insight* 592–95.

num, fiunt media quibus cognoscimus non solum corpus sed psyche, sed intelligentiam, sed voluntatem, sed modum existendi.[54]

(c) Sensus est conditio possibilitatis tum communicationis tum cooperationis humanae.

(d) Sensus pertinet ad ipsam constitutionem institutorum. Sine sensu non haberentur vel familia proprie dicta vel societas, moralitas vel educatio, status vel ius, oeconomia vel technologia.

(e) Sensus denique pertinet ad ipsam constitutionem omnis linguae, literaturae, operis artis, symboli, scientiae, philosophiae, historiae, religionis.

3 Sensus et Historia

(a) Circa ipsum evolventem contextum, alibi ubi de historia.

(b) Evolutio sensus termini technici, e.g., persona. In analysi litteraria graeca explicabatur Homerum tali loco in propria persona loqui, tali alio loco in persona Diomedis, etc. In exegesi psalmorum Origenes saepe difficile duxit determinare in quanam persona (sua? Dei? hominis iniqui?) locutus esset psalmista. In contextu trinitario Hippolytus agnovit duas personas et tertiam gratiam Spiritus sancti. Tertullianus tres posuit personas. In symbolo dicitur 'qui locutus est per prophetas.' An persona est qui loquitur? Augustinus definivit personam heuristice. Pater, Filius, et Spiritus sanctus sunt tres. Non tamen tres sunt dei, tres patres, tres filii , tres spiritus. Quid tres? Dicimus personas ut respondere possimus. Boethius, Richardus a S. Victore, Aquinas personam definiverunt. Scotus, Capreolus, Caietanus, Tiphanus, Suarezius theorias ontologicas de constitutione personae voluerunt. Postea, persona investigata est sub aspectu psychologico (conscientiae) et sub aspectu phaenomenologico (ego et tu).

(c) Covariatio sensus et rei. Ubi res per sensum vel totaliter vel partialiter constituitur, evolutio sensus etiam est evolutio rei. Si evolvitur sensus terminorum, evolvitur ipsa scientia. Si evolvitur notio status, notio iuris, notio matrimonii, non tantum theoretice in libris politicis, iuridicis, ethicis, sed etiam secundum apprehensionem sensus communis, tunc non solum mutantur opiniones privatae sed etiam realitates obiectivae. Ita aetas moderna novum mundum, novum hominem, efformavit, quia pede-

us; and as these objectifications rise from one level to another, there occur the means by which we know not only our body but also our psyche, our intelligence, our willing, our way of existing.[54]

(c) Meaning is the condition of the possibility of both human communication and cooperation.

(d) Meaning is part of the very constitution of institutions. Without meaning there would be no family in the proper sense, no society, no morality or education, no state or law, no economy or technology.

(e) Finally, meaning is part of the very constitution of every language, literature, work of art, symbol, science, philosophy, history, religion.

3 Meaning and History

(a) Concerning the developing context itself, see where we treat of history elsewhere.

(b) Development in the meaning of a technical term – person, for example. In the analysis of Greek literature, Homer is said to be speaking in his own person in one place, but in the person of Diomedes, etc., in other places. In his exegesis of the Psalms, Origen often found it difficult to determine the person in which the psalmist was speaking, whether in his own, in the person of God, or of a sinful man. In a trinitarian context, Hippolytus recognized two persons and one grace of the Holy Spirit. Tertullian posited three persons. In the creed it says, 'who spoke through the prophets.' Is a person one who speaks? Augustine defined person heuristically. The Father, the Son, and the Holy Spirit are three. Yet they are not three gods, three fathers, three sons, or three spirits. Three what, then? To be able to answer we say 'persons.' Boethius, Richard of St Victor, and Aquinas all defined 'person.' Scotus, Capreolus, Cajetan, Tiphanus, Suárez wanted ontological theories on what constitutes a person. Later, the notion of person was investigated under its psychological aspect (consciousness) and under its phenomenological aspect ('I and thou').

(c) The co-variation of meaning and thing. When a thing is wholly or partly constituted by meaning, a development in meaning is also a development in the thing. If the meaning of the terms evolve, the science itself evolves. If the notion of the state, of law, of matrimony, evolve not only theoretically in books on politics, law, or ethics, but also according to a commonsense understanding, then not only private opinions but also the objective realities change. Thus has the modern age produced a new world,

---

54 [The Latin words 'sed modum existendi' are handwritten in the autograph.]

tentim novae opiniones de institutis sunt disseminatae, evolutae, acceptae, applicatae.

(d) Unde concludes: genus humanum ad Deum convertere est novos sensus hominibus communicare; unde momentum verbi Dei revelati, traditi, conservati, ad diversos contextus transpositi, semperque praedicati et omnibus adiunctis applicati. Etiam concludes: aliud evangelium evangelizare praeterquam evangelizatum est, novam ecclesiam introducit; haereses.

4 Sensus et Interioritas

(a) Sponte opinamur sensum potius in exterioritate quam in interioritate inveniri. Quid 'album,' 'paries,' 'aedificium,' etc. Brevissime respondetur, Ecco! Quo tamen praetermittitur cooperatio intelligentiae et iudicii. Si modo stupido agam, supponam te velle dicere 'parietem' significare colorem, 'album' significare partem aedificii.

(b) Res in clariori luce sistitur ubi interpretatio libri fit. Ibi ex parte exteriori non habentur nisi signa conventionalia tali et tali ordine disposita. Quidquid in interpretatione dicitur praeter repetitionem eorundem signorum eodem ordine dispositorum, ex experientiis, memoriis, actibus intelligendi et concipiendi, reflectendi et iudicandi, ipsius interpretis proveniunt.

(c) Si distinguuntur sensus derivati et sensus primitivi (quibus derivati exponi possunt), si ad primitivos unice attenditur, equidem dicerem unumquemque eo melius, plenius, exactius, sensus possibiles cognoscere quo melius, exactius, plenius ad propriam interioritatem attendit. Secundum I, 88, 2, 3m: 'anima humana intelligit se ipsam per suum intelligere, quod est actus proprius eius, perfecte demonstrans virtutem eius et naturam.'[55] Sed sicut actus interior intelligendi demonstrat naturam et virtutem animae, ita etiam demonstrat ea quae virtute animae fiunt.

(d) Sunt denique termini quibus sensus fundamentalis non est nisi sensus qui in interioritate apprehenditur. Quid vita? In primis cognoscitur quatenus conscie et crescente conscientia vivimus. Quid amor, being-in-love?[56] Includit actus voluntatis qui amorem confirmare vel pedetentim destruere

a new man, because gradually new opinions concerning institutions have been disseminated, developed, accepted, and implemented.

(d) We conclude, then, that to turn the human race to God is to communicate new meanings to people. Hence the importance of the revealed word of God, handed down, conserved, transposed to different contexts, constantly preached, and applied in all circumstances. We further conclude that to preach a gospel other than that which has been preached means to introduce a new church: heresies.

4 Meaning and Interiority

(a) We automatically think that meaning is to be found in exteriority rather than in interiority. What is 'white' or 'building' or 'wall'? We simply answer, 'Look!' Such an answer overlooks the cooperation of understanding and judgment. If I were to act stupidly, I should suppose that according to you 'wall' means a color and 'white' means a part of a building.

(b) This matter becomes clearer in interpreting a book. All that is there exteriorly are conventional signs arranged in a certain order. In interpreting the book, whatever is said beyond repeating those same signs in the same order will come from the experiences, the memories, the acts of understanding and conceiving, reflecting and judging of the interpreter.

(c) If we distinguish between derived meanings and primitive meanings (by which the derived meanings can be explained), and if we attend only to the primitive meanings, I should say that the better, the more exactly, and the more fully one attends to one's own interiority, the better, more fully, and more exactly will one know the possible meanings. In the words of Aquinas, 'The human soul understands itself through its own act of understanding, which is the act proper to it, perfectly demonstrating its nature and power.'[55] But just as the interior act of understanding demonstrates the nature and power of the soul, so also it demonstrates whatever is done by the power of the soul.

(d) Finally, there are terms in which the fundamental meaning is only the meaning that is apprehended in interiority. What is life? It is known above all insofar as we live consciously and with increasing consciousness. What is love, being-in-love?[56] It includes acts of the will that can strengthen

---

55 Thomas Aquinas, *Summa theologiae*, 1, q. 88, a. 2, ad 3m. [A key text for Lonergan; see, for example, *Verbum* 90 and note 147, 225 and note 148; '*Insight*: Preface to a Discussion,' in *Collection* 142–52, esp. 142–45.]

56 [The English expression 'being-in-love' is handwritten in the autograph.]

possunt. Sed actus voluntatis se habent ad amorem, fere sicut gubernaculum ad navim. Aquinas enumerat effectus amoris, ubi amor intelligitur passio quaedam animae.[57] At eiusmodi thematizatio et analysis non supponuntur, ubi secundum usum communem de amore fit sermo; sed potius ipse amor expertos suos effectus includit et per eos quasi constituitur. Quid religio? Sicut amor est experta, intellecta, agnita, electa unio unde amicus fit dimidium animae meae, ita religio est alia quaedam experta, intellecta, agnita, electa unio et quasi communio cum toto cosmico, cum eiusdem elemento vel parte prima, principali, finali. Quid praesentia Dei? An Deus sistitur ex parte obiecti ut imaginibus vel categoriis conceptualibus apprehendatur? An potius 'Qui *habitat* in adiutorio Altissimi, in protectione Dei caeli commorabitur,' 'Dominus regit me et nihil mihi deerit,' etc.[58]

or gradually destroy love. But acts of the will are to love somewhat as the rudder is to a ship. Aquinas lists the effects of love, where love is understood as a passion of the soul.[57] But that sort of thematization and analysis is not supposed when one is speaking of love in the ordinary way; rather, love itself includes its experienced effects and is as it were constituted by them. What is religion? Just as love is an experienced, understood, acknowledged, and chosen union whereby a friend becomes 'half of my soul,' so religion is another experienced, understood, acknowledged, and chosen union and, in a way, a communion with the total cosmos, with its first, principal, and final element or part. What is the presence of God? Is God on the side of the object so as to be apprehended in images or conceptual categories? Or rather is it a matter of 'He who dwells in the shelter of the Most High will abide in the protection of the God of heaven' [Psalms 91]. 'The Lord is my shepherd, there is nothing I shall want' [Psalms 23 (22)] etc.[58]

57 Thomas Aquinas, *Summa theologiae*, 1-2, q. 28, q. 27, a. 1.
58 [Lonergan adds by hand a fifth heading: 'Meaning and Metaphysics. See Lonergan, *Insight*, p. 502.' He would seem to be referring to chapter 16, §3.3, 'The Nature of Metaphysical Equivalence,' which in the 1957 edition of *Insight* begins on p. 502 and goes to p. 507. In the CWL edition of *Insight*, the pagination is 526–30.]

Index

Abbé de Saint Pierre, 335
Abelard, Peter, 5 n. 6, 21, 159, 571, 577, 593 and n. 4, 599, 657
Abstraction: and concepts, 125; operatory a., 301, 303, 309; and thing-in-itself, 475–77; and understanding, 125, 127
Acacius of Caesarea, 23, 191
'Accept Responsibility for Judging,' see Precepts of method
Action and passion: and motion, 85
Acton, Lord (John Dalberg-Acton), 273, 281
Adaptation, 340, 367–69
Adoptionism, 193, 603
Aeby, G., 11 n. 16
Aeterni Patris, 659, 677
Aëtius, 195
Agent intellect, 131, 133, 253, 341, 641
Albert the Great, 599, 683
Alcuin, 21, 599
Alexander of Alexandria, 191
Alonso-Schökel, L., 205 n. 139
Altaner, B., 421 n. 70
Ampère, A.-M., 251

Anachronism: and inauthenticity, 411
Analysis, way of, see Discovery, way of
Analytic principles, 89–91
Ancyra, Pseudo-synod/Council of, 63 n. 48, 133, 195
Anomoians, 23 n. 25, 191
Anselm, 15 and n. 21, 157, 159, 163, 597, 633, 655, 657
Answers: ordering of theological, see Ordering(s) of theological answers
Antioch, Dedication Council of, 191
Antiochene exegesis, 13, 191
Antitheses: of worlds, and theological problematic, 395–403
Apologetics/Apologetic theology: and dogmatic theology, 155, 675; and positive theology, 575
Appearances: and judgment, 485–87, 497
A priori: and a posteriori in rules of method, 207; and historians/history, 197–201, 326; and transcendental method, 386
Archaism: and inauthenticity, 411
Archimedes, 119
Arian, Arianism, 11, 13, 23, 43, 63, 133,

Integration: and circles of operations, 316, 349; and development, 429, 441; and differentiation, 429, 431, 561, 567, 569; of positive and speculative theology, 43; and specialization, 318, 338, 349; of theology and science, 167; and wisdom, 445; of worlds, 411–15, 431, 433

Intellect: as able to make or become all things, 109, 131, 338; and being, 109, 131, 397, 627, 645; formal and proper object of, 371; grasps intelligibility in sense data, 443; human i. potential, 445; and intelligible species, 435; potential human i. and solution to methodological problems, 79, 641; as related to faith and theology, 529–31; and rules of method, 157, 177; and sense, 69, 71, 79, 107, 635 (*see also* Chasm); and speculative intellectual habits, 49, 79, 619, 623, 629–31. *See also* Agent intellect

Intellectualism, 409

Intellectus quaerens fidem, 25

Isomorphism: and operations and results, 301; structural i., 509, 511

James, W., 123 and n. 91, 281, 337
James of Metz, 217
Jansenius, Cornelius Otto, 47, 165
Jaspers, K., 111 n. 83, 149 and n. 111, 207–209 and n. 141, 326, 349, 373 n. 17, 399 n. 47
Jerome, 195
Jerusalem, First Council of, 602
Joachim of Fiore, 25, 155
John Chrysostom, 193
John of the Cross, 399, 573
John of St Thomas, 27–29, 599 and n. 18
Jonas, H., 75 and n. 59
Josephus, 275

Judgment: accepting responsibility for, 207–17, 227; and absolute positing, 489; and being, 324–26, 343, 485, 497; and concrete, 145; and contexts, 457; different types of, 147; and extrinsicism, *see* Extrinsicism; and faith, 209 (*see also* Faith); and immanentism, *see* Immanentism; modal j., 447 n. 95; and perception, 323–24; personal aspect of, 147, 151; and questions 'Is it?'/ 'Is it so?' 103; and reduction to intellect and sense, 119; and truth, 121, 143, 209, 215, 343, 344, 573; and verification, 133; and virtually unconditioned, 133, 147; and wisdom, 51, 53, 61, 65, 67, 91, 215, 445–51, 457, 527, 621

Julius I, Pope, 193
Jung, C.G., 71, 101 n. 76, 329, 395 n. 43, 681
Justin, 7–9 and n. 8, 181, 593

Kant, I., 71, 141, 147, 149, 219, 221, 239, 259, 269 n. 33, 281, 323, 326, 337, 342, 353, 385 and n. 34, 387, 399, 427, 439 n. 90, 449–51, 483 and n. 134, 485, 525, 639 and n. 56, 661, 675, 689
Keller, H., 699
Kepler, J., 87, 161, 251
Kerygmatic theology, 47, 425, 575, 617, 669
Kierkegaard, S., 71, 281, 337, 411
Kilwardby, R., 215
Kirch, K., 195 n. 132
Klubertanz, G.P., 323, 343
Knowledge: as accumulation of acts of understanding, 119; and belief, *see* Belief; both spiritual and bodily, 444; compared to faith and theology, 527–33; descriptive and explanatory k., 83; distinctions within unity of, 501–99 passim; distinguished from faith,

Montanists, 157
Morel, G., 401 n. 48, 681, 683 n. 34
Motion: and action and passion, 85;
  and Aristotle's categories, 83, 85; and
  Aristotle's notion of science, 83, 91,
  187, 237, 659–61; and modern science, 417, 659–61
Movements from below and above, 131,
  207, 251–57, 267, 271, 273, 289, 338,
  347
Mutual self-mediation, 555 n. 184
Mystical body: church as, 93, 155; and
  history, 155; and systematic conceptualization, 155. *See also* Mediation: and
  theology
Myth: as mentality, 71–75, 97, 103, 181,
  219, 316, 318, 319, 326, 331, 340, 347,
  354, 397, 399, 415, 635, 639 n. 56; and
  logos, see *Logos*: and *mythos*

Nag Hammadi, 248 and n. 19
Names: and essences, 83; and feelings,
  109; importance of in ancient world,
  103; and proper nouns, 107
Nationalism, 316, 331, 339
Naturalism: and historicism, 287, 328,
  335, 336, 337; as *Weltanschauung*, 316
Nature: at Chalcedon, 15, 45, 121, 181,
  183, 193, 271; and grace, 55, 163, 165,
  623, 675; and person, 45, 181, 183,
  193, 271, 415, 587, 595, 657; pure n.,
  167, 241, 419, 461, 673; as remote
  principle of operation, 477; as technical term, 45
Necessity: absolute and hypothetical,
  93, 95, 147, 385, 439, 441; and fittingness, 55; metaphysical, moral, and
  physical, 95; and science, 63, 91–94,
  147; and theology, 439, 441
Neoplatonism, 107
Nestorians/Nestorius, 157, 181, 553,
  583, 603

Newman, J.H., 143 and n. 107, 151, 447
  and n. 97, 455, 677
Newton, I., 23, 71, 87, 119 and n. 89,
  125 n. 92, 141, 161, 165, 185 and n.
  125, 187, 189, 219, 221, 251, 271, 332,
  336, 352, 401, 475, 639 and n. 56, 655,
  663
Nicea, Council of, 19, 133, 181, 189,
  191, 193, 195, 433, 441, 443, 567, 617
Nicholas of Autrecourt, 77
Niebuhr, B.G., 247 and n. 17, 281
Nietzsche, F., 71, 281, 285, 335, 337, 701
Noetus, 11
Nominalism, 171, 569
Noncontradiction: principle of, 344
Notion of being, *see* Being
Nouns: common and proper, 107–11
Novatian, 13 and n. 18, 593

Objectivity: absolute o., 453; and charity, 322; experiential o., 453; normative o., 453; and rational judgment,
  387
Object(s): acts specified by, 521, 671;
  considered from methodological
  viewpoint, 377–81; and criteria of
  authenticity, 379; and division and
  development of sciences, 379; of
  faith, 519–25, 529; formal o. *de iure*
  and *de facto*, 379; formal o. of intellect, 371, 529, 645; formal and material o., 377–79; formal o. and science,
  153; formal o. of will, 371; o. of Greek
  and modern sciences contrasted, 237,
  241; o. of history, 249, 265, 409; and
  human good, 685; immediate and
  mediated o., 367; o. of natural and
  human sciences contrasted, 677–79;
  o. of natural knowledge, divine faith,
  and theology, 529; o. of natural
  theology and dogmatic theology
  contrasted, 663–67, 669, 671; and

Peckham, J., 215, 217

Peinador, M., 419 n. 70

Pelagians/Pelagianism, 15, 157, 161,
183, 553, 567, 595, 603

Perennial philosophy/philosophies, 37,
223, 345

Periodic table, 23, 87, 251, 253, 271, 475

Person: history of notion of, 421, 703;
and nature, *see* Nature: and person

Personalism, 344, 345, 391, 421

Perspectives: historical p. and questions, 31, 249, 255, 257; and perception, 99, 103, 328; and truth, 317–20;
see also Perspectivism

Perspectivism: 332; and relativism, 257.
See also Perspectives

Petavius, 443

Phantasm: and understanding, 119,
133, 221, 267, 435, 445, 647

Phenomenology: 291, 321, 323, 337,
391, 411, 421, 423, 433, 435, 437 n.
86, 493

Philip the Chancellor, 21, 45, 135, 163,
599

Philology, 41, 205, 661

Philosophy: and axial period, 101;
Christian p., 153, 273, 355, 357, 433,
551; distinguished from common
sense and natural science, 507; history of as science, 257–71; Indian p.,
107; modern p. and method, 115,
117; p. of philosophies, 259 n. 25, 269
and n. 33, 289; p. of religion, 321–22;
regression of in modernity, 79; and
science, 153, 221, 336, 655; and theology, 3, 163, 273, 355, 551, 655; and
wisdom, 81, 325, 461. *See also* Interiority; Perennial philosophy

'Philosophy of ...,' 153, 321

Photian schism, 15

Photinus, 193

Piaget, J., 231 n. 1, 305 n. 78, 311, 315,

326, 337, 340, 383–85, 367 nn. 5 and
7, 379, 687 n. 36

Pius XII, 581, 671

Pivotal point: and theological understanding, 25, 27, 69, 201, 635

Planck, M., 177

Plato/Platonism, 51, 73, 113, 115, 259,
317, 323, 356, 417, 433, 455, 469, 577,
583, 603, 621, 635

Plotinus, 475, 621

Polymorphism: in philosophy, 321, 323

Polybius, 239 and n. 7, 275

Porphyrian tree, 59, 65, 81, 627

Positions: and counterpositions, 143,
325, 511–13 (*see also* Counterpositions); 'develop p.,' 119, 137, 143,
171–207, 225

Positive theology, 41, 43, 155, 179, 203,
207, 337, 389, 501, 561, 573, 575, 577
n. 204, 581, 615, 637, 667

Positivism: and authorities, 533;
Christian p., 531; and foundations,
615, 675; and historicism, 279 n. 50;
perennial p., 223; and science, 441;
and systematization, 316

Positivists: linguistic p., 89

Posterior Analytics, 239 and n. 7, 277, 445
n. 93, 479 n. 107

Potency-form-act, 133, 135, 137, 145,
501, 503, 509

Praepositinus of Cremona, 163

Precepts of method, 117–217 passim,
342

Preconceptual, 51, 77, 119, 169, 295,
495

Preface of Holy Trinity, 433

Premature systematization, 339–41

Premotion: Aristotle on, 91; Aquinas
on, 91–93

Priestly, J., 251

Prior, A.N., 33 n. 32, 607 n. 27

Proclus, 185